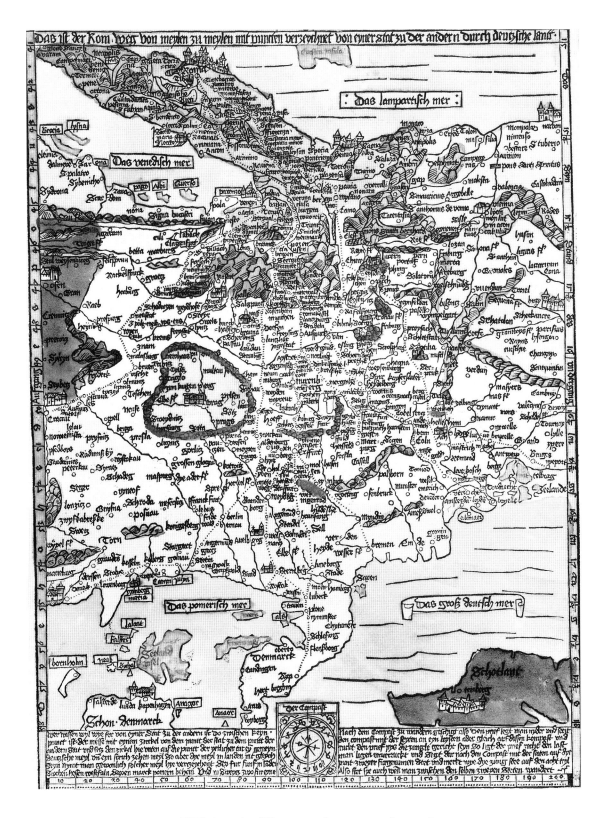

With 265 illustrations, 29 in color

POWER AND PROFIT
THE MERCHANT IN MEDIEVAL EUROPE

PETER SPUFFORD

For Marc Fitch and Bridget Spufford

Page 1 (half-title)   *For a sea port to use a sailing boat on a seal was perfectly normal, but finding this on a Paris seal makes one pause to think of the importance of river transport on the Seine in 1412 when this new seal was cut for the city's provost of merchants. We tend to think of watermen sculling with passengers in small boats on the Thames, but, as the seal illustrates, French watermen operated on an entirely different scale, using the Seine and its tributaries to bring goods to Paris from Burgundy in one direction and from the sea in the other.*

Frontispiece   *In 1500 in his* Romweg Karte *(map of roads to Rome), Erhard Etzlaub of Nuremberg set out for the first time in graphic form a traditional set of pilgrim itineraries, most of which were, of course, also the key commercial routes from the rising economic centres of Germany to the old established centres of Italy. Since the convention of putting the north at the top did not yet exist, Rome is logically put in that position. It is possibly the earliest attempt at drawing a land map to scale, with the distances between towns indicated by the number of dots on the road. Every dot, as he explained, represents a mile.*

Title page   *The* speculum *or mirror was a favourite late medieval didactic form, reflecting not only how things are, but also explaining how they ought to be. Since 'mirrors' were aimed at the sons of princes and the greatest nobility, they are frequently lavishly illustrated, as is this* Miroir d'Humanité *(a mirror of human life) produced in 1462 for a client at the Burgundian court. It is an interesting comment on how far notions of wealth had changed by the mid-fifteenth century that the 'rich man' should be illustrated by a merchant counting his money, not by a landowner surveying his property.*

Picture research by Georgina Bruckner

First published in hardcover in the United States of America in 2003 by Thames & Hudson Inc., 500 Fifth Avenue, New York, New York 10110

thamesandhudsonusa.com

Library of Congress Catalog Card Number 2002103867
ISBN 0-500-25118-5

Printed and bound in Hong Kong by C&C Offset Printing Company Ltd

Contents

This brisk fourteenth-century sketch of the attributes of a merchant emphasizes his
calibrated rod for measuring cloth, and his pair of scales, here shown as hand scales for
weighing small quantities of precious commodities. To be a merchant is to weigh and to
measure. The strong element of satire in medieval writing, and its accompanying
illustrations, is often hard for modern readers to pick out. Are his clothes the most up-to-
date fashion of the day? Or do they caricature the aspirations of the nouveau riche?

Cessolis ms, German, fourteenth century

Preface

Tˢ HIS BOOK has been a very long time in gestation. I had the original idea
for it in the mid 1970s, as a spin off from the work that turned into
Money and its Use in Medieval Europe. After a great deal of background
reading it became apparent that the book could not be written without visiting many of the places involved. I would therefore like to begin by thanking
the University of Keele, where I was then a Reader, for a sabbatical term.
However, such extensive fieldwork required resources as well as opportunity.
My deepest thanks go therefore to the late Dr Marc Fitch, whose enthusiasm
and generosity made it possible to spend so many months in the spring and
summer of 1978 following some of the routes set out in the late medieval
Itinéraire de Bruges in over a hundred short stages, from Bruges itself to the
cities of medieval Tuscany, and thence onwards to the mining areas of central
Europe, and then back to Flanders again, by way of the fair sites of Champagne, the passes of the Alps and the Apennines, 'new towns' like Pietrasanta
on the Francigena, and the rising cities of fifteenth-century Swabia and
Franconia. As well as such major seaports as Genoa and Venice, I was also
enabled to visit minor ones as far apart as Sluys, Aigues Mortes and Porto
Venere, as well as river-ports like Troyes, St-Jean de Losne, Signa, Brescello
and Maastricht.

The fieldwork turned out to be very much a family affair. We crossed as
nearly as possible from Sandwich to Calais to travel down several of the alternative routes given in the *Itinéraire* from Bruges to Florence in the smallest
size of van adapted to sleep four people. The children were ten and thirteen.
It began cold, and had rained so much that the whole of north-western
Europe was like a sponge. We were very happy. We discovered two universals.
Camp-sites, over a hundred of them, were very much the same, wherever we
were, unless the water in the showers was warm, which was very unlikely. We
remember Pontarlier in the Jura with deep affection for this reason. The
other universal was the Mass, whether in Flemish, French, Italian, Croat,
German or even Latin. Our daughter Bridget had recently had a kidney
transplant, but was utterly undeterred. It was admittedly a little hard on the
children, normally travelling rather slowly on an old road, now demoted to
'B' or 'C' status, not far from a newer, faster, 'A' road, a railway line, a motorway and sometimes even a canal as well, each reflecting good medieval
judgement in the choice of routes. It also took them a little while to adjust to
the pretence that all buildings put up after 1500 were invisible.

After Easter, our son Francis returned to school in England, sadly for us
and for him, but Bridget, who had just passed her 'eleven plus', then the

examination for going to grammar school, stayed on. For the next three months while I did archival work, mostly in Florence, she helped my wife do the shopping in a small town in the Chianti hills, naturally picking up the language at her age a good deal faster than my wife. She also started to learn about pictures. She, with my wife, developed the horrible, but useful, habit of peering into the backgrounds of late medieval paintings in the Uffizi and elsewhere, looking both for travellers and for 'realistic' landscapes. As a result of all this she later dazed her oral examiner in French at 'O' level, then the public examination at sixteen, by telling her about Uccello's odd use of perspective. It was Bridget who found a relevant painting of copper mining hung in an obscure corner of the Uffizi (p. 365). She also particularly delighted in the furnishings and fabrics in the Davizzi (now Davanzati) palace. Perhaps most of all she enjoyed spending her pocket-money in small shops in Venice, on buying, with squeaks of delight, her own little sample boxes of representative spices, which are still stuck into her diary of the trip. Even as tolerant a hospital as Guy's felt that perhaps blood-tests could not be regularly carried out for Bridget and the results transmitted sufficiently fast from central Europe. So when it came to the time to travel into Slovenia and onwards, she and my wife in their turn sadly turned for home.

However, one of my oldest friends, Alasdair Mackinnon, who is the most superb linguist I know, fluent in Italian, Slovene, Croat, Magyar and German, and by transposition also able to cope in Slovak, Polish and Czech, took their place. On this occasion I did not need his Dutch, Swedish or even his Gaelic. Without his astonishingly extensive knowledge not only of the languages, but also of the people and the idiosyncracies of communist rule, it would have been impossible to zigzag across modern borders through Slovenia, Croatia, Hungary, Slovakia, Spiš, Poland, Austria and Bohemia, to see the cattle roads at Ptuj and Koc, the port of Senj, the new planted towns at Zagreb and Karlovac, the mining towns of Kremnica, and Banska Stiavnica, Jihlava and Kutna Hora, besides the Luxemburg capitals at Buda and Prague, let alone Esztergom, and the staple-towns-cum-capitals at Cracow and Vienna, at points where major land-routes crossed major river routes, the new fifteenth-century pass through the Carpathians from the Hron valley to that of the Vistula, and the older route under the castle of Spis, and sleepy Varazdin too, where they still had Christmas decorations in July and wished us a Happy New Year.

My wife suffered from mild anxiety during our period in central Europe, a decade before the Wall collapsed. My uncle had been prominent in British clandestine 'information gathering' activities in central and eastern Europe, and I was specifically told not to reveal my mother's real, rather unusual, maiden name if questioned, or even in filling up simple forms. My wife felt, with a certain amount of reason, that to be crossing the modern borders of an anachronistic Czechoslovakia, superimposed on medieval Bohemia, Moravia, and Slovakia, no less than six times, whilst taking photographs of strategic points like old bridges, might seem a little more than mildly eccentric if my mother's family name had somehow slipped through. However, nothing worse befell us than the impossibility of communicating Alasdair's Welsh place of birth, which was required a multiplicity of times for Czechoslovak camp-sites. The combination of consonants was as impossible to the Czechs and Slovaks as their languages were to me. We, on the other hand, probably made one of the worst days in the life of a fresh young Slovak border guard, when his superiors set him to itemize the contents of our camping van, which of course contained all the necessary bibliographical material, much of it stowed in Tuscan terracotta plant troughs, as well as mere means to live. His new uniform issue cap was too large, and, all through the several hours for which he inspected us, kept falling over his eyes, as he, ideologically most unsoundly, muttered 'Jesu, Maria' at increasingly frequent intervals. His first suspicious find came when he discovered, by dint of careful measurement, a large space at the back, suitable for contraband or a smuggled refugee, which then unfortunately turned out to contain the engine. However, all his spirits revived when he discovered a 'hidden document' secreted under a seat cushion. It turned out, poor man, to be our mislaid copy of the map of the city of Bruges drawn by Marc Gheerarts in 1562.

In Germany our son Francis rejoined me and took over the navigation. He guided me from Nuremberg to the Danube in flood at Regensburg, which lapped at our feet as we lunched, from Augsburg over the Brenner and back, and finally through the Rhineland to Brabant and Flanders. His keen perceptions and indefatigable curiosity led him to ask all the right questions at fourteen, as he has continued to do ever since.

And so many people gave us hospitality and advice on the journey and took us to see buildings, artefacts and documents that we would otherwise have missed – Victor and Esther de Waal in England at Canterbury, on the road from London to Sandwich; Wim and An Blockmans in Flanders, with their memorable tour of medieval industrial Ghent; John and Nicoletta Day in Paris and what little could be seen of the Valois capital; Aldo and Mariele De Maddelena in Visconti and Sforza Milan; Vlado and Charlotte Ivir in Croatia at Zagreb; Kristina Samperl in Ptuj; Andras and Erzebet Sugar, Istvan Gedai and Lajos Huszar in Buda; Jozef Gindl in Slovakia at Banska Stiavnica; Zbigniew Zabinski, Zdzisław Kapera, and Stanisłava Kubiakowa in Jagellon Cracow; Stefan Kazimir back in Slovakia at Bratislava; my cousin Elizabeth in ducal Vienna; Mme Mucilova in Bohemia at Kutna Hora; Mme Haskova and Karel Castelin in Prague; Anne Neundorf and Franz and Ursula Kuhn in the Palatinate at Heidelberg; and Madeleine de Heusch in Brabant at Brussels. How properly to thank so many at so long a distance of time? And how to thank the numerous academic colleagues who have enriched my knowledge over so many years. Most appear appropriately in the footnotes, but some do not, like Bjorn Poulsen of Aarhus who talked to me about the Danish cattle trade or Susan Rose of Roehampton who talked about Mediterranean shipping, and, above all to John Munro who provided the sharpest and most detailed and useful report of any publisher's readers I have seen, and saved me from numerous pitfalls.

As well as libraries, buildings, paintings and continuing landscapes, my understanding of medieval manufacture, necessity, luxury and survival has been enriched over the years by museums from the Victoria and Albert to the Bargello, the Cloisters to the Cinquentenaire, Cluny to the Antwerp Vleeshuis, as well as specialist museums like the Gutenberg and Plantin printing museums.

The book itself has been written and rewritten in many different places. It was begun with the first version of Chapter 3 at Greve in Chianti in the middle of looking, and was continued slowly, between other writing, at Haddenham in the English Fens. It took a great leap forward when I was given a sabbatical year by the University of Cambridge and Queens' College, which I spent partially on the very edge of Tuscany, outside Cortona, where Germaine Greer, with typical generosity, lent us her lovely retreat in the hills, in which to write in peace. Large parts of Chapters 4, 5, and 6 will always be associated with the orange of Umbrian oaks in winter and the overspilling banks of violets in the spring that followed the snow. Chapter 2, which emphasized the importance of power in medieval trade, largely took shape in the autumn at Island Bay in New Zealand, outside Wellington. Everything was rewritten at Leuven whilst I was Visiting Professor there at the invitation of Herman van der Wee. The first part of Chapter 8 was prepared as a lecture for delivery in Lübeck. The rest of Chapter 8 and, finally, Chapter 1, which emphasized the compelling motive of profit, were added in the fifteenth-century hall of the parish guild of St John the Baptist at Whittlesford. The writing and rewriting of a book, which is by now three times the length originally intended, has meant an immense amount of typing, and I have incurred extraordinary debts of gratitude, for so many thousands of words, to Carolyn Busfield at Keele who began on my manuscript, to Louise Rambaut in Saint Ives to whom I sent handwritten chapters by post from Cortona and Wellington, and above all to Anne Simpson, assisted by Margaret Hennessy, at the Netherlands Institute for Advanced Study, who took the burden of a virtual retyping of the whole book when I was a Visiting Fellow there.

Amongst all these thanks I am not mentioning my wife, Margaret. She is too close to me, and to the book. We have always read and commented on everything that the other has written, but she has been so closely involved with this book, from its conception to its completion, that it is more nearly hers than anything else that I have written.

Over all the years since the initial fieldwork, Marc Fitch continued to be remarkably supportive, but, like Bridget, he was not able to see the finished product, which I dedicate to them.

Peter Spufford
Cambridge
Pentecost 2002

1

The transformation of trade

THIRTEENTH-CENTURY EUROPE saw an enormous expansion in the scale of trade, local, regional, national, international and even inter-continental. In certain places, and on certain routes, there was a radical alteration in the way commerce was carried on, which was intimately linked to this expansion in scale. This change in the methods of trade has sometimes been called a 'commercial revolution', on the analogy of the 'industrial revolution' in the methods of manufacture in the eighteenth and nineteenth centuries.

The commercial changes of thirteenth-century Europe were largely made possible by very substantial increases in population and an enormous growth in the money supply, to such an extent that early fourteenth-century Europe was both overpopulated in relation to agricultural productivity and also nearly everywhere accustomed to the general use of coined money, supplemented by credit. In most parts of Europe the early fourteenth-century population levels were not equalled again until the seventeenth century, or surpassed until the eighteenth. The money supply was also at a high point, not to be reached again for several centuries. In England, for instance, over 800 tons of silver was circulating as coined money by 1319 under Edward II, at least a twenty-fourfold increase since the mid-twelfth century. However, at the end of Queen Elizabeth I's reign, some three centuries later, only the equivalent of 500 tons of silver was circulating as coined money, gold and silver together[1].

Except in this introduction I shall not say much directly about these major transformations in commerce of the thirteenth century. I shall, of course, refer to them incidentally throughout the book, but my present purpose is to write about the patterns of trade that had evolved in that commercial revolution of the thirteenth century, which continued throughout the rest of the Middle Ages into the Early Modern period. I shall therefore focus on the fourteenth century, but will extend the time-span backwards to 1200, or even earlier, and forward to 1500, and occasionally a little later. Fourteenth-century Europe itself saw not only shifts in the routes of trade, both inside and outside Europe, but also a major reversal in many of its economies from expansion to contraction. This contraction, sometimes called the 'economic depression of the Renaissance', was associated with an extraordinary drop in the population of Europe, brought about by climatic deterioration and famines, followed by a long sequence of waves of bubonic plague. At the same time there was a radical shrinkage in the means of payment, whether in money or in credit, ultimately going back to the exhaustion of the silver mines of central Europe.

*Until 1344, when Edward III
began striking a gold coinage, only
silver coins were minted in
England. The gold noble (top),
one of the largest coins of late
medieval Europe, effectively
double the internationally used
florin of Florence, became the
standard gold coin for late
medieval England. Outside
England it circulated widely in
Scotland, and in Flanders,
England's principal trading
partner, and along the Hanseatic
commercial routes into the Baltic.
To emphasize his claim to
independent sovereignty over
Aquitaine, Edward III also struck
small numbers of gold coins there,
including the guyennois (below)
in 1360. Although magnified here
to the same size as the noble, it was
actually a much smaller coin.*

The longer time-span from before 1200 to after 1500 naturally comprises more long-term trends, starting early in the period of general expansion, and continuing beyond the period of general contraction into a fresh period of general expansion from the mid-fifteenth century onwards. These very long-term trends, it must be said, are more visible to us looking back at them than they were to contemporaries. Men do not generally think in such long time-spans. The longest that they can feel is their own life-time. The economist J. M. Keynes once commented on such over-long trends: 'In the long run we are all dead'. What concerned contemporaries is what concerns us now, the shorter-term booms and recessions, lasting only a few years. They, too, had trade-cycles. They, too, experienced over-production for markets that turned out to be not as large as they had expected or hoped. They, too, experienced competition for markets from foreign rivals, who seemed sometimes to have unfair advantages in manufacture, cheaper labour, or the ability to extend credit. They, too, gained or suffered in the short term from the actions of particular governments. Government policies were then much more rarely geared to economic ends, except in a very few states like the Venetian Republic. Nevertheless, some policies, particularly war, taxation and debasement of the coinage, often had considerable consequences for trade and industry.

Even more than these short-term movements, lasting a few years, and affecting different places in different ways, contemporaries were concerned with the annual cycle of agricultural production. In most developed countries today we are largely cushioned from glut and dearth in a way that our ancestors never were, and our contemporaries in less developed countries still are not. The relative success or failure of the wheat harvest on the American prairies still makes annual ripples on the markets of the developed world, but this is nothing compared with the effects of harvests in fourteenth-century Europe. Crop failure in northern Europe in 1316, on top of that in 1315, brought about widespread famine, disruption and death from Ireland to Poland. Famine meant death. One in every ten of the inhabitants of Ypres in Flanders, then a major manufacturing city for luxury woollen cloth for international markets, died in only four months in 1317, pauperized by starvation, and had to be buried at public expense.

Geographically this volume will be concerned largely with those places in Europe most influenced by the commercial revolution of the thirteenth century. These were, firstly and above all, the capital cities of Europe, in which were concentrated both the demand of huge numbers of ordinary people for food, and the desire of small numbers of very wealthy aristocrats and courtiers for high-priced luxuries, which two demands together created the trade of Europe. Secondly, there were the manufacturing and commercial centres of northern Italy, the southern Netherlands and later also southern Germany, which supplied many of these needs. Finally it will bring into focus, in a way that is often ignored, the mining regions of central Europe which provided the silver and gold without which a money-saturated economy could not have existed.

Beyond the capital cities, the commercial and industrial centres and the regions of Europe in which precious metals were mined, the scope of this volume extends outwards to encompass trade in grain from the Baltic and Black Sea coastlands, in cattle from Denmark and the Hungarian plain, in wool from the hills of England and the central plateau of Castile, in furs from Russia and Ireland, in ivory from African or Indian elephants, in silk from Sicily and China, in slaves from the Steppes and western Africa, in dyestuffs from Portugal and Java, in falcons from Iceland and in pearls from the Persian Gulf, in alum from Asia Minor and in pepper from southern India. In other words it will extend to all the places that supplied the basic materials for industry, as well as the foodstuffs necessary to keep the inhabitants of the cities alive, and the precious objects required to satisfy the aspirations of the most fastidious, or the most quixotic, of the nobility.

The genesis of this book lay in a study of the flows of bullion from those mining areas outwards, and some traces of its origin survive in a preoccupation with the routes of trade, particularly land routes, and with the scale and imbalances of trade between different regions of Europe, and between Europe and other parts of the world. For the purpose of writing *Money and its use in Medieval Europe*, I had already started looking at the balances of payments and the movements of silver and gold. It then became clear to me that, although political and religious factors played a part in the movements of bullion, trade was in the long run far more important. Only in the short run did political, or occasionally religious, actions have greater effects than trade balances on the large-scale movement of silver and gold, coined and uncoined. Trade balances, however, provided the basic and overwhelming reasons for normal and continuous movements of gold and silver, both within late medieval Europe and between Europe and other continents. Even when, as in the commercial relations between the most important centres in western Europe, individual transactions were paid for by bills of exchange, the ultimate imbalances were settled by movements of bullion. In regions of less balanced trade, for example in the Baltic or between central Europe and northern Italy, or between northern Italy and the Levant, immediate payments for goods were still most often made in precious metals.

The book begins, as medieval trade itself did, with consumers, and in particular with the concentration of consumers in the capital cities of western Europe. It brings out the importance of such cities as Paris and Milan, Avignon and Florence, London and Naples, Brussels and Rome as focal points for trade as well as for government and politics.

From the consumers, on whom medieval trade and industry were focused, attention will turn to the suppliers, and in particular the great multinational business houses with their holding companies in Tuscany, and later in southern Germany. The route from Paris, the greatest of the capital cities, to Florence, where so many medieval multinational companies had their head offices, will be looked at in detail. I shall next turn to various helps and some hindrances to trade, road improvements and bridge-building, the provision of inns and carrying services, as well as tolls, brigandage and state interference in trade.

I shall then look at some particular commodities in much more detail.

Two distraught caricature figures of merchants from an illuminated Bible to illustrate the passage from the book of Harley Apocalypse (English, thirteenth century): 'Fallen, fallen is Babylon the great!...And the merchants of the earth weep and mourn for her, since no-one buys their cargo any more, cargo of gold, silver, jewels and pearls, fine linen, purple, silk and scarlet, all kinds of scented wood, all articles of ivory, all articles of costly wood, bronze, iron, and marble, cinnamon, spice, incense, myrrh, frankincense, wine, olive oil, choice flour and wheat, cattle and sheep, horses and chariots, slaves – and human lives.... The merchants of these wares, who gained wealth from her, will stand far off, in fear of her torment, weeping and mourning aloud "Alas, alas...in one hour all this wealth has been laid waste!"'

Firstly I shall examine a range of industrial products, particularly fabrics and metal goods from the southern Netherlands, northern Italy and southern Germany, and then such luxury goods as Venetian glass, Faenza majolica, and Arras tapestries. An examination of various different industries brings out how very frequently new industries began as the production of substitutes for goods previously imported. After manufactured goods, I shall treat raw materials and foodstuffs, including wool and iron, cotton and copper, raw silk and spices, beer and wine, grain and timber, fur and leather, alum and dyestuffs and even pearls and jewels.

Only then will I turn to my original preoccupation with the imbalances in trade and the movements of gold and silver about Europe and look at the consequent importance of mining, or the failure to mine, precious metals, particularly in central Europe.

I shall conclude by looking at the changing geographical patterns of trade in the later Middle Ages. In the thirteenth century, the road and river network was dominated by a triangle of land routes, between a Bruges-focused Netherlands, a Florence-focused Tuscany and the Bohemian silver mines.

The fourteenth century saw a diffusion of land routes and the greater importance of sea transport, in a period of uncertain land travel. Late fifteenth-century European trade saw a return to road and river transport, as sea travel in the Mediterranean in turn became increasingly uncertain. At the same time, there was a new emphasis on south German merchants and manufacturers, who made the Antwerp–Nuremberg–Venice routes the new spine for European trade.

The commercial revolution of the thirteenth century

The major transitions in the methods of commerce in the thirteenth century are the vital background to the whole book. These changes were initiated by merchants from the great trading cities of northern and central Italy. In northern Italy, merchants from Genoa, Venice and Milan took the lead, followed by those from Asti, Piacenza and Bologna. In Tuscany and Umbria it was not only merchants from Florence who were involved, but also those from Lucca, Siena, Pisa, Perugia and even smaller cities like Prato. The extraordinary developments of the 'long thirteenth century' in such fields as banking were not lost in the succeeding period of contraction. There was no going back once these innovations had taken place. Indeed some developments, like the holding company and marine insurance, belong to the period of contraction. Furthermore the commercial techniques developed in northern and central Italy began to spread across the Alps to southern Germany at this very time. However, the continued importance of less advanced business methods, regional fairs and the restraint of trade through staple-rights (see below, p. 47), must be stressed, alongside the most sophisticated north Italian developments in international banking, commercial insurance and accounting.

The thirteenth-century increase in the demand for luxury goods was backed up by newly liberated quantities of ready cash, arising from a revolution in rents. By the end of the century landlords essentially collected their

rents in money in place of a mixture of goods, services and coin, amongst which coin had been the least important. It is no wonder that this demand for distant luxuries brought about an enormous quantitative change in the volume of international trade. Moreover, as business became focused on a limited number of particular places, or rather along a limited number of routes between those places, a critical mass was reached, so that qualitative as well as merely quantitative changes in the nature of commerce began to take place. This vital transformation could only happen when the concentrated supply of money, and consequently of trade, rose beyond a certain critical point.

Up to that point, on any particular route, all that occurred was an increase in the volume of trade within the traditional framework. Italian merchants, for example, merely added extra mules loaded with goods to the mule-trains that accompanied them when they ventured northwards across the Alps. However, once the critical point was reached, the scale of enterprises allowed for a division of labour.

After that point, businesses became large enough and continuous enough to maintain three separate parties: the sedentary merchants remaining full-time in northern Italy, who specialized in the financing and organization of import-export trade; the specialist carriers, whether *vectuarii* by land, or shipowners by sea, who took the goods from the principals to their agents; and thirdly the full-time agents themselves, resident overseas or beyond the Alps, who devoted their energies to sales or purchases according to the instructions sent to them by their principals.

Such a threefold division of labour naturally took place first on the routes along which demand was most concentrated at an early date, i.e. on those which ran from the ports of northern Italy to the Levant. From the twelfth century colonies of Venetian, Genoese and Pisan agents came to live permanently at Acre, Alexandria and Constantinople. Only a little later, similar north Italian colonies began to be found in Rome, Naples and Palermo and at the fairs of Champagne. At the same time colonies of agents from other cities settled within the cities of northern Italy itself. Later still, by the end of the thirteenth century, they existed in the northern capitals of Paris and London, and also at some of the greater ports with wealthy hinterlands, such as Bruges, Seville, Barcelona and Montpellier.

Often these merchant colonies were very loosely organized, but in other places they were strictly regimented, either by their own wish or because of the insistence of the host community. The very large Genoese community at Pera, outside Constantinople, described by contemporaries as a 'second Genoa', was one of these. At Acre the quarters given over to the Venetians, Genoese and Pisans took up so much of the town that it was virtually another Italian city.

The Christian enclaves within Islamic lands were particularly tightly controlled. Here the host community set aside a segregated part of the city,

Giovanni Arnolfini, painted here by Jan van Eyck after 1434, exemplifies the large number of Italian businessmen resident for long periods in other parts of Europe. He was the most prominent member of the large 'nation' of merchants from Lucca resident in mid-fifteenth-century Bruges, and much involved in the import of luxurious silk fabrics from Italy. He was already sufficiently established by 1422–3 to be able to supply the ruler, Philip the Good, with six expensive tapestries, for sending to Pope Martin V 'so that his holiness would maintain the duke in his favour'.

The merchant who did not travel

Merchants abroad

Francesco della Chiesa was another Italian businessman resident abroad. He was a member of the Genoese community resident in Valencia in the late fifteenth century. Like Arnolfini he turned to a prominent local painter when he wanted a triptych to send home, and had himself painted in as the donor. This detail is from B. Bermaja triptych of the Virgin of Montserrat.

In De' Barbari's view of Venice in 1500, the 'Fondaco dei Tedeschi', the accommodation provided by the state for German merchants, can be seen on the right of the Rialto bridge, labelled 'fontego dalamanj'. Immediately on the other side of the bridge was the main financial quarter of the city, the 'Island of the Rialto'.

known as a *funduk*, in which there was residential accommodation for western merchants, warehousing for their goods, Latin Christian chapels for their worship, and sometimes even bath-houses for their exclusive use. Some of these quarters, like those of the Italian communities in Alexandria, were very considerable. Such large communities had consuls who represented the home government to the residents, and kept law and order within the *funduk*, bargained with the authorities of the host state for privileges, and registered protests against breaches of such privileges. The succession of consuls appointed to have oversight of the large Venetian community at Alexandria has been established from 1302 to 1498. They had vice-consuls to look after the smaller Venetian community at Damietta, itself a fairly considerable port on another mouth of the Nile. The Venetian communities in Syria came under the jurisdiction of a different consul based in the fifteenth century at Damascus, not on the coast. Those at Beirut, the port for Damascus and at Tripoli, the port for Aleppo, were looked after by vice-consuls of the Damascus consul. These consuls were often drawn from the grandest families of the Venetian nobility and included members of the Mocenigo, Morosini, Dandolo families which also produced Doges.[2]

Other *funduks* were tiny and cramped, like some in the Maghreb. In the mid-fourteenth century there were colonies of merchants from Pisa, Florence and Genoa in all the major north African ports on the Barbary coast from Safi (in modern Morocco) to Tunis. There were also colonies of Catalan merchants from Barcelona in at least some of them, like Bejaia (Bougie) and Tunis. Some of these communities were very long lasting. Tunis is a good example. Here, the Genoese had a church of their own in the late twelfth century. In 1261, the consuls of the Catalan community were not only administering justice to the resident merchants and providing a notary to register contracts, but, within their quarter, had a bakery to lease out as well as a tavern and several shops. The king of Aragon provided their permanent chaplain. By 1351 the Pisans had a bakery, and their own cemetery as well as a

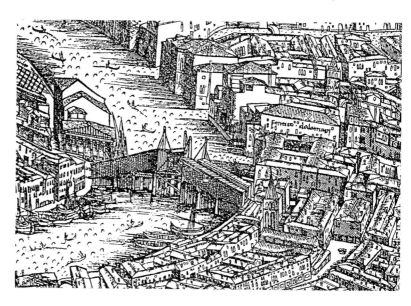

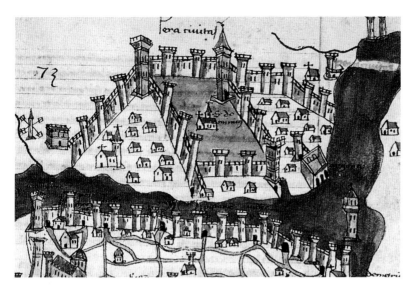

The largest group of Italians abroad was the Genoese community at Pera (Galata) opposite Constantinople on the north side of the Golden Horn. The complex of walls in this late fifteenth-century map shows not only the initial thirteenth-century walled colony, but also the fortifications of the new suburbs of its fourteenth-century expansion. Their bitter rivals, the Venetians, had wharves on the city side of the harbour.

church. At the same time, the Florentines were numerous enough to support their own customs official.[3] Despite all these facilities, conditions were still very closed-in and fairly unnatural in these small émigré communities, made up predominantly of young men. The lack of women was particularly marked, although some Genoese had wives and concubines with them in Tunis. Relations with the host community were often precarious. When the Venetians and Genoese walled in and fortified their enclaves in Tabriz, in the hope of providing some protection for their nationals, it so aggravated their Persian hosts that they were expelled instead.

The *funduk* formula was adapted by the Venetians for the 'German' merchants who came to Venice from across the Alps. The city provided them with warehousing and residential accommodation in the 'Fondaco dei Tedeschi' (see below p. 352). It was not only in the Mediterranean that such particular foreign groups had separate accommodation. The Hanseatic merchants in northern Europe also had communal accommodation on a grand scale, as in the enclosed 'Peterhof' in Novgorod and the 'Steelyard' in London, at two of the end points of their trading activities, and on a smaller scale, and unenclosed, at their 'Kontor', with its warehouses on the dockside in Bergen, smaller still at their warehouse in King's Lynn on the east coast of England. Even this last still combined chambers for goods with chambers for people, and opened at the one end to shipping at the quay, and at the other on to one of the main streets of the town.

Even where commercial inns, or rented property, were normally used by foreign merchants, and fully equipped warehouses and residential accommodation were not provided for a particular national group, they often had some sort of consular building of their own, as the Venetians, Genoese, Florentines and English all did at Bruges.[4] William Caxton, later famous as England's first printer, was head of the English community at Bruges. Over time, some of these consular houses grew more complex. Some of the *panden* (courtyard houses) of the foreign merchants in sixteenth-century Antwerp, the English

The figures on the Campo dei Mori, made more enigmatic by the later addition of turbans, are supposed to represent members of the Mastelli family. Their palazzo nearby has a camel on its façade, as an allusion to the camel caravans which brought to the ports of the eastern Mediterranean the oriental goods that they imported into Europe.

One of the routes of the Itinéraire de Bruges *of use to both merchants and pilgrims was that from Bruges up the Rhine and across the Alps to Milan, Florence and Rome. The* Itinéraire *is divided up into numerous short sections. The three sections shown from this route (opposite) are from Cologne up the road on the west bank of the Rhine to Basel; from Basel over the St Gotthard pass to Como; and from Como south towards Rome through Milan, Bologna and Florence. The distances north of the St Gotthard are given in leagues, but those south of the pass in miles. North of Milan this was the route used by the Florentine couriers who carried the* scarselle fiorentine *to Bruges.*

house for example, seem almost as large and well equipped as a fully blown Hanseatic warehouse or Italian *funduk*.

In addition it was very common, even within Europe, for foreign merchants to have a place of worship of their own. The Catalan and Lucchese colonies in fifteenth-century Bruges had their own chapels in the Carmelite and Augustinian friary churches in the town, whilst the Florentine colony in late fifteenth-century Lyons had its chapel in the Dominican church.[5]

Jews, as foreigners everywhere, lived under more or less restricted circumstances, freely or tightly bound depending on the attitudes of their 'hosts'. Sometimes a Jewish quarter was closed off in the same way as a *funduk*, like the 'Call' in Majorca.[6] Sometimes Jews were free to live anywhere in a city, as in Venice, but this liberty ended early in the sixteenth century, when they were compelled to live in a specifically Jewish quarter by the foundry, the *ghetto*.[7]

This transformation of commerce, by which the peripatetic merchant moving about western Europe and the Mediterranean with his goods was replaced by several different men with specialized functions, only became possible in turn in those areas in which a sufficient amount of money and a sufficient scale of demand came to be concentrated. Even on these routes, merchants trading on a smaller scale continued to travel with their goods. Even in the 1320s over 150 Catalan merchants still made an annual trip from Barcelona to Barbary, even though there had been communities of resident Catalans in some of the cities of the Maghreb for a century or more. In the second half of the thirteenth century, one of the consuls of the Catalan community had been living there continuously, as consul, for twenty years.

The byproducts of this revolutionary commercial division of labour have been increasingly understood by historians since the Belgian businessman and scholar Raymond de Roover first pointed out its essential elements at a meeting of the American Business Historical Society in 1941.[8]

Trading companies

Partnerships and financing, which had previously lasted only for a single voyage, took on a more permanent aspect in the thirteenth century, lasting for terms of several years, and often renewed on a similar basis for a further period.[9] In Tuscany, in particular, partnership was extended enormously. The capital of one of the largest companies, the Bardi of Florence, when renewed for twenty-one years in 1310, was divided into as many as fifty-six shares.[10] Such shares were transferable without breaking up the partnership. They were held not only by members of the families of the founders, and by the principal employees, who were encouraged to invest their own savings, but also by other rich men, who were not at all involved in the actual running of the company.

In addition to the *corpo*, that is, the capital raised by the shareholders when a company was formed or re-formed, additional capital could be put in later, by shareholders, by employees and by outsiders. Such *denari fuori del corpo* carried fixed rates of interest, like modern debentures. Many Tuscan companies from the thirteenth century onwards used short-term borrowing at low fixed interest, *fuori del corpo* or *sopracorpo*, beyond or above the *corpo*, to increase their resources. The extraordinarily extensive way in which rich Florentines invested in the *sopracorpo* of trading companies is clearly revealed by their returns of capital for tax purposes in 1427. International Italian trading companies seem to have been prepared to accept deposits at any of their branches. In the first half of the fourteenth century great English noblemen placed appreciable funds with the London branches of Florentine companies. The Earl of Lincoln had money with the Frescobaldi, the Earl of Hereford with the Pulci, and the younger Despenser with the Bardi and Peruzzi. One of the most remarkable examples of the extent to which medieval Italian companies relied on such extra funds is the Medici company at Rome, which in the mid-fifteenth century was not only run entirely on deposits, without any share capital of its own after 1426, but was also able to provide operating capital for other companies in the Medici group.[11]

The sedentary merchant at home was thus no longer a simple individual capitalist. As head of a company he was also a manager responsible to his shareholders, and to his depositors.

The evolution of the company with transferable shares had certainly taken place by the early fourteenth century, and probably already by the mid-thirteenth. It is not entirely clear how this had been accomplished. In the early thirteenth century the most common form of arrangement had still been, as in the mid-twelfth, for an investor to enter into a *commenda* contract with a merchant, by which he commended a sum of money to the merchant for a particular trading venture. Any profit made by trading with the money was split between the merchant and the investor. Inventories after death, drawn up by notaries, reveal both merchants with many investors in their enterprises, and investors dividing their money between many different enterprises.

The evolution from this multitude of bilateral short-term investment arrangements to shareholding over a longer term coincided with, and seems to have been intimately bound up with, the other aspects of the so-called commercial revolution of the thirteenth century. In the early fourteenth century, the greatest companies of Florence, such as those of the Bardi, the Peruzzi, the Acciaiuoli and the Buonaccorsi, were all modelled in this new way. They all had speculative capital, the *corpo* of the shareholders, tied up for time-spans of up to twenty-one years. In the fifteenth and sixteenth centuries in southern Germany the great trading companies followed the Italian pattern, although often for shorter periods in the first instance. Some are known that were set up for as long as twelve years, but most were for only five or six years. The Meuting firm in Augsburg, for example, was set up in 1436 for a five-year term, and the great Ravensburg company in 1386 for six years, and so were the Welser companies of Augsburg and Nuremberg, and the Fugger company of Augsburg in 1494 and again in 1502, although later renewals were for eight years at a time.[12]

Many, but far from all, of these shares were held by family members, and companies were not necessarily even run by members of the families whose names they bore. By the 1340s the key figure in the Buonaccorsi company, the fourth biggest in Florence, was not a Buonaccorsi, but Giovanni Villani. Shares or fractions of shares could already be sold without breaking up the company. When the contracted period had elapsed, capital and accumulated profits were nominally distributed to shareholders, but most shareholders seemed to prefer that their money be re-invested at once in a fresh company for a further period. The Ravensburg company, the 'Grosse Ravensburger Gesellschaft', was repeatedly renewed in this way for successive six-year terms from 1386 to 1524. At the end of the fifteenth century there were eighty shareholders involved in one of these reconstitutions.[13]

Similar companies with shareholders were also created for owning and operating other enterprises which lasted for more than a short period, like mines, mills and ships. Even the companies which leased and operated the Venetian galleys had a capital divided into shares, normally twenty-four.

As well as the expansion of firms at home, which mobilized such large amounts of capital, there was an equivalent expansion of the scale of enterprises abroad. It was perfectly possible to repeat the principal–agent relationship over and over again, with agents of the same principal in many different places. The earliest such multi-branched companies, for example the Chiarenti of Pistoia,[14] or the Cerchi and Velluti of Florence, came into existence in the middle years of the thirteenth century. The Velluti soon had branches at Pisa, the papal curia, Bologna, Milan, Genoa, Paris and London.[15] By the 1340s the Peruzzi and Acciaiuoli of Florence had branches in nearly a score of places, from Bruges and London to Rhodes and Famagusta, including permanent factors in the Florentine *funduk* in Tunis, besides being in correspondence with agents in numerous other cities in the Mediterranean and western Europe.

The 1340s saw many of the largest multi-branched firms in western Europe forced into bankruptcy. Whole companies collapsed when affairs went wrong at single branches, because they were unitary enterprises. These included the three largest, the Bardi, the Peruzzi and the Acciaiuoli of Florence, whilst the fourth biggest, the Buonaccorsi, went into liquidation under suspicious circumstances for which its managing director, Giovanni Villani, spent time in prison. The consequence of this wave of bankruptcies was the creation of groups of companies. In these, every branch or enterprise was separate, each with its own capital and shareholders, although there was a holding company which dominated them all. The earliest tentative move towards such a group structure of which we are aware was that of the Alberti in the third quarter of the fourteenth century. In the early fifteenth century the Datini group had this sort of structure. So did the Medici group in the mid-fifteenth century.[16] None of these company groups, however, surpassed the Bardi or Peruzzi in overall size until the Fugger group did so in the sixteenth century. This type of structure remained the way to manage large international enterprises until the nineteenth century. The enterprises grew bigger, but the structure remained the same.

The transferability of shares goes back to around the time when companies first began to be set up for a fixed time-span, and was a natural corollary of it. From the early fourteenth-century records of the Florentine Bardi company, we know when and to whom shares or parts of shares were transferred, for this concerned the company, but not for how much, nor how the sale was arranged. At about the same time a market for state bonds came into existence in Venice, Genoa and Florence. Shares in the *monte*, the consolidated debt, of these states were traded sufficiently commonly for historians to be able to reconstruct the market price per hundred florins or ducats of *monte* obligations over long periods of time. The earliest quotations for Venice are from the second half of the thirteenth century. How far arrangements to purchase shares in companies and shares in the *monte* were carried out in the same way is unknowable, but at some point, maybe even at the very beginning, they came together as a single market. Until the seventeenth century such evidence as we have relates mostly to the market in government stock, not in company shares. The recording of the transfer of shares was not a problem for a company with relatively few shareholders. The Bardi could do it easily.

Commercial correspondence, which had been unnecessary when the merchant had his own goods under his own eyes and struck personal bargains with sellers and buyers, became much more prolific, and courier services developed between the main commercial centres in the thirteenth century. From 1260 onwards we have scattered evidence that regular and dependable courier services had already, probably fairly recently, come into existence between the commercial centres of Tuscany and the fairs of Champagne.[17] Their name *scarselle* literally meant the leather pouches in which couriers carried the correspondence. In the fourteenth and fifteenth centuries these services became more and more organized. In 1357, in the period of reconstruction after the crashes of the 1340s, seventeen Florentine merchant companies agreed together to found a common courier service, the *scarsella dei mercanti fiorentini*. The implication is surely that, until then, the companies had run their own individual services. Running a regular courier service was an expensive business. It involved not only the payment and maintenance of an adequately sized group of couriers for each route, but also access to an enormous numbers of horses, which had to be available for frequent changes of mount at suitable intervals all along the routes. That so many courier services developed in the later Middle Ages indicates how much the Italian business communities valued them.

By the early fifteenth century there were a number of important regular commercial courier services. The two *scarselle fiorentine* consisted of regular services from Florence and Pisa to Barcelona and to Bruges. There were two services to Bruges, one by way of Milan and Cologne, the other by way of Paris. The *scarsella lucchese* ran from Lucca and Pisa to Bruges. The two *scarselle genovesi* ran from Genoa to Bruges and to Barcelona, and sometimes on to Seville, whilst the two *scarselle catalane*, in the opposite direction, ran from Barcelona to Bruges, and to Pisa and Florence. There are also some

Commercial correspondence and couriers

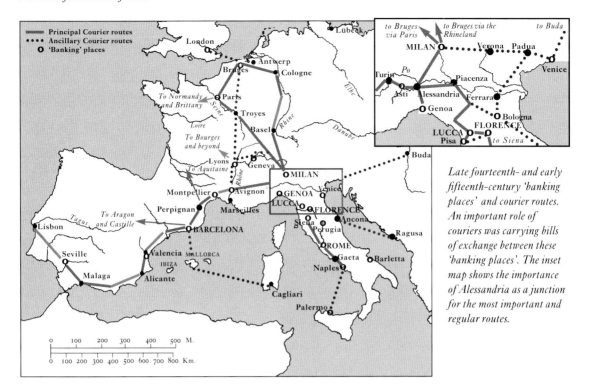

Late fourteenth- and early fifteenth-century 'banking places' and courier routes. An important role of couriers was carrying bills of exchange between these 'banking places'. The inset map shows the importance of Alessandria as a junction for the most important and regular routes.*

The couriers, normally mounted but shown here delivering a letter, maintained regular services used by merchants. The letter-bag, scarsella in Italian, which gave its name to some of the Italian courier services, is very evident. Woodcut by Hans Guldenmund of Nuremberg, sixteenth century.

indications of a *scarsella dei lombardi*, between the Lombard cities and Barcelona. Later in the century, there were *poste di Milano* joining Milan to Naples by way of Florence and Rome.[18] As well as these longer-distance courier services there were numerous and frequent shorter-distance services within northern Italy. The twice-weekly service between Venice and Lucca is revealed in a letter of Giovanni Lazzari in Venice, replying to one from Guisfredo Cenami, a silk manufacturer of Lucca, on 7 March 1375, which begins: 'You say that in the space of two days you have received four letters of mine. I am sending them in the usual way every Wednesday and Saturday.' Cenami's own letter had taken a week to arrive.[19] In addition to these standard services there were numerous other couriers on the road. Some were hired for particular occasions. In 1425–26, when Rinaldo degli Albizzi spent six months in Rome as Florentine ambassador to Pope Martin V, he was in frequent correspondence with the priors and the committee for war in Florence. He used his own personal servant as a special courier for important letters, but normally relied on the regular weekly postal service between Rome and Florence, which arrived in Rome on Fridays and left for Florence on Sundays. His letter-book also reveals that the leading Florentine business houses in Rome still maintained their own private messengers in addition to the *procaccio* couriers, and Rinaldo degli Albizzi sometimes consigned his official letters to them as well.[20] Some courier services were organized as businesses by commercial *maestri dei corrieri*. The courier firm run by Antonio di Bartolomeo del Vantaggio was operating on a vast number of routes, including a weekly service leaving Florence every Saturday for Venice in the 1470s.

In the early 1420s Giovanni da Uzzanno recorded in his notebook that commercial couriers from Florence were expected to reach agents in Rome, nearly 300 km away, in 5 or 6 days; agents in Naples, nearly 500 km away, in 11 or 12 days; agents in Paris in 20 to 22 days; in Bruges, nearly 1,400 km distant, in under 25 days; and in Seville, nearly 2,000 km away, in under 32 days.[21] The Italian times suggest an average of around 50 km a day. Once the Alps had been crossed, it was possible to travel rather faster across France. A courier who travelled from Chalon to Paris in 6 days in 1400 was averaging well over 60 km a day. Phenomenal speeds could be achieved if pressed. A fourteenth-century papal courier once managed to average 150 km per day from Avignon to Paris, as fast as the young Florentine nobleman Buonaccorso Pitti claimed when he was an exile in France fighting for the king of France. With self-conscious pride he remembered in his book of *ricordanze* that he had once covered the 153 km from Troyes to Paris in a single day.[22] These speeds can be compared with around 30 or 40 kms a day normally covered by pack animals and carriers' wagons (see below pp. 200–1).

The quantity of post being carried may be gauged from the fact that the surviving letters and account books of the companies of the Datini group, from the last years of the fourteenth century and the first years of the fifteenth, produced clear evidence for 320,000 dates of despatch and receipt of letters and bills. From these Professor Melis and his pupils were able to work out the pattern of courier services and the normal times taken.[23]

Their analysis showed that, although Uzzanno's expectations may have been more or less correct, in real life the delivery times for individual letters could be extremely variable. The 17,000 letters between Florence and Genoa normally took 5 to 7 days to deliver, as did the 7,000 letters between Florence and Venice. Outside northern Italy delivery times were not so consistent. The 13,000 letters sent between Barcelona and Valencia normally took between 3 and 6 days to arrive. If a greater distance was involved, including travel by boat, the times taken were even more variable. The 348 letters between London and Naples varied in delivery times from 27 to 75 days, although most arrived between 32 and 54 days after despatch. This should be compared with Uzzanno's note that letters from Florence to London (over 1,500 km plus the Channel crossing) should take under 30 days. Real couriers could travel faster than expectations, as well as a great deal slower. Water could be faster than land, for most of the 493 letters between Venice and Constantinople were delivered in 34 to 46 days. It was possible for most Datini managers, agents and correspondents to communicate with head office at least weekly and with each other scarcely less frequently, and the Datini group of companies seems only to have been unusual in that the letters were preserved. This phenomenal degree of contact, and the continual flow of business information between members of north Italian commercial groups gave Italian entrepreneurs an edge over non-Italian competitors. Florentine, Lucchese, Pisan, Venetian, Genoese and Milanese businessmen abroad were able to bargain in the light of accurate knowledge of their markets and have supplies sent to them to meet specific known demand.

Dürer has caught something of the urgency with which armed couriers traversed the roads of late medieval Europe. Since couriers carried paperwork, not valuables, they were not a target for brigands, and a sword, well used, was enough to deter the casual robber.

This Austrian playing card shows a late fifteenth-century courier (Bott) delivering a sealed document. At this time the archduke of Austria was also Emperor, so it was natural for an Austrian playing card to show one of the imperial couriers, complete with badge of office, run for Maximilian by the Taxis family.

In the fifteenth century, south German cities imitated this Italian 'postal' organization, like so many of the other Italian commercial innovations. The increasingly important commercial and industrial communities in these cities became intensely conscious of the importance for business of up-to-date information and frequent contact. By the end of the century, the centre of this new communications network was the courier service that joined Nuremberg to Augsburg in each direction three times a week. In addition, Nuremberg couriers regularly travelled the road to Venice, and Augsburg couriers presumably already did the same, as they certainly did in the sixteenth century. The Augsburg courier ordinance of 1555 stipulated that a courier should collect letters in the city every Saturday for delivery in Venice the following Saturday. Fifteenth-century Augsburg couriers certainly went once a week to Regensburg, and also to Strasbourg, which also maintained its own courier services under an *oberbote* (head courier), appointed by the city.[24] All this fifteenth-century activity was confined to the south of Germany. It was not until the sixteenth century that Hamburg organized the first regular courier services in the north of the country.

Courier services run by business communities and by their cities were not the only ones. Religious orders maintained them to keep in touch, like the *bryff-jongen* (letter boys) of the Teutonic order. With the development of a pattern of resident ambassadors in the fifteenth century, courier services came to be maintained by various states to keep the ambassadors in contact with their Secretaries of State at home. The letters home of the Milanese ambassadors at the Burgundian court in Brussels reveal that state correspondence could be entrusted to commercial or ecclesiastical couriers when there were no official ones available[25]. This worked reciprocally, so that commercial letters were carried in state or ecclesiastical pouches. For example, commercial letters were carried by the state courier service run, from around 1489, by the Taxis family for the archduke Maximilian, initially between Innsbruck in his ancestral Austria and Brussels or Mechelen (Malines) in his son's Burgundian state. These were the beginnings of the extensive Habsburg imperial post. According to the Memmingen Chronicle in 1490 there were post-stations every 30 km all the way from Innsbruck to the Netherlands, with accommodation for men and horses. By changing both men and horses, greater speeds could be achieved. When pressed, distances of up to 200 km could be covered in a single day, although 100 to 140 km a day was more normal. In the early years his postal service cost Maximilian up to 5,000 gulden a year. However, by 1516 so many 'private' letters were being carried by the Taxis postal system that it could afford to carry imperial letters free of charge, and still make a handsome profit.[26]

With such courier services available it was possible for those who took the trouble in any of the key commercial centres of Europe to find out what was going on in the others. North Italian business letters survive from the mid-thirteenth century onwards conveying such knowledge, e.g. Tolomei, 1265, Champagne to Siena. At the end of the fourteenth century, Datini, and his contemporaries with initiative, had *listini dei prezzi*, which enabled them to know the prices of a range of commodities in a wide variety of places. In the Datini papers *listini* survive from the years 1383–1430 from places as widely separated as Damascus and London. The tradition continued into the Fugger newsletters, and on to printed commercial newsletters. A printed commodity price current was certainly published in Antwerp in 1540, but earlier publication has been suggested for Venice and, perhaps, even before 1500, for Lyons, continuing in the tradition of the manuscript *listini dei prezzi*. As well as commodity prices, rates of exchange were essential information. In sixteenth-century Antwerp they were not only officially determined, but officially promulgated in 1540, and had perhaps already been in the 1530s.[27]

Commercial accounting, which had also been rudimentary, and even largely unnecessary, when the merchant could deal with his customers personally, came to be essential and indeed complex, as business firms had to deal with shareholders, suppliers, customers, multiple branches and associated companies over long distances and long periods of time. Any sizable company needed many different sets of books, with different functions. That double-entry bookkeeping had developed by the end of the thirteenth century is undisputed. What is debated is whether it was a Genoese or a Tuscan innovation. It was certainly the most significant of advances in accounting, and when, later, adopted elsewhere, was often described as 'Italian'. The early modern dissemination of Italian double-entry bookkeeping followed on from the publication of Luca Pacioli's *Summa de Arithmetica*, the first edition of which was printed in Venice in 1494.[28]

The huge numbers of letters sent and received, and the large numbers of different account books that needed to be kept, demanded that the whole business class was thoroughly literate and numerate. The Italian cities which led the commercial revolution were also leaders in numeracy and literacy. There is a lack of surviving documentation from the thirteenth century itself, but those sources that do still exist hint at the extensive availability of suitable teaching in the key cities. In around 1200 Fibonacci of Pisa went off to the Arabic world, and on his return wrote a mathematical text book, which was widely copied, that made Hindu-Arabic numerals available to north Italians, by itself a huge step forward for commercial accounting.[29] In 1221, a Genoese father hired a notary, who also taught a school, to board and instruct his son for five years; in 1248, a Genoese banker had a teacher for his two sons. A lay teacher of boys, the first of many, appears in a Florentine document of 1275, and a Venetian teacher in 1287. There is more complete information from Milan. In 1288 it had not only eight 'professors of grammar' but also seventy or more teaching lower levels. As well as teachers of reading, writing and grammar, teachers of commercial arithmetic are also known from the thirteenth century.

Secular, vernacular education was well established by the early fourteenth century. In the new flood of surviving documentation after 1300, there appears also a flood of schoolteachers, in Liguria, Lombardy, the Veneto and

Bookkeeping, literacy and commercial arithmetic

Fibonacci's Liber abbaci, *which made the use of Arabic numerals accessible to Italians, allowed more complex problems in commercial arithmetic to be solved than could be managed before. Calculating exchange rates, translating weights and measures from one place to another, and even reckoning compound interest, as here, were now manageable.*

Tuscany.[30] In the commercial and industrial city of Lucca, the home of the earliest large-scale Italian manufacture of silken fabrics, the commune itself, in the 1350s, funded not only an elementary reading and writing teacher and an arithmetic and geometry instructor, but also a grammarian, a teacher of notarial skills, and a master of logic and philosophy. The first record of the commune paying for an *abbachista*, a teacher of commercial arithmetic, comes from 1345. He also taught bookkeeping, and served as an accountant to the commune, with a rent-free house. The rationale for the commune's expenditure was that the citizens of Lucca were 'much engaged in business, which can hardly be carried on if one is ignorant in arithmetic and abacus'. The commune's provision of part of the appropriate educational infrastructure no doubt helped to keep Lucchese businessmen prominent in international trade through the fifteenth century into the sixteenth.

As well as the possession of a knowledge of commercial arithmetic by those engaged in running businesses, there was also a much wider basic ability to read in these cities. Giovanni Villani's figures for Florence in 1338 have been interpreted to mean that 37–45% of the school-age population were then receiving basic schooling. These figures have been disputed, and, unlike most of Villani's figures, may be somewhat exaggerated. Even though the extent of mass reading ability in mid-fourteenth-century Florence may be questioned, its existence is not – most artisans in Florence were certainly literate. In the shrunken Florence of the 1480s at least 28% of boys aged 6–14 still attended formal school.[31] Villani also reported the existence of six active *abbaco* schools there, and of these there is no doubt. A sizeable minority of Florentine boys attended these specialized schools after they had mastered reading and then writing. When Master Benedetto took over one of these *botteghe del'abbaco* in 1440, after the death of his master, he claimed that he was the successor to a long line of named arithmetic teachers stretching back to the very beginning of the fourteenth century, all teaching on the same site, by the Trinità bridge and church, where the *abbachiste* had their own chapel.[32] A much smaller minority went on to acquire a Latin education, which did not have the same practical advantages.

The evidence from fifteenth-century southern Germany is even more tantalizing than that from thirteenth-century northern Italy, but suggests that the south German cities exactly reflected the earlier Italian model of a drive towards literacy and numeracy for commercial purposes of both merchants and artisans.

The Libro di Mercatantie, *put together in Florence in the 1420s (see p. 53), became the prototype for merchant manuals elsewhere, first naturally in Nuremberg and other parts of southern Germany. The message conveyed by the cover of this south German manual is quite clear: the successful merchant calculates and keeps account books carefully.*

Insurance

Another of the consequences of the threefold division between sedentary merchant, carrier and agent was the development of insurance for goods whilst in transit, when they were outside the control of either the merchant at home in Italy or his distant employees or trusted correspondents abroad. When merchants had travelled with their goods, they could attempt to protect them, and when they could not, as when a ship foundered, they were at risk of perishing too. The sedentary merchant wished to spread the risks of transit, particularly at sea, and to achieve this security insurance was devised.

Primitive methods of spreading risks were tried out in the thirteenth century, when the 'insurance loan' was developed. In this system a shipowner advanced to a merchant, who was shipping goods with him, a sum which covered the value, or more usually a part of the value, of the goods being shipped. If the goods failed to arrive the merchant kept the advance as some compensation for his loss. If the goods arrived safely, the merchant repaid the loan along with charges for freight and for risk (*per nolo e rischio*). Such an arrangement certainly discouraged dishonest shippers, but was not altogether adequate.

Insurance, as we understand it, does not seem to have begun until some date in the first half of the fourteenth century.[33] The oldest surviving indisputably clear policies of marine insurance go back to 1350, when, by a notarized contract *ex causa assecurationis*, a Genoese merchant in Palermo, Leonardo Cattaneo underwrote a shipload of wheat being sent from Sicily to Tunis. He was paid a premium of 54 florins, *pro qua securitate*, to insure the wheat, worth 300 florins, *super omni risicum, periculum et fortunam dei maris et gentium* ('against all perils or misfortunes from the sea or from men'), and promised to pay 300 florins one month after receiving certain news of the

Although Luca Pacioli (1445–1517) was a Franciscan friar, he led a far from humble life. He was a flamboyant self-publicising professor of mathematics who prided himself on the aristocratic audiences who flocked to his lectures in virtually every Italian university and court from Naples to Milan. His Summa de Arithmetica, *Venice, 1494, was a vast encyclopaedia of mathematics and commercial arithmetic, which printed for the first time many of the most commonly available mathematical works of late medieval Italy, including a treatise on double-entry bookkeeping which has become associated with his name. This portrait is by Jacopo de' Barbari.*

cargo's complete loss, and a proportionate amount if the loss was only partial.[34] Since Palermo was not at the centre of commercial innovation and the form of contract appears already fully developed, we can only assume that Cattaneo was engaging in an underwriting activity already being practised at home in Genoa, and presumably developed either there, or in Venice, Pisa, or Florence. This assumption is reinforced by hints, a generation earlier, in the account books of the Peruzzi in Florence in 1320, and of Duccio de Banchello in Venice in 1336, that premiums were being paid for insurance. The old 'insurance loans' continued, however, alongside the new 'premium insurance' contracts, until the 1360s at least.

As with exchange contracts, which were first notarized and then merely entered in the books of the bankers involved, so, by the end of the century, insurance policies in Pisa were being drawn up in Italian by insurance brokers rather than in Latin by notaries. The brokers were engaged in forming syndicates of underwriters who shared in the risk. In 1396, for example, the Pisan firm in the Datini group was one of fourteen underwriters for 1,250 florins worth of wool and leather being shipped from Majorca to Venice. No single underwriter bore more than 200 florins of risk. In 1400 Datini wrote to his Majorcan agents, reprimanding them for breaking his self-imposed rules: he had shared in underwriting more than a thousand policies, and on principle had never borne more than 150 florins of risk at a time. He also insisted that all his own goods should be insured. Many of these policies were underwritten by his Pisan firm on cargoes being shipped from Porto Pisano, the outport of Pisa. In 1384 one of its memorandum books noted rates of 4% on cargoes shipped from Porto Pisano to Naples, Palermo, Tunis and Barcelona. In the 1430s Jacomo Badoer, a Venetian at Constantinople, noted insurance rates of 6% for cargoes on the longer journey from Constantinople to Venice. The rate of premium varied not only according to distance, but also according to the season of the year, conditions of war or peace, and whether pirates were known to be active. Giovanni da Uzzanno, in his notebook, compiled in the early 1420s, noted that the premium from London to Porto Pisano was 'normally between 12% and 15% of the value, but occasionally even higher when there were rumours about dangers from pirates or otherwise' (*sempre e da fiorini 12 in 15 per 100 di valuta, e quando piue, secondo i pericoli che sentono o di corsali o daltro*). The account books of Bernardo Cambi, who was underwriting in Florence from 1450 to 1477, suggest either that Uzzanno was unduly pessimistic, or that conditions had improved. He shared in insuring cargoes in Genoese *nefs* from Southampton to Porto Pisano for 7%, 9% and 10%, and in the Burgundian galleys operated by the Medici for 6%. He also shared in underwriting goods on the comparable journey from Sluys, the outport of Bruges, to Porto Pisano for 5%. What is clear from the Cambi account books is that insurance premiums for goods shipped by galley were always appreciably less than for goods in other sorts of ship.

Like Francesco Datini at the beginning of the century, the Medici later insisted that their managers in Bruges and London saw to it that goods were always insured in transit, unless shipped aboard the armed Florentine or

Gold and silver being transported with an armed guard. On occasions when bills of exchange were not usable and which could not be insured, reliance had to be placed on an adequate troop of cavalry to provide safety en route. Here the troops of Baldwin, Archbishop of Trier, are escorting treasure wagons on their way to the Alps in 1310, for the Emperor Henry VII's journey to Rome for his coronation. From the manuscript Kaiser Heinrichs Romfahrt, c. *1340.*

Venetian galleys. The Medici firms themselves engaged in a little underwriting. In 1445, for example, the manager of the Bruges business, Bernardo Portinari, underwrote a cargo of mixed goods, including tapestries, linens, furs and mercery from Sluys to Porto Pisano. In the middle of the fifteenth century the principal centre for marine insurance was Venice.[35] The Medici firm there therefore arranged underwriting for other businesses in the group. In 1455, for example, it arranged for a syndicate of fifteen Venetian underwriters to provide cover for the Medici firm in London, for 1,600 Venetian ducats worth of cloth, wool and lead being shipped from London to Porto Pisano. This was arranged at a premium of 7%. These goods were being carried in a sailing vessel. Like Cambi's, Medici accounts indicate that lower premiums were charged whenever goods were carried by galley, since the risks of both accident and piracy were much lower. Thus, in the same year, only 3% was charged on another policy, also arranged in Venice, for shipping 1,200 ducats worth of wool from Southampton to Venice, since it was in a galley.[36]

As well as marine insurance there was a certain amount of insurance on goods being carried overland. The earliest surviving policies from Pisa or Florence on river and road trade date from 1382. The Cambi account books record several such cases: for example, in 1453 he insured several loads of merchandise being taken from Bologna to the Geneva fairs by *vetturali*, and the next year of goods being sent overland from Lille to Geneva and of velvet being sent from Florence to Geneva.

Insurance is yet another aspect of the medieval Italian 'commercial revolution' that spread to other parts of Europe and continued unchanged into modern Europe. By the mid-fifteenth century marine insurance could be arranged in Barcelona[37] and in Bruges, and shortly thereafter elsewhere in the Netherlands as well. As early as 1489 an underwriter in Kampen was insuring white wine belonging to Norman and Picard merchants which was being shipped in a Kampen-owned ship, with a Danzig master, from La Rochelle to

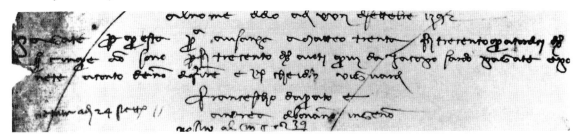

A bill of exchange made out on 22 October 1392 by the Genoa company in the Datini group to the Pisa company, by which Jacopo Sardo in Genoa could send 300 Florentine florins abroad to Matteo Trento in Pisa, without coin needing to be transported.

Le Crotoy at the mouth of the Somme. In the sixteenth century there was a lively insurance market in Antwerp, regulated by a Kamer van Assurantie. The forms of the policies being written well before the end of the fourteenth century were already essentially the same as the master policy of Lloyds of London of 1776, whilst the case law on insurance contracts built up in Italian courts was applied in the fifteenth century in Bruges and Barcelona, and in the eighteenth century in London.

International banking

A further consequence of the regularity and scale of trade was the growth of mutual confidence amongst international merchants, and between them and their suppliers and customers. On the basis of this confidence credit sales could take place, so effectively anticipating and increasing the supply of money, and, as a consequence, enabling a greater volume of business to be transacted.

The most important result of this growth of mutual confidence between merchants was the use of various instruments of payment out of which the bill of exchange was gradually perfected. No longer did every prospective purchaser or returning vendor need to carry with him large and stealable quantities of precious metals, whether in coin, or in bars of silver or in gold by the ounce, in small bags, depending on the trading area. Instead the static manager could send and receive remittances from his factors and agents by bills of exchange. The bill of exchange seems to have evolved into its definitive form by the end of the thirteenth century. It had begun over a hundred years earlier with the notarized *instrumentum ex causa cambii*. The surviving Genoese notarial registers include some such instruments from the late twelfth century, mostly involving transactions between Genoa and the Champagne fairs. In the thirteenth century the Champagne fairs were not only the principal bullion market of Europe, but also the principal money market as well, and the forcing house for the development of the bill of exchange. By the first half of the fourteenth century it had become normal to make commercial payments by bill of exchange between a wide range of cities in western Europe. The merchant banking network was focused on the great trading cities of northern Italy, particularly of Tuscany. It extended westwards to the papal curia when it was at Avignon, to Montpellier, Barcelona, Valencia, Seville and sometimes Lisbon, and northwards to the Champagne fairs, until they faded from importance at the end of the thirteenth century. It also extended to Paris, Bruges and London and reached southwards to Naples, Barletta and Palermo[38] (see map p.26).

One of a sequence of figures personifying the liberal arts, Arithmetic *demonstrates her art to men who need to use it. Since this is a north European tapestry from Tournai, she is showing how to calculate by laying out reckoning counters, rather than by using Arabic numerals, as in Mediterranean Europe. Reckoning with counters continued in the north until the seventeenth century. For reckoning, the table or its covering cloth was ruled with a pattern of lines, which the tapestry weavers have failed to put in.*

Arithmetica

Monstrat ars numeri que virtus possit habere
Explico penunueru que sit proportio rerum

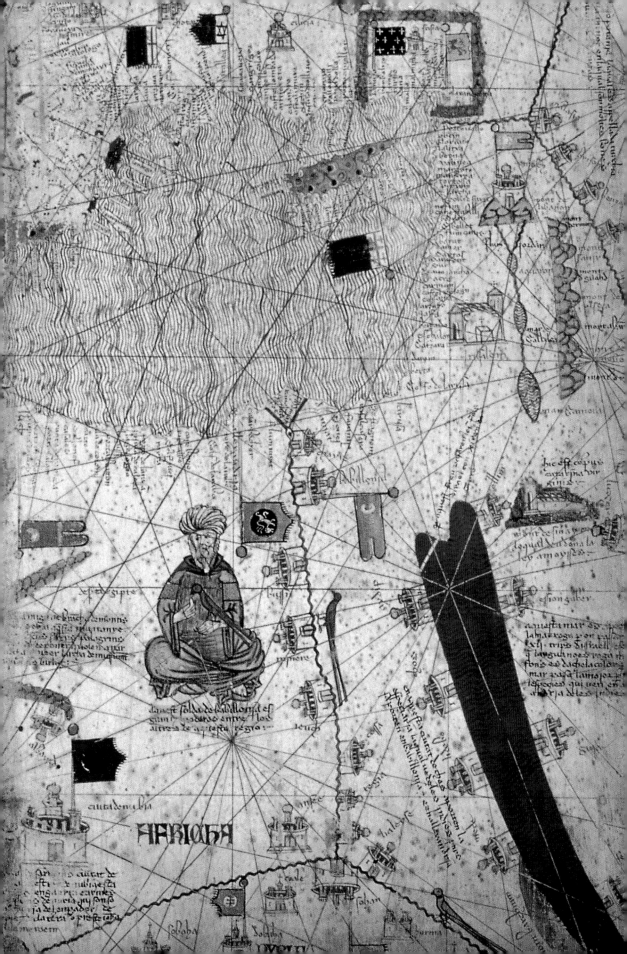

Even between these cities, although the majority of transactions could be carried out by bill of exchange, any eventual imbalance had ultimately to be settled up in gold or silver. When an imbalance between two banking-places became too great, the rate of exchange rose (or fell) to such an extent that it passed one of the specie points. In other words, it temporarily became cheaper to transport bullion, in one direction or the other, with all its attendant costs and risks, than to buy a bill of exchange. The net quantity of silver transported from Bruges to London or Paris to Florence, or of gold from Seville to Genoa did not diminish as a result of the development of bills of exchange, but the amount of business was increased out of all proportion. The bill of exchange multiplied enormously the supply of money available for international transactions between these cities. Although bills of exchange were developed by merchants for merchants, they very quickly came to be used by non-merchants as well. Successive popes were their most considerable non-commercial users. Papal collectors in England and the Low Countries, northern France, the Spanish kingdoms and Italy normally used bills of exchange to transmit the money they had collected to the apostolic camera at Avignon in the first half of the fourteenth century. Bishops travelling to the curia no longer needed to ensure that their chamberlains were loaded down with an adequate quantity of mark bars of silver.[39] Noblemen, whether on pilgrimage or representing their princes on embassies, could also avail themselves of bills of exchange. There were, however, limits. Certain international political payments, such as wages to keep whole armies in the field for protracted periods, subsidies for expensive allies, or royal ransoms and dowries, could easily prove too large for the normal commercial system to handle, and so had to be transmitted largely, or wholly, in silver, or gold. For example, when John XXII needed to pay 60,000 florins to the papal army in Lombardy in the summer of 1328, he had to send it all in coin. That episode provides an excellent example of the risks involved in carrying coin, for, despite a guard of 150 cavalry, the convoy was ambushed, and sumpter animals carrying over half the money were seized by the Pavese on the way. Furthermore, many of the cavalry were captured and had to be ransomed and recompensed for the loss of their armour and riding horses.[40] It was much cheaper and safer to send money by bill whenever possible, and it is hardly surprising that by the early fourteenth century a very large proportion of normal payments within this network of cities was made by bill of exchange.

However, outside this range of banking places, even ordinary international payments had still to be made primarily in bullion. Where there was a large and continuous imbalance of trade, as there was between the mining centres of Europe and the commercially advanced areas, a bill-of-exchange system had little chance of developing. In the fourteenth century, papal collectors in Poland still had to take bullion to Bruges or Venice before they could make use of the west European banking system, by acquiring bills of exchange to remit to the curia.[41] At the very end of the fourteenth century bills of exchange began to be occasionally used by south German merchants, but until well into the fifteenth century even the most prominent trading cities

The Mediterranean section of the famous Catalan Atlas (Majorca, fourteenth century) is an elaborately decorated version of the practical portolan charts carried on shipboard (see p. 55). From the portolans it derives the navigational lines for use with a compass and the names of a huge number of places along the Mediterranean coasts. For courtly interest a figure of the Mamluk sultan has been added immediately to the west of the Nile, and Cairo marked with his flag. The Red Sea is painted red, and St Catherine's monastery on Mount Sinai, a destination for western pilgrims, appears east of its northern tip. Above 'Jerusalem' is the church of the Holy Sepulchre, even more important for pilgrims. In the north-eastern corner of the Mediterranean the Christian kingdom of Armenia can be seen, still safely walled in by mountains. It fell to Egyptian arms in 1375, the very year the Atlas was being drawn for Charles V of France.

elsewhere in Germany, such as Lübeck, basically remained outside this network of exchanges.

Between Christian Europe, Muslim north Africa and the Levant, the use of bills was little developed. This was so even though the scale of trade was very large, and the division of labour between manager, carrier and factor developed early, for here there were not only chronic imbalances of trade, but also decided differences in the values given to gold and to silver in the three areas concerned. Since Europe was a silver-producer and Africa a gold-producer, silver was less valued in Europe than Africa, and gold less valued in Africa than Europe. When this disproportion in value was sufficiently great to overcome the risks and costs of the voyage across the western Mediterranean, it occasionally became worthwhile to take European silver to Africa in order to purchase African gold. Much more frequently, it was common sense to carry additional silver southwards and gold northwards along with other more ordinary merchandise. The balances both between Christian Europe and the Levant, and between Muslim north Africa and the Levant, were strongly in favour of the Levant, and were consequently settled by sending enormous quantities of European silver and African gold. As a consequence of the long-running and continuous imbalance between the Maghreb and the Levant, all payments from one to the other were made in coin, although a number of banking instruments had already evolved within the central countries of the Muslim world. The *suftadja* there was the nearest equivalent to the European bill of exchange. Although the *suftadja* evolved some two centuries before its western counterpart, there is no convincing evidence that it had any direct influence on European developments. Indirect influence is possible, but too nebulous to pin down, for considerable numbers of eleventh- and twelfth-century Italian merchants must have become aware of the banking instruments used, between themselves, by the Muslim merchants with whom they traded in the cities of the eastern Mediterranean.[42] The Near East itself had a generally unfavourable balance with the Middle and Far East, so that much African gold and European silver continued further into Asia. Such circumstances were the very antithesis of the more balanced trading conditions in which the bill of exchange evolved.

Local banking

Local banking developed at the same time as international banking.[43] Within certain of the leading commercial cities, moneychangers extended their activities from manual moneychanging to taking deposits, and then to transferring sums from one account to another on the instructions of the depositors. In Genoa, the most precocious centre for such local giro banking activities, the notarial register of Guglielmo Cassinese (1190–92) indicates that local payments could be made not only by transfer between accounts within the same bank, but also by transfer between accounts in different banks in the city. This was possible because the bankers maintained accounts in each other's banks. In this way interlocking banking systems came into existence. The largest of these was that at Florence, where there were reputedly as many as eighty banks by the early fourteenth century. By then it had become customary amongst merchants within a limited number of cities to make payments as far as possible by assignment on their bank accounts (*per ditta di banco*). Such assignment was initially normally made by oral instruction by the account holder in person at the bank. In the course of the fourteenth century, written instructions, or cheques, supplemented and eventually supplanted oral instructions. The earliest surviving cheques are Tuscan, from Pisa and Florence. Similar written orders to pay came into use in Genoa and Barcelona, but Venetian banks continued to insist on the presence of the payer, or of an agent with a notarized power of attorney, to give oral instructions. The word 'cheque' almost certainly derives from the earlier Muslim *sakk*. It is not clear how direct the connection was, but both were essentially written orders for payment made through the banker with whom the drawer had an account. Similar orders can be found in pre-Muslim Egypt and Palestine under Byzantine rule.[44] The earliest surviving Florentine cheque so far discovered was drawn on the Castellani bank by two patrician Tornaquinci in November 1368 to pay a draper, Segnia Ciapi, for black cloth for a family funeral. Within a hundred years cheques were in use there by very modest men for modest purposes. In 1477, a Florentine haberdasher wrote a cheque to pay for the emptying of a cesspit.[45]

By 1321 it was apparent that some Venetian bankers were reluctant to pay out cash, instead of making transfers between accounts, for in that year the Great Council had to legislate that bankers were to be compelled to pay out cash within three days if asked to do so. Another habit, of which the bankers' account holders complained, in Barcelona and Genoa as well as Venice, was to send them to other banks to look for cash.

By allowing overdrafts and thus letting their cash reserves fall below, and often well below, the total of their deposits, such local deposit bankers were not only facilitating payments, but also effectively increasing the money supply.

In Venice, so much unminted silver came in the course of the thirteenth century that it had become normal practice by the fourteenth century for merchants to be paid for the bullion that they brought to the city by crediting them with its value in a bank account. Its importers could then immediately pay for their purchases of spices and other merchandise by assignment on their bank account.

As well as these current accounts, on which no interest was paid, money-changer banks also ran deposit accounts on which interest accumulated. These were suitable for sums of money that were not required for several years, the dowries of orphan girls for example, and could therefore be invested by the banker in long-term enterprises. Some Venetian bankers invested directly in trading voyages. A complete round trip, from Venice to the Levant, back to Venice, onwards to Flanders, and back to Venice again, took two years. To make an investment in such a voyage the banker had to be certain that his depositors would not call for their money suddenly. Such transfer banking developed much more quickly in Genoa than in other cities. In Venice, for example, the earliest direct evidence of a moneychanger running bank accounts is as late as 1274, and even then it is not clear if they were current or deposit accounts. Indirect evidence, however, suggests that such banking activities had by then already been going on for several years.

Outside Italy, the earliest evidence is a little later still. The Privilege of Barcelona in 1284 implies that current-account banking, with credit transfer between accounts, already existed there at that date. It probably had done so since at least the 1260s. There is evidence for moneychangers acting as local bankers at Valencia by 1284, in Palma by 1288, in Lérida by 1301, and in Bruges also around 1300. Later evidence suggests that moneychangers were also acting in this way in the course of the fourteenth century in Avignon, Liège, Strasbourg and Constantinople, but not in London where money-changing remained a royal monopoly associated with the mints. Where they were available, such local banking facilities were used by a surprisingly large number of people. It has been suggested that in Bruges around 1400 one in forty of the total population, perhaps one in ten of the adult males, had bank accounts.[46] A slightly higher proportion has been suggested for Venice around 1500, when as many as 4,000 out of a total adult male population of 30,000 had current bank accounts, and a high proportion, precisely half, were not patricians. If the wealth and tax structure of Venice in 1500 was anything like that of Florence in 1457, these 4,000 account holders would have enjoyed three quarters of the taxable income of the city. Nevertheless, even in Venice, by far the most commercially sophisticated city in Europe in 1500, a vast number of small transactions had still to be carried out with actual metallic coins. In less advanced cities the use of coin remained dominant.[47]

Bank accounts were quite clearly part of the money supply by the end of the 'long thirteenth century', and legislation was introduced to protect those who used them. In Venice a guarantee of 3,000 lire was required in 1270 before a moneychanger banker was allowed to set up in business. In Barcelona, from 1300, book entries by credit transfer legally ranked equally with original deposits among the liabilities of bankers. Those who failed were forbidden ever to keep a bank again, and were to be detained on bread and water until all their account holders were satisfied in full. In 1321 the legislation there was greatly increased in severity. Bankers who failed and did not settle up in full within a year were to be beheaded and their property sold for the satisfaction of their account holders. This was actually enforced. Francesch Castello was beheaded in front of his bank in 1360.[48]

International banking and local banking soon came to be combined, where that was possible. At least in Genoa and Venice, Barcelona and Bruges, bills of exchange could be bought by debiting a bank account and their proceeds credited to a bank account. A late, but vivid, example of how important this combination of the two forms of banking became comes from fifteenth-century Genoa. An account-book of the Piccamiglio records the receipt of payments from abroad by bills of exchange between 1456 and 1459, totalling 159,710 Genoese lire. Of these only 11,753 lire worth of bills were paid to them in cash. All the rest, over 92.5%, were met by transfer in bank.

The number of moneychangers in the Netherlands had already begun to

In 1490, when Piero Pacini printed the standard Italian Merchant Manual, as Il libro di tucti echostumi, *first compiled in Florence in the 1420s (see p. 53), he added woodcuts, in this case of a busy bank in Florence in his own day. Is it a cheque that the cashier on the left is holding?*

shrink in the last quarter of the fourteenth century. In Brabant a partial solution was provided by the setting up of municipal exchanges, or *stadwissel*, by such towns as 'sHertogenbosch, as early as 1378, and Brussels, Leuven and Antwerp. There is no evidence, however, that these combined banking with exchange functions. In the fifteenth century the numbers of moneychangers continued to decline in the Netherlands, as elsewhere in Europe. In Germany, even at Frankfurt and Nuremberg, the number dropped sharply. Eventually, the combined role of changer and banker was suppressed in the Netherlands, since the demand for guarantees and tighter regulation had failed. When a common coinage was introduced for the newly united Netherlands in 1433, the regulations also stipulated that in future moneychangers were not allowed to receive money on deposit for merchants or make payments for them.[49] A few moneychangers survived and, despite Burgundian legislation, some continued to act as bankers. In Antwerp in 1480 only one changer, who had sureties for 10,000 crowns, was thought by the city to be sound, but he too disappeared in the next wave of bankruptcies in the mid-1480s. When the coinage was renewed in 1489, after Maximilian's civil war debasements during Philip the Handsome's minority, the 1433 prohibition of changers acting as bankers was reiterated, and this time the prohibition was observed. The sixteenth-century Antwerp moneychangers kept away from deposit banking, as did their Amsterdam successors in the seventeenth century. In France, such deposit banking run by moneychangers was so reduced that it only survived at Lyons.

In sixteenth-century Antwerp such banking needed to be reinvented. Here men other than licensed moneychangers began to act as *kassiers* (cashiers) for merchants, keeping their money on deposit, accepting payments on their behalf and making payments to their order. They came to perform many of the same functions that the moneychanger bankers had earlier performed, transferring funds from one account to another for clients, and to other *kassiers*. They also received payment for bills of exchange into their clients' accounts, or accepted and paid bills of exchange on behalf of their clients.[50]

In London too there was a similar need for deposit bankers that had never been met by moneychangers, since there were no private moneychangers in medieval London. From the fifteenth century onwards London goldsmiths were beginning to engage in deposit banking, but it was only at the end of the seventeenth century that they, together with some of the loan- and mortgage-broking scriveners, effectively developed an extensive and effective deposit banking system. The influence of the *kassier* bankers of Antwerp and Amsterdam on this evolution was marked.

In Mediterranean Europe when private bankers fell on hard times in the crisis years of the late fourteenth century and the fifteenth, alternative arrangements began to be considered. Instead of either demanding heavier guarantees, or the traditional tightening of regulations, some cities and states began to take an active part in the provision of a service so important to the business community. Such action was discussed in Venice in 1356 and again in 1374, but the first, and longest lived, of these public banks to come into existence was the 'Taula de Canvi' founded by the city of Barcelona in 1401, which, having surmounted a number of crises in the fifteenth and sixteenth centuries, survived until it became a part of the Bank of Spain in 1853. Other attempts to found public banks in the kingdoms of the crown of Aragon were, however, short lived. The 'Taula de Canvi' of Valencia only lasted from 1408 to 1416. The 'Taula del General' of Palma de Majorca which was operating by 1454 did not survive the fifteenth century. Plans to set up municipal public banks in Tarragona and Gerona in 1416 and 1443 never got off the ground. In Italy in the first half of the fifteenth century, the 'Casa di San Giorgio', the association of state bond-holders in Genoa, which collected most of the state's taxes which had been assigned to them, amongst many other activities, ran a public deposit bank in Genoa from 1407 to 1444, but with little long-term success. After further experimentation more durable state institutions were created in the sixteenth century.[51]

It will be apparent that bank money and other additions to the money supply did not develop where the money supply was generally poor, but, on the contrary, in some of the places where the money supply was already most abundant. The silver mined in Europe largely ended up in Asia. Much of it passed through wide areas of the European countryside and through the capital cities of the west on the way, but a great deal of it concentrated in its passage through Europe in the great commercial cities. It was the middlemen of these cities who took the largest profits and added most to the value of the goods passing through their hands. In consequence, it was in their cities, and in certain areas of primary production, like wool-growing England, that the largest accumulations of silver were to be found. The middlemen of the Middle East did not seem to have the same success as their west European counterparts, particularly the Italians, in detaining a large proportion of this silver on its way to India or China. It was therefore only in a limited number of cities, many of them in northern Italy, that the money supply built up to an adequate level for transfer banking to develop. Once it did so, it increased the money supply still more and allowed further developments to take place.

Among the natural consequences of this revolution in the use of money and the increased possibilities of productive investment was a radical change in attitudes towards lending. Coin and ingots, instead of being hoarded for safety, or only lent reluctantly at rates of interest that were very high, to compensate for the risks involved, were commonly mobilized for investment. A great dethesaurization of precious metals added further to the supply of money and its velocity of circulation. In Italian cities it is easy enough to find examples of investment rather than hoarding. When a moderately well-to-do Genoese nobleman, Guglielmo de Castro, died in 1240, his executors discovered that, apart from his house and domestic goods, all his assets, some 1,100 Genoese lire and 440 *bezants*, had been invested by him and his wife over the previous six years in two dozen separately notarized *commenda* contracts. A generation later, in 1268, the executors of the extraordinarily rich Venetian doge, Ranieri Zeno, discovered that he had no less than 22,935 Venetian *lire di piccioli* invested in 132 *colleganza* contracts, very similar to *commenda* contracts (see above p. 23), compared with only 3,388 lire in actual coin. Less than 7% of his enormous wealth was liquid, whilst 46% was invested in the commercial enterprises of others.

The same phenomenon of wide investment is equally striking when seen from the other end, and on a much smaller scale. The executors of a Genoese businessman, Armano, who died in Bonifacio in Corsica in 1239, found that he had managed to persuade twenty-six men and women to finance his business, exporting hides, by commending small investments to him, to a total of 1,201 Genoese lire. He also had a partner who had put 400 lire into the business. By the end of the century small investors, rather than putting their money directly into business ventures, were in some cities able to choose to deposit it instead, in greater safety, in banks, which took the risk of the eventual commercial investments. By combining investments, some very small indeed, in this way, quite enormous sums could be mobilized. A striking, although rather late, example of this is provided by the Aiutamicristo bank of Pisa, which was able to lend 100,000 florins of its depositors' money to the Sancasciano company of Pisa, for purchasing cloth, between 1354 and 1371. Large investors, on the other hand, continued to invest directly in business ventures.

Usury and interest rates

As commercial loans became an ordinary part of north Italian economic life, so north Italian canonists reworked the ecclesiastical doctrine of usury to make the payment of interest acceptable under certain circumstances. The old approach, developed from the ninth century onwards, condemned loans at interest, with biblical and classical precedents, because in a largely non-commercial age such loans had primarily been for immediate, crisis, spending on food, drink and other short-term common necessities. The problems of repayment trapped the borrowers in a downward spiral of misery. A new approach was needed to cope with productive loans that enabled the borrower to expand the scope of his business. The key to the new approach was *lucrum cessans*, the profit the lender would have made himself if he had kept the money to trade with, but had in fact forgone in order to lend it to the borrower so that he could trade with it instead. The most significant of the early writers along these lines was the Lombard canonist Henry of Susa. In 1271 he wrote: 'If some merchant, who is accustomed to pursue trade, and the commerce of the fairs, and there profit much, has...lent (me) money with which he would have done business, I remain obliged from this to his *interesse*, to recompense him for the profit he would have made had he engaged in the business himself.' Innocent IV concurred, but many canonists disagreed. However, by the early fifteenth century Bernardino of Siena had gone further: 'Money has not simply the character of money; but it has beyond this a productive character, which we commonly call capital'. Borrowing capital therefore was like borrowing a plough, which had a use separate from itself, not like borrowing wine, which did not. A price should therefore be paid for borrowing capital, provided it was a just price.[52]

As men felt freer to invest rather than hoard, commercial interest rates dropped, particularly in those places where the money supply was most plentiful, like the cities of northern Italy, to a level at which a great many undertakings could be profitably financed that would have been impossible at higher rates of interest.

In Genoa in 1200 bankers were making commercial loans at 20% per annum, in Florence in 1211 at 22%, and in Venice Pietro Ziani, doge from 1205 to 1229, lent at 20%, as his father had done before him. Funds accumulated in the hands of pious foundations and lent to those engaged in the Levant trade had also paid 20% in twelfth-century Venice. Commercial interest rates were still the same as those for personal loans. The loans on the security of land in central Italy in the third quarter of the twelfth century were also at 20% per annum. A hundred years later things were very different. In the first half of the fourteenth century commercial loans in Genoa could sometimes be obtained for as little as 7%, although they were generally rather higher. In Florence the Peruzzi bank in the first quarter of the century was paying its depositors 8% and charging 2% more for loans. In Pisa in the 1350s the Aiutamicristo bank was still lending to the Sancasciano company at this same average rate of 10%. In Venice money was cheaper still. In the 1330s, the banker Francesco Corner was only paying his depositors 5% and 7%, whilst loans were being made to shopkeepers and craftsmen at 8%, which was the standard rate for *colleganza* within the city in 1330, but rates were still dropping. They were down to 5% after 1340. Pious foundations had only been getting 5% on funds invested in the Levant trade since the previous century.

Late thirteenth- and early fourteenth-century Italian city states replaced direct taxation by compelling their richer citizens to lend money to the state when it needed large sums suddenly, as in wartime. Until they could be repaid these forced loans, *prestanze*, paid interest, but at even lower rates. The rights to repayment and to the interest, could be sold, like modern government bonds. The Venetian state nominally only paid 5% on forced loans from 1262. Since this was well below the market rate, the shares in the public debt changed hands at well below par. Between 1285 and 1316 their price fluctuated between 60% and 78%, giving a return of 6.5% to 8.5% on the market price. When the rate of interest on bank deposits fell to 5% in the 1330s, the shares rose to par. Cities, however, had to pay the market rate when they wished to attract voluntary loans. The Venetian government offered 8% to 12% in the late thirteenth century, but this rate too dropped to 5% or under by the mid-fourteenth century.[53]

Princes, noblemen and other private individuals, who were all bad risks, still had to pay high rates, whether to loan sharks, or even to reputable bankers who sometimes extended their operations into these grey areas. Like loans to cities and city states, loans for commercial purposes, and also, by analogy, those for industrial purposes, largely escaped the condemnation of the usury laws in the later Middle Ages. The concept of 'usury' remained for consumption loans, which were largely, in the later Middle Ages, in the hands of *usurarii manifesti* (pawnbrokers) who were frequently licensed outsiders – 'Cahorsins' in England, 'Lombards' in the Low Countries and France, Tuscans at Mestre outside Venice, Jews in Tuscany. Those working on a small scale accepted the cooking vessels and bedding of the poor as security for loans. Those on a large scale accepted the crowns of impecunious monarchs. For example in 1297 a group of Lombards from Asti advanced 4,600 *livres tournois* to King Edward I of England, in the Low Countries, on the security of jewels and plate with an estimated worth of 7,015 *li.tur*. Eight months later he redeemed them, and paid interest of at least 560 *li.tur*. In other words he had paid interest equivalent to a rate of at least 18.3% a year. If this was all he paid, it was very cheap for a non-commercial loan, particularly in northern Europe. Two generations later his grandson fared much worse, when Simon de Mirabello took the great crown of England in pledge from King Edward III, and charged 35% a year. The Leopardi of Asti also lent him money on security and charged him 42%, but that included a penalty for late repayment.[54]

In the course of the thirteenth century a gulf opened in Italy between the low interest rates charged on commercial and industrial loans, and the high interest rates charged on others. It is not surprising that the term 'usurious' gradually acquired the meaning of 'at a high rate of interest', in other words at an exorbitant, unjust rate. Professor Luzzatto showed that in late medieval Venice, when loans for commercial purposes could be had for 5%, loans at moderate interest, below 12%, were still regarded as lawful and just, whilst those at immoderate rates, above 12%, were regarded as usurious.[55] In the Early Modern period governments were frequently prepared to specify rates of interest above which loans counted as usurious. The differential between commercial and non-commercial loans is clearly illustrated in the correspondence of the Vicente company in 1260. 'Money here', they wrote from Siena, 'is priced at five and six denari per lira between merchants, and for those who

In the second quarter of the twelfth century, when this dramatic capital in Autun Cathedral was carved, Avaritia, Covetousness, *was regarded as one of the Seven Deadly Sins. The medieval commercial revolution made the naturally acquisitive human instinct into a virtue, within limits. But even today we feel the unacceptable face of capitalism looks like this – untrammelled Greed.*

are not merchants at ten and twelve denari per lira'. ('*Che Sapi ch'e denari ci sono valuti, da uno merchatante ad altro, cinque d. e sei libra, e altri che ne siano merch[at]anti sono valuti diece d. e dodici in chorsa*'). Interestingly they regarded even the commercial rate that they were quoting as abnormally high, on account of the war with Florence.

The falling of commercial interest rates in the principal cities of Italy in the course of the thirteenth century, from 20% per annum and more to 10% per annum and less, is a very clear indication of the change in scale of the money supply. The decades when interest rates fell have not yet, to my knowledge, been pinpointed. It is, however, noticeable that the dei Boni only paid 7% at Pistoia on money invested with them, *fuori del corpo*, as early as 1259. Once having fallen, at some date between 1211 and 1259, commercial interest rates in northern Italy remained below 10% until the seventeenth century, frequently going as low as 5%.

Low interest rates have always given the edge to those who could raise money cheaply. They could undercut their rivals by accepting low profit margins, or waiting longer for a return on their investment, or by reversing the normal pattern of credit. Buyers who could borrow at low interest rates could extend credit to sellers, rather than the usual extension of credit from seller to buyer. An early example of this was the way in which, in the second half of the thirteenth century, Tuscan merchants, borrowing at under 10%, were able very largely to oust Flemish merchants, who still had to borrow at 16% or over, from two of their principal trading areas, England and the Champagne fairs. Earlier in the century Flemish merchants had been purchasing English wool in England to carry back to Flanders for Flemish cloth manufacturers, but they found it increasingly hard to compete with Italians who were prepared not only to contract to buy wool in England in advance, but to put down the money for it even before it was grown. Similarly, members of the Hanse of Flemish towns had been buying high quality Flemish woollen cloth to take to the Champagne fairs for sale. By the end of the century they could no longer compete with the prices that the Tuscans, backed by cheaper credit, were able to offer to the cloth manufacturers in Flanders for export direct to Italian and other markets. Although money in the Netherlands was much more expensive than in northern Italy in the later Middle Ages, it was still probably less expensive than anywhere else in Europe until the fifteenth century. It may even have dropped below 16% (approximately one sixth) above 10% in the fourteenth and fifteenth centuries.

Not surprisingly interest rates fell to north Italian levels in southern Germany in the course of the fifteenth century. By the end of the century the Hochstetter of Augsburg were only paying 5% for additional short-term funds. In the sixteenth century interest rates followed suit in Antwerp.

Centre and periphery   The leaders of the new organization of trade were the international, multi-branched companies, with many shareholders, which were prepared to trade in anything and everything, and engaged in international banking, insurance, manufacture and even retailing as well. It is, however, important to remember that, in parallel with these gigantic companies, there was a whole range of less complex businesses. Even in Tuscany there were many smaller, specialized, single-branched companies, with a head office in a Tuscan city and one branch abroad, which were engaged in trading in a single commodity. There were also companies in Tuscany, or individual merchants, who traded on too small a scale to establish any branches abroad at all, but who could still engage in long-distance trading by using correspondents amongst the residents abroad, who were themselves independent merchants, acting in conjunction with a variety of different businessmen at home. There were also, of course, even more numerous merchants who travelled with their goods. This traditional method of engaging in trade was still more or less universal, until the fifteenth century, in non-Mediterranean Europe, north and east of a line from Bruges to Venice. When Buonaccorso Pitti and Matteo Tinghi wished to sell Italian saffron in Buda in 1376, they went with it themselves.[56] Any direct European commercial contacts with the outside world also involved merchants travelling with their own goods. Although Francesco Pegolotti was an employee of one of the largest and most complex of Florentine enterprises, he nevertheless described the road to China in terms of individual merchants accompanying their own linens on the outward journey and their own silks on their return journey. The Venetian traders who purchased precious stones in fourteenth-century Delhi had also gone there themselves.[57] For all such journeys outside the limited area of well-organized business in western Europe and the Mediterranean, and within it for much, smaller-scale, trade, short-term, individual journey, *commenda* contracts went on being used as the means of supplementing self-financing. Merchants from everywhere else all went on accompanying their goods until the larger south German companies also reached a size where they could emulate the techniques employed by the larger north Italian companies.

Staple towns

There were a number of geographical bottlenecks through which the rapidly growing trade of the thirteenth century had to pass, and local traders, backed by privileges from their rulers, naturally tried to capitalize on their position. The most common form that such rights took was the denomination of a particular town or city as a 'staple'. In such a place foreign merchants were compelled to offer their goods only to sworn burgesses and only to buy from them. London was one such privileged place, the principal port of entry to England, inheriting from antiquity a position at the focus of the country's road network, and within a few miles of the centre of government at Westminster. By the fourteenth century long-distance traders saw the Londoners' privileged position as a burdensome restraint on their ability to trade within the country. There was continued tension over such a right throughout the century. The crown was repeatedly petitioned for freedom to trade more widely by powerful groups of foreign merchants, who wished to trade into England through London. Whenever the crown succumbed to the financial blandishments of Hanseatics or Italians and withdrew or modified the citizens' privilege, the city instantly counter-petitioned and offered large sums for the restoration of the monopolist and monopsonist position of those admitted as citizens. The compulsory intrusion of such a group of middlemen naturally increased transaction costs and could divert trade. Because of London's privileges it often made more sense for Italians to land goods at Southampton, or Hanseatics at Lynn, because they could then take them direct to English fairs and customers.[58]

The duke of Austria had given a similar privilege to the citizens of Vienna, so that Italian and Bohemian merchants on the north–south road or south German and Hungarian merchants on the Danube could not sell to each other, but only to Viennese. By the fourteenth century this was much resented. In 1327 the kings of Bohemia and Hungary made an agreement to promote trade between themselves and cut out the Viennese, so that trade from Hungary to southern Germany would pass through Bohemia, and from Bohemia to Italy through Hungary or southern Germany. In the same way the counts of Holland made Dordrecht a staple town, so that everything that came up or down the Rhine and Meuse had to be offered to its privileged burgesses.[59] A modified version of such a staple right was the obligation of foreigners to involve local brokers in all transactions, as at Bruges.

From the second half of the twelfth century to the first half of the fourteenth rulers throughout Europe granted the right to hold a market to many thousands of towns, some very small. Towns leased plots for setting up stalls once a week, where the produce of local artisans, pottery in this illustration from a Flemish manuscript of about 1460, could be sold alongside rural produce, eggs and vegetables here. The covered stalls should have been closed down at the end of the day, but some never were and, over time, turned into permanent shop buildings.

Fairs   Although I concentrate on the largest scale of long-distance trade, it is important to remember that most late medieval European trade was local and regional. One of the key features of the expansive thirteenth century was the development right across Europe of a vast interlocking network of myriad local weekly markets and of annual or biannual fairs.[60] This network grew up with the penetration of money into the European countrysides, and joined at numerous points to the arteries of long-distance trade. With the fourteenth- and fifteenth-century contractions in population, money supply and arable agriculture, many of these local markets, particularly in areas like eastern Germany which had specialized in grain production, fell out of use. Lost markets became as ubiquitous as lost villages, and were concentrated in much

The right to hold a fair every June in the great open space in front of the royal abbey of Saint Denis was granted in the middle of the eleventh century. The fair, later known as the 'Lendit of the plain of St-Denis', grew from a local fair into an occasion of international commercial importance in the period after the decline of the Champagne cycle of fairs. The illustration from a French manuscript of the fourteenth century of the opening of the fair by the Bishop of Paris shows semi-permanent booths, set up for the weeks that the fair lasted. As well as a major occasion for selling manufactured goods, like bales of cloth, it still remained an agricultural fair as well. The miniaturist has shown a flock of sheep for sale.

the same parts of Europe. However, the regional fair structure seems to have survived rather better. Some fairs not only survived, but even grew more important in the last century-and-a-half of the Middle Ages,[61] like that at Stourbridge on the Cam below Cambridge, which, beginning as a venue for the annual sale of local barley, grew to become a major regional fair for eastern England.

Moreover, above these regional fairs, there were a handful of fairs of international importance which continued to flourish. Many of these were held at the intersections between the long-distance commerce dominated by 'Italian' ways of business, and less complex methods of trading. 'German' as well as 'Italian' merchants were particularly noticeable at many of them. The Champagne fairs had performed this role in the thirteenth century (see below pp. 144–50). The international fairs of the fourteenth and fifteenth centuries are therefore sometimes described by historians as 'successor' fairs to those of Champagne. Like them, they were generally held beside navigable rivers and so were accessible both by road and by water. South of Champagne, the most important were, in turn, those at Chalon on the Saône, at Geneva on the Rhône, and at Lyons at the confluence of the two rivers.[62] West of Champagne, the old Lendit fair at St-Denis, on the Seine below Paris, achieved a new lease of life.[63] East of Champagne the main fairs were at Frankfurt on the Main, where 'German' merchants purchased the products of the Low Countries, principally woollen cloth.[64] To the north of Champagne were those at Antwerp and at Bergen-op-Zoom on the Scheldt, where Hanseatic,

Rhineland and south German merchants met not only Netherlanders, but also men from many other nations.[65] There were also a few other fairs of considerable importance elsewhere, like those at Leipzig, and and at Medina del Campo in northern Castile.

In the course of his lengthy travels through Europe in the late 1430s the Castilian Pero Tafur visited a number of these fairs. 'I have seen other fairs, at Geneva in Savoy, at Frankfurt in Germany, and at Medina in Castile, but all these together are not to be compared with Antwerp.' What had caught his very un-mercantile eye? 'Pictures of all kinds are sold in the monastery of St Francis; in the church of St John they sell the cloths of Arras; in a Dominican monastery all kinds of goldsmith's work, and thus the various articles are distributed among the monasteries and churches, and the rest is sold in the streets. Outside the city at one of the gates is a great street with large stables and other buildings on either side of it. Here they sell hackneys, trotters and other horses, a most remarkable sight…Hungarians and Prussians enrich the fair with their horses….' There is no impression that the principal activity of the Antwerp fairs had anything to do with the sale of various qualities of woollen cloth. His interests were those of the noble consumer of the rare and exotic: 'The Duke of Burgundy comes always to the fair, which is the reason why there is so much splendour to be seen at his court.' He naturally noticed his own countrymen: 'as for Spaniards they are as numerous, or more numerous, at Antwerp than anywhere else. I met merchants from Burgos who were settled in Bruges, and in the city I found also Juan de Morillo, a servant of our king.' He did, however, enumerate people of other nationalities whom he encountered – Germans, English, and French. He also observed in the Scheldt the carracks and galleys of Venice, Florence and Genoa, which were apparently tied up to the city walls.[66]

Exchanges and brokers

In the course of the fifteenth century Antwerp evolved from a place notable for its regular, but temporary, fairs into a city in which business was continuously being transacted. In the 1480s, a period of civil war in the Netherlands, Antwerp replaced Bruges as the principal permanent international marketplace for north-western Europe. The 'nations' of foreign merchants, Venetian, Genoese, Florentine, Lucchese, Milanese, Spanish, Portuguese, Breton, English and Hanseatic, moved there.[67]

The focus of business was the exchange, at which specialized brokers of various sorts were to be found, at fixed hours of the day, ready to introduce to each other buyers and sellers of particular commodities, borrowers and lenders, shippers and underwriters and to put deals together between them. The first exchange building in northern Europe specifically built for brokers to meet in was the *Beurs* or *Bourse* put up by the city of Antwerp in 1517.[68] Arcaded galleries with similar functions already existed in southern Europe, for example the Lottja, or Lonja, in Barcelona, completed in 1392, and the Loggia dei Mercanti put up on the Piazza of the Rialto in Venice as early as 1322, and rebuilt in 1459.[69] Before buildings were put up for them, brokers had congregated, as in Antwerp, in particular squares which were gradually

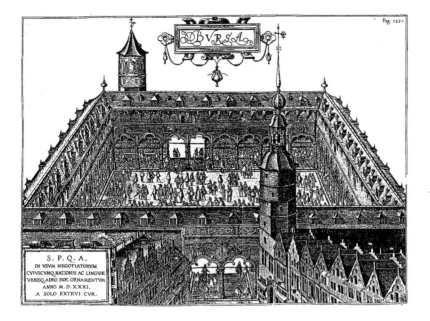

S. P. Q. A.
IN VSVM NEGOTIATORVM
CVIVSCVMQ.NATIONIS AC LINGVÆ
VRBISQ.ADEO SVÆ ORNAMENTVM
ANNO M. D. XXXI.
A SOLO EXTRVI CVR.

The new Antwerp Bourse, with arcaded galleries on four sides, erected by the city authorities in 1531 was much the grandest expression so far of the principle of a publicly provided gallery, in which brokers were available at fixed times every day to bring merchants together to conduct business, regardless of the weather. It was the culminating point of a sequence of such arcades set up by the great commercial cities of Europe, since the first Loggia dei Mercanti of 1322 in Venice. Engraving after L. Guicciardini, 1581.

set aside for their use, like the Piazza dei Banchi in Genoa, the Plaça dels Canvis de la Mar in Barcelona, the Place du Change in Lyons,[70] or the square in Bruges named after a wealthy family of innkeeper-brokers, the van der Beurse, or de la Bourse. As well as the inn of the van der Beurse family, which, after 1450, became the consular house of the Venetian 'nation' at Bruges, the consular houses of the Genoese and Florentine 'nations' were also on the square, whilst that of the Lucchese 'nation' was just round the corner. Brokers, particularly exchange brokers, met in the arcaded gallery in front of the Florentine house, so as not to be disturbed by traffic or rain. When a purpose-built exchange was erected by the city in Antwerp in 1517, it not only borrowed the name *Bourse* or *Beurs* from Bruges, but also took the form of a small square with arcaded galleries. When it was replaced in 1531 by a spacious new building, that too took the form of a square, a much grander one, surrounded by arcaded galleries.

The city's decision to build a new *Bourse* provoked a frenzy of petitioning and counter-petitioning. On the one hand it was argued 'that the Bourse standing in Wolstrate was too small, on account of the much greater numbers of merchants dealing in the city and the Bourse than in former times'[71] and should therefore be moved to another site. The counter-petition, by the German, Spanish, English, Sicilian, Genoese, Florentine, Lucchese and Milanese nations 'that the present Bourse lies in the most suitable position for the convenience of merchants. It is in the central part of the town, close to the churches, the market, the town hall, the weighbridge, and the foreign consular buildings, and not far from the waterfront',[72] was too late to be of effect. It was made several months after plans had been laid, a week after Charles V had approved the translation of the Bourse to the new site, and a fortnight after work had begun! Seven months later Charles, not surprisingly, turned it down. One of the most interesting features of the counter-petition was that it enumerated other existing bourses. It said 'that merchants would rather have it placed nearer to the waterfront, just as the bourses in other great merchant cities are placed, as in Venice, Genoa, Naples, Palermo, Lyons and particularly Bruges',[73] whereas the new site was outside the centre of the town and far from the waterfront.

Despite all forebodings, the new Antwerp Beurs of 1531 was highly successful and became the model in its turn for the *Burse*, later called the Royal Exchange, in London, as well as for the *Beurs* in Amsterdam.[74]

Information

The extraordinary complexity of the trading world of the later Middle Ages could be very confusing. There was a need to know a very great deal of information, not merely the latest news conveyed by merchant letters week by week, but background information about all the places with which trading was being carried out, or might be carried out. It is no wonder that from the late thirteenth century onwards it became habitual for young Italians entering a business career to jot down useful information in private notebooks for their own use, to add to them over the years, and sometimes to make a fair copy later in life. They became guides to the weights and measures and the currency in use in various places, the commodities to be found in particular places and how to distinguish different qualities (like that of steel in Brescia) the dates of fairs, the customs duties to be paid, minting arrangements, and the expected times for couriers and bills of exchange to pass between places. Such notebooks are almost as useful to modern historians as they were to their compilers.

Quite often, however, the compilers incorporated parts of the notebooks of older men in their own, or even copied them out wholesale, with a minimum of updating. Sometimes they openly declared what they were doing, as did Antonio da Pescia, then a factor of Giovanni de Bicci de' Medici in Florence, who, when he began his own notebook on 1 December 1416, said that he was copying from a notebook (*quaderna*) made in 1396 by another Florentine, Saminiato de' Ricci in Genoa, although he knew that some measures and currencies had changed in the previous twenty years.[75] Often the compilers did not declare their sources. From the point of view of the historian this can sometimes be confusing, because it is not clear to what date a particular piece of information relates. Presumably the compilers themselves did not suffer from this confusion. Some fifteen such notebooks have been published, in whole or in part, ranging in date from around 1270 to the early fifteenth century. The earliest considerable notebook is the Venetian Zibaldone da Canal from around 1311.[76] At least another five remain to be published. Their contents overlap with the much more numerous books of arithmetic designed for commercial purposes. The notebook compiled in the 1380s by Nicolo di Bona, who later worked with the Datini firm in Pisa, ends with Seville material dateable to 1385–86. However it also contains not only matter relating to trade in Provence from before 1344, but also part of a commercial arithmetic book, the *Algorism* of Messer Jacopo of Florence, ostensibly compiled in Montpellier in 1307, which Nicolo only partially updated.[77] By the fifteenth century compiling, or at least copying, notebooks, had become a regular part of the process of commercial education for aspiring businessmen. Many seem to have been compiled by young Tuscans, particularly Florentines, serving abroad as factors for multi-branched businesses. The creation of these notebooks was perhaps a natural by-product of such companies and of the likelihood of a rising merchant, like Francesco Pegolotti, spending time in many branches of his firm, at different stages of his career.

In the fifteenth century a standard text became available for copying, and I believe it would be proper to use the term 'manual' rather than 'notebook' for this educational standard text and to distinguish it from individual personal compilations. It was probably put together in Florence in the 1420s. No fewer than eight manuscript copies of this *Libro di Mercatantie* survive, ranging in date from 1444 to 1496, and the various filiations of these manuscripts suggest that they are the survivors from a very much larger number. It looks as if from the beginning this text was intended to be what it clearly became, the standard manual for young fifteenth-century men of business, and was fuller and more comprehensive than any of the individual notebooks that have survived, as if it had been designed as a 'manual'. Its dominant position was confirmed by its being printed on three separate occasions before the end of the fifteenth century.[78] It was, in addition, incorporated in 1494 into Luca Pacioli's influential *Summa de Arithmetica*. It too was copied by young Tuscans overseas, like the copy made in 1458 by Giorgio Chiarini, for Ricciardo di Viero del Bene of Florence, in a house in Ragusa (Dubrovnik) rented by Martino Chiarini for the Pazzi firm in Barcelona.[79] Like the Bardi, the Alberti, the Medici and the Strozzi, the Pazzi were a noble Florentine clan, members of which engaged in international business on a large scale in the fifteenth century.

In contrast to the dominance of this standard manual within the commercial world of the fifteenth century, modern historians have preferred to quote most often from Francesco Pegolotti's notebook, which is the most detailed of the fourteenth-century examples. Francesco (di Balducci) Pegolotti, who worked for the Bardi, the largest of the four giant corporations that dominated international trade up to the bankruptcies of the 1340s, recorded in his notebook, made up over his working life, from around the beginning of the century to about 1340, something of its various activities. His notes on places range from the prime sheep-raising monasteries of England to the spice markets of Egypt and Persia, from the ports of the Moroccan coast to those of the Crimea, and even, although his own firm did not trade beyond the Black Sea, to practical details of the silk road from Cathay. His notes on products range not only over all the materials used in the manufacture of cloth, from the different qualities of the wool on the English monastery-owned sheep to the different qualities of the alum from various parts of Asia Minor, but also over a vast range of products which had nothing to do with woollen cloth. These included both high-value, small-volume products like silk and spices and low-value, bulky, everyday necessities like grain and oil and wine. They also included less probable commodities like cheese from Apulia and little wooden boxes from Cyprus.[80]

It was also necessary for those who travelled to know where they were going, as well as what conditions they would find on arrival. If they were travelling by sea in the Mediterranean this was provided, by the middle of the thirteenth century, by port books, which listed ports along the coasts, port by port, with the distances between one landmark and the next. By the end of the century these port books began to be supplemented by port-maps or portolans, designed to be used with the compass, which was then being adopted as a practical navigational tool. The oldest to survive, drawn up in Pisa, Genoa and Venice, are the earliest maps, of any known, which were drawn to scale. They were made to be hung up on board ship for navigation, and showed the coasts with myriad named places along them, with compass point rays to assist navigation between them. Reckoning tables were also prepared for use alongside them. In the fourteenth century Venice, not surprisingly, produced many portolans, and some of the Venetian map makers can be identified as having served at sea themselves, like Marco Pizzigani, who was patron of the Cornaria, which sailed into Venice from Tana in December 1330.[81] Similarly a Genoese map of 1403 says that it had been checked against the 'efficacious experience' and information of seamen. They were not only made for use by those sailing from the great north Italian ports. Peter IV of Aragon insisted in 1354 that all ships from his kingdoms should carry not one but two maps, and by the middle of the fifteenth century they were even being drawn up in London, admittedly by Italians. In addition to practical use on board ship, rather more ornate portolans were also used by merchants and it is these that have mostly survived. They sometimes exist bound up in groups, like the *Medici Atlas*, which opens with an almanac for 1351.[82] Palma da Majorca became particularly known for the production of such ornate portolans in the mid-fourteenth century, and over thirty are known.[83] The earliest of these, produced by Angelino Dulcert in 1339, was the first to map outside the Mediterranean and Black Sea, and showed coasts as far north as the Baltic, and as far south as Europeans then knew of the coast of Africa.

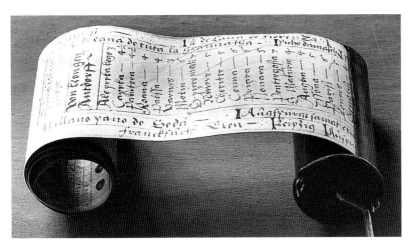

The standard method of finding the way by road across medieval Europe was to use an itinerary set out on a long roll on which the places to be passed through were arranged in order, with an indication of the distances between them. The survival of such rolls is extremely rare. The tradition of long map rolls is suggested by the layout of the maps on the pages of John Ogilby's Britannia, i, 1675, where the strip maps are drawn as if they curled over at top and bottom.

Portolan maps also formed part of a late fourteenth-century Venetian *Tavola per riconoscere tutte le terre e luoghi* (Handbook for recognizing all lands and places), which included both maps of the coasts, and also considerable verbal descriptions of ports and how to enter them. It looks as if it was originally made for the master of a vessel. However, the partial copy which survives was made a century later, in 1482, by a Florentine for a member of the Strozzi family, not a mariner but a patrician merchant banker, on the largest scale. The surviving section takes the user round the coasts and ports of Europe from Bruges to the Aegean, but the index indicates that the original extended from the entrance to the Baltic round to the Black Sea.[84] Yet grander than these were the highly decorative portolans produced for courtly markets, with vignettes of mountains and cities, wild life and rulers. The best know of these courtly cartographers was a Majorcan Jew, Abraham Cresques, who became '*Magister mappamundorum et bruxolarum*' to the King of Aragon, for whom he produced maps in the 1380s. He was probably also responsible for the famous *Catalan Atlas* of 1375, which was in the library of Charles V of France at the time of his death. As well as two sections covering Europe and Africa from the Atlantic to Jerusalem, the *Catalan Atlas* has a further two sections covering Asia from Jerusalem to China and Sumatra, incorporating the best information brought back by Italian travellers earlier in the century. Abraham's son Jahuda succeeded him as '*Magister cartorum navigandi*' to the Aragonese court, and can probably be identified as the Majorcan cartographer recruited by Prince Henry of Portugal, 'the navigator', in 1419 to supply maps to his sea captains. In the fifteenth century Lisbon and Barcelona joined Genoa and Venice as the principal places in which portolans were drawn. For those travelling by land there was nothing as sophisticated as a portolan. The normal means of finding the direction for travel was from manuscript road books, or sometimes long rolls, which give lists of places on the way, with distances between them, exactly like the port books which preceded the portolans. When printing came in, these manuscript road books were replaced by printed itineraries giving the same information. In England the earliest printed itineraries to survive are those at the end of the 1541 edition of the much reprinted *Chronycle of years*, but obviously compiled at some time before the Reformation, since it gives the route to the Marian shrine at Walsingham.[85] In Germany the earliest to survive is also printed with a chronicle, Sebastian Brant's *Chronik über Teutschland* in 1543, although equally patently compiled earlier. In France the earliest is Charles Estienne's specific *Guide des chemins de France* entirely devoted to routes; and in Italy the equivalent was a guide printed by the Genoese postmaster Cherubini de Stella in 1563.[86] One of the most comprehensive of the manuscript road books was that compiled some time between 1375 and 1425 in or around Bruges and therefore known to historians as the *Itinéraire de Bruges*. We only have a fair copy, full of blunders, commissioned by one of Philip the Good's bastard sons, the Abbot of St Bavo at Ghent, Raphael de Mercatelis, which is now in the library of the University of Ghent. As a prestige production for a grand library, it is beautifully presented like the grand portolans drawn for the same market. Like the earliest English printed itineraries, the Bruges *Itinéraire* combines mostly commercial roads with some pilgrim routes, such as the road from Bruges to Compostella. It was probably because of the pilgrim routes that the bibliophile abbot had it copied, although it might just have been sheer curiosity.[87] Whatever his reason I am particularly grateful to him, for his *Itinéraire* provided the framework for my own investigation of late medieval land routes. As well as itineraries, land maps also existed in the Middle Ages, and a very few survive – the Gough Map, for example, which shows English roads around 1360, and a slightly earlier Italian map.[88] Erhard Etzlaub of Nuremberg's *Romweg Karte* (Map of roads to Rome) of 1500, is a traditional set of pilgrim itineraries innovatively set out in graphic form, with the distances between towns indicated by the number of dots on the road on the map. Every dot, as he explained, represents a mile: '*der Rom-Weg von meylen zu meylen mit puncten verzeychnet von eyner stat zu der andern durch deutzsche lantt*'. It is possibly the earliest attempt at drawing a land map to scale.

Careers in business

We can get some idea of the sort of ideal career structure in business hoped for by young Italians, from the success stories of Giovanni Benci and Francesco Sassetti, who spent their entire careers with the Medici group of companies, and ended as general managers, in 1443–55 and 1463–90 respectively.[89]

Giovanni, the son of Amerigo Benci, came from a family of moderate means, which in the Florentine tax returns of 1427, the *catasto*, already owned a house in town and a small farm in the country. After completing his schooling, he began his commercial career at the age of 15 when he went to the Rome company of the Medici in 1409 as an office boy. He had become the head bookkeeper there before 1420. In 1424 he was sent to Geneva to prepare for the opening of a Medici company there, and when it opened he became its manager and a shareholder. In 1433 he opened a temporary branch in Basel, when the papal curia was effectively there during the general council of the church. In 1435 he returned to Florence as assistant general manager of the whole enterprise and ran the banking side of the business. In 1443 he succeeded as general manager, and presided over a period of considerable growth. He did not fail to enrich himself. In 1451, when the company structure was reorganized, he had been able to invest 18,000 florins in the holding company. The 1457 *catasto* shows that he had been able to leave his heirs property assessed at more than 26,000 florins, over a fifth of the declared wealth of the Medici themselves. His heirs had 7,400 florins on deposit in the Medici businesses, considerable investments in real estate, both farms and urban property, and a large holding of stock in government securities. By this time the Florentine state no longer expected to repay separate *prestanze* (forced loans) within a short period and had consolidated them into a perpetual mountain of debt, known as the *monte commune*. Shares in it had come to be regarded as a very secure investment, providing a regular fixed income. If their investments yielded 5%, they produced an unearned annual income of

1,300 florins, at a time when skilled workmen earned 25 to 30 florins a year. No wonder they were able to live in a palatial house.

Francesco, son of Tommaso Sassetti, was left an orphan at the age of four on the death of his father, a moneychanger in the Mercato Nuovo in Florence. He did not join the Medici until 1440, when he was nearly twenty, as a factor in Geneva. Within seven years he had risen first to be assistant manager and then manager of the Medici firm there, and became a shareholder both in the Geneva company, as later in its successor at Lyons, and in the Avignon firm. In 1459 he too returned to Florence as assistant general manager, and succeeded as general manager in 1463, only to preside over the decline of the commercial fortunes of the Medici, which was at least in part due to his own incompetence. He too enriched himself, perhaps not altogether scrupulously, and, at the height of his fortunes, was twice as wealthy as Benci had been. At this point he was able to build a new chapel for his family in the church of Santa Trinita in Florence, and to commission Domenico Ghirlandaio to fresco the walls and ceiling. The lunettes at the corners of these frescos celebrate four of the places in which he had worked. However the collapse of the Medici branch at Lyons shortly afterwards ruined him, and he died a relatively poor man in 1490.

Boccaccio, one of the most famous Florentine authors of the fourteenth century, came from a minor noble family of the subject city of Certaldo. His father worked for the Bardi, and, after *abbaco* school, he himself began a commercial career at the age of thirteen in 1326, working with his father in the Bardi branch in Naples. After what he considered 'six wasted years' in the Ruga Cambiorum (Bankers' Row), where the Bardi had their offices in the heart of the business district of Naples, and a further spell as a student of canon law, he was eventually able to escape into a literary life. His most celebrated work, *The Decameron*, a hundred stories ostensibly told over ten days during the first visitation of bubonic plague in 1348, is full of merchants. Although the plots of many of his tales are very old, and imported, through the Arabic world from Indian traditional collections of stories, he retold them in contemporary terms with extensive and elaborate commercial settings ideally suited to his Florentine audience, at the time when Florence was still the leading commercial–industrial city in Europe. The stories nominally told on just one day, the second, include Genoese carracks returning from Constantinople, highway robbers, horse dealers in Naples, Genoese pirates falling on Pisa, galleys going to Alexandria, slavers and domestic slaves in Genoa, Catalan boats at Rhodes, Cypriots trading in Armenia, Florentine merchants in England and Lombard merchants from Piacenza trading in Paris and Alexandria.

This Italian merchant seems to be working out how to cope with some emergency revealed in the letter he is reading. Perhaps it tells him that a ship had been set upon and robbed, in which he was sending hundreds of florins worth of pearls and other merchandise to Valencia, uninsured. Buonaccorso Berardi received just such devastating news in a letter from Gregorio Datini September 1393.

There were a number of factors in all leading commercial societies that worked together to encourage capital accumulation. No one with initiative was precluded from active participation in business or manufacture. This demanded social attitudes that saw no derogation in the involvement of the elites in commerce and industry, and the investment in trade of resources

Climate for growth and capital accumulation

drawn from land-owning. Conversely Florentine, Venetian, Nuremberg, and Augsburg merchant patricians, like Dutch Regents and British industrialists after them, took pleasure in noble pursuits. In Florence there was jousting on the square in front of Santa Croce, and in Venice on the square in front of St Mark's. Successful merchants put their money into land, despite the relatively low returns, not only because of the security of such investments, but because of the social dimension of land ownership. The Bardi and the Medici, the Stromeir and the Fugger put such a high proportion of their profits into land not only for security and income, but because they and other successful businessmen came to think of themselves as noble (and going back to the no derogation theme, many of them were of noble origin), and wished others to think the same.[90] The possession of landed estates and castles, rural villas, and grand country houses was an essential part of living nobly.

In these societies the involvement of dominant political individuals, mostly nobility, in business meant a consequent political preoccupation of the government with the economy, unlike most medieval states. The late medieval Venetian state has been likened to a gigantic joint stock company, but that could never be said of the kingdom of France. The leading commercial centres of Europe all gave themselves favourable taxation systems, and showed a willingness to invest public money in the infrastructure. They all came to possess variants of a common taxation system. The main emphasis was on indirect taxation. This was the case in fourteenth-century Florence, where the gate taxes on essentials coming into the city, and, as Florence took over other city-states, coming into those cities too, produced a large share of its regular income. In the fifteenth-century Burgundian Netherlands the finances of the cities relied heavily on excise duties, a tradition inherited by sixteenth- and seventeenth-century Holland. Such an emphasis on indirect rather than direct taxation favoured saving and accumulation rather than spending. It also bore more heavily on the poor than on the rich, for such taxation was levied most frequently on necessities – bread, wine, beer – rather than on luxuries. Internal excises on necessities provide an easily collectable and reasonably regular income, not easily disturbed, like customs revenues, by foreign war or blockade. Even when war did make mammoth demands for additional funds, there was, as far as possible, a deliberate avoidance of direct taxation of the rich. In Florence, over a hundred years, many of them not at all peaceful, elapsed between the expiry of the thirteenth-century direct tax, the *estimo*, and the use in the fifteenth-century of the detailed declarations of wealth, the *catasto*, as a basis for direct taxes as well as loans. In between the rich did not pay for wars, they lent the necessary money for wars to the state, and received interest on their loans from it. That interest was paid for by the indirect taxes levied on goods consumed by the poor. The money loaned to the Florentine state still counted as part of the capital of the lender, as the obligations of the state were resellable, and a good investment. In the Burgundian Netherlands in time of war the central government was granted taxation, but, in so far as this fell on the cities, they raised it by selling *renten*, negotiable fixed-interest annuities, rather than by taxing their citizens directly. Once again the rich were able to escape direct taxes, and the interest on their *renten*, and sometimes the redemption of their capital too, was paid for by excises.

The increase in the supply of money may not have been directly a cause of the late medieval commercial revolution, but it was a necessary pre-condition for it. Without an adequate money supply available in the countryside, even if only seasonally, the landlords could not have taken advantage of the pressure that growing population was enabling them to put on their tenants and bring about the revolution in rents that they desired. Without such a revolution in rents the landlords could not have achieved an enhanced standard of living and obtained a variety of choice of purchases that had not been available before. The demand generated in the mining areas might have initiated commercial and industrial expansion, but it was the strong and sustained demand from the rulers and landowners that acted as the stimulus to continuous commercial and industrial growth almost uninterruptedly for a century and a half. Without the concentrated force of that demand in capital cities, rather than scattered between rural castles throughout western Europe, merchants could not have operated on an adequate scale for the revolutionary division of labour in commerce to take place, with all its ancillary changes.

An example that elegantly ties together a number of these strands is provided by the accounts of the Trésor du Louvre. Philip IV of France, in need of money for his war with Aragon, was granted permission by Pope Nicholas IV to tax the revenues of the French clergy. In 1289 one of the largest international business houses in Florence, the company of Musciatto and Albizzo di Guido di Figline, commonly known as the 'Franzesi' on account of the amount of business they did for the king of France, were nominated as receivers of this tax, a tenth, in the Auvergne. The company sent out three men, led by Noffo Dei, their resident agent at the Champagne fairs, who collected it in ready cash and transported it by cart to the May fair at Provins, where the coin was used for loans and the purchase of goods.[91] At one stroke coin was drawn out of rural Auvergne directly into the mainstream of international banking and trade.

From rural rent to courtly living, from banking and international trade to public revenue and military service, the long thirteenth century of the commercial revolution witnessed a series of fundamental transformations, each associated with a complete change in the scale of, and attitudes to, the use of money. The whole period from this commercial revolution to the industrial revolution of the eighteenth and nineteenth centuries possessed an economic unity, the basis of which was established by these radical transformations arising from the new uses of money. These fundamental changes lay behind and underpinned the whole fabric of medieval European trade to which this book is devoted.

Money supply and economic change

These fifteenth-century leather purses are rare survivals of once familiar objects. They were so common that there were even guilds of purse-makers. Their regulations stipulated that no apprentice might be qualified until he could produce purses from which the smallest coins in circulation would not escape, and some medieval coins were very small indeed.

2

Courts and consumers

This fifteenth-century French miniature appears to show subjects bringing in their tax payments in bags and boxes to a royal figure in person, with an office in the background, but this was no longer literally the case in the fifteenth century. The whole process had been highly bureaucratic for two centuries. In France tax payments were made locally to royal officials and transmitted by them to the royal Trésor, *and audited either by the* Chambre des Comptes *or* Cour des Aides, *depending on the type of tax. The nearest that coin came to royal hands was in the tiny sums handed Charles VII in person, for such purposes as gambling, by his* Argentier *Jacques Coeur.*

IN THE SIXTEENTH CENTURY Giovanni Botero neatly summed up the importance of the capital city in his time:

> It doth infinitely avail to the magnifying and making cities great and populous the residency of the prince therein according to the greatness of whose empire she does increase for where the prince is resident, there also the parliaments are held, and the supreme place of justice is there kept. All matters of importance have recourse to that place, all princes and all persons of account, ambassadors of princes and of commonwealths, and all agents of cities that are subject make their repair thither; all such as aspire and thirst after offices and honours rush thither amain with emulation and disdain for others. Thither are the revenues brought that pertain unto the state, and there are they disposed of again.[1]

Giovanni Botero's description of the capital cities and their size and importance in 1588 could equally have been used at any time since the remarkable growth in government in the thirteenth century, when capital cities first sprang into prominence. Just as Fernand Braudel wrote of a 'long sixteenth century', I have written of a 'long thirteenth century', stretching from the 1160s to the 1330s.[2] From the 1160s on, there was a continuous series of newly opened-up mines in Europe producing silver on an increasingly large scale. As money increased in quantity, it could be used more freely for a wide range of activities in which it had previously played a minimal role. It was only from the late twelfth century that rulers began to be able to draw considerable and regular money incomes from their subjects.

In the first place, rulers became freer, from the second half of the twelfth century, to choose where they would live. Hitherto they had had to perambulate incessantly between places to which the produce of their estates could conveniently be brought for consumption, literally living off domain production and rent paid in kind on the spot. When the proportion of the produce of their estates received in money rather than in kind increased rapidly, it became much easier for them and their courts and administrators to remain static for long periods. In this way each of the patchwork of formerly feudal states that made up twelfth-century 'France' was able to develop a 'capital' in which its ruler, or at least his administration, was permanently to be found – for example at Paris, Provins, Poitiers or Toulouse. Round the palaces of the rulers clustered the houses of their nobles, for this same liberation from the necessity of living in the countryside was also experienced by the landowning

y commence le liuxe Intitule de
[ri]chesse. Et premierement comē
[ri]chesse empesche souuent le sau
[ue]ment

ostre sauueur ihū
crist en son euuan
gile ou viiᵉ chᵖᵣe
de saint mathieu
Je vꝰ dy feablement
ue vng richs home diffialement
u a paines entrera ou Royaume
es cieulx. Et en cest mesmes chi

dune aguille que vng riche nentr
rõit ou Royaume du ael. Translatez
Ces deux auctoritez icy ont bien
mestier de expoficiõ pourae que
quant a la premiere il est bien a
noter que mõ sauueur ne dist
me que ce soit impossible dung
riche hõme estre sauuez mais dist
que cest difficile. Car cest bien diffi
ale de posseder richesses et de top esae
en lamour dicelles escrirez et dete[nir]
et non estre en lamour dicelles accu[ez]

HI PRAEFVRVNT ÆRAR HI VERO KT IVLII M CCCCLXVIII
IO KT IAN MCCCCLXVII ANDREAS CAPACIVS
ANDREAS D XPHORI MANNVS BARTHOLOMAEI VTEL
CAPACIVS CAM LONVS SIACOBVS PETRI HV
NICOLAVS BAPISTAE MIDVS KATHERINVS NANN
VENTVRINVS IS NERII NICOLAVS PIC
THOMMAS VRBA COLMINI PICCOLMINEVS
NI IOANNELVS MATHEVS PINOCII SCRIP
DINVS BERTOCI MARTVS SARDVINVS LEONAR
ALOISIVS OLDOBRANDI DI ARDVINVS TAB
CERETANVS MATHEV
S PINOCII SCRIPSATO
NIVS IOANIS BALNEARVS TB

classes in general. From the time that they were liberated in the thirteenth century from preponderantly living on their estates, by the commutation of goods rents and labour rents into money rents, many of them chose to spend at least part of the year 'at court', living in newly built, noble town houses in or near the capital of their ruler. At Provins, the *hôtels* of some of the nobility of Champagne still survive in the upper town beside the palace of their count. Such noblemen brought their rural incomes with them, or had them remitted to them there by their stewards. Their time 'at court' was a time for great spending, on, for example, conspicuous extravagance to emphasize political importance, or on foreign luxuries only available in such cities.

As well as the 'revenues that pertain to the state', of which Botero wrote, the revenues of the greater subjects were therefore also brought to the capitals, there to be 'disposed of again'. It was generally in the capitals that they chose to spend the major part of their rent rolls. It was the disposing of the revenues of states and of their greater subjects that made capital cities such magnets of demand. In a society in which commerce was so much more dominated by consumers than today's producer-oriented economies, capital cities were therefore of the utmost importance in generating local, regional, national, international and even inter-continental trade. The greater the state, the greater was the power of demand for the commodities of trade generated in its capital.

In the second place, rulers also became freer to hire and fire both their civil officials and their troops. Feudal society, strictly defined, had been one in which there had been a great devolution of power, since rulers had had to maintain both their military and civil officials by grants of land. The term *feuda* or fief, properly applied to the office, had been gradually transferred to the land used to support the official. As both their office and land had tended to become treated as hereditary property, such officials had become immovable and hence uncontrollable. For instance, counts, castellans or knights, who were responsible for counties, castles or fighting on horseback were all paid with land. In the same way chamberlains, responsible for royal or noble finances, were equally paid with land. Hereditary officials, who treated their fiefs, counties, castles and chamberlainships and the land that went with them as inalienable, exercised their offices in their own interests and no longer in that of their rulers. For rulers to be able to control their officials once more was a radical innovation.

In the last quarter of the twelfth century, money-fiefs – *fiefs rentes, feoda de bursa*, fiefs paid not in land, but in money – very suddenly became common in the Low Countries. From 1190 the same swift increase in such grants took place in England, and from 1200 in France and Germany. It was only when rulers regularly had enough money in hand that money-fiefs could replace enfeoffments with land as the normal means of paying knights and also, occasionally, other officials.[3] At the same time, it became normal to pay salaries in money to the general run of non-military officers in the service of rulers of western Europe. The availability of adequate and regular money incomes allowed for a revolution in the government of states.

The covers of the principal registers of the Provisores, *overseers, of the* Biccherna, *Lords of the Treasury, the financial magistracy, of the Sienese state, were frequently painted with scenes of their activities. That in 1468 shows officials paying out sums of money. On the right, payment is being made to a war captain and a token number of soldiers. On the left payment is being made to some of the principal servants of the state. In peace and war alike the Sienese state paid a huge range of officials, from the* podesta *who was in charge of law and order throughout its territories down to those who ensured that the city streets were cleaned every Saturday. As well as sums paid out to the numerous members of the city fire brigade and those who maintained bridges and fortifications in the countryside, the state also supported health and education: hospitals in the city and spas in the countryside, and the university of which it was so proud. Every activity had to be meticulously recorded, every expenditure authorised and justified, a perpetual flood of correspondence kept up, and a huge number of courts and tribunals staffed. Many of the consequently large secretariat on the state payroll were highly qualified and expensive notaries.*

Castellans and knights paid with money did not become hereditary as their land-paid predecessors had done, nor did 'civil servants' paid with money. Henry the Liberal was able to reorganize the local administration of his county of Champagne into twenty-nine *prévôtés*, each administered by a *prévôt* who was paid in money, not land. Thus the first post-feudal states could emerge.

Such enormously increased money incomes of cities, princes and kings quickly affected the conduct of war and politics. The use of money in politics and war is well illustrated by the 40,000 marks of silver that John of England sent to pay for the Bouvines campaign of 1214.[4] Indeed their enlarged money incomes allowed kings and princes the possibility of running their states and maintaining power by the payment of regular salaries in money, without prejudicing the future by grants of land to maintain officials or soldiers.

When, in the course of the thirteenth century, the kings of France acquired so many of these twelfth-century states, Paris came to absorb the attributes of their lesser capitals into itself. Paris thus became the greatest single focus in France, not only for political activity, but also for consumer demand, whilst Provins and Toulouse died as capital cities. It was therefore in thirteenth-century Paris that Professor Strayer found the 'medieval origins of the modern state' as far as France was concerned.[5]

It was also in the thirteenth century that the problem of financing post-feudal war began to be solved. When the size and regularity of their money incomes was sufficiently assured, and when banking had evolved to an adequate scale, rulers were able to use their regular incomes as security for borrowing large lump sums. Such possibilities of anticipating their regular incomes gave them a much greater freedom of action in emergencies. In this way post-feudal armies could be paid in wartime, just as post-feudal administrations could be paid in peacetime. Sienese bankers gave this sort of help to Frederick II, Florentine bankers to Charles of Anjou, and a variety of Tuscan bankers to both Edward I and Philip IV in their wars with one another.[6]

All these developments depended on the development of a market-oriented economy in the rural west. The initiative was always that of the landlords, but it was not possible for the transformation to take place fully until there was a market, and money available for the peasant to obtain by selling his produce. Professor Fossier has shown how payment in money rather than in work was an increased burden on all but the most prosperous tenants. To have his labour returned to him and to be expected instead to provide a money- or goods-rent out of the produce of a holding that he had hitherto farmed to sustain himself and his family, without the size of the holding being increased, meant the handing-over, or compulsory sale on the market, of a large proportion of the produce that he and his family had previously consumed, and so a radical diminution of their standard of living. It was the availability of markedly increased supplies of coined money, combined with population pressures, that enabled landlords to push their often reluctant tenants into a market economy, by demanding increasing quantities of cash from them.[7] The transition from an economy in which money had

had a relatively minor role to one in which it was the measure of all things was not without difficulties, even for landlords.[8] Yet kings and princes, as the greatest landlords in their territories, stood to gain, like other landlords, from the increased possibilities of compelling their tenants to pay rents in money. Many other traditional sources of 'income' in goods and services were equally transformed into money. The counts of Flanders, for example, had systematically imposed this conversion to money by 1187, and in royal France a similar transformation was largely brought about early in the thirteenth century by Philip Augustus.

In addition, the widespread availability of money in the hands of a numerous peasantry also allowed for the imposition of direct taxation on a much larger scale than anything attempted since antiquity. This was yet another of the novelties of the long thirteenth century. In England direct taxation began even at the end of the twelfth century. The thirteenth century therefore saw the reappearance of 'large' cities in the west for the first time since the eventual break-up of the Roman world. Their emergence depended on the development of a market economy in the rural west.

One very crude measure of the importance of these cities is the wealth of the princes around whom they grew up. We have scattered information about some early fourteenth-century rulers,[9] but its significance depends on the proportion of the wealth of the country that they ruled. The accounts of Philip VI of France, surviving for 1329, reveal an income, before the outbreak of the prolonged war with England, equivalent to 785,912 Florentine florins.[10] At the same time the annual income of Robert of Naples (1309–43), who was ruling over the mainland part of the older Kingdom of Sicily, has been estimated as equal to 600,000 Florentine florins,[11] whilst that of Edward II of England, between 1316 and 1324 averaged the equivalent of 546,000 florins a year. I have no figures for the income of James II Aragon (1291–1327), the brother of the king of Sicily, but the Florentine chronicler, Giovanni Villani, said that both their incomes were lower than that of the city state of Florence.[12] On these grounds alone Paris should have been the most important royal capital in western Europe, followed by Naples, Westminster (when combined with nearby London), Barcelona and Palermo. The kings of Bohemia and Hungary had even lower royal incomes, despite their royalties on the mining of silver and gold. Prague and Buda, although growing fast in the fourteenth century, consequently lagged in importance as centres of demand. Poorer still were the kings of Poland, Portugal, Denmark, Sweden and Scotland. The kings of Castile strangely remained itinerant long after other kings had settled down, so that in the fourteenth century there was still no capital to the relatively wealthy kingdom of Castile.[13] As a consequence, although there were a number of relatively large cities in late medieval Castile – Seville, Cordoba, Toledo, Valladolid and Burgos – there was none that was overwhelmingly large until the rapid growth of Madrid from the late sixteenth century onwards. The emperors had no capital either, since their office was still elective. In the fourteenth century, the imperial crown was most

The wealth of rulers

frequently worn by members of the Luxembourg, Habsburg and Wittels-bach families, who ran the impoverished vestiges of imperial administration from their own family lands and never created an imperial capital.

There were, however, uncrowned princes with greater incomes than many kings. In northern Italy the Visconti rulers of Milan have to be reckoned amongst the richest rulers of fourteenth-century Europe. The Visconti power in northern Italy was temporarily eclipsed by the Della Scala rulers of Verona, who in the 1330s controlled no fewer than thirteen city states. Giovanni Villani reckoned that in 1336, Mastino Della Scala of Verona had an annual income equivalent to 700,000 Florentine florins, which he recognized was only exceeded by that of the king of France. For most of the century it was the Milanese rulers who had that sort of income. Giovanni Villani knew what he was talking about. He was not only managing director of the third biggest business in Florence, but also one of the city's commissioners for coordinating its successful war effort against Della Scala expansion. In 1343, when the war was over, the city chamberlains of Florence accounted for revenues of 942,000 lire, approximately 314,000 florins, which corresponds to Villani's estimate of the income of the city in 1336–38 of normally 300,000 florins, sometimes more, sometimes less. Florence had at this stage barely embarked on the series of acquisitions that were to make it the veritable capital of Tuscany by the fifteenth century. (By then in all of Tuscany only Siena and Lucca remained independent, and that not for want of attempts to subdue them on the part of the Florentines.) This greatly expanded Medicean Tuscan state, with Florence as its capital, was still in the future in Villani's time, but even the smaller Florentine state of his own days disposed of an income greater than several kings, the emperor, or even the pope. John XXII (1316–34) aggressively expanded papal revenues from all parts of Latin Christendom to pay for the expensive armies that he fielded in his vain attempts to reconquer the papal states, but his annual income was no more than the equal of 228,000 Florentine florins. Avignon, then the papal capital, consequently ranked far behind Paris and Milan, Venice and Naples, London and Barcelona, Palermo and Florence as a centre of consumption.

Venice is in this list, since it too counted as a capital city in the first half of the fourteenth century, even though the republic did not yet rule any territory in mainland Italy. Apart from the city itself the Venetian state then consisted of extensive but scattered territories overseas. By the early fifteenth century, Venice had rapidly acquired lands in Italy as well, conquering Verona and almost all the territories that the Della Scala had ruled, so that by the 1420s it was possibly the richest capital in Europe.

Outside northern Italy, the richest non-royal principalities were to be found in the southern Netherlands. The counts of Flanders were particularly wealthy, followed at some distance by the dukes of Brabant and the counts of Hainault-Holland. Although the counts of Flanders could not rival the Visconti in Milan or the richer kings, they possessed incomes larger than the poorer kings. Ghent, Brussels and Valenciennes were proportionately important as capitals. When in the 1430s Philip the Good of Burgundy acquired all

This detail from a Franco-Flemish altarpiece of 1475 shows the old Louvre, built in Paris in the 1360s for King Charles V. It was a moated residence for the king and his household, a strong, but comfortable rebuild of Philip II's dour twelfth-century fortress. At that time Louis XI was based at Plessis near Tours and only visited Paris occasionally. Since he and other fifteenth-century kings spent their resources on grand palaces along the Loire, they left Charles V's Louvre virtually unchanged for over a century-and-a-half.

these principalities, their combined revenues made him the wealthiest ruler in Europe, surpassing even the Venetian Republic, the richest kings and the Duke of Milan.

There were a myriad other principalities scattered through Europe, particularly in the Empire, most of which had a static prince and a miniature capital. A few of them had some importance as magnets of demand. The dukes of Austria liked to compare themselves with the kings of Bohemia, but were probably not even as rich as the kings of Poland, so that Vienna was probably less a centre of consumption than Cracow.

The money incomes of rulers that I have quoted from the second quarter of the fourteenth century represent an end point to a long period of growth that went back to the second half of the twelfth century. It is hard to measure the extent of this growth, not only because we lack detailed information on royal incomes at an earlier period, but also because it is harder to compare currencies before the middle of the thirteenth century. From Florence we have partial accounts from the city chamberlains for 1240 which suggest an annual income of around 26,000 Florentine lire. A century later it was 942,000 Florentine lire. Taking account of the fall in the value of Florentine money, a reasonable suggestion might be that the real income of the city state increased elevenfold over the century. These figures are merely suggestive, but do lead us to believe that the real incomes and hence the purchasing power of some kings, princes and cities increased very largely indeed in the course of the thirteenth century.

Apart from war, and the maintenance of a paid civil service, the most important use of their vastly increased incomes made by rulers in the later Middle Ages, and indeed well into the Early Modern period, was for building. Successive rulers built themselves grander, or at least more up-to-date, palaces than their predecessors, to house not only themselves, but also their organs of government. This was still as true of Philip II's Escorial and of Louis XIV's Versailles as it was of Henry III's Palace of Westminster. In Paris at the beginning of the thirteenth century Philip II was still living in the bleak donjon of the Louvre and it was there that the foundations of the French administrative

The palaces of rulers

state were laid. In the middle of the century, his grandson, (St) Louis IX, began the rebuilding of a much earlier palace on the Ile de la Cité. From this complex of buildings, the palace chapel, the Sainte Chapelle, designed to house the King's most precious relic, which he believed to be the 'Crown of Thorns', still survives as one of the finest and most lavish examples of mid-thirteenth-century architecture. The building and rebuilding of this palace continued through the reigns of his son and grandson, and it was only finished to the satisfaction of Philip IV near the end of his reign, when there were grand celebrations lasting two weeks to mark its completion.[14]

The palace contained not only the apartments in which the king lived, the *logis du roi*, but also the main departments of government, finance, justice, and the chancery, which, little by little, had not only become permanently settled in Paris, but were brought back within the palace itself at the time of Philip IV's rebuilding.

The most recent arrival was the Treasury, together with a house for the Treasurer. The Treasure had previously been kept by the Knights Templar at their Temple in the north of the city. The Treasury had only been brought into the palace under Philip IV by his finance minister, Enguerrand de Marigny, who had helped plan the palace.[15] The Treasury joined the separate auditing department, the *chambre des comptes*, which was already established there, staffed by professional *maîtres des comptes*, with a keen eye for financial irregularities among local revenue collectors. The principal law courts of the country, the *parlements* of Paris, were also established there, and the great hall built by Philip IV for the formal sessions of the Parlement still stands. No longer was justice commonly given out immediately by the king himself, although St Louis had still given some personal judgments. One such occasion, when he sat giving judgment under an oak at Vincennes, was nostalgically recorded by Joinville in his old age. However, by the reign of Philip IV, the central administration of justice was in the hands of *parlements* staffed by professional lawyers organized in three chambers.

The Chancery, which had evolved from the royal writing office, was the core of the permanent royal administration in the palace, run by professional university-trained bureaucrats. It was through the Chancery that royal commands reached the localities and that the country was governed. Next to the palace chapel were the muniments, in the *trésor des chartes*, which were the filed archives that gave the government the teeth of precedent and the knowledge to encroach on other jurisdictions and to defend itself against the encroachments of others. Until the thirteenth century such muniments as the kings had possessed had been peripatetic with the king. By the beginning of the fourteenth century the royal palace in the Ile de la Cité thus already contained just such a grouping of departments of state as Botero was writing about in the sixteenth century. A continuous and increasing stream of people had been coming to Paris throughout the thirteenth century to deal with these officials.

The palace in which they worked was built at vast expense, and rows of houses had been destroyed to make way for it. Nevertheless by 1350 architec-

tural fashion had changed, and the new king, John II, felt that Philip IV's palace was hopelessly out of date. He chose instead to live in the Hôtel de Nesle, opposite the Louvre, when in Paris, but preferred to spend his time in the château he had rebuilt and elaborately decorated for himself at Vaudreuil in Normandy, three days' journey out of Paris. His son, Charles V, used his greatly increased income not only to pay his father's ransom in the 1360s and to drive the English out of France in the 1370s, but also to build himself grander new palaces, at Vincennes much closer to Paris, and to rebuild the Louvre in the city itself, which he finished in 1371.[16]

He handed his father's Hôtel de Nesle over to his younger brother the Duc de Berry. The older palace on the island in the Seine was left to the administrators. Eventually the lawyers took over the whole of it and adapted it for their purposes – and much of it went up in flames in the seventeenth century. Fifty years later Charles V's own renewed Louvre was abandoned in its turn. His son Charles VI regarded it as old-fashioned and last occupied it in 1418. He moved out to the other end of the city, to the Hôtel St-Paul, which, despite the civil war, he had expensively modernized and much enlarged. Charles VI remained there for the length of his reign and his widow lived there until her death in 1435. There was then no royal residence in Paris until the sixteenth century (below pp. 136–7). The Louvre became in turn a prison and an arsenal before its Renaissance rebuilding as a royal palace once more.

St Louis' youngest brother, Charles of Anjou, was also a palace builder in his newly conquered kingdom of Sicily (known as the 'Regno' and including most of Italy south of Rome). To keep a grip on his new lands he toured them relentlessly, and most of his civil servants had to travel with him. However, some parts of his administration were given permanent bases, and these were in Naples rather than Palermo. The Treasury, for example, was given a fixed seat in Naples in 1277, in the Castel dell'Ovo. In the years immediately following, 1279–83, he built himself the Castel Nuovo there as an impressive formal residence, in the place of both the Castel dell'Ovo and Frederick II's

Castel di Capua, which he regarded as old-fashioned. Charles was surely mindful of the fate of Pope John XXI, who had died in 1277 when the ceiling fell on him as he worked in the study in the too flimsily built extension he had just had constructed for his palace in Viterbo. Charles, therefore, built the Castel Nuovo very robustly. Nevertheless, only his palatine chapel survived the successive rebuildings of the Aragonese period. It is because of this mania for rebuilding, for regarding buildings of fifty years before as hopelessly out of date, that so few complete medieval palaces survive.[17]

When St Louis was rebuilding on the Ile de la Cité in Paris, his contemporary, Henry III of England, was also extensively rebuilding the 150-year-old palace at Westminster. The medieval English state had very similar institutions to the French, some of them rather older. The auditing department, the Exchequer, went back to the twelfth century. The much earlier Treasury, formerly at Winchester, later joined it at Westminster. At the very end of the century Hubert Walter remodelled the Chancery under John, and in 1215, Magna Carta provided that lawsuits should no longer follow the king. The English high courts, the court of King's Bench and the court of Common Pleas evolved over the following years and were housed in Henry III's palace at Westminster.[18] Of Henry III's extensive building, nothing survives, although the twelfth-century great hall, magnificently re-roofed in the fourteenth century, still exists. It was here that the sessions of the courts of Common Pleas, King's Bench and Chancery were held. Much of Henry III's palace was remodelled out of existence by later kings. When Edward II rebuilt it some years after the fire of 1297, a distinction began to be made between the 'Great Palace' which housed the institutions of government, and the 'Privy Palace' in which the king himself lived. After the fire of 1512 Henry VIII built himself a new palace in Whitehall and abandoned the old one to parliament.

Only at Avignon does a fourteenth-century palace survive virtually unchanged, and that was small compared with those of Paris and Westminster. The papal palace was redesigned and greatly extended by Clement VI in

Detail of a fresco in one of Clement VI's private rooms.

The plan (below) of the papal palace at Avignon makes it clear how much this was built as a seat of government. The buildings shaded in grey were added by Clement V.

1. Stables. 2. Woodstore.
3. Kitchens. 4. Buttery and pantry.
5. Great Dining Hall.
6. *Below:* Camera Apostolica;
Above: Pope's Audience Chamber.
7. *Above:* Library.
8. 'Angel Tower'. *Ground floor:* Treasury. *First floor:* Chamberlains.
Second floor: Pope's private chambers.
9. *Below:* lavatories and baths. *Above:* Pope's study. 10. *Above:* Pope's private dining room.
11. *Above:* Pope's private kitchen.
12. Chapel of Benedict XII.
13. Grand staircase.
14. Wing for members of the Papal household. 15. Consistory. Grand reception hall. 16. *Below:* Papal guards. *Above:* Senior Bureaucrats. 17. Great Gate of Clement VI.
18. *Below:* Tribunal of Chancery.
Above: Chamber of Cardinal Chamberlain.
19. Main staircase of honour.
20. *Below:* Principal Law Court.

the 1340s. Fifty years later, when it would normally have been vulnerable to rebuilding, the papacy had split in two and Benedict XIII (Peter de Luna), the Spanish pope resident in Avignon, was almost without supporters and could not afford to rebuild it. It was soon abandoned for good. It is still possible to see the rooms in which the papal administration of well over six hundred people worked in the 1340s.[19] This administration had developed early, because the nature of papal resources and obligations, stretching across the whole of Latin Christendom, demanded a greater degree of organization if they were to hold together at all. At Rome, where the popes were mainly based in the twelfth and thirteenth centuries, a papal Chancery developed early. There was also a papal auditing department, the Camera Apostolica, and papal law courts, the Great Audience or Rota, and the Lesser Audience, to which appeals came in enormous numbers from all parts of Europe. In the fourteenth century the popes were mainly based at Avignon, although most of them expended a great deal of energy in attempting to return to Rome. Whilst it was at Avignon Pope John XXII radically overhauled the machinery of papal government. It is still possible to visit the rooms in which the new streamlined Camera Apostolica, the Treasury, the Chancery and the law courts conducted their business and to get the feel of how a medieval administration was articulated, in a way that is impossible in Paris or Westminster. It is even possible to see the giant slots for concealing treasure chests beneath the stone slabbed floor of the Lower Treasury. It is also, most improbably, possible to see the private apartments of pope Clement VI himself, complete with their original wall paintings. These rooms are most precious, since the

John XXII, a very capable administrator, spent the resources of the papacy on a series of bloody but unsuccessful wars in Italy so that he could return to Rome. His austere and pious successor, Benedict XII (1334–42), an ex-inquisitor, thought this improper. So he bought the palace of the bishop of Avignon, had it pulled down and had a practical permanent headquarters for the papacy built there, around a cloister, with each building specifically designed for the department that it was to house. The strong 'Angel Tower' rising above the rest of the palace in the centre of the view above, had the Treasury at its lowest level. His huge palace already dominated the city, but his successor, the flamboyant Clement VI (1342–52), added a huge grand court, and had the whole palace magnificently re-frescoed.

private apartments of a ruler were naturally the most vulnerable to modernization and survived only because they were deserted – and dry.

A huge mixture of administrators and lawyers, gaolers and couriers, as well as those attending on the pope himself, worked, and many also lived, within the palace. These included in 1320, for example, a hundred and eight young noblemen as his squires, as well as physicians, launderers, and staff for the kitchen and stables. Specialists came for a time, like the team of painters, headed by Matteo Giovanetti of Viterbo, who came from all over Europe, from 1343 onwards, to refresco the palace as it was rebuilt for Clement VI. Courts always provided plenty of work for painters. John II of France, for example, commissioned Jean Coste in 1350 to paint frescoes at Vaudreuil in emulation of Clement VI's new frescoes which he had recently seen at Avignon.[20] Two years earlier the Emperor Charles IV had begun having his great rural retreat at Karlstejn in Bohemia decorated, whilst successive doges were having the palace in Venice frescoed in the same decade.[21] As well as the works of art that have survived in churches, there were once many more that have not survived in palaces. These ranged from frescoes (which were usually overwhelmed by new fashion, as in Venice, or perished from damp, as at Vaudreuil), to panel paintings (which being portable were a trifle more likely to survive, particularly portraits in increasing numbers from the mid-fourteenth century onwards) to ephemera, painted often by very distinguished artists for occasions of pageantry, royal weddings, coronations and ceremonial first 'entries' to capitals, which were never intended to last for more than the instant of celebration.

From the fifteenth century the palace of Federigo da Montefeltro, the first duke of Urbino, also survives intact, through the happy accident for the historian that, on the expiry of the Montefeltro dynasty, the duchy was taken over by the papacy and there were no more resident dukes to rebuild the palace. It was most appropriate for Castiglione to set *The Courtier* in the circle of Federigo's cultivated daughter-in-law, Isabella, which gathered in the duchess's apartments in this palace. The whole magnificent building focuses on the dramatic and dominant balcony from which Federigo could survey his principality and show himself to his people. Here too there are rooms not only for those who ran his household and managed his estates, but also for those who staffed the government departments of his tiny state. It also housed accountants, cooks, masters in Chancery and men to look after the vast ducal stables, as well as famous, and less famous, painters who came to Urbino from the Netherlands and Spain and many parts of Italy, like Piero della Francesca, Botticelli and Justus of Ghent. Since so much of their work was on panels, far more of it survives than from the patronage of any comparable fourteenth- or thirteenth-century ruler, including a notable portrait of the patron himself. The scale and splendour of such a palace, built in so minor a principality, albeit for an aesthete of a prince, enriched by his military expertise, can only hint at the still greater splendour of the palaces of major rulers that no longer survive.

The situation in Brussels is much more normal. Only the footings of the

With his distinctive nose, the cultivated Federigo da Montefeltro, Count and then Duke of Urbino, (1444–82), shows himself, behind a rich oriental carpet, as he wished to be seen, not wearing armour and holding a sword, but in princely clothing pensively holding a volume from his celebrated library. It is a propaganda picture of a ruler who greatly enriched his tiny state by selling his services as a leader of mercenaries.

great hall can be seen today of the palace on the Coudenberg of the dukes of Brabant which was inherited by Philip the Good of Burgundy. Here he maintained the most lavish court in Europe and twice remodelled and extended the palace, particularly to cope with the ceremonial of elaborate receptions. Everything else has vanished. The modern palace of the kings of Belgium, laid out on a different axis, which overlays a part of it, provides an appropriate continuity in use of the site, but that is all. A few tantalizing manuscript miniatures show us just a little of what once existed.

It is so easy to think of great medieval architecture in terms of churches, which took so much longer to build and were so much less vulnerable to changes of fashion, but much of the greatest secular architecture is no longer to be seen. We can admire the grand fireplaces built only for the guards at St Louis' port of Aigues Mortes – but what of the fireplaces that St Louis and Philip IV built for themselves in the palace of the Ile de la Cité? Yet in their day, they not only existed in magnificence, but of course generated a demand for stone and timber, sometimes quarried or felled at considerable distances. The trades in stone and timber are ones that are often overlooked. Within the palaces, the furniture and furnishings were even more prone to fashion than the buildings themselves and even less likely to survive. All the furniture has

The city of Urbino rises to a ridge on which the counts had their fortress. From the 1440s to the 1460s Federigo used some of his wealth as a successful condottiere to rebuild the castle of his ancestors in the new Renaissance style. The great state rooms around the courtyard face away from us, but between the two turrets on the right of the picture are the private apartments of Federigo from which he could look out westwards over his city and across his principality to the ridge of the Apennines.

Federigo commissioned the Florence workshop of Baccio Pontelli to create the famous trompe l'oeil *inlays for his private study from drawings by the greatest artists of the day, to illustrate his many interests, here astronomy and music. They were finished in 1476.*

vanished from the palace at Avignon. It is surprising to find still surviving at Urbino the bed enclosure which gave the duke and his duchess some privacy in those vast rooms and the inlaid woodwork of the ducal *studiolo*. Normally we are reliant on paintings to offer us any sense of the interiors.

Kings had to be seen to die richly as well as to live richly. The royal mausoleum gave as much prestige to a dynasty as the audience halls and grand reception rooms did to its living head. Henry III spent as lavishly on rebuilding Westminster Abbey as he did on his new palace alongside. He particularly lavished attention on the shrine of his saintly predecessor, Edward the Confessor, who had died two hundred years before. In so doing he emphasized his own descent from the Anglo-Saxon kings. He also did so by giving his eldest son the Anglo-Saxon name Edward, and used the sanctity of the earlier Edward to increase the sacred aura of his own kingship.

In France the tombs of the Capetian kings, like their Carolingian and Merovingian forebears, were at the abbey of St-Denis, almost as near Paris as Westminster to London. The twelfth-century royal rebuilding of St-Denis had created the first major piece of Gothic architecture in Europe. Royalty had to be as up-to-date in death as in life. Louis IX largely rebuilt the basilica a century later. When his grandson, Philip IV, succeeded in having Boniface VIII canonize Louis IX, he did not rebuild St-Denis yet again, but he did reshuffle the tombs of the seven centuries of kings to give pride of place to St Louis, so that he too could use the sanctity of his grandfather to enhance the 'religion' of kingship with which he was trying to surround himself in his new palace.

Here was work for generations of masons and sculptors. The shrines, furthermore, provided a market for gold and jewels which the London and Paris goldsmiths sold to their respective kings for their adornment. It is difficult in the twenty-first century to envisage the richness of these royal shrines, since the Reformation in England and the Revolution in France stripped them of their gems. The nearest thing to survive is that of Saint Mark, treated like an ancestor by the Venetian Republic. The almost vulgarly gem-encrusted Pala d'Oro enables us to picture the reliquary-tombs these kings built for their ancestors and their own prestige.

Princely town houses

In addition to the revenues of the ruler, the capital saw a great concentration of the revenues of his greater subjects, who came, in the course of the thirteenth century, to build their own great houses around the palace of their monarch (see map opposite).

By the fourteenth century, Paris boasted a score or so *hôtels* of the greatest of the territorial princes of France, houses which themselves were small palaces.[22] The Hôtel d'Artois, which in the fourteenth century came into the possession of the dukes of Burgundy, was the headquarters of the administration of the lands of the dukes until they made Brussels their own capital in the fifteenth century. It was not from Dijon, or from Lille, that the affairs of Flanders and Artois and the two Burgundies were run at the end of the fourteenth century, but from Paris. The same could be said (amongst others) of

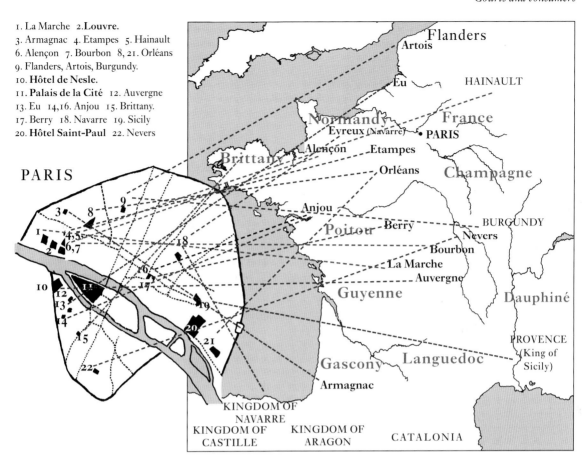

Key to map:
1. La Marche 2.**Louvre.**
3. Armagnac 4. Etampes 5. Hainault
6. Alençon 7. Bourbon 8, 21. Orléans
9. Flanders, Artois, Burgundy.
10. **Hôtel de Nesle.**
11. **Palais de la Cité** 12. Auvergne
13. Eu 14,16. Anjou 15. Brittany.
17. Berry 18. Navarre 19. Sicily
20. **Hôtel Saint-Paul** 22. Nevers

Princes and their Paris palaces c. 1400. On the left the hôtels *of some of the great princes are shown within the walls of Paris. The royal palaces are marked in bold in the key. On the right are the areas ruled by these princes. Their presence in Paris made the city a centre of consumption that drew on princely revenues from immense areas of territory, including principalities that were not at that time within the Kingdom of France: the Kingdom of Navarre, which was entirely independent; and the counties of Provence, Burgundy and Hainault, and part of Flanders which were all then quite clearly within the Empire, not France. Taxpayers in Navarre or Hainault had the mortification of seeing their taxes spent in Paris, not in Pamplona or Valenciennes!*

the dukes of Orléans, the dukes of Anjou, (who were also counts of Provence), the dukes of Berry, the Bourbons, the Alençons, the Armagnacs, the La Marches, and the dukes of Brittany. In other words, Paris had become the capital not only of France, but also of the great principalities of France. And it was the revenues not only of the king that came to Paris, and were to be disposed of again there, but those of these great magnates, whether from their own rent rolls or from their pensions from the crown.

Alongside the score or so *hôtels* of the great princes of the blood, and the descendants of the great feudatories of France, there were also twice as many *hôtels* of the great ecclesiastics of France. Not only did archbishops like those of Sens, of Rheims and of Rouen have their *hôtels* in Paris, but also lesser bishops like those of Le Mans and Laon and a whole range of abbots from those of Cluny, St-Denis and Clairvaux downwards. Whereas most of the lay magnates had their palaces on the north bank of the Seine, the ecclesiastics were mostly on the south, the university left bank. Some of them were as large and sumptuous as any of the *hôtels* of the great lay magnates. We still have part of the late fifteenth-century mansion of the archbishops of Sens, in whose archdiocese or province Paris lay. Most interesting of all is the Paris house of the abbots of Cluny, the richest monastery in Europe, which today houses the Musée de Cluny. As it stands it is also a late fifteenth-century rebuilding, for the great magnates, like their kings, rebuilt and rebuilt. A

The famous Musée de Cluny is housed in the Paris hôtel *of the abbots of Cluny, one of the finest extant examples of a great medieval house. A large number of bishops and abbots built prestigious houses in Paris, where they lived for a considerable part of the year, so long as it was the city where the king of France lived. After 1422, when the king no longer lived in Paris, these major ecclesiastics stopped using their Paris houses too, and most sold them (below p. 137). It was very strange of an abbot of Cluny to choose to rebuild his Paris house in the 1490s in the latest style of Gothic, while the king, Charles VIII, was lavishing attention on his château at Amboise. The clue to this odd behaviour may lie in the fact that the abbot was a member of the Amboise family, from whom Charles VII had confiscated the castle that Charles VIII was now aggrandising.*

glimpse of these houses gives some impression of the scale of households that they contained, the members of which were numbered by the hundred. They were small royal palaces in themselves. Eudes Rigaud, a thirteenth-century archbishop of Rouen, for example, although a Franciscan and possibly therefore more modest than many prelates, was nevertheless accustomed to travel between Rouen and Paris with no fewer than eighty horsemen. The revenues of these bishoprics and abbeys also came to Paris, and were spent there.

Of the Parisian *hôtels* of the great lay lords even less survives. There is part of the *hôtel* belonging to Olivier de Clisson, a new member of the greater nobility, who was constable of France at the end of the fourteenth century. There are only a few fragments of the Hôtel d'Artois, as rebuilt at the end of the fourteenth century by Duke John the Fearless of Burgundy. For what life looked like inside these *hôtels* we have to rely, as with royal palaces, on paintings. The Limburg brothers painted John, Duke of Berry, dining with a visiting bishop in his *hôtel*, and we have here perhaps idealized glimpse of his furnishings, his plate, his tapestries, his food and his servants in an action snapshot.

The building up of a society in which the greatest magnates clustered around their king in Paris was something new of the thirteenth century. Some of this focusing on Paris was by the independent choice of the great magnates themselves, some of it was to meet the wishes of the kings. Philip IV, for example, exerted himself to try to ensure, by trickery and force if necessary, that princes from frontier territories, like the counts of Flanders, of Bar and of Burgundy, whose lands straddled the border between France and the Empire, should be his clients and should live in Paris. It was made easier for him to do so as, with the failure of central monarchy in the Empire, there was no rival pole of attraction there. The pattern of tiny principalities, each with its miniature capital, which was cut short in France, continued to develop in the Empire into the fourteenth century and beyond.

It was also in the course of the thirteenth century that in England the archbishops and bishops, the greater abbots and great lay lords began building themselves aristocratic town houses, frequently known as 'inns', in London, or along the Strand, the riverside road that joined London and Westminster. Thirty ecclesiastical town houses were built in the thirteenth century, including the 'inns' of seven bishops along the Strand. Some fragments still survive, for example the rose west window of the great hall of the bishops of Winchester's 'inn' in Southwark and parts of Ely House, the 'inn' of the bishops of Ely, from which the lordship of the Isle of Ely as well as the bishopric could be run, and show what complex establishments these palaces were, with their own miniature administrative departments. The palace of the medieval archbishops of Canterbury, in Lambeth, is still occupied by their present day successor, although it has naturally been much changed and rebuilt over the centuries.[23]

As well as the considerable establishments of the great ecclesiastics of England, there were in London, as in Paris, those of the greatest lay magnates, some of whom, but not so many as in France, were related to the royal house. The greatest of these royal cousins in the fourteenth century, the counts, later dukes, of Lancaster, had the palace of the Savoy in the Strand, next door to the 'inn' of the bishops of Worcester. Further along the Strand were the vast homes of other lay magnates. Yet others had their 'inns' scattered in and out of the back streets of London itself.[24] One visitor said that if all these great houses were pulled out from the back streets and put together, they would make London the finest city in Europe.

In France and in England therefore, by the fourteenth century, the greater nobility and ecclesiastics were spending a considerable proportion of their lives in Paris and in London, and concentrating much of their expenditure in these cities. Even when they were not present themselves in their town houses in the capitals the stewards of their households frequently purchased luxuries for them that were not available elsewhere. It was from his 'inn' in Southwark that amber and furs from the Baltic were purchased for the bishop of Winchester. This expenditure by king and magnates made these cities key markets for the long-distance luxury trade of Europe.

Exactly the same was true for most of the other kings. In Sicily and the Regno the monarchical capitals of Palermo and Naples attracted the nobility to build their own *alberghi* around the palaces of their Hohenstaufen, Angevin and Aragonese rulers. Naples thus became the great consumption centre for all of southern Italy, as well as the political focal point for the murderous rivalries between the 'bloody cousinhood' who disputed for power after the death of King Robert in 1343.[25]

The rent rolls and royal pensions of those members of the Angevin royal house who dominated the politics of the Regno – the princes of Taranto, Bari, Eboli and Durazzo – were spent in Naples, if not on luxuries for themselves, then on swarms of armed hangers-on. They, in turn, created a market. Of all the monarchs of Europe, only the kings of Poland really failed to bring their greater nobility to live around them in Cracow.

The same was happening in the non-royal capitals of northern Italy as the nobility increasingly chose to live in the cities, whether under republican or signorial constitutions. Indeed some of the cities obliged the nobility of the *contado* to spend a certain proportion of each year within their walls. For example, from early in the thirteenth century the commune of Florence, which was itself an association of nobles, tried to ensure that *all* the nobility of the Florentine state spent part of the year in Florence itself. Many of the men who ran the industry and commerce that made it a boom town in the late thirteenth and early fourteenth centuries came from lineages that must be called 'noble' from landed origins. Those who did not have such origins, far from producing a new 'bourgeois' culture, put their profits into land, bought castles and sought to live nobly. Even at the time of Florence's fastest commercial and industrial expansion, the late thirteenth century, there was no slackening in the attempt to maintain an aristocratic way of life. It was at this time that Dante Alighieri, the son of a successful businessman, was most attracted as a young man to the 'set' around the poet Guido Cavalcanti, a

The west end of the great hall of Winchester House, the bishop of Winchester's inn in Southwark, is all that remains above ground of a truly palatial group of thirteenth-century buildings, constructed on a seven-acre site beside the Thames, with its own dock, mills and prison. Beneath the splendid rose window, three doorways can be seen leading to the pantry, kitchen and buttery. Excavations have revealed much detail of buildings for so long covered by warehouses, now converted to luxury flats. Documentary work has added more detail, and shown how much the bishop lived there, how he used it for administering his diocese and as a base for selling the produce of his estates on London markets. In 1220–1, for example, deliveries included 106,000 herrings and 306 pigs ready fattened up for slaughter.

member of a distinguished family of rural nobility. As an older man Dante spent his exile at the courts of princes and in his writings was a forceful advocate of a renewal of imperial government in Italy. His 'bourgeois' origins are not at all visible in his way of life, and indeed he believed himself to be descended from a knightly family and married into a minor branch of the noble Donati. His 'inspiration', Beatrice, came from one of the richest families in the city, the Portinari. She married into the very richest family of all, the Bardi, who owned castles in the *contado* and were soon to run the largest commercial and banking enterprise in Europe.

Up to the mid-thirteenth century to live 'nobly' in a Tuscan city meant to live in a tall castle-like tower house within the city, and to carry on vendettas from it against rival noble families. In the mid-thirteenth century many of these vendettas focused in the faction-fighting of Guelfs and Ghibellines. First one party was successful and drove the other into exile, destroying or cutting down their opponents' tower houses, then the exiles returned and did the same. In Florence, Guelf towers suffered in 1260 and Ghibelline towers in 1266. Eventually a compromise was reached, in which it was decreed that no towers, except those owned corporately by the commune, should exceed a prescribed height. Since they could no longer build upwards and express their power in the height and strength of their impregnable stone towers, the patriciate began to build outwards and to express their wealth in the luxurious appointments of their *palazzi*. One of the earliest, possibly the earliest, of such new-style palaces was that built for the Mozzi, which was thought a fit place to put up popes and foreign rulers when they passed through the city. Other patrician families rapidly followed their example, like the Frescobaldi, whose late thirteenth-century *palazzo* also still survives and the Portinari, whose *palazzo* disappeared in two later rebuildings. Those who are prepared to look can still see numerous examples of the truncated older tower houses amongst, and often incorporated into, the *palazzi* of the Florentine nobility. The remains of similar noble towers can be found in Siena and many other north Italian cities. Later myth gave to Verona seven hundred such towers, a quite unbelievable number.[26] Only in one state, the very small one, focused on the little city of San Gimignano, was there no legislation to lop down the towers of the nobility, and here a handful of towers can still be seen rising to their full height. Even by the fifteenth century their survival was sufficiently distinctive for painters such as Taddeo Bartolo (1362/3–1422) or Ghirlandaio to use them to symbolize the city. Elsewhere in Tuscany the new *palazzo* became the hallmark of patrician life.

These *palazzi* clearly rivalled the *hôtels* and 'inns' of the nobility in the capital cities of northern Europe. With their country villas and castles in the *contado*, Italian patricians were as at home in the hunting field as their northern counterparts. Northern visitors were astonished that Italian communes conferred knighthood on their citizens. Florentine patricians, who were brought up on the same traditions of courtly literature, in French until Dante's time, could meet noblemen from other parts of Europe on an equal footing on social occasions, in diplomatic negotiations, or even on the battle-

Louis, Lord of Gruuthuse and Earl of Winchester, commissioned this lavishly illuminated four-volume manuscript of Froissart's Chronicle in Bruges. The scenes that it purports to portray relate to the 1380s, but the figures are dressed in the costume of the 1470s. Here the courtly party (on the right) of nine-year-old Louis of Anjou, titular King of Sicily and Jerusalem, accompanied by his domineering mother, is being welcomed by a group of Parisians (on the left), after his coronation in Naples in 1387. The miniaturist's imagined Paris can be seen in the background, not recognisable apart from the towers of Notre Dame. The great city that the miniaturist actually knew was Bruges, and the court that at Brussels, to which his patron was attached. In the 1380s the boy king Louis II had only ruled Naples very briefly. Such wealth and power as he had came from ruling Provence, just outside France. He spent much of his life at the court of his mad cousin, Charles VI of France, based in the Paris hôtel marked 'Sicily' on the map on p. 75.

E Duc de bretai
gne sen vint a
baugency sur
loirre ꝛ sa ordõn
na vne partie de sés besoithes
poure de nir vers paris. En cel
lui mesines temps entra a
paris auant ce que se Duc de
bretaigne y entrast la royne
de secille ꝛ de iherusalem qui
femme anoit este au Duc dã
iou qui nomme sestoit en sés
titstres seigneur de naisce ꝛ
aussy roy. Et pour ꝛy que la

dame pour ce en faicte men
tion amenoit son ieune fils
loys en sa compaignie legl
on nommoit ia par toutte
france roy des terres dessus.
En ceur compaignie estoit
iehan de bretaigne frere a la
dame ꝛ venoient a paris.
Auant que la dame entrast
a paris elle sisuiffia aux
Ducs de berri ꝛ de bourgoigne
quelle venoit et pour enter
a paris ꝛ amenoit son ieune
fils loys en sa compaignie se

field. The young Florentine nobleman Buonaccorso Pitti led troops in battle in France under Charles VI.[27] Until the sixteenth century Florentine noblemen did not perceive involvement in business as any derogation to their nobility, provided always that it was the right sort of business. As we have seen, it was perfectly consonant with noble status to engage in the management of a bank, of a wholesale import-export house, or of a large-scale cloth manufacturing business. Buonaccorso Pitti in his later years ran a most successful woollen cloth firm, besides representing his city in diplomatic negotiations at princely courts and acting as *podestà* (virtually governor) of subordinate cities.

At the same time that the patriciate of Florence was enlarging houses on a new more spacious scale, it was corporately enlarging its city. The later years of the thirteenth century saw an attempt to improve its face by deliberate town planning. As in the houses, so in the city, the emphasis was on space. New squares were deliberately created by pulling down houses. The major streets were broadened. Embankments to carry riverside roads were created along the Arno. A whole new quarter to the north-east was laid out on a regular rectangular grid. Some of this work had a practical intention, like the new, especially broad, Via Larga (now Via Cavour) parallel to the old narrow Via San Gallo, designed to make it easy for the carts which brought in the grain from the Mugello to reach the grain market in the centre of the city. However, most of these improvements were designed for the greater beauty and honour of the city.[28] 'Noble' aesthetic considerations dominated, not 'bourgeois' practical ones – if, that is, such an antithesis has ever existed except in the fevered imagination of historians whose class-consciousness has run to excess.

The great men of the city were great men in the country as well, and vice versa. Even great rural landowners from old noble families like the Ricasoli, who had no share in Florentine industry or commerce, nevertheless had a

When Anton Koberger published Hartmann Schedel's Liber Chronicarum *in Nuremberg in 1493, it became justifiably famous for its handsome printing and lavish illustrations (see below p. 283). This woodcut gives a very recognisable picture of fifteenth-century Florence. The great houses of some of the Tuscan aristocracy can be picked out: the square palazzo of the Ricasoli at the left hand end of the nearest bridge, the fortress of the Spini at the left hand end of the next bridge, and the new mansion of Luca Pitti on the right of the picture.*

In 1329, a time of acute food shortage, the captain of Colle, capital of a miniature state near Florence, agreed to sell that city 1,600 mule-loads of grain, but when the Pisans offered a better price he let them have it instead. This picture (opposite), a copy of a fresco, expresses the Florentines' indignation. Their mules leave Colle empty on the left, the Pisans', laden, on the right. A year later the Florentines took a bloody revenge and incorporated Colle into their state.

great *palazzo* in the city as well as their ancestral castle of Broglio in the borderlands between the Florentine state and the Sienese, where they had owned vast estates for centuries. To this day the Ricasoli still draw immense wealth from the celebrated Chianti produced around Broglio.

As the Florentine state stretched its tentacles across Tuscany, the greater families of the subjugated city states, of Prato, of Pistoia, and eventually of Pisa, came to live in Florence as their capital. The patriciate of Medicean Florence was closer than ever to the image of a nobility surrounding a prince. Florence was more than ever a centre of consumption of luxury goods.

It was this handful of very rich men of the newly enlarged Florentine state, the Pazzi, the Pitti, the Strozzi, the Rucellai, and above all the crypto-princely Medici themselves who were among the first to patronize humanists, painters and sculptors and, of course, to build, or rebuild, their *palazzi* in the new 'antique' fashion of the early Renaissance.[29] By the fifteenth century all these were old nobility, some of them very old. The Pazzi and the Pitti had been feudal lords before they came into the city in the thirteenth century, the Strozzi and the Medici had become noble by the end of the thirteenth century.

The other capital cities of northern Italy were also full of factious noble consumers. In Milan, two noble parties for long struggled for power, that led by the della Torre and that led by the Visconti. Power alternated between these two groups until the Visconti and their noble supporters eventually achieved a lasting *signoria*. Venice was a city packed as full of noblemen as Florence or Milan. Political power was exclusively in the hands of the nobility. The city was dominated by twenty to thirty great families, and the richest of these noble clans, like the Dandolo, Contarini and Morosini, and later the Gradenigo and Mocenigo, each produced several doges.[30] Even in the tiny Ligurian state, the great landed aristocracy, like the Fieschi, the Spinola, the Doria, the Adorno and the Grimaldi, who are still rulers of Monaco, lived in Genoa, dominated city politics, and spent their rural rent rolls there.[31]

The papal monarchy too drew magnates to itself. In Rome in the thirteenth century the lay nobility of the papal states, the Patrimony of St Peter, like the Colonna, the Orsini, the Caetani and the Savelli had *palazzi* scattered among the ruins of ancient Rome. The Frangipane and the Annibaldi in turn adapted the ruins of the Colosseum as their palace. The Roman nobility too had lived in a forest of multitudinous towers, like their north Italian counterparts, until Brancaleone d'Andolò supposedly destroyed 140 of them in the 1250s.[32]

Around the papal palace in the Lateran were the *palazzi* of the cardinals, the 'nobility' of the Western Church itself. When the popes moved to Avignon the lay nobles remained behind, but the cardinals moved with the pope. Like him, they first rented accommodation for themselves, but when it became apparent that the papacy was going to remain at Avignon for some time they followed the papal example and built themselves palatial new *livrées*. Some clustered about the new papal palace itself, others faced it on the French bank of the Rhône, from Villeneuve-les-Avignon.[33] The view of Vil-

Nearly all of the very tall noble towers of the twelfth and early thirteenth centuries were severely cut down in the second half of the thirteenth century. Of the few that have survived intact, two are in Bologna. The Torre degli Asinelli and the unfinished Torre Garisenda are reminders of a vendetta-riven society in which a family's influence and safety lay in the possession of a taller and stronger tower than rival noble families.

leneuve across the Rhône still looks like a perfect survival from a fourteenth-century book of hours, preserved, just as the papal palace itself is, by abandonment. The richest of the cardinals were comparable in income to the wealthiest noblemen of any secular court, so much so that Petrarch scathingly commented, 'Instead of the Apostles who went barefoot, we now see satraps mounted on horses decked with gold and champing golden bits, and whose very hoofs will soon be shod with gold, if God do not restrain their arrogant display of wealth.' Petrarch knew what he was criticizing. His own patron, Cardinal Colonna, was probably the richest of all. Before building a palace for himself, Cardinal Arnaud d'Aux is reputed to have rented thirty-one houses for his retinue and Bernard de Garves had rented fifty-one. The combined households of the twenty-four cardinals contained over a thousand people. Here again was a huge market.[34] In 1420 Martin V, himself a Colonna, managed with great difficulty to recover Rome for a reunited papacy. Although his successor, Eugenius IV, had to spend many years exiled in Florence, by the middle of the fifteenth century Rome was again the established

Looking eastwards down the via dei Bardi in Florence the truncated stump of the ancient fortified tower of the Mozzi can be seen rising on the right. The Mozzi, Guelf magnates, had the upper storeys of their tower destroyed by the victorious Ghibellines in 1260 and their adult males sent into exile. After their return in 1266, they built an extensive new palace beside and behind it (the façade can be seen to the left of the tower). It was the grandest house in Florence when Pope Gregory X stayed there in 1273 during his abortive attempt to reconcile the two factions.

capital for the papacy, with the popes themselves now in their new palace on the Vatican surrounded once again by the *palazzi* of both Cardinals and lay magnates.[35]

When Philip the Good came to rule a greater Netherlands in the fifteenth century, consisting of not only the modern kingdoms of the Netherlands and Belgium but also the grand-duchy of Luxembourg and several *départements* of modern France, the nobility of the whole area joined him in living in Brussels. However, as well as the greater nobility of his own group of principalities, like the Croy, Brimeu, Lalaing and Lannoy, and prince-bishops like those of Utrecht and Liège, other independent princes built themselves houses in Brussels too, like the Duke of Cleves, and their Ravenstein cadets, the dukes of Guelders and their Egmont cadets, the dukes of Julich and the counts of Nassau and Wurttemburg, all from the Empire, and Burgundian cadets like the counts of Nevers and Etampes from France, and even the dukes of Bourbon and the princes of Orange. Of these only the *hôtel* of the Ravensteins and the chapel from that of the Nassaus survive. It is no wonder that Brussels was so considerable a centre for luxury consumption in the mid-fifteenth century.[36]

The composition of court cities

Before considering the overall size of these new capital cities of the thirteenth century it is worth considering the composition of the huge clusters of people that quickly gathered round a ruler and his court.

The clearest indication of the difference that becoming a 'capital' could make to a city is provided by the meteoric growth of Avignon at the beginning of papal residence there in the early fourteenth century.[37] Before the arrival of the pope, Avignon had about 5,000 people, a moderately large provincial town by the standards of the time. Within ten years, it had grown to over 40,000. This is not a large city by twentieth-century standards, but in the first half of the fourteenth century it was only exceeded anywhere in Europe by some ten others. How was this growth made up? We have already seen that there were well over 600 people working in the papal palace, and over 1,000 people working in the households of the cardinals. In addition, there were nearly 2,000 other clergy resident there, each of whom had his own household. These were mostly small, but some were rather larger, like that of Petrarch. He was a highly successful pluralist who rarely resided in any of his many benefices, although he was reputed to be able to travel from Avignon to Ravenna spending each night in a different living of his own. The money that these clergy drew from their benefices was mostly spent in the city. In addition, there were over 1,300 students at the curial university, which had moved there with the pope, and many of these students, already in orders, were also maintained by money from distant benefices.

However, the largest group in the additional population was made up of those who had come to supply goods and services to the pope and the cardinals, to the resident clergy and the university. Such suppliers of goods and services, many of them Tuscans, had families and households of their own and accounted for some 20,000 immigrants. Of 1,224 tradesmen and artisans

who were members of the confraternity of Notre Dame in 1376, over 1,100 were Italians, including not only goldsmiths and jewellers but also armourers, leather-workers, weavers, carpenters, stonemasons and sculptors. Avignon had become a city of opportunity for craftsmen and businessmen, like Francesco Datini, the best-documented businessman of the Middle Ages. It had also become, as Petrarch drily commented, a city of opportunity for a host of 'adventurers, usurers, thieves and prostitutes'. Such people, of course, swelled the population of all capitals.

Again like all capitals, Avignon also became a city of innkeepers who catered for the immense throng of visitors, litigants in the courts, and petitioners for favours. Just as Botero described, 'all such as aspire and thirst after offices and honours' did indeed 'rush thither amain with emulation and disdain for others'. Many stayed in the inns along the street leading up from the bridge.

Because the papal capital had moved, the difference that being a capital city made is most visible in Avignon, but the same emphasis on the supply of goods and services is visible in all the capital cities. In London, the largest livery companies, or guilds, each with over fifty members at the end of the fifteenth century, were nearly all ones concerned with retail trade, with delivering goods to the customer at the end of a chain of supply that might reach back hundreds or even thousands of miles to distant producers. They were tailors and drapers, grocers and mercers, fishmongers and brewers, skinners and goldsmiths.[38] Every capital city had a network of retail shopkeepers, prepared to supply, at a price, every need or fashionable whim of the ruler and his court. Those who were selling the same range of goods frequently had their shops close to one another. Drapers were to be found together in one place, vintners in another, butchers in another, fishmongers in another, and mercers and grocers in yet other places close to each other. The same was true of such manufacturing as went on in the these cities. Goldsmiths, for example, were to be found together in the city centres, whilst tanners, because of the odious smell, were together on the periphery. In Venice the tanners were not even on the main islands, but on the Giudecca, just as the glass-makers, because of the fire risk, were on another island,

The Florentine state raised most of its tax revenues from indirect taxes, including a gabelle on retail sales. The fourteenth-century scribe who wrote up the register of tax rates enjoyed himself putting in rough sketches of each type of business alongside the rates of tax to be paid. On the left above is a woman selling delicatessen/ charcuterie, and on the right two goldsmiths at their counter, ready to sell noblemen their most expensive wares, with jewelled belts and purses hanging up behind them. The drawings are from the Libro di gabelle fiorentine.

Murano. Only a few trades, like bakeries, were scattered, each serving a neighbourhood.[39] This tradition of dealers in the same commodities clustering together still survives in Delhi and in dozens of Islamic cities from Marrakesh and Cairo to Istanbul and Karachi. This is true not only for older trades, like the dealers in old clothes, but also for new specialisms – bicycles, car-parts, photographic equipment and even electronic gadgetry. It is a living, growing tradition. We have already mentioned the armies of masons, sculptors, carpenters and fresco painters who, under the direction of supervising architects, were at work on the perpetual building and rebuilding of palaces for ruler and nobility alike. In cities like Florence in the thirteenth century, Avignon in the fourteenth century, or Brussels in the fifteenth, they were also building whole new quarters for the mushrooming population.

Notaries were also exceptionally busy and numerous in Avignon, as in most capital cities, for all contracts and agreements needed licensed notaries to record them in official registers to make them legal and binding.

Where 'the supreme place of justice is kept' a corps of professional lawyers necessarily comes into existence, to plead in the courts on behalf of the litigants from all corners of the state. Such litigants, as well as the petitioners for favours, brought yet more money to the capital, spending freely not only on lawyers and innkeepers, but also on greasing the palms of all those whom they thought might assist them.

For many of the offices in the new departments of state some sort of training was necessary. Avignon was not the only capital to have a ruler-sponsored university whose best graduates walked into civil service jobs. Paris, with a twelfth-century university, was perhaps the archetype. The university at Naples was founded by the Emperor Frederick II in 1224 specifically with the aim of feeding the civil service of the Regno with candidates for jobs.[40] So was that at Lisbon. In the fourteenth century, state-sponsored universities were created at Prague and Cracow and Vienna. In the fifteenth century, they were joined by universities in the capitals of many other, lesser, principalities, like Heidelberg. However, not all capitals had such universities. The Burgundian university for the Netherlands was at Leuven, not Brussels; the Visconti university was at Pavia, not Milan; the English universities were at Oxford and

Booksellers (left), were to be found in all capital cities, although not every city had as many as Florence. There was a ready sale amongst a highly literate aristocracy for sumptuously produced manuscripts of history and political literature as well as for devotional works, light romances, poetry and practical legal textbooks. Furriers (on the right), like goldsmiths and booksellers, also aimed their garments and trimmings at a rich and aristocratic market. Even the basic furs were expensive since they had to be imported great distances, mostly from the further shores of the Black Sea or the Baltic.

Cambridge, not London or Westminster, although London did have Inns of Court in which lawyers received their professional education.

Physicians and surgeons, barbers and apothecaries were also numerous in capital cities, for the rich provided the best patients. Some of these medical men had a great deal of insight, like Guy de Chaulliac, doctor to Pope Clement VI, who wrote accurately and perceptively on bubonic plague, but others were mere quacks, intent on fleecing their patients.

Then, as now, there was also an 'entertainment industry' focused on capital cities, of very mixed prestige and cultural value. At the top end of the spectrum were the musicians, maintained in varying numbers, which were often considerable, by the rulers themselves, and also by many individual nobles too. Much lower in the spectrum were players, and popular entertainers like bear-wards. At the bottom end of the spectrum, and most numerous of all, were the prostitutes. These varied in quality from wealthy courtesans to common drabs. Like members of other trades, prostitutes often worked close to one another, and there were 'red-light' quarters in medieval capitals, like the Glatigny, next to the bishop's palace, in the heart of Paris, which shared the Ile de la Cité with the royal palace, and the cathedral of Notre Dame. It was from all-too-rich experience in his short life, that François Villon wrote that everything in fifteenth-century Paris ended up in the alehouse or the brothel:

Chausses, pourpoins esguilletez
Robes, et toutes vos drappilles
Ains que vous fassiez pis, portez
Tout aux tavernes et aux filles.[41]
('So that you may behave badly, take your
hose and your tight embroidered jackets,
your robes and all your clothing,
everything to the taverns and the girls.')

Brothels were often licensed and regulated and some were even provided by the state. In its fight against homosexuality, the priors of Florence 'desiring to eliminate a worse evil by means of a lesser one' set aside 1,000 florins in

The scene from Ghent (opposite) by Pierre Pourbus shows that, although the style of architecture had changed, mid-sixteenth-century shopkeepers were, like their medieval predecessors, still arranging a selection of their wares outside their shops every day to lure customers in.

Overleaf
Between 1337 and 1340 Ambrogio Lorenzetti painted his justly famous Allegory of Justice and the Common Good, around the walls of the meeting hall of the Nine, the elected rulers of the Sienese state. It is one of the earliest examples of purely secular painting to survive, loaded with a very complex symbolism, about which scholars are still arguing. Its intention was to keep the fruits of justice and injustice before the eyes of the rulers. Eighty years or so after it was painted, one of the most popular preachers of the fifteenth century, (St) Bernardino, said 'When, outside Siena I was preaching on War and Peace, there came to my mind those pictures painted for you. When I turn to the picture of Peace I see merchants buying and selling, I see dancing, the houses being repaired, the workers busy in the vineyard....' The complex symbolism may have been lost, but we can see clearly some of the fruits of just government. The symbiotic relation between the city and the rest of the state is expressed by the device of the linking road. Inside the gate pack animals can be seen coming in to be unloaded as the focal point of busy scenes of commercial activity. Against the backdrop of a fruitful countryside, with well cared for vineyards, peaceful citizens are riding out of the gate, meeting a pig being driven in for sale, to join the flock of sheep already within the city. The message is clear, justice brings prosperity to merchants and farmers alike.

1415 for the construction and furnishing of two more public brothels in different quarters of the city, in addition to the one that already existed.[42]

As well as recognizable groups of occupations, there was a multiplicity of hangers-on difficult to categorize, not only Petrarch's 'adventurers' and thieves, but men in or out of livery, idling about porters' lodges, mere thugs, armed men hired, or waiting to be hired for an occasion, men to carry torches at night, to catch rats, or to empty private cesspits.

The cities themselves employed whole armies of people to perform menial occupations, like the men who ran night-soil carts in and out of London, or their opposite numbers who took municipal sewage boats round Venice by night from the thirteenth century onwards.

As well as the cities themselves there were numerous institutions within them that provided employment and maintenance. At around the same time, for example, charitable foundations provided hospitals for the poor, the sick, and the aged, as well as the traveller.

The numbers pile up. It has been estimated that Paris, the capital of the largest and richest state in Europe, grew from around 20,000 inhabitants at the beginning of the thirteenth century to some 200,000 at the end. It kept such a population through the fourteenth century into the early fifteenth century despite the enormous death toll from the repeated waves of plague. As long as the king and the court were resident in Paris, there was always hope of fortune there to attract newcomers in from the country, and from the lesser towns of the kingdom. The streets of every capital were 'paved with gold' in the mythology of its country, and the 'Dick Whittington' and 'Long Meg' myths of the poor boy or girl who made good were potent in luring in the optimistic and youthful poor from the countryside. The few who actually made it to great wealth fed the myth. The many who failed were ignored and forgotten. Beneath the economy of the rich lay the enormous economy of the poor. Historians have estimated that a quarter of the inhabitants of many cities were normally destitute, with many more being thrown into acute poverty from time to time.[43] This is not very different from the 30% or so below the poverty line in less developed countries today. Many an optimistic youth ended as a beggar, or picked over refuse for a living, and died, all too soon, in the unhealthy shanty town suburbs that surrounded all such capitals.

In every capital city, as in every large town, there were also houses of mendicant friars, often not only Dominicans and Franciscans, but also Austin (Augustinian) Friars and Carmelites, and sometimes more exotic groups like the Crutched Friars and Friars of the Sack. In the thirteenth century Bonaventure, as head of the Franciscans, directed his order to concentrate their work on the towns not only for idealistic reasons, but also because it was easier to exist on alms there. It was not only the well-to-do who had renounced their property and voluntarily embraced poverty for Christ's sake who found it easier to obtain alms in towns. Those who were involuntarily poor also found it easier to beg. Every capital city was therefore thronged with beggars, crippled and sick, widowed, unmarried mothers, unemploy-

SENÇA PAVRA OGNVOM FRANCO CAMINI
E LAVORANDO SEMINI CIASCVNO
MENTRE CHE TAL COMVNO
MANTERRA QVESTA DONNA I SIGNORIA
CHEL ALEVATA AREI OGNI BALIA

Two scenes from a French fourteenth-century manuscript. Above: stalls under an arcade are selling a range of luxury goods to well-to-do customers. At the stall on the left, boots are for sale with the immensely elongated and pointed toes so fashionable in the 1450s and 1460s. The posture of men in some miniatures suggests that they may have been hideously uncomfortable and impaired the ability to walk freely. At the stall on the right, domestic plate is for sale, shown off on a sideboard, just as it might be by its noble purchasers in their own castles or city houses. Right: by contrast to its luxurious side, there was also the concentration of beggars in every city.

able, or merely the great mass of unemployed and underemployed whose expectation of doing well in the city had been frustrated by not finding work, or at least not finding enough work. On top of the huge numbers of deserving poor, there were, then as now, a small number of cunning and undeserving men and women who deliberately made their living by exploiting the charity and compassion of the well-to-do. The diatribes poured out, then as now, against such cheats, must not lead us to underestimate the huge amount of genuine misery in medieval capital cities, represented by the abandoned or widowed women with young children covered with genuine running sores, not ones simulated or induced to move the pity of the rich. The enormous number of confraternities, hospitals and other charitable foundations helped to alleviate this misery, most effectively in those cities like Florence where the populations were so greatly reduced by the fourteenth- and fifteenth-century waves of plague.[44] Nevertheless, the extent of human suffering in capital cities was immense. Nowhere was the disparity between the richest and the poorest so apparent, and if this book must necessarily concentrate on the richest as giving the greatest stimulus to long-distance trade, readers ought not to be unaware of the poor, as omnipresent in medieval Paris or London as in present-day Calcutta or Bombay.

The table on page 94 gives some idea of the range of size of the largest cities in western Europe in the later Middle Ages. Even the largest of these, Paris, with some 200,000 inhabitants, was much smaller than classical Rome. It was smaller even than Constantinople had been from classical times until the eleventh-century collapse of the Byzantine Empire, or than the largest of the contemporary cities in China, like Hangchow, which late thirteenth- and early fourteenth-century European travellers marvelled at for their size. Since classical antiquity no city in western Europe, not even Lombard Milan, had exceeded around 30,000 inhabitants until the late twelfth or early thirteenth century. The new opportunities for rulers and their nobility of living on money incomes away from their rural estates made the growth of cities possible again in the west for the first time for three quarters of a millennium.

The size of court cities

Many of these figures are very tentative and some are greatly disputed. Some of the capital cities that I have discussed changed size quite rapidly. Avignon, for example, had not started to grow in 1300, and had shrunk again by 1400. The same is true of Prague. Brussels had not started to grow by 1400 and had shrunk again by 1500. The Duke of Burgundy, with some of his greatest nobles, was by then in his wife's kingdom of Castile. There was then no longer a court in the Netherlands, and its administration was in Malines (Mechelen). Some of the disappearances are just as interesting as the new appearances. The county of Flanders had no capital of its own after the fourteenth century. It was run from Ghent in 1350, but from Paris in 1400 and from Brussels in 1450.

The numbers for the population in the capitals and the figures for the incomes of the rulers do not always correlate in any obvious way. In some cases the incomes of the rulers (above pp. 65–6) did not reflect the wealth of

	1300	1350	1400	1450	1500
c. 200,000	Paris	Paris	Paris		
100,000 –200,000	Milan Venice			Venice	Venice Naples Milan
60,000 –100,000	Florence London Genoa Seville	Milan Venice Florence London Genoa Avignon Seville	Milan Venice Seville	Milan Paris London	Paris Tours London Florence
c. 50,000	Naples Palermo Rome Ghent Bruges Verona? Barcelona? Cordoba? Bologna? Siena?	Naples Palermo Rome Ghent Bruges Barcelona Prague Verona?	Naples London Florence Genoa Bruges Avignon? Rome?	Naples Florence Genoa Bruges Brussels Seville Rome	*20 cities including* Lisbon Palermo Rome Genoa Antwerp Lyons Brussels Seville

Suggested changing populations of the largest cities in western Europe 1300–1500. It is possible to discern not only the effects of political developments discussed in the text on the previous page, but also the effects of the overall decline in Eurasian population during the waves of plague which began with the black death of 1348–9, as well as of shifts in commerce and industry, which accelerated the shrinkage of Genoa and Florence, but not of Venice and Milan.

their kingdoms, in others the size of the cities owed a great deal to other factors than the presence of an administration and a court.

As far as incomes are concerned, a comparison of France and England reveals some anomalies. Philip VI, as king of 20,000,000 Frenchmen, did not have an income over three times as great as Edward II, the king of 6,000,000 Englishmen, as might be suggested by the populations of the two kingdoms, nor was it over twice as large, as might be suggested by the relative size of Paris and London. It was barely 40% larger. This disproportionately low income was because the kings of France, except for Charles V in the 1360s and 1370s, had a relatively poor system of national taxation until Charles VII collected the *taille* in the fifteenth century.[45] In marked contrast by the end of the thirteenth century the kings of England had already developed an extremely successful system of taxation, consisting of the regular levy of customs duties on imports and exports, particularly wool, supplemented in times of war by parliamentary grants of subsidies, effectively direct taxes on income.

Some of these capital cities, like Venice, Florence or Barcelona were also of considerable commercial importance. Others, like Ghent, Milan and again Florence, were important industrially.

City and country

It will have become apparent already that princes and their governments were enormous consumers of luxury goods, and so were the lay nobility and higher clergy who chose to live close to their prince. It may be rather less apparent that the greatest problem in medieval cities was supplying the population as a whole with food, drink and fuel. The bulk carrying trades of medieval Europe grew up in response to these needs. The growth of bulk carrying trade, in some cases over very long distances, expanded at the same time as the growth of the cities. Unless transport had developed, and unless agricultural producers had been able to respond to demand, the cities could not have grown to the size they did. Even so the inhabitants of the great cities were always vulnerable to food shortages.

One of the prime preoccupations of city governments was to see that the poorer inhabitants did not starve to the point of rioting over the price and supply of bread. The support they gave could take the form of subsidizing bread, as in Florence, during the great south European famines of the 1340s, when the city authorities imported grain in bulk from long distances and sold at a subsidized price to the city's bakers. It could alternatively take the form of outright giving to the poor. While John XXII was pope (1316–34) he paid for the distribution of an average of 67,500 loaves of bread each week to the poorer inhabitants of Avignon.

Reciprocally, without the demand from the cities, the rural inhabitants would not have had a market for their products, and without such a market they would not have been able to pay the rents and taxes in cash that enabled the rulers and nobles to live and spend in the cities. The thirteenth century therefore saw not only the reappearance of 'large' cities, but also the development of a market-oriented economy in the rural west. It was the availability of markedly increased supplies of coined money, combined with population pressures, that enabled landlords to push their often reluctant tenants into a market economy, by demanding increasing quantities of cash from them.

The relationship between city and country was essential for both. Ambrogio Lorenzetti has expressed this relationship in the allegory of good government which he painted for the Palazzo Publico in Siena. It shows not only the city, but also the *contado*. He has joined the two together by a road running across the countryside through a city gate into a piazza.

However, even after the fundamental 'monetization' of the rural economy in the thirteenth century, the use of money in the city and the country was quite different. The thirteenth century witnessed the creation of a great seasonal flow and ebb of coined money, into and out of the countryside. In rural society, the procession of the seasons was of primary importance. In urban society much can be done at any time of year, but rural society is geared to an annual 'harvesting'. I use 'harvest' here in the most general sense, not only the reaping of wheat, barley, rye and oats, but also the gathering in of grapes and olives and the seasonal readiness for marketing of cattle and sheep, dairy products and wool. The timing of the flow, or flows, of money depended on the nature of the principal product, or products, of any particular region. Peasant producers had a great deal to offer for sale, but their sales were generally made all at once. This frequently happened at only one time of year, when the grain had been threshed, the grapes, olives or cheeses pressed, the sheep sheared, the cattle fattened or the woad balled.[46]

As the concentration on production for the market increased during the long thirteenth century, so specialization increased, so that the most suitable products for a region tended to become the only products. Vineyards took the place of fields of grain in parts of France, like the Bordelais and the Auxerrois at the same time as vineyards disappeared in England. Specialized products were increasingly sold at regular fairs, which brought enormous sums of money into the countryside very suddenly. In the grain-growing areas of eastern England annual sales took place round Michaelmas (29 September) at, for example, the Stourbridge fair near Cambridge. In Apulia, where cheese and oil were the principal products, there were two sets of fairs, one in late April and early May, the other late in the autumn.[47] The dating of the establishment of medieval European fairs is illuminating. In England royal charters approving them began to be granted in the 1180s and were common by the 1220s.

The existence of an extensive network of small, weekly markets from the thirteenth century onwards implies a more modest use of money throughout the year, when the minor products of the countryside, such as eggs, could be sold and the money spent on urban products, or at least on products, such as salt, that were distributed through towns.

At fair-time, however, very much larger amounts of current coin, usually good silver, suddenly reached the purses of the peasantry. At these times, the richer peasant paid such labour as he employed. Those who hired full-time labour, such as shepherds and ploughmen, paid their annual wages then. Those who only employed casual labour by the day did so for specific jobs. The most numerous of these were related to 'harvesting', and so were paid for at 'harvest' times. The additional hands for grain-harvesting, sheep-shearing and grape-picking, the great labour-intensive operations of the farming year, thus earned their wages then.

The major peasant purchases of manufactured goods, such as ploughshares and other iron tools, also took place at these times of year when the purchasers could afford them. They were frequently bought at the same fairs at which the produce of the countryside was sold to the city. At 'harvest' times the poorer peasants also paid off such debts as they had contracted, whether to richer neighbours, or to specialized lenders, who multiplied as the thirteenth century progressed. The new wave of urban moneylenders to be found in thirteenth-century France – Jews, Cahorsins or Lombards from Asti and thereabouts – expected repayment by peasants at fixed times of year. In the Ile de France loans by Jews to peasants had to be repaid at All Saints (1 November) by a royal ordinance of 1230. Jewish loans of grain to peasants were repaid in money at Carpentras in the autumn, and at Perpignan in August and September.

Payment of tithe, sometimes also commuted for money, naturally took place at this time of year, as did the payment of taxes in money, another of the new impositions of the long thirteenth century made possible by its availability. In England, for example, the thirteenth-century subsidies exacted by Henry III and Edward I were based on a proportionate levy, frequently a fif-

teenth part, of the 'goods' of the peasantry, that is of their produce as available for sale at Michaelmas. The tradition of assessing rural taxation at Michaelmas continued in England at least until the hearth taxes of the late seventeenth century. Seasonal direct taxation of production thus came to be the typical form of rural taxation throughout the later Middle Ages and the Early Modern period. By contrast, the dominant form of urban taxation much more frequently took the form of year-round, indirect taxation of consumption, for example by gate taxes on goods passing into the city. This difference in taxation reflects the essentially different use of money in town and countryside.

Such money as remained in peasant purses was saved against the great expenses of peasant life, most notably the accumulation of dowries for daughters or the purchase of additional land. However, saving did not necessarily mean the hoarding of coin, although it often did. Peasants very frequently also lent money one to another, against the security of their tenements. The majority of hoards of coins that have been discovered from the Middle Ages were secreted in the countryside rather than the town. Equally, the labourer tried to save, and hoard, against the great expense of setting up as a peasant tenant, and of the marriage that went with it. Despite these aspirations, little of the coin that reached the purses of the peasantry at these seasons of harvest had any chance of remaining there. Most of it returned to

Weekly markets in towns all over Europe made possible the sale of local products of every sort all round the year from the thirteenth century onwards. In this French scene, from around 1400, a woman by the market cross has brought in vegetables from the country, as have farmers their cattle and other livestock. On the left a basket-weaver has his stall, and in the centre two covered stalls are selling pieces of fabric, which might be locally woven cloth, or represent the final end of a chain of sales stretching across Europe.

the city within a few weeks. Some returned at once from purchases at the fairs themselves, some almost at once as loans, tithes and taxes were collected in, but the larger part was concentrated into the hands of the landlords and their stewards.

Rent-day was fixed to coincide with the sale of harvest. In southern England, for example, most cash-rents were paid at Michaelmas (29 September) immediately after the grain harvest was sold, although in some cases minor payments were also due at Easter, presumably after the spring sale of lambs. In Bohemia, where the harvest is slightly later, rent-day was normally 16 October. In Lorraine the cycle was differently timed again: major payments of money-rents were made at Martinmas (11 November) and minor payments on St John's Day (24 June). When, and where, direct cultivation of the demesnes was still practised, the seasonal pattern was very little different. In such cases it was, instead, the landlords' stewards who received the proceeds from the sales of produce, who paid out the wages, the tithes and in some cases the taxes, and purchased the ploughshares and so forth, before remitting the balance to the landlords.

Within weeks of being filled with good silver the purses of all but the richest peasants were almost empty and remained so for the rest of the year. Some of the money had already returned to the city, in the purses of urban casual labourers who had come out for the harvest, or in the purses of urban moneylenders, or in those of the men who sold urban products at the fairs, or in the coffers of tax collectors. Some was in the hands of the clergy, some remained with the richest peasants, but most had been paid to the nobility or their stewards. This, too, returned to the city in due course, since so many noblemen came to be resident there for all or part of the year and had their revenues remitted to them by their stewards.

The net effect of this rapid, seasonal cycle of money payments was the temporary wide diffusion of coin followed by its sudden re-concentration, as the city sucked the countryside dry again of the cash that it had sent out. By and large, the countryside was denuded of all but the smallest of small change from one 'harvest' to the next. It has been suggested that this seasonal pattern of ebb and flow between city and country, established in the long thirteenth century, continued throughout the pre-industrial period, and, in rare cases, even up to the present. As late as the sixteenth century, most of the money in England was to be found concentrated in London and the seaports, and in seventeenth-century Sicily it was found in Palermo and Messina. A study of the Sarakatsan shepherds of Zagori in Greece in the 1950s revealed a rural community that then still used money only seasonally. In rural northern India today, marriages, which are expensive in terms both of dowries and of feasting, and major purchases, like tractors, still take place mainly in the period after the great grain sales in March and April.

Only in the hinterland of the great cities in the southern Netherlands or northern Italy did a semi-urban pattern of using money all the year round develop in the later Middle Ages, since there was scope there for market gardening, or for town-dependent occupations such as spinning at piece-rates.

Albrecht Dürer has captured for us a south German peasant and his wife at the beginning of the sixteenth century with a representative selection of the produce of their smallholding

The urban pattern was quite different. Money was used in cities throughout the year. The seasonal nature of its use in the countryside obviously had an effect on urban life, as did the seasonal nature of certain long-distance travel, but these were rhythms within a continued use of money as a day-by-day urban phenomenon.

Urban wages were more generally day-wages or piece-work wages, paid all the year round, rather than annual wages. Urban rents might be annual, but they might also be paid monthly. Townsmen bought bread by the loaf, whereas the countrymen bought, or sold, grain by the bushel. Loaves need repeated purchase, grain can be bought once a year. Townsmen bought meat by the pound, whereas countrymen bought, or sold, whole animals. The countryman therefore needed his money less often, in fewer, larger sums than the townsman, who used his money throughout the year for a myriad of minor transactions, just as we are accustomed to do in our industrialized society.

How were particular cities fed? Paris, as the largest capital, ought to have presented the largest problem. In 1328 a hearth-tax was taken, of which the records survive, which have led historians to believe that it was then a city of over 200,000 people.[48] The majority of these people bought their bread ready-made from bakers. The principal point of sale of grain in the city was the Halles, where there were no fewer than twenty-four official measurers to oversee the sales of wheat in the *halle au blé* established under Philip II. There were another eighteen official measurers at the Grève, and twelve in the Jewry and the Ile de la Cité. The grain was ground in Paris itself by an impressive number of small watermills in the Seine. In 1323 no less than thirteen floating watermills were moored under the arches of the Grand Pont, now called the Pont au Change, between the royal palace in the Ile de la Cité and the north bank. Over fifty further watermills were to be found within a mile upstream.

The Paris markets were largely supplied by the Seine and its tributaries, although some grain reached the city by road. River transport had a great cost advantage over road transport for such heavy goods. A high proportion of the grain came by water from the cereal-growing lands along the Oise and the Marne.

The main road-axis of Paris was from the north-east to the south-west. Beyond the forest belt that immediately surrounded the city there were grain-growing regions in both directions, Picardy and Artois to the north-east and Beauce to the south-west. Grain from both these regions was carried to Paris by road (see map p. 103).

It may surprise some readers that so large an area of northern France was tied up with feeding Paris when its population was so small by modern standards, and indeed that there should have been any worry at all about feeding a city of 200,000 inhabitants. The problem existed because of the much lower yields of grain in the Middle Ages. In the first half of the fourteenth century yields of wheat even in the rich grain lands of Artois and the Ile de France

Feeding court cities

could be as low as eight times the seed sown, and much lower elsewhere.[49] With as much as an eightfold yield, one eighth needed to be set aside for seed, and up to another quarter might be sent to be milled to make bread for the peasant family's own consumption. Thus, even in normal years, only 60% was a marketable surplus. In years of poor harvests and in less productive regions, the figure was a third or less. Furthermore, until seed drills were invented that allowed regular and intensive sowing, the amount sown per acre or hectare was very much lower except where that was done painstakingly by hand in rows, as in Flanders. The problem was aggravated further in many areas by having a third or even a half of the land fallow and unsown. This meant that the yields per acre or hectare were overall proportionately even lower than the comparison of yields per seed sown suggests. It is in relation to that sort of productivity that Paris was so hard to feed, and that 200,000 Frenchmen were too many.

Paris lay in the wine- rather than the beer-drinking part of Europe, and drank a very great deal of it. Like its grain, the wine of Paris also came by water from as far away as Poitou, the Loire valley and above all Burgundy.[4] In Paris there was a special wharf for wine boats from Burgundy, within the 'port de Grève', on the north bank of the Seine, by the Place de l'Hôtel de Ville, formerly the Place de Grève. We traditionally think of the wine of Burgundy as that from around Beaune. However, late medieval Frenchmen distinguished two wine Burgundies, *Basse Bourgogne*, defined as stretching from Sens to Cravant 17 km (11 miles) south of Auxerre, and *Haute Bourgogne*, defined as 'above Cravant' and including all the famous vineyards from Dijon to Macon.[50] In the later Middle Ages, nearly all of the Burgundy that reached Paris came from the Auxerrois and could be shipped directly down the Yonne (below p. 295). An early fourteenth-century miniature shows wine being unloaded, where today *bateaux-mouche* tie up to unload visitors, whose

Just as cattle were brought to the city on the hoof to be slaughtered there, so grain was brought unground to be milled there. Paris was not atypical in having over sixty small floating mills, driven by waterwheels, moored under its bridges, to grind the grain shipped down the Seine and its tributaries to feed the city. The early fourteenth-century miniaturist has taken the opportunity of showing how the grain was taken to the mills in small rowing boats.

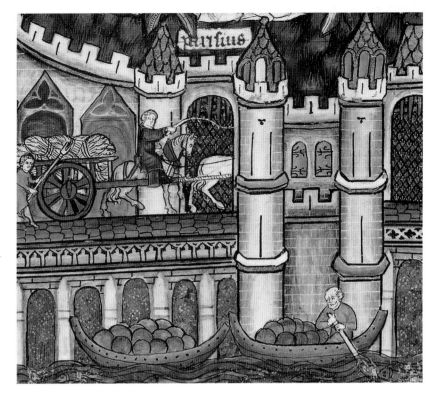

Another of the splendid vignettes of Paris, painted in 1317 at the foot of scenes from the life of Saint Denis, shows how provisions were brought into Paris both by boat on the Seine and by two-wheeled carts. Not only were many of the streets of Paris paved by the early fourteenth century, but the main roads of the Ile de France had also been sufficiently improved to allow the passage of wheeled vehicles.

tourist-eye view of the modern quaysides of Paris can give them no impression that these were once the lifelines by which the city received its food and drink. The wine still came by water in the seventeenth century, when Brother Laurence sadly noted in his *Practice of the Presence of God* that from his monastery in Paris he had been 'lately sent into Burgundy to buy the provision of wine for the society, which was a very unwelcome task for him, because…he was lame, and could not go about the boat, but by rolling himself over the casks'.[51]

As well as bread and wine, the inhabitants of Paris also needed salt in enormous quantities for preserving as well as seasoning food. This came from saltpans around the Bay of Biscay, particularly from the Bay of Bourgneuf and the south coast of Brittany and was shipped up the Seine from Rouen. A sales-tax of a *denier* on every *livre* value of salt was paid by both buyer and seller. In 1293 the city bought the right to collect this tax for the next eight years for 10,000 *livres parisis*. If we can assume that this sum was related to the actual proceeds of the tax, it suggests that total salt sales in Paris were expected to be of the order of 1,200,000 *livres parisis*.

The Seine not only brought wheat, wine and salt, but also wood in great quantities, from both upstream and down, for daily use in heating and cooking, and also for construction and reconstruction of ordinary houses. As well as wood from the immediate vicinity, carried along the lower Seine, the Oise, the Marne and the Aisne, timber from the distant forests of the Morvan was rafted down the Yonne to Paris. It is no wonder that the guild of watermen was the most important in the city. When, in the 1350s, Etienne Marcel attempted to take over the government of France through the estates-

Apart from the breeches made in Bruges, little ready-made clothing was traded in medieval Europe. People therefore normally chose their own cloth and took it to a tailor to be made up. It is therefore not surprising that hundreds of small tailors' shops were to be found in every capital city of Europe, as in this French example, where garments were cut out and made up for customers.

general, his power-base was Paris, and inside Paris, the guild of watermen of which he was provost.

The Seine also carried goods to Paris by way of the Lendit fairs, a little downstream at St-Denis, but not all goods travelled in that way, nor indeed could any goods travel more than a limited distance by water. Every river has a head of navigation; beyond that point no vessels can go and all goods had to be fed to the river system by road.

Ordinary people ate relatively little meat before the improvement of their diet in the fifteenth century, but even 'relatively little' for 200,000 people added up to a considerable amount, especially when augmented by the great quantities consumed by the court and the nobility. Before refrigeration, beasts were generally slaughtered where they were to be eaten, so that large numbers had to be driven into Paris on the hoof, to be killed and sold at the Grande Boucherie near the Châtelet at the northern end of the Grand Pont. The cattle eaten in Paris were mostly reared to the west of the city in Perche, Maine and the adjacent bocage areas of southern Normandy.

The late medieval church in the west forbade the eating of meat on Fridays and in Lent, and this prohibition seems to have been generally observed. Meat-eaters then ate fish. Most was salted and some of this came a considerable distance, from the North Sea and the Baltic. River fish were sold fresh at the Porte de Paris, which was also near the Châtelet.

Whereas countrymen grew their own vegetables, city dwellers had to buy them. Vegetables grown in market gardens round Paris were also sold at the Porte de Paris. A century later, in the first half of the fifteenth century, an anonymous Parisian, who put down his purchases as well as political events in a vivid notebook, recorded buying turnips, peas, beans and leeks as well as apples, peaches and walnuts, besides butter and cheese.[52]

The bulk of the population also needed enormous quantities of cheap clothing. Some of this was provided by the clothing of the better off, handed down to those in their service or sold to cobblers of old clothes who made and remade it over and over again. Some was made new from cheaper qualities of woollen cloth, most of which was woven on the spot. At the beginning of the fourteenth century there was a considerable group of weavers of cheaper woollen cloths in Paris itself, particularly congregated in the faubourg St-Marcel. More was woven in the nearby town of St-Denis which clustered around the royal abbey and the Lendit fairground. Its quality depended on local wool. The Paris and St-Denis cloth not only satisfied the bulk market for cheap cloth at home, but some was of a quality to enter into international trade (below p. 240).[53] Linen of all qualities was principally obtained from Champagne, but was also imported from Artois and Lombardy.

What was the case for Paris was also the case, to a lesser extent, for other capitals. Some, like London or Naples or Palermo, could basically be provided with the necessary food, drink and fuel by their own countries. Others could not be so provided for and were responsible for the growth of long-distance trades in bulk commodities.

London, which is now thought to have been a city of around 80,000 people in the first half of the fourteenth century, drew on foodstuffs from all over southern and eastern England. Like Paris it relied heavily on foodstuffs brought by river. All the river ports on the Thames from Oxford downstream, particularly Henley, shipped grain, much of it wheat, to London. Some foodstuffs came by road, vegetables, barley and malt from Hertfordshire. Unlike Paris, a great deal came via coastal shipping, which brought grain, much of it barley, not only from Kent ports like Faversham and down the Medway from Maidstone, but also round East Anglia from Yarmouth, from the small ports of the Norfolk coast, and the larger ports of the Wash, like Lynn, Wisbech and Boston. Wheat came down the Nene from Northamptonshire to Wisbech, and barley came down the Ouse from Bedfordshire, Huntingdonshire and Cambridgeshire to Lynn. Cattle came from the west midlands, and were driven across to the Fens, or the Essex marshes, where they were fattened up before being driven in to London, along with pigs, sheep and geese.[54] Both ale and wine were drunk. The brewers' livery company had more members than most at the end of the fifteenth century. Their ale was brewed from the same barley that made London's bread, but London's wine had mostly to come from overseas, since southern and eastern England produced inadequate quantities of wine. London's wine came mostly from Bordeaux. At the beginning of the fourteenth century some 20,000 tuns were shipped in a normal year. However, with the collapse of the Gascon wine trade in the middle of the century, the era of cheap wine came to an end.[55]

By contrast with Paris or London, which could essentially be fed from France or England, the cities of the Netherlands and northern Italy had often

The map shows the principal sources of grain, wine, cattle, salt, fish and wood used for provisioning late medieval Paris. As can be seen, the river system was vital for shipping much of the grain, wine and timber to the capital. The French fifteenth-century woodcut above shows wine being examined ready for shipping downstream.

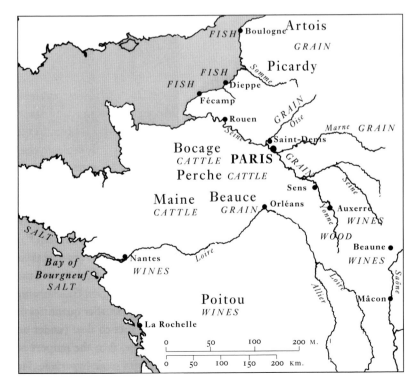

to be fed from great distances. None of the individual cities of the southern Netherlands, not even Ghent, the residence of the counts of Flanders, approached the size of London. However, because of the concentration of both capital and industrial cities in a belt running from the coast to Cologne, it was frequently impossible to feed more than a small proportion of their inhabitants locally, despite hand sowing of wheat to get maximum yields per hectare.[56] In the first half of the fourteenth century the combined population of the towns of Flanders alone exceeded that of Paris. This gives some idea of the scale of the problem of feeding them. A great deal of grain from Picardy and Artois was therefore sent northwards as well as southwards to Paris. Grain was also brought down the Rhine and the Meuse, and from further afield by sea, some from southern England, but mostly from the new grain-lands on the southern shores of the Baltic opened up in the thirteenth century. This trade temporarily collapsed with the decline in population, and therefore of demand for grain in the late fourteenth century. In the mid-fifteenth century the combined urban populations of Flanders, Brabant and Holland again reached 470,000 and by the end of the century Baltic grain was again needed to feed these cities. Until the late fifteenth century, Bruges was the most significant port of entry for the whole region, but some grain and salt from the Baltic came in, in increasing quantities, through Antwerp and Amsterdam and thence by internal waterways to the cities that needed it. Ghent, as the largest city in the region, and consequently the principal consumer of grain, attempted to establish a monopoly over all grain imported into Flanders except through Bruges.[57]

In the later Middle Ages those who lived in the cities in the industrial belt between Calais and Cologne largely relied for supplies of meat on cattle raised to the west of the Zuider Zee in the Oversticht of Utrecht and in Friesland. They were first walked to north Brabant and fattened up around 'sHertogenbosch and then driven on to the big cities for slaughter. In the fifteenth century additional cattle were reared in Denmark for the urban markets of Flanders, Brabant and Holland. After being sold at the cattle fairs at Hamburg, they too were driven to the cities by way of north Brabant. Herring was the ordinary fish of the Low Countries, and was given to the poor in large quantities in Lent. In the late fourteenth and early fifteenth centuries the poor of Lier, a not very considerable town, had between 10,000 and 20,000 herrings distributed to them each Lent. They could be either wet i.e. preserved with salt, or dry, preserved by smoking. Until around 1420 they came exclusively from Scania, packed in barrels. However, in the fifteenth century they were gutted and cured in Antwerp and Malines (Mechelen).[58]

As far as drink was concerned, the Low Countries, besides growing their own wine in limited quantities, relied heavily on Iberian wines, and, until the destruction of the vineyards in the mid-fourteenth century, on Gascon wine too. This was all imported through Bruges, along with smaller quantities of wine from the Loire valley and Poitou. In 1213 a French fleet (under an admiral called Savary de Mauléon) captured Damme, then the outport of Bruges. He reported back to his master Philip II with some hyperbole. He had found wealth beyond all his hopes, brought in by ship from all parts of the world, which included 'those true berries which, when planted on all sides, clothe the whole joyful countryside in crimson, are sent hither with rafts, laden with the wine pressed in Gascony, or the countryside around La Rochelle'. An early fourteenth-century description adds Rhenish wine 'from the Kingdom of Germany' to the wines available in Bruges. It was brought down the Rhine from the Rhineland vineyards in large quantities. However, in the course of the later Middle Ages the inhabitants first of the northern Low Countries, and then of the southern too, changed their habits considerably from wine-drinking to beer-drinking.

Northern Italy had an even greater concentration of population than the southern Netherlands and its problems of feeding itself were correspondingly greater. The number of people to be fed was many times greater than that for Paris. The countrysides of Tuscany and Lombardy, although very rich, could not, with medieval yields, even begin to feed the cities there. Grain had to be imported from other parts of the Mediterranean through Venice, Pisa and Genoa, as had wine and oil. Meat for the cities north of the Appenines was supplied by cattle raised in Hungary and driven round the eastern end of the Alps, re-fattened in the hinterland of Aquilea, and then driven on for slaughter in the cities of northern Italy themselves. Hungary also supplied beef to the cities of southern Germany in the same way. In Tuscany mutton was more important. Huge flocks of sheep were driven from southern Italy, and some individual entrepreneurs are known to have brought 7,000 or 8,000 sheep and goats in a year for sale at the cattle market on the banks of the Arno, outside the walls immediately upstream from Florence. In the 1330s Giovanni Villani reckoned that altogether 50,000 sheep and 20,000 goats were brought to the city each year. Many sheep were raised in Apulia where they were important for providing wool and *pecorino* (ewe's milk cheese) for Tuscany as well. The Apulian sheep were gathered at Foggia for their five hundred kilometre walk north. At Aquila, in the central Appenines east of Rome, they were joined by sheep from the Abruzzi, and then driven north, passing, to the annoyance of the inhabitants, through the streets of Perugia and Cortona and then alongside the Arno down to Florence itself. Smaller flocks were similarly driven to Siena, Lucca and Pisa.[59]

The growth of some of the cities of northern Italy had taken place remarkably fast, like that of Paris. In Florence, for example, when the line of a broad new circuit of walls was laid out, and gates built, at the end of the thirteenth century, to take in the new suburbs that had grown up, it enclosed an area eight times that of the previous walls built just over a hundred years before. By the time the military preoccupations of the early fourteenth century dictated that the walls were actually built even newer suburbs had grown outside the gates of the 1280s. By the 1320s it had become the third largest city in Italy. Not far short of a 120,000 people lived within the new walls, or immediately outside the gates, until starvation, and the killing diseases which follow from it, reduced the population in the famine years of the 1340s, despite the best efforts of the government to keep the city fed. This turned out to be the highest point of population of these north Italian cities, and the problem of feeding them, although often difficult, was never so severe as in the 1340s. Wave after wave of plague struck Florence from 1348 onwards, and, despite enormous migration from the countryside, the overall population shrank enormously. After the sixth wave of bubonic plague, in 1400, the population of the city was at last stabilized, but at a level of less than a third of the population of the 1330s. Much of the area within the new fourteenth-century walls was not inhabited again until the nineteenth century. Just as Florence had outstripped many other north Italian cities in its rate of growth in the thirteenth century, so its population fell faster in the second half of the fourteenth.[60]

Even Milan and Venice, which became politically so much more important, ceased to grow after the 1340s. The problem of feeding the cities was reduced, not only because some of them had shrunk in size, but also because of the improved methods of keeping them fed. The increase in size and efficiency of bulk-carrying ships, particularly carracks, made it easier to bring in food from a distance. Great government-sponsored grain warehouses kept a reserve against years of poor harvests; and government-sponsored drainage and irrigation works tried to increase local food production, for example, by growing rice to feed Milan. This was attempted even though local food production in some cases fell, as the inhabitants of the countryside deserted food production to seize the opportunities they believed were offered in the cities by taking the places of those who had died of plague. They did this despite the tax reductions, and even tax exemptions, which some governments offered as incentives to those who would settle, or even remain, as cultivators within the boundaries of their states. The very desperation of these tax incentives shows the straits to which city authorities were sometimes reduced in their attempts to feed their citizens.[61]

Court cities and the trade in luxuries

It is not the demand for basic commodities, however, which makes such a striking impact on the modern reader, but the demands of the ruling and noble minority for luxuries, which merchants travelled vast distances to satisfy. Wealthy households wished to be better served, better housed, better fed and better clothed than others, not counting all the conspicuous consumption that went with 'living nobly', and the magnanimous extravagance that distinguished the nobility from other people. In attitude the higher clergy were at one with the lay aristocracy, and were indeed most often drawn from it. The nobility, secular and ecclesiastical, provided the consuming focus that activated so much of medieval and early modern long-distance trade.

Henry Ford maintained that he was himself responsible for the change in attitudes that gave developed economies in the twentieth century a producer emphasis rather than a consumer emphasis. He liked to point out that until he set out to mass-produce them, car-manufacturers waited for orders, and only made them as and when and how the customer wanted. This was all very well for a luxury market, but he wanted to make more than fifty highly-priced, individually custom-built cars a year as his predecessors had done. Instead, he made a standard article in very much larger numbers at a much cheaper price and set about selling it after it had been made. Henry Ford, of course, exaggerated greatly, but there was a large element of truth in what he wrote. At no earlier time could the ordinary family have expected to ride in the equivalent of its own coach and horses. Standard products were not, however, Henry Ford's invention. They existed in many fields in the nineteenth century, and in some cases went back to the Middle Ages. Vigorous attempts were made to ensure that many medieval woollen cloths, for example, came in rolls of standard width and length, colour and quality. Nevertheless for the later Middle Ages, Henry Ford was largely right that it was the customer who called the tune, and particularly the noble customer with his demands for better housing, better food and drink, better clothing and for conspicuous display articles and all that goes with an aristocratic, military, way of life.

Better housing we have already considered. We have seen that noble town houses, like royal palaces, were constantly being built and rebuilt, and demanded an enormous number of masons and carpenters and workmen perpetually keeping them in good order. We have not emphasized that such noble houses, like royal palaces, for long stood out from their neighbours, since they were generally of stone or brick, when the majority of houses in cities were half-timbered, or at best a single storey of stone, with half-timbering above. Little by little, in reaction to fires, many great cities insisted that all new housing be of stone or brick, but noble housing continued to stand out by its grandeur, if not by its material. Building in stone stimulated trade in stone, sometimes from quite considerable distances. The quarries at Barnack in Lincolnshire in England, near Caen in Normandy, and at Carrara in Tuscany all sent high quality stone for prestigious buildings in distant cities.

Something of the appointment and furnishing of these great houses can be gleaned from the fourteenth-century Davizzi (later Davanzati) palace in Florence, which has been lovingly restored and furnished and is now Italian state property (illustration overleaf, p. 108). Most of the ground floor is taken up by a spacious loggia around a central courtyard. The three upper floors contain some magnificent rooms culminating in the great kitchen, which was on the top floor. The best rooms were once hung with tapestries, but these have long vanished, and only the hooks on which they were hung survive. The walls of the second-best rooms, however, were frescoed to resemble tapestry, and these fourteenth-century frescoes survive. They are some of the earliest secular frescoes to do so. The formal dining room has frescoes which represent a diapered tapestry in which a parrot motif is dominant. The best guest bedroom has a similar tapestry fresco in which peacocks predominate. The main bedroom on the second floor is decorated with frescoes which illustrate the courtly Burgundian love story of the Châtelaine de Vergy, and the best bed now has on it a superb fourteenth-century Sicilian cream linen bedspread sewn with the courtly love story of Tristan and Isolde. This was formerly in the *palazzo* of the Gianfigliazzi, another Florentine patrician

Hardly any of the sparse furnishings of even the grandest medieval houses have survived in situ. In the grand reception room at the front of the fourteenth-century palazzo *built for the Davizzi family in Florence there were wall hangings, possibly imported tapestry. On the opposite side of the courtyard the dining room (above) was painted to imitate a fabric woven in a diaper pattern of reds and greens with a parrot motif. The fabric in the reception room has long since perished, but the painted hangings still survive, with painted trees in painted panels above them. The coffered ceiling was also picked out in reds and greens.*

family. The furnishings of the city *palazzi* of these southern patricians could clearly rival the houses of the landed nobility of northern Europe.[62]

The furnishings of noble houses thus involved tapestries or, even in *palazzi*, elaborate but cheaper pretences, like frescoes to resemble tapestries, since the latter were very costly. Even rulers and great magnates had so few really good tapestries that they were prepared to have them carted about between their country castles, and from the country to their city houses and back again. As well as the cities of the southern Netherlands that specialized in tapestry-weaving, tapestry workshops were to be found in capital cities themselves (below pp. 276–8). Between 1377 and 1382 the leading tapestry workshop in Paris, that of Nicolas Bataille, produced a series of six gigantic tapestries on the theme of the Apocalypse for Louis, Duke of Anjou, one of the brothers of Charles V, designed by Jehan or Hennequin de Bondolf of Bruges, the king's painter. Each of the six panels was nearly 24 metres long and 6 metres high. Together with a more than life-size upright figure at the right, each tapestry had no fewer than fourteen separate, and very lively, scenes, making 84 scenes and six large figures in all. Jehan Bondolf had derived the scenes from '*une Apocalypse en françois toute figuree et ystoriee*', which Charles V had lent his brother from the royal library specifically '*pour faire son beau tapis*'.[63] Bataille's workshop wove another series, on the theme of the Nine Heroes (three classical, three old testament and three Christian heroes) for his younger brother Jean, Duke of Berry. For their elder brother, Charles V, Bataille produced, in conjunction with Jacques Dourdin, one of the other great Paris tapestry-makers of the period, an immense tapestry entitled the 'Jousts of St Denis'. Shortly before Bataille's death in 1399, his workshop wove a tapestry of 'Theseus and the Golden Eagle' for Charles' younger son Louis, Duke of Orléans. Other favoured fourteenth-century topics for tapestries were scenes from the Charlemagne and Arthurian cycles, the Trojan war, the Crusaders' conquest of Jerusalem, the *Romance of the Rose*, and amorous scenes suitable for (?masculine) bedrooms.

When Brussels became a centre of tapestry-weaving in the middle of the fifteenth century, it too was a capital city, so that there was a court to hand as a 'domestic' market for its products. Charles the Rash, for example, himself ordered a series of tapestries on the life of Caesar. He too had his tapestries carried about. For his marriage to Margaret of England in 1468, he took to Bruges a considerable number of tapestries, some with possibly appropriate historical subjects like the marriage of Clovis the first Christian king of the Franks, and his grandfather John's victory over the Liègois in 1408. Charles had tapestries sent ahead from Brussels to create the right atmosphere for his interview at Trier with the Emperor Frederick III in 1473, at which he expected to be made a king. Besides his 'Alexander' tapestries, he had his 'Fleece' tapestries sent: one series which told the story of how Jason acquired the Golden Fleece, and another which told the story of Gideon, regent of Israel, and his fleece. Charles also had tapestries with him on campaign against the Swiss, and many of them fell into Swiss hands after his defeat at Grandson in 1476 and were distributed among the Swiss cantons.[64]

Carpeting noble houses generally involved the import of carpets from the Near East. The taste for 'Persian' carpets had already begun. In 1398 Charles VI's brother, Louis Duke of Orléans, and his Milanese duchess, Valentina, imported a dozen '*tapis de peluche*' from Turkey. They purchased another of 'saracen' origin.[65] Alternatively carpets, used for floors, walls and tables, could also be bought from the Low Countries, where European substitute versions of oriental carpets were manufactured and exported through Bruges to capital cities throughout Europe.

The furniture in the houses of the very rich seems to have been heavily concentrated in their private rooms, whilst the large public rooms seem to have been relatively sparsely furnished.[66] There is a fairly large stock of grand late medieval furniture scattered around the world in such museums as the Cloisters in New York, the Cinquantenaire in Brussels, the Cluny in Paris, the Bargello in Florence, the German National Museum in Nuremberg, and the Victoria and Albert in London. Chests are the most common items to survive, and among these marriage chests, finely painted or finely carved, are some of the most spectacular pieces that we still have. Tables, elaborate benches, and finely panelled cupboards of various sorts have also lasted through the centuries, together with very occasional chairs. The finest pieces are naturally the ones most likely to survive changes of fashion intact. The nearest we have to arrangements of furniture in rooms is the furniture collected in the Davanzati palace in Florence, and the Flemish room at the Cloisters which has been set up to mirror the furnishing in a fifteenth-century painting within the room. Our only real evidence for furnishing is in the backgrounds of such fifteenth-century paintings as the Fouquet minia-

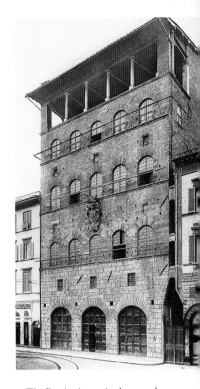

The Davizzi were in the second rank of nobility, behind the six dominant families of Florence. They hardly had an opportunity to enjoy their palace. Barely had they finished building it, late in the fourteenth century, than they were exiled, and then involved in unsuccessful conspiracies to overthrow those who had exiled them. From the 1420s their palace became the head office for assessing taxation throughout the Florentine state, by then most of Tuscany. In the sixteenth century they had to sell out to their more politically astute neighbours the Davanzati, who added the loggia at the top. The façade conceals a series of large rooms ranged round a courtyard (see dining room opposite), refurbished since the nineteenth century to evoke the domestic life of an aristocratic family in late medieval Florence.

The six huge tapestries illustrating the book of Revelation were already known to be remarkable while they were being woven for the duke of Anjou, between 1377 and 1382, in the Paris workshop of Nicolas Bataille (see p. 108). For long they were hung around the local cathedral, but they have now been expertly restored and enjoy a purpose-built museum for themselves in Angers. The six-metre-high army of lively horsemen riding down their victims (above), only fills the extreme left of fourteen panels on one of these enormous tapestries.

The demand for luxury food and drink

ture of the birth of John the Baptist in the Book of Hours he illuminated for Etienne Chevalier. Pieces of fine furniture were obviously objects of prestige and expense, but they generated virtually nothing in the way of long-distance trade since they were made in the capital cities themselves.

The nobility wished their better houses to be lit up more often and more fully and for longer hours than other houses, and with sweet-smelling beeswax candles, rather than foul-smelling tallow candles. Royalty used only fresh wax candles, so there were immense perquisites in unused candle-ends for those attached to royal households. Chandlers made their candles in the capital cities themselves, but the wax to make them sometimes had to travel over very long distances, as the demand in capital cities greatly outstripped what was available locally. Wax was imported into fourteenth-century Bruges, for example, from as far away as Russia, Hungary and Bohemia (below pp. 304–5).

As well as better housing and furnishing, itself a stimulus to both local industry and long-distance trade, noble consumers demanded better food. Being fed better in many cases simply meant being fed more, and in particular eating more meat, much more meat than other people. A half of the expenditure on food in noble households for which we have surviving accounts was quite simply on meat and on fish. This was very different from what their poorer neighbours could afford, who consumed a preponderantly cereal diet, until the improvements in ordinary diet of the fifteenth century. The rich therefore had an incredibly high protein diet, taking in perhaps as much as 4,000 calories a day. It was as unhealthy a diet as that of the poor, or possibly even more unhealthy, for the rich probably ate fewer vegetables.[67] Such descriptions as we have of the gargantuan feasts laid on for special occasions, like the relation in loving detail by Olivier de La Marche of the Burgundian feasts which he arranged, emphasize the eating of course after course of different sorts of meat.[68]

We know something of the way some of these dishes were prepared from the *Forme of Cury*, a recipe book prepared around 1390 at the request of King Richard II of England. Nearly two hundred recipes reveal how extensively the culinary arts, as practised in the kitchens of royal and noble households, relied on the heavy use of spices to differentiate the meat.[69] Italian recipes bring out the same emphasis on spices in noble kitchens. Most of the pepper and cloves, nutmeg, cinnamon and ginger imported into Europe from Asia ended up in noble kitchens, as did European spices such as saffron and coriander.

As well as simply eating a great deal more meat and eating it highly and variously spiced, the nobility also ate a wider variety of food. Hunting in all centuries has been a noble – in many places for long periods of time an exclusively noble – occupation. Game of all sorts therefore appeared on noble

The only way we can have any impression of medieval interiors when furnished is from looking at paintings. The picture of Elizabeth having newly given birth to John the Baptist from the Milan Book of Hours (Flemish) shows us, quite incidentally, the furnishings of a comfortable bedroom in an affluent house in mid-fifteenth-century Flanders, with its curtained bed, its chest for books and family papers, a handsome table, ewers, plates, and a candlestick of brass from Dinant in the Meuse valley, besides pet dogs. At the back is a view through to an equally comfortable living room.

Paris shops in the first years of the sixteenth century, from a French manuscript. The barber in the stone shop, hung with barber's bowls, is busy shaving a customer, but next door the three furriers in a half-timbered shop, who are hopefully displaying a cloak of vair, have totally failed to catch the attention of the potential customers in the foreground.

tables as it did not, or at least normally should not have done, on commoner tables. Wild boar and venison, swan and pheasant were royal and noble food. Fish were kept in noble fishponds, and rabbits were reared in warrens for noble tables. The skill of the kitchens often consisted of such mechanical ingenuity as stuffing one bird inside another to confuse both sight and taste. However, not much of this consumption provoked trade, particularly long-distance trade. The game consumed in Paris came from the forest belt that encircled the city. There were, however, some notable exceptions. Although most people living away from the coast, in so far as they could afford to eat fish at all, ate salted herring, or river fish caught locally, there was a small luxury market for fresh saltwater fish away from its place of origin. In Paris, from St Louis' time onwards, fresh sea fish could be obtained by those who would pay the price at the Halles. Fishing ports all along the Channel coast from Fécamp in upper Normandy (i.e. north of the Seine) to Boulogne rushed their catches to Paris for this market. What was ordinary at the sea coast was extraordinary in Paris. Some luxury fish, however, came from much further afield. When Pero Tafur visited Kaffa in the Crimea in 1438, he went on a revealing excursion:

> While I was there I went to see the Don…. In this river there are many fish which they load on ships, especially great quantities of sturgeon…a very good fish, both fresh and salted, and they can be met with in Castile and even in Flanders, whither they are carried…. They put the eggs into casks and carry them all over the world, especially to Greece and Turkey, and they call them caviare.[70]

Much of the consumption of food by the nobility that did provoke trade was of this sort. The eating of rice or oranges in northern Europe, or using olive oil there for cooking, was exotic and luxurious. In the south all this was commonplace and unremarkable. Such goods might have to pass through many hands to reach the eventual noble customer at the other end of Europe. For example Swedish nobles bought a mixture of south European, African, Levantine and Oriental foods and spices from Hanseatic merchants in Stockholm.[71] The Hanseatic merchants who sold these goods to them had patently not gathered them together themselves, but had bought them in Bruges, where they had been brought by other merchants from various countries. The most important groups of overseas merchants in Bruges were from Italy. Amongst them the Venetians, the Genoese, the Florentines, the Lucchese and the Sienese were most noticeable. It was merchants from these Italian states who dominated so much of European trade until the fifteenth century. By the first half of the fourteenth century the major capitals of Europe had their own colonies of resident merchants from these Italian states, but the minor capitals did not provide a big enough market in themselves to warrant Italian firms sending permanent representatives to them.

In the Low Countries none of the princes of the individual principalities had enough purchasing power, even with their nobility, to warrant the presence of large colonies of Italians in their capitals. But their combined purchasing power was of a different order. Bruges acted as a focal point for this, so that it was worthwhile for Italian firms to maintain permanent representatives there. It was equally worthwhile for the Venetians to send their heavily manned galley fleets, so expensive to run, laden with oriental spices, to Bruges, although it was not a capital city. From there spices were bought by the counts of Flanders, the dukes of Brabant and the counts of Hainault-Holland and their nobilities. In addition Rhineland merchants, like those of Cologne, came to Bruges to buy spices to carry to many of the minor capitals of what is now western Germany. Furthermore, Hanseatic merchants, particularly from Lübeck, came to Bruges to buy and carry away spices to many of the minor capitals of what is now northern Germany, as well as to the capitals of the Baltic states, like Stockholm. When Pero Tafur visited Bruges in 1438, he wrote of it:

> Without doubt the goddess of luxury has great power there, but it is not a place for poor men who will be badly received, but anyone who has money and wishes to spend it will find in this town alone everything which the whole world produces.

He went on to enumerate some of these products vividly, naturally concentrating on those luxury foods that interested him:

> I saw there oranges and lemons from Castile, which seemed only just to have been gathered from the trees, fruits and wine from Greece, as abundant as in that country. I saw also confections and spices from Alexandria, and all the Levant, just as if one were there.[72]

As a Castilian, from Cordoba in Andalusia, he naturally picked out first the fresh citrus fruit from his homeland. Citrus trees – lemons, limes and sour (i.e., Seville) oranges – were one of the groups of plants introduced from India into the Mediterranean world by the Arabs. They had reached Pero Tafur's southern Spanish homeland by the tenth century, and continued to be grown there after the Christian *reconquista*. The sweet, Chinese, varieties of orange were not to reach western Europe until the sixteenth century. Finding such exotic foodstuffs as fresh lemons in fifteenth-century Bruges is a fascinating addition to the numerous commodities which we know were traded in, but surely not significant either in bulk or in value. In 1421, when Charles VI of France had a high fever in the last year of his life, his doctors wished him to eat oranges and pomegranates. There were none available in Paris, so they wrote to Philip the Good, then Count of Flanders, who was able to have '*cinq quarterons (125) de pommes d'orange et trente pommes de grenade, bien enfardelés*' sent from Bruges.[73] More important were the Greek fruits that Pero Tafur next noticed, which were undoubtedly the dried grapes or raisins that appear, from the late fourteenth century, in two Italian merchants' notebooks and in the standard fifteenth-century *Libro di Mercatantie* as *uve passe*, and *racino seco*, along with dried figs. They noted Greek *uve passe*, packed by the *modius*, being shipped from Chiarenza and Patras, up the Adriatic to Ancona and Venice, and also available in Florence. By the 1430s Venetians or

On the awning over his shop in the same street the spice seller is advertising 'bon Ipocras' as a tonic, an infusion of cinnamon and other spices in wine. On his counter he has a sugar loaf ready to cut up and other spices in two open bowls and a closed box. Yet more spices, ranged in jars on the shelves behind him, could only be there because of a spice trade that stretched to Paris from across the Indian Ocean.

Florentines were carrying them onwards to Bruges to catch Pero Tafur's attention. The trade in raisins and currants to the north was one that continued into the sixteenth and seventeenth centuries, and greatly expanded in the hands of the English and the Dutch.

A very similar range of goods is described a hundred years earlier by an anonymous writer, writing about the trade of Bruges early in the fourteenth century:

> These are the kingdoms and the lands whence cometh merchandise to Bruges and the land of Flanders, to wit, the goods hereunder set forth. From the kingdom of Jerusalem, the kingdom of Egypt, the land of the Sudan cometh pepper and all manner of spices. From the kingdom of Armenia cometh cotton and all the spices afore mentioned.

The anonymous author was right to pick out pepper as the single spice to be named. It was the cheapest of the Indian spices used in Europe, and the one used in the largest quantities.

The generic heading of 'spices' as imported by Italians from Alexandria and the Levant to European capitals, and sold there by grocers or *speziali*, was then much broader than our narrow modern definition of culinary spices. Foods such as sugar then counted as 'spices'. The Venetians and Genoese first brought sugar to northern Europe from Muslim Egypt and Syria, and then grew it in their own sugar cane plantations in east Mediterranean islands like Cyprus and Crete. It was sold in the capitals of Europe in the form of conical loaves and much preferred to honey as a sweetener in noble households. Furthermore, it had the enormous advantage that the most elaborate subtleties, complex edible edifices, could be constructed of it as set pieces for grand dinners. It was also used in preparing candied fruits for such occasions.

Not only were foods such as sugar counted as spices, but so were many of the ingredients used in medicine. In Florence *speziali* and *medici* formed a single *arte* or guild. The spices priced highly enough to be worth the cost of transport in Venetian galleys ended up in the shops of apothecaries as well as those of grocers. The dried root of the giant rhubarb of eastern China used as an aperient, and the compound ingredients of *thiriacum*, the panacea treacle, were imported as 'spices' along with pepper and cloves.

With their 'better' food, royalty and nobility drank 'better' too. Better drinking, like better eating, essentially meant being able to afford more, often much more. The wine that the rulers and nobility drank so freely generally came from the same areas as that drunk by more ordinary people. In London, for example, until the mid-fourteenth century, the nobility of England, like the generality of people there, derived much of the wine that they drank from Gascony. However, within the vast quantity of claret imported into London, there were then, as now, superior and inferior wines, although they were not as distinctly categorized as they have been since the nineteenth century.

In London, a ward of the city, the Vintry, was largely given over to vintners, wine importers who, like merchants in so many other trades, worked alongside each other. Some effectively dealt with *vins ordinaires*, others with superior wines, like Jean de Gisors, who from 1240 had his own wharf, recently excavated, and numbered the king of England himself, then Henry III, amongst his regular customers. Leading vintners, like other leading suppliers to the king, not only grew richer on the court connection, but also more powerful. De Gisors was an alderman for twenty years, including a time as sheriff of the city, and twice mayor of London. When the era of cheap claret came to an end, in the opening phase of the Hundred Years' War, the nobility continued to drink superior claret and began to develop their taste for some of the better Spanish and Portuguese wines. By the fifteenth century, as still in the twentieth, the wines from around Jerez and from around Oporto were much appreciated in London.

Similarly in Paris, the king and court drank wine from the same areas of France as the more ordinary people, but there was a greater emphasis on that from the most famous vineyards of the Côte de Beaune. These prestigious Burgundies also found their way to the counts of Flanders and their nobility in Ghent, or their fifteenth-century descendants in Brussels. They were also carried to Avignon in the fourteenth century, where the popes and their cardinals could afford both great cellars and developed palates.

There were a few wines which were too expensive for consumption by any but the rich. The most prestigious was malmsey, produced in limited quantities in southern Greece and exported through Monemvasia in the Peloponnese. Some of the vines, transplanted to Madeira in the fifteenth century, produced an even more highly prized wine in their new habitat (below p. 293).

The nobility naturally wished their better food and better drink to be served to them in superior vessels. Their considerable quantities of silver plate and their very occasional gold plate seems to have been kept more for ostentatious display than use. The actual tableware used in their households often consisted of pewter or brass *dinanderie*. As its name suggests the latter mostly came from Dinant and other places in the Meuse valley in the bishopric of Liège, and was taken through Flanders to Bruges to export. Later, in the fifteenth century, brassware from Malines (Mechelen), Antwerp and Nuremberg took its place on noble tables (below p. 269).

Besides pewter and brassware, noble tables also carried superior pottery, for example, majolica, a tin-glazed earthenware. This was first developed in the Muslim world and continued to be manufactured at Manises in the Valencia region after the Christian reconquest. From there it was exported to many noble families sometimes made to order, painted with their own coats of arms. In time the potters of Faenza first imitated Spanish ware, then took over the north Italian market, and eventually the whole European market with faïence, only to be supplanted in their turn, by native potters elsewhere who developed products that took its market away. By the sixteenth century it was the potters of Delft who had most of this market (below p. 272).

On their tables the nobility had drinking glasses, and other glassware. Originally this too came from the Levant, particularly from Syria, and was imported and distributed through Europe by the Venetians. Very soon the Venetians themselves were making the glass, improving on Syrian patterns and distributing their own products instead. In due course south German merchants who had been importing glass from Venice for German use began making similar glass themselves (below pp. 270–1).

The demand for luxury clothing

The largest market of all provided by rulers and their nobility was for clothing and furnishing. The great lords of France and England supported armies of tailors. The tailors responded to the whims of fashion, and fashion in clothing changed very much faster than in building.[74]

Whatever the fashion of the day, great men and women were very visibly differently and better dressed than their poorer contemporaries. This differentiation in clothing that marked off the nobility from their contemporaries was from time to time reinforced by sumptuary legislation specifically designed to prevent emulation of the clothes of the great by those of humbler station. This acute visible distinction between social ranks only disappeared when mass-produced cheap copies of fashionable garments became available in the twentieth century.[75] Whatever the fashion, tailors for the nobility did not use cheap home-spun fabrics, but expensive ones brought long distances. For long the most important of these were the heavy and extraordinarily costly woollen fabrics of the Low Countries and their imitations early in the fourteenth century from Tuscany, and later from England. Even more expensive were the silks. The most expensive of these were the silks of China itself, like the 'satins' of Zaitun. These were imitated first in Byzantium and the Muslim Middle East, where such fabrics as 'damasks' were made in Damascus, and then in Europe itself. The silk weavers of Lucca were the first to produce European imitations of these oriental fabrics, but their products in turn were imitated and in some cases improved on in Bologna, Florence, Venice and Genoa, so that mercers in capital cities could carry a vast array of satins, damasks, velvets, brocades and cloth of gold from Italian suppliers. Fabulous fabrics could be made yet more fantastically expensive by embroidery. The broderers of London produced *opus anglicanum*, the finest and most sought-after embroidery of all, usually worked on silks imported from Italy. It was so expensive that only rulers and their families and the very greatest of the nobility, whether lay or ecclesiastical, could afford it.

For under-garments and lighter wear, tailors could use the finest linens of Champagne or lower quality linens from Artois and Lombardy, which were imported for the purpose, along with cotton fabrics from Syria, or their Lombard imitations. They also used mixed linen and cotton fabrics, the fustians of Lombardy, or their south German imitations from around Ulm.

As well as drapers, mercers and linen drapers, there were specialist furriers to supply tailors with high quality furs from Ireland or northern Russia for their noble clients; skinners and cordwainers to supply kid gloves and soft shoes made after the method of Cordoba, from Norwegian and other goat skin; and other superior leather-wear from Pisa (below pp. 334–8).

The drapers, like broderers and butchers, vintners and prostitutes, were to be found clustered together. In Paris the oldest part of the Halles was one such place where drapers congregated. In Paris the mercers acquired a

When Giovannino de' Grassi and his workshop illuminated a copy of the Tacuinum Sanitatis, *for the duke of Milan, they used a contemporary tailor's workshop in 1390s Milan to illustrate their page on 'woollen clothing'. The tailor is cutting out garments with shears on his giant worktable, and three assistants, one of them cross-legged on the table, are making them up. Finished clothing waits on a rack for fittings. Another copy of the* Tacuinum *shows a customer having a fitting. The text points out that the best woollen clothing uses the finest cloth from Flanders, and adds that the roughness of wool on the skin can be remedied by wearing linen under it.*

section of the Halles by 1263, and the skinners and cordwainers another over the next two decades, under Philip III. The clustering together of merchants or craftsmen of the same sort should have been beneficial to customers, but there were always risks or sharp practice. Regulations were frequently made to prevent unfair competition. For example the statutes for the drapers of Rome, made in the mid-thirteenth century when it was still the papal capital, included a chapter entitled 'How customers should be taken through the shops and how they should be shown cloth'. This stipulated that:

> If one merchant takes his cloth out to show it better to a customer no other merchant is to try to show the customer his cloth until the first merchant's cloth has been fully looked at, rerolled, bound and carried away. Only one merchant at a time was to move the customer from the dark shops to the light; cloths were not to be compared, and customers not to be stolen.[76]

Our finest descriptions of the clothing of medieval rulers and their courts are fictional, and the problem arises of how much we can trust them. Professor Raymond van Uytven has sagely pointed out:

To captivate an audience a work of fiction must seem real. A writer may idealise persons, things or situations and his imagination can be hyperbolical, but the concrete representation of his images will always reveal features of the real world around him. His casual remarks and comparisons will reflect the common opinion of his public and other generally acknowledged facts of the time. The knights of an epic are doubtless richer and bolder than they usually were, the ladies lovelier and more elegant, but for them to be seen in this way the author has to dress them in the richest clothes he actually knew.[77]

In Béroul's *Tristan*, the oldest surviving version of the story, Yseut, the heroine, queen of King Mark and lover of Tristan, is described as 'wearing robes of silk brought from Baghdad lined with white ermine. Her hair fell over her shoulders in a linen headscarf worked with fine gold.' When King Mark was visited by King Arthur with his private household, Béroul heightens the effect: 'Little coarse cloth was worn there, almost everything was of silk. Of the cloths what shall I say? There were garments made of the finest wool, dyed scarlet. No one ever saw two richer courts.' A little later Chrétien de Troyes in his *Eric et Enide* tried his hand at describing the clothing at Arthur's court. 'Puissant and lavish was the king: for the mantles he bestowed were not of serge, nor of rabbit skins, nor of cheap brown fur, but of heavy silk and ermine, of spotted fur and flowered silks, bordered with heavy and stiff gold braid.' On the occasion of Eric and Enid's marriage Chrétien's Arthur 'ordered a hundred knights to be bathed whom he wished to dub knights. There was none of them but had a parti-coloured robe of rich brocade of Alexandria.'[78] The real life courts that Chrétien knew were those of his patron, Mary, Countess of Champagne, at Provins, and of her father, Louis VII, King of France, at Paris.

Real life could be as ostentatious as fiction. Clement VI, by far the most lavish of medieval popes, the same who had had his new walls frescoed with nightingales in Avignon, and who is reputed to have said 'my predecessors did not know how to be pope', ordered no fewer than 430 ermine skins for a cape for himself in 1347, and another 310 for a mantle, besides 362 for five hoods. The same year he had another cloak lined with sable and purchased forty rolls of gold and coloured cloth from Damascus, besides many other fabrics including gold brocade from Venice, superior heavy woollen broadcloth from Brabant, and fine linen from Champagne.[79] Real life expenditure on clothing for members of a court was always scaled according to rank. In the fifteenth century Philip the Good of the Netherlands dressed his court with different qualities of fabric from the Chancellor Rolin and his rival the Great Chamberlain Croy downwards. He himself conspicuously preferred to wear plain Italian black velvet. His son Charles the Rash, at his interview with the Emperor Frederick at Trier in 1473, seems to have tried to dress his followers to outshine Kings Mark and Arthur at their interview.[80]

Popes in Avignon bought cloth from Tuscans, such as the young Francesco Datini, the rising son of the innkeeper Marco Datini of Prato, who was able to supply at one time 'white linen from Genoa, fustian from Cremona, scarlet *zendadi* from Lucca, white, blue and undyed woollen cloth from Florence, besides silk curtains, with curtain rings, table cloths and napkins'.[81]

The rulers in Brussels bought equally from Tuscans, who were based in Bruges. Pero Tafur in his description of that city in 1438 commented:

> Here was all Italy with its brocades, silks and armour and everything which is made there, and indeed, there is no part of the world whose products are not found here at their best.[82]

The anonymous description of goods available in Bruges a hundred years earlier lists vairs and greys (sorts of fur) from the kingdom of Russia and notes that 'from the kingdom of Tartary cometh gold cloth, and diverse kinds of silks.' In other words, the fabrics of China that had been carried across the whole breadth of Mongol Asia by enterprising merchants, some of them north Italians.

Fabric was normally carried unmade up to its final destinations, there to be used by local tailors to suit the clients' tastes. Ready-made clothing does not seem to have generally been available anywhere much before the seventeenth century, but there was one medieval exception. Geoffrey Chaucer, writing at the court of Richard II of England at the end of the fourteenth century, produced a parody of contemporary romances, Sir Thopas, in which the hero's clothing was described:

> His shoon of cordewane,
> Of Brugges were his hosen broun,
> His robe was of syklatoun,
> That coste many a jane.

'Hose', or serge trousers from Bruges, appear in literature as items of luxury clothing in epics, romances and fabliaux back to the thirteenth century.[83] In real life they could be purchased in Paris from mercers.

The demand for plate and jewels

As well as a demand for better housing, better food and drink and better clothing, there was also in every capital city a prodigious demand for conspicuous display articles such as gold and silver plate, or bronze and enamel from the Meuse valley, the Rhineland and Limoges, pearls from the Persian Gulf, or diamonds, rubies and other gems from India. Most of these were sold to royal and noble customers by goldsmiths, who made up most of the precious objects to their customers' requirements in their own workshops in the capital cities themselves. Paris, as the largest and wealthiest court city of Europe from at least the mid-thirteenth century onwards, naturally had the largest and most prestigious group of goldsmiths. From documents we know that, as with many other types of business, they clustered together, principally on the Grand Pont which was then built up with houses. The Parisian goldsmiths were already established there in the 1250s, when St Louis' envoy to the Mongol khan was understandably surprised to find in Caracorum, at the further end of Asia, a goldsmith, William Buchier, whose brother, Roger, was a goldsmith on the Grand Pont.[84]

Some of the finest pieces of medieval goldsmiths' work to survive were made by Parisian craftsmen. One of the most exciting pieces of jewelry to survive is the delicate crown, made in the 1370s either in Paris, or by Parisian goldsmiths working elsewhere, possibly at Prague, the court city of the Emperor Charles IV. It seems to have come to England with the Emperor's daughter, Anne 'of Bohemia', when she became Richard II's first queen, and went out again in 1402 with Blanche, the daughter of King Henry IV, when she went to become the ten-year-old bride of Ludwig, son of the the newly elected ruler of Germany, the Count Palatine Rupert of Wittelsbach. It is now in Munich. It is an elaborate twelve-part circlet of gold, from which rise twelve golden lilies. The twelve sections of the base are themselves delicate tracery hexagons, set with jewels and enamelled in blue, red and white. The lilies are set with many more sapphires, rubies, diamonds and pearls, all imported from Asia.[85]

Some goldsmiths' work was, however, made elsewhere than in court cities. From the mid-thirteenth century to the late fourteenth century, Siena was well known for its goldsmiths, whose work was distributed throughout central and northern Italy and beyond. It is not surprising that, when the papacy established a new capital at Avignon, Sienese goldsmiths should feature noticeably among the large number of specialized migrants who came from Italy. At Avignon some of the goods on offer were rather different. In 1335 a Tuscan goldsmith, Bonaccorso de Vanni, not only had in his shop there the usual loose precious stones and some gold and silver ornaments, but also jewelled crucifixes, an image of Our Lady with crown, and a jewelled mitre, offered for sale at 280 florins, or about ten years' wages for a weaver, and still over a year-and-a-half's wages for a knight.[86]

In the second quarter of the fifteenth century Philip 'the Good' of Burgundy, the ruler of what is now Belgium and the Netherlands, became the richest sovereign in Europe and held Europe's most prestigious court at his new 'capital', Brussels. His territories naturally became key centres for the production of luxury objects both for home consumption and export. In some fields, for example tapestry, painting, manuscript illumination and goldsmiths' work, they took over and developed the leading role previously played by Paris. Philip the Good himself built up a remarkable collection of jewelry and plate.[87] His son Charles had much of the plate melted down and minted to pay his troops, but purchased yet more jewelry. Since he was never king, Charles had no crown, but he made up for it by creating a jewelled hat that was richer than many crowns. He had it with him when he was defeated by the Swiss and it ended up as part of the booty which was displayed in public.

In 1449, during the reign of Philip the Good, Petrus Christus painted St Eloi or Eligius, the seventh-century goldsmith-moneyer-minister of King Dagobert, who became bishop of Noyon in 641, and was canonized after his death in 660. He became the patron saint of goldsmiths and moneyers. This

'portrait' executed in Bruges, presumably for a goldsmith or guild of goldsmiths shows what M. J. Friedlander, the historian of Netherlandish art, has called 'a painstakingly accurate representation of a goldsmith's shop'. Two customers, who by their lavish and fashionable costume, are of the higher nobility, are to be seen purchasing pearls by weight, presumably either for making up into jewelry or for embroidery onto rich clothing to make it yet richer still. In the background are more pearls, precious stones and some ready-made gold rings.

Very little of the goldsmiths' work created for the rulers of the Burgundian Netherlands survives. One of the few pieces to do so is the remarkable St George created in 1467 for Charles by Gerard Loyet, his most favoured Brussels goldsmith, and given by him to the cathedral church of St Lambert at Liège in 1471.[88] It has survived in the cathedral treasury.

Such survivals are exceptional. This is hardly surprising since, when the fashion for particular jewelry changed, as it frequently did, the constituent parts were too precious to be discarded or abandoned like out-of-fashion clothing or housing. Instead they were broken up and remade into fresh jewelry in a newer fashion.

Other examples are known only from paintings, like the pearl necklace worn in the 1470s by Elizabeth the wife of King Edward IV of England. Paintings also give us many more examples of the use of pearls for embroidering clothes than have survived. We can see the pearl-embroidered clothes

In his painting of St Eloi (Eligius), Petrus Christus shows us the
interior of a goldsmith's in 1449, with rings on spindles, an open bag
of pearls, precious stones, coral, amber and some ready-made
brooches for sale.

worn by the young Guidobaldo, son and successor to Federigo da Montefeltro, the Duke of Urbino, when he was painted at the age of four or five by Pedro Berruguete in 1476 or 1477. At about the same date the Venetian painter Carlo Crivelli (*c.* 1435–*c.* 1495) produced a fantasy painting of St Mary Magdalene wearing a small fortune on her sleeve, which on close examination can be seen to be embroidered not only with gold thread, but with numerous fine pearls. Such extraordinarily expensive detachable sleeves existed in real life and can be found in inventories, priced as if jewelry in themselves.[89] Among the earliest still extant secular garments sewn with pearls is the wedding dress worn by the Netherlands princess Mary when she married Louis/Lajos of Hungary in 1521.

Every capital had goldsmiths, but Paris alone developed a major line in ivory-carving. Developed first to supply the home market provided by the French court, the Paris ivory-carvers developed unmatchable skills that meant that the nobility from all the courts in Europe bought Paris ivories. The Duchess of Burgundy, who presided over the court in Beaune, had a dressing-table set of Parisian ivory. It was only when the supply of ivory to carve dried up at the end of the fourteenth century that any substitutes for Paris ivories were traded in (below pp. 280–1).

The most luxurious goods of all were bought from goldsmiths, but some of the other goods bought by the nobility ran them close in price. A whole roll of the finest Brussels woollen cloth sold for around the same price as 800 grams of gold or as 1 diamond, 5 rubies and 5 emeralds. In this league, even spices were cheap. Thirty kilos of pepper could be bought for the same money.[90] The finest products on offer from medieval booksellers were not cheap, however, for the finest products demanded the deployment of immense numbers of hours of work by highly skilled and gifted illuminators. In every capital there were booksellers or stationers. They had some standard works in stock, ready written, but the most luxurious were commissioned by their clients themselves, after lengthy discussions, with very exact specifications. Many works therefore came in both a standard form and in luxurious illuminated versions. The best known of these are Books of Hours, religious office books for private lay devotion, which were produced in ever increasing quantities from their first compilation in the 1240s onwards. The most magnificent were created in Paris and Bruges for members of the ruling houses of France and the Netherlands. Less well known are the *taqwîm* or tables of health written in Arabic by Ibn Botlan of Baghdad in the mid-eleventh century and translated into Latin for King Manfred of Sicily two hundred years later. Numerous plain unadorned manuscripts of the Latin text survive from the fourteenth and fifteenth centuries, but nine abbreviated, but lavishly illustrated, versions of the *Tacuinum Sanitatis* were also created in the 1380s and 1390s for members of the Milanese and Veronese court circles. It is from some of these that a number of illustrations have been drawn for Chapter 6.[91] In the fifteenth century stationers were purveying printed books as well, and some were turning into publishers, a few on a large scale for an international market, whilst the remainder ceased to create books, but only

In the 1470s princely children could be weighed down by their pearl-embroidered clothes like the young Guidobaldo, future Duke of Urbino, wielding his miniature sceptre, seen here in a detail from Berruguete's portrait of his father Federigo da Montefeltro.

Opposite: In 1467 Gerard Loyet, valet de chambre and official goldsmith to Charles, the ruler of the Netherlands, created this spectacular miniature sculpture of his master in gold for the palace chapel in Brussels. Charles, kneeling in armour on an elaborate cushion, holds a relic, supported by a standing St George, also in full armour, with almost identical features. The same year Charles rewarded Loyet by appointing him general master of the mints of the county and duchy of Burgundy, and two years after that general master of all mints in the Burgundian Netherlands, a post he held until 1494 in the reign of Charles' grandson Philip.

Great princes did not need to visit goldsmiths in their shops. The goldsmiths came to them. In this French miniature of about 1410, two goldsmiths on bended knee are offering jewels and rings from a casket to the elderly John Duke of Berry, seated in state. A ducal counsellor is making suggestions and two guards stand at the door. By 1410 he was the only surviving uncle of Charles VI of France. He was as well known as a collector of fine jewels, which have not survived, as of richly illuminated manuscripts, many of which have.

sold them. Printing was also used for other purposes. Governments used it for printed proclamations and placards. Printed forms rapidly came to be designed, for example for indulgences. Printing was also used more frivolously, as with playing cards. All these had manuscript precursors. Behind the stationers in the chain of production, both of manuscript and print, stood the makers of parchment, vellum and paper. Paper was yet another product imported into capital cities in considerable quantities, not only for books, but also for use in great amounts by government, and in lesser amounts for the administration of noble estates and the running of businesses. Government accounts were frequently drafted on paper, and a fair copy only made on parchment when the audit was complete. Paper once imported into Italy and then distributed by Italians, was gradually replaced by paper made by Italians, until in their turn the men of Nuremberg ceased to import Italian paper and began to make their own, first for themselves, and then to export in place of Italian paper (below pp. 255–8).

Ecclesiastical institutions as well as rich individuals were also customers for goldsmiths' work. Around 1350 Ramsey abbey commissioned this elegant silver gilt incense box for use in the abbey church. It is of the traditional boat shape, with a ram's head at each end, as a punning allusion to the name of the island in the English Fens where the abbey was sited.

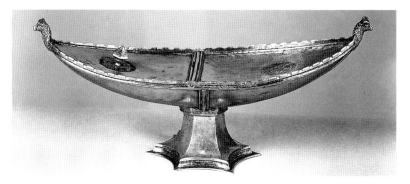

*In the 1470s an earlier (French) husband and wife team than
Quentin Massys' (see p. 13) run a large goldsmiths shop with a
similar range of goods to Petrus Christus' St Eligius (see p. 122).*

This marvellous little gold horse and groom enamelled in white and blue stand beneath a pedestal on which a Madonna and Child are being worshipped. A Paris goldsmith created this present for Queen Isabella to give to her husband Charles VI of France on New Year's day 1404. It is now in the Treasury of Altötting, Bavaria.

Left: The cut of this beautiful padded French doublet, made up from fine Sicilian silk lampas woven with gold thread, reveals that it was produced after the innovations in tailoring around 1400. It was for long believed to have belonged to Charles of Blois, duke of Brittany (1345–64), and preserved because of the reputation for sanctity which caused him to be beatified.

There were a great many other luxuries that were available for purchase in most capitals. Some of these were amongst the 'dry goods' that might be purchased from mercers, along with silks and haberdashery. In 1446 the 'dry goods' that the mercers of Venice were selling included knives and scissors, pewter and imported candlesticks and other brassware from 'Flanders' i.e. *dinanderie*.[92]

Some luxuries, like soap, were not to be found amongst the mercers' dry goods. Naturally the nobility preferred the imported white olive oil-based soap of Castile, or its perfectly satisfactory Venetian imitation, to the black wood ash-based soap of northern Europe (below p. 273).

Military demand

In addition to noble demand for domestic and personal consumables, there was a huge market for commodities specifically related to the warlike way of life of a still very military aristocracy, for arms and armour, and for war horses, both for war itself and for the tournament.

Every capital city had its own armourers. However, in one capital, Milan, the armour-makers, catering firstly for the domestic market created by the aggressive and expansionist Visconti, developed an export industry which supplied many of the needs of other rulers (below pp. 259–60). Milanese armour could be bought in other capitals, for example, in Avignon, where the young Francesco Datini started up in business as an importer of Milanese armour. In 1367 he had in stock 45 basinets, 3 *chapeaux de fer*, 10 *cervelieres* (steel skull caps), 20 cuirasses, 60 breastplates, and 12 hauberks (coats of mail). The following year he supplied 50 cuirasses, 50 *cervelieres*, 12 basinets, and 12 pairs of gauntlets for the defence of Avignon.[93] When he had a shop of his own he assembled swords for sale there from foreign components, using sword blades from Germany, where Sölingen by then produced better steel blades even than Toledo, and sword handles and scabbards from Italy.

In London the nobility mostly bought armour imported from Milan, and later Germany. In 1322 the wardens of the London armourers were marking imported armour before it was sold. Specialized milliners were selling Milan goods, both imported Milanese armour itself and the padded clothing to be worn under it, particularly under the helmets. The fraternity of linen armourers was also providing padded clothing.

The price of armour gradually rose as it became heavier, reaching a maximum weight soon after the middle of the fifteenth century. In Paris in 1300, under Philip IV, simple armour for an ordinary knight cost six l*ivres tournois* at a time when a knight's wages were five *sous* a day. By 1450, under Charles VII, when the *livre tournois* had permanently lost a great deal of value, a knight's armour cost thirty *livres tournois*, at a time when a knight's wages were ten *sous* a day. In terms of a knight's wages, the cost of his armour had increased from just over three weeks' pay to two months' pay. In terms of gold the cost had almost exactly doubled. This increase in cost reflects the growing complexity of armour. In 1300 knights wore only mail shirts and helmets and carried shields. In 1450 they were encased in plate armour. The trade in armour as well as increasing in value also greatly increased in

In his sharply individual style, Carlo Crivelli has painted St Mary Magdalene (opposite) with controlled eroticism as a highly successful courtesan, suddenly converted, coming, hopefully but slightly apprehensively, to offer her Lord the box of precious ointment, which she holds with long and delicate fingers. Her body is still revealingly and richly clothed in some of the accumulated earnings of her profession, with a small fortune in her extraordinary detachable sleeve alone, embroidered not only with gold thread, but with numerous fine pearls (see p. 123).

Only small quantities of luxury arms and armour survive in museums, but a great quantity of ordinary mass-produced arms and armour from Milan and Brescia once existed. A group of guards are relaxing (above) in an early sixteenth-century guardroom with some of the equipment of ordinary soldiers hanging above them for use as needed – breastplates, helmets, crossbows, pikes and a drum. This is one of a series of wall paintings in the Castello di Issogno, Val d'Aosta.

volume, as war continued and proliferated for over a century and half, from the wars of the 1290s up to the final battle of the 'Hundred Years' War' at Castillon and the peace of Lodi, in 1453 and 1454 respectively, which brought peace at last to France and Italy. It is little wonder that the armourers of Milan prospered, and that it was a market that the capitalists of Nuremberg were eager to break into.

As well as ordinary armour which any knight might wear, the most elaborate, chased and gilded armour was produced for rulers and the greatest nobles. Piers Gaveston, greatly favoured by Edward II of England, and elevated by him to the earldom of Cornwall in 1307, had such an elaborate suit of armour, with pearls on the shoulders.

Even in peacetime, there was a continuous market not only for armour, but also for warhorses, both for use in tournaments and to be available in case of war. Edward I of England expected his knights to own their own warhorses ready to bring with them on campaign, although he was prepared to replace those that were killed. The horse rolls from his Scottish campaigns list all the horses brought by individuals when the army set out, together with agreed values in case they needed replacing. The value of these horses varied enormously. By then the best warhorses were the 'great horses' that came from Lombardy. During the war between Philip IV of France and Edward I, 2,500 Lombard horses were sent from Italy into France. When Lombard warhorses had first arrived in England in 1232 they made a huge impact.[94] Henry III reputedly asked the mayor of London to try to damp down the market in them so that they did not become too expensive for royal purchase!

Until the 'new' great Lombard horses arrived, the English nobility had been improving their own bloodstock by importing stallions from northern Castile, which were bred by religious houses along the pilgrim road to Compostella. Béroul had made his Tristan come to a tournament with two fine Castilian horses. North Italy as well as exporting horses, also imported them. In 1376 the young Buonaccorso Pitti, returning from Buda, congratulated himself on having safely managed to bring horses from Hungary and sell them at a considerable profit in Florence.[95]

As well as warhorses, great households used many other horses too, for riding and for drawing carriages. We have already seen Eudes Rigaud travelling up to Paris from Rouen with eighty horsemen. When Pierre de Banhac returned from Rome with Urban V he had to rent ten stables in Avignon for his horses. How many they held altogether is not clear, but four of them held thirty-nine horses. Many of these less exotic horses were bred locally, but

Pisanello's warhorses and armour. Some of Pisanello's meticulous sketches which he made in preparation for his paintings have survived in the Louvre. They show his acute and accurate powers of observation, particularly of animals, like the heavy, realistic, stallion, on the left, complete with mark of ownership. Very similar warhorses, seen from the same angle, occur in his paintings and on his medals. However his fantasy painting of St George, above, from his St Anthony Abbot and St George of c. 1340, with his cropped curly hair, looks like a more handsome, idealized, version of one of Pisanello's medal portraits of his patron, Lionello d'Este, the Marquess of Ferrara, dressed up in a floppy sunhat and with rather flimsy cardboard armour over his red-cross surcoat.

some were sent long distances, like the Danish palfreys that could be bought in Bruges early in the fourteenth century.

If rulers kept horses by the hundred, and great lords by the score, large capital cities altogether accommodated horses by the thousand, including all those used for carrying goods and drawing wagons. Such horses all needed food and harness. The feeding of so many horses added to the demands made by capitals on the countryside and particularly for hay.[96] Burgundian government accounts from the fifteenth-century Netherlands make the same daily allowance for feeding and stabling a horse as they do for board and lodging for a man.

The quality of harness naturally varied according to the rider. The finest was exceedingly expensive. In *Eric et Enide* Chrétien naturally gave his hero the best that real life could afford, or perhaps a little better:

> Of the bridles, breast straps and saddle I can surely say that the workmanship was rich and handsome…the saddle was covered with a precious purple cloth. The saddle bows were of ivory, on which was carved the story of how Aeneas came from Troy. A skillful craftsman spent more than seven years on carving it.

A fictional fantasy maybe, but fit to set beside the many thousands of intricate surviving examples of the Parisian ivory-carvers' skills.

Chrétien's hero was, on this occasion, riding out hunting, not to war or the tournament. He caused them to have 'taken with them rich falcons, both young and moulted, many a tercel and sparrow hawk'. Many capitals, like Paris, were set in good hunting country, and in the capitals all that was needed for hunting could be bought, not only the horses, but also the dogs and the falcons and even their jesses. King Philip IV of France, passionately addicted to hunting as he was, kept formidable kennels and mews and was an exceptionally good customer. The best hawks were gerfalcons which originated in Iceland, where they were captured and trained. When the nobility of the principalities of the Low Countries bought them at Bruges they were described as from the kingdom of Norway. From Bruges some reached the courts in London and Paris, and from Paris some were carried to Avignon, where many of the higher clergy hunted despite express prohibitions, and others were taken over the Alps for sale to members of Italian courts.

Italian suppliers of luxuries

Although the nobility, or their stewards, might need to visit a number of different types of retailer to make their purchases, there were in all the larger capitals resident Italian businessmen who belonged to multi-branched import-export houses, that dealt with the whole range of commodities that the rich would wish to buy, as well as with bulky necessities. Most of the merchant notebooks of the fourteenth and fifteenth centuries were compiled by men who worked for such omnicompetent businesses and have left us a clear record of what was brought to the capital cities and where it was brought from.

In later chapters I will also discuss in detail the sources of many of both

By far the best documented merchant of medieval Europe was Francesco di Marco Datini (c. 1335–1410). He looks out at us from the Palazzo Communale in his home city of Prato, a shrewd and successful businessman yet also, from his letters, clearly a slightly philistine nouveau riche very humanly apprehensive about death and the afterlife.

the bulky necessities and the luxuries referred to in this chapter. In Chapter 5 I shall examine manufactured goods, and in Chapter 6, foodstuffs and raw materials.

The career of Francesco Datini, from 1350 to 1410, shows us the build-up of one of these businesses. From modest beginnings in Avignon, we have already seen him beginning to trade in the import of armour and arms from Milan and Germany. He then added to this the import of spices and next that of cloth. The trade in cloth came to be the core of his interlinked group of companies. Having installed a manager in his business in Avignon, he moved back to Tuscany, to his father's home town of Prato, where he not only organized the despatch of goods to Avignon, but also himself became a cloth manufacturer, with two separate cloth-making companies. He ran a dye works there as well. He also started companies in Spain from which the wool for his cloth mostly came, and gradually built up a group of businesses that spanned the whole of the western Mediterranean and which traded in practically every possible commodity, from sending goldsmiths' goods and works of art to Avignon, to diversifying into banking and insurance. Documents relating to these firms have survived by a curious chance. Because he died without an heir, he left his fortune to a charity which he founded, and which still exists. When his executors wound up his affairs, they preserved his complete business papers, which still remain in the lavish house he built himself in Prato. They lay bare to us the meteoric career which made him one of the most successful self-made 'multi-millionaires' of the later Middle Ages, ending his days in Florence running the holding company for an interlocking group of west Mediterranean businesses, whose activities stretched from the English Cotswolds to Arabia, and from Castile to the Crimea.[97]

Francesco Datini can exemplify for us both the opportunities for success in business in capital cities and also the way in which Italians dominated the supply of luxuries to the rulers, the lay magnates, the higher clergy, and all the other noble and rich of the capital cities. Only those capital cities that in themselves could generate enough to support imports on a large enough scale had established and organized groups of resident north Italian merchants.

In southern Europe there were organized communities of north Italian merchants in such capitals as Naples, Palermo, Barcelona and Avignon, and in Rome before the papacy moved to Avignon and again afterwards. In northern Italy itself there were colonies of merchants from other cities in the capitals there, such as Florence, Milan and Venice. Outside Mediterranean Europe the number of capitals that had well organized Italian merchant communities was much more restrained. Effectively only Paris and London did so, together with Bruges, which acted as a focus for the purchasing power of many minor capitals.

The lack of an effective central monarchy in Germany meant that, since there was no single great capital, demand was too diffused for any single route to carry enough trade to warrant the new commercial division of labour. As a consequence the trade of the Hanseatic cities, northwards and eastwards from Bruges, did not reach the critical volume in the Middle Ages, and that of the south German cities was still equally primitive in its organization until the very end of the fourteenth century. Until then Germany and central Europe, with one exception, were not yet ready for the commercial revolution. Only at Prague, where the last Premyslid and the first Luxemburg kings of Bohemia ran a centralized monarchy, as well as enjoying mining-revenues, was there a capital large enough for the scale of demand generated in it to warrant even a small resident Italian business community around 1300. It was only later, in the second half of the fourteenth century, that the Angevin monarchs of Hungary, supported by the new gold from Kremnica, managed in the same way to make Buda a focal point for the nobility of Hungary and hence also for Italian businessmen.

It was worthwhile for Italian companies to maintain branches in London from the mid-thirteenth century through to the end of the Middle Ages. The first resident Italian merchants were living in London by 1250, and by 1277 at least seven companies already had representatives there. In the fifteenth century four nations of Italians resident in London had formally organized groups: the Venetians, the Genoese, the Florentines and the Lucchese. Their statutes of 1457 survive. A generation later Dominic Mancini sets his *Usurpation of Richard III* in perspective for his Italian readers with a description of the wharves and the commercial area behind it, as far back as Lombard Street, the Mercery, West Cheap and the Goldsmithery:

> On the banks of the Thames are huge warehouses for imports, and numerous cranes of remarkable size to unload merchandise from the ships. From the district on the east, adjacent to the Tower, three paved streets lead towards the other quarter in the direction of the walls on the

Opposite: London was one of the places where the Italian merchants who dominated Mediterranean trade could link with the Hanseatic merchants who dominated the trade of the Baltic. For both, London was a far flung destination. Hanseatic merchants were based at the Steelyard, marked 'Staelhof' by Van Wyngaerde on his panorama of London of c. 1540. On the waterfront, the Steelyard had one of the 'huge warehouses' commented on by Mancini and one of his 'cranes of remarkable size'. Its buildings stretched back to Thames Street. Through the Steelyard Hanseatic merchants imported many of the staple commodities which Mancini said were to be found in Thames Street, the paved main street closest to the river.

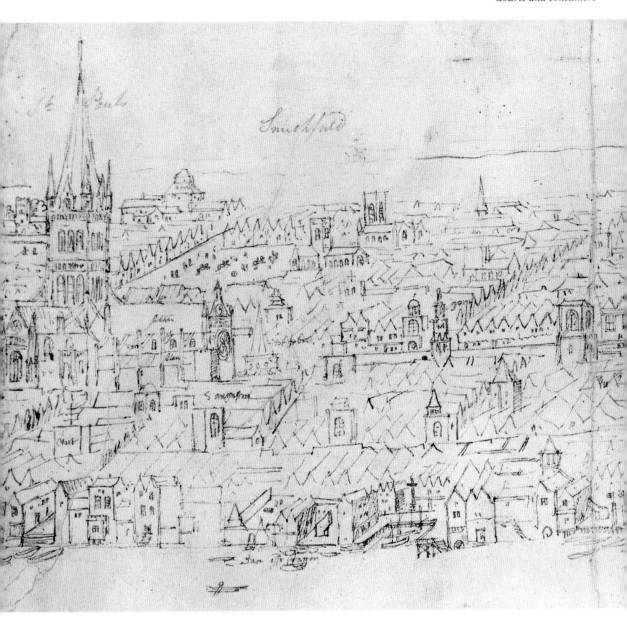

west: they are almost straight and are the busiest streets in the city. The one closest to the river, below the others, is devoted to various staple commodities, both liquid and solid – minerals, wines, honey, pitch, wax, flax, robes, thread, grain, fish, and other rather sordid goods. In the street running between the other two you will find hardly anything for sale except cloths. And in the third street, which is level and touches the centre of the town, the traffic is in more precious goods such as gold and silver cups, dyed stuffs, various silks, carpets, tapestry, and much other exotic merchandise.[98]

Resident Italians possibly arrived a little later in Bruges, but by 1290 the local manager of the Buonsignori of Siena was doing business with the court of Flanders and in 1306 the branch manager of the Gallerani of Siena became Receiver of Flanders. In the fifteenth century the focal point for international business in Bruges was the Place de la Bourse, where the Venetians, Florentines and Genoese all had their consular houses.

It was also worthwhile for Italians to maintain branches in Paris, beginning at the same period, but ending with the abandonment of Paris as their capital by its kings in the fifteenth century. The 1292 tax returns reveal the residence of representatives of twenty Italian companies in Paris, mainly at that date from Florence, Siena and Piacenza. Six of the seven highest tax payers in Paris were then Italian businessmen, the highest taxed of all being Gandolfe degli Acelli ,the Paris representative of the famous Burri company of Piacenza. At the end of the fourteenth century the men of Lucca were the dominant group in the city, followed by those of Asti. There were representatives of thirty Lucchese business houses in Paris.

From the cities in which the international Italian business houses had branches, or agents, luxury goods were carried onwards, by others, to cities in which they did not maintain a presence. At an international level, this meant Hanseatic merchants carrying Mediterranean, Levantine and oriental goods from Bruges to Stockholm and other consumption centres that could be reached through the Baltic; and Cologne and south German merchants carrying similar goods from Bruges and Venice to the numerous small court cities of the Empire. At a national level, this meant English and French merchants carrying similar goods from London and Paris to the regional centres of provincial England and northern France, particularly to sub-capitals like York or Rouen which had important administrative functions, but also to lesser centres, county towns like Lincoln or Stafford. Whereas the great magnates of a kingdom built themselves palatial aristocratic town houses in the capital, the gentry or lesser nobility built themselves humbler town houses in regional centres, and purchased goods for consumption by their households there. Much provincial trade was, of course, purely local, but some part of it had to link into the arteries of long-distance international trade. Thus in 1444–45 John Hopton, a comfortably off Suffolk gentleman, with an income of £300 sterling a year from his lands, sent his bailiff, Nicholas Greenhalgh, to Norwich to stock up not only with oats and malt, meat and fish which presumably originated in East Anglia or along its coasts, but also to purchase salt, saffron and candles which may or may not have done so, and pepper,[99] which had been sent out from London, whither it had been brought by Italians, most probably by Venetians in galleys. Therefore the town houses and 'shopping' of the lesser nobility or gentry affected provincial centres much as royal and magnate residences affected court cities on a very much grander scale.

The clearest indication of the importance of the residence of a king and his greater nobility to the economy of a city and to the trade drawn to a capital by the court is provided by what happened quite suddenly when Paris ceased to be the capital of the kings of France after 1422, when Charles VI died in the Hôtel de St Paul.

No king of France lived in Paris again until 1575. With the abandonment of the royal palace, the nobility themselves also ceased to live in Paris. A few followed Charles VII to Bourges; a few followed Henry VI's regent, the Duke of Bedford, to Normandy. Most retired to their own territories. From the second quarter of the fifteenth century the greatest of the princes of the blood, the dukes of Burgundy from Philip the Good onwards, were based in their own capital at Brussels, in their Netherlands' principalities, and no longer lived in Paris. The dukes of Anjou, still nominally kings of Sicily, no longer lived in Paris, but held their own court at Tarascon on the Rhône in their county of Provence. Charles III, 'the Noble', Count of Evreux and King of Navarre, bought houses and land to expand his palace at Olite in Navarre, and moved there from the Hôtel de Navarre, in Paris, formerly the Hôtel d'Evreux, where he and his ancestors had lived and focused their political activities since 1317. After his death in 1425 his daughter and successor continued to hold court at Olite surrounded by the nobility of Navarre.[100] The dukes of Brittany ran their administration and held their court at Rennes, and their Paris hôtel collapsed in ruins. The dukes of Bourbon lived in their own principalities, except when they were at the Burgundian court, and the other magnates did much the same.

For many years the only considerable magnate at Charles VII's court was the Count of Maine, the younger brother of René of Anjou, whose revenues were not very significant. Later in Charles VII's reign more magnates gathered round him. Even more gathered round his successors. They re-gathered, however, in the Loire valley, not in Paris. The most favoured royal residence changed at least once in every generation. This was no longer movement from one part of Paris to another, but from a castle or palace in one town to that in another. As soon as he could leave Bourges, Charles VII spent many years at Chinon below Tours. His son, Louis XI, preferred Langeais and Plessis, closer to Tours. Louis' daughter, Anne of Beaujeu, ruled as regent from Gien above Orléans. Her younger brother, Charles VIII, when he succeeded, chose to live at his mother's château at Amboise, between Orléans and Tours. Charles' cousin and successor, Louis XII, chose Blois.

It is not surprising that by the end of the fifteenth century all but ten of the great ecclesiastics had ceased to keep up their establishments in Paris. Over three quarters of the bishops and abbots had sold their Paris town houses, and that of the Archbishop of Rouen fell into ruin.[101] Although the university, once by far the largest in Europe, did not leave Paris, it shrank very greatly as a result of the departure of kings and princes. Rival administrations set up their own universities for their own states which drew many students who would formerly have gone to Paris. The Duke of Bedford founded one at Caen for Plantagenet France and Charles VII one at Bourges for Valois France. The greatest of the princes of France also founded universities for their own semi-independent states, as the Duke of Brittany did at Rennes. These defections were not the only wounds that the university of Paris suffered. Quite independently of the kings living elsewhere, Paris also ceased to draw large numbers of students from the Netherlands, Germany and central Europe, which had in the past all sent them to Paris. Now they

When the French court moved from Paris in the 1420s, first to Bourges and then to the Loire valley, opportunities opened for Jacques Coeur, who ran an Italian style multi-branched company from Bourges. He made a very considerable fortune from his many activities, particularly from supplying the French court with luxuries. He used his wealth and influence to obtain the archbishopric of Bourges for his son Jean and began to build himself a pretentious Gothic mansion in the city in 1443. Like all his other assets it was seized by the king in July 1451.

had their own state-sponsored universities, from Leuven to Cracow. Yet another group had stopped spending nearly so much money in Paris. With neither noble nor academic customers, the Paris manuscript-writing work-shops collapsed. In fifteenth-century France the most important centre of manuscript production was no longer at Paris, but at Tours near the royal court.

The most important people left in Paris were those lawyers who still kept some parts of the royal administration going in Paris. It was such *gens de robe* who bought up the deserted *hôtels* of the lay aristocracy and higher clergy cheaply.

Inevitably the population of Paris dropped vertiginously. It had remained the same through the second half of the fourteenth century, despite six waves of plague, and was still much the same size at the end of the century as it had been at the beginning. Yet the disappearance of a resident king and his court eventually halved the population. Already by the end of the 1420s it had dropped by 20% and went on sinking. Half the population in Paris could no longer be supported without the king and the magnates and the revenue that they brought in. The butchers and the grocers, the tailors and the drapers, all suffered, as well as the stationers. Goldsmiths moved from the Grand Pont to Bourges or Tours to be nearer their aristocratic clients, and makers of belts and purses for less well-to-do customers replaced them. The enormous quantity of inns and hostelries that there had been in the fourteenth century, to cater for the numbers of people who were coming to Paris, to the court and the administration, were deserted, closed down and sold, and ceased to exist. The overall surplus of accommodation in Paris was such that rents dropped to a tenth of what they had been at the beginning of the fifteenth century.

With the collapse of the market, Paris ceased to be important for international trade. Jacques Coeur, the greatest French merchant of the middle of the century, who was based in Bourges, did not even possess a branch in Paris. The Italian merchant communities in Paris all dispersed.

The collapse of Paris after the departure of the kings was as remarkable as the growth of Avignon after the arrival of the popes. Both underlined the importance for trade of rulers and their resident magnates, with their demands for housing and furnishing, fuel and lighting, better food and drink, superior clothing, jewelry and other highly priced luxuries, for horses and armour and all the rest of the panoply of war. In every capital of Europe these demands were repeated on a larger or smaller scale, and in all the larger capitals it was Italian import-export houses that ultimately provided for many of these demands. It is now time to pursue our trail from the court and its conspicuous consumption to the head offices of these Italian business enterprises. Let us take the road from Paris, as paradigm of all such capitals, to Florence where so many of the multi-branched companies were based.

In Bruges the Italian communities clustered round the square which took its name from a wealthy family of innkeeper-brokers, the van der Beurse or de la Bourse. Their consular houses were still recognisable when Sanderus published his Flandria Illustrata *in 1641. The building with the arcade facing us across the square was the consular house of the Florentine 'nation'. The Venetian 'nation' was on the left hand side of the square, in the house furthest away from us, whilst the Genoese, separated from them by a narrow street, occupied the next building towards us. Although the Lucchese 'nation' was not on the square, it was just round the corner.*

3

From court to counting house

THE COSTLY LUXURY GOODS that came into Paris at the height of its prosperity while the king and his great nobles and their households were resident there mainly came by road. Water transport was for the bulky necessities. Many of these luxury commodities came from northern Italy.

The roads from Paris and Champagne to northern Italy were very varied. One of the two most important was the road which ran to Lombardy in a more or less straight line, passing through the Jura and the Alps at the Jougne Pass and the Great St Bernard. The other followed the road which split off from the first at Dijon or Chanceux and ran down the Rhône valley. The traveller then went on by sea to Genoa or Pisa. Less important variants crossed the Alps by other passes than the Great St Bernard, or reached the Mediterranean other than by the Rhône valley.

From Paris to Dijon

Matthew Paris, a monk of St Albans, added telling sketches to his voluminous writings. Around 1254 he illustrated the land route from London to Apulia, dividing his itinerary up into sections a day's journey in length, setting out from London at the bottom of the first column, where the spire of old St Paul's can be seen. Two-and-a-half days' journey brought his traveller to Dover at the top of the column, where he labels the castle 'the key to the rich island of England'. The narrow sea-crossing took his traveller to Calais and Boulogne at the foot of the second column. He then provided alternative routes: one from Calais to Rheims by way of Arras, then the financial centre of north-western Europe; the other from Boulogne to Beauvais via Montreuil, then still an important port. This alternative continued through Paris and followed the route discussed in the text.

From Paris to Dijon the early fifteenth-century *Itinéraire de Bruges* recommended the following route (map p. 144).[1] (The original distances in leagues are approximate; mine in kilometres are accurate.) The traveller was to leave Paris by the Porte St Antoine in the walls completed in 1370 under King Charles V:

Paris		
Cuertel	iii leagues	(Créteil 11 km)
Bri conte Robert	iii leagues	(Brie-Comte-Robert 9 km)
Guines putem	iii leagues	(Guignes 15 km)
Grand puys	iiii leagues	(Grand Puits 14 km)
Provin	v leagues	(Provins 27 km)
Nougant	iiii leagues	(Nogent-sur-Seine 17 km)
Maringi	v leagues	(Marigny 22 km)
Grand pavillon	iii leagues	(Le pavillon Ste Julie 13 km)
Troyes	iv leagues	(Troyes 16 km)
Bar sur Seyne	vii leagues	(Bar-sur-Seine 33 km)
Castillon	v leagues	(Châtillon-sur-Seine 35 km)
Maignillambert	v leagues	(Magny-Lambert 25 km)
Chanseus	vi leagues	(Chanceux 25 km)
Saint Songe	iii leagues	(Saint-Seine 12 km)
Dygon	v leagues	(Dijon 26 km)

Merchants coming through Rheims from Bruges and the other commercial and industrial cities of Flanders and Brabant joined this route at Troyes.

A century-and-a-half earlier, around 1254, very much the same routes

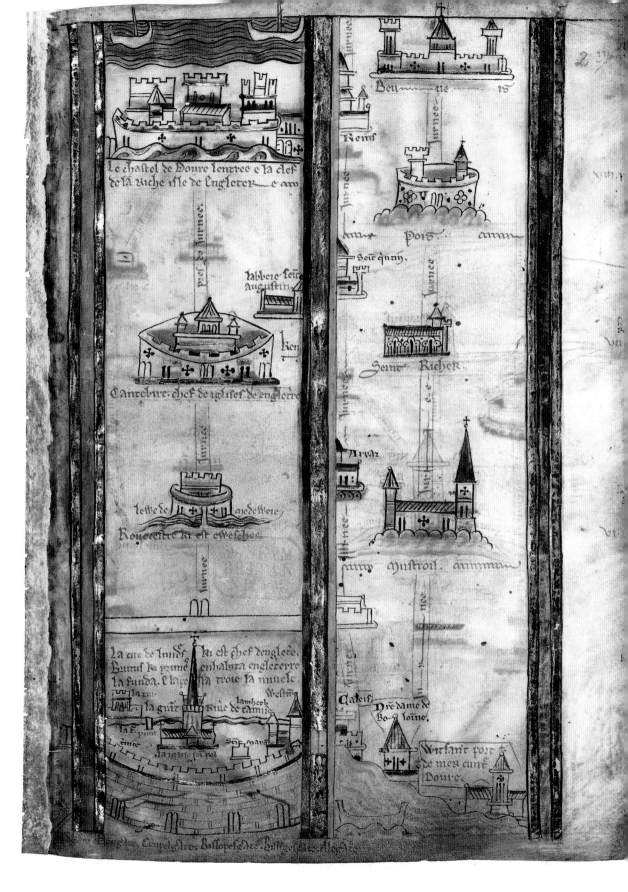

Le chastel de Doure lentree e la clef
de la riche isle de Engleter · e an

pref de iurnee

labbere feint
auguftin

Cantebire · chef de iglifes de engletere

iurnee

teste de ayedeuere

Roueceftre ki est euefches

iurnee

iurnee

La cite de lunds · ki est chef denglere
Burut ki prime enhabita engleterre
la funda · e laço la troie la nuuele

la tur   Weftm̃
       la grãt   lãbeth
la k̃e punt   riue de tamife
çmar
           la iglife fci pol   fci mars

Bounnie   15

Reins

Pors

Seit qntin

Seint Richer

Arraz

Quiftroil

Cateis   Dredame de
              Bo-loine

Wtfãt port
de mer cunt
Doure

from Paris and Flanders were recommended by Matthew Paris (ill. p. 141).[2] In that year Eudes Rigaud, archbishop of Rouen, travelled to Rome along this road in winter with his entourage.[3] Some of his stopping places were rather different from those available to more ordinary travellers. He spent his first night just outside Paris at the famous Benedictine abbey of Saint-Maur, whilst other travellers passed through Créteil, at the other end of the bridge across the Marne. His second night was spent at his brother's château of Courquetaine, whilst others would stop at Guignes, not far away. His third night he spent in Brie at the house of the Knights Templars at Rampillon, not at nearby Grandpuits or Nangis. Whereas the archbishop could put up at the houses of Templars, Benedictine abbeys and the castles of the nobility, the merchant traveller and the carrier had to be content with inns and commercial hostelries and the occasional hospice.

The first, or in Archbishop Rigaud's case, the second, day's journey from Paris took the traveller through the thick forest belt which surrounded the capital. This belt of forests was much beloved by kings and nobles for the marvellous hunting that it provided. The succession of famous castles and palaces that ring Paris – Vincennes, Fontainebleau, Versailles and Chantilly – all began as hunting lodges. Indeed, one French historian even went so far as to suggest that the Capetians fixed on Paris as a capital because of the quality of the hunting available.[4] An inexhaustible reserve of wild beasts within a day's ride of the capital may have been an enormous asset from an aristocratic point of view, but it was not necessarily so when seen from the angle of the ordinary citizen of Paris. One early fifteenth-century citizen of Paris recorded in his famous, but unfortunately anonymous, journal how on several occasions in bad winters, wolves from the forests haunted the area immediately around the walls of Paris, ready to devour the unwary who ventured outside the gates alone. Occasionally wolves even managed to get into the city itself, roaming the streets, and spreading terror.[5] The journal vividly records the pleasure felt by the citizens when one particularly savage beast was killed, and how its body was carried round the city and a collection taken up for the benefit of its killer.

The first day's journey out of Paris was a dangerous one, but the greatest danger lay not in the packs of wolves, but in the bands of brigands who

By the 1430s Pisanello was already famous for the amazing fidelity and power of observation of men and animals shown in his paintings and drawings, and so gives us an accurate picture of life and death in and around Verona, Mantua, Ferrara and Milan where he worked. In the background of his mural of St George he shows us the fate of captured robbers hanging on a gallows outside one of these north Italian cities (?Verona) and in a sketchbook one of the wolves that haunted the forests of the Alps and Appenines, just as they did the forest belt around Paris.

lurked in those forests and sallied out to prey on the travellers on the roads in and out of the city. Such robbers were a menace that rulers unsuccessfully tried to eradicate from the twelfth century onwards. Measures to protect travellers were taken, the forest margins were cut back, and at the end of the thirteenth century a public gibbet was put up by Enguerrand de Marigny, the finance minister, in a prominent position near the Porte Saint Antoine, so that the rotting corpses of robbers should deter others. The finance minister ended his notable career by being hanged on it himself. Yet there was still little likelihood that ordinary thieves would be found and brought to justice. Even in the eighteenth century, highwaymen and footpads were still relatively numerous along the roads out of Paris.

The medieval traveller did not leave the forest behind at any single precise moment, for the edge of the forest belt was always poorly demarcated. The enormous expansion in population in the twelfth and thirteenth centuries saw a tremendous diminution in forests and wastelands. New hamlets sprang up in clearings in the forest, and existing villages extended their arable fields into hitherto uncultivated land. The decline in population in the fourteenth and fifteenth centuries saw much of this relatively recently cleared land revert to waste. First rough scrub and then, surprisingly rapidly, mature forest, covered lands that had been under the plough for a couple of centuries.

Brie and Champagne

Once the main route from Paris to the south had emerged from this dangerous forest belt the merchant reached comparative safety in the rich, open, cultivated grain lands of Brie. But he had also reached a different country from Paris in another sense. For much of the Middle Ages 'France' meant little more than the Ile de France, and the rest of what we today consider to be 'France' was thought of as a group of more or less independent states. With the collapse of the Carolingian Empire in the ninth and tenth centuries, particularly under the impact of the ruthless invasions of the Normans, there came about an almost total breakdown of public administration. The protection of the rural population and any enforcement of law and order fell into the hands of a great variety of local feudal lords. From the tenth and eleventh centuries onwards, some of these lords, particularly the descendants of those who had been most active in stopping the invaders, came to exercise a great deal more power than others and by accumulating to themselves lands and castles, rights and obligations, built up quite extensive principalities. In the Ile de France itself, the Capetian counts of Paris did just this, but their effective rule extended no further to the south-east than the forest belt immediately around Paris. The other side of the forest lay the 'state' of the counts of Brie, with their 'capital' at Provins. By the twelfth and thirteenth centuries, the counts of Brie who also ruled the county of Champagne, with its 'capital' at Troyes, were amongst the richest and most powerful rulers in what is now France. They were allied by marriage to the other ruling families of the kingdom. The court of Champagne, which seems to have been most frequently at Troyes in the twelfth century and Provins in the thirteenth,

attracted to itself not only the nobility of the counties of Brie and Champagne, but also the sons of noblemen from many parts of western Europe. The attractiveness of Champagne lay in part in the character of its rulers. Count Henry was nicknamed 'the Liberal', and his ess Marie was amongst the most celebrated patronesses of early French literature. In the 1170s, she was the patroness of Chrétien de Troyes, the most successful and sensitive writer of the new style of romances, which in the second half of the twelfth century succeeded the old epic *chansons de geste*. The tortured, suffering figures of Lancelot and Tristan, adulterous lovers as well as brave knights, came to replace the simpler heroics of the faithful Roland and Oliver. At the same time, Andreas, a chaplain, possibly Marie's, in his mock-learned *Art of Courtly Love* started a new genre in literature. The satirically humorous handbook for courtly lovers, enshrined the complex 'laws' of love which evolved in the 'courts' of love held by such great ladies as Marie of Champagne herself, or her mother Eleanor of Aquitaine at Poitiers. In these courts, the ladies and the young unattached noblemen parodied the new law courts which were so arduously being created by their husbands and fathers with the aid of their legal advisors.

The *ville haute* of Provins in the twelfth and thirteenth centuries contained not only the older fortified keep of the earlier warrior counts but the extensive new palace, which was more suited both to the administration of a state and the leisured life of a court. Around it, the noblemen of Brie and Champagne competed with one another in displaying their own wealth by building great stone houses with wide romanesque portals. The more solid and impressive these were the better; as with the rich heavy garments of the thick and incredibly expensive Flemish cloth that they so much liked to wear.

The provisioning of such a new capital with goods and services brought together many more people. As well as the free-spending count and countess, their nobility and the even more freely spending youths (who, in the fashion of courtly youths, were wealthy one day and poverty-stricken the next, until the next instalment of money arrived from their fathers) there was also a host of servants and hangers-on. The whole social group was in turn maintained by craftsmen and retailers, tailors and mercers, goldsmiths and grocers. All of them needed to be fed, ensuring that a strong regional market for primary necessities was built up. The fairs at Provins, however, came to be of much more importance than merely for the sale of local agricultural produce, or even of the not inconsiderable local production of woollen and linen cloth. The geographical position of Champagne gave to its fairs, for a century-and-a-half, an important international position quite different from those of the vast number of other local and regional fairs that had been springing up all over Europe at the same time. The specialized cloth-dealers of the so-called 'Hanse' of Flemish towns were prepared to make the week-long journey to bring their valuable and prestigious cloth here to sell alongside the local cloth. The Genoese, and later, other Italians, were prepared to spend the best part of a month bringing Italian goods and those they imported from Levant to Champagne. In return, they carried off unfinished cloth for finishing in Italy

Routes from Paris to Dijon recommended by the Itinéraire de Bruges, *both going through Provins and, alternatively, avoiding it. Many goods were also carried down to Paris on the Seine. The map also indicates the various principalities, and the forest belts that the route passed through.*

and re-sale. They were so important for Italian merchants that those who jotted down details of these fairs in their notebooks called them simply *the* fairs, *I Fieri*, without any qualification. Not only the suppliers of the local courts at Provins and Troyes, but also the suppliers of the even more rapidly growing court in Paris, found it convenient to purchase at the Champagne fairs the luxuries of Flanders, of Italy and the East, on which their princely and noble clientele increasingly wished to spend the revenues from their growing rent rolls.

A map of the clientele of the Champagne fairs shows a considerable number of places in Germany, as well as Italy, northern France, and Flanders, from which merchants came to the fairs. They too were primarily customers, rather than suppliers of goods. The Germans paid for the goods they took away by bringing large quantities of ingots of newly-mined silver. In the second half of the twelfth century this silver was particularly that from the recently discovered, and very rich, silver mines at Freiberg in the Margraviate of Meissen.

In Provins the fairs were first held on the fortified rock spur, outside the old castle of the counts, and later in the great open space that lay in front of the church of St Ayoul below the spur. Gradually a whole lower town, the *ville basse*, grew up between St Ayoul and the foot of the hill on which stood the *ville haute*. The fairs, once established, themselves gave employment and prosperity to the growing town. Enterprising men set up as innkeepers to

In the nineteenth century, the small local market of Provins only took up a tiny part of the huge site of the thirteenth-century international trade fairs in front of the church of St Ayoul. There were two such fairs every year, each lasting two months. The wealth that the fairs had brought to the town is reflected in the scale and grandeur of the church itself.

provide accommodation for the visiting merchants, their beasts and their goods. Some of the inns still survive. Those who could not find accommodation within the town had to camp outside the ramparts.[6]

Symbols of the importance of the fairs are provided by the money of Provins and the weights of Troyes. When a mint was established at Provins in the tenth century it struck coins for local use. However, with the expansion of the fairs from regional to international importance, the coinage of Provins became not only the dominant currency of eastern France, but also travelled in great quantities to Italy. By the 1170s, it had also become the dominant currency of central Italy (ill. p. 149). In the same way, the weight standard of Troyes, which was originally purely local, was adopted as an international standard, 'troy weight', for weighing commodities in London as well as Paris. It is significant that the money, partially representing the imbalance of payments for goods, travelled southwards, whilst the weight standard moved northwards with the goods.[7]

The first half of the thirteenth century saw a continuous growth in the importance of the fairs, which, as the amount of business expanded, lasted longer and longer. Eventually each of the six most important fairs came to be held for approximately six weeks. As a consequence, the separate fairs developed into a continuous cycle throughout the year, so that there was almost always an international commodity fair being carried on in one or other of the four towns, Provins, Troyes, Lagny and Bar-sur-Aube. The cycle began at harvest time on 14 September with the fair of St Ayoul at Provins. This was followed on 2 November by the fair of St Remy, the so-called 'cold' fair, at Troyes. The Lagny fair began on 2 January, and the Bar-Sur-Aube fair on the Tuesday before mid-Lent. The two most important fairs concluded the cycle in the summer, when the Alpine passes could be easily crossed. These were the May fair at Provins, which started on the Tuesday before Ascension Day and the 'hot' fair, or St John's fair, at Troyes, from the first fortnight in July onwards.[8]

The fairs flourished under the patronage and protection of successive counts, who shared in the prosperity they generated. The return the counts received from levying tolls, even at a low rate, increased greatly with the amount of business done. The counts negotiated with other princes, like the dukes of Burgundy, or the counts of Flanders, to ensure protection for merchants and their goods coming to, and returning from, the fairs. A whole organization of overseers and courts for the fairs gradually evolved, so that cheap and rapid justice was available to settle commercial disputes, and enforce the payment of debts contracted at them. It eventually became expected that payment of debts contracted at the fairs would be enforced not only at the fairs themselves, but also in the principal commercial cities of the Low Countries and Italy. This sort of confidence in the certainty of being able to collect the money involved, was the necessary pre-condition for the earliest and most tentative beginnings of merchant banking. It became possible for Italian merchants to extend credit to their customers from one fair to the next. It also became possible for Italian merchants with funds to spare, after they had sold their goods, to make loans to others from one fair to the next, and in turn to be repaid not at a future fair, but in Italy. Merchants in Italy could also arrange for money to be sent to Champagne. Even private individuals used these nascent banking facilities for moving money about.[9]

An early example is Giraldus Cambrensis, Archdeacon of Brecon, who, on his outward journey to Rome, in the autumn of 1203, bought a sort of traveller's cheque from some Bologna merchants at the Troyes fair, which he was able to cash in Faenza when he reached Italy. On his return journey he himself was able to repay at Troyes money which he had borrowed in Bologna.[10]

For much of the thirteenth century, the counts continued the traditions of their ancestors. Thibault IV, the grandson of Henry I and Marie, was himself a noted writer of love songs. After he inherited the kingdom of Navarre in 1234, he still generally resided in Provins.[11] Provins enjoyed its period of the greatest prosperity under Thibault IV and his sons, when the revenues of both Champagne and Navarre were spent there. However in 1274 his grand-daughter, heiress of both Champagne and Navarre, then carried them to the crown of France by her marriage to Philip, the heir to the throne of France. After 1284, when he became king as Philip IV, Champagne never again had a resident count with a freely spending court. Whereas earlier counts had expended their lavish benefactions in their county, building churches and hospitals in Provins and in Troyes, their successors' charity was given in Paris. It was in Paris, not in Provins, that they founded the prestigious College de Navarre. Paris had completely absorbed the attributes of a capital which Provins, and Troyes, had possessed in the twelfth and thirteenth centuries.

The upper town at Provins died, and has been preserved as a fossil. After 1284 it was no longer worth spending money on the palace of the counts or the grand houses of their nobility. Unlike most buildings of this period elsewhere, which have been rebuilt by prosperous later generations and adapted to their tastes, many have survived at Provins. Poverty is a great preserver.

The disappearance of a resident court and its considerable purchasing power was only one of the changes which brought about the gradual decline of the Champagne fairs over the next four decades. Philip IV, as well as causing the court at Provins to come to an end, also severely disrupted trade northwards from Champagne by his wars with Flanders from 1297 onwards, and, to help pay for his wars, increased the rate of taxation on the goods sold at the fairs. The fairs could surely have recovered from war and heavy taxes if they had been otherwise flourishing.

More important than the actions of Philip IV was the opening of a commercial sea route from the Mediterranean to Bruges in the last quarter of the thirteenth century, made possible by navigational improvements and the Castilian conquest of Seville and Cadiz. The first Genoese galleys had made the journey in the 1270s, and by the early fourteenth century frequent fleets were setting out for the north from Venice and Barcelona as well as Genoa.

Italians were able to purchase unfinished cloth in Bruges, and bring it back by sea. As a consequence cloth sales at the Champagne fairs fell off radically.

The most important cause of the decline, however, seems to have been in part a consequence of success. As the scale of business increased between the Italian cities and the Champagne fairs, it reached the point at which a division of labour became feasible, as it had already done on the sea routes from Italy to the Levant. The more considerable merchants began to remain behind in Italy, in Siena, or Lucca or Florence, whilst they entrusted sales and purchases at the fairs to agents or partners who followed the cycle of fairs from place to place within Champagne. They kept in touch with one another by frequent correspondence whilst their goods were transported by specialized carriers. This division of labour, by ensuring a permanent presence at the fairs for the larger Italian enterprises, greatly increased their opportunities for business. Under these conditions it was perfectly possible for bargains to be struck without the goods in question actually being present. An Italian could agree in Champagne to purchase a certain number of rolls of Flemish cloth of a specified quality, and they could be transported directly from Flanders to Italy, without necessarily passing through the town where the sale took place. Similarly, spices could be sold from Italy to Paris at a fair, whilst they were still in Italy. The amount of business transacted at the fairs thus continued to increase, whilst the quantity of goods brought to them began to diminish. The next development, however, was altogether ruinous to the fairs. The larger Italian business houses began to supplement, and eventually replace, their representatives at the fairs, with representatives living in Paris, London and Bruges, the cities with which they did most business. This mass desertion sounded their death-knell (above pp. 134–6).[12]

Just as the predominance of the money of Champagne symbolized the importance of the fairs at their apogee, so the relative unimportance of its money later on symbolized their decline. When Champagne and Brie became royal, the Provins mint ceased striking the distinctive money *provinois* and instead struck royal money *tournois*. The *denier tournois*, although quite different in appearance, was in fact of the same weight and fineness as the *denier provinois* so that the royal succession to the counties made no difference in this respect. Philip IV moved the mint from Provins to Troyes, which did not lose its prosperity so fast after the end of the direct line of counts. The last moneyer from Provins lived on until 1336, and was buried in the church of St Firmin. When the Champagne mint was at Troyes it was no longer of much importance. Accounts survive from eight royal mints in operation in France in the four years between 1309 and 1312. The quantity of coin struck at Troyes was, by then, the smallest but one of any of them.

However, even after the fairs had declined in importance for the sale of actual goods, they still retained a lingering value as money markets, as times and places at which loans could be raised, payments for goods sold elsewhere could be made, and buyers and sellers of bills of exchange could be sure to find one another. The fair-ground at Provins for long retained the name of 'Place des Changes', and the road leading from it out of the town towards

Nogent, Troyes and eventually Italy, still bears the name 'Rue des Changes' and passes out of the walls into the woods through the 'Porte des Changes'.

Eventually these exchange functions disappeared and Provins became merely a stage on the road from Paris to Italy. By the time the *Itinéraire de Bruges* was compiled, around 1400, or perhaps a little earlier, it could even be bypassed. The traveller who wished to do so was advised that he could leave the old route near Nangiz (Nangis), cross the Seine at Bray, and rejoin the old route at Marigny. The compiler reckoned that this new route was more direct. Even so, it did not last, and is harder to follow on the ground today than the old one which was so important from the twelfth to the fourteenth century.

So the main road has now reverted to the same course that it followed when the fairs were in their heyday. The distance onwards from Provins to Troyes, some 73 kilometres (43 miles), was about three times the distance that normally separated market towns in a heavily-settled countryside. The two intervening market towns on the road were Nogent, where the route crosses the Seine, and Marigny.

From Provins to Troyes was thus a journey that it was possible to make in a single day, although it was obviously more comfortable to take a day-and-a-half over it, as Archbishop Eudes of Rouen and his men did, in 1254. They broke their journey at the Paraclete, not far from Nogent. In 1254 the Paraclete was a flourishing Benedictine nunnery, where the archbishop's sister was one of the nuns. When the theologian and philosopher Peter Abelard was driven from the schools of Paris in 1121, he first found refuge with the monks of St Ayoul by the fairs of Provins, and then set up a cell for himself at the Paraclete, which rapidly grew to a monastery, before being handed over to Heloise as a house of nuns. Abelard had set up his oratory there to retreat from the world, but that retreat was not total. It was well-chosen to keep him in touch with events. The main road from Paris to Rome, and so the main ecclesiastical news, as well as many leading churchmen themselves, passed his door. It lay almost exactly half the distance from Clairvaux to Paris, where his principal scholastic opponent, St Bernard, would have had the doubtful satisfaction of passing him most frequently.

Troyes, the next town of great importance, has not been preserved like Provins, because it has gone on living, whereas Provins is in many ways as it was when the counts left it in the thirteenth century. Troyes, too, went into a decline with the collapse of the fairs in the fourteenth century, although not so marked as Provins. Unlike Provins, Troyes always commanded considerable river traffic on the Seine. In addition, in the twelfth century it became a much better centre for communication by road.[13] It stood where the main routes from Flanders, including the one through Rheims, joined the roads from Paris towards Italy. Other important roads were focused here. It was easy to travel westwards to the Loire valley at Orléans, or south-westwards, along the surprisingly commonly-used route over the Massif Central to the Mediterranean ports through Nevers, Clermont and Le Puy. Similarly well-used roads led eastwards into Lorraine and Strasbourg and through the

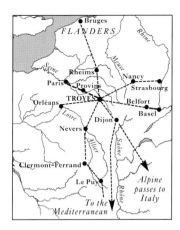

In the thirteenth century the fairs of Troyes were centrally placed for traders coming from the Low Countries, Germany and Italy as well as many parts of France.

In the twelfth century and the first half of the thirteenth, the silver *deniers* of Champagne, minted at Provins and hence known as *provinois*, were not only the standard coins of the Champagne fairs, but also the principal currency of eastern France and circulated as far away as Rome. Magnified four times.

Belfort gap to Basel and the upper Rhineland. Such a key centre of communication maintained a certain vitality even in the great depression of the late fourteenth and early fifteenth centuries. When European commerce revived in the late fifteenth century, Troyes revived with it, and this revival blotted out the remains of an earlier Troyes by 'up-to-date' rebuilding. 'Old' Troyes today is what is left over from the revival of business from the late fifteenth century onwards. Even much of the evidence of this middle period of prosperity was destroyed by nineteenth- and twentieth-century prosperity. By the beginning of the sixteenth century, there were already *bonnetiers* in Troyes. In the course of that century, it became the key city in France for the manufacture of ribbons and haberdashery. Its marvellous situation at the heart of a network of roads made it an ideal centre from which pedlars and hawkers could travel outwards with their packs full of the haberdashery of Troyes. It is not surprising that in the seventeenth century Troyes also became the key town for the printing and distribution of cheap popular literature, which the hawkers and pedlars also carried to a newly literate rural public. Nor is it surprising that from an early stage in the industrial revolution, Troyes should have been notable for its cotton mills and stocking frames. This repeated later prosperity has totally destroyed all secular evidence of the earlier, medieval, prosperity. Nothing remains. Even the castle of the counts has disappeared. There is no trace of the fairs themselves, held in the market place and all the surrounding streets. All that is left are the names of the *quais* along the Seine, and perhaps a single warehouse.

The other two fair towns, Lagny and Bar-sur-Aube, had only one fair a year, not two, like Provins and Troyes. Neither of their fairs, at Lagny in January, and at Bar-sur-Aube in Lent, could compare with the great May fair of Provins and the 'hot' fair of Troyes in July. Medieval Lagny, like medieval Troyes, has enjoyed, and suffered from, later prosperity, and therefore, as at Troyes, nothing remains.[14]

At Bar-sur-Aube, once the capital of the county of Bar, before it was absorbed by marriage into the county of Champagne, there has been no great later prosperity. The town is still today the quiet market town that it has been since the fair died. As at Provins, the fair began around the castle of the courts and spread through the growing town. The Benedictine Priory of St Pierre still preserves its 'Halloy' around the west and south sides of the priory church. This is a covered gallery, mostly of wood, but partially of stone, in which merchants gathered at fair-time. It once gave directly on to a large market place. However, over the centuries most of the triangular marketplace, which was once as large as the Place des Changes in front of St Ayoul at Provins, has been filled in by buildings. Today only a relatively small marketplace survives, separated from St Pierre by a row of later buildings, including the modern covered market.

The great international commerce based on 'the fairs' was supported by an intense local traffic in the products of Brie and Champagne themselves. From time to time some of these goods entered into longer-distance trade as well. The cheese of Brie was already well known in the Middle Ages and trav-

elled at least as far as Flanders. Around 1369 a Bruges schoolmaster wrote a successful conversation manual for teaching French, which he called the *Livre des Mestiers*, and from which his Flemish speaking pupils learnt to say the names of familiar products in French. Of the three sorts of cheese he named, one was '*Froumage de Brie*'. Today we connect Champagne with its distinctive wine, but the *vin mousseux* of Rheims and Epernay was not invented until the late seventeenth century. Champagne instead was known for its grain. This was grown in the great open fields which were so typical of the region that the description 'champagne' or 'champion' country was applied to other parts of Europe characterized by similar, vast, grain-growing common fields. Champagne provided much of the grain which fed the people of Paris. The roads of Champagne were therefore crowded in the autumn with grain carts lumbering slowly towards Troyes, loaded up with great barrels of grain for shipping down the Seine to Paris.

Up to the middle of the thirteenth century, Champagne was also known for the high quality of its woollen cloth, and this was certainly a commodity which was sold at the fairs. Early notarial registers at Genoa and Marseilles indicate how much of it was already exported to the Mediterranean countries in the second half of the twelfth century. However, in the middle of the thirteenth century, the woollen cloth of Champagne, like that of England, was eclipsed by the even higher quality of the luxury cloths of Flanders which drove them off the international market. Unlike woollen cloth-making in England, which experienced a dramatic revival a hundred years later in the middle of the fourteenth century, the woollen manufacture of Champagne never recovered.

The arcaded gallery or Halloy at Bar-sur-Aube is one of the few physical remains to survive of any of the Champagne fairs. It gave all-weather covering for merchants to meet and strike bargains during the Lent Fair held every spring in March and April. It was rebuilt in its present form in the early fourteenth century just as the fairs were declining. In some ways it was the primitive and remote ancestor of the arcaded galleries of the Antwerp Bourse illustrated on p. 51.

The manufacture of linen cloth in Champagne, mostly in the north around Rheims, was much more resilient. In the early fourteenth century, a Latin–Cuman–Persian phrase book, the *Codex Cumanicus*, written for Genoese and other Italian merchants going to Asia, distinguished between different sorts of European linens to offer to Persian customers. The list began with 'linen of Champagne' and proceeded to particularize 'linen of Rheims', before other western linens. The highest qualities of linen were fabrics worth carrying over very long distances indeed. Whereas heavy luxury woollen cloths might suit the nobility of Europe, lighter linen cloth was much preferred in the markets of Asia. The successful Florentine merchant, Pegolotti, in the second quarter of the fourteenth century, noted down that when travelling overland to China, it was advisable to take linen for the first part of the journey and to sell it at Urgenj in central Asia, although he suggested that it might even be worth while to carry a few bales of the very finest linens all the way to China.[15]

Burgundy

South and east of Troyes great tracts of forest closed in the southern and eastern frontiers of Champagne, just as they had between 'France' and Brie. In these directions, Champagne was perceived as a physical entity, 'cut off' from the outside world. Modern travellers by rail or motorway lose this sense of *pays*. From Troyes, the main road followed the Seine up through the forest to Bar-sur-Seine, and from Châtillon-sur-Seine to the hills, which so strikingly appear to divide Champagne and Burgundy. However, this divide was more apparent than real, for by the beginning of the thirteenth century, Burgundy already stretched across it into the upper Seine valley. Châtillon-sur-Seine was an outpost of Burgundy, as one thirteenth-century traveller found to his cost. In 1203, Giraldus Cambrensis described how, coming home from Rome 'by long hard stages we traversed Burgundy and neared the French frontier'. Burgundy was quite clearly not 'France' to the archdeacon, although oddly Champagne was. His narrative bears witness to the occasionally fortuitous efficiency of a medieval frontier service. Gerald had been maliciously informed against by another traveller, and his description had been circulated. It had reached the garrison of the Duke of Burgundy's border castle at Châtillon, which controlled the bridge over the loop in the Seine over which all travellers on this route had to pass. Gerald relates how,

> as we came within sight of Châtillon-sur-Seine, the lieutenant of the castle there came out with his suite to meet the seneschal of the duke of Burgundy. By chance he encountered us. The archdeacon, bringing up the rear as was his custom, was noticed by the brother of the lieutenant's wife. The youth scrutinized his face under the rain-hood and bade him wait... the lieutenant hastened back...and order was given that he...be arrested and taken to Châtillon...the youthful brother of the lieutenant added that he had recognised the archdeacon by the description, partly by his height and partly by his large and bushy eyebrows – especially the eyebrows.[16]

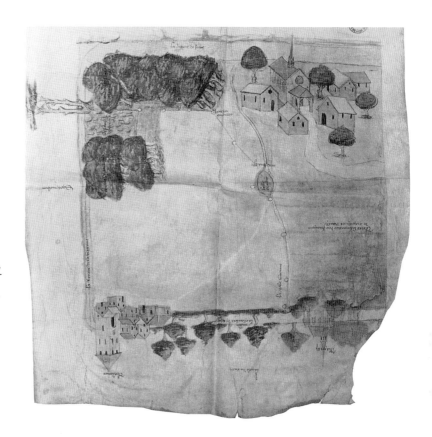

Despite nominal peace between Philip of Burgundy and his poorer cousin Charles VII of France after the Treaty of Arras in 1435, there was frequent friction between their officials along their borders. The clarification of one such boundary problem provoked the creation of this map in 1460 showing how the frontier ran between one village in 'France' and another in 'Burgundy'. Nothing makes clearer that what is now modern France was made up of different countries in the later Middle Ages.

We tend to know much more about tolls and customs dues than about frontier guards, for the simple reason that the collection of tolls had a high chance of leaving a permanent record, whilst safe conducts, or passports, were allowed to perish when the relevant journey had been completed. However, an elaborate system of safe-conducts did exist. For example, the counts of Champagne saw to it that merchants coming to their fairs had safe-conduct for travel through Burgundy.

So Burgundy stretched over the natural divide into Champagne in a way which was not surprising on grounds of military defence. In the same way, the Milanese state from the mid-fourteenth century did not end at the Cisa pass on the ridge of the Apennines, but stretched a little way down the western, or Tuscan, side to Pontremoli. Similarly, the Florentine state, lying on the other side of the hills, did not stop at the top of the Futa pass, but stretched down the northern slopes of the Apennines, where it founded the fortified new town of Firenzuola in the 1330s. In our own day, the Israeli state cannot comfortably be content with the ridge of the Golan heights as its frontier, but, for reasons of security, wishes to occupy a little of the 'Syrian' slopes too. All states must wish to secure their land frontiers in this sort of way, but only the stronger state is actually able to do so.

From Burgundian Châtillon 'in Champagne' the road ran south-eastwards alongside the now tiny and unnavigable Seine, until around Magny Lambert, the 'Rue Haute' climbed out of the steep valley of the Seine to run across the high limestone plateau between the heads of side valleys which cut

The Chambellans were by origin a Dijon family, like their near neighbours the Sauvegrains. They made their first fortune as cloth manufacturers. To this they added ducal service, investment in vineyards, and successful marriages, eventually being ennobled. As well as making money in the city, such families also spent lavishly there. In the fifteenth century the Chambellan family built an impressive house in the rue des Forges, immediately behind the ducal palace, in the late Gothic Flamboyant style. Its fine spiral staircase has a central column rising to a grape-picker carrying his basket, which supports an extravagantly sculpted palm tree vault.

sharply into it from either side. Here and there the road dipped suddenly where such valleys cut across the road. It did so, for example, at St Seine, where Archbishop Rigaud put up at the abbey that nestled in the valley bottom, or at Val Suzon, where the limestone gorge contained one of the minor hospices linked with the mother-hospice on the Great St Bernard pass. Only after another belt of hill and forest did the road eventually come out into the rich lands of the northern part of Burgundy proper, around Dijon. Whereas in Champagne the rivers flow northwards into the English Channel, in Burgundy they flow southwards into the Mediterranean.

These forested limestone hills, although not a major barrier by comparison with the Alps or even the Jura, were nevertheless a crucial watershed between north and south, and a very real divide between the two 'countries'. Burgundy looked southwards, but Champagne looked towards Paris.

Dijon, the first important town on the road inside Burgundy, was a junction for routes. This was so even before it acquired a political significance when the dukes of Burgundy moved their administration there from Beaune in the fourteenth century. Many of the buildings of Dijon reflect this 'political' significance. The dukes themselves built their own palace in the centre of the town. They also built their lavish foundation of a Charterhouse at Champmol outside it, partially as a family mausoleum. Their officials, too, built themselves fine stone houses in the same late Gothic, flamboyant, style as their masters. The *hôtels* of the Chambellans or the Sauvegrains are surviving examples. Dijon, however, was never the 'capital' of the extraordinarily wealthy 'state' of the fifteenth-century Burgundian rulers. Until the 1420s the Valois dukes ran their 'state' from their Paris *hôtel*, and then from Brussels. Their Dijon palace was only an occasional residence for these rulers. Dijon remained their administrative centre, for the duchy and county of Burgundy, and the focal point for their nobility and as such was a regional centre of importance. However, little survives to show it as a late medieval consumption centre save for a single fifteenth-century retail shop, the Maison Millière, in the shadow of the church of Notre Dame.

Even before the Valois dukes made it one of their residences, Dijon was one of the points at which a choice had to be made by the traveller bound for Italy. In high summer, when the passes of the Jura and the Alps were clear of snow, the main road led straight ahead through the Jougne pass and the Great St Bernard. The alternative was to turn south down the Rhône valley. Later choices had to be made further along either route. After passing through the Jura the traveller to Italy could choose to cross the Alps either by the traditional Great St Bernard pass, or the newer Simplon pass. If he chose to go down the Rhône valley, he had later to choose whether to cross the Alps by the Mt Cenis pass or to go on to take ship at Aigues Mortes or Marseilles.

The choice to use any of the Alpine passes could, however, only be made for a relatively limited time in the year. In the twenty-first century the Great St Bernard is not open to modern wheeled traffic until June,[17] and sometimes quite late in June. It closes up again in October. With pack animals a passage could be forced, often with great difficulty, over a rather longer period each year. This was particularly true in those longish spells of time, such as in the medieval warm period around the twelfth century, when the climate was generally milder than it is now. Nevertheless the direct route across the mountains was most usable, and most used, in the height of summer. It was not surprising that the 'hot' fair in July and August at Troyes was able to attract so many more merchants from Italy than the other fairs.

From Dijon this direct route ran across the flat open fields of ducal Burgundy to St-Jean-de-Losne, where the broad waters of the Saône made as real and impressive a barrier between Burgundy and Franche Comté as the hills and forests between Champagne and Burgundy. It was a remarkable feat to construct a bridge here, and, when it was built, it was as easy a passage to control as a mountain pass. If merchants wished to follow this main trade route, their goods were obliged to cross this bridge. Only its modern successor survives. Flood, war, and improvements have made medieval bridges one of the rarest survivals (below pp. 176–80). The dukes of Burgundy drew a rich revenue from this monopoly situation. The tolls at St-Jean-de-Losne could not easily be avoided by taking any alternative road nearby, for there was none. The surviving receipts from the tolls emphasize the importance of Italian merchants, bringing warhorses, fustians, furs and mercery from Lombardy and returning with wool and cloth. Most of the merchants were from Milan, but others came from a variety of places, including several from Venice, not generally a city known for merchants who sent goods overland.[18]

The Great St Bernard and Simplon passes

The Saône was, of course, as it still is, a highway as well as a barrier. Modern barges still make great use of the river. The medieval quayside at St-Jean-de-Losne was one of the three principal points at which goods were transferred from road to river in order to travel south. Further upstream, goods which had travelled due east from Troyes on the road to Belfort and Basel could be unloaded on to the Saône at Port-sur-Saône. Downstream, they could be unloaded at Chalon-sur-Saône.

From St-Jean-de-Losne the direct road to Italy continued across the flat open fields of the French Comté, so like those on the Burgundian bank of the Saône. The *Itinéraire de Bruges* picked out Giveri (Gevry) at the Doubs crossing, as the next stage on the journey. It marked the limit of the flat and open plain. The terrain changed abruptly there, and the *Itinéraire* next mentioned La Loye, at the edge of the Forest of Chaux on a slight ridge above the Loue valley. Neither Gevry nor La Loye is more than a village today. Indeed, this part of the route is hard to follow on the ground. This is one of the very few parts of a medieval trade route in western Europe where the same line is not followed today by a motorway, or even a trunk road. The exercise of tracing out the routes followed by medieval carts or pack animals is normally carried out in a fog of exhaust fumes.

Just before Salins-les-Bains the route again coincides with a modern major road. Salins itself was, and is, a long narrow town, lying in the bottom of a winding limestone gorge, leading up into the vastly different landscape of the Jura above. Its name betrays its past importance. A brine well was exploited there as early as the sixth century, but its great expansion only dates from the thirteenth.[19] By the beginning of the following century, according to the local tradition, which was, no doubt, greatly exaggerated, no less than six hundred carts a day passed through the town, either bringing wood to burn to evaporate the salt, or else transporting away the salt itself. The salt was frequently carried in the form of crystals, packed loosely into great barrels of pine wood, each of which contained no less than a quarter of a ton. Alternatively it was dispatched in the form of round blocks, or loaves, which were made of different weights according to the market for which they were intended. They varied from just over one kilo to nearly six. As well as *gros sel d'ordinaire* for sale in Dôle, the medieval 'capital' of Franche-Comté only 45 kilometres away, there was also 'sel Fribourg' and 'sel Lombard' for more distant destinations.

The town took its name and its importance from the great fortified enclosure of the 'salines' or saltworks. The visitor today can still be taken down into the twelfth- and thirteenth-century galleries into which the brine was pumped up. The brine was then boiled down to crystals. Unfortunately, the medieval boiling houses have all disappeared, and only the eighteenth-century ones can still be seen.

Salins was also one of the towns which stood on the boundary between mountainous regions where transport primarily depended on the horse or mule, and the easier lands to the north and west in which wagons could be used. In such towns the inns and innkeepers were of particular importance

and prospered accordingly (below pp. 203–8). Goods which had come by wagon were unloaded and unpacked here, and often temporarily stored by the innkeepers, until they could be re-packed in smaller quantities as suitable burdens for trains of animals to carry onwards into the mountains.

The mountains of Jura already rise on either side of Salins, and the road at once climbs steeply from the gorge in which it lies. It goes on rising almost continuously for 60 kilometres (nearly 40 miles) through Pontarlier, to the top of the mountains at the Jougne pass, which is at over 1,000 metres, or some 3,300 feet, above sea level.

Inns could be found at Pontarlier and Les Clées, some 15 and 20 kilometres from either end of the Pass. Near the summit was another of the series of hospices linked with that on the Great St Bernard. It was burnt down in the eighteenth century, but its memory is preserved in the name of the surviving hamlet of 'Les Hôpitaux Vieux'.

When the ridge of the Jura had been crossed, the route left Franche-Comté behind, and entered yet another new 'country', the Vaud. In the later Middle Ages, this was among the territories ruled by the counts (from 1416, dukes) of Savoy. Some travellers followed the track high up on the north side of the Orbe valley when they were descending from the Jougne pass. Most took the track in the valley bottom. The rulers of Savoy established two customs posts with identical tolls, at Lignerolles and Les Clées, respectively, because of the split in the route, so that no traveller should escape payment at one or the other.[20]

The details of the tolls collected for the rulers of Savoy at the customs posts at the end of the Jougne pass survive in a mid-fifteenth-century list for Les Clées.[21] This incorporates a much earlier toll list. Despite the decline in overland trade early in the fourteenth century, it still gives first place amongst the goods to be expected on the road to rolls of high value, export quality, French and Flemish cloth, and to bales of wool, particularly those from England. In the opposite direction, the key goods coming from Lombardy were described as *averi ponderis*, or goods sold by weight. These were particularly 'spices'. There were also graded tolls on the horses from Lombardy

First used by the Romans, the brine wells of Salins became one of the most important inland sources of salt in late medieval Europe. The boiling houses, where the newly pumped up brine was evaporated in immense cauldrons over wood fires, lead down to extensive underground galleries. Workings and equipment survive from many periods since the twelfth century.

157

which were taken to France for sale, rising steeply from mere *bestia equina* to *magna equina* and the even more heavily taxed warhorses. The various sorts of birds of prey, equally for sale eventually to noble customers, were various sorts of falcon (*asturcone* and *gilfaudo*), tercelets, and sparrowhawks. Also for noble use, in a more round-about way, were the sacks of Lombard woad commonly used to dye luxury cloth the blue so often illustrated in Flemish paintings of the Virgin's cloak. Amongst other goods listed were herrings, on which toll was paid by the thousand, supplied from the Baltic for Friday and Lenten fare at rich men's tables throughout Europe. The *chinallata* of *frumenti* or *siliginis* (different sorts of wheat) which were being sent up to the mountains from the grain lands of Burgundy were more ordinary, and only attracted a particularly low rate of toll. There is no mention of a special rate of toll for loaves of salt, so they must have been included in the general heading for other merchandise taxed by the *fardello*. Each *fardello*, which was presumably a mule-load, had to pay nine old *deniers* of Lausanne as toll, much more than a *chinallata* of *frumenti*, but much less than any of the other goods listed for the Jougne pass.

Those who sought to evade the customs posts at Lignerolles and Les Clées, by taking the higher and more difficult Col des Etroits through the Jura a few miles to the north-east of the Jougne pass, found themselves confronted at Vuiteboeuf by a third customs post at which the rulers of Savoy exacted the same tolls. For those who wished to travel between France and Italy along this route, there was no avoiding the Savoyard toll collectors at one place or another. Indeed, there was no avoiding the Savoyard toll collectors anywhere in the western Alps. Those travellers who continued southwards from Dijon through Burgundy down to Lyons and then turned westwards for the Mont Cenis, which shared the bulk of the Alpine traffic with the Great St Bernard, were equally confronted by the collectors at the bridge over the Isère at Montmélian.

A few miles below the Savoyard customs posts, the various tracks down from the Jougne pass joined together to run down through 'Borsenie' to Lausanne and Vevey on Lake Geneva. At Vevey a route from 'Germany' joined that from 'France'. As Nicholas Seemundarson, a mid-twelfth-century Icelander, who had travelled his *romavegr* through Schleswig, Hannover, Mainz and Basel, put it: '*ibi junguntur viae quibus Alpes transituri Romam petunt variarum gentium peregrinantes, scilicet: Franci, Flaemingi, Galli, Angli, Saxones et Scandinavi.*' ('Here the roads join together for pilgrims to Rome who seek to cross the Alps from various nations, namely French, Flemings, Welsh, English, Saxons and Scandinavians.')[22] From Basel he had reached Vevey through Solothurn and Avenches. The road runs along the shore of Lake Geneva to Villeneuve, which, its name suggests, was a deliberately founded new town.

The founding of new towns in large numbers throughout western Europe was a marked feature of late medieval economic expansion, particularly in the thirteenth century. Many of these new towns became just what was expected of them, fresh local market centres which would serve their neigh-

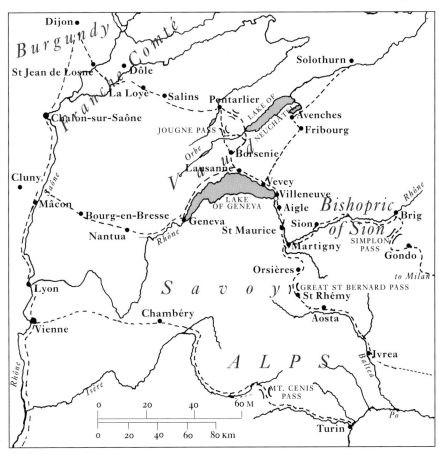

Routes from Burgundy and the Rhône valley to Lombardy, showing where goods crossed the Jura and the Alps. At the end of the thirteenth century the main route between Burgundy and Lombardy still crossed over the Jougne and Great St Bernard passes, although much trade also used the Mont Cenis Pass. However, the newly opened Simplon Pass route was growing in importance and led more directly to Milan. The surviving records of the tolls collected by the rulers of Savoy at the entrances to the passes in the later Middle Ages give a great deal of information about the scale and nature of the trade which crossed the mountains. The hospices on or near the summits of the passes, primarily intended for pilgrims, also catered for carriers and other travellers.

bourhood and bring in for their landlord a higher return in rents than he could expect from a purely agricultural use of the land. Others did much better than could possibly have been anticipated, and grew into cities like Ypres, Liverpool, Bilbao, Zagreb, Stockholm or Berlin.[23] Yet others failed more or less completely, and are today no larger than hamlets. The main roads of Europe had a natural attraction for landlords who hoped to found such new towns, and a long sequence of 'Villeneuves' grew up along them. This one is no more than a small village today. From Villeneuve, where yet another toll was taken,[24] the route given by the *Itinéraire de Bruges* followed the upper Rhône valley through Aylle (Aigle) and Saint Maurius (Saint-Maurice) to Martigny and then up into the Alps along the steep-sided valley of the Durance through Sanbranster (Saint Branchier) and Sorsières (Orsière) to the Great St Bernard Pass.

Some travellers, particularly in the fourteenth century, continued up the Rhône valley from Marigny through Sion and Brig, and then crossed the Alps at the Simplon pass. The Simplon pass had the advantage over the Great St Bernard of being much lower, 2,010 metres, (6,590 feet) against 2,473 metres, (8,110 feet) and therefore of being closed by snow for much shorter periods of the year. On the other hand, the road on the Italian side was very difficult and dangerous, particularly in the Gondo gorge. The Simplon route took travellers directly to Milan, whilst the Great St Bernard route came out through Aosta into western Lombardy. Despite its height, and long periods of closure, the Great St Bernard seems to have had more travellers. The use of the Simplon seems to have opened up in the mid-thirteenth century. There was no hospice on it until 1235. In the fifteenth century much of the traffic that it had had in the fourteenth century seems to have reverted to the Great St Bernard route again.

The economic interests, as well as the piety, of the counts of Champagne had much to do with the endowment of the series of hospices which gradually came into existence along the main route from Champagne to Italy. This ensured that pilgrims from Champagne could reach Rome, and at the same time that Italian contingents could be assisted in coming to their fairs. The richest and most famous of these was the hospice on the Great St Bernard Pass (below pp. 210–12). The hospice in Troyes itself, the *Domus Dei,* was, from the mid-twelfth century, run by the same Canons Regulars who ran the hospice at the pass. Other endowments came from both emperors and popes, and from grateful travellers, so that eventually the hospice on the Great St Bernard had possessions scattered from England to Sicily, as well as in Champagne and the vicinity of the pass itself.

Many of the other hospices on this route, as well as the one in Troyes, were also connected with the foundation on the Great St Bernard, like the hospice near the summit of the Jougne pass in the Jura. By the end of the twelfth century further hospices were to be found between Troyes and the Jougne pass at Bar-sur-Seine, Val Suzon, and Salins, and between the Jougne and the Great St Bernard at Lausanne and Vevey.[25]

In the height of summer, the passage of the Great St Bernard was not difficult. A north German, Albert of Stade, who crossed the Alps in 1236 referred in his *Annales* not only to the Great St Bernard and the Brenner, but also to the Mont Cenis, the St Gotthard and the Septimer passes. He suggested that the best time for crossing the Alps was:

> about the middle of August, since then the air is mild, the roads are dry, it is not wet, streams and rivers do not overflow everywhere, the days are long enough for travelling, and the nights for resting the body, and the gathering of the new harvest means there is no dearth of provisions.[26]

However, travellers did pass through the Alps at times that would seem to us most unpropitious. The abbot of St Truiden (St Trond), in what is now Belgium, returning home, found the small village of St Rhémy, which was the last inhabited place on the Italian side of the Great St Bernard, overcrowded by throngs of travellers at the beginning of January. He goes on to tell how Alpine guides, or *marones*, approached the travellers of their own accord and 'offered, for a large price, that they should try to open a path so that the travellers might follow on foot, their horses following in turn'. He explains how they set about doing so:

> The *marones* wrapped their heads round with felt because of the intense cold, put rough mittens on their hands, pulled on their high boots, the

soles of which were armed with iron spikes on account of the slipperiness of the ice, took in their hands long staves to sound for the path buried deep under the snow, and boldly set out along the usual road. It was very early in the morning.[27]

Although these guides were fatally overwhelmed by an avalanche and the travellers had to turn back to wait for 'fine weather', they succeeded in hiring fresh guides, only a week or so later, and managed 'now crawling, now stumbling' to get over the pass, some eight miles away, and nearly 3,000 feet above St Rhémy. Guides appear to have been expendable.

In 1188, John de Bremble, a monk of Christchurch, Canterbury, equally managed to cross the Great St Bernard in February. His account of the terrors of the crossing in winter is justly famous:

> …on the one hand looking up to the heaven of the mountains, on the other shuddering at the hell of the valleys. 'Lord,' I said, 'restore me to my brethren, that I may tell them not to come to this place of torment.' Place of torment indeed where the marble pavement of the stony ground is ice alone, and you cannot set your foot safely; I put my hand into my scrip, to scratch out a syllable or two – behold, I found my ink-bottle filled with a dry mass of ice. My fingers too refused to write; my beard was stiff with frost, and my breath congealed into a long icicle. I could not write.[28]

This then was the direct route from Paris and Champagne to Italy, going onwards from Dijon by way of the Jougne pass, and culminating in the terrors of the Great St Bernard. From St Rhémy, where the counts of Savoy took yet another toll, the road eventually descended into upper Lombardy through Aosta, Ivrea and Vercelli.

The travellers who chose to travel southwards from Dijon to cross the Alps by the Mont Cenis, or to travel down the Rhône valley to the mouth and onwards by sea, had first to traverse the rich agricultural lands of the Duchy

When Konrad Witz painted Christ calling Peter to be his disciple for the Cathedral at Geneva he increased the impact and immediacy of the painting by placing the boat from which Peter was fishing not on the Sea of Galilee, but on the lake immediately outside the city. He has thus given us the opportunity to share the view seen by travellers setting out on the road along the north shore of Lake Geneva in 1444.

Rhône valley routes to Italy

of Burgundy. From Dijon nearly to Chalon, the names of the villages strung along the road read like a wine list: Gevrey-Chambertin, Vougeot, Vosne Romanée, Nuits-St George, Aloxe Corton, Pommard, Volnay, Meursault, Puligny and Chassagne Montrachet. In the heart of these famous vineyards lay Beaune. Then, as now, it was the focal point of the Burgundian wine trade. It was also, until they moved to Dijon in the fourteenth century, the preferred residence, when in Burgundy, of its dukes. Ducal residence made of Beaune a court town, and a centre for the consumption of luxury goods. The vineyards made it a centre for the sale of wine. The two are most fittingly combined today by the wine museum which is housed in the former ducal palace. A great array of old wine-presses are preserved in the adjacent four-teenth-century press-house of the duke, a building in itself as large as a tithe barn. The wine of Beaune travelled greater distances than the salt of Salins. Apart from the papal market at Avignon in the fourteenth century, merchants then primarily carried it northwards, as they do today. Vast barrels of the precious wine were carefully bound or 'pantalooned' with hoops of willow to prevent damage on the rough journey by cart along the main road through the hills and forests to Champagne, and then, with great relief, transferred to boats where they could be shipped down the Seine to Paris. In his book of *ricordanze*, the Florentine nobleman Buonaccorso Pitti, recalled how in 1395, when he was a young man travelling through Burgundy on the way from Paris to Avignon in the entourage of the Duke of Orléans, brother of Charles VI, he had sold three very grand warhorses to the Duke of Burgundy. He had bought the horses in Italy, and invested the proceeds from the sale in wine, which he sold on his return to Paris, not only more than doubling his money, but also retaining ten casks of wine, each of around 400 litres, for his own use. He concluded 'Thus I was lucky with two of the chanciest of all commodities: horses and wine.'[29]

Some of the wine of Burgundy went on from Paris to Flanders and Brabant where it competed with the wine of Bordeaux. This transit should have taken place by river and road through the royal toll station at Bapaume, but it was cheaper and safer to take it, illegally, down the Seine and around the northern French coast.

From Beaune the route to Chalon-sur-Saône runs below the slopes on which grapes ripen to make the most famous wines. At Chalon, as at St-Jean-de-Losne, or Port-sur-Saône further north, many merchants transferred their goods to boats to travel southwards. For a time at least, Chalon was more than a mere staging point on the route southwards, or even a key place for the transfer of goods from road to river. In the fourteenth century, it became the venue of one of the most important international trade fairs in Europe.[30]

After the collapse of the fairs of Champagne in the late thirteenth and early fourteenth century, much long-distance trade was carried on by seden-tary merchants at home in Italy, with resident factors in the principal cities outside Italy. However, certain sorts of business could still most conveniently be carried on at fairs. The annual sale of a local product, whether grain, or cattle, or cheese, or horses, could always be best managed at a local fair.

However, at a number of places international fairs were carried on, principally for the benefit of merchants further to the east, who had not yet developed a system involving resident factors elsewhere. For two centuries or more after the collapse of the Champagne fairs there was always one fair town of international importance halfway between Paris and Italy, which was also within reach of German traders. For much of the fourteenth century, it was Chalon. In the first half of the fifteenth century, Geneva took its place. In its turn, Geneva was supplanted by Lyon in the second half of the fifteenth century.

From Chalon, the Saône, with the road on its west bank as an alternative, flows down through Tournus to Mâcon. The *Itinéraire de Bruges* provides a third option to either the river, or the riverside road, in a rather more westerly route from Chalon to Mâcon, by way of Cluny.

The roads of the late Middle Ages carried many ecclesiastical travellers as well as merchants. Far too much of our evidence of travel comes from ecclesiastical sources. Churchmen were more prone to leave narratives of their journeys than merchants, who, in their notebooks and *ricordanze*, took travel itself for granted. An archbishop of Rouen, the abbots of St Truiden and Stade, an archdeacon of Brecon and a monk of Canterbury have all been quoted already. Many of the focal points of the Christian world of late medieval Europe lay along major routes and helped to shape them. At Rome, the papacy could be reached by roads that continued the trade-routes southwards from Tuscany, and at Avignon the papal court was astride the major route down the Rhône Valley. At Paris, the schools of the university were the theological heart of Latin Christianity. Great scholars like St Thomas Aquinas followed the road between the university and the papal *curia* innumerable times.

Here in Burgundy, part way along the road from Paris to Rome were some of the main centres of west European monasticism. Cluny provided the great impulse to monastic reform in the tenth century. Indeed, in the eleventh, it provided part of the inspiration for the general reform of the whole of the

Looking south-west down the Saône to the medieval bridge at Chalon in 1649. In the fourteenth century the fair, held for two months every year on the river bank below the city, attracted merchants from southern Germany who paid tolls to cross the bridge of St Laurent to reach it. Those coming from north and south brought their goods either on the river itself or on the roads on the west bank.

Latin church. The Cluniac order was the first to acquire a European-wide organization. Cluniac houses were founded from the kingdom of England to that of Sicily, and from Castile to Westphalia. The constitution of the order required frequent visits from the hundreds of daughter-houses to Cluny. The abbots of Cluny were themselves great travellers too. Indeed, it was public reaction to the capture by Saracens of one of its abbots, St Maiolus, while he was returning over the Great St Bernard in the summer of 972 from an interview with the reforming Emperor Otto I in Italy, that brought about the clearance of the Saracens from the western and central Alps. The Saracens had controlled the passes from their base at Fraxinetun for eighty years or more. This clearance of the Saracens from the Alps encouraged the revival of commerce at the end of the tenth century.

In the twelfth century, the abbey of Cîteaux, 23 kilometres south of Dijon, a few miles east of the main road at Nuits St Georges, and its principal daughter-house, Clairvaux, 14 kilometres south of Bar-sur-Aube, provided a similar impetus to that which Cluny had given two centuries earlier. St Bernard, abbot of Clairvaux and the principal propagandist of the Cistercian movement, was an indefatigable traveller, perpetually on the road between Clairvaux and either Paris or Rome.

Even in our own day, this area seems to have an ecclesiastical importance. The ecumenical community at Taizé, only 10 kilometres north of Cluny, had a key place in the liturgical renewal of Latin Christianity in the twentieth century and draws to itself each year many tens of thousands of visitors from all parts of Europe. They frequently travel the same roads that their precursors trod to Cluny a millennium before.

Of the great abbey of Cluny little remains, but with its vast lands and its international administration, Cluny came to be something of a 'capital' in itself. Since it was the richest abbey in Europe in the later Middle Ages, there was certainly a great concentration of spending power in the hands of the abbot and the obedientiaries. The town of Cluny flourished in the shadow of the abbey, as Provins or Beaune did, in the shadow of a secular court. Over two hundred Romanesque town houses of stone still survive from the second half of the twelfth century and the first half of the thirteenth. The distinctive form of these houses, with a solid vaulted chamber on the ground floor open to the street through a wide arch, suggests that they were built for use as shops or workshops, and the number surviving implies considerable trade and manufacture.[31] One of them is reputed to have been the local mint. It was worthwhile for some merchants, as well as many ecclesiastics, to step aside a short distance from the main road to call on such valued customers. Like secular rulers, the abbots gravitated to Paris in the course of the thirteenth century, so that much of their spending power was transferred to Paris and the town of Cluny developed much more slowly than it had earlier. In the fifteenth century successive abbots rebuilt both their Paris *hôtel*, which now houses the Musée de Cluny, and their palatial residence in Cluny itself.

The traveller who had made the detour to Cluny returned to the Saône at Mâcon. Here, the medieval bridge of St Laurent still survives. It is an impos-

The rivers and roads of Europe formed an integrated transport network for carrying goods. In this French woodcut goods are being transferred between road and river transport on the Seine at the very end of the fifteenth century, but very similar scenes were to be found at Chalon or Mâcon on the Saône, or indeed on the Po, the Danube, the Rhine or the Thames.

ing structure of twelve arches in stone brought from Bresse. Although it was restored in the nineteenth century, it is still basically the same bridge that was first built in the fourteenth century. It makes of Mâcon a cross-roads, where the north-south route, by river and by the road on its west bank, is crossed by an east-west route from the upper Loire valley to Lake Geneva and thence to southern Germany.

The journey due south from Mâcon down the valley of the Saône and the Rhône was long and tedious, although not difficult. The *Itinéraire de Bruges* lists no fewer than sixteen stage points between Mâcon and Avignon. The modern traveller too, finds this journey tedious and boring. Much of the east bank of the Rhône south of Lyon lay in the Dauphiné of Vienne. This was another independent principality until 1349, when it was purchased by Philip VI of France. It was sufficiently economically important to become the principal inheritance of the eldest sons of the kings of France. The Dauphiné stretched from the Rhône to the Alps, and, until the fifteenth century, its 'capital', Vienne, vied with Lyon as the most important city of the Rhône valley. From Vienne, as well as from Lyon, therefore, roads led eastwards upwards to Chambéry, and on, by way of the Maurienne valley, to the Mont Cenis pass and so to Turin and Asti. This was the main route to Italy for the traveller who wished to travel on southwards from Dijon through Burgundy before making the Alpine crossing.

The Mont Cenis shared the bulk of the traffic across the western Alps with the Great St Bernard and Simplon passes. None of the other passes seems to have rivalled them in importance. The Little St Bernard, which had been so important to the Romans, was largely neglected, and so was the old Mont Genèvre route.

The Mont Cenis route to Italy

One of the earliest accounts of a crossing of the Mont Cenis was written in the late eleventh century. In January, 1077, the weather was particularly bad, and it needed all the persuasiveness of the formidable Henry IV to get his imperial expedition to Italy over the pass. Lampert of Hersfeld, who probably had his account from a member of the emperor's suite, wrote afterwards:

> The winter was severe, and the mountains to be crossed were of immense extent…. Certain natives were hired who knew the region and were accustomed to the steep slopes of the Alps. They were to precede the party on the steep places and through the masses of snow, to do what they could to make the passage of those behind easier. Led by these men they climbed with great difficulty to the highest point in the mountains, but there seemed no way of going any further. Any attempt to make a descent was apparently impossible because the slope was precipitous and, owing to the ice, slippery. Then the men tried to the utmost of their ability to avoid the danger, now crawling on their hands and feet, now supporting themselves on the shoulders of those in front; now and again, as their feet slipped, falling and rolling. The guides installed the queen and her ladies, who were in the rear of the party, in ox-hides, and slid them down the slope.

John XXIII, the most widely supported of three rival popes, resigned at Constance in May 1415. He was based in Italy, and so had made several winter crossings of the Alps in the months since the Council opened there. On one occasion he attempted to cross the Arlberg Pass in a carriage, but was ignominiously toppled into the snow on the way. This was hardly surprising, since none of the Alpine passes was really made fit to take wheeled traffic until later in the fifteenth century. This woodcut is from Ulrich von Reichenthal's Concilium zu Constanz, Augsburg, 1483.

Some of the horses were lowered on various contrivances, others were dragged down with their feet tied. Many were killed in the process, many were maimed, only a few came through whole and unharmed…. At last after the greatest peril, they reached level ground.[32]

The Mont Cenis has the modern advantage of not being closed to wheeled traffic for as long as the Great St Bernard. Even so, it only opens in April, and closes in November. It is quite astonishing to see the quantity of goods that went over the pass in the fourteenth century, at a time of year when it is now considered impossible to cross. The toll records of Montmelian show that between 9 January and 16 April 1302, no fewer than 1,373½ loads of taxable goods went over the pass. One donkey-load was reckoned as the half of a horse-load. Two winters earlier, the traffic at the same unseasonable time of year was even more intense. Between 22 January and 1 May 1300, 2,226½ loads of taxable goods passed by. All this was the 'mere' routine of business. The *vectuarii*, the haulage contractors who transported the goods of merchants, reckoned that, despite the additional dangers of a winter crossing, it was worthwhile to accept goods for carriage, even at this season. Presumably, despite their keen financial sense, they could not have been enticed to carry goods over the pass in the sort of weather Henry IV had encountered in 1077.

The counts of Savoy were the principal beneficiaries of the tolls of the Mont Cenis route, as they were of the Vaudois tolls on the Jougne route through the Jura and of the St Rhémy tolls below the Great St Bernard. As the Savoyard 'state' grew in the later Middle Ages, more and more of the Alpine tolls fell into their hands.[33] On the Mont Cenis route their principal toll was exacted at the bridge over the Isère at Montmélian, which was most suitably placed for toll collection. The main streams of traffic from Vienne and Lyon, had been joined at Chambéry by a minor trickle from Mâcon through Bourg en Bresse, and the small amount of trade going over the Little St Bernard had not yet left the valley.

Unfortunately the accounts of the tolls at Montmélian do not survive until the very end of the thirteenth century, when certain of the more important types of trade were already in decline. In 1295, the Count of Savoy tried to attract back the trade in French, and most particularly Flemish, cloths by reducing the rates of toll, from 7 *sous* and 6 *deniers* of Vienne, to 3 *sous*. A further lowering in the rate of duty in 1300, from 3 *sous* of Vienne to one *sou* coincided with a tiny temporary revival in the trade. Over 4,000 horses laden with cloth passed through Montmélian between January 1302 and May 1303. Even this was relatively insignificant, at a time when as many as 100,000 rolls of cloth were being produced annually at Ypres, and rather more at Ghent. However, it was impossible to halt the decline in the cloth trade through the Alps merely by lowering the rate of duty at one toll station, even if it was a major one. These years of the early fourteenth century saw a radical decline in the quantity of Flemish and French cloth sent by road over the Alps, as the sea voyages of the Genoese and Venetian galleys and round ships to Bruges became increasingly regular and important.[34] Never again, after 1305, did

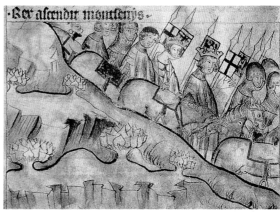

more than 500 horses laden with cloth pass through Montmélian, with the single exception of the year 1337, when there was considerable disruption in trade by sea, because of the opening of hostilities between Edward III and Philip VI.

Second in importance to woollens in the toll lists were other fabrics. In 1302–3, nearly seven hundred horses laden with *grosses toiles* – coarse hempen stuff, passed through Montmélian, as well as a much smaller quantity of finer white linen of Rheims and Champagne. The carriage of these hempen and flaxen cloths by road dropped off at more or less the same time as that of the woollens.

No fewer than 500 loads of alum passed through Montmélian in 1303 in the opposite direction. This alum came from Asia Minor and was extensively used as a cleansing agent and a dye-fixative by woollen cloth manufacturers. After 1303, it ceased to be taken to Flanders overland. It too went by sea.

After 1305 or thereabouts, all that was left to travel by road, apart from horses, were certain small quantities of spices and of wax from the Italian end, and of salt herrings and bronze wares from the French end. Mercery still travelled in both directions, but the trades in 'cordovan' leather and in furs from Genoa to Champagne had come to an end.

The trade in horses, however, was always erratic. Apart from a regular sale of fifty or so Lombard and Romagnol destriers, the warhorses so much prized by the nobility of France, which travelled to France every year, the horse trade depended very much on peace or war. In times of war, or even of threatened hostilities, as many as four or five hundred great warhorses could be sent across the pass for sale in France in a single year.

After both the terrors of the mountains and the expense of the tolls had been overcome, the travelling merchant was not out of danger. One party of merchants from Lille was set upon in 1222 when it had safely reached Italy. The goods of which they were robbed throw a particular light on a worthwhile consignment of the period. They were carrying fine and expensive cloth from Lille, Ypres and Beauvais, together with much-esteemed breeches from Bruges.[35] These last had a reputation for quality which spread amongst the whole nobility of Europe.

*In 1310 Henry VII crossed the Mont Cenis on his way to coronation as Emperor in Rome. The vivid pictorial record made afterwards for his brother Baldwin of Trier (*Kaiser Heinrichs Romfahrt, *c. 1430) shows the king and queen on horseback, closely accompanied by Baldwin, in his archiepiscopal skullcap, and Amadeus V Count of Savoy. They are shown first ascending through the Savoy lands to the pass and then descending to Susa. The wagons, that had accompanied them up to this point, are shown being taken away on level ground.*

Even after the steep descent to Susa at the Italian end of the Mont Cenis there still remained two days' relatively easy journey down the Valle di Susa to Turin, the 'capital' of Piedmont, which fell into the hands of the counts of Savoy as early as 1060. From Turin the road ran on to Chieri and Asti. These are today towns of relatively little importance, but they were once prosperous and independent city states. It was the men of these cities, who, with their Genoese neighbours to the south, were the first to make considerable use of the Mont Cenis pass and this route to Champagne in the twelfth century. It was because they were first that they made the French, and then the English, think of Italian businessmen as 'Lombards', even when, later, far more of the Italian merchant communities in Paris or London were, in fact, Tuscan by origin. The Tuscans in Paris in the 1290s were taxed as 'Lombards' and the main street of Italian merchants in London was not called 'Tuscan Street', but Lombard Street. The men of Asti and Chieri, besides their own dealings in Champagne, also provided many of the *vectuarii* who transported the goods of merchants of other cities across the Alps. In addition, the Astigiani also fanned out from the 'French' end of the Mont Cenis pass to settle in innumerable small towns and even in villages as small-scale moneylenders and pawnbrokers. However, not all the men of Asti worked on so small a scale. When the four greatest Florentine banking houses went into liquidation in the 1340s, Clement VI was left without a papal banker. He turned to the Malabayla of Asti as the only surviving bank with an international organization sufficiently widely spread to cope with the needs of the papacy to transfer large sums of money to Avignon from all parts of Europe. For a generation the Malabayla was the leading banking house in Europe, until the Alberti brought the primacy in banking back to Florence.

The main road between Rome and the Great St Bernard Pass, marked here by a solid line, was known to medieval Italians as the Francigena, *the French Road. Other important commercial roads between Tuscany and the passes in the western Alps have also been indicated, together with the passes by which they crossed the Appenines, and also some of the ports from which it was possible to ship goods to the mouth of the Rhône.*

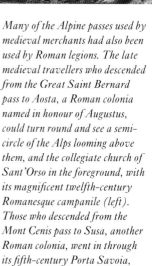

Many of the Alpine passes used by medieval merchants had also been used by Roman legions. The late medieval travellers who descended from the Great Saint Bernard pass to Aosta, a Roman colonia named in honour of Augustus, could turn round and see a semi-circle of the Alps looming above them, and the collegiate church of Sant'Orso in the foreground, with its magnificent twelfth-century Romanesque campanile (left). Those who descended from the Mont Cenis pass to Susa, another Roman colonia, went in through its fifth-century Porta Savoia, considerable fragments of which still survive (right).

From Asti the main road led on to Tortona. This was a major road junction, where an important road across the Appenines through the Boccheta pass from Genoa came in to join the roads which spread out to Pavia and Milan, and above all, to the key crossing of the river Po at Piacenza. At Piacenza those who crossed the Mont Cenis pass rejoined those who had crossed the Alps by the Great St Bernard. They could then go down to the lower Po valley and Venice by water or cross the Po and through the Appenine passes leading to Tuscany, and so, eventually, if they wished, on the via Francigena to Rome.[36]

The alternative to facing crossing the Alps was to continue down the length of the Rhône valley to the Mediterranean, and then onwards to Italy by sea. This route from Lyon and Vienne ran through the vineyards of l'Hermitage and Châteauneuf-du-Pape, and the towns of Valence, Montélimar and Orange to Avignon. One of the earliest of the great bridge-building enterprises was that begun at Avignon in 1177, reputedly in response to a vision by the young priest Bénézet, who was later canonized. He succeeded in building the bridge with the aid of extensive alms from laymen. He also had the

Sea routes to Italy

assistance of a confraternity of brethren who were devoted to the good work of bridge-building in much the same way that the brethren of the St Bernard were dedicated to the maintenance of hospices. When the bridge was completed, it stretched for nearly a kilometre, and was crowned with a chapel significantly dedicated to St Nicholas, the patron saint of merchants. Because of its early bridge, Avignon had already become a town of moderate importance by the standards of the early fourteenth century. Although it had only 5,000–6,000 inhabitants, this was probably more than any city in England apart from London, York and Bristol. Since it possessed the most southerly bridge across the Rhône, it was thus in direct contact with the rich coastlands around Montpellier, as well as the equally fertile and prosperous county of Provence. Avignon itself was not then in France, for the Rhône marked the frontier. However at the far, eastern, end of the bridge, the French founded a new town, Villeneuve-lès-Avignon, to participate in the prosperity brought by the bridge, and built a frontier fortress to defend the crossing.

In 1309, Pope Clement V, unable to return to Rome because of the civil war there between the Colonna and Orsini factions, put up temporarily at the Dominican friary in Avignon. Thirty years later, the papacy was still 'temporarily' there. Benedict XII, an austere and peace-loving Cistercian, reacted against the policy of his predecessor, John XXII, who had stretched the vast resources of the papacy to the very limit to send huge armies into Italy in a series of hopeless attempts to recover control of Rome. Benedict disbanded the armies and, instead, decided to face the reality of the situation by making a permanent home for the papacy in Avignon.[37] The papal palace that he built and that his successor Clement VI extended, stands as a witness to that decision to acknowledge Avignon as the 'capital' of Christendom. There were many, like Petrarch, who disapproved of this decision. To them, Avignon was the sinful city of 'Babylon', a new place of exile beside the Rhône, only fit for lamentation and for comparison with the ancient Jewish exile beside the waters of the Euphrates. Petrarch wrote in 1357:

The most southerly bridge across the Rhône, begun as early as 1177, contributed greatly to the growth of Avignon. Like many early bridges, it was a religious foundation with a chapel on it.

Now you see with your own eyes and feel with your own hands what this new Babylon really is – boiling, seething, obscene, terrible…. Whatever perfidy and fraud, whatever cruelty and arrogance, whatever shameless-ness and unbridled lust you have heard of or read of, whatever impiety and immorality the whole world holds or has ever held – all this you may see heaped up there.[38]

By this date Innocent VI was already preparing to return to Rome and had put the rebuilding of the Lateran palace there in hand. Despite all the plans and polemics, Avignon remained the reluctant capital of the Popes for nearly another fifty years. When the Great Schism began in 1378, so that there were two rival Popes in existence at one time, one of them maintained his *curia* at Avignon. It was not until 1403, when Benedict XIII fled from the city, nearly a hundred years after Clement V's arrival for a short stay, that Avignon lost its character as a papal capital. Until then, the merchant traveller to the city was visiting one of the capital cities of medieval Europe. Very likely he was intent on making a profit from the opportunities it offered. Now the modern trav-eller may well be intent on examining a fourteenth-century capital which has been preserved. Just as the abandonment of Provins led to the preservation of a twelfth- and thirteenth-century princely capital with its Romanesque houses, castle, palace, and fair-site, so the papal plans to return to Rome in 1353 and their eventual abandonment of Avignon in 1403 led to the preserva-tion of a mid-fourteenth-century capital city. Only the tourist trade really flourishes in Avignon today. The traveller intent on leaving even that behind has only to cross the river to Villeneuve-lès-Avignon, which was a favourite dwelling place of the cardinals. It now seems, in April, to be more heavily populated by the nightingales singing in the evenings above the beds of iris round the central citadel than by other foreign visitors.

From Avignon to Italy it was possible, with some difficulty, to travel through Provence and along the coast road to Genoa, even though the moun-tains drop precipitously into the sea for most of the distance between Nice and Genoa and do so even more forbiddingly to the east of Genoa. The *Itinéraire de Bruges* lays out a route from Avignon through Aix-en-Provence and Nice. This winding, minor inland road amongst sage brush and small settlements is again one of the few sections of medieval route which is not adopted by modern major roads. From Nice and Savona, the road leads to Genoa. From Genoa, the *Itinéraire* suggests travelling by boat along the Italian coastline to Porto Venere, near La Spezia, or Porto Pisano in Tuscany as the Emperor Henry VII did in 1312.

This piece of coast has probably only been followed by land with any ease since the opening of the motorway which traverses it in a series of dizzying viaducts from spur to spur, alternating with lengthy tunnels through the spurs. The traveller with vertigo will still find it easier, as it was in the later Middle Ages, to travel from Avignon to Italy by sea. Until the mid-thirteenth century the main choice of ports was between Marseilles in the independent county of Provence, and Montpellier, then in the hands of the kings of Aragon.

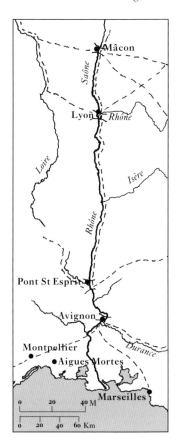

The Rhône-Saône was both a great artery of trade and an obstacle to it, until a sequence of bridges was built that enabled goods to be carried across it. These bridges linked Italy and southern Germany on the east with Spain and the Loire valley on the west. The ports at its mouth provided further means of conveying goods to east and west.

In 1241, (St) Louis IX of France, whose father had lately acquired this corner of France for the royal domain, caused a new royal port to be built in his own lands at Aigues Mortes. He embarked there for his ill-fated crusades. It was not a popular move amongst the other ports of southern France. These had to pay additional taxes for building a rival port, which had the most up-to-date equipment, and also enjoyed royal favour and patronage. For a century or so Aigues Mortes, even though it was an artificial creation, became one of the principal ports of southern France. It was laid out on an irregular grid pattern for St Louis, within a parallelogram of walls of the 1260s which survive in their entirety, complete with their gates and original guard-houses. Very little expense was spared; the guard-houses on the walls boast fireplaces fit for small châteaux, and their ceiling bosses are beautifully sculpted. The pious instigator of the crusade against the infidel would certainly have approved the way the money was spent, but those taxed to provide the where-withal did not. Today, the small walled town, isolated from the sea behind the silt beds and sand-flats, which killed it as a port, remains almost untouched, another almost perfect fossil, preserved again by poverty, and practically unvisited by any but the French, pausing briefly on their way to the tourist beaches of the Mediterranean beyond the modern salt pans.

In the early fourteenth century, however, when Aigues Mortes was very much alive, the Florentine merchant Francesco di Balducci Pegolotti, of the Bardi house, put in his notebook a breakdown of the costs of bringing English wool most cheaply to Florence. His preference was a combination of land routes and sea routes. From England the wool was to be sent in returning

From the air St Louis' new crusade port of Aigues Mortes at the mouth of the Rhône now looks like an inland town. The sea which once came up to the walls on the southern, left hand, side has retreated far out of sight. No expense was spared in the 1260s on the magnificent fortifications which can clearly be seen surviving in their entirety, but the wharves that were its raison d'être have vanished without trace.

Sea trade reached late medieval Tuscany through Porto Pisano, the outport of Pisa. This twelfth-century marble relief in the Campo Santo at Pisa suggests that it then possessed a harbour with two entrances closed with chains, and was highly defensible against marauders from the sea, whether Saracen or Genoese.

The Genoese nevertheless captured it at the end of the thirteenth century and controlled it for over a hundred years.

wine-boats to Gascony, and then carried overland to Aigues Mortes for shipping on to Porto Pisano, then the most important port of Tuscany.

Porto Pisano is no longer to be found on any map. It has been superseded since the sixteenth century by the nearby village of Livorno (Leghorn) which has now grown into a great industrial and commercial city. Porto Pisano was the home port of the galley fleets of Pisa from the time when it ceased to be practicable to take sea-going vessels up the Arno direct to Pisa itself until Pisa's naval might was destroyed by the Genoese at the battle of Meloria in 1284. Porto Pisano remained the most important port of Tuscany, but was served by Genoese shipping until after Pisa was conquered by Florence in the early fifteenth century. The Florentines attempted to revive the merchant marine of Pisa. In the 1430s their galleys rowed out from Porto Pisano to ports as far away as Southampton, Bruges and Alexandria.[39]

These then were the principal medieval routes from Paris to Tuscany. The traveller arrived over the Great St Bernard at Aosta and Vercelli, over the Simplon at Milan, or over the Mont Cenis at Asti, and then by Italian roads across the Appenines to Tuscany, or else he came by sea, from Marseilles, Montpellier or Aigues Mortes via Genoa to Porto Venere or Porto Pisano. He could then begin to discover the nature of Tuscany that had produced the commercial revolution, and was the home of so many merchants, whose goods travelled the roads of Europe for their profit.

4

Helps and hindrances to trade

MY DESCRIPTION OF THE VARIOUS ROUTES between Paris and Tuscany raised a number of points about the ease or difficulty of getting goods from one place to another. In this chapter I would like to look further at some of these issues: the replacement of ferries by bridges, the replacement of mule tracks by wagon roads, the opening of new mountain passes, the canalization of rivers, the growth in importance of carriers and watermen, the provision of inns and hospices, attempts to cope with brigandage, and the burden of tolls and charges levied to pay for improvements and security.

In Europe west of the Rhine and south of the Danube the barbarian kingdoms of the Dark Ages inherited a network of Roman stone bridges and paved roads. They also inherited the consciousness that it was a public responsibility to maintain bridges and roads. However the resources at their disposal frequently did not match up to their consciousness of responsibility so that, despite their efforts, roads, and more particularly bridges, began to fall into decay, rapidly or slowly according to circumstances. The Carolingians retained this sense of responsibility and transmitted it to their successor kings, dukes and counts of the next centuries. Where these acted with any dynamism Roman roads in some cases took several centuries to fall out of use. But by the twelfth century few remained usable, and many had been replaced by winding roads that joined adjacent settlements. For example, the great Appian Way, the main road running directly southwards from Rome itself, was abandoned a few miles from the city when the Roman drainage system of the fertile Pontine plain collapsed and the plain degenerated into marshland. The paved Roman road was replaced by a hill road, fit only for pack animals, that staggered lengthily southwards from *castrum* to *castrum*. Where routes crossed rivers they relied on fords and ferries where once there had been bridges. There was no bridge across the Rhine at Cologne from the collapse of the Roman bridge until the building of the nineteenth-century railway bridge.

The twelfth century probably witnessed the nadir of the European road system. Little survived from classical antiquity beyond a vague sense that there was some public obligation to look after roads and bridges. This obligation had in practice generally devolved to such a level that it resolved itself into the duty of the inhabitants of particular parishes or estates to care for local stretches of road. Even where the will to fulfil their duties existed, the peasant inhabitants normally lacked the resources or organization to do anything more than sketchily patch up what had survived and slow down the process of decay.

In some places individuals or ecclesiastical corporations had been enfeoffed with the office of caring for particular roads. The cathedral chapter of Speyer, for example, had been enfeoffed with the function of maintaining the main north-south road along the west bank of the Rhine between Speyer and Rheinhausen. It was paid for by a toll at Speyer.

Under such circumstances long-distance land trade was extraordinarily slow and cumbersome and almost everywhere dependent on pack animals.

Bridges

The bridges were always the weakest links in the road network and the most difficult for occasional local labour to maintain. In the course of the twelfth century local efforts began to be supplanted by a more powerful organization of resources, often of a charitable nature.

Hugh, Bishop of Grenoble from 1080 to 1132, was one of the first to treat bridge-building as a charitable activity. As well as providing his old master, Bruno, and his companions with the first Charterhouse, his other claims to sanctity (he was canonised only two years after his death), included founding a hospital at Grenoble and building a stone bridge over the Isère.[1] Grenoble stands on the Isère on one of the approach roads to the Mont Cenis pass. In 1130, Thibaud, Count of Blois, the brother of King Stephen of England, built a bridge over the Loire 'for the salvation of his soul', but not many individuals could build a whole bridge themselves. There was nevertheless a considerable wave of bridge-building, from the twelfth century into the thirteenth, which reflected an attitude that saw it as a charitable enterprise, a 'good work' of religious importance.[2]

Only a few years later the 'Steinerne Brücke' was built across the Danube at Regensburg in only eleven years, between 1135 and 1146. The bridge across the Main in Würzburg and the 'Judith Brücke' in Prague (1169) were built in the same period.[3] Of the great charitable bridge-building enterprises the best known is probably that begun at Avignon in 1177, in response to a vision, by the young priest Bénézet (see p. 170). Similar impulses to that which moved St Bénézet to build his bridge moved men to build bridges all over France in the following decades. One of the last of these bridge-building confraternities began the largest of all these charitable bridges in 1265 near Mondragon, 50 kilometres (30 miles) up the Rhône from Avignon. The twenty-five arches of the bridge, with the necessary accompanying works, took over forty years to complete. The bridge still survives, even now an

Until the confraternity of the Holy Spirit completed its bridge (below) in 1309 there was no bridge across the Rhône for over 140 miles between Lyon and Avignon. Their task was enormous, since the river, which was so slight in the summer, filled a kilometre-wide bed in the winter months. It needed twenty-five arches to cross it. River traffic passed under the larger arch at the western, right-hand, end to reach the wharves at the small new town of Pont St Esprit. The bridge, once built, enabled traffic which came from central France through the Cevennes, down the road in the Ardèche valley, to cross the river to reach all the Rhône valley towns strung out along the main north–south road along the eastern bank, and to gain access to the road that wound its way to Italy over the Montgenèvre pass.

immense and memorable monument to the vision of the bridge-builders. At its western, French, end another new town was planted, named Pont St Esprit after the bridge, which, with its accompanying hospitals, was dedicated to the Holy Spirit.

The work was particularly complex as the bridge was sited only half a kilometre below the confluence of the turbulent Ardèche with the Rhône and the water level was consequently liable to rise precipitately. The bridge itself acted almost as a dam when the Rhône was in flood and it was necessary to erect ten kilometres of dikes against floods besides reinforcing the imperial bank with piles for 2,500 metres above the bridge so that the river should not '*delaisse son ancien cours et mecte ledit pont en isle*' (make a new course for itself around the eastern end of the bridge). It was an extremely expensive enterprise to maintain, for, as well as the bridge itself, the dikes and banks needed perpetual attention. The *Oeuvre hospitalière du Pont Saint Esprit*, whose rectors looked after the bridge, possessed, inter alia, two quarries of its own, from which the bridge had been built, and from which it was maintained, and a *mouton*, a military machine adapted to be a pile driver, which needed to be replaced from time to time, in the spring of 1474 for example.

It was normal for a toll to be levied from those using such a bridge, and sometimes, as at the Pont St Esprit, from those using the river under it, to help pay for its upkeep and repair. However, tolls by themselves were not adequate to maintain a bridge. Those who planned to build one did not simply have to look for enough funds to build it in the first place, but for an adequate permanent endowment in land. The first years' rents from the bridge's lands paid for the initial building. The fact that the Pont St Esprit and its associated

In the 1440s Jehan Wauquelin's team of miniaturists at Mons provided a series of vivid illustrations for the history of the county of Hainault, which he translated into French for Philip the Good. By then Hainault was criss-crossed with a series of roads fit for wheeled traffic. Here two towns, on the left and the right of the picture, are being joined by a new road. The whole process is sketched out graphically yet economically, from cutting a way through a forest and grubbing up the roots of the trees, to paving a newly constructed bridge.

works took forty years to complete was not because medieval masons could not work any faster, but because it needed forty years' income to pay them. The endowment was then intended to pay for the maintenance of the fabric, of the brotherhood and of their chapel.

It was common for a chapel to be built on a bridge, as on the Rhône bridges at Pont St Esprit and Avignon, the Florentine bridge over the Arno at Signa and the bridges over the Avon in England at Bristol, over the Ouse at St Ives, and over the Thames at London.[4] Alternatively a chapel might be built at one end of it, as by the Medway bridge at Rochester in England, or by the Ponte Nuovo over the Arno at Pisa. The confraternities and charitable corporations who looked after such bridges normally had a bridge house at one end. The *logis* of the *Oeuvre hospitalière du Pont Saint Esprit* was at the French end.

Endowments included both large single gifts, like the considerable estates given by the Bishop of Rochester for the building of the Medway bridge there, and numerous smaller gifts.[5] Ninety-eight of the 632 wills entered in surviving Genoese notarial registers from the period 1155 to 1253 left tiny legacies for bridges, principally but not exclusively the bridges across the Bisagno to the east of the city and the Polverra to the west. Both these streams could change suddenly from small trickles to violent torrents and needed robust bridges. At the end of each was a church or chapel and the house at which tolls were collected and from which the fabric and the endowment were looked after. The wills speak of 'the church of Santa Margarita and the bridge' and 'the bridge of priest Berardo', clearly indicating the religious importance of bridges to the testators. As well as the numerous small bequests to specified bridges, other wills in these registers also included lump sums left generally to 'churches, bridges, hospitals and the poor' to be distributed at the discretion of the executors.[6]

Some bridges built in city centres were able to help pay for themselves in other ways besides tolls. The Ponte Vecchio in the middle of Pisa, the Grand Pont in Paris,[7] and London Bridge, all had houses and shops built on them as the Ponte Vecchio in Florence still does. The rents from their houses and shops helped pay for the upkeep of the bridges, in the same way that rents from houses and shops built between the buttresses of city centre churches increased the endowments of the churches concerned.

Many bridges were fortified in the Middle Ages, lest what was intended to improve travel for merchants and pilgrims should instead give access to armies of soldiers. Fortification was particularly necessary in frontier zones. In the disputable borderland on the edge of Aquitaine, Cahors (above) changed hands, between English and French, several times in the thirteenth and four-teenth centuries, until it became definitively French in 1369.

In many cities the sides of the bridge were leased out for houses and shops so that rents would help pay the costs of bridge maintenance. The houses and shops on the Ponte Vecchio, across the Arno in Florence, improbably survive (right). The corridor over the top was only added in 1564.

Endowments for bridges were always vulnerable, not only to the maladministration of those in charge or to the rapacity of powerful lords, but also to the excessive costs of major rebuildings or to the drop in landed incomes suffered by most landlords at the end of the Middle Ages. Those in charge of the Pont St Esprit had to go out on *quêtes*, missions to beg support in the neighbourhood for the bridge works. Most endowments for bridges have consequently vanished long since, but some have survived, like the Bridge House estates of London Bridge, or the Rochester Bridge charities. These are amongst the oldest surviving charities in the world.

A second surge in bridge-building, from the thirteenth century into the fourteenth, was a consequence of such a strong re-emphasis of the older attitude of bridge-building as a public concern that it again had a practical effect. New life was breathed into the attenuated legacy of Rome.

Bridges were often defended along with the towns with which they were associated. During a truce in the Hundred Years' War, the Pont St Esprit over the Rhône was seized, for extortion, by temporarily unemployed *routiers*, companies of contract soldiers. Afterwards, to prevent this happening again, the French royal seneschal of Beaucaire deliberately extended the fortifications of the royal town at its west end to enclose the end of the viaduct leading to the bridge, and erected three towers on the bridge itself. The *tour du roy*, on the first pier in the river from the western bank, effectively closed the bridge with two shuttable gates and a guardhouse. The central tower contained not only the bridge chapel, of St Nicolas, but also a prison beneath, whilst the eastern tower *devers l'empire* was equipped with a drawbridge so that it could be closed at that end as well. The very grand Scaliger bridge which entered the city of Verona across the Adige was also fortified, as was London Bridge and the bridge across the Lot at Cahors, as well as smaller bridges like that across the Monnow at Monmouth on the border of Wales, and across the Greve on the Florence–Siena road. Jan van Eyck incorporated such fortified bridges into the backgrounds of some of his pictures, for example the Madonna and child that he painted for Nicholas Rolin, the Burgundian Chancellor. Although the identification of Van Eyck's bridges, despite decades of effort by art historians, has proved impossible, they nevertheless represent clearly the ideal bridge to be hoped for in the mid-fifteenth century.

The exquisite, but now detached, bridge chapel at Pisa, Santa Maria della Spina (above), so richly decorated when rebuilt in 1323, once stood at the end of its bridge, but was moved stone by stone in 1871.

Since so many bridges were charitable enterprises in origin, they often had chapels incorporated in them, like this one from Sebastian Münster's Cosmographia, *Basel, 1545.*

The maintenance of bridges was such a moral imperative that a broken bridge was a potent metaphor, here reinforced by the sorry state of the traveller approaching it.

Until the great surges of bridge-building from the late twelfth century onward, merchants had had to rely on ferries to cross the major rivers of Europe. The enormous increase in trade between the late twelfth century and the early fourteenth was enormously assisted by the great programmes of bridge-building carried out in these centuries. Not only were bridges immensely quicker to use than ferries, but bridge tolls were much lower than ferry dues. Those whose livelihoods in running ferries were ruined by a new bridge had to be compensated from the bridge's funds. Where there were few new bridges, hereditary ferrymen remained in possession of their rights and obligations. In Slovenia a farm was usually assigned for their maintenance.[8] Bridge tolls were frequently appropriated by rulers or great lords, although a proportion was supposed to be used to help maintain the bridges. However, tolls never made bridge-building a profitable proposition. It always remained a good work, a charitable enterprise for public benefit, whether undertaken by religious bodies or by princes and communes.

Of all the road improvements of the long thirteenth century, bridge-building made the greatest difference, not only by speeding up and cheapening trade along existing routes, but sometimes even by opening up totally new routes.

Even in the fourteenth century, when the great era of medieval bridge-building had come to an end, there was only a limited number of permanent stone bridges across major rivers. On the Saône and Rhône they were at St-Jean-de-Losne, Chalon and Mâcon on the Saône, at the confluence of the two rivers at Lyon, at Pont St Esprit and finally at Avignon. Altogether there were only some half-dozen bridges scattered over the 500 or more kilometres (more than 300 miles) between St-Jean-de-Losne and the sea (map p. 171).

These rare bridges were built both at nodal points to trade, and came to reinforce them. At St-Jean-de-Losne, the river was crossed by the key road from Champagne to the Great St Bernard. At Chalon, the Rhône crossing came at the point where a route from the upper Loire came down to the Rhône; at Mâcon, the bridge carried another road from the upper Loire valley to Lake Geneva and thence to south Germany or to the Mont Cenis pass and thence to north Italy; at Lyon, the main valley road itself crossed from the west bank of the river to the east; and at Pont St Esprit, the river was crossed by the roads which penetrated the Massif Central by the Ardèche valley, and the Alps by the Mont Genèvre pass. At Avignon, it was crossed by the road from Spain, Toulouse and Montpellier, to Marseilles and Provence. At each of these points the bridge focused and enlarged trading activities.

Important medieval bridges, then, were always few in number. Fewer still survive. Their numbers have been reduced by accidental destruction by flood. The bombing of strategic routes in the Second World War has reduced their number still further. However the worst enemy, as with every other historical monument, has been progress. 'Improvement', which created the bridges in the first place, has, over successive centuries, reduced their number to a mere handful.

In the 1170s the Frederick I made peace with the Pope, the King of Sicily, and the Lombard League and gained control of Tuscany and Spoleto. He could then re-organise the imperial administration of Italy, with an increased number of administrative centres (hollow triangles), and toll stations (solid triangles) The latter define the principal roads on the eve of the road revolution, although it is not clear how much the tolls were for the upkeep of the emperor rather than the roads.

The road revolution

In the thirteenth century the revival of 'public' interest in bridges went hand in hand with a revival of public interest in roads.

In the 1220s the *Sachsenspiegel* of Eike von Repgow contains the earliest German road ordinances and distinguishes between 'Königs Strassen' and other roads. From his stance on the north German plain he assumed that the 'Königs Strassen' were already fit to take wagons, and says that they should be wide enough for two wagons to pass. Later evidence indicates that the road to Italy over the Brenner was regarded as such a 'Königs' or 'Kaisers Strasse'. Eike von Repgow also provided a sort of 'highway code', describing which had priority at bridges and narrow places – laden wagons, unladen wagons, those on horseback and pedestrians.[9] In 1236, Frederick II made arrangements for the maintenance of roads.

By the early fourteenth century the public concern for the maintenance of roads in England had reached such a point that when the coast road to Bridlington in Yorkshire disappeared into the sea, together with the cliffs along which it ran, the inhabitants of Bridlington petitioned the king in Parliament. A line for a new road was laid out as a result and arrangements were made for the compulsory purchase of the necessary land to build it.

Whereas in Germany, France, England, Castile and Sicily, it was emperors, kings and princes who took up again the dormant public obligation to care for roads and bridges, in north Italy it was the city states which did so. In some cases their schemes of road improvement began as early as the twelfth century, but it was really in the thirteenth that the most marked changes took place.

The map on the previous page shows the range of imperial roads in Italy, between Rome and Bologna, in the second half of the twelfth century. Many of these roads were in a very poor state, fit only for pack animals. A few of them still ran firmly along Roman routes, despite suffering from the best part of a millennium of degradation. However, many of them had left low-lying ground, as bridges and embankments had collapsed and not been repaired, and reverted to circuitous pre-Roman routes on higher ground. Over a long period of time the road system had gradually become more and more primitive, as each section of any road became effectively the concern of the local community alone. Imperial oversight was negligible, and any such regional oversight as existed was frequently in the hands of bishops who delegated their responsibilities to the local *pieve* (central baptismal churches serving several parishes, like minsters in Dark Age England). In the twelfth century each of the rising city communes began to take an interest in the principal roads in its *contado*, and it was their activity that transformed the roads of Tuscany and Lombardy in a way that has been called the 'road revolution of the thirteenth century'.

Pisa and Florence provide contrasting examples of how this improvement in roads was carried out in the course of the long thirteenth century, in ways that made a massive difference to the speed and costs of transporting goods. The city of Pisa improved five main roads in its *contado* and Florence twelve *strade maestre*.

In the twelfth century the Pisans began by replacing the old road to Lucca, then still the most important city in Tuscany. This was a hill road across the Monte Pisano, fit only for pack animals. They replaced it by a new road on the level around the edge of the Monte Pisano suitable for carts. This new road was under construction in 1162 and was in use by 1184. It was appropriate that the first road improvement in Tuscany should connect its then principal city to its principal port.

In the 1190s, the Pisans reconstructed their collapsed Ponte Vecchio across the Arno, joining Pisa proper to Kinsica on the south bank. A second bridge, the Ponte Nuovo, followed soon after. At more or less the same time, the Pisans began to make a road fit for carts to use from this south bank quarter to their new out-port, Porto Pisano, which is now part of Livorno. This involved building three stone bridges and throwing up an embankment across the intervening swamps. The embankment was stabilized by planting trees along it every four feet (see map). By 1233 they had begun to resurrect that part of the old Roman Via Aurelia which ran northwards across the swamps to join the Via Francigena, the *strata francorum*, which carried pilgrims and merchants to and from 'France'. Again bridge-building and embankments were the order of the day. The Lucchese founded a new town, Pietrasanta, in 1342 at the junction of these roads.

Around the same time the Pisans started to improve the old road to Florence on the north bank of the Arno, but in 1262 they decided to start an

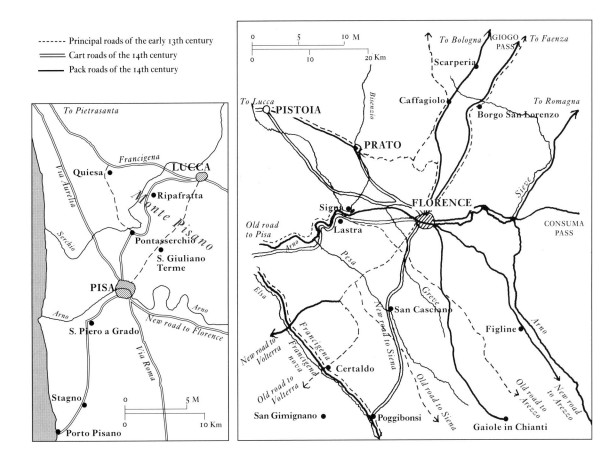

The maps of the road networks around Pisa and Florence clarify road improvements made between the twelfth and fourteenth centuries by these two cities.

altogether new road instead. This began with a new bridge to replace the old ford across the Arno immediately above Pisa itself. It continued along a broad elevated dike, again stabilized with numerous trees, along the south bank of the Arno. The new road, however, progressed very slowly for, after all, the old, unimproved road already existed, and most heavy goods went in barges on the Arno itself as far as Signa, the 'port' of Florence. In the 1280s a great effort was made at last to finish it, and this coincided with an upgrading of main roads by paving rather than gravelling them. Just as the first, late twelfth- and early thirteenth-century, stage in road improvement allowed the use of two-wheeled carts instead of pack animals, so this next stage allowed for an increase in cart size. In 1299 a single four-wheeled cart was able to bring the 2,500 pound chain, designed to close the harbour mouth at Porto Pisano, by road from Pisa.

The paved Pisan roads of the late thirteenth century were 12–15 feet (3.7–4.6 m) wide to allow two of the new large carts to pass. Widening preceded paving in at least one case, the Via Romea, the 'coastal' Maremma road to Rome southward from Pisa. It had presumably done so in other cases as well. The Via Romea was the longest of the roads out of Pisa to be improved by the city, for Pisan territory extended far to the south of the city to include much of the Maremma. This huge southern extension of Pisan territory took in the lands of the Gherardesca counts of Donoratico. The Gherardesca at times dominated the city and it was presumably their interest that gave an unexpectedly high priority to the improvement of a road that would otherwise not have warranted such treatment. Most travellers to Rome still went inland on the Via Francigena through Siena, and even improved land transport cannot have been cheaper than the sea-going barges in which the wine of the Maremma was traditionally shipped to Pisa. The Via Romea ran through Pisan territory for 85 miles (137 km). The Via Romea had been widened for 60 miles, when Ugolino dei Gherardesca, then ruler of Pisa, made arrangements in 1286 for the remaining section to be widened. The next thing to do was to pave it, or rather re-pave it, for this road also ran along part of the line of the Roman Via Aurelia. By 1308 paving had already advanced 25 miles from Pisa and was continuing. It was astonishing to consider paving such an enormous distance when the paving of the main streets inside cities was relatively novel and many were as yet unpaved. Was this unexpected emphasis on the Via Romea really to create a Gherardesca military road, as Roman roads had been, or as General Wade's military roads were to be in post-1745 Scotland, or Hitler's *autobahnen* in 1930s Germany?

Whereas Pisa stands on the Arno where it issues into a swampy coastal plain, Florence sits in a vast hollow surrounded on all sides by hills. The Pisans were able to create roads usable by carts by building embankments across their swamps and laying relatively flat paved roads along the tops of them. What the Florentines could do was to bridge the tributaries of the Arno again and again to produce shorter and more passable roads for pack animals. The key to road improvement for the Florentines then was a mammoth programme of bridge-building and the laying out of new roads along easier routes. Of the ten main roads out of Florence by 1285 only three followed the same lines as their unimproved predecessors at the beginning of the century.[10] Two more *strade maestre* were added in the fourteenth century.

Many of the old roads had wound about, following the ridges on the tops of hills to avoid crossing streams, but the new ones had no hesitation in following, or crossing, the bottoms of the valleys. Along the new *strade maestre* a score of large bridges, mostly in stone, crossed the major tributaries of the Arno, like the Elsa, the Pesa, the Sieve and the Bisenzio, by the end of the thirteenth century. They were supplemented by numerous *ponticelli* over tiny streams, perhaps half of them built of wood. Professor Charles de la Roncière has found records of some seventy bridges of various sizes built for the Commune of Florence between 1280 and 1380. By 1380 many wooden bridges from the beginning of the century had been replaced by stone ones.[11]

Whereas the Pisans built their main roads on embankments, the Florentines dug out drainage ditches, which were supposed to be a *braccio* (55 cm) deep, at the sides of theirs.

Pack animals could certainly travel much faster on the improved roads, but the terrain meant that very few of the new Florentine roads could be improved enough for wheeled vehicles. By the end of the thirteenth century the only roads for carts were those laid out along the Arno to Signa, the port of Florence and the new road to Prato, across the marshes between the two cities, which was paved in 1282. This was a more important road than it might seem, for outside Florentine territory it led on from Prato through Pistoia to Lucca, following much the same line as the modern motorway. From Lucca, carts could travel through Pisa to the sea at Porto Pisano, or northwards along the Francigena to Pietrasanta. The first stage of the new road south to Siena was also paved. This was usable by carts only as far as the ford at San Casciano, a mere 11 miles (18 km) from the city. Beyond that, even this important road was only fit for pack animals. The Pesa ford at San Casciano was not replaced by a bridge until 1300, and the Greve ford on the same road for a few more years. The section onwards to Poggibonsi, on the Florentine border, was eventually widened to twelve *braccia* (6.5 m) in the 1320s and partially paved at the same time. The way in which paving still only extended for a limited distance from a city can be seen in one of Ambrogio Lorenzetti's frescoes painted in 1337 in the city hall at Siena (ill. p. 90–1).

Road improvement continued out of Florence in other directions in the fourteenth century. A totally new road, usable by carts, was constructed across low-lying ground to Pistoia in the first twenty years of the century. The priors of Florence next decided to upgrade their new thirteenth-century road along the south bank of the Arno to make it fit for carts. As well as improving the roadways themselves, the Florentines also made their *strade maestre* more convenient, by constructing fountains and wells for drinking water for men and beasts. The Sienese did the same on the stretch of the Francigena that passed through their territory. The Florentines also set up boundary stones along the roads. These were designed to mark the passage from one community responsible for road maintenance to the next, but were also of assistance to travellers.

By the beginning of the fourteenth century successive Florentine 'captains of the people' were sending out three commissioners in May each year to inspect the previous year's damage to the *strade maestre*. These commissioners had to arrange for the necessary repairs, particularly those to bridges, to be done by the local communities of the *contado*, who still had to carry most of the burden for the upkeep of roads. Their instructions were supposed to be acted on at once, and the commissioners returned two months later to see if their orders had been obeyed. In the middle of the fourteenth century a permanent office was set up, with funds of its own, to oversee roads and bridges continually under elected '*uffitiali delle strate, vie, ponti e pontizelli del contado di Firenze*'.

Sometimes repairs took place as fast as was intended. When the bridge over the Sieve, at Borgo San Lorenzo on the main road across the Appenines to Faenza in the Romagna, was swept away by a sudden summer flood in June 1347, the city arranged for it to be rebuilt urgently in July so that the grain from the coming harvest in the Romagna could get through to feed the city 'because a great multitude of people were accustomed to come by this way to the city of Florence from the Romagna with wheat and corn and other indispensable foodstuffs'.[12] On the other hand repairs could equally drag on for a very long time indeed. The most inefficient case was what happened when the bridge was destroyed over the Elsa, where the new thirteenth-century road to Pisa left Florentine territory. It was not rebuilt for forty years! The Mercanzia of Florence, the corporation made up of the five principal trading guilds of the city, ran a ferry across the Elsa for over twenty years, at the very time that this road to Pisa was being upgraded to be fit for carts! The new bridge across the Elsa was finally finished, in stone, in 1347, and it became possible at last to take goods by cart all the way to Pisa without either using a ferry or going round through Prato, Pistoia and Lucca.

Road improvements in the Florentine *contado* took place much later than in the Pisan, not only because of the difference in terrain, but also possibly because of the slowness of decision-making in a democracy, particularly one with frequently changing office holders. Even when a decision had been reached to make a new road or a new bridge, or even to improve or repair an existing road or bridge, there could still be long delays, whilst the financing of the works was partitioned amongst the inhabitants in the vicinity. A seigneurial regime, like that of Ugolino della Gherardesca in Pisa in the 1280s, could act much more decisively. The Pisan section of the new riverside road to Florence was consequently paved half a century before the Florentine section.

To a greater or lesser extent all the city states of northern and central Italy followed these patterns. Each city picked out for special attention a limited number of routes which were important to it. Siena picked out nine such principal roads, and from the 1270s appointed six supervisors under a *iudex viarum* to care for them.[13] Amongst the tasks entrusted to the *podesta* of Vicenza in 1264 was the maintainance of *vias publicas*, particularly that from Padua. Like the monarchies with their *viae realae*, even the small commune of Tivoli had a Via Maior which it paved, or rather re-paved, for their *via silicata et lapidea* had been the Roman Via Tiburtina. Embankments carrying new roads were thrown up in low-lying lands, innumerable bridges were built across rivers and streams, main roads were widened and either gravelled or paved. The area in which wheeled transport could operate was vastly enlarged, even in a region as broken up by hills as northern and central Italy. The speed and ease of transport by pack animals was greatly increased. Even

Another vivid detail, by one of Jehan Wauquelin's team of miniaturists working at Mons in the 1440s on the history of the county of Hainault (see above p. 177), shows the paving of a road with neatly squared blocks of stone. By the 1440s a limited number of main roads, like that in Hainault between Mons and Valenciennes, had long been paved.

in southern Italy road improvement and bridge-building became a concern of government in the thirteenth century. Charles I (1266–85) ordered the repair and improvement of three of the principal roads out of Naples: that to Salerno; the Via Degli Abruzzi running northwards through Capua, Sulmona and Aquila, which led to Umbria and Tuscany, where it joined up with roads being improved by the governments of city states; and that running eastwards through Avellino and Foggia to the key grain-growing lands of Apulia and to the Adriatic seaports, which he also ordered to be reconditioned and enlarged.[14]

Johan Plesner used the words *rivoluzione stradale* (road revolution) for what happened in the thirteenth-century Florentine *contado*, but the term might properly be applied much more widely, not merely to most of northern and central Italy, but also to large areas of western Europe outside Italy. In the southern Netherlands the interests of the mercantile cities were as strong as in northern Italy. The Duke of Brabant conceded to his *chefs-villes* the right to ensure the maintenance of the roads in their own parts of the duchy, since it was the merchants of the *chefs-villes* who needed them to be in a fit state for trade. One of these *chefs-villes*, Brussels, had a separate administration called 'la Chaussée' by 1326, which acquired its own lands and had other revenues from *weg-geld*, dues for the use of the crane and the weigh-house, and levies made on goods arriving at the wharves and at some of the gates. This was used to maintain particular roads out from the city to a standard fit for *chars* as well as *charettes*.[15] One is strongly reminded of the care of *strade maestre* in northern Italy.

Mountain passes

The only activity to be able to claim even comparable importance to the medieval road system as bridge-building was the improvement of access to mountain passes. Very few totally new routes were opened in the later Middle Ages, for most of the major Alpine passes then used were already known and used in pre-historic times, as well as by the Romans. A Roman temple to Jupiter stands very near where the medieval hospice was later built on the Great St Bernard. The only really major new passes to be opened through the Alps were the Simplon and the St Gotthard connecting Milan with the Rhineland. The key to opening the latter was the building of a precarious road alongside the river Reuss. Below Andermatt the Reuss rushes through the narrow Schöllenen gorge, a smoothly polished granite defile, that until around 1225 defeated all attempts at road-building. Even then all that could be managed was to hang a wooden way, for men and pack animals, by chains from the side of the gorge. When this last link was open, the route was still exceedingly complex and not to be undertaken lightly. The easiest part of the journey was from Milan by road to Sesto at the southern end of the Lake Maggiore. Goods then went by water the length of the lake to Magadino. They continued by pack animal past Bellinzona up the Ticino valley (the Val Levantina), over the St Gotthard, with its hospice and shrine to St Gotthard, then down the Reuss valley, through the terrible Schöllenen Gorge to Flüelen on the southern end of Lake Luzern, where goods had to take to the water again to Luzern, and on by boat down the Reuss, Aare and Rhine to Basel. It seems a perfectly ghastly route and the central sections were not made fit for wheeled transport until the 1820s. It was nevertheless used quite extensively in the later Middle Ages.[16]

However, although new routes were few, many of the roads leading to the passes were improved quite considerably. These improvements were partially competitive. After the opening of the St Gotthard a great deal of traffic left the older Septimer pass route, which in the Roman period and the earlier Middle Ages had been the principal pass through the central Alps, connecting Milan and the Rhineland. As on the 'new' St Gotthard route, goods had been carried for part of the journey by water, along the length of Lake Como. On the north side of the Septimer pass the route came down to the upper Rhine valley at Chur, and then followed the Rhine down to Lake Constance. In 1387 the Bishop of Chur had the very top of the pass paved, from Casaccia on the south side to Bivio on the north, in an unsuccessful attempt to lure some of the lost traffic back.

The road on the south side of the Brenner pass was improved in two stages, like some of the roads around Florence. At the beginning of the fourteenth century, in 1314, one Kunter, a private citizen of Bolzano, paid for the improvements that enabled the old ridge road north of the city to be brought down into the valley of the Isarco. The new 'Kunter' road was still only fit for pack animals. However in 1480, when the Brenner had become the most used pass in the whole of the Alps, a further set of improvements was made, which turned it into a road fit for wheeled vehicles.[17]

In 1490 the Brenner was the most used pass in the Alps. When he went to Italy for the first time in 1494/5 Albrecht Dürer made detailed sketches of buildings and landscapes all along the Brenner road from Innsbruck to Verona. This detail from his engraving of Nemesis, *based on one of his sketches, shows the road at Chiusa (Klausen) on the Italian side of the pass on the way down the Isarco valley to Bolzano. As its name suggests, Chiusa was a place where the road could be closed for the levying of tolls.*

Little of this late medieval mountain road-building survives, but if Joachim Patinir's pictures are to be taken merely as exaggeration rather than pure fantasy, some of it may have been quite as exotic as modern cliff-hanging motorway construction in the same Alpine regions, except that the fantastic precipice-clinging constructions were in wood rather than reinforced concrete. The landscape of precipitous over-dramatized rock formations and the crazy, slatted paths and bridges that circumnavigate and surmount them look so surrealist and unreal that it comes as a shock to see, in the landscape round the painter's own home town of Dinant, which was itself once overwhelmed by the collapse of one of these precipices, that the painter was in fact producing mere plodding, representational pictures of his own locality. If his landscapes were true to life, there is at least a possibility that the paths, tracks and roads that attempted to subjugate them were also in some sense accurate representations of the 'roads', reminiscent to our eyes of the contemporary crossings of Nepali gorges. They bring home the hindrances that fourteenth- and fifteenth-century merchants had to battle with to pursue their trade. Such exotic creations of the road-builders' art were always fragile and vulnerable to collapse and destruction by avalanche. How much had to be re-created each spring?

The little that does survive of these mountain roads is limited to things like the few stone slabs by which the medieval mule tracks crossed small torrents on the way up to the Great St Bernard pass. In Alpine passes, perhaps more than anywhere else, the nature of the ground has meant that later cart roads and even modern motorways have followed the same lines and swept

Joachim Patinir's surprisingly realistic early sixteenth-century road rises sharply from the plain into the mountains across a wooden bridge that does what modern railway and motorway engineers have done in stone and concrete. This detail is from his 'Penitent Magdalen' in Dijon.

away virtually all traces of their predecessors. A small part of the fourteenth-century paving over the Septimer pass survives near Casaccia, perhaps precisely because this is not followed by any modern main road.

New passes were also opened elsewhere in Europe, like the Giogo pass connecting Florence and Bologna (see p. 216). However, compared with Alpine passes this one across the Appenines seems exceedingly tame. It is by no means even as difficult as the Cisa, the traditional pass for crossing the Appenines from Lombardy to Tuscany, and it is also slightly lower. The highest point on the Giogo route is 968 metres, or 3,146 feet, and on the Cisa route, it is 1,039 metres or 3,375 feet. These passes are at the same sort of height as the Jougne pass through the Jura of 1,070 metres or 3,283 feet, but half the height, or even less than half, of the passes through the western Alps. The Great St Bernard is 2,473 metres high (8,037 feet) and the Mont Cenis 2,084 metres (6,773 feet). For comparison, for British readers, the summits of Snowdon and Ben Nevis are only 3,560 feet (1,095 metres) and 4,406 feet (1,356 metres) high respectively.

The medieval heyday of opening new passes, like building new bridges, was in the long thirteenth century. Both processes slowed down in the second half of the fourteenth century and the first half of the fifteenth. The Regno provides a good example. With the breakdown in central government after the death of King Robert II in 1343 there was a failure to organize improvement and even maintenance of the road network, which inevitably led to a general degradation over time. The fifteenth century saw a renewal in road maintenance and improvement including the opening of new passes.

In northern Spain the roads through the Cantabrian mountains from Burgos to the Biscay ports were vigorously improved in the fifteenth century to facilitate the rapidly increasing export of high quality wool. Instead of mules, it became possible to use long narrow ox-drawn carts, each carrying four mule-loads as far as Vitoria, and then smaller carts, drawn by two mules, each carrying three mule-loads through the passes themselves. The costs of improvements were shared between Burgos and the port towns.[18]

Perhaps the most significant pass to be opened, in terms of its commercial consequences, was not in the Alps at all, but in the Tatra. In the late fifteenth century a route was finished through the mountains from the mining areas of Slovakia into southern Poland. This had very considerable local importance in that it offered a much more direct route between Buda and Cracow, the capitals of Hungary and Poland, than the much more easterly old roundabout road through Spis (Zips). However, its real importance was that it became possible for a large proportion of the expanding production of copper in Slovakia to be taken to the Vistula, where it was shipped downriver, along with a great deal of grain, and out through Torun and Gdansk to Antwerp. As a very distant consequence, Antwerp came to replace Venice in a few years as the principal copper market of Europe. The mines, and indeed much of the trade, continued in the hands of the same south German entrepreneurs, like the Thurzos and the Fuggers, but now, as in other fields, the principal orientation of their activities shifted from Venice to Antwerp.

When a group of merchants had an interest in a particular route they were not content merely to let the local authorities get on with its maintenance, or not, as the case might be. They took positive measures to see that something was done. This was relatively easy if the relevant authority was their own government. The Mercanzia of Florence could petition the priors to improve the roads that interested its members with some expectation of action being taken. The Mercanzia itself ran a ferry across the Elsa when the bridge was destroyed, and also acquired the oversight of the *vectuarii*, the carriers, within the Florentine *contado*.

Even at the end of the Middle Ages many mountain roads were no better than this pilgrim path to a hilltop shrine: another woodcut from Münster's Cosmographia.

Commercial pressure for improvement

When another government was involved, effective pressure for maintenance or improvement was more problematic and demanded patient negotiation. The merchants of Milan had a strong interest in the upkeep of the Simplon pass road. From the end of the thirteenth century onward, they sent syndics at intervals to negotiate with the bishop of Sion who was overlord of the Valais, the upper Rhône valley, from below Martigny to Simplon. The earliest set of negotiations for which records survive was in 1271–73. What the syndicates could offer the bishop and his steward was money, lump sum payments and consent to increased dues of various sorts. What they wanted of the bishop in the first place was that he should change his system of providing for road and bridge maintenance. In 1271 the bishop had recently been enfeoffing local lords with the job of looking after short stretches of road, in one case only 10 km (6 miles) long. In return he granted them the right to levy a toll on their section. The merchants much preferred to pay one large toll to the bishop and his steward to cover the whole distance through his lands, rather than a tiny toll every couple of hours. The bishop agreed and began buying back the fiefs, but the road was still not as the merchants wanted it. In 1275 Pope Gregory X, returning that way from Lausanne to Rome, could still complain of dangerous bridges. The Milanese were not satisfied, and further negotiations took place in 1291, 1321, 1336 and 1351 at least. At about the same time, in 1286, the Venetians were similarly trying to put pressure on the Count of Gorizia to keep up his section of the 'Hungarian road', that ran along the route of the old Roman *via publica*, across Slovenia to Hungary through Ljubljana and Ptuj.[19]

Occasionally when merchants could not get authorities to maintain roads to their satisfaction they took direct action themselves. For example, in 1469 when the bridge at Houtand near Pontarlier on the main road from Salins through the Jura was in danger of collapse, the Grande Saunerie at Salins first sent inspectors to see what was needed, then they applied pressure for the necessary works to be done, and eventually when it became apparent that nothing was going to be done by those responsible, they paid to have the bridge rebuilt, in wood. Having established such a precedent it is no wonder that when a sudden flood destroyed the bridge at Pontarlier the following year, the cost and work of its replacement also fell on the Grande Saunerie. They found that, as well as their traditional responsibilities for the maintenance of the roads and bridges within 15 km of Salins, they had made themselves perpetually liable for the more distant bridges at Houtand and Pontarlier. In 1502 the Grande Saunerie rebuilt the bridge at Houtand in stone.

Roads, rivers and lakes

As the new St Gotthard pass route and the Septimer pass route that it replaced both illustrate, no clear distinction was made between travelling by road and travelling by water. Medieval merchants and carriers saw road and river, or lake, as complementary to each other. We have already noted how important the Saône–Rhône river system was for the carriage of goods and identified three of the key places, Port sur Saône, St-Jean-de-Losne and

Today punting is thought of as a frivolous diversion in Cambridge and Oxford, but formerly it was a practical way of getting people and goods about, and not only in the English Fens. In many low-lying parts of Europe, it was as natural to take grain to be milled by punt as by mule, as in this fifteenth-century sketch.

Chalon, where goods were commonly transferred from different roads to the Saône. We have also noticed how the political role of the watermen of Paris depended on their economic significance as the most important group of water carriers on the Seine river system.

We have described one way that the wines of Burgundy might reach their Flemish consumers by a mixture of road and river transport. An alternative route, equally a mixture of road and river transport, was to take the wine from Beaune by road to Cravat on the Yonne, then to carry it by river boat *down* the Yonne and the Seine and *up* the Oise to Pont L'Evêque, then to take it by cart through Peronne to the Lys, and eventually to bring it down to Ghent by water again.

We have already picked out the importance of the *quais* on the Seine to the fairs of Troyes. This combination of road and river access was similarly important for many fairs. Of the Champagne fair towns only Provins did not have immediate access to an easily navigable river. Lagny lay on the Marne and Bar on the Aube. In the same way almost all of the network of successor fairs to those of Champagne were accessible by water. In the south the fairs of Chalon, Geneva and Lyon lay on the Saône and Rhône. In the north those of Antwerp and Bergen-op-Zoom both lay on the Scheldt, with access to the Rhine and Meuse river systems and the range of internal waterways into the northern Netherlands leading as far as Amsterdam and the ports of the Zuider Zee. In the centre the old Lendit fairs at St-Denis took on a new lease of life after the decline of the Champagne fairs. They were held between the abbey and the Seine. To the east, the fairs of Frankfurt were held by the Main, with easy access to the whole Rhine–Main river system.

In England one of the most important fairs was the Michelmas fair at Stourbridge, held on the Cam near the head of navigation at Cambridge and with access to the whole complex Ouse river system that ran through the Fens to the Wash, with the port of King's Lynn at its mouth.

The continent of Europe was deeply penetrated by a large number of navigable rivers, which were used as fully as was practicable. Professor Bautier, in his discussion of the complementarity of road and river in medieval France, has fascinatingly brought out how there was a general preference there for river transport where it was available, except for commodities of the highest value. Many roads therefore acted as feeders to river traffic. In France as well as the systems we have already noticed there was also an important Loire system in the west. In England, as well as the Ouse system, there was a Thames system with its head of navigation at Oxford. In the Empire, as well as the Rhine system of rivers, there was also an Elbe system, and a Danube system which ran out through central Europe into the Black Sea. As in France, the roads that joined the river systems were of particular importance. Nuremberg owed a great deal of her importance to her position at the junction of the roads from Würzburg and Bamberg on the Main with those from Donauwörth, Ingolstadt and Regensburg on the Danube, so linking the Rhine and Danube river systems and making a continuous route from the North Sea to the Black Sea. In Lombardy, the Po was the main artery, and many of the goods that crossed the Appenines or the Alps had been shipped up the Po from Venice and transferred to road transport at various points, most importantly at Piacenza. Venice was not at the mouth of the Po, but at that of the Brenta, which joined Padua directly to Venice. However, it was easy for river vessels to make the short coastal journey from the Venetian lagoon to one of the mouths of the Po.

Many of these river systems had a major port at the point at which it was sensible to transfer goods from sea-going vessels to river boats, like Hamburg on the Elbe, Torun on the Vistula, or Bordeaux and Libourne on the Garonne and Dordogne respectively, which came to be the key sea ports for shipping Gascon wines onwards to England or Flanders. Local authorities quite deliberately made improvements to make such transfers easier. At Bristol in England a new harbour was created in the 1240s by a mammoth excavation of the mouth of the River Frome where it flowed into the Avon below the town.[20] The complementarity between roads and river transport on the one hand, and sea transport on the other, and the changing balance between these is explored extensively in the conclusion (Chapter 8, pp. 395–408).

This sort of ready interlinking between sea-going ships, river boats, four-wheeled carts, two-wheeled carts and pack animals continued into the Early Modern period. Dr Frearson has found it in his work on corridors of communication in seventeenth-century England. Too often earlier English historians had emphasized river or coastal travel as an alternative to road travel, in competition with it. It now appears that in England, as elsewhere, they were complementary and intermeshed. Indeed such interlinking still survives into the modern world, where for example, there are integrated transport systems for containers between road, rail, river and sea, or where bus, passenger train and aeroplane services are seen as linked and complementary, rather than as competitors.

As a consequence of such a view, improvements were frequently made to both road and river at the same time. When the new bridge was built at Pont St Esprit from 1265 onwards, not only was the passage of river traffic on the Rhône catered for by a particularly large arch, but means of transferring from road to river were provided. Similarly road and river improvements went hand in hand at Warneton in Flanders where the main road from Ypres to Lille crossed the Lys. At the beginning of the fourteenth century the men of Ypres paid for paving to make the road fit for carts from Ypres to the count's bridge and his new *quais* at Warneton.[21] This was only one example of a long tradition of cooperation between cities and rulers in Flanders and Brabant for investment in the linked infrastructures of cart-roads and canals or canalized rivers.[22] In the same way, at the end of the fifteenth century, when the Emperor Maximilian I was involved with bridge-building at Linz, he was also involved at the same time with the adjacent harbour works on the Danube.[23]

At Pisa, for long the sea port at the mouth of the Arno, the wharves lay along the river between the bridges, for ease of interchange between sea and river and road transport. When Porto Pisano replaced Pisa itself as the sea port of Tuscany, the Pisans had a road built to Porto Pisano on an embankment wide enough for two large carts to pass. But a considerable quantity of goods came round to Pisa from Porto Pisano in sea-going barges 30 feet long and 8.25 feet wide. Such barges were not only used for grain that had been shipped great distances into Porto Pisano, but also for other bulky commodities, and for wine grown further south in the Maremma. At Pisa there were two customs houses, one downstream of the bridges, and one up, and two boat-building yards, one downstream and one up. Many goods continued upstream by water. It took barges six days to Signa, the head of navigation, 14 km (9 miles) downstream from Florence. The Arno itself formed the principal artery of Tuscany in so far as it was navigable. It was the preferred route for heavy goods, iron, wood, fish, wine, oil, salt and above all grain, so much needed to feed the population of the inland cities, as well as the raw materials to manufacture Tuscan fabrics, wool and cotton and silk, alum and dyestuffs, since Tuscan industry was almost entirely dependent on products which were not indigenous. Downstream came manufactured goods, particularly woollen cloth in the fourteenth century and damask, brocades and velvets in the fifteenth. On rivers, as on roads, transfer from one sort of transport to another was common. The largest size of barges, *piatte*, could be towed only as far as Empoli. Their cargoes were then transferred to *scafe*, half the size, which could be towed as far as Signa. Only very tiny boats, *noccoli*, a tenth of the size of *scafe*, could go further upstream. Most goods for Florence were in practice 'delivered to Signa'. The carriers registered the goods, for payment of *gabelle* to the commune, and left them on the wharf, or had them warehoused. There was a prodigious number of inns at Signa. It was the responsibility of the purchaser to see to it that the goods were brought by cart along the paved road into the city, and this was the case whether it was a private individual, a commercial firm, or even the city of Florence itself. The communal officials of the Abbondanza, responsible for feeding the city, bought wheat and salt and paid a price for it 'delivered to Signa'. Upstream of Signa the river was navigable only by the tiny *noccoli*, not merely because it was too shallow, but also because it was impeded by dozens of mills most of which also had their own fish weirs (*molendinum cum pischaria*). With a great deal of difficulty, and rather slowly (see above) a riverside road between Pisa and Florence was constructed along the south bank by the two communes. The utility of the river itself meant that this road was not as pressing a priority as those in other directions. The river of course risked drying up in summer and overflowing in spring, so that barges could not be towed, and at the same time the riverside road was flooded. There was a third route, longer, but more certain, that hugged the lower slopes of the Appenines, like the modern motorway running up from Pisa to Lucca, through Pistoia and Prato to Florence. This longer route, by the joint efforts of the communes in its path, was made fit for wagons much earlier than the riverside road on the south bank. The choice of what combination of road and river to use to get goods from Porto Pisano to inland Tuscany depended not only on the time of year, but on the value and bulk of the goods themselves and how quickly they were needed. Carriers and watermen were available on all routes inland from the sea. All set off from the same place, the bridges at Pisa and the wharves between them.

And naturally there was, at the same period, investment in harbour works on the coast as well as on rivers, to provide larger safe havens, as at Antwerp or Genoa,[24] or by management of the lagoon at Venice. Totally new harbours were also created and maintained, as at Sluys and Porto Pisano and even Hvar on the Dalmatian coast, where the Venetians constructed a main mole with an enclosed anchorage in the mid-fifteenth century.[25] Lighthouses were similarly erected and manned to guide shipping into harbours, as at Calais.

Local carriers and watermen

There seem to have been two sorts of carriers involved. There were the ordinary carriers and watermen from the communities along the main routes, each of which had local monopolies over particular stretches of road, river or lake. The development of these local carrying services was most important in enabling the expansion and transformation of trade in the thirteenth century. In addition there were a certain number of longer-distance carriers.

Quite a lot is known about local carriers in the fourteenth century because of disputes between different communities that have left legal records. In 1396, for example, there was a lawsuit between Prato and Faido on the St Gotthard pass route, and in 1380 another between Aosta and St Rhémy on the Great St Bernard route. When the Count of Savoy in 1380 granted the inhabitants of Aosta a monopoly of carrying services from Ivrea through Aosta to Saint Rhémy, the last 'town' on the south side of the Great St Bernard pass, the inhabitants of Saint Rhémy and its neighbour Etroubles instantly dis-

puted the legality of such a grant. They claimed that they already possessed an immemorial monopoly of carrying services from Ivrea upwards. Over the pass itself they shared the monopoly with the inhabitants of Bourg St Pierre, the first town on the north side of the pass. They claimed that 'their livelihoods depended on the carrying trade since, unlike the inhabitants of Aosta, they had no vines, meadows or fields, their natural soil being arid and mountainous terrain, which gave them no means of subsistence, and they would be compelled to emigrate if their monopoly was infringed'. They were essentially succeeful. Two hundred years later the inhabitants of Saint Rhémy still had the monopoly of carrying services from Aosta up to the pass.

In the fourteenth century the different groups of ordinary carriers can be picked out along the Simplon pass route, between France and Milan. Ordinary carriers of Sion, in the upper Rhône valley, carried goods upwards only as far as Leuk (Loèche) 26 kilometers (16 miles) away. Those of Leuk carried goods downwards as far as Sion, and upwards as far as Brig, 28 kilometers (17.5 miles) further on. Those of Brig carried goods downwards as far as Leuk and upwards for 32 kilometers (20 miles) over the pass to Simplon on its south side. The next stage on was at Domodossola another 32 kilometres (20 miles) down. These sections of road were known as *Longeria*, *Logeria* or *Logaria*. At Leuk, the carriers from Sion or Brig delivered the goods they were carrying to a *souste* outside the town. This was a public warehouse. A new *souste* was built in 1336, at the request of the Milanese merchants whose goods followed this route. They had bargained with the bishop of Sion for secure *soustes* to be built to protect their goods; for him to impose regulations to ensure that they were not ripped off by the *vectuarii* of the diocese; for the right to choose who unpacked and repacked their goods, not necessarily the local *ligator*, at Brig, where valley bottom transport changed to mountain pack animals; and for a say in the appointment of the chief weigher at Brig.

The emphasis of the new *souste* was on security. It was built entirely of stone, from foundations to roof, and had two strong gates, both closed with bolts and locks. It stood apart from other buildings and was big enough for

Road and river transport were truly complementary, as this printed ordinance of 1500 for Paris demonstrates. Both grain and wine reached Paris in barrels on the Seine, after being carried to the river by road from the places where they were grown (see pp. 99–103). In the woodcut, above left, a horse is bringing long barrels to a river bank to be transferred to the waiting boats, for transport to Paris. In the 1460s Bonozzo Gozzoli depicted camels to add a fantasy element, as befitting the journey of the Magi, to an otherwise realistic portrayal of a mule train (above right) plodding through the Apennines.

200 bales, mule-loads, of wool to be deposited and manoeuvered. When it was new, the commune of Leuk put it under the charge of a citizen of Milan who collected the *droit de souste*, three *oboles* (1.5 d.) per bale entrusted to his charge. Carriers of Leuk who were looking for loads had to be ready at prime to load up their mules or mule (they each seem to have had only one or two mules). The *paritor* appointed by the commune had to see that when there was not enough work for everybody, the loads were divided fairly among the carriers on a rotation system. Similar arrangements to share the work were made elsewhere on this route, and, also on other Alpine routes, *per roatem*, *per partitam*, *zu Teil*. At Vogogna, the next place below Domodossola, on the Simplon road, the division of work in 1374 was between *carratores*. Short-distance carriers, being bound to a locality, could be, and were, regulated and supervised by public authority, whether it was the bishop of Sion in the upper Rhône valley, or the Mercanzia in the Florentine *contado*. On the other hand they could also band together, in more or less powerful corporations, for joint action, like the Watermen of Paris or the associations of muleteers and watermen, 'Schiffer – und Säumer – genossenschaften' on the St Gotthard route.

Longer-distance carriers

Monopoly short-distance carriers had provided the normal carrying services that had so assisted the thirteenth-century expansion of trade and continued to do so for the remainder of the Middle Ages. However, alongside this arrangement to '*conducere merchanzias per ordinem*', whereby carriers from one privileged community handed on goods to those of the next, or next but one, there were in the fifteenth century an increasing number of carriers who took goods for longer distances. Such longer-distance carriers took goods the whole way from Sion to Domodossola, *four* ordinary stages, on the Simplon pass route; from Flüelen on Lake Luzern to Bellinzona over the St Gotthard pass on the route from the Rhineland to Milan; and from Chur to Chiavenna over the Splügen pass on the route from Nuremberg and Augsburg to Milan.

Beyond and behind these carriers there were, at the end of the fifteenth century, transport entrepreneurs who organized carrying services over even longer stretches of road. On the complex St Gotthard pass route one of the most active of these was a Genoese, Petrus Gambarus, who was based in Luzern from at least 1484 to 1510. He and his Genoese associates in Basel organized carrying services from Italy right through the Rhineland. Although the most active, Gambarus was not alone in Luzern. From at least 1493 to 1520 another Genoese, only known in Luzern as 'Stefan of Genoa', was also organizing overland transport from Genoa to Antwerp.[26]

Luzern was not the only place in which long-distance carriers were to be found. Salins, already noted for its salt, was another such place (above, pp. 156–57). As well as carrying the local salt both northwards across the Burgundian plain by cart and southwards across the Jura on mules, and bringing the wood to the salines, Salins carriers were also prepared to arrange the transport of other mens's goods both by mule over the mountains to Italy, and by cart far into France. Long-distance carriers were also to be found at Aosta, where the mountain road over the Great St Bernard came down to the valley floor and carts could be used again, at Asti and Chieri on the way down into Italy from the Mont Cenis pass, and in Hesse, south of Frankfurt where carriers were based by the end of the fifteenth century who covered the whole distance from southern Germany to Antwerp. After the road improvements of the thirteenth and fourteenth centuries the roads in large areas of what is now France could be traversed by carts of one sort or another. The only parts of France in which pack animals still dominated were the Jura, the Alps and the Pyrenees, although pack animals were also used extensively in the Massif Central (see Gascon map). At the end of the fifteenth century goods were brought to and from the fairs at Lyon by long-distance carters from as far away as Chatillon, Bar-sur-Seine, Troyes and Nogent on the Seine, as well as from Roanne on the Loire, by long-distance muleteers from Susa and Turin on the other side of the Mont Cenis pass; and by boatmen from Chalon, St-Jean-de-Losne, Auxonne and Gray on the Saône.

Carters and watermen worked together. The carters from Roanne carried goods collected from, or destined for, watermen on the Loire, just as those from Troyes and Nogent carried goods collected from or delivered to watermen on the Seine, and just as the watermen on the Saône carried goods collected from, or destined for the carters working on the roads across Burgundy.

Whilst a large part of France was country for carters, and goods could be carried relatively long distances without change in the means of transport, in northern Italy the difference in terrain meant that goods had more often to be transferred between carts and pack animals. By the fourteenth century gravelled (pack animal) roads in the mountains alternated frequently with paved (cart) roads in the newly drained valleys and plains.

A packhorse was expected to carry a *charge* of cloth, skins or mercery weighing four quintals or 400 pounds, (about 195 kg). A two-wheeled *charette*, drawn by two or three horses, could carry between three and four times that weight, whilst a four-wheeled wagon, a *currus sive car*, normally with six horses, could carry 1300–1500 kg. This means that the 2,500 pound harbour chain carried to Porto Pisano in 1299 was not exceptionally heavy, although it was a dramatic load (above, p. 183). The development of the mobile front axle improved carts still further. In France oxen do not seem to have been used for pulling long-distance wagons, except perhaps in the south west. The lighter two-wheeled cart was used over shorter distances, for carrying grain, single barrels of wine, and some building materials. The heavier four-wheeled wagon could normally carry three, or occasionally four, *queues* or *fûts* of the wines of Burgundy, each containing 365 modern litres; or thirteen to sixteen *charges* (each of around 100 kg) of salt from Salins; or fifty to one hundred rolls of woollen cloth; or a ton-and-a-half of newly quarried stone. When the roads had improved enough to take them, the heavier four-wheeled wagons were preferred for long-distance haulage. With iron-rimmed wheels and iron axles, and with so large a team of horses, and the harness for them, each

Loads, speeds and costs of carriage

wagon was an expensive investment for a carrier. A successful haulage business then, as now, needed a great deal of capital.

Where the roads had been improved enough to take the heavier four-wheeled *currus*, they were also good enough for specialized wagons for people, primitive coaches, to be developed. For women and children, the elderly and infirm they replaced single-person covered litters slung between horses. Illustrations sometimes show these primitive coaches as gigantic multi-passenger litters swinging from the framework of wagons that scarcely differed from those used by commercial carriers. Others were extremely luxurious. In the 1330s Edward III of England spent £1,000, the value of a herd of 1,600 oxen, on a carriage for his sister Eleanor, complete with carpets and cushions. In some parts of Europe they were much used, but their swinging motion was acutely uncomfortable for some travellers. In 1438 Pero Tafur crossed Brabant, and between 'sHertogenbosch and Mechelen observed:

> The people here are accustomed to travel in carts, but I could not suffer it, for I would far rather be at sea. I continued to ride, while my people followed in the carts.[31]

In the sixteenth century St Teresa and her nuns, when they travelled round Castile in such a covered wagon, also complained of the discomforts of inadequate suspension.

The normal distance travelled by any type of carrier in one day seems to have been in the region of 30 to 40 km. The stages for pack animals over the Simplon pass were a little more than 30 km apart. From Mergozzo on Lake Maggiore, up the Ossolo valley to Domodossola is just over 30 km, from Domodossola onwards up to the village of Simplon is 32 km, and from Simplon over the pass to the town of Brig in the upper Rhône valley is another 32 km. Further along the route north, heavy four-wheeled carts on the roads between Salins and Paris also covered 30 or 40 km a day, although the lighter, shorter-distance, two-wheeled carts seem only to have been capable of covering under 30 km a day. If moderately loaded packhorses were used on these easier roads between Salins and Paris, as they sometimes were for special loads, they were able to travel longer distances, over 40 km a day. Indeed a convoy of four men and six horses did the journey from Dijon to Paris in six days in January 1412, averaging 50 km a day. No doubt they travelled so exceptionally fast because they were carrying money. This was coming up to the speed of couriers (Chapter 1, pp. 27–8). The distances covered by non-commercial travellers were not very different from the normal speeds of carriers. Archbishop Eudes Rigaud and his retinue averaged 33 km (20 miles) a day between Paris and Dijon in 1254. In practice their day's journey varied in length between 20 and 45 km, but the archbishop was taking it slowly, visiting friends and acquaintances all along the way. It is remarkable how, despite using much more prestigious accommodation, so many of the stages of the archbishop's journey coincided neatly with the stages listed for more ordinary travellers a century-and-a-half later in the *Itinéraire de Bruges*. On the Paris–Dijon section the stages seem to be either

11–14 km, 22–27 km, or 33–35 km apart – one third, two-thirds, or a whole day's travel respectively for a carrier using large four-wheeled carts.

Transport was not cheap. Only the most expensive commodities were worth transporting by road. Professor Sapori found that when the del Bene company bought the finest French cloth at the Troyes Fairs in 1319 and had it carried back to Florence, the costs of transport, packing, tolls and insurance added an average of 16% to the initial costs, and in one case over 20%.[28] At the end of the thirteenth century the predominant form of transport between the Champagne fairs and Italy was still the pack animal. Road improvements made the use of the four-wheeled *char* possible on many French roads and this was very much cheaper. For the occasional packhorse journeys between Dijon and Paris, Professor Dubois has calculated a price of 4s 7d–6s 1d *tournois* per tonne per kilometre both in the 1390s and again in the 1440s, both periods of monetary stability, whilst that for carriage in a four-wheeled wagon was charged at 9d–1s 8d *tournois* per tonne per kilometre. The advantage of the wagon over the packhorse was evident. It was much cheaper, bulkier loads could be carried, and it was not much slower. However, its use did depend on adequate roads, and the road revolution in France, beginning with bridge-building, was accomplished in the fourteenth century. It transformed much of France from a land fit only for packhorses to a land in which the major roads could take four-wheeled wagons.[29]

However, where rivers suitable for the transport of goods existed, they were even cheaper to use. Professor Dubois has been able to put together some late fourteenth-century charges for the transport of wine and grain from Chalon by the Saône and Rhône to Avignon and of wine from Cravant by the Yonne and the Seine to Paris. By converting those charges into *deniers* per tonne per kilometre he has calculated that watermen charged around one seventh of the sum that wagoners charged for taking the same goods on the

What better way to show how important a relic was in the early thirteenth century than to put it in a reliquary of rock crystal and gold in the form of a coach, when such a coach was the very latest, and prodigiously expensive, way of carrying about the most exalted people At that date the road from Paris to Orléans, where this reliquary is to be found in the church of St-Aignan, had recently been made fit for royalty to travel in primitive coaches.

parallel journey by riverside roads. English evidence, from charges to sheriffs made for carrying goods they had purveyed for the crown between 1296 and 1352, suggests that under such circumstances English wagoners charged slightly less than French, whilst English bargemen, operating smaller barges on smaller rivers, charged around double their French counterparts. The saving to be made by using barges, rather than wagons, for as much of a journey as possible, was still enormous, even if much smaller than in France. In England a yet bigger saving was to be made by using coastal vessels, rather than either wagons or barges. The advantage of using a combination of river with road wherever possible, rather than road alone, was very striking and often made it worthwhile to take a longer, slower, route using the maximum length of river and the minimum of road, rather than a more direct route by road alone.[30]

In view of the comparative cheapness of river-borne traffic, it is not surprising that, as well as road improvements, there were also river improvements, which were particularly cost-effective. For example, the woollen cloth-producing town of Zoutleeuw in Brabant, which owed its prosperity to its position on the new late twelfth-century main road from Bruges in Flanders to Cologne in the Rhineland, deliberately increased its potential in the thirteenth century by making the tiny river Gete navigable, so that water-borne traffic could come and go to Antwerp and the sea.

On a much larger scale, the citizens of St Omer, Ypres and Bruges in the twelfth century organized the cutting of channels suitable to bring vessels inland from the new coastal towns of Gravelines, Nieuwpoort and Damme respectively.

The Gravelines–St Omer canal was the biggest of these, and could take sea-going boats of up to six hundred tons. The amount that such canals were used may be gathered from a stray account covering 122 days in the winter of 1296–97, which shows that 3,250 barges and 87 larger vessels then paid toll on arrival at Ypres from Nieuwpoort. An even larger canal than any of these was the Lieve canal built in 1259 by the city of Ghent to join it to the already canalized Zwin at Damme, so giving it water access to the expanding Bruges market. Even more than roads, canals demanded continuous and expensive maintenance, particularly dredging and the upkeep of retaining dikes. The costs generally greatly exceeded the revenues from tolls, and even cities of the stature of Bruges and Ghent felt the strain of keeping up their canals.[31] Even larger than any of the Flemish waterways was the canal cut from the Elbe to Lübeck. The arrival of the first boats in Lübeck in 1398, after eight years of work, was greeted with great public rejoicing and festivity.

For bulky commodities, even relatively cheap transportation by river could still add appreciably to their cost. In 1284 a *staio* of salt imported into Pisa cost 3 li. 10s. *piccioli* of Florence there. However, the six-day barge journey on the Arno to Signa, plus the short road journey into Florence cost a further *lira*, adding over 28% to the cost of salt by the time it reached Florence. To have taken commodities like salt and grain the whole distance by road would have made them prohibitively expensive on arrival. There were

Drawing on his experience of grand inns in the southern Netherlands, the miniaturist shows travellers arriving at an inn, recognisable as such by the bush outside. Inside, two of its multi-bedded rooms are the mise en scène of one of the stories told at the court of Philip the Good and collected as the Cent Nouvelles Nouvelles *(This is an English fifteenth-century illustration of it.) The naked men getting into bed with the women are not their husbands, who are safely asleep in the right-hand room. Many large beds to a room was normal provision in inns. Privacy was provided by bed curtains, which are here pulled back and sketched in very slightly for the sake of showing off the characters in the story.*

indeed clear limits on the sorts of commodity that it was worth carrying by different means of transport. High quality Italian or Castilian white soap for example, was probably the cheapest commodity, by weight, that it was worth transporting across the Alps from Venice to Nuremberg at the end of the fourteenth century.[32]

Inns

The complexity of frequently changing means of transport and of paying all the tolls for road, bridge and river maintenance demanded organization. Where they existed long-distance carriers saw to all this for their merchant clients, but more often it was innkeepers who took this responsibility, as well as providing warehousing at crucial points on the journey.

The number and importance of the inns at Salins, as at Brig or Libourne (see above) tied in with the carriers, for at all these places the means of transport changed and it was at the inns that the goods were unpacked and repacked in an appropriate form for the next means of transport.

Inns were as essential as carriers and watermen to the flow of goods along the road and river routes of Europe, and were intimately connected with them. Innkeepers were vital to the arrangements that merchants made for sending goods from place to place. Pegolotti brought out the importance of innkeepers when he made a note of the costs of transporting wool from England to Florence. This passage seems to be one of the later entries in his notebook and can be dated to around 1336. The wool was sent by the London

Inns, as well as providing accommodation for people and their animals, also offered them food and drink. This waiter at a south German inn, bringing a jug of wine to the guests, appears on a fifteenth-century playing card.

branch of the Bardi to a known innkeeper at Libourne on the Dordogne in returning Gascon wine boats. It was packed in gigantic English cart-size wool sacks, each containing wool from the shorn fleeces of around 200 sheep and was accompanied by a 'swain' from London, who handed over responsibility at Libourne to the innkeeper. After the wool had been carried from the ship to the inn, the innkeeper had it weighed and stored it for the time being, stacked in piles at his inn. He had each of the gigantic sacks broken down into two bales suitable to load onto pack animals, including even purchasing the necessary ropes for the bales. He then arranged for and paid a carrier to take the wool to an inn at Montpellier. The innkeeper at Montpellier took it in and arranged for, and paid, another carrier to take it on to another inn at Aigues Mortes. The innkeeper at Aigues Mortes kept it until there was a galley ready to go to Porto Pisano in Tuscany. As soon as a galley was available he organized and paid porters and small boats to take the wool out to it.[33] The Bardi needed to correspond only with the innkeepers, whom they paid for storage and service and reimbursed for their expenses.

Inns therefore provided far more than simply lodging and food for those travelling and stalling for their horses. Except in the few places where there were locked public warehouses, *soustes*, it was inns that provided the safe overnight storage for goods, and, as the Pegolotti example shows, at places where the means of transport changed, like Libourne and Aigues Mortes, Salins and Signa (above, pp. 156–7 and p. 195), they might provide for storage for much longer periods of time, until ships, river boats, carts or pack animals were available to take the goods onwards. They then had them appropriately repacked for the journey onwards, and coped with paying toll collectors and officials like weighers, and with organizing carriers and watermen and paying them.

It was patently necessary to have a great deal of capital to run such an inn: innkeepers on this scale had to be wealthy to begin with, and became wealthier still. They came from a wide range of backgrounds. Priests, notaries and even nobles went into innkeeping in France as well as men who had already been successful in a variety of trades.[34] In Bruges innkeepers came from some of the wealthiest patrician families in the city, like the van de Buerze family, which gave its name to the Exchange. Inns, of course, came in many sizes, and not all of them could provide the whole range of facilities that merchants might need.

Different customers were treated differently, and the accommodation provided varied according to social status. One of the salacious mid-fifteenth-century stories in the Burgundian *Cent Nouvelles Nouvelles* makes it clear that even noble customers would not get a room to themselves, although they would probably have a bed to themselves. The only element of privacy was that women might have their beds in a different chamber from men, and that superior beds would be curtained. Poorer travellers had to sleep several to a bed with total strangers. In 1385, an inn at Arezzo which had four beds and a mattress put up 180 overnight guests in nineteen days. On the busiest night the four beds were shared by fifteen travellers. It was hardly surprising that they were also frequently shared by bed bugs as well. Paumgartner of Nuremberg said of Italian inns that all the beds were full of bugs: '*alle bett voller wantzen seind*'. There were clearly as many qualities of inn in late medieval Europe as there are modern hotels.

In some places there were great concentrations of inns. Naturally, large numbers of inns were to be found in all the places to which merchants and their agents came in large numbers, even more than at the places at which the means of transport changed. National capitals, international fair towns, international trading cities and regional centres of consumption were the most obvious such places. Paris had a huge number of inns, 4,000 according to one exaggerated early fifteenth-century estimate, so did London, and so did Tours later in the fifteenth century, when the kings of France were living in the Loire valley. In their heyday the Champagne fair towns had had large numbers of inns, a few of which still survive, and so did the towns where successor fairs were held: Antwerp and Bergen-op-Zoom, Frankfurt, and the succession of Chalon, Geneva and Lyon. The more temporary the selling place the more likely the merchants and their agents would stay in inns, or even, if necessary, camp in tents outside the fair town, as happened at thirteenth-century Troyes. The more permanent the selling place the more likely that merchants and their agents would acquire premises of their own. Tommaso Portinari, for example, rented the whole of the huge Bladelin house in Bruges as offices, warehousing and residential accommodation for the Bruges company in the Medici group. This was unusual. At Bruges, visiting merchants normally used the inns.

Innkeepers were expected, in fourteenth-century Bruges, to see that their guests complied with local regulations. They also functioned as brokers, introducing buyers to sellers, foreigners who were lodging with them to

Around 1430 Robert Campin, then running a workshop in Tournai, placed this small isolated roadside inn on a hillside into the background of his 'Adoration of the Shepherds', now in Dijon. Such small inns were to be found on roadsides everywhere in western Europe. They had stabling (on the right), a tavern room (on the left), and one large bedchamber with several beds (upstairs), which the innkeeper's family shared with the guests.

natives or even to other foreigners. Inkeepers in Bruges had to be freemen of the city (*poorters*) and consequently members of a guild. Innkeepers and brokers had a common guild, that of *hosteliers en makelaars*.

One of the key introductory functions of innkeepers in Bruges was to link visiting merchants in to the local network of moneychanger bankers.[35] Professor James Murray has recently shown how closely bankers and inn-keepers worked together. Innkeepers naturally had accounts with the local bankers. From the surviving ledgers of one moneychanger banker in Bruges, Colard de Marke, between April 1366 and December 1369, it is apparent that sixty-eight of the Bruges innkeepers had accounts with him, besides a handful of innkeepers in other cities. Colard de Marke was only one of fifteen authorized bankers in the city, and far from the largest of them. In the other direction, bankers put up some of the large capital needed to run an inn. Colard de Marke invested in the businesses of two, or possibly three, of his innkeeper customers. Three of the fifteen moneychanger bankers actually ran inns themselves. This sort of close interrelationship with bankers made it possible for innkeepers to stand surety for their guests, exchange coins for them, accept coin on deposit, and arrange for them to be able to make pay-ments through book transfer. Book transfer, of course, extended to clients of any of the banks, for banks within the city had accounts with each other. Colard de Marke and Willem Ruweel, one of the other Bruges bankers, trans-ferred money between each other's accounts 152 times in the year from October 1367 to October 1368, effectively on every other working day. In addition Bruges bankers kept reciprocal accounts with some moneychanger bankers in other cities in the Low Countries. Colard de Marke had such accounts with changers in Ghent, Antwerp, Tournai, Douai, Valenciennes and Mons. He also transferred money by bill of exchange to London and Paris. Coin was constantly being carried back and forth between inns and banks, so that foreign guests could have whatever coin they wanted when they needed it. No individual innkeeper could hold the range of coin that a banker like Colard de Marke carried. When the German merchants who imported considerable quantities of bullion to Bruges had to send it to the Flemish mint to be coined, they did so by way of their innkeepers, who in turn passed it on to their own bankers. Colard de Marke then sent bullion that had come to him to the mint in Ghent, using a Ghent innkeeper as his intermediary.

Innkeepers in Bruges frequently specialized in taking in merchants of a particular nationality, and naturally had regular customers. Jakop van le Fine, for example, one of Colard de Marke's innkeeper customers, specialized in hosting Spanish and Portuguese merchants. In the mid-fourteenth century, the Bruges schoolmaster teaching French to his Flemish pupils, had them learn to say how Oliver, his innkeeper, specialized in taking in '*les Alemans qu'on nomme Oesterlincs*', in other words, Hanseatic merchants, but did not take in other nationalities like Lombards, Genoese, Florentines or Lucchese. The Celys, London wool exporters, regularly used the same inns in Calais and Bruges in the fifteenth century.

In these cities, to which merchants came in large numbers, inns often clustered together. Professor Wolff has plotted the whereabouts of some seventy inns in mid-fifteenth-century Toulouse, which was the administrative centre for the whole of the Languedoc and the greatest regional commercial centre in south-western France. It was then still a city of some 25,000 inhabitants, even after so many waves of plague. Fifty of these seventy inns were concentrated in four places, particularly by the two bridges over the Garonne. In Montpellier, the inns were concentrated in three places, particularly by the two principal gates; at Aix in two places, particularly by the gate for Marseille;[36] in Siena, they clustered in Camollia, near the northern gate where the Francigena came into the city; and in Avignon they were concentrated in two places, particularly along the road inside the gate giving out on to the famous bridge across the Rhône.

Suitable facilities of various sorts for travellers were frequently to be found close by these large groups of inns. At Avignon we know that one of the principal 'stews', Turkish baths, was in the same street as all the inns by the bridge. At Lille we know that the red light district was close to the largest group of inns. In Southwark – the town which grew up at the south end of the bridge across the Thames into London where the main route came in from Canterbury, Sandwich and the short Channel crossing from the continent – all three (inns, bathhouses and brothels) were found concentrated together, close by the Bishop of Winchester's magnificent London palace.[37] Inns were also found strung out in the places through which merchants and their goods passed, not merely at their ends, and at the nodal points where one form of transport was changed for another. Accommodation was needed at a distance of a day's journey. In the Florentine *contado*, a ring of inns was to be found in the mid-fourteenth century in all the small towns a day's journey out from Florence, for example at Scarperia on the main road across the Appenines to Bologna, or at Figline on the main road up the Arno valley to Arezzo. The only major concentrations of inns in the Florentine *contado* less than a full day's journey from Florence were at Signa where the river barges docked, and at San Casciano on the road south to Siena and Rome, which was the point where the cart road from the city gave out and goods had to be transferred from carts to pack animals before going on. Inns with their warehousing were patently needed there.

As well as overnight accommodation a day's journey apart, men and beasts needed feeding between. The stages along the roads of late fourteenth-century Europe set out in the *Itinéraire de Bruges* are thus at intervals of one third of a day's journey, some 11 to 14 km (7–9 miles) apart. This fits conveniently with the normal distance between market towns in the more densely settled parts of Europe, but in the less densely settled parts of Europe there were tiny settlements along the main roads that barely seemed to exist apart from their inns, like those strung out along the road through Apulia to the ports of Bari and Brindisi. They survived on lodging and feeding travellers. On the Simplon pass route there were also intervening stopping, or feeding, points between each of the stages with *soustes* I have picked out on p. 197. Fifteenth-century notes of advice for travellers across the Alps to Venice comment that these were *viel gudt herbergen* on the Brenner route, and travel advice from Venice in 1492 picked out specific inns as worth staying in, like the great roomy 'Krone' in the tiny village of Sterzing just below the pass itself.[38]

Sterzing was indeed one of the places that lived on the passing trade, and such places were frequently to be found a little way down on either side of a pass, like Les Clées and Pontarlier on the Jougne, or St Rhémy and Bourg St Pierre on either side of the Great St Bernard.

The innkeepers at St Rhémy and Bourg St Pierre not only arranged for the *marroniers* who were essential for guiding groups of travellers over the pass, but also had numbers of mules ready to rent out in bad weather to travellers on horseback, whilst their own less sure-footed horses were led over the pass. We learn this from the account of a traveller who crossed the pass in 1486, in conditions he considered atrocious, late in February.

Hospices

On the passes themselves charitable hospices were to be found rather than commercial inns, but merchants and carriers did not normally stay in them – although they were very glad to do so when conditions were bad.

Hospices or hospitals were essentially charitable and catered for poor and benighted travellers and, above all, for pilgrims. Some *hospits* or *hospitalia* did, of course, care for the sick, but the same words were also used for the much more numerous houses which took in travellers.

The author of the guide for pilgrims to Compostela of 1139 wrote that 'Hospices have been set up where they were necessary; they are sacred places, houses of God to give comfort to holy pilgrims, to give rest to the poor and consolation to the sick…'. The guide was here specifically describing three great pilgrim hospices of the twelfth century. 'Three columns necessary above all for the support of his poor, have been established by God in this world': the hospice of St Christine on the Somport pass on the way to Compostela, the hospice of St Bernard on the way to Rome and Jerusalem, and the hospice of St John in Jerusalem itself.[39]

Endowed early in the fourteenth century by Sancho VII, King of Navarre, the canons of Roncesvalles maintained a spacious hospice (below left) high up on the south side of the Ibañeta pass, for pilgrims (below right) on the road to Santiago de Compostela. They also put up non-pilgrim travellers on the most important commercial road through the western Pyrenees from France to Spain. This relief is from Pistoia Cathedral, whose bishop had acquired part of St James's body.

Was the author perhaps exaggerating the importance of his own pilgrim route in placing the hospice on the Somport pass alongside the other two? The Somport pass through the Pyrenees had been important when Jaca, on the river Aragón, to which it led, had been the primitive centre for the young kingdom of Aragon. As Aragon grew, and incorporated Barcelona and the county of Catalonia, Jaca lost its importance and so did the Somport pass. It is not even mentioned in the *Itinéraire de Bruges*. By then the pilgrim route for Compostela ran through the Pyrenees further west, at Roncesvalles, where there was also a hospice .

It was an expensive undertaking to go on one of the great pilgrimages, to the shrine of St James in Compestella, to the tombs of the apostles in Rome, or, most expensive of all, to the holy places in Jerusalem, and, even beyond Jerusalem, to Mount Sinai.[40] There were of course numerous lesser shrines throughout Christendom that drew pilgrims, like the tomb of Thomas Becket at Canterbury in England, the shrine of Our Lady at Hal in Hainault, that of the Three Kings at Cologne, the supposed tombs of Mary Magdalene and of Lazarus at Vézelay and Autun in Burgundy, or the shrine of St Nicholas at Bari in the Regno. These generally drew pilgrims from much

Soon after the St Gotthard pass was opened in the 1220s for traffic from Milan to the Rhineland (see pp. 187–8), a hospice was built near the summit for the use of travellers. When this print was made around 1800, it was quite correct to show goods being carried on mules, since the pass was still not usable by wheeled vehicles.

shorter distances and were therefore less expensive as pilgrimages. Nevertheless, the *Itinéraire de Bruges*, alongside its commercial routes, not only gives pilgrimage routes from Bruges to Compostela, Rome and Jerusalem, but also to St Nicholas of Varangeville in Lorraine, to the Marian shrines at Rocamadour and Le Puy on the edge of the Massif Central of France, to La Sainte Baume in Provence, and even to St Nicholas at Bari.

Pilgrimage could, of course, be not merely an act of voluntary devotion, but also be imposed as an ecclesiastical penance for sin, or even as secular penalty for crime. In such cases the distance required was strangely not graded according to the severity of the sin or crime.[41] The distance to be travelled determined not only the time to be spent in expiation, but also the expense. Despite the existence of hospices, travelling was expensive. Pilgrims had frequently to pay for their food and their lodging, and for putting up their horses and servants if they had them, at ordinary commercial inns along the way. A late fifteenth-century guide for south German pilgrims to Compostela gave details of both hospices and inns along the way, with comments on the innkeepers and whether their prices were reasonable, as well as the costs of using bridges and when to change currency.[42] Even the allegorical pilgrim in Baudouin de Condé's poem carried with him not only the pilgrim's famous staff and scrip, but also a good cape, hat and shoes 'and money of which I had need'.[43] The sometimes astonishingly large sums of money which pilgrims to Rome had with them in the 1400 Jubilee year were revealed when they sickened of the plague at Siena on the way, and had to be admitted to the great Hospital of Santa Maria della Scala, and deposited their property with one of the clergy.[44]

Hospices on pilgrimage routes, like inns everywhere, had to be able to cater for pilgrims, and indeed other travellers, of all ranks and stations in life, according to their status. When an emperor or a pope passed that way, he and his suite put up at the hospice on the Great St Bernard, as Napoleon did many centuries later. Such visitors were exceptionally grand and occasional, but they were not alone in giving generously to hospices. Groups of men who had been on the same pilgrimage formed confraternities like the Jerusalem brotherhood at Haarlem, which also acted as channels of giving to hospices on the way to the shrine of their patron.

The cumulative effect of large and small gifts over many years was that the Hospitallers of the hospital of St John of Jerusalem came to own extensive estates all over western Europe, particularly after the majority of the lands of the dissolved order of the Templars was given to them.

The canons of St Bernard were only poor in comparison with the Hospitallers of St John. By any other standard the hospital of St Bernard, and its vast chain of associated hospices, was very well endowed. They came to own considerable estates along the roads northwards and westwards from the pass as far as Metz and Rheims, and along those southwards and eastwards from the pass as far as Turin and Novara, besides outlying lands in England, Apulia and Sicily. By the second half of the fifteenth century there were no fewer than twenty-nine associated hospices, mainly close to hand in the dio-

The St Gotthard pass over the Alps acquired its name from the church there dedicated to the saint, a reforming and philanthropic eleventh-century bishop of Hildesheim.

ceses of Sion, Lausanne and Geneva to the north of the pass and in those of Aosta and Turin to the south.[45]

The principal hospice, on the Great St Bernard pass itself, was founded around 1050 by Bernard, Archdeacon of Aosta. He made his reputation as a charismatic itinerant preacher in north Italy in the dioceses of Aosta, Novara and Pavia. He also founded the hospice on the Little St Bernard at about the same time, although the two remained separate until 1466. Like Anselm, the famous theologian, who became Archbishop of Canterbury, and was also canonized, Bernard was himself part of the extended princely family descended from the kings of Arles that was already deeply entrenched in the western Alps as counts of Savoy and viscounts of Aosta. After his death he became known as St Bernard of Mont Joux, after the mountain above the hospice. The hospice itself was originally known as the hospice of Mont Joux, but was already being called *Bernardshospits* by 1154. Its early endowments came principally from his relations, and included the old monastery at Bourg-St-Pierre north of the pass, and its possessions, which had been appropriated to their own use by the counts of Aosta in the tenth century after the Saracens had been driven out. Bernard's new hospice was the successor to an earlier hospice, run from the old monastery. He constructed it in part with stone from a Roman temple to Jupiter. It was run by men called initially merely 'clerks' or 'brothers', but from the end of the twelfth century known as canons, and following the Augustinian rule. By the time that the whole network of hospices had been set up it had become a small order of canons. Its head was a provost and beneath him were ten priors at the most important hospices, including that on the pass itself. The prior at the hospice in the pass was deputy head of the order. As well as the counts of Savoy and Aosta, benefactors included emperors, counts of Champagne, one of whom gave half the toll (*péage*) on linens at the Provins fairs, a king of England, and many nobles and other laymen, bishops of Aosta and other clergy. Most of the gifts came in the twelfth century, but they were never enough to maintain the whole network of hospices. Inns, properly run, made good profits and their owners became rich. Hospices, even when properly run, were always in financial difficulties. Consequently, like the confraternities which ran bridges, such as that at Pont St Esprit, and indeed many other ecclesiastical bodies, the canons had to send out *quêteurs* on begging expeditions or 'quests' to raise extra funds. These begging expeditions went out backed with papal approval. For example in 1225 a papal bull addressed to the Archbishop of Sens and his suffragans (who included the Bishop of Paris), offered indulgences to those who gave financial aid to the *quêteurs*.

As well as the buildings, which demanded a huge amount of upkeep, particularly those in exposed situations, on the Great St Bernard itself, and on the Jougne pass, the order supported *maronniers*. They guided travellers without payment – unlike those attached to the inns at St Rhémy, who had to be paid fees – acted as a rescue service and provided fixed ropes to aid travellers on the steepest parts. The *maronniers* also took a share in keeping up the road itself, together with the counts of Savoy, the innkeepers of St Rhémy,

Pilgrims were fed, and given beds, on the way to their destination. This fourteenth-century wall-painting of a pilgrim meal comes from the cathedral at Lérida, which lay on the road from Barcelona to Santiago de Compostela. One of the pilgrims has the cockleshell of St James on her hat.

and the entirely independent hospice of Saint Job at Fotiates. The hospice, between St Rhémy and the summit, besides giving every traveller a ration of bread and wine, also looked after '*les perches*', the sign posts which showed the traveller the direction to follow. The St Bernard network of hospices was open to help all travellers, including even merchants and carriers, even though their specific function was to aid pilgrim travellers, whether rich or poor.[46]

There were also hospices at the tops of the passes on the main alternative routes to and from Italy. The hospice on the Mont Cenis pass had also been refounded in the eleventh century and richly endowed by the counts of Savoy. The new passes of the thirteenth century, the St Gotthard and the Simplon, also acquired hospices soon after they were opened.[47] (illustration p. 209) By the end of the thirteenth century popes and other ecclesiastical travellers, as well as merchants, preferred the Simplon. However, at a later date pilgrims, as well as such trade as still went over the western Alps, reverted to the Great St Bernard. It was particularly busy with Rome-bound pilgrims in the years of papal jubilee in the fifteenth century.

Hospice-founding continued into the fourteenth century. The Arlberg pass, an east–west pass, linking the head of the Inn valley with a side valley running down to the upper Rhine below Chur, was relatively unimportant both for pilgrims and for long-distance trade. Consequently it did not acquire a hospice in either the eleventh century or the thirteenth. However it did have considerable local significance, particularly in joining the extreme west of Austria, the Vorarlberg, with the rest of the country. Fourteenth-century Austrians complained that the settlements on either side of the pass were so far apart that men became lost in snow, storm and cloud and perished. Eventually Heinrich Findelkind, with the active support of Duke Leopold of Austria, founded a brotherhood to set up and run a hospice, with a chapel dedicated to St Christopher. The foundation stone was laid on 24 June 1386 and *quêteurs* were sent out not only into Austria, but other parts of the Empire too, and into Italy, Hungary and Poland as well, to solicit gifts, including relics for the chapel. Donors had their names inscribed in the book of brotherhood, to be prayed for, and, by the end of the fifteenth century, four thousand donors had been so inscribed.

There was another large, well endowed hospice, not mentioned in the Compostela guide, at Altopascio in Tuscany, south-east of Lucca, on the via Francigena, the 'French Road' through Italy from the Alpine passes to Rome. It was the largest and most successful of the many hospices along this 'road'. By 1192 there were already fifty or so pilgrim hospices along the road or in Rome itself. Eventually there were 23 hospices run by canons in the Val d'Elsa alone, between the river crossing of the Arno and Siena.[48] The via Francigena left Lucca by the Porta San Gervasio, the new east gate in the walls of 1260. It then swung south eastwards across the low-lying, but tolerably firm, ground between the lakes and marshes of Bientina and Fucecchio before entering the desolate forest of Le Cerbaie. Even in the eighteenth century it was described as

…the vast forest called Cerbaia [where] the thick trees made it dark even at mid-day, and the narrow winding roads within it became a labyrinth in which many travellers often lost their way and ended up dead, and often too they were robbed and murdered by thieves.

Today much of the area is still forest. The soil is too thin and too poor to support anything else. On the northern edge of the forest, from the eleventh century until the fourteenth, there was at Altopascio the famous fortified hospice of San Jacopo. Unlike most hospices on the Francigena, which were run by canons, the Altopascio hospice was maintained by a mixed order of clergy and laymen, the brethren and knights of Altopascio. They not only provided food and lodging to those on the road, particularly to pilgrims bound for the holy places, but also maintained the road itself, and its bridges, and defended travellers from the bandits of the forest. Like the canons of St Bernard, the order of Altopascio acquired dependent houses and vast lands, which also stretched from north-west to south-east, from England and Flanders to Sicily, strung out along the great central highway of Europe in the central Middle Ages. Altopascio also acquired scattered lands in Germany and Spain and closer to hand in Piedmont and Istria. Pilgrims going to Rome by land from all these places naturally passed through Altopascio. It remained active well into the fourteenth century. In the middle of the century Boccaccio featured the vast cooking cauldron of Altopascio in one of the stories in his *Decameron*. However at the end of the century it was sacked and burned down by Pisan soldiery. Today the remains of the three courtyards and two of the great gates of the medieval fortified hospice can still be seen, entangled with the town hall and parish church of the modern town of Altopascio. The romanesque chapel provides two transepts for the present nineteenth-century church, with the thirteenth-century bell-tower beside it. In the bell-tower hangs the bell called 'La Smarita' (the lost one) which, when the hospice was still active, was rung for an hour every night, between one and two hours after sunset 'so that those who were lost in the forest could save themselves by following the sound of the bell' and 'could be sure to find haven and spend the night with tranquility, safe from assassins and creatures of the wild'.[49]

Unfortunately the success of these hospices in accumulating endowments made them, like other ecclesiastical institutions, vulnerable in the fifteenth century to secular depredation. In 1459 Francis, the eleven-year-old son of the Duke of Savoy, was appointed by Pope Pius II as provost of the order of St Bernard, *in commendam*, and enjoyed its revenues, including even the gifts collected by the *quêteurs*! Since this was his first benefice he became known as 'Monsieur de Mont Joux'. Successive popes gave him other benefices, to keep in with the Savoys, and he gradually accumulated two priories, four abbacies, the bishopric of Geneva and the archbishopric of Auch. He was succeeded in turn by two great-nephews, when they were three and four years old respectively.[50]

In some places late medieval roads continued to follow their Roman precursors. This outcrop of the Appenines meant that at Terracina the late medieval road from Rome to Naples had to take the same line as the Roman Via Appia and run in a very narrow passage between the mountains and the Gulf of Gaeta (right). In this illustration from Braun and Hogenberg's Civitate Orbis Terrarum (Antwerp, 1515) travellers are leaving an inn there (marked G) in the Naples direction. Gaeta, a useful port as well as a centre of soap-making, lay a day's journey ahead of them.

The lands of Altopascio were similarly covetable, and various Florentines tried to get their hands on them before they were finally taken over by members of the Capponi family in the fifteenth century.[51] The combination of burning by Pisan soldiery and secularisation by the Capponi destroyed the order of Altopascio for ever. The order of St Bernard, however, survived the depredations of members of the house of Savoy in the fifteenth century and the early sixteenth. More surprisingly still it was one of the very few ecclesiatical institutions in the lands conquered by Napoleon not to be dissolved by him in conformity with the tenets of the French Revolution. On the contrary, having brought an army over the pass, and understood its utility, he increased its endowments. The order survives to this day, operating a mountain rescue service, and indeed training other mountain rescue teams.

As well as these great and famous hospices there were very many tiny hospices to be found along the roads of medieval Europe. Such *hospitalia* were very numerous by the mid-fourteenth century. Professor de la Roncière has uncovered evidence for the existence of no fewer that 136 in the Florentine *contado* alone, excluding Florence itself, by the 1370s. The oldest of them went back to the eleventh century at least. Only two of these were hospitals for the sick, the remainder were for the poor. Some only offered food, but most offered accommodation, particularly for the poor or benighted traveller, although most of them were very small with only a few beds. A quarter of them clustered around the city, to receive those travelling in to it, but the largest number, over half, were a day's walk from it, many of them strung out along the *strade maestre*. They were thus often established in exactly the same places as inns. There were, for example, seven *hospitalia* at Figline, a day's walk from the city on the road up the Arno valley to Arezzo, just as there were numerous inns there. There were five *hospitalia* at Poggibonsi, a long day's walk from the city towards Siena, and three at Empoli, a day's walk towards Pisa. Quite often they were established at places of difficulty, or potential difficulty, along the road, at passes, or above all at bridges. At Peretola where the main roads to Prato and Pistoia divided, the hospice was on the bridge and both were run by a single confraternity.[52] Like a gift to a bridge, a gift to a hospice was a charitable work. A hospice demanded an endowment. Often the initial endowment for its foundation was provided by a gift of lands by a great patrician family or an existing religious community. However, in the Florentine *contado*, the endowments were increased by innumerable small bequests from very ordinary people. The general legacies in twelfth- and thirteenth-century Genoese wills also linked hospices with bridges, as well as with churches and the poor.[53]

However, apart from exceptional places like the Great St Bernard and Altopascio, and not always even there, travelling merchants and the carriers who conveyed merchandise were not put up in these *hospitalia*, but in commercial inns. At the height of the medieval population rise in the early fourteenth century, there were many vainly seeking work in the great cities of Europe, where even those in work were generally impoverished, being paid low wages at a time of high prices. There was much need for *hospitalia* for the poor.

Something that concerned pilgrims, merchants and carriers alike was safety on the road. All over Europe the main roads had to pass through forested places like the Cerbaia, which provided all too good shelter for robbers. In a great many places the forests were a very real danger to travellers and their goods. Pickings were of course particularly good for bands of robbers in the vicinity of capital cities, and we have already noticed the unsuccessful attempts made by the kings of France to eradicate them in both the late Middle Ages and the Early Modern period. The armed knights of Altapascio were not the only providers of security along the way.

Paris was not alone as a capital city in being ringed by wild country in which gangs of thieves abounded. Travellers on the road out of London to Canterbury had to pass through the empty heathlands above Greenwich. While they were crossing Blackheath, or as they lumbered up Shooter's Hill, they were liable to be set upon. Similarly the Great North Road from London was not safe beyond Potters Bar and Barnet.

The main road from Naples into Apulia passed through badly guarded forests, and in the fourteenth century the ancient road through Terracina to Rome was virtually abandoned because of brigandage, and communication

Brigands and robbers

between the two capitals continued largely by sea until the second half of the fifteenth century.[54]

Outside Rome, on the main road north, no less a person than Anthony Woodville, the brother of the English queen, was set upon in 1476, and robbed of jewels and plate worth 1,000 marks. His party contained an earl, a baron, a knight, four esquires and a king of arms, with the appropriate number of servants, which must have been very large.[55] Such a party was not unable to defend itself. Merchants, by comparison, were relatively defence-less, so the forest belts through which they had to travel must have represented terrifying risks to them. The efforts of the knights of Altopascio to provide for the security of those passing through the Cerbaia were only unusual in having a charitable basis. Elsewhere cities and princes took upon themselves the protection of travellers and their goods with more or less success. Cities with large merchant communities of their own had a very strong motivation to make roads secure for trade.

There was, for example, known and constant danger on the roads through the wooded Appenines. As well as the most common westerly route over the Cisa pass, there were a number of other passes in the central Appenines between Tuscany and Emilia, for example the Poretta Pass between Pistoia and Bologna, and the Futa Pass between Florence and Bologna. To the Florentines the route northwards over the Appenines to Bologna ranked only second in importance to the route to the sea. A great deal of attention was given in the fourteenth century to the protection of this route, for its users were constantly threatened with violence by predatory feudal lords like the Ubaldini, who lurked in the Appenines with their armed retainers and made brigandage their business for several generations. The Florentines deliberately moved the route ten kilometres eastwards from the Futa to a parallel pass known as the Giogo, in response to the problem, and in 1306 founded a new fortified township at Scarperia where the new route took off. The dangers lay, of course, in the woods, for the roads, after rising strongly on the Tuscan side to the high grazing land near the passes, dropped down gradually on the northern side through woods which are still very extensive, and which were once even more extensive, as settlement names like 'Madonna dei Boschi' suggest. It was at the beginning of the long, and generally slow, descent towards Bologna that the greatest risks lay. The Florentines therefore set up a second fortified township, Firenzuola, little Florence, at the most dangerous point on the north side of the pass in 1322. The garrison was expected to provide adequate protection to travellers on the road. Its efforts were only partially successful, for on two occasions, in 1342, and again in 1357, the Ubaldini captured and burnt Firenzuola itself, besides closing the road in other places in 1351, 1352, 1360, 1361, 1373 and finally in 1377.[56]

The advantage of the new road was not speed, for the terrain was much the same as the Futa, but, despite the Ubaldini, comparative safety. By the time the *Itinéraire de Bruges* was compiled, the Giogo route was described as the principal alternative to the Cisa route as the means of getting from any of the Alpine passes to Rome.

By 1335 carriages had evolved slightly from that illustrated on p. 225. By now the bodies of coaches were slung from the chassis on great leather straps, to absorb some of the jolting of the wheels on pavé. Like covered wagons on the great nineteenth-century treks, they had cloth stretched over hoops for protection against rain or sun. In this case it could also be let down to cover the 'windows'. This German four-horse carriage (opposite), crammed full of women and children, was to illustrates a biblical passage in Judges about the tribe of Dan journeying to find a place to settle. This is why they are accompanied by their flocks of sheep and goats and have a cock on the roof and why the men riding behind are bearded and wearing distinctive Jewish hats.

The opening of an entirely new pass and the creation of a complete new road with two new fortified townships, was the most dramatic provision of the Florentine state against brigands, but it was far from the only one. Six other *castelli* were created on key roads. Two of these were on another road through the Appenines, that to Faenza, slightly further east of the routes to Bologna. Here it was the counts Guidi and their marauding retainers whose depredations on travellers were to be resisted by the armed patrols based on the *castelli*. Three *castelli* were set up on the road south-east from Florence up the Arno valley to Arezzo and onwards to Rome. The noble predators here were the Uberti. As on the Bologna road, the actions of the city were only partially successful. The Uberti and their noble allies, the Pazzi and the Tarlati, sacked the market town of Figline in 1352. The *castello* at Montalpruno, planned in 1329 at the Consuma pass on the road eastwards to the Casentino, was designed as a fortified place 300 *bracchia* by 600 *bracchia*, with two gates, one towards the city, the other towards the Casentino. In other words, the *castello*, as at Scarperia and Firenzuolo, sat astride the main road, which passed right through the new walled and guarded refuge from one side to the other. As well as the garrisons in the eight *castelli*, the republic set up a number of vicariates within their state, from the 1290s onwards. The responsibilities of the 'vicars' included the use of the troops committed to their charge for suppression of brigandage. The city deliberately captured, and razed to the ground, the castles of the rural nobility which they had used as bases for seizing merchandise. In this way two of the castles of the Cavalcanti and one of the Gherardini were destroyed on the road to Siena in 1302 and 1304. In 1303 the Florentines seized the *rocca* of the counts of Gangalandi at Lastra opposite the port of Signa in the Arno on the route to the sea.

Thus, even one of the greatest trading cities of Europe had difficulty in protecting merchants and their goods within its own territories, despite very considerable efforts. But in the 1360s, just as the Florentines seemed to be finally winning, an even greater menace was let loose. The new military companies of *condottieri*, when not being paid to fight wars, and, sometimes even when they were, kept themselves alive by pillage.

The Alps were not only higher and more desolate than the Appenines, but they held even greater human dangers. Whilst the Florentines had to set about creating fortified settlements in the early fourteenth century, the counts of Savoy already had long-standing fortified *clusae* to shut the Alpine passes. There was one at St Rhémy on the south side of the Great St Bernard pass, for example, and another, the Chiusa di S. Michele, above Turin on the way up to the Mont Cenis pass.[57]

In their attempts to pacify the Regno, its Norman rulers had given local officials the task of providing soldiers to accompany travellers, and in return authorised them to collect tolls variously known as *guidaggio* and *salvinaio*. As time passed many of their successors continued to collect the tolls assiduously, but refrained from escorting travellers. King Robert abolished these abusive levies in 1321, but after his death they were soon collected again.

In the aftermath of war, unemployed mercenaries frequently turned brigand and preyed on trade.
It was so in north-eastern Italy after the brief war between Maximilian I and the Venetian republic. Stefan Praun, a Nuremberg merchant trading with Italy, commissioned the altarpiece on the opposite page, in 1511, from the workshop of Paul Lautensack in Bamberg, in thanksgiving for the rescue of his goods, by divine intervention, from a surprise attack by mercenaries. His goods were in a boat on lake Garda, on the route between the Brenner and Milan. The discomfited mercenaries can be seen fleeing bottom right. In the boat, centre, the sailors are pleading for help to the Virgin, at the top, who is in a surprisingly comfortable bed in the stable at Bethlehem, with Joseph winding wool, rather belatedly, to make baby clothes for the newly born Christ child in the manger. The donor himself is kneeling bottom left, with both his coat of arms and his merchant mark on shields.

Armed escorts

Many unauthorised tolls were added, particularly in the disorderly years of the first half of the fifteenth century, and the rates levied increased so enormously that they acted as a considerable restraint on trade. In 1455 and again in 1466 King Alfonso and his son Ferrante set enquiries in motion into 'the grave disorders deriving from the widespread levying of *diritti di passo* and the negative repercussions on domestic trade' asking 'whether or not the places in which the toll was collected were really dangerous'; and 'whether the collectors had an adequate number of armed persons'. They discovered that many who collected tolls did nothing to watch over the places assigned to them, to improve the roads or to accompany wayfarers through suspect areas.[58]

In Germany the emperors had frequently delegated the ancient royal duty to care for roads, by enfeoffing individual lords with the office of caring for particular roads. Those enfeoffed took on the responsibility for the safety of travellers on it as well as the physical maintenance of the road. In the periods of general breakdown of public order in Germany this could become very difficult. The most frequent method was not to clear the area of predators but to provide an armed escort for each separate caravan of goods. The bishop of Sion, as well as erecting lockable *soustes,* for the overnight safety of goods (see above, p. 197), also provided escorts along the upper Rhône valley and onwards as far as the cross of Ott at the summit of the Simplon pass.

Since armed men were always expensive to maintain, travellers themselves naturally had to pay for the privilege of an escort. Indeed they were then forbidden to travel without one. An escort ordinance, for the Luxemburg–Strasbourg road, of Philip, Duke of Lorraine in 1394 suggests a certain fusion of roles, that of escorting and that of carrying. It talks about the necessity of making connections with safe inns at places on the way for the '*Fuhrleute, ihre Pferde, Wagen und Geschire, worin der kaufleute Gut gefahren wird*' ('escorts, their horses, wagons and harness, so that merchants may travel well').

In Germany too, just as in south Italy, the armed escort, *conductus* or *geleit*, which had begun as a protection, in the end often became, from the merchants' point of view, an additional burden and restraint on trade. From the lord of the road's point of view it had become a legitimate source of extra income to be exploited as lucratively as possible. If the cost of any one route became too expensive, merchants naturally sought alternative routes, and lords naturally responded by making particular routes compulsory. It is quite extraordinary that trade could ever develop on any scale in Germany. In order for it to do so those cities that were to develop into considerable commercial centres in the fifteenth and sixteenth centuries had to enter into horrendously complex negotiations. The city of Nuremberg ended up by having to make agreements about escorts with some hundred lords and other cities. The fifteenth-century *Geleitbuch*, a handbook for Nuremberg merchants, laid down which route was to be followed to reach which place, and what escorts were to be provided along the way, and what fees were to be paid for them. Between Nuremberg and Frankfurt, merchants going to the fair set out with an escort provided by their own city, but soon changed it for an escort provided by the margrave of Brandenburg, then for another provided by the bishop of Würzburg, then for others provided by the count of Wurtheim and the elector of Mainz, and finally for one provided by the city of Frankfurt itself. Besides the money paid to the lords, the escorts themselves expected extra money from those they guarded, for drinks, and also took kick-backs from the inns to which they led men and goods, just as modern tour guides do from the hotels to which they bring their coach-loads.[59]

The numerous leagues of cities and princes in fourteenth- and fifteenth-century Germany managed to suppress brigandage in the areas in which they operated, but highway robbery remained a very real risk in many places into the Early Modern period. In 1495 Maximilian I optimistically included security of goods and persons on the roads of the Empire in his everlasting public peace, the *Landfriede*. A group of merchants, assembled in Frankfurt in 1521, quoted its terms back against his son Charles V in their supplication against highway robbers:

> Everyone, and particularly the common craftsman, who moves along the imperial highways (*Reichsstrassen*) should have cheap, trustworthy and safe use of them, and also free trade and travel. However, up to now, the public peace has been commonly broken, not only against the magistracy, on whom we depend, but also against our persons, lives, possessions and goods.

The cause of their supplication was a spate of dramatic and violent highway robberies, which they recounted in lurid detail, perpetrated on the goods and persons of merchants in various parts of the empire, including one that had just happened two miles outside the city to someone attempting to come to the Frankfurt fair. The roads to great international fairs, like those running in to capital cities, provided good prey for brigands. As well as eloquent supplication for public action, merchants backed up their words by boycotting the fairs. In the end it was the Swabian League that accomplished what neither Charles V nor Maximilian had been able to do. The League sent its army into the wilds of Franconia destroying up to twenty-three castles and chasing their predatory lords from the land.[60]

Reprisal

As well as the capricious and thoroughly illegal violence of highway robbery and brigandage, there was also a survival from an earlier period of the custom of legal 'reprisal'. By this custom it was possible for someone who had been defrauded or unpaid by a foreigner to sue in a local court to have goods up to the value in question seized for his benefit from any person of the same origin as the person who had failed to pay him. The person who had had his goods seized in this way was then expected to go home and recoup his money from the original defaulter. From one point of view it was a thoroughly sensible procedure until an international commercial law could be developed. However, it rendered every honest merchant abroad vulnerable to the consequences of non-payment by any of his less scrupulous compatriots. With the enormous extension of trade in the thirteenth century such a custom was no longer tenable. The possibilities of reprisal were gradually eroded both by individual safe conducts and by group privileges. The *Carta Mercatoria* of Edward I of England in 1303, nominally addressed to all foreign merchants, but in practice purely for Hanseatic merchants, provided that goods of foreigners could only be seized from those who were individually responsible for particular debts, or from those who had personally and explicitly guaranteed that particular payments be made.[61] Such attitudes became very general, but, unfortunately not universal. Nearly two centuries later, in 1490, some Milanese merchants trading with England had their goods seized in the Rhineland by the count palatine and the margrave of Baden *ratione reprissaliarum*. Gian Galeazzo Maria Sforza, then Duke of Milan, was sufficiently outraged to write about the problem personally to the King of England, Henry VII. Henry VII replied at once, saying that he had received the Duke's letter, '*non sine gravi et molesti anime*', and went on 'since we have forbidden these reprisals, so that merchants can do business in our realm, to come and go, to stay and rest, wherefore we are greatly surprised that the emperor or any other prince has done what they have done.' He had therefore written immediately, in the strongest terms, to the emperor, the count palatine and the margrave, that they should release the said merchants and merchandise without delay. At the same time he sent the Duke copies of what he had written.[62] Reprisal patently only survived in a few 'backward' areas.

War

Guard towers and armed escorts and punitive and exemplary actions might deter or prevent highway robbery and banditry, and reciprocal privileges might mitigate legal seizures, but some sorts of disorder and violence were impossible to cope with. In northern Italy, the uncontrolled armies of unemployed *condottieri*, or in France the great companies of well armed soldiers, suddenly discharged whenever truces were made in the Hundred Years' War, could not be restrained. Any goods in their way were simply appropriated without redress. When they were out in force, everyone, from the humblest countryman to the richest and most exalted cardinal, fled for safety to the nearest walled town, and stayed there until the army had pillaged its way past, and even then they were not entirely safe, for even some walled towns fell to such professional armies on the rampage and were systematically looted. Avoidance was the only security in such cases. The same was generally true in time of overt and public war.

When the Florentines were at war with Pisa, before they captured it in 1406, and then with the Genoese for another decade or more, until they wrested control of Porto Pisano from them, there was great difficulty in getting goods in and out of Florence by sea. Florentines imported French and Catalan wool in an extraordinarily long and roundabout way through Venice and then across the Appennines; Datini sent cloth from Prato, by then a subject city of Florence, westwards to Spain along the same expensive and circuitous route eastwards through Venice; and grain from Sicily, necessary to make Florentine bread, was temporarily imported through Talamone, a

tiny port on the Maremma coast south of Grosetto. The grain was carried at enormous expense on mule tracks over the hills that passed through Volterra, and carefully avoided enemy-held territory, or that of the unfriendly Sienese. Avoidance, however expensive, was normally the only response to war.

Very occasionally, the deliberate diversion of trade was made a part of the conduct of war itself. When the Emperor Sigismund of Luxemburg, as King of Hungary, was at war with Venice at the beginning of the fifteenth century, over territory on the east coast of the Adriatic, he tried to impose a boycott on south German and central European commerce with Venice, clearly recognizing that such trade was vital to Venetian interests. He hoped that trade through Milan and Genoa would be able to supply everything that was needed, and ruin the Venetians. Unfortunately for Sigismund, the Genoese no longer had access to the resources that the Venetians did. They could therefore not meet all the demands put on them. They could not, for example, obtain raw cotton in the quantity or quality that the Swiss, the Swabians and the Slovaks had been accustomed to receive from Venice for their considerable manufacture of fustians. Sigismund's subjects consequently resumed trading with Venice by way of Milan, even though he kept the Brenner and Tarvis passes shut. War then generally only diverted trade rather than prevented it, unless the diversion was so much more expensive that particular lines of business ceased to be worthwhile.

One of the principal consequences of any war was an increase in taxation of some sort. Some forms of taxation had greater consequences for trade than others. Some, such as customs duties, affected trade directly; others, such as currency debasements, did so indirectly. Normally the effect on trade was unintentional. The vastly increased rates of customs placed by Edward III on the export of wool from England in the 1330s were imposed purely as a fiscal

Customs dues

measure to help meet the enormous costs of the general Anglo-French war
that developed out of the defence of Gascony against Philip VI. Such high
rates of duty maintained through two decades of war – and continued even
after peace was signed – had the totally unintended effect of protecting a re-
nascent English cloth manufacture and converting the export of raw wool
into an export of unfinished cloth.[63]

Occasionally there seems to have been some logic in customs dues. At the
very end of the fifteenth century the government of Maximilian I in his Austrian territories seems to have had some principles by which it regulated
customs dues. Imports were to be taxed lightly, since any tax on them
increased domestic prices; whilst exports and transit goods were to be taxed
heavily since foreigners effectively paid the tax. Cattle imported from
Hungary were free of tax, so that the price of beef did not rise for nobility, or
for the miners who were also apparently great consumers of beef. On the
other hand, Hungarian cattle that were driven through the Habsburg lands to
the cities of southern Germany or those of northern Italy were taxed heavily.
The only imports to be taxed at all heavily were foreign wines that might
compete unfavourably with native ones.

Tolls

From the point of view of the merchant, customs dues were not very different from the numerous tolls that had to be paid en route. In theory, tolls were
paid for the maintenance of bridges, roads and passes. In practice, they could
either prove totally inadequate for the purpose, like many bridge tolls, or else
provide a substantial revenue for their recipient. In the Empire many tolls
had been granted as the means of supporting fief-holders enfeoffed with the
offices of caring for particular roads. In 1235 the Emperor Frederick II had
turned this round, and generalized it, when he had specifically laid down that
taking a toll on a road made the recipient responsible its maintenance. As time
went on, however, many lords came to treat tolls as part of the revenues of
lordship, less and less connected with any responsibility for road maintenance, and eventually virtually indistinguishable from customs dues. This

was not always the case. The great road improvements of the thirteenth and fourteenth centuries were essentially funded out of tolls. The counts of Savoy, who took so many tolls in the western Alps, spent heavily on road maintenance. The accounts of the counts' receiver of the *péage* at Villeneuve-de-Chillon, on the north shore of Lake Geneva, paid by those using both the Great St Bernard and the Simplon passes, show how large a part of his receipts were spent, all through the fourteenth century on 'repairs to the roads…along which bales of wool and other merchandise are carried by those from whom the *péage* at Villeneuve is levied'.[64] Similar expenditure is constantly recorded by another of the counts' receivers at the same time on the road through Maurienne, and particularly on the bridge over the Ain, on the way up to the Mont Cenis pass.

Such surviving toll accounts are, of course, invaluable for the historian, for they give us glimpses of the actual traffic on particular roads at particular times, like the quantities of fustian, spices, mercery, paper, iron lances and tallow, which passed, in carts, through Villeneuve-de-Chillon on the way to the fairs at Geneva in 1423–24.[65] Such tolls, when first imposed when a road was improved or a bridge built, were seen as a reasonable price to pay for the cheapening of transport brought about by the improvements. However, as time passed, what had once seemed reasonable and beneficial came to be regarded as oppressive and burdensome, particularly in the empire where the tolls were so often backed up by the compulsion to use particular roads. Sometimes regulations seemed oppressive at once, as when the Bishop of Chur, having paved the road over the Septimer pass to attract traffic back to it, sought to recoup his expenditure by acquiring from the Emperor Charles IV a privilege requiring merchants to use his new paved road and pay the tolls on it. Charles IV himself used some of his considerable revenues in Bohemia on road improvements, but he too wanted to see a return on his expenditure. He therefore required the merchants of Görlitz, to their own disadvantage, to use, and help pay for, one of the new roads that he had had constructed, that from Lausitz southwards through the gap in the mountains at Zittau to Prague.

Elsewhere, however, specific attempts were even made to reduce tolls. The Florentines, as they enlarged their state in the fourteenth century, slightly reduced the number of internal tolls on their roads. Other owners of tolls, even the Ubaldini, were deliberately bought out and the tolls concen-

When and where suitable roads existed, great ladies travelled in coaches rather than litters, (see p. 200). Below is a much grander and slightly earlier carriage than that on p. 217, from Sir Geoffrey Luttrell's psalter, c. 1310–20. Such carriages were entered from the rear. The sides are emblazoned with imperial eagles, and the hooped superstructure is covered with very superior fabric, but it does not yet have any sort of hanging suspension to save the four crowned queens riding inside from the jolting of the road. It is drawn by five (pairs of) horses with two riders, and a mounted escort rides behind. Can the illuminator have been alluding to the four daughters of the Count of Provence who all became Queens? One of them married Richard of Cornwall, King of the Romans (i.e. Emperor elect), uncle of Edward I, whom Sir Geoffrey served.

trated at the frontiers. This was a tentative and precocious beginning of a move towards the payment of a single toll at the border for the use of all roads within the state.

The priors of Florence were not alone in seeing the reduction of tolls as an advantage for trade. In 1346 the Visconti brothers went further. They came to an agreement with the central group of the city-states that they ruled, Milan itself, together with Como, Lodi and Cremona, by which the individual states agreed to give up local privileges to form a unified customs system. Formal agreement was one thing, practical implementation was another. Local authorities dragged their feet, so that it was not until the reign of Francesco Sforza, Duke of Milan from 1450, that a regional free trade area actually came into existence for all his territories, much to the advantage of Lombard manufactures and internal trade, as well as the ostensible aim of the original agreement, which had been to promote transit trade across Lombardy from the Alpine passes to Genoa.[66]

In the reduction of customs dues, as in so many other fields, the cities of southern Germany saw the advantages of what was being done in northern Italy, and adapted the idea to their own very different circumstances. The city government of Nuremberg also sought to reduce the costs of trade for its citizens. It entered into reciprocal agreements with other lords and cities, so that its merchants, when sending merchandise, could pay reduced tolls and sales taxes or even be exempt from them. In this way they could have goods shipped on the Danube between Regensburg and Passau, over a hundred kilometres downstream, without paying any of the intervening tolls. In granting reciprocal rights to citizens of other cities it still demanded that they, like its own citizens, pay a small road- and bridge-maintenance duty at its own city gates of 1 heller on a two-wheeled cart, and 2 heller on a four-wheeled wagon. [67]

Quicker, cheaper and safer transport	The overall impression is that between the great commercial revival of the thirteenth century and the end of the Middle Ages the transport of goods became both quicker and cheaper and, with flagrant exceptions, even safer. The ubiquitous trains of packhorses and mules, often still accompanied by the owners of the goods that they were carrying, gave place at varying dates in many parts of Europe, including even some of the mountainous areas, to two-wheeled and then four-wheeled wagons run by professional carriers organized from a network of inns that provided warehousing and packing facilities. Underlying this change was a revolutionary improvement in the width and surface of roads and the building of countless bridges. Some of the impulse for this, particularly in its earliest stages, came from pious motives, particularly the building of bridges on pilgrim routes and the provision of hospices for pilgrims, poor travellers and those in difficulties in remote and isolated places. As the 'road revolution' gathered momentum, the provision of good roads, fit for primitive coaches as well as wagons, became more and more an object of public policy, particularly in places with commercial interests. Improvements elsewhere were in part a response to pressure from

merchants from such places. Expenditure on the improvement and maintenance of roads could, at least in part, be defrayed by the tolls paid by users
who could, because of the improvements, carry more goods, more cheaply.
As costs dropped, by volume and weight, the range of goods worth carrying
over any specified distance increased. Cheaper textiles, as well as the dearer
luxury fabrics, became worth carrying over long distances. The ability to
carry goods economically over longer distances in its turn encouraged greater
specialization, as well as increasing the volume of trade in many areas of
Europe, even at a time like the late fourteenth and fifteenth centuries when
the general cataclysmic drop in population would lead the historian to expect
a universal contraction in trade.

The great leap forward in transport, of the thirteenth and fourteenth centuries, was followed by a continuous sequence of minor road improvements
from the fifteenth century into the Early Modern period. The next major
wave of road improvements did not come until a spate of new paved roads
was laid out in many countries in the eighteenth century. In countries like
France or the Austrian Netherlands the *steenwegs* were laid out by public
authority. In England the comparable turnpike roads were a product of
private enterprise. Until then Europe had essentially been served for four
centuries by the road network produced by an earlier 'road revolution'.

*The via Francigena, the 'French
Road' from the passes in the
western Alps to Rome was much
used as a road for trade in the
Middle Ages, as well as for
pilgrims. In this section, near
Montefiascone, about 70 miles
from Rome, the medieval road
made use of the ancient Roman
via Cassia which had been so well
made and maintained that it was
still in a fit state to carry wheeled
traffic at the end of the Middle
Ages.*

5

Trade in manufactured goods

Industrial regions

IT IS TIME to turn from the consumers and the means and manner of trade to the goods actually produced and carried. Although simple homespun fabrics, whether in wool or linen, simple pots, and simple ironwork were made all over late medieval Europe, the sorts of textiles, pottery and iron goods that extended into more than local trade originated in a very few places. The concentration of manufactures for long-distance trade was particularly noticeable in the southern Netherlands, northern Italy and, in the fifteenth century, in southern Germany.

The southern Netherlands was in some sense the industrial heartland of medieval Europe. An extraordinary range of goods was made in a broad cigar-shaped pattern of cities and towns stretching from Calais and Sluys on the coast to Cologne on the Rhine. Until the fifteenth century the area was intensely politically divided, so that industry was to be found in the counties of Flanders, Hainault, and Namur, the duchy of Brabant, the prince bishoprics of Cambrai, Liège and Cologne, the cities of Tournai and Aachen, and to a certain extent a little to the south in the county of Artois and to the north in the county of Holland. Here the finest woollens in Europe were manufactured, and also of a great deal of cheap woollen cloth and linens. The finest tapestries in Europe were made here, as well as poorer ones, and carpets. The greatest centre for brass-working was here. So also was some iron-working, including armour and the finest swords. Pewter too was made here, and the only coalfield to be exploited on a significant scale in the Middle Ages was here as well. Here was one of the great focal points for artists in Europe. Some of the greatest of medieval painters and miniaturists worked here, but in the context of a large production of cheaper art and book production. This continued and expanded when printing from moveable type was invented.

Italy, north of a line from Siena to Perugia to Ancona, formed a second industrial area. An equally extraordinary and overlapping range of goods was made here. This area was split into two by the Appenines. It was also politically fragmented, although by the fifteenth century the three states of Milan, Venice and Florence controlled much of it and had absorbed a large number of hitherto independent city states. Here there was to be found the manufacture of luxury woollens, only surpassed by the best from Flanders and Brabant, and also a great deal of cheap woollen cloth, of cottons and linens and fustians and the most astonishing range of superlative silk fabrics, besides leather-working. Working in iron in northern Italy included the principal armour manufacture in Europe. The most important glass manufacture, the finest pottery, and an extensive manufacture of soap and

In the still life opposite, from an Altarpiece of the Virgin, a pupil of Rogier van der Weyden enjoyed himself catching shadows, contrasting textures and playing with perspective. He gives an intimate glimpse of a library niche, with its curtain pulled back to reveal untidily piled books, with open clasps and a protective cover hanging loose. The niche also contains a ewer and bowl for hand-washing, with the towel hanging on an ornately carved rail. In 1460s the objects he chose were all manufactured within the industrial region of the southern Netherlands: brass bowls and ewers in the Meuse valley, particularly Dinant (see p. 269), books in Bruges, and fabric of all sorts in many places.

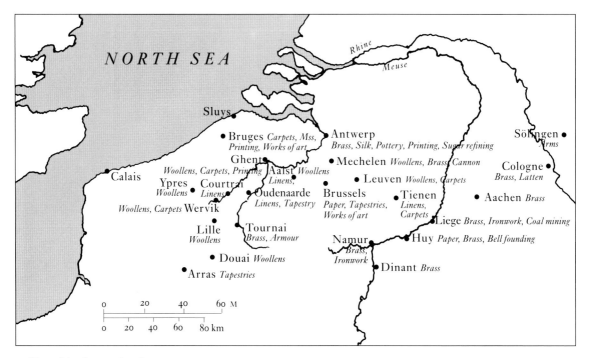

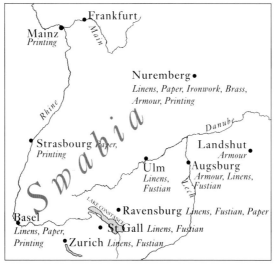

Most of the places and products mentioned in this chapter appear on these maps of the three key industrial areas of Europe. In northern Italy, the most important commerce of late medieval Europe depended on, and encouraged, manufacture (facing page). More concentratedly industrial was the band of cities from Ypres to Cologne (above). From the fourteenth century onwards a south German area (right) was of increasing industrial importance.

paper were also to be found. Here, too, was the other great focal point for artists. Most of the other great medieval painters worked here, once again in the context of large production of cheaper art, much of which was exported, and of books. Here too, book production continued and expanded when printing from moveable type was invented.

In the third area between the Alps and the Main, industry came relatively late on the scene, but shared many of the products of the other two areas. Once again there was an important production of textiles, for the most extensive production of linens and fustians grew up here. At the end of the Middle Ages this area was coming to be the most important centre of metal-working in Europe as well. There was a growing and significant brass industry, whilst the iron industry of the Upper Palatinate made it a late medieval Ruhr. Both fine and mass-produced armour were made. Here, too, a manufacture of paper began. The art of printing with moveable type was invented and had its first diffusion. Woodworking was important and a whole host of lesser industries, leather, glass, pottery, contributed something to trade.

The three areas were joined together by the Rhineland, by the Rhône valley and by the ever growing and improving network of Alpine passes. Together they formed a broad band from the North Sea to the Mediterranean, stretching from Umbria to south Holland, which to a large extent coincides with Jan de Vries' early modern urban belt, or the 'blue banana' of the urban fabric of contemporary geographers (see pp. 389–90). Outside this broad band, much industry was to be found in capital cities, like London which still lay outside the band to the north, Paris to the west, and Rome, Naples and Palermo to the south. All capital cities, whether inside this band or not, were to some extent industrial cities, since the court market stimulated luxury industries, either on the spot or in the immediate vicinity. The importance of such domestic court markets made for the growth of some luxury industries which later became export industries. The broderers of *Opus Anglicanum* in London, the ivory-carvers of Paris, the armour-makers of Milan, the tapestry-weavers of Brussels all catered in the first instance for a domestic, court, market, but then exported all over Europe. Other aspects of court demand also stimulated local industry. Every capital had its own goldsmiths and silversmiths. Other aspects of these capital cities also stimulated specialist demand, like the parchment-makers who were so numerous in the university quarter of Paris.

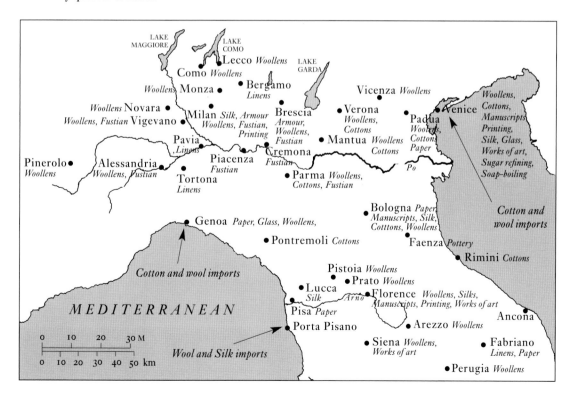

Since the Arte della Lana (the guild of cloth manufacturers) of Florence depended entirely on wool from sheep, it seemed entirely appropriate that a sheep, in the form of the Lamb of God, should feature prominently in their corporate coat of arms on the Orsanmichele.

The presence of large numbers of consumers for luxury articles provided a market near home. For example, the luxury woollens of Tuscany, the silks of Lucca, the majolica of Faenza, all sold first and foremost to the nobility of northern Italy, and then to those elsewhere in Europe. The noble market of the principalities of the southern Netherlands had equally been important in the original growth of the manufacture of luxury woollen fabrics in Flanders. When that noble market was concentrated in the Burgundian court in the fifteenth century it continued to provide an important stimulus to manufacturers. The port cities of Bruges and later of Antwerp engaged in the processing of imports for the court at Brussels. The refining of imported sugar, the weaving of imported silk, the cutting of imported diamonds, the making-up of imported furs all found a place in Antwerp at the end of the fifteenth century, along with the production of majolica as a substitute for imports from Italy.

I would now like to look in turn at some of those industries in detail, beginning with the production of textiles, woollens, silks, linens, cottons and fustians and of paper, continuing with the working of metals, of iron, particularly armour, and of brass, and with the making of glass, pottery and soap, and concluding with the creation of works of decorative art, tapestry, embroidery, ivory-carving and manuscript illumination as well as painting and sculpture.

Woollen cloth

Woollen cloth of various qualities was made in many parts of Europe from the Iberian peninsula to Poland. The most luxurious cloths, which could only be afforded by emperors, kings, popes and their courtiers, by bishops and princes and by the very richest of the *magnati* of the great cities, were, however, only produced in a very limited number of places. Despite this, it was not only the most expensive qualities of woollen cloth that entered into international trade, for some of the lower qualities also had a wide distribution. Until the end of the thirteenth century Mediterranean Europe imported large quantities of cheap cloth from the Low Countries and England.[1]

The dominant area of Europe in which luxury cloth was produced in large quantities was the southern Netherlands. The heyday of the production of heavy woollen cloth here was in the late thirteenth and early fourteenth centuries, but even in the 1390s the Lombard illuminator of the *Tacuinum Sanitatis* illustrated 'woollen clothing' by a tailor giving a customer a fitting, with the legend 'the best is this kind from Flanders'. In 1438 Pero Tafur visiting Bruges, which was then the commercial focal point of the whole area, commented: 'The products of the whole world are brought here, so that they have everything in abundance, in exchange for the work of their hands. From this place is sent forth the merchandise of the world, woollen cloths of which there is here a great abundance.'[2]

In the twelfth century, the key towns for the woollen cloth industry of the southern Netherlands were Arras, Douai and Lille in Flanders, Valenciennes in Hainault, Cambrai and Tournai. Arras was then the principal commercial centre, with Montreuil as its port. Much of this woollen cloth was already

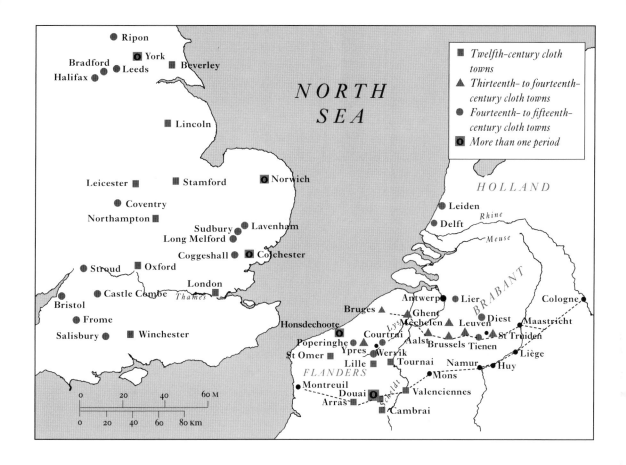

The map brings out how frequently the places on which the weaving of woollen cloth was concentrated changed in north-western Europe between the twelfth and the fifteenth centuries. The key arteries of communication from Cologne to the coast are also indicated, since many twelfth-century cloth towns were on the southern route to Arras and Montreuil, whilst most later cloth towns were closer to the more northerly route to Bruges. Some of the smaller centres have not been named.

being made from wool imported from England, although at this period the English had a flourishing woollen cloth industry of their own. Englishmen, in places like Stamford, Lincoln and Oxford were making up English wool into both cheap and luxury cloth for export to much the same markets as the Flemings were dealing with themselves. However, early in the thirteenth century, the woollen cloth industry shifted northwards to centre on Ghent and Ypres in Flanders, although Douai remained important. At the same time the principal artery of communication across the Low Countries also moved northwards, as did the principal commercial centre, from Arras to Bruges, where it remained, until it was supplanted by Antwerp at the end of the fifteenth century. However, the key places in which the woollen cloth was actually made went on changing considerably over these three centuries.[3]

The scale of manufacture in north-western Europe increased enormously in the course of the thirteenth century, and reached its highest point at the beginning of the fourteenth century. Although the export of English cloth to the south was already shrinking in the 1290s, that from Ghent and Ypres went on growing for longer. The sales of their cheaper cloth then declined quite suddenly around 1320. Ypres was especially hard hit and a whole quarter of the town fell into ruin. The manufacture of cheap cloth for domestic markets naturally continued, but only a few fabrics went on being made for export, like worsteds in Norwich and sayes in Hondschoote, but largely for a Baltic rather than a Mediterranean market. The manufacture of the most luxurious

After the papal takeover of Perugia, new statutes were imposed on the guilds of the city in 1536. When those of the cloth manufacturers were elaborately written up for the statutes of the Wool Merchants' Guild (opposite), they were headed by a crowned griffin standing on a properly baled and firmly corded roll of cloth ready for export.

The scale of cloth manufacture in and around medieval Ypres was embodied in the scale of its Cloth Hall. In 1304 it took the form in which it survived until its destruction in the First World War. There was no need or opportunity to enlarge or modernize it in-between, because the huge woollen cloth industry in the area collapsed soon after its completion, and never recovered. If the fifteenth-century Wool Hall at Lavenham (below) did indeed perform the same function, its scale underlines the difference between the city-based cloth industry of thirteenth-century Flanders and the dispersed small-town manufacture of fifteenth-century England.

cloths for sale overseas continued until the end of the Middle Ages, particularly in Ghent, but on a diminished scale.[4] The political crisis that afflicted the Flemish cloth industry did not affect that in neighbouring Mechelen (Malines) and in the Brabant towns like Brussels and Leuven, which had already grown markedly in the 1270s and 1290s. On the contrary, the quantity produced there again increased rapidly in the 1320s for a generation. In the later fourteenth century the production of luxury woollens for export began again in England, protected by the heavy customs duties on English wool imposed from the opening of the Hundred Years' War onwards. The cloth-manufacturers of Brabant and England drew on the skills developed in Flanders and encouraged the migration of skilled men. However, a considerable amount of English cloth was exported unfinished, to be finished and dyed in the Low Countries, particularly at Antwerp where the English sold it. This reliance on superior continental finishing skills continued until the seventeenth century. The amount of value added by finishing, sometimes as

In nomine scē in-
diuidue trinitatis
pris et filij i spūs
scī amē. anno dñi ōmillio qua
tricentesimo tertio. Indictiōe
undecima tp̄: dñi bonifacij

much as 50%, caused much resentment in England. At the same time, the weaving of heavy woollen cloth in larger quantities also returned to Flanders. However, the dramatic increase in production was focused on small towns like Wervik (Wervicq) and Courtrai in the Leie (Lys) valley, rather than on the cities of Ypres and Ghent, the former centres for cloth-manufacture. The 'new draperies' of these Leie valley towns used short, carded, wheel-spun wool for both warp and weft, which allowed them to produce high quality cloths at under half the cost of the traditional 'old draperies'.[5] It is no wonder that, with the promotional activities of the Alberti group of companies and other Tuscan entrepreneurs, Leie valley broadcloths, known there as 'vervins' conquered 'Mediterranean' markets, from Lisbon and Tunis to the Black Sea and Alexandria. At the end of the century Datini's firm in Barcelona (with its branches in Valencia and Majorca) by itself handled over 1,600 'vervins', slightly more than the number of rolls of cloth it sold from Prato and Florence.[6] The same pattern was repeated in Brabant. Cloth-production increased markedly in small towns like Lier and Diest and further south Zoutleeuw (Leau) and Tienen (Tirlemont) whilst it declined in the larger centres like Brussels and Leuven. In 1425, the Leuven cloth hall was already so little used that it was handed on to the new university which still keeps its central administration there. In the fifteenth century, it was the turn of small towns in south Holland like Leiden and Delft to grow.[7] Much of the revived English cloth industry was similarly focused on small towns, like Stroud and Castle Combe in the Cotswolds, Long Melford and Lavenham in Suffolk, or Ripon and Halifax in Yorkshire.[8]

The other great luxury cloth-producing area of medieval Europe was Tuscany. Woollen textile manufacture dominated the economies of cities like Prato, Pistoia, and Siena and even Arezzo and Volterra, but the key manufacturing city was Florence. Shortly before the middle of the fourteenth century Giovanni Villani described Florence as having the form of a cross, and delighted to emphasise that at the centre point of the cross was the Arte della Lana, the guild headquarters of the woollen cloth-manufacturers. This he felt most properly symbolized the way that the manufacture of woollen cloth lay at the heart of all the city's concerns. According to him no fewer than 30,000 people depended on the cloth industry, and that at a time, the 1330s, when the total population of the city cannot have been much more than 100,000. Something over 100,000 may not now seem a large population, but, in the early fourteenth century, it was a size equalled only in Europe by Venice and Milan, and most probably by Genoa. It was exceeded only by Constantinople, and by Paris. In this Florence then, an immense city by fourteenth-century standards, a third of the population lived by a single activity, the manufacture of woollen cloth. And what cloth it was too! Much of it was the highest quality of luxury cloth designed for the aristocratic market. Some 80,000 rolls of cloth were produced each year in the 1330s, and according to Villani were worth no less than 1,200,000 gold florins. This was approximately equal to the combined annual incomes of the kings of England and of France.

When, shortly after 1450, Master Etienne Chevalier, Treasurer of France to Charles VII and Louis XI, had himself painted at Tours by Jean Fouquet, the finest painter in France, he dressed carefully in his best red woollen gown (opposite). At the same time, Petrus Christus was painting St Eligius, as a rich Bruges goldsmith, in a very similar pleated gown of the finest scarlet cloth (see p. 122). Such scarlet cloth was only exceeded in price by the finest velvet, such as the king of England or the duke of Burgundy might wear (see pp. 246–6 and 250).

This production of luxury cloth was a new development in Villani's own lifetime.[9] At the beginning of the fourteenth century Florence had actually produced more cloth than in the 1330s, but it was of considerably less value. The mass-production of relatively cheap cloth was first developed on the basis of the wool from the local sheep which grazed in the Appenines, in the Chianti hills and fed on the hay from the meadows of the Arno valley and the Prato Magno, the great plateau meadow above the woods of Vallombrosa. Its manufacture was expanded on the basis of wool imported from many parts of the western Mediterranean, particularly where transhumant pasturage was practised.[10] This cheap cloth was widely traded in the thirteenth century. It was on sale in Venice by 1225, in Palermo by 1237 and at Ragusa (Dubrovnik) by 1252, and competed increasingly successfully for Mediterranean markets with the cheaper cloth of the Low Countries and England.

The growth of the manufacture of luxury woollen cloth in Florence did not, however, develop directly from the mass-production of cheaper cloth. Instead, it came about as a development from the activities of Florentine import-export merchants, who were grouped in the Calimala guild. In the thirteenth century they became increasingly involved in the import of luxury *panni franceschi*, which they initially bought at the Champagne fairs. Although they were all generically called 'French', because acquired in 'France', most of these were from the southern Netherlands and sold in Champagne by Flemish merchants. As the thirteenth century progressed, Tuscan merchants went increasingly often to Flanders and Flemish merchants consequently travelled less often to Champagne to sell their wares. The cloth-manufacturers instead sold their cloth direct to Italians in the great cloth halls of the cities of the southern Low Countries themselves. The late thirteenth- and early fourteenth-century cloth hall in Ypres, destroyed in the First World War, was the most impressive of them. Cloth for the whole of the southern Netherlands was offered for sale in the cloth hall at Bruges. At the beginning of the fourteenth century, firms such as the del Bene in Florence, whose partners belonged to the Calimala, made their livelihood almost exclusively out of the continued repetition of a highly successful formula. The managing partner in Florence sent orders to their permanent representative in 'France' for the purchase of *panni franceschi*, together with the necessary bills of exchange to finance their purchase. Some of them were sold in Florence itself, and the rest despatched to the firm's permanent representative in Naples, the capital of one of the richest kingdoms of Europe and a key export market for Florentine businessmen. Almost invariably the del Bene factor in Naples did nothing more than remit the proceeds of his sales back to Florence by bills of exchange. He was as specialized a salesman, knowing his way round the Neapolitan court and the cloth retailers of Naples, as his colleague in 'France' was a specialized buyer. The most expensive cloths that the del Bene sold in Florence were those of Douai, Mechelen and Brussels. The next most costly were those of Châlons-sur-Marne in Champagne, the nearest to a truly 'French' cloth that they sold in their higher price bracket. Then, in descending order of price, were cloths of Ghent, of

Ypres (the better quality), of Lille and of Alost. Even these were expensive cloths. At the same time as the del Bene were selling Flemish and Brabançon cloth in Florence, the Bencivenni were buying much cheaper Florentine cloth there for export to Venice. The dearest Florentine cloth that the Bencivenni bought was cheaper than the cheapest cloth of Lille and Alost that the del Bene company sold, or even the second quality *couverture* of Ypres. Most of it was less than half the price.

In the thirteenth century, Italian merchants, many of them Florentines, had already supplanted Flemings as purchasers of wool in England. They bought it direct from English abbeys, or noble owners of sheep ranches, like the earls of Hereford and Lancaster, and sold it in Flanders. When the crisis of the 1320s destroyed the Flemish cloth manufacture and with it the market for English wool there, enterprising Florentine firms, including the Bardi and Peruzzi, made up for their lost market in Flanders by importing the expensive fine quality English wool direct to Florence itself. This was used by Florentine cloth-manufacturers to produce imitations of the luxury quality Low Countries cloth which was becoming increasingly hard to buy. These imitations were generically known as *panni alla francesca*. The most expensive of them was described as *a moda di Doagio*, since the most expensive imported cloth had been that of Douai. It was followed in price by that *a modo di Mellino* and that *a modo di Borsella* or *a Borsella*, in imitation of the cloths of Mechelen and Brussels respectively. Cloth-workers from Flanders and Brabant moved to Florence in sufficient numbers to sustain a confraternity, that of St Barbara, which still had several hundred members in the fifteenth century.[11]

The import of the cloth from the Low Countries itself continued in an attenuated form. Giovanni Villani reckoned, in the 1330s, that 10,000 rolls of such cloth were still being brought into Florence each year by the merchants of the Calimala guild, against the 80,000 rolls woven in the city. Giovanni Villani knew what he was writing about, for he, like his father before him, was a member of the Calimala guild, and for long one of its most successful members.

Thereafter Florence produced two distinct qualities of woollen cloth. On the one hand there was that for the luxury markets of the Mediterranean world, manufactured with fine quality English wool. It soon ceased to be thought of as an imitation, but was regarded as a luxury fabric in its own right. It was increasingly known as *panna di San Martino*, from the neighbourhood where its manufacture was concentrated. On the other hand, there was *panna di garbo*, the traditional cheaper mass-market fabric made from poorer Mediterranean wools. Textiles, particularly woollen cloth, remained at the heart of Florentine trade.

In this Florence was not alone, it was merely the largest and most successful of the Tuscan cities, all of which engaged to a high degree in cloth-manufacture and in the international trade that went with it. As in Florence, the import of French and Flemish cloth preceded the large-scale manufacture of cloth from foreign wool in Siena. Some of the earliest surviving Sienese business letters, those of the Tolomei, concern the purchase of foreign cloth by the firm's permanent representatives at the Champagne fairs in the 1260s for sending back to Siena.[12]

Prato, the city next to the west of Florence in the Arno valley, was the home city of Francesco Datini, the best documented of all medieval merchants, who made his fortune in the adverse business conditions of the late fourteenth and early fifteenth centuries. At the centre of his business empire were the two cloth-manufacturing concerns and the dyeworks that he maintained in Prato itself.[13] The records of these companies reveal just how extensively Prato, and not only the city of Prato, but the surrounding countryside also, were dependent on the manufacture of woollen cloth. Prato still remains today a city dependent on textiles. The present association of textile manufacturers goes on meeting in the former building of the medieval Arte della Lana. With remarkable continuity the Italian state has its technical college for the textile industry, the 'Istituto Tullio Buzzi' at Prato, which keeps alive and develops the modern equivalents of those skills that made medieval Tuscan textiles so desirable from the thirteenth century onwards. The historian is tempted to rub his eyes.

Although the southern Netherlands, with England, and Tuscany, dominated the production of luxury woollen cloths in late medieval Europe, some was made in other places. The cloth of Châlons, for example, was sold at the Champagne fairs in the thirteenth century, and exported to Vienna, as well as Florence, in the early fourteenth. Luxury cloth was also made in Normandy in the second half of the fifteenth century. The cloth of Rouen, for example, was a passable imitation of that of Brussels.

Besides these extremely high-priced luxury fabrics, there was a continued production of less luxurious woollens which also entered international trade. Even in the thirteenth century much of this production was carried out in the same areas as the higher quality fabrics, although Paris and St-Denis produced some medium-priced fabrics, known as *biffes,* which sold beyond the domestic market of the capital, through the Champagne Fairs, to southern Europe. In the thirteenth century they could be bought in Tuscany at Siena, Florence and Pisa; in northern Italy at Venice, Bologna and Genoa; in Spain at San Sebastian and Perpignan; and in Portugal. They were priced at about a quarter of the price of the finest scarlets, half the price of good cloth of Ypres or Douai, but more than double the price of really cheap cloth from Valenciennes, St Omer or Florence.[14] The production of really cheap cloth in the southern Low Countries virtually disappeared in the first half of the fourteenth century,[15] unlike the the manufacture of the traditional massmarket *panni di garbo*, which survived in Tuscany in greatly diminished quantities. What has not been mentioned so far is the even larger manufacture of cheaper woollens in the Po basin. Whereas the manufacture of cheaper woollens in Tuscany continued to shrink from the fourteenth century into the fifteenth, that in Lombardy continued to thrive until the midfifteenth century, when the supplies of Spanish wool on which it relied were interrupted.[16] A considerable production of cheaper woollens also developed

along the Mediterranean coast from Provence to Catalonia, particularly around Perpignan.[17] However, hardly any other areas of Europe than these produced woollen fabrics that had more than a local market in late medieval Europe. One of the few exceptions was Silesia. Walloon weavers who migrated to Wroclaw (Breslau) in the thirteenth century produced cloth that was widely used in eastern Europe.

Before raw wool could be transformed into a roll of cloth ready for sale it had to pass through a large number of different processes. In the production of the highest qualities of cloth, fit to compete in the export markets of Europe, there was an extreme division of labour.[18] Each process was undertaken by different groups of people with specialized skills. With lower qualities of cloth the division of labour was much less. The production of luxury cloth was dominated in each centre by a relatively small number of entrepreneurs with a considerable investment in working capital. Although 30,000 people depended on the cloth manufacture in Villani's Florence, the whole industry was controlled by the members of the Arte della Lana who numbered only 200. It was these wealthy entrepreneurs who bought the raw wool and many months later sold the finished cloth. Although they did not own the means of production, they continued to own the material which was being worked on throughout the many processes involved, paying out fees along the way to the carders, spinners, weavers, fullers and dyers who did the actual work. The entrepreneurs' expertise lay in purchasing the best wools, in selecting the most skilled subcontractors, in maintaining consistent standards, and in marketing finished fabrics.

The first thing that had to be done to the fleeces when they reached the cloth-manufacturer's warehouse was to sort and beat the wool and clean it, beating the wool began the process of making the fibres fit to spin. However, if too much of the natural greases had been washed out of the wool in the

As the necessary preamble to cloth manufacture in all ages, sheep had first to be sheared, and the position of the twentieth-century sheared sheep almost exactly echoes its fourteenth-century counterpart in the Florentine Libro di gabelle.

The manufacture of woollen cloth

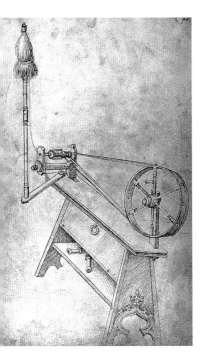

This accurate late fifteenth-century drawing by the Master of the Housebook of a sturdy German model illustrates how spinning wheels had gone on evolving since they were first introduced over two centuries earlier, becoming more and more able to produce superior yarn. Such wheels were still turned by hand, not with a treadle.

process of cleaning it, it had to be re-oiled to make it manageable. Having been sorted, cleaned and oiled by men in the warehouse, the wool was sent out to be prepared for spinning by combing or carding according to the type of wool and the use to which it was to be put. The coarse long-fibred wools were most amenable to combing with long tined combs, and the finer shorter wools were more suitable for having their fibres separated between wooden cards with numerous short spikes. Cards seem to have evolved in the twelfth century in southern Europe, probably in the Iberian peninsular. A hard-surfaced fabric, like a worsted, was best produced entirely from combed wool, whilst a soft-surfaced woollen, with a raised nap, was frequently produced using combed wool for the long, warp, threads on which the fabric was woven and a carded wool for the cross, weft, threads with which it was woven.

When the combers and carders, usually women, had teased out the fibres of the wool, it was returned to the warehouse ready to be sent out again to the spinners. The number of spinners needed was enormous, and much was done in the countryside surrounding the cloth-manufacturing cities. One of Datini's cloth-manufacturing businesses employed no fewer than 770 spinners in and around Prato, nearly all of them women.[19] Even in the fifteenth century some spinning was still done by hand, using a drop spindle, or spindle whorl, as this method was thought to produce better yarn. However, in the thirteenth century spinning wheels had evolved from the wheels already in use for spooling silk, cotton and woollen yarns. This produced yarn three times as fast, and thus at a third of the cost of yarn spun on the traditional drop spindle. Since wheel-spun yarn was not thought to be so good, the most luxurious cloths continued to use only hand-spun wool throughout the Middle Ages, whilst slightly less luxurious cloths used hand-spun wool for the warp and wheel-spun wool for the weft. The spun yarn was then returned to the warehouse and the spinners paid according to the weight of yarn brought in.

Before it was sent out to the weavers, the long, warp, threads had to be prepared and measured out to the exact length of the piece of cloth to be woven. This was done on a warping frame (ill. p. 248). The lengths of cloths were standardised according to the types of cloth and the places in which they were woven. The preparation of the yarn for the warp could involve not only measuring, but also twisting two or more threads together.

It was only then that the yarn, warp and weft in the right quantities, could be sent out to the weavers, most, but far from all, of whom were men. The warp was sent out first, as it took some time to set up a broad loom, threading upwards of 1,200 warp threads through the heddles ready for weaving. Some of the most luxurious cloths, for example Brussels scarlets, are known to have used over 3,000 warp threads in the fifteenth century. The horizontal treadle loom was probably originally a tenth-century adaption of Middle Eastern silk and cotton looms, although the large two-man version of it used by thirteenth-century professional weavers for double-width broadcloth evolved later. The horizontal treadle loom made it possible to weave long pieces of cloth.[20] The standard lengths laid down for late medieval rolls of cloth were generally between 30 and 40 metres (32 to 43 yards), although some were much longer, and half-length pieces were sometimes allowed. Weavers owned their own looms, which were exceedingly expensive. The dearest ones could cost as much as a small cottage. The capital needed may in part explain the preponderance of men over women as weavers.[21] Weavers sometimes bought their looms on an instalment system. Giotto, in the early fourteenth century, invested some of his income from painting and sculpture in a business selling looms to weavers on hire purchase. Can the loom that appeared on his campanile in Florence have been particularly meaningful to him? There were, of course, many fewer weavers than spinners. The broad looms, producing cloth over two metres wide, needed a second person as an

Since he well knew that weaving was primarily a male occupation (he sold looms on hire-purchase), it is surprising that Giotto should have incorporated a female webster in his design of the bas relief that Andrea Pisano carved for the Campanile in Florence (above). Perhaps she is the weaving queen Penelope, and the standing figure Odysseus.

The fifteenth-century English illuminator was evidently more comfortable sketching the weaver, with shuttle in hand, at work on his expensive and complex horizontal treadle loom, than he was at drawing the ancillary operations. His spinning wheel cannot possibly work, but he has produced a vivid, if rather confusing, impression of straightened wool-fibres being teased apart (bottom left), with what look like rakes, but are probably intended to represent cards rather than combs.

assistant, more often a woman than the master, to share in operating them, with a child working with them as well, to put the wool on to the shuttles ready for them to use. It normally took about a fortnight to weave a long roll of broadcloth including the highly skilled setting up, which took several days in itself. Since weaving of fine cloths by candlelight was forbidden, they took longer to weave in the shorter daylight hours of winter. Putting summer and winter working together, production of fine cloths seems to have averaged 25–30 rolls of cloth per loom in a year. Weavers were paid a lump sum at the end for their work. Master weavers were, in some sense, self-employed subcontractors. They owned their own means of production, once they had finished buying their loom. A fair proportion acquired a second loom, and the most successful, despite prohibitions, a third and even a fourth. Even those with a single loom were by no means as badly off as the poor labourers employed in the warehouses on such menial occupations as the sorting, beating and washing of the raw wool. The weavers of Ghent had a powerful guild, and those of Florence greatly resented that, despite their importance, they had no independent guild of their own, except briefly after the Ciompi revolt of 1378.

After being woven, the fibres of the cloth needed to be felted together by fulling. The newly woven cloth was put into shallow vats containing a solution which included fuller's earth. This was then beaten, either by 'walking' it, treading it underfoot, or slapping it repeatedly with the palms of the hands. This was a very time-consuming operation and for a long roll of cloth took many man-hours. Early in the eleventh century it was discovered how to mechanize this process. Water-powered fulling- or 'walk-mills' were widely diffused in the course of the twelfth and thirteenth centuries. They were constructed by entrepreneurs along streams in the countrysides around the cloth-producing towns, or sometimes even on the rivers that flowed through them, although the wooden blocks or hammers were apparently sufficiently noisy for some places, like Barcelona in 1255, to forbid the use of fulling-mills in or close to the city. Water-powered fulling was quicker than foot-fulling, and, since it was much less labour-intensive, much cheaper.[22] However, there was a reluctance to use fulling-mills, like the reluctance to use spinning-wheels, for the very highest qualities of cloth, which continued to be fulled by human 'walkers'.

When the fibres had been adequately felted together, the pieces of cloth had shrunk, often very unevenly, by up to a third of their length and by as much as a half of their width. They therefore needed to be stretched on tenter-frames, to which they were attached by tenter-hooks, to bring them back into shape, as they dried. To be effective this needed to be done slowly. In northern Europe this was done out-of-doors. Tenter-grounds were to be found around the cloth-manufacturing towns and appear in old paintings of Ghent or Stroud. In southern Europe the sun was too fierce for tentering to be done in the open air. Instead, stretching-sheds were used. Many of these were of wood, but others were of stone. One such *tiratoio*, or stretching-shed, that exists today is in Siena. It is a rare survivor of a species of building which was once so prominent a feature of Tuscan cities. Such vast buildings repre-

Rare examples survive in Gubbio (left, at the bottom in the foreground) and in Siena (below) of the multi-storey stretching sheds that were used in southern Europe to stretch the long rolls of newly fulled woollen cloth whilst it dried out.

sented an enormous capital outlay. In Florence most of them were corporately owned by the Arte della Lana, but a few were in private hands, like that owned by the Pitti family, already wealthy from cloth-manufacturing. The appearance on early paintings of Florence of these large buildings, not dissimilar to some of the textile mills of the industrial revolution, led some early economic historians to believe that the medieval cloth industry of Tuscany was organised on a factory system. This was not at all the case. The manufacturer merely maintained a range of warehousing facilities, in which only a few simple operations were performed, and from which the wool, as it was transformed into cloth, was sent out again and again to combers and spinners and weavers who worked in their own homes, or to subcontractors with specialized buildings like fulling-mills or stretching-sheds. Datini's account books regularly record the fees that he paid to have his cloth stretched in Prato. Neither sketches nor physical remains survive of any of the Prato stretching-sheds, although the archives reveal that a series of *piazze* are now to be found where they once stood. The *tiratoio* in Siena still exists only because it is now the convent for the Dominican nuns devoted to the upkeep of the sanctuary of St Catherine of Siena on the opposite side of the Vicolo del Tiratoio. Holiness is as potent a cause as poverty for the survival of buildings. It is five storeys high, over 140 feet (*circa* 44 metres) long and nearly 50 feet (*circa* 15 metres) broad. When in use as a stretching-shed, as many as thirty rolls of cloth could be stretched in it at one time.

After stretching, the cloth was returned to the warehouse, where it was examined minutely and imperfections repaired by hand by knotters, who were usually women. The stretched cloth was not, of course, the same size as it had been before fulling. The rolls of cloth that were eventually sold were often only three-quarters of the length and breadth that they had been on the loom, but were, of course, proportionately thicker and more compacted.

However, tentering was not the end of the manufacturing process, although cloth could be sold, unfinished, at this stage.

The nap of woollens, although not of worsteds, was laboriously raised with teasels and then sheared to produce an appealing smooth surface. This was an extremely delicate operation and the skill of the shearing could make or mar the quality of a cloth. The finest qualities of cloth, from the best English wool, were subjected to a second round of napping and shearing, or even a third.

At some stage cloth had also to be dyed. The raw wool could be dyed at the very beginning, even before spinning. Such dyed wool was used in the Florentine *tintallano* fabrics, and in the famous blue cloth of Ypres. The yarn could be dyed, and mixed colours of yarn could then be used, different for weft and warp for example. In this way, Florentine *mescolato* cloth, English and Flemish *medleys*, striped or rayed cloth and even chequered cloth could be produced. Most commonly, however, the finished rolls of fabric were dyed at or near the end of the manufacturing process. A combination of dyes was used to attain colours like black or green that no single dye could produce, or to obtain delicate differences according to changes in fashion. Sometimes cloth was dyed twice, once with woad at an early stage, and again with other dyes 'in the piece' at the end. The costs of dyeing varied enormously according to the colours. It could be an extravagant and luxurious operation, and for the finest woollens represented at least a quarter, and sometimes as much as half, of the total production costs.

Siena has a surviving dyeworks, also preserved, like the *tiratoio*, not by poverty, but by the accident of sanctity. The sanctuary of St Catherine of Siena is a complex of oratories built in and around the house of her father, Jacopo Benincasa, a successful fourteenth-century dyer. Few of the multitude of pilgrims who come to worship in the lower chapels, on the ground floor of the house, can realise that these two high vaulted rooms, each of two bays (one of which is disguised by the insertion of a later floor), are probably the only medieval dyeworks to survive anywhere.

Dyeing was probably the most skilled of all the cloth-making processes, and as well as skill, required very considerable capital. This was not only fixed capital represented by buildings and vats, but above all working capital, for many of the dyestuffs came from great distances and were very costly. The most expensive of them all was 'grain', which crushed and mixed with water produced a 'vermilion' dye. It was used alone for the most brilliant and expensive red fabrics, but because of its expense was often used in combination with other dyestuffs. All woollen fabrics dyed with 'grain', even partially, were known as scarlets. In this way it was possible to have not only 'vermeille' scarlet but also various 'sanguine' scarlets, 'violete' scarlet, 'murrey' (mulberry) scarlet, brown 'scarlet', and even black and dark perse-blue scarlet which were very fashionable at the end of the fifteenth century. Most surprising of all were green and white scarlets. The latter seems to have described undyed cloth of a quality worth dyeing with 'grain'. It was only worth using so expensive a dye on the most expensive fabrics, made from the finest quality English wool from the Welsh Marches or the Cotswolds. They were often also the largest fabrics which were sheared several times. All this made them

This fifteenth-century Flemish miniature shows an idealized and far too clean version of a dye-works where the most splendid cloth, such as that made up for Etienne Chevalier to wear for his portrait (see p. 236), is being expensively dyed scarlet. Undyed cloth is stacked ready at the bottom left, waiting its turn in the vat.

yet more expensive. Scarlets in Ghent in 1362–3 cost over four times as much as the cloth that the city bought to clothe its militiamen, and that was by no means the cheapest cloth. In Cracow at the end of the fourteenth century, scarlets imported from Brussels and bought by the Polish royal court cost sixteen times as much as the common cloth brought into the city which had been woven in the surrounding villages.[23]

Most dyestuffs, including 'grain', needed alum to fix them. Alum also acted as a mordant and removed grease and oil from the fabric. Just how much there was in the wool is revealed by the estimate that shearing and cleaning with alum could together reduce the weight of a fabric by 40%. Since wool needed to be greasy to be worked up into cloth, alum could not be used until the final stages. Dyes which needed alum as a fixative could therefore only be used at the final stages of production, which meant that much dyeing was carried out 'in the piece', and dyeing in the wool, or in the yarn, was limited to dyestuffs, like woad, that did not need fixing with alum.

Dyers were commonly men of substance like Jacopo Benincasa. In parts of northern Europe they even came to dominate the manufacture of cloth, but in Tuscany they were normally independent subcontractors to each of whom many different cloth-manufacturers sent their wool, their yarn, or their made-up cloth, according to the stage at which they wished it to be dyed. Sometimes men with a multitude of interlocking interests, like Francesco Datini, owned both cloth manufacturing firms and dye-works, but they were treated as completely independent entities, with an entirely

separate series of accounts. The unique surviving dye-works of Jacopo Benincasa and the adjacent *tiratoio* stand in a quarter of Siena which developed
rapidly in the thirteenth century and was almost entirely devoted to the production of woollen cloth.

The luxury woollen cloth industry established in Tuscany in the 1320s
grew very rapidly indeed until a sequence of calamities in the 1340s put a
brake on Tuscan, particularly Florentine, commerce. The fall in the production of luxury woollens was as sudden as its rise. The scale of production on
which Giovanni Villani had commented in the 1330s had shrunk so far by
1378 that it was hard to find purchasers for even a third of the number of rolls
of cloth. Some compensation for this violent fall in the production of woollens was to be found in the following century in new production of silk
fabrics, taffetas and brocades, damasks and velvets.

Silk fabrics

By the beginning of the fourteenth century Lucca had already been long
established as the dominant silk-weaving city of western Europe.[24] The raw
silk used in the Lucchese industry was partly imported from Sicily and Calabria but much came from further afield, for example that brought by the
Genoese from Asia Minor. A very little raw silk was provided locally for the
Lucchese from the Lunigiana, which was the first area to produce silk in
Tuscany. The silk fabrics woven in Lucca were carried to all parts of Europe
by Lucchese and other Tuscan merchants, who sold them along with fine silk
stuffs made in the Levant and even finer ones that had been carried all the
way from China. The Lucchese fabrics began as substitutes for Middle
Eastern fabrics, themselves originally substitutes for Chinese.

Cendal, a light fabric, was the commonest type of silk cloth, which was
extensively used for garments and their linings, for furnishings and even for
banners. It was available in many plain colours and was woven in all the silk-
weaving areas of Asia and southern Europe. Lucca cendal was well known in
England from the thirteenth century. Sactant and taffeta were related to
cendal. Both were of eastern origin, but they were also woven in Europe.

*The use of the horizontal loom
demanded that warp threads
should be the same length. By
the beginning of the thirteenth
century the upright warping frame
provided an efficient way of
achieving this. With its legs a
standard distance apart, and pegs
set at regular intervals, it allowed
a single worker to wind threads
from a number of bobbins at once,
zigzagged over the pegs in a set
pattern until the length of warp
needed was reached. The warp
threads could then be cut exactly
and despatched to the weaver to
set up his loom. The text on p.242
describes the use of warping frames
in the manufacture of cloth from
wool, but they were used equally
for linen, cotton and, as here, silk.*

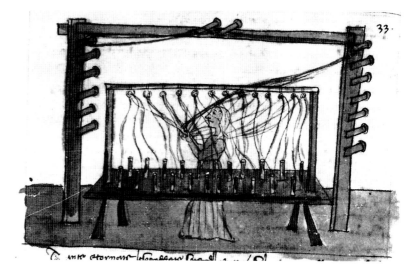

The silk-throwing machine, reputedly invented in Bologna in 1272 (see p. 250), was one of the most complex of the many applications of water-power to manufacture that took place in the thirteenth century. The rotary motion of the water wheel was used to make a number of horizontal bars turn, which drew the silk off a huge number of cocoons at once (visible at the top). The thread was then passed on to an equivalent number of rotating bobbins (at the bottom). Only a handful of workers were needed to replace the bobbins when full, and to replace cocoons when emptied, starting to unwind the thread from the next cocoon. Both sketches are from the Maestre dell' Arte della Seta, *fourteenth-century, Florence.*

Taffeta takes its name from the Persian *tafta*. Samite was a heavier, more lustrous silk, mostly used for dress and furnishings. It was generally plain, but patterned samites were also woven. Satin was glossiest of all plain silks, and was made in imitation of fabric believed to have been imported originally from Zaitun in China. Lampas was the most common category of patterned silk, often with fanciful patterns of animals and birds. In the course of the fourteenth century Lampas was supplanted by the heaviest and most luxurious of the silk fabrics, patterned damasks and velvets, which although oriental in origin, were refined by the Lucchese and other Italians, particularly in the fifteenth century. 'Damask' came to be applied to all Damascus-style fabrics, with their symmetrical patterns of stylized plants, not merely those imported from Damascus.[25]

The extraordinary complexity and depth of the patterns involved in many fabrics meant that silk-weaving was much more complicated than woollen-weaving. The same range of dyestuffs was used as for wool. Most of the richer silks were not of single colours. The use of different colours, or at least different shades of the same colour, meant that such silks had to be dyed as thread, not as a finished product. Brocades, and brocaded velvets were further enriched by the use of 'silver' or 'gold' thread, which was actually silver or silver-gilt string wound spirally on a silk thread. All this meant that the eventual customers for such fabrics were limited, like that for the most luxurious woollens, to rulers and their families, and the richest of magnates.

The accounts of the English royal wardrobe give some idea of the relative values of the finest silks and woollens in the first half of the fifteenth century.

The prices English kings were prepared to pay for the dearest scarlets of fine wool (up to 19s sterling a yard) consistently exceeded what they would spend on the finest damasks and satins (up to 13s 4d and 11s 8d respectively), but was surpassed by the cost of the finest velvets (up to 30s a yard). This was at a time when the wages of skilled craftsmen in the building industry in England had newly increased to 6d a day. A single yard of such velvet cost the same as employing a carpenter or a mason for sixty days.[26]

Some Lucchese silk workers were already working in other cities in the second half of the thirteenth century. One such, Borghesano, is attributed with the invention of the water-powered silk-throwing machine at Bologna in 1272, with which four workers could do the work of hundreds of throwers or spinners of silk. After 1314 the silk industry declined in Lucca itself, when many of the citizens fled the city to life in exile, some to Florence and other guelf cities of Tuscany, but many more carried their skills across the Appenines to join their compatriots who had already established silk industries in Bologna and Venice.[27] For much of the fourteenth century the European silk industry was concentrated in Venice, Bologna and Lucca itself. At the end of the century the Florentine industry was beginning to grow, and in the fifteenth century some Lucchese craftsmen also established themselves in Milan and Genoa. The Genoese, along with the Venetians, were the principal importers of raw silk, but much of the silk that they imported was landed at Porto Pisano for use in Bologna (via the Appenine passes) and Florence.

By the second half of the fifteenth century Venice, Bologna and Florence had become the three principal heirs of the Lucchese silk industry. In Venice from the middle of the century onwards, members of the aristocracy, the Mocenigo, Dandolo, Loredan, Tiepolo, Foscarini and Querini, who were already great landowners and overseas merchants, invested heavily in silk-manufacture. Despite legislation, which was supposed to limit any one owner to no more than six silk looms, some manufacturers owned twenty, thirty or even forty by the end of the century. Under these circumstances the silk-weavers themselves were no longer independent subcontractors, but had become mere employees.

Although silk-workers from Lucca were first to be found in Florence in the fourteenth century, the great increase in the manufacture of silk fabrics took place there in the 1430s and 1450s. The activities of Andrea Banchi, one of the more important Florentine silk-manufacturers in this period of expansion are well documented. Banchi specialized in brocaded fabrics.[28] It was also at this time that the Medici invested in the manufacture of silk fabrics as well as woollens. The new manufacture of silken cloth in Florence did something to offset the decline in the manufacture of woollens there. Nevertheless even by the end of the fifteenth century the silk industry was still quantitively less important in Florence than the shrunken remains of the woollen industry, and this despite the deliberate fostering of silk by the Medici regime. Legislation enacted in 1441 prescribed that, 'throughout the *contado*, every countryman who dwells in his own *podere* (a substantial farm), should plant five mulberry trees each year until he has fifty'. How much contribution silkworms fed on local mulberry trees made to the Florentine silk industry is not clear, but government sponsorship of mulberry-growing was a precedent to be followed elsewhere, in other parts of northern Italy later in the fifteenth century, in France in the sixteenth century and even in England in the seventeenth. Most silk still came from further afield. The silk industry in Genoa, recently established in 1439 by émigré workers from Lucca, partially used raw silks brought in by Genoese merchants from Calabria in southern Italy and from the Moorish kingdom of Granada in southern Spain, but a large part of it came from Asia Minor, sent by Genoese merchants established in Chios and Rhodes.

As well as the pieces, and occasional garments, of silk fabric that survive, silks can frequently be seen in paintings of the fifteenth century, since 'Flemish', as well as Italian, painters delighted to incorporate such rich fabrics to emphasize the wealth or importance of their subjects.

At the very beginning of the fourteenth century, the compiler of the *Codex Cumanicus*, who was probably a Genoese, put into his Latin–Persian–Cumanic dictionary words and phrases that would be useful for Italian merchants trading into Persia and central Asia, where Cumanic was the *lingua franca*. One of the key European commodities that Italians took to Persia and central Asia was linen. The compiler of this trilingual book thought it worthwhile to distinguish some of the different places from which export quality linen came. In doing so, he pinpoints for us most, but not all, of the important places in which export quality linen was manufactured by the beginning of the fourteenth century. Some of his categories, 'linen of Lombardy', 'linen of Champagne', and 'linen of Germany' covered whole manufacturing areas, others like 'linen of Orleans' or 'linens of Fabriano' related to individual places. Some of his particular places fall within his general areas. Within his general category 'linen of Lombardy', he picked out for particular mention 'linen of Bergamo', and similarly, 'linen of Rheims', within 'linen of Champagne'.[29] Other evidence suggests that this dictionary was based on actual practice. An early fourteenth-century eulogist of the linen of Milan prided himself that it was exported '*usque ad Tartares*'.[30] When the Florentine magnate, Leonardo Frescobaldi, passed through Egypt in 1384 on pilgrimage he observed Egyptian women actually wearing what he recognized to be 'linen of Rheims'.[31]

The dictionary compiler was, of course, writing from the point of view of an Italian exporting to the east. A different, northern European, point of view is given by the Customs Account for the port of London for 1390. Of something over 12,000 pieces of linen, each 50 ells long, imported into London, around 6,000 pieces had come from Westphalia, and around 5,500 pieces from the Netherlands, mainly from the county of Flanders. This indicates the two principal areas producing high quality linen in northern Europe, the area around Osnabruck in Westphalia, and a 'Flemish' area very close to the region producing woollens at the same time. It stretched from Artois, across the southern part of the county of Flanders, around Courtrai,

Linens, cottons and fustians

Oudenaarde and Ath, northwards through Alost into the Pays de Waas along the lower Scheldt and eastwards through the county of Hainault into the southern part of the duchy of Brabant.

Linen-making and flax-growing were to be found very much in the same places, for linen-weaving was an industry which grew up in the countryside itself. By the early years of the sixteenth century half the peasant households in the Oudenaarde area had looms. Flax-growing and linen-weaving were much favoured by smallholders, for the cultivation and propagation of flax were very labour-intensive. The returns were commensurately worthwhile. A hectare sown with flax could yield enough fibre to make around 1,200 ells of linen. In addition the seed could be used for oil. The linen excise at Courtrai suggests that the production of linen in that region grew continuously from the fourteenth century onwards, rising particularly fast in the 1430s and 40s, and only interrupted by the civil wars of the 1480s.

The compiler of the *Codex Cumanicus* did not pinpoint what part of 'Germany' was producing the linen he thought likely to be sent to Asia. It was patently not the distant Westphalian linen-weaving area, but rather the large flax-growing region of Swabia, centring on Lake Constance, which was already partially in the Swiss Confederation at the end of the Middle Ages. It stretched for 250 km, from the Lech on the east to Basel in the west, and from the Alps northwards to beyond the upper Danube. Linen from this area was carried through the Alps and so became available for Genoese exporters.

In these specializing areas, the manufacture of linens fit to export, like that of woollens, was in the hands of merchant entrepreneurs, who oversaw the various processes involved, and ensured that the linens produced conformed to fixed standards of size and quality. The manufacture of linens from Swabia and Lombardy for export went back to the twelfth century and in Flanders possibly even earlier, if the strange eleventh-century poem, the *conflictus ovis et linis* (the strife between wool and flax) can be used as evidence.

Once woven, linen and fustian were bleached in a lye of wood ashes, sometimes with added lime; they were then washed and stretched out in the fields to dry in the sun for eight to sixteen weeks according to the fabric and the weather. Because this stage in the process was so dependent on the weather, the production of linens and fustians had to be very seasonal. Drying grounds, with their striking contrast between the brilliant artificial white of the fabric and the darker colours of nature, could be found around many towns. This sixteenth-century painting shows some still in use around St Gall, just south of Lake Constance, near the centre of the Swabian flax-growing region. St Gall lay just off the main route from Nuremberg and Augsburg to Milan. In the last quarter of the fourteenth century its merchants began importing raw cotton to mix with their native flax to make their own fustian.

After his death in 1464, Rogier van der Weyden's workshop continued to produce outstanding portraits in the style that he had made famous. This portrait, of a lady whose identity has now been lost, has his same marvellous feel for the texture of fabric. The most expensive linen, which was popular in Burgundian court circles for headdresses in the 1460s, was so fine as to be transparent. The painter emulates the skill of the master himself in representing such a transparent headdress over her cap and forehead.

As with other fabrics, there was a very considerable range in the price of different linens. Champagne linens commanded the highest prices everywhere from the Levant to England. In Damascus in 1379 Champagne linen of 'Rheims' was priced at over five-and-a-half times Swabian linen of 'Constance', and ten times Italian linen. It was only exceeded in price by the very finest Florentine woollens. The Wardrobe accounts of Henry VI of England for 1438–39 indicate that the finest Rheims linen cost over seven times as much as some of the Brabant linen. Purchases for a royal Wardrobe naturally did not include the cheapest linens. In the 1430s the fine Rheims linen cost well over the average price for English woollen broadcloth at the time.[32]

Thirteenth-century Lombardy not only produced large quantities of linen and of cheaper woollens, but also began to engage in the manufacture of cotton fabrics as well. This rapidly growing Lombard cotton industry depended on increasing quantities of cotton imported through Venice and Genoa from Asia Minor from the thirteenth century, and particularly from

Syria where the best cotton was grown in the Middle Ages from the twelfth century onwards. Cotton-cultivation was also taken up in Sicily and Calabria, but unlike silk, cotton could not be grown in northern Italy itself. The cotton fabrics of Lombardy were exported throughout Europe and the Mediterranean, including some, bizarrely, sent back to Syria itself. This is really no odder than the re-import into England in the early fourteenth century of Flemish textiles made of English wool, or a hundred years later into Valencia of Tuscan textiles made of Valencian wool. The centres for the manufacture of cotton in the Po Basin were in many cases identical with those for the manufacture of linens and of cheaper woollens from Piedmont down through Lombardy proper, to Emilia, the Romagna and the Veneto.[33]

As well as the production of fabrics of a single fibre, there were many cross-fibre fabrics – silk-cotton, wool-cotton, hemp-cotton, linen-wool and linen-cotton. The most important of these by far was the manufacture of fustians, the linen-cotton mix, with the stronger linen as the warp and the lighter cotton as the weft, thus combining the durability of linen with the fineness and softness of cotton. The manufacture of fustians in 'Lombardy' grew particularly fast in the fourteenth century at the expense of both pure linens and pure cotton fabrics. South German merchants who were increasingly trading across the Alps to northern Italy were carrying back with them northern Italian cottons and fustians. However, by the 1370s merchants from Ulm, Augsburg and Nuremberg were instead buying raw Syrian cotton in Milan and Venice, and fustians were being manufactured in southern Germany itself, within the traditional linen-producing area of Swabia. The centre for the production of fustians was Ulm and the small towns between Ulm and Augsburg, although some was produced in a whole range of places, like Zürich, throughout the broad Swabian flax-growing region. By the end of the fourteenth century, Augsburg and Nuremberg merchants were taking Ulm fustians to Frankfurt and Cologne. In the fifteenth century, Swabian fustian spread northwards and north-westwards to capture the whole north- and west-European market from Spain, to England, to the Hanseatic customers in the Baltic. By the beginning of the sixteenth century, around 50,000 pieces of linen were inspected and stamped at Ulm. So were over 100,000 pieces of fustian. Linen and fustian were the key products which enabled the Grosse Ravensburger Handelsgesellschaft to grow and flourish for so long. It was based in the small town of Ravensburg, north of Lake Constance, and its trading tentacles stretched all across western Europe. This vast production of fustian in Swabia not only deprived the Lombard fustian-makers of their overseas markets, but even began to impinge on their home market in north Italy. As early as 1417, the doge of Venice, Michael Steno, attempted to protect the fustian-manufacture of the Venetian *terraferma* by imposing crippling import dues on German fustians. Venice later tried to prohibit their import altogether. Despite similar protectionist legislation throughout the whole Po basin, the Lombard cotton-fustian industry went into a marked decline in the fifteenth century, apart from the very highest quality cotton fabrics which went on being manufactured in Cremona and

Milan. Other, less important, flax-growing areas also added the making of fustian to their pre-existing linen-weaving in the fifteenth century, like those in Silesia or in Slovakia around Kosice (Kaschau), which primarily supplied the Hungarian and Polish markets. In the latter case the cotton did not come through Venice or Genoa, but was imported through the Black Sea by way of Lvov.[34]

As well as the materials used being mixed, techniques used in one fabric came to be used in another. In this way the term 'damask', originally applied to a particular sort of patterned silk fabric from Damascus, having first been transferred to Damascus-style Italian silk fabrics, was eventually used for Damascus-style patterned fabrics made of other textiles, particularly linens.

Besides fustians, there were also much coarser fabrics, *grosses toiles*, coarse hempen stuffs, and even some of these entered into international trade. Up to the early fourteenth century the rough hempen fabrics made in the Rhône-Saône valley were carried to Italy across the Mont Cenis pass. Later, they were carried down the Rhône and shipped to Italy from Aigues-Mortes (see pp. 167 and 401). The *bombasine* of Marseilles, a mixed hemp-cotton fabric, which used 'Burgundian' hemp from the Rhône-Saône valley and cotton imported from the Levant, was much used for sailcloth.

Paper

Closely allied with the production of linens from the thirteenth century onwards was the making of paper in Italy, France and Germany in turn. Until the enormous thirteenth-century increase in the use of the written word, western Europeans had been slow to take up the use of paper. Western Europeans first met paper in Constantinople and consequently initially called it '*pergamena graeca*', Greek parchment, even though all the paper used in the Byzantine Empire was imported from neighbouring Muslim countries. For long all the paper used in western Europe was also imported from various places in the Muslim world, from Syria to Andalusia. However, paper began to be made in western Europe itself when the demand for writing material leaped prodigiously in Europe from the thirteenth century onwards, with the growth of record-keeping of every sort. Central governments, particularly that of the papacy, led in this, but they were soon followed at every level of local government in church and state, and by ecclesiastical institutions and land-owning laity in their records of estate management. The keeping and auditing of accounts became a regular feature at every level from that of the *Recette Générale* of a kingdom to the humblest hospital. In addition there was an explosive use of the written word in business, not merely for ledgers and for the regular weekly letters sent to head offices in Tuscany from branch managers abroad, but also for the flood of notes on tiny pieces of paper written by cloth manufacturers when communicating with their spinners or weavers, or even their bankers. The literate nobility and entrepreneurs of the thirteenth century were joined in the fourteenth by literate artisans in the cities of northern Italy and the southern Low Countries, and by those else-where in the fifteenth. More widespread literacy in itself provoked a greater demand for reading matter. Traditionally west Europeans had written both documents and books on parchment, but the supply of parchment could not keep pace with the fast-growing demand, and paper was increasingly used instead. There was initially some resistance to this trend and doubt about the durability of paper. The Emperor Frederick II, for example, insisted that his Sicilian chancery always use parchment. However, the earliest surviving deliberations of the General Council of Siena, from 1248, were already recorded in paper volumes. Paper generally took over for everyday use in Italy in the thirteenth century, in France in the fourteenth and in Germany in the fifteenth. The highest quality illuminated books naturally continued to be written on parchment, as were important or formal documents, together with the grandest accounts, which, once audited, were still fair-copied on to parchment, in a few cases to the end of the Middle Ages and even beyond. However, in Siena, even the main series of Biccherna accounts, the central accounts of the income and expenditure of the state, were kept on parchment only up to 1302. In the late thirteenth century the Sienese 'civil servants' were buying paper by the ream of 480 sheets, and parchment by the quire of four sheets. Furthermore the paper that they bought was much cheaper. By 1278–81 they had to pay over seven-and-a-half times as much per sheet for the limited amount of parchment that they used, as they did for paper, which they could buy at less than 1.75d sienese a sheet.[35]

Although paper was made in Italy from the thirteenth century onwards, the first papermill north of the Alps (above) was not established until 1390. It was at Pegnitz, just outside the walls of Nuremberg (see p. 258), and was still working when Hartmann Schedel had his woodcut made in 1493.

Making paper from rags was yet another Chinese innovation, which, like the manufacture of silk fabrics, was slowly taken up in many parts of Asia. The use of paper spread ahead of its manufacture. Although paper was in use in Palestine by the seventh century, it was not yet made there. The story is told that paper-making was introduced into the Caliphate when two Chinese paper-makers were amongst the captives taken when Samarkand was captured in 751. Over the next three centuries paper-making gradually spread through the Muslim world to Baghdad, to Damascus, to Cairo, to Tunis, and eventually to Toledo in central Spain. There was naturally an active trade in paper between regions that were already making it and those that were using it but not yet making it. In the first half of the tenth century, for example, paper was exported from Morocco for use in Muslim Spain. In the second half of the century craftsmen from north Africa were making paper in Spain in Andalusia and in linen-making Valencia. By the twelfth century Muslim Spain had become an exporter of paper, to southern France and northern Italy, where it was not yet being made.[36] In the middle of the twelfth century the register of the Genoese notary Giovanni Scriba, which has proved so useful for historians of Italian trade, was written on imported paper.

The thirteenth century was the key period for the development of both the use and the manufacture of paper in Christian western Europe. Not only did paper continue to be made in Spain after the Christian reconquest, particularly at Jativa in Valencia, reconquered in 1238, and around Barcelona, but paper also began to be made, in the first half of the century, in northern Italy, most notably in the small town of Fabriano, high up in the Appenines above Ancona, in the centre of a linen-weaving area. Fabriano linen had been of sufficiently high quality to appear in the *Codex Cumanicus*. Whereas

Spanish paper continued to be made in the Muslim tradition, various technical innovations took place in northern Italy. Rigid metal frames were used, which enabled sheets to be standardized, and animal gelatine was used for sizing the paper, so that ink did not run. Finally, by 1276 at Fabriano, the fast-flowing Appenine streams were harnessed in water-mills for the pulping of linen and hempen rags with hammers. The process was similar to that for fulling woollen cloth or crushing mineral ores (see pp. 244 and 364). Although such mills demanded considerable capital outlay, the paper that they produced was much cheaper, and of a much more uniform quality, than that produced in the Near East and Spain with pestles and mortars. In less than fifty years Italian paper not only dominated the home market, but ousted Spanish paper from the French market and in the fourteenth century supplanted Spanish paper in Spain itself.

In due course master paper-makers from Fabriano moved to set up paper-mills elsewhere in Italy, carrying their skills with them, like Lucchese silk-manufacturers. By the end of the fourteenth century there were some thirty paper-mills in northern and central Italy to which paper-making had spread from Fabriano. In due course master paper-makers from Fabriano moved to set up paper-mills elsewhere in Italy, carrying their skills with them, like Lucchese silk-manufacturers. By the end of the fourteenth century there were some thirty paper-mills in northern and central Italy to which paper-making had spread from Fabriano. The expansion of paper-making in Italy continued into the fifteenth century. At the beginning of the century, for example, they opened paper-mills in the Leira valley above Voltri, immediately to the west of Genoa, Fabriano and Fabriano-derived paper not only dominated the European market, but was also exported by Venetians and Genoese in all directions, much of it, ironically, to the Muslim world, to North Africa, Egypt, Syria, and Ottoman Turkey, as well as to Constantinople and, through the Black Sea, to Russia. Imitative Italian paper had become cheaper and better than its Middle Eastern prototype.[37]

In France paper had been used in increasing quantities in the thirteenth century. It was largely imported from Spain in the first half of the century and from Italy in the second. In the fourteenth century the market in what is now southern France was increased by the move of the papacy and its bureaucracy from Rome to Avignon. The needs of the papal curia were largely met by Italian merchants. It is therefore not surprising that in the fourteenth century Italians not only imported Italian paper to Avignon, but set up at least nine paper-mills nearby in Provence to supply the large curial market for paper. As well as meeting local demand, Provençal paper was then itself exported by sea, and began to compete with north Italian paper in Spain, Portugal and England. In the fourteenth century paper-mills were also set up in France itself, beginning at Troyes in the heart of the Champagne linen-weaving country around 1330 not far from the Paris market. In 1334 John II of France granted the University of Paris pre-emption rights on Troyes paper. Shortly afterwards paper began to be made in the Auvergne. Champagne and Auvergne paper was then exported and began to compete

In 1568 Jost Amman's woodcut managed to show many of the processes of making paper, which were virtually unchanged since the thirteenthth century. A waterwheel can be seen turning outside the window, which operates the trip-hammers breaking up the fabric fibres in the trough in front of the window. The fibre-loaded liquid is being shaken down into paper in a framed fine metal sieve over the tub in the foreground. Watermarks were built into the paper, by putting a pattern into the metal. Before the damp paper is entirely dry, it is made quite flat in the screw press in the background.

with north Italian papers in the continually expanding markets for paper in Germany and the Netherlands.[38] Before the end of the fourteenth century, paper-making was also transplanted, like fustian-weaving, from northern Italy to southern Germany. The first paper made in Germany came from a mill on the Pegnitz just outside the walls of Nuremberg which was converted for this purpose in 1390 by Ulman Stromer. He was at the time managing director of the Stromer import-export house, which was by then already fifty years old. It was one of the first wave of large south German business houses. It grew up on trade with north Italy and Flanders combined with the exploitation of mineral wealth, first of the Upper Palatinate, and then of all Central Europe, and by 1390 was doing business as far away as Barcelona and the Crimea, Lübeck and Rome. The firm had, of course, been importing paper, with many other commodities, from Italy, and therefore had a market ready for it in southern Germany. Paper was thus added to the many other types of manufacture borrowed by south Germans from Italy. The Nuremberg paper-mill continued to be run by members of the Stromer firm until 1463, when it became the property of the city of Nuremberg.[39] By that time there were more paper-mills north of the Alps, at Ravensburg and Basel for example in the Swabian linen-manufacturing area, and at Chemnitz in the Slovak linen-manufacturing area. The Grosse Ravensburger Handelsgesellschaft traded in paper as well as linen and fustian. There were yet other paper-mills at Strasbourg on the Rhine, at Metz and Epinal on the Moselle, at Huy on the Meuse, and even at Mons in Hainault and at Uccle near Brussels. By that time too, European printing had moved on, from the block books of the 1420s to printing with moveable type from the 1450s. This enormously enlarged the demand for paper once more. Johannes Gutenberg himself printed 35–40 copies of his famous Bible on vellum, but over 150 copies on paper. In Basel in particular the growth of printing greatly expanded the market for local paper (see p. 283). Soon more and more old linen shirts were sent off to paper-millers all over Europe to meet the rising demand for paper.

Metal working

Foodstuffs and textiles were the most important commodities in medieval trade, but metals came not so far behind. Much of the trade was in the form of bars or plates of iron, copper, lead and tin sent outwards from the areas in which they were mined, and generally only made into objects of consumption, horseshoes or nails, plough-shares or prickets, as and when and where they were needed. Most of the iron mined in northern Spain was exported as bar iron, but a little was sent out in the form of anchors, cross-bows, wool-combs and even nails.[40] However, some manufactured metal goods were regularly traded over long distances, particularly fine steel blades and scissors, armour, locks, high-quality tools and brass wares.

Arms and armour

Arms and armour were the principal range of goods manufactured from iron to enter into international trade. Much was made in royal armouries in the capital cities of Europe. However, there were some places which specialized in this manufacture for trade. The finest steel sword blades (and also superior steel knives) were originally largely made outside Christian Europe, in Toledo and Damascus. However, just as west Europeans imitated, and soon improved on, Near Eastern cotton and silk fabrics, so they also imitated and improved on the steel blades of Toledo and Damascus. Within Europe the best sword blades and cutlery were made at Sölingen outside Cologne, and examples of Sölingen steel blades, often fitted with local handles, can be seen in museums from London to Zagreb.[41] Cologne itself was also noted for its swords from the twelfth century onwards, and by the thirteenth was also producing helmets and hauberks (mailshirts) in considerable quantities. When plate armour developed, from around 1300, Cologne produced that too, concentrating on large quantities of low- and medium-quality munition armour, that is armour for ordinary soldiers, which was bought ready-made, in bulk.

It was not, however, the Rhineland, but northern Italy which became the principal supplier of the armour so consistently required by the crowned heads of Europe, their nobles and their gentlemen, for the serious business of war, and the less serious, but important, pastime of tournaments. The armour of Milan and Brescia had the highest reputation of any in Europe, particularly in the fifteenth century, when armour was at its heaviest and most necessary. The iron for it was mined in many valleys in the southern flanks of the Alps from Savoy to Friuli, but particularly from the Alpine valleys above Como and Brescia.

Milan and Brescia produced both cheap ready-made armour in bulk for common soldiers and also the most extravagant made-to-measure suits of parade-armour for rulers, and every quality in between. In 1295, Frederic the Lombard delivered one such bulk order of north Italian armour to Philip IV of France, for his war with Edward I of England. It consisted of 4,511 mail shirts, 5,067 coats of plates, 2,853 helmets, 1,374 gorgets for protecting the neck, 751 pairs of gauntlets and 6,309 round shields.

Milan was by far the most important production centre for armour in medieval Europe, but Brescia ran it a close second. Both had access to locally-produced iron, to large quantities of charcoal from Alpine stands of timber, and to the fast-flowing streams needed to operate tilt hammers and polishing-

The later fifteenth-century gala helmet (left), not made for fighting in, and the complete suit of armour from around 1400 (above) are representative of the fine made-to-measure armour from Milan and Brescia which has survived so much more frequently than the cheap ready-made armour produced there in bulk.

mills. Bonvesin de Riva's famous description of Milan in 1288 included an account of its armourers just at the moment when the first beginnings of plate armour were being added to the established production of mail hauberks, helmets and swords.

Brescia had a chequered history. Although its independence as a separate state came to an end when it was taken over by Milan in 1355, the Visconti promoted its manufacture of armour. There was much movement of crafts-men between the two cities, and some manufacturers maintained workshops in both Milan and Brescia. The dukes of Milan then had lordship over much of the production of armour for sale in Europe for three generations, until the Venetians captured Brescia in 1426. The scale of the production of armour may be gauged by the fact that in 1427, after yet another defeat by Venice at the battle of Maclodio, the Duke of Milan, Filippo Maria Visconti, was able to order from the Milanese armourers 4,000 sets of cavalry armour and 2,000 sets of infantry armour, to replace what had been lost, and have it supplied within a few days. Milanese armourers went on being able to supply in this sort of quantity. Henry VIII of England was able to order 5,000 sets of light armour in 1513, and get them at a very competitive price.

The armourers of Brescia meanwhile found that their Venetian con-querors had become their best customers. In 1478, the Venetian government ordered 10,000 cuirasses and 10,000 sallets (helmets) for refitting out their standing army. This sort of bulk production was partially achieved by a degree of specialization. The large-scale merchant armourers subcontracted to workshops that made only one part of a suit of armour. One workshop made only shoulder and arm defences, another made cuirasses, back and breast plates, a third made helmets, and so on.

At the end of the fourteenth century the armourers of southern Germany began to compete with those of Milan and Brescia, just as the Ulm fustians competed with Lombard fustians, and south German merchants emulated north Italian business techniques. Until the 1420s there had been an international style in armour, dictated from Milan, and evolving in much the same way everywhere. Until this time, the armour makers of south Germany had been producing only imitations to supplement the armour imported across the Alps from Milan and Brescia to sell to German princes for themselves and their armies. From the 1420s, south German armour replaced north Italian armour in south Germany and gradually began to encroach on other European markets. From this point onwards there was a distinctive German style to the armour made in Nuremberg, Augsburg, Landshut and Innsbruck. Nuremberg became the key centre for this south German manufacture of armour, as it already was for the production of locks and of other small and complex pieces of iron work (see p. 324).

Nuremberg specialized in ready-made munition armour and, as in Milan, there was a considerable degree of specialization. Guild regulations were so framed that workshops had to remain small. Until 1507 no more than the master himself, two qualified journeymen and a single apprentice were sup-posed to work in a single workshop. It is not surprising that such tiny

When Benozzo Gozzoli set out to fulfil Piero de' Medici's commission to paint the procession of the Magi on his chapel walls, he emphasized that they were kings, rather than wise men, and consequently portrayed them in the most luxurious way he knew, using the finest products available in 1460s Florence. Everything that the Magus opposite wears is of superlative quality, from the oriental fantasy of his crown to his gold spurs. His superb Florentine silk gown, trimmed with fur, is only surpassed by the even finer silk sleeve which protrudes from it, and the bejewelled trappings for his horse. It used to be thought that the model for this king was a recollection of the Byzantine emperor John VIII Palaeologus who made a great impression when he came to the Council of Florence over twenty years earlier. There are indeed some similarities to Pisanello's portrait medal of him made when he was in Ferrara in 1438.

This group of objects, standing against a background of fifteenth-century north Italian gold brocade (see pp. 250–1), effectively represents many of the luxury trades of late medieval Europe. Most fine ivory bought throughout Europe was carved in Paris (see pp. 280-1), like the fourteenth-century Virgin and Child. The most highly prized pottery in mid-fifteenth-century Europe was Manises ware from Valencia (see p. 262), like the jar on the right. The contemporary blue and white glazed earthenware from Florence, like the apothecary's jar in the centre, seems crude in comparison, and was not traded so widely. The expensive brass wares enamelled in Limoges, like the reliquary on the left, were widely purchased in the twelfth and thirteenthth centuries, but then fell out of fashion. However the brass wares from the Meuse valley (see pp. 266–9), like the twelfth-century brass aquamanile in front, continued to have a huge sale until the fifteenth century.

workshops each concentrated on supplying single items of armour – gauntlets, leg harness, breast-plates, or arm-defences for example – to the merchants who put them together. In 1363 it was already possible to put together 1,816 sets of armour for the Emperor Charles IV, and a century later much larger quantities were put together for Matthias Corvinus of Hungary for his wars against the Turks.

Outside Milan, Brescia and Cologne, and later Nuremberg, the only places which attempted to produce considerable quantities of ordinary armour in the fourteenth century were Tournai and Bruges, and they were hampered by a lack of local iron, a lack of charcoal, and a lack of fast-running water.

There were no major production centres for armour elsewhere in Europe, not in France, nor in the British Isles, nor in Scandinavia, nor in Eastern Europe, nor in southern Italy, nor in any of the kingdoms of the Iberian peninsula. The French armies wore Italian armour and in the fifteenth century increasingly wore Nuremberg armour sent through Basel. English armies did the same, although they took some of the production from Tournai and Bruges. Spanish armies, like Italian ones, naturally wore armour from Milan and Brescia. Francesco Datini started by selling Italian armour in Avignon as a young man and went on dealing in it along with so much else, all through his life (see p. 129). Thirty-five years later, he reckoned on a 15% profit on armour he was sending from Italy to Barcelona. East European armies, on the other hand, naturally wore German armour.

Armour of the highest quality, specially made to measure for rulers and great noblemen, was produced in an overlapping range of places. Milan and Brescia could make both munition armour and parade armour. Milanese armourers, as well as making suits of armour for the dukes of Milan themselves, also made armour for the kings of England and France, and their close relations and for the dukes of Burgundy. Brescia armourers supplied the Montefeltro dukes of Urbino, the marquesses of Ferrara and Mantua and the Ottoman Sultan Bāyezīd II. The largest manufacturers even did both, like the Missaglia firm in Milan. In 1430 the firm sent off 5,000 lire worth of ready-made armour speculatively for sale in Tuscany and the Romagna and in 1436 it was collecting debts from Catalonia, Aragon, Navarre and Galicia. However, the head of the firm, Tomaso, was also personal armourer to the last Visconti Duke of Milan, Filippo Maria, who knighted him in 1435. In 1450 the first Sforza duke, Francesco, renewed his appointment as personal armourer. The firm not only made armour, but also leased iron mines and owned several polishing-mills. It made enormous profits and the next head of the Missaglia firm, Antonio, sank some of his share of the profits in the purchase of a noble fief in 1472.

For high-quality luxury armour it was not Nuremberg but Augsburg, and to a lesser extent Landshut and Innsbruck that tried to rival Milan. The Helmschmid firm was the most prestigious in Augsburg, and like the Missaglia in Milan continued for several generations. Lorenz Helmschmid made armour for the Emperor Frederick III in the 1470s. At Landshut there

As well as verdure tapestries woven speculatively and despatched for sale without individual clients in mind, figured tapestries commissioned for particular rooms were among the most expensive forms of art to be sent across Europe. St John (opposite), gripping his book of Revelation, while gazing intently at the souls of the martyrs, comes from one of the famous Apocalypse tapestries specially woven in Paris between 1366 and 1382 for hanging in Angers (see pp. 108 and 266).

was a home court market after the division of Bavaria created a separate Duchy of Bavaria-Landshut in 1425. As well as the local dukes, personal customers for Landshut's finest armour included the Duke of Saxony and Matthias Corvinus of Hungary.

The armourers of Mühlau, just outside Innsbruck, where there was fast-running water for polishing-mills, also had a home court market in the counts of Tyrol, who not only wore Innsbruck armour themselves, but also sent it as prestigious presents to other rulers, like James III of Scotland or Matthias of Hungary.

At Bruges the manufacture of high-quality armour was added to the existing production of munition armour when Philip the Good came to live largely in the Netherlands from the late 1430s. In successive generations the rulers of the Netherlands, Philip the Good, Charles the Rash, and Mary's consort Maximilian all had armour made for them in Bruges. The manufacture of first class armour similarly began at Tours when the kings of France came to live in the Loire valley in the 1430s.

Many of those other centres for the manufacture of armour drew on craftsmen and entrepreneurs from Milan. The first Milanese armourer arrived in Tours as early as 1425, and under Louis XI there was a small colony of them there. Milanese armourers also participated in the high-quality production at Mühlau–Innsbruck, Landshut and Bruges.

Despite the growing number of armourers in or near courts, many rulers went on buying armour of the finest workmanship from great distances for themselves. However there was a very real problem in producing well-fitting made-to-measure armour for far away customers. At the prodigious prices paid for it, it needed to be well-fitting. In 1386 the accounts of Louis, the brother of Charles VI, then Duke of Touraine, but later Duke of Orléans, reveal that he bought three ells of fine Rheims linen to have a doublet made to send as a pattern to his armourer.

When the Earl of Derby, later Henry IV of England, ordered armour from Milan, four armourers came with it to give him a fitting, before finishing it and hardening it. In 1464 Francesco Missaglia came personally from Milan to measure Philip the Good and two years later he went to France to measure Louis XI for a set of the finest Milanese armour, despite the existence by then of high-quality armourers in Bruges and Tours. The Missaglia firm's products were simply regarded as the best that could be obtained. It was not until the sixteenth century that the solution was reached of modelling the customer in wax. Charles V was then able to send wax models of the imperial legs from Spain to the Helmschmids in Augsburg.

Some of the armour produced for rulers demanded the cooperation of goldsmiths with armourers. In 1385 the parade armour made for John I of Castile had a gold and jewelled crown attached to the *bacinet*, whilst in the 1460s Philip the Good simply had a *gorget* (collar) made of gold. The next ruler of the Netherlands, his son Charles, had his superb court goldsmith, Gerard Loyet, enamel his steel *gorget*.

Brass

Across four centuries workshops in the Meuse valley cast an extraordinary range of brass objects from Renier de Huy's early twelfth-century font for Liège (left) to the candelabra painted into the Arnolfini marriage portrait by Jan van Eyck in 1434 (right).

Brass, an alloy of copper and zinc, was used very extensively in the later Middle Ages. Although in the final product there is much more copper than zinc, to achieve this result much more zinc ore (calamine) was needed than copper ore. Sometimes the quantity of calamine used was four times as much as that of copper ore. The largest brass industry of medieval Europe therefore grew up in the vicinity of calamine deposits rather than those of copper. The principal calamine deposits worked in medieval Europe lay in the hills to the east of Liège, from near Aachen in the north to Givet in the south. These fed brass-manufacture not only in Aachen and Liège, but also in the Meuse valley at Huy and Dinant, further west at Malines (Mechelen), and in the Rhine valley around Cologne. The copper used came from the deposits in the Harz mountains around Goslar in lower Saxony and a less important brass industry therefore did grow up in lower Saxony itself. Latten, a variant on brass, also incorporated a quantity of tin, much of which was obtained from Cornwall in England.

There was a continuous tradition of brass-founding of large objects in the Meuse valley from the twelfth century onwards. One of the earliest and most dramatic of its products is the spectacular brass font at Liège, cast around 1110 by Renier de Huy. Bell-founding was in continuous demand in the later Middle Ages , and there was also a market for other church furnishings in brass. Brass lecterns, for example, were exported in considerable numbers. Around forty-five standard 'eagle' lecterns, exported to British churches, still survive, mainly in East Anglia. The lectern in King's College Chapel in Cambridge is a remarkable, if rather late, example of a more complicated pattern. Monumental brasses, supplied in the form of complete plates of latten, had considerable commercial success and were sold to customers from the Iberian peninsula to Scandinavia and Poland.[42] England, as well as importing 'Flemish' memorial brasses, particularly from the *tombiers* of Tournai in the mid-fourteenth century, also had its own monumental brass workshops. English marblers imported unengraved latten plates and cut out effigies and inscriptions to make composite memorials of latten and Purbeck marble (or sometimes Derbyshire alabaster) for an English market focused on the royal court in London. Several thousand of these composite memorials still survive. Nearly all were made in London, where at any one time only one or two firms dominated the craft from the late thirteenth century onwards.[43]

In the course of the fifteenth century more efficient cannon began to be cast, like church bells, in bronze rather than forged in iron. The early iron cannon appear to have been more of a danger to those who fired them than to those they were aimed at. Charles the Rash provided a considerable home market for the new, more expensive, longer-barrelled cannon, but cannon from Mechelen were also widely exported.

As well as such large objects, there was also a wide international market for domestic brassware. From the thirteenth century brass cauldrons, with three or four legs and a handle for carrying and suspension, began to replace earthenware. By the fifteenth century brass kettles were being produced as well. Brass mortars, used domestically for grinding spices, or in pharmacy, replaced stone ones. Brass candlesticks were exported extensively for domestic as well as church lighting, whether made to be attached to the wall or stand on tables. Socketed brass candlesticks came to supplant the pricket form from the end of the thirteenth century.

Brass water-containers, whether conventional ewers or the exotic aquamanile animal shapes so fashionable in the thirteenth century, replaced pottery ones. In a pre-fork society, in which people used their fingers for eating much more than we do, these were regularly used for pouring water for

About 1500 the Flemish 'Master of St Augustine' had a splendid time painting a whole range of brass objects in the saint's chamber, such as were by then being made in many towns from Brussels, Mechelen and Antwerp eastwards to Cologne. He mostly painted items to be expected in a bedroom like a washing set, a candlestick, a lantern, a small bell and a bucket, but also what appears to be a censer for liturgical use.

hand-washing after meals, in conjunction with broad deep dishes. These hand-washing sets were only a part of the extensive use of brass for all sorts of tableware. Brass tableware was for long more popular than pewter, for those who wanted something better than treen or coarse pottery, but could not rise to silver plate. Dinant was the most important centre for the production of such brass tableware, which was consequently known as 'Dinanderie'. Dinant brassworkers drew their calamine from the mines of Körnelimünster and Gressenich. Dinanderie was exported throughout Europe and pieces are to be found in display in museums from London to Cracow. The quantity sent out could be enormous. The customs accounts for Hull, not one of England's most important ports, show that seven shiploads of brass 'pots' were imported in 1310–11, one of which consisted of 11,400 items.[44] After the capture and burning of Dinant in 1466, Philip the Good of Burgundy ordered his receiver general from Namur to have men search through the ruins and appropriate what metalwork could be found. In the ruins 2,950 pounds weight of brass objects was recovered, besides a large quantity of calamine. The quantity of 'copper' objects, some half made, was only small in comparison with the brass. They included a considerable number of cauldrons, and several batches of candlesticks, including 141 in one batch and 85 in another. Pewter was also being made in Dinant, for plates, spoons and other objects of 'tin' were recovered. Although the total weight of worked 'tin' found, 350 pounds, was very much less than that of brass, there was also 760 pounds of unworked tin from England waiting for use, besides 1,000 pounds of lead, and 160 pounds of lead and tin ready mixed in the proportion of 2 parts of lead to 3 of tin. The same men were involved in both trades, for more than 12 hammers, large and small, belonging to *batterie* were recovered, which since they were marked with a sign of ownership, were sold back to their previous owner, described as a coppersmith, along with a quantity of objects of both 'copper' and 'tin' which also bore his mark.[45]

Dinant never recovered. Its brass-workers were scattered and brass-working, already important at Mechelen and Aachen, became yet more important still and developed at Brussels, Namur and Antwerp. The church of Zoutleeuw ordered an eagle lectern in brass from Antwerp in 1469 and an absolutely enormous brass paschal candlestick, 5.68 metres (18 feet 5½ inches) high from Brussels in 1482. Brass-working also developed, much more surprisingly, at Nuremberg, which, unlike other brass-producing centres (Dinant, Aachen or lower Saxony), was near neither calamine nor copper deposits. The merchants of Nuremberg, however, were active traders in copper and shared in the control of exploitation of the newly discovered copper deposits in Slovakia. The Nuremberg brass industry was a by-product of this control. The metal-working skills developed in fine iron-work were applied to brass wares, made, under mercantile control, for export markets.[46]

Dinanderie and pewter were, of course, not the only prestigious tableware manufactured in Europe. There were also specialized producers of luxury glass and high-class pottery, which were worth carrying, despite their

Although brass manufacture was initially concentrated in the Meuse valley, similar products were made at an early date at Aachen and in the Rhine valley around Cologne. This brass water jug in the shape of a lion was made in one of these nearby German centres as early as the thirteenth century.

Glass

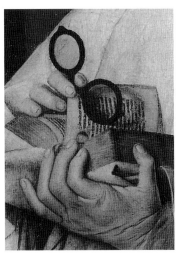

From the thirteenth century onwards mirrors and spectacles from Venice were sent all over Europe. They both found a place in fifteenth-century Flemish paintings. In the 1430s Jan van Eyck put a mirror in his portrait of the Arnolfini (left), and spectacles in the hands of Canon van der Paele (right).

fragility, over vast distances. In the later Middle Ages the Venetian Republic had for long been the foremost producer of glass in Europe. Glass was no longer produced in the city itself: because of the fire hazards in the closely built-up central islands of thirteenth-century Venice, the glass makers' furnaces had been banished across the lagoon to the island of Murano in 1291. Like European silk, cotton and paper, European glass-manufacture began as an import substitute. The glass-making skills of Venetian artisans were ultimately derived from Syria. Inferior glass had long been made in Venice, in Torcello as early as the eighth century and in Venice itself by the tenth. The transition to superior glass came in the thirteenth century, with the import of the peculiarly appropriate alkaline ash, rich in sodium, from Syria in place of ash obtained from burning local plants (see pp. 273–4). The Venetians had a near-monopoly of this import. It was one of the key ingredients of the superiority of Venetian glass over that made elsewhere. Suitable sands from the lagoon itself and from the Adige, and plentiful fuel cheaply shipped in across the Adriatic were among the other advantages enjoyed by the Venetian glassmakers. Ordinary cups and bottles, clear window glass and mirrors were sent out in enormous quantities, as well as the prestigious and expensive polychrome bowls and vases, sometimes exotically enamelled, which are so much better known. As well as exporting Murano glass northwards and westwards, Venetians also exported it eastwards, to Egypt by the 1310s, to Greece, Constantinople, Rhodes and the Black Sea coasts by the 1340s, and in the fifteenth century even to Syria, where the native glass industry was totally eclipsed. In the first half of the fifteenth century an improved method of purifying the ashes to obtain a high grade alkali carbonate was discovered, presumably in Venice, and this allowed for further developments, like the invention of *cristallo*, glass that imitates rock-crystal.

From the end of the thirteenth century spectacles were another Venetian speciality, since the glass industry was able to provide the precisely moulded and highly polished clear glass lenses that were needed. Spectacle-making spread across Europe from Venice in the later Middle Ages, and reached as far as England before the middle of the fifteenth century. The earliest known spectacle-maker there was a German, taxed in 1441–43 in Southwark, on the south bank of the Thames immediately opposite London.[47]

The reputation of Murano glass-makers was such that attempts were made to lure them to other Italian cities, beginning as early as the end of the thirteenth century. The Venetian government strenuously tried to keep a monopoly of superior glass-making, and forbade craftsmen to go abroad, as well as preventing the re-export of Syrian ash. However, from time to time some craftsmen did succumb to foreign enticement, and a few small glass-works were set up elsewhere, including Florence and Ancona. Venetian opposition was more effective in preventing most other glass-makers from obtaining Syrian ash than from obtaining skilled craftsmen. Only the established glass-making tradition at Altare in Liguria was able to benefit from Syrian ash, which had been imported through Genoa. Altare glass, however never enjoyed the same reputation as Venetian.

Venice was effectively able to maintain its position as the unrivalled maker of superior glass to Europe and the Mediterranean world until the end of the Middle Ages. In the fifteenth century ineffective attempts were made to improve the cruder glass being made in France, the Low Countries and particularly in south Germany by bringing in craftsmen from Altare and Murano. Some unimproved glass had a market of its own by the fifteenth century. A glass industry had developed in Bohemia in the fourteenth century, reputedly under the patronage of the Emperor Charles IV (King of Bohemia 1346–78). On the eve of the Hussite Wars in the 1420s there was a score of glass workshops in Bohemia known to historians that produced not only stained glass for church windows and plain window glass for affluent houses, but also greenish-yellow utility glass tablewares. This had not only a home market, but was also exported to Silesia by the 1470s, and indeed throughout central Europe. Examples of Bohemian glass of this period have been found in excavations as far away as Lübeck. Meanwhile the Bohemian nobility imported Venetian glass, and Bohemian glass was not improved in imitation of Venetian until the 1570s.[48]

Pottery, like cloth and iron goods, was made everywhere, but just as there was luxury cloth and luxury ironwork made in a limited number of places which entered into international trade, so there was luxury pottery. There was a whole hierarchy of potteries across Europe that supplied more than local needs, like those of Saintonge in western France and Aardenberg in the Netherlands. Wares from both these potteries have been found in excavations in Yorkshire in northern England. At the top of the hierarchy, the most favoured was tin-glazed earthenware of Muslim, eventually Persian, origin. In the early fourteenth century Majorca was key to the distribution of the glazed earthenwares of Valencia and Andalusia, hence its name *majolica*. Around 1320 *majolica* was being sent to England and Flanders.[49] By the early fifteenth century the most important place of manufacture for this lustrous Hispano-Moresque tin-glazed earthenware was Manises in the hinterland of

Oriental influences are evident in some of the glass wares produced on Murano and exported all over Europe. The finest, decorated with gold and enamel, like this late fifteenth-century jug, could compete with plate for the tables of the aristocracy.

Pottery

As well as importing glazed earthenware from the Muslim shores of the Mediterranean, potters in Pisa, Arezzo, Siena and Florence began producing rather primitive and derivative 'maiolioca arcaica' by the end of the thirteenth century. In the fourteenth century this Tuscan pottery evolved alongside the more successful wares being produced in the Romagna at Faenza. By the second quarter of the fifteenth century the most skilled potters in Florence were able to produce much more sophisticated majolica fit to grace the tables of Renaissance nobility, like this two-handled tin-glazed jar decorated in cobalt blue.

Valencia. Until the middle of the fifteenth century, Manises ware was exported to all parts of Europe, even to Italy, where a rival version of majolica was being produced at Faenza in the Romagna for use at table, and for spice jars, apothecary's pots, tiles and decorative pieces. Like cottons and silks, glass and paper, the Italian manufacture of majolica had begun as another import substitute. Fine late fourteenth-century examples of Faenza majolica are known, and by 1410 there was a separate majolica guild in the city with its own statutes. After capturing the home markets of Italy from Manises and Muslim wares, Faenza majolica was widely exported, particularly at the expense of Manises ware, in the second half of the fifteenth century, to the nobility of other parts of Europe, amongst whom it became generally known as *faience* from the French form of the city's name. Just as Lucchese silk-workers and Fabriano paper-makers spread through Italy, setting up silk-looms and paper-mills where they settled, so, from the mid-fifteenth century, Faenza majolica potters set up majolica potteries in other parts of Italy, particularly in the Romagna and Tuscany. Its manufacture eventually spread to France and the Low Countries where potteries made their own majolica. It is yet another case of the substitution wheel coming full circle. The exported Italian import-substitute had been substituted for.

Soap   Just as Italian majolica-makers took over from Spaniards, so did Italian soap-makers, particularly in Venice. The Castilians had succeeded in developing a white, olive-oil-based, soap alongside the traditional black soap, which was also made in Castile. This white soap was the luxury soap *par excellence* of thirteenth-century Europe. Castile exported it particularly to the nobility of northern Europe by sea. They also exported the black soap to northern

Europe for the woollen cloth industry for cleansing the cloth before finishing. White soap cost over three times as much as black.[50] White Castilian soap depended not only on abundant supplies of local oil, but also on the availability of suitable plants to burn to produce alkali-rich ash. Once Venetians, Genoese and Provençal merchants started importing suitable 'soda ash' from Egypt and Syria, soap-making could be transformed in Italy and Provence as well. South Italian olive oil was the other key ingredient. Apulian olive oil was shipped across and up the Adriatic to supply the soap-makers of Ragusa, Ancona and above all Venice, whilst on the west coast soap was made in the south itself at Naples and, above all, at Gaeta, and further north at Savona and Genoa. In the fourteenth century, the Venetians and Genoese competed directly with the Castilians for the north European market. They also exported soap to the Near East, to Frankish Greece, Constantinople, Turkish Asia Minor, Rhodes, Cyprus, and in very considerable quantities, back to Syria and Egypt, whence the ash came. At an earlier period northern Syria and Palestine had produced considerable quantities of fine soap themselves. There seems no evidence to suggest that imitative Italian soap, unlike Italian paper, was markedly better than its Levantine original.[51] All this trade was carried by sea, but with the much higher costs of land transport, it was problematic how far it was worth carrying such a heavy product by road. In the late fourteenth century this luxury white soap was about the cheapest commodity for its weight that it was worth carrying across the Alps (see p. 354).

As we have seen, the alkaline properties of 'soda ash' made it essential for the famous Venetian glass industry, and also for the manufacture of high-quality soap. It was obtained by burning *salsola* and other related small bushes that grew only in Syria. They were gathered from the fringes of the desert and the sea coast, where they flourished in the saline soil. The plants were called *kali* by the Syrians, and their ashes were normally called *lumen*, although *kali* was sometimes applied to the ashes too. The Venetians used the term *lume* and *kily*, but sometimes added the article to the noun, so forming *allumen* and *alkali*.

Soda ash

The first report of the import of *allumen* into Venice dates from 1233, and in 1275 the re-export of Syrian ash from Venice was forbidden for the first time. The ashes were principally obtained in Tripoli, although some were bought at Aleppo and Beirut, and, during the papal interdiction on direct trade with the Mamluks in the first half of the fourteenth century, from the Christian kingdom of Lesser Armenia. They were relatively cheap in Syria, but were heavy. Shipping costs were therefore considerable, and could exceed the original cost, even when they were used to ballast Venetian cotton cogs, when the costs of sailing were largely covered by the cotton. They were certainly not something to ship in a galley. They were very profitable to carry, because although cheap in Syria, they were much in demand in Venice. The shippers could apparently make as much as a 200% profit on their initial outlay. It is difficult to gauge the scale of the trade. Fragmentary evidence includes the isolated fact that 1,200 *migliaia*, each of a thousand Venetian pounds, around 570 tonnes, sailed with the Venetian spring convoy in 1395. Other information is expressed in 'sacks' but suggests that this might have been rather a large half-year. The Venetians tried, as far as possible, to keep a tight grip on the Syrian ash and tried to prevent it reaching other glass-makers, elsewhere in Italy, or in the fifteenth century in Germany. They even tried to prevent it reaching majolica-makers.

As well as Syrian ash there was also Egyptian ash, from similar plants, which could be bought at Alexandria and Damietta. However, according to Pegolotti, it was only a third of the value of the Syrian. Venetian glass-manufacturers found it totally unsuitable, although it was perfectly usable for making soap. Venetians took it in quantity to the soap-makers of Gaeta, as well as to their own.

Merchants from Genoa, Ancona and Provence also shipped Egyptian, and to a lesser extent Syrian, ash into Europe. This was mostly used for soap-manufacture in Genoa and Savona, Ancona and Ragusa, Gaeta and Naples and Provence, and even occasionally Flanders and England. The Spanish, however, were able to use ash from similar plants which grew in Spain itself. All this was 'sweet' olive-oil-based soap, but north Europeans could only make inferior 'speckled' tallow-based soap. To supply north European soap-making there was a separate, but also quite considerable trade in potash, which was brought to Bruges from Denmark and Germany. The potash did not originate in Germany, for the Germans of the Hanseatic towns them-selves imported potash from Russia, where it was obtained from burning a quite different range of plants.

Trade in 'works of art'   The glass of Venice and the majolica of Faenza were certainly bought for their decorative value as much as for their practical use. They shared, there-fore, in the trade in works of art that developed in late medieval Europe. Some of these were produced in the capital cities of Europe, like *Opus Angli-canum* in London, or the ivories of Paris, but most were made in the textile-manufacturing areas of northern Italy and the southern Netherlands. Is it more than a strange coincidence that so many paintings of the fourteenth and fifteenth centuries were produced in Ghent and Brussels, Florence and Siena? Some of the greatest of these were specifically produced for export, like the triptych that Hugo van der Goes painted in Ghent in 1474–75, for Tommaso Portinari, the manager of the Medici branch in Bruges, to send back to Florence for the high altar of S. Egidio, Florence, the church of the great Hospital of Santa Maria Nuova, founded nearly two centuries earlier by his ancestor Folco Portinari. Italian works of art went in the opposite direc-tion, for example the tomb made in Florence for a bishop of Tournai by Andrea della Robbia. The order was placed through the Medici firm in Bruges.

Paintings by well known artists of the fifteenth-century Renaissance, like van der Weyden and Bouts, Masaccio and Botticelli, form only the most visible, prestigious and appreciated tip of a vast invisible artistic iceberg. Beneath them were the large number of men whose names we no longer know, but who have been dignified by art historians with the soubriquet of 'The Master of…', like 'the Master of the view of St Gudule' who, from the scale of his surviving output, must have run a very large workshop in late fifteenth-century Brussels, specializing in the production, after a well tried formula, of vast altarpieces for export.

Beneath these again was a host of inferior workshops, like those in Florence around 1400 who supplied the philistine Francesco Datini with third-rate pictures of sacred subjects which he cynically bought in bulk at cheap rates to purvey, with many other lines of business, to Avignon, where one of the rival popes still kept his curia, and where there was consequently a lively market for such works. In 1387 his Avignon agent wrote to him 'You say you can't find panels at the price we want, because there aren't any at such low prices. You should only buy them when the master's hard up. So, if you're looking around and find a master who's in need of money, then come to terms.' When he had been in Avignon himself ten years earlier he had written back to Florence in similar terms.[52]

There is documentary evidence of the movement of painters from Constantinople to Crete before 1453, and in the second half of the fifteenth century Crete became the most important centre of art in the Greek world. Once again as well as prestigious works of art there was a huge outpouring of third-rate pictures which simply counted as merchandise. Notarial documents from Candia (now Heraklion) record numerous bulk orders by Venetian merchants from icon painters there, for export to western Europe, particularly Flanders. One such commission, in 1499, was for 700 paintings of the Virgin to be delivered in forty-five days: 200 were to be icons in the Byzantine tradition (*in forma greca*), but 500 were to be in a western style (*in forma a la latina*). Under these conditions originality was necessarily lacking, and technical perfection at a premium. Surviving fifteenth-century icons illustrate the repetitive use of successful and established iconographic formulae.[53]

Professor van der Wee has gone so far as to suggest that the creation of an export trade in works of art in the same centres as the manufacture of luxury textiles was no coincidence at all, but part of a *conscious* restructuring of the economy of these cities when their luxury textile manufacture was in decline. What is clear is that once a painting tradition was established in a place, young men born elsewhere were attracted to it. Hans Memling, for example, was drawn to Bruges from Seligenstadt near Mainz, and Gentile da Fabriano to Florence from Fabriano. Once a tradition was established more than merely native talent was soon involved. But what established a tradition? The home demand apparent in capital cities is sufficient explanation for the growth of the London broderers and the Paris ivory-workers, but what of the textile cities? I have already suggested that in the absence of a capital, until Philip the Good as ruler of a united Netherlands settled in Brussels in his latter years, Bruges acted as the consumption centre for the rulers and nobility, rural and urban of the Low Countries, and that Florence, Milan and Venice were, by the fifteenth century, effectively the capital cities of rich and

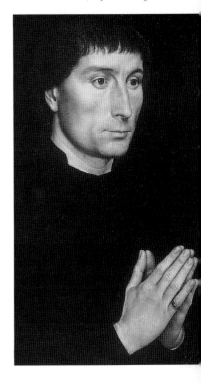

Before he commissioned the triptych from van der Goes to send to Florence, Tommaso Portinari had himself painted in Bruges by the newly established German painter Hans Memling.

A carpet imported into Italy from the Near East, and laid neatly down some steps, lends a touch of comfortable realism to Domenico Ghirlandaio's painting of the Virgin with Child. It is just part of his meticulous and convincing view of life in Florence at the end of the fifteenth century. He was not alone in incorporating carpets into paintings, either in Italy (see pp. 268–9, illustration p. 72) or the Netherlands.

prosperous states, as well as commercial and industrial cities. As such they were great centres of consumption. The wealth of their manufacturers was only one part of the home demand in such places, and it is clear, at least for well known and famous artists, that the larger part of their work was for the home market, van Eyck for the lord of Pamele, van de Weyden for Philip the Good and members of his court, Benozzo Gozzoli for the Medici, Bramante for the Sforza, and the Bellini for the upper nobility of Venice. For these artists the export market was an addition to the demand from the ruler, the great officers of state, and the nobility at home.

Tapestries and carpets

Tapestries and *Opus Anglicanum* are products where painting and textiles did meet. Every tapestry had an artist to design it before the tapestry-weaver could begin, and some tapestries had fashionable painters to design them. Rogier van der Weyden, for example, designed tapestries for Alfonso V of Naples and Lionello d'Este of Ferrara.[54]

Tapestry-weaving was yet another skill imported into Europe from the Middle East. In 1262 it was already appropriate for one of the proctors of Henry III of England at the court of Louis IX of France to be seeking in Paris for a suitable tapestry for the hall of the English chancellor.[55] What is not clear is whether the tapestries that he looked at had been imported from the Middle East or had been made in Paris itself. By the middle of the fourteenth century tapestry-weaving was clearly well established in Paris itself, where the court provided a prodigious market, as well as in Arras. The French royal family were themselves lavish purchasers. John II bought at least 235 tapestries between 1350 and 1364, and his sons, Charles V and the dukes of Burgundy, Anjou and Berry continued the tradition (see pp. 108–9). In 1364, Louis of Anjou, by the age of 25, had already acquired 76 tapestries, and went on spending lavishly on them all his life, including the famous Angers *Apocalypse* tapestries, which were woven in the Paris workshop of Nicolas Bataille on a gigantic loom six metres wide (ills. pp. 110 and 264). Tapestry-weaving was enormously labour intensive and proportionately expensive. The duke paid Bataille a thousand gold francs for each tapestry.[56] With the same money he could have employed ten master masons or carpenters, with forty assistants, on a building project for a whole year. By 1400 it was his wealthier elder brother Philip the Bold of Burgundy who was said to have owned the finest collection of tapestries existing in Europe. In the next generation Charles VI's brother, Louis Duke of Orléans, and his Milanese duchess, Valentina, also bought tapestries on a grand scale, woven for them both in Paris and Arras.[57] Charles VI, however, was the last king to live in Paris for well over a century, and Paris collapsed as a centre of consumption. With the removal of the court market, Parisian tapestry-weaving came to an end around 1425.

In the fifteenth century, after the failure of tapestry-weaving in Paris, it was heavily concentrated in the southern Netherlands. Until its capture by Louis XI in 1477, Arras was the centre of the industry and gave its name to the product – 'arras', 'arras cloths', 'arazzi'. However it was not alone. There were already tapestry weavers at Bruges and Tournai in the fourteenth century. Tournai was almost as important a producer as Arras by the beginning of the fifteenth century. In the middle of the century, Brussels, with the court market, rapidly increased in importance. A number of other centres, like Oudenaarde, made cheaper tapestries. Such tapestries were also woven in the rural areas around Oudenaarde and Geraardsbergen from the mid-fifteenth century as linen-weaving declined. The Oudenaarde tapestry-weavers were sufficiently numerous to have a guild of their own in 1441. Shortly afterwards tapestry-weavers formed guilds in Ghent and Bruges, where 114 tapestry-weavers are known from the fifteenth century.[58] Tapestries were naturally sold through Bruges and later through Antwerp, where some were also made. From there they were distributed throughout Europe. The less expensive sort, called *verdure*, greenery, had repetitive foliage patterns, and could safely be sold speculatively, but the most expensive tapestries were ordered specially by individual clients, who asked for particular stories to hang in particular rooms. In the second half of the fourteenth century Philip the Bold of Burgundy had already commissioned numerous tapestries to be sent from Arras to Paris. In the next generation, Louis of Orléans also had tapestries sent from Arras to Paris. He sometimes had them carried out from his Paris hôtel for use at his new castle at Pierrefonds, where the tapestry hooks still survive, although, alas, not the tapestries themselves. At the same time one of the sons of Edward III of England, John of Gaunt, Duke of Lancaster, also had Arras tapestries woven for hanging in his palatial 'inn' on the Strand between London and Westminster. In the mid-fifteenth century a Lille tapestry-maker was commissioned to make two sets of tapestries to send to Florence for Giovanni and Piero, the sons of Cosimo de'Medici. Giovanni's set represented the 'Triumphs of Petrarch'. The Medici firm in Bruges also supplied other Italians like Gaspare, Count of Vimercato, a courtier in Milan, and Astorre Manfredi, Lord of Faenza, who purchased a set representing the story of 'Sampson'. At about the same time, Federigo da Montefeltro had Flemish tapestries woven for the throne room of his new ducal palace at Urbino, and so did the king of Poland for his palace at Cracow. Federigo sent the designs from Italy to be woven in Tournai. The tapestry workshops of Arras were already a sight for discerning travellers to wonder at. When he went out from Bruges to visit them in 1438 Pero Tafur concluded:

> It is a pleasant place, and very rich, especially by reason of its woven cloths and all kinds of tapestries, and although they are made in other places, yet it well appears that *those which are made in Arras have the preference*.[59]

At the end of the fifteenth century the southern Netherlands still remained the centre for European tapestry-weaving. The current vogue was for *millefleurs* tapestries, in which the figures were placed on a flowery ground on dark blue and red backgrounds. The finest surviving examples are those that form the series of six tapestries of the 'Lady of the Unicorn', woven for Jean le Viste of Lyons, Lord of Arcy and, at his death in 1500, President of the French Cour des Aides. Other unicorn tapestries of this period also survive as well as a series of 'Scenes from Courtly Life'.

On his visit in 1438 Pero Tafur joined to woollen cloths, as the key manufacture of the hinterland of Bruges, not only 'arras cloths' but also 'all kinds of carpets'.[60] The weaving of carpets, for covering tables and benches and walls as well as floors, was yet another replacement for a hitherto imported oriental luxury. Europeans had been importing carpets from Asia Minor since the late thirteenth century. Marco Polo believed it was the Armenians and Greeks living amongst the Turks in such cities as Konya (Iconium), Kaisarieh (Caesarea) and Sivas (Sebasteia) who wove 'the choicest and most beautiful carpets in the world'. The carpets with figurative motifs that appear in some fifteenth-century Italian paintings are believed to be these Anatolian carpets. In fifteenth-century Europe a mania developed for oriental carpets, not only 'Turkish', but also Persian and even Indian.[61] A secular, non-figurative carpet is to be found under the throne of Ludovico Gonzaga, in Mantegna's frescoes in the Camera degli Sposi in Mantua, and carpets hung from balconies abound in Vittore Carpaccio's paintings for Venetian confraternities. When carpets were being imported into Europe in some quantity, it is little wonder that European imitations began to be made. Carpet-weaving was taken up in the fifteenth-century Netherlands in a number of large and medium sized towns, such as Ghent, Leuven and Wervik, particularly when traditional cloth-making was in decline. Tienen (Tirlemont) in south

Brabant, was one of the small towns where woollen-manufacture had begun to prosper in the second half of the fourteenth century. At the end of the century Hanseatic merchants were sending its cloths from Bruges through the Baltic to Gdansk and Prussia, and onward up the Vistula via Torun to Cracow, Silesia and Slovakia. When its markets shrank in the mid-fifteenth-century depression, Tienen turned to weaving carpets, which were carried in waggon-loads for sale at the Bergen-op-Zoom fairs. By 1470–71 the proceeds of the excise on the growing manufacture of carpets was already nearly 60% of the shrinking excise on woollens.[62]

Opus Anglicanum
and ivory

In the first half of the thirteenth century we know that *Opus Anglicanum*, embroidery in silks and gold thread on various fabrics, but usually on linen, was purchased by Henry III of England. English royal accounts for the next two centuries continue to show the kings of England and members of their families as customers of the London 'broderers', as the embroiderers of *Opus Anglicanum* were called. Other rulers followed suit. In the mid-thirteenth century, popes Innocent IV, Alexander IV and Urban IV all ordered *Opus Anglicanum* for themselves. Most of the surviving examples are ecclesiastical, elaborate copes and chasubles embroidered with religious subjects. By the end of the century Boniface VIII's treasury contained no fewer than 113 items of English embroidery.[63] Documentary evidence, however, indicates that there was a considerable secular market as well, although little survives. Embroidered robes once existed in quantity, as worn, for example, by Edward III, his Queen, and his son the Black Prince, and also embroidered sets of bed furnishings – with matching coverlet, tester, cushions and hangings. Like tapestry, every piece of embroidery needed an artist to sketch its design before the broderers began work. The broderers and their designers formed a close group, living and working in a particular area of London.[64]

Although pre-eminent in the thirteenth and fourteenth centuries, English broderers were not alone. There was a privileged group in Paris from the end of the thirteenth century. At the end of the fourteenth century Florentine embroideries were being sold from Avignon to Philip the Bold, Duke of Burgundy and regent of France. In the course of the fifteenth century a prestigious group of broderers emerged, along with the tapestry-weavers, in the shadow of the Burgundian court, who also served a wider market. When the import-export merchant's guild of Florence, the Calimala, wished to provide a prestigious set of heavily embroidered liturgical vestments for use on major feast days in the city's baptistery, they commissioned a major local artist, Antonio del Pollaiuolo, to design them. However instead of sending his sketches to the Low Countries, they imported a team of broderers in 1466 led by a man from Mechelen whose name was italianized as Coppino. Coppino and his team were still working on the cycle of embroidered panels of the life of Florence's patron saint, St John the Baptist, in 1480.[65] Just as the broderers in the English capital for long held something of a monopoly in the supply of the highest quality embroidery to the rulers and nobles and the greater prelates throughout Europe, the ivory-carvers of Paris did much the same.

Secular survivals from the vast output of Paris ivory-carvers are rarer than religious ones. This lively fourteenth-century scene on the end panel of a small ivory box is entirely secular: a hunter galloping out of his castle gateway blowing his horn, with his basset hound beside him.

There was a large home market to support the Paris ivory-carvers, but they also found markets throughout Europe. Of the 2,000–3,000 examples of medieval European carved ivory in museums throughout the world the overwhelming majority are from Paris. Only a handful were carved in other places, at most 60 in England, and rather more in Italy.

Almost all the surviving ivory objects can be dated between 1270 and 1400. It is not clear whether this chronology mainly relates to fashion, or to political events that affected the home market in Paris, or to trading conditions outside Europe. Elephant tusks were bought in Acre, Alexandria and Lajazzo by Italian merchants, who shipped them to Marseilles, Aigues Mortes or Bruges for transmission to Paris, where several guilds were involved in a veritable ivory-carving quarter of the city. As with *Opus Anglicanum*, most of the surviving ivories are religious, not only small devotional carvings, but pyxes for the host and heads to pastoral staffs. However, documentary evidence again reveals that secular boxes of ivory, combs, mirrors and cups, chess-men and dice, counters for draughts and backgammon once existed in considerable numbers, let alone knife-handles and writing tablets.

By the end of the reign of St Louis, when ivory-carving began to be on a considerable scale, Paris had been a fast growing capital for some time, and the leading artistic centre in Europe. At the end of the century, his grandson, Philip IV, was actively encouraging yet more princes and nobles, even some from strictly outside the borders of his kingdom to spend part of their lives in Paris. This built it up as a consumption centre for such luxuries as ivory. Although Parisian ivory-carving came to an end during the troubled reign of Charles VI, which saw the breakdown of Paris as the centre for the nobility of the whole kingdom, the collapse in the consumption of luxuries does not seem an adequate explanation, as it does for the end of tapestry-weaving, since ivory-carving had ceased in Paris during a period of relative prosperity more than twenty years before the death of the king, and even a decade before the breakdown of government in the civil war of Armangnacs and Burgundians. Furthermore the carving of ivory, unlike the weaving of tapestries, did not shift elsewhere when it ceased in Paris. An explanation must be sought rather in the supply of ivory itself. It is probable, but by no means certain, that Indian elephants provided the bulk of the ivory. Trading across Asia was certainly becoming easier in the 1270s, which fits with the increase in Parisian ivory-carving. Although direct trade between Europe and India had broken down long since, it was still continuing in the second half of the fourteenth century through a sequence of intermediaries. However in the 1390s the trade routes were greatly disrupted by the rise of Timur, who not only overran Persia and Iraq, but entered India itself, sacking Delhi in 1398, and ravaging further into India the following year. The Embriaci of Genoa produced substitute animal bone ivories, just at the time that true elephant ivories ceased to be made, which does suggest that disruption in the supply of the raw material was the key to the ending of ivory-carving in Paris around 1400. In France itself Jean, Duke of Berry, bought 'Embriaci ivory', as did Gian Galeazzo Visconti at Milan.

Manuscripts and printed books

The production of manuscripts for the market was at the same time utilitarian and part of the world of works of art. On the one hand there were the strictly utilitarian multiple copies of standard texts made to sell to those students who did not make their own. On the other were the lavishly illuminated volumes commissioned individually by rulers. Between lay a whole range of copies of different qualities for a vigorous book trade. Much of the commercial production of books in late medieval Europe was therefore concentrated in university cities like Bologna, Paris, Oxford and Cambridge, capital cities like Paris and London, and commercial cities like Bruges and Florence. However a number of devotional works, like Books of Hours, some in Dutch, were produced outside a strictly commercial context by the Brethren of the Common Life in the fifteenth-century Netherlands and had a surprisingly wide sale.

Commercial production of books in Latin had emerged in Paris by the beginning of the thirteenth century, concentrating on books for university and other ecclesiastical patrons. However a court market for works in French developed as well around the middle of the century and grew rapidly. From the mid-century the book trade was run by professional bookseller-publishers, *libraires*. There were some two dozen families of them, clustered in the Rue Neuve in the Ile de la Cité between the Royal Palace and Notre Dame, convenient for serving both lay customers and clergy. *Libraires* were essentially entrepreneurs. They bought parchment and paper from stationers and employed the scribes, illuminators and book-binders who actually produced the books. In the course of the thirteenth and fourteenth centuries they produced huge numbers of French romances, didactic works particularly law books, devotional works, legends and such lengthy historical works as the *Grandes Chroniques* for their wealthy clients, but the vernacular bible was their best seller by far.[66] As well as the home market in Paris, they also exported books in French to all the parts of Europe where the nobility wanted to read them.

The royal house of France was particularly notable as a buyer of books in the late fourteenth and early fifteenth centuries. Charles V built up an extensive library, including several of the works of Aristotle specially translated into French for his own use by Nicolas Oresme. His brothers the dukes of Berry and Burgundy followed suit. With fewer resources at his disposal, Jean Duke of Berry naturally built up a smaller library than his eldest brother, but he had it even more lavishly illustrated. By the time of his death he had acquired 41 histories, 38 chivalric romances and a small number of other secular works including Marco Polo's *Travels* and other cosmographical books, but his most beautifully illuminated manuscripts were his religious works. For no considerable practical purpose can he have needed 16 psalters as well as 14 bibles, or for worship as many as 6 missals, 18 breviaries and 15 Books of Hours! It seems that as soon as his artists had finished one lavish Book of Hours for him he wanted another, yet more lavish than the last. At the end of his life he lived largely at Bourges, but until then he had been mainly based in his Paris Hôtel de Nesle and it was miniaturists working in

A rare glimpse of manuscript book-production in Bruges comes from a miniature of Charles the Rash's visit to David Aubert, who was writing a copy of the Histoire de Charles Martel *for him in 1463–5.*

nia bona. lauf:honoz: virtuf
potétia: ꝛ gratiaꝛ actio tibi
chꝛifte. Amen.

Viue deũ fic ꝛ vines per fecula cunc,
cta. Prouidet ꝛ tribuit deus omnia
nobis. Proficit abfque deo nullꝰin
oꝛbe laboꝛ. Illa placet tellꝰin qua
res parua beatũ. De facit ꝛ tenues
uꝛuriantur opes.

Si foꝛtuna volet fies de rhetoꝛe conful.
Si volet hec eadem fies de côfule rhetoꝛ.
Quicquid amoꝛ iuffit nó eft côtédere tutũ
Regnat et in dominos ius habet ille fuos
Vita data é vtéda data é fine fenere nobis.
Mutua: nec certa perfoluenda die.

Ufus ꝛ ars docuit quod fapit omnis homo
Ars animos frangit ꝛ firmas diruit vꝛbes
Arte cadunt turres arte leuatur onus
Artibus ingenijs quefita eft gloꝛia multis
Principijs obfta fero medicina paratur
ꝛum mala per longas conualuere moꝛas
Sed propera nec te venturas differ in hoꝛas
Qui non eft hodie cras minus aptus erit.

*Having made a success of printing
in Venice, including the first
edition of Euclid's* Geometry,
*Erhard Ratdolt decided to go
home to Augsburg in 1486 and set
up a press there. In preparation
for his return, he printed an
advertisement to show potential
customers the fourteen different
founts (including a Greek one)
that he had available for printing.
Above are four sizes of his Gothic
fount.*

Paris who illuminated his library. These were not necessarily Parisians by birth. His principal miniaturists were Jacquemart de Hesdin, a native of Artois, and Paul and Jean de Limbourg from Nijmegen in Guelders. The latter produced for the Duke of Berry what is probably the most celebrated single manuscript of the later Middle Ages, his *Très Riches Heures.* The Limbourg brothers had previously worked for one of Jean's other brothers, Philip the Bold, Duke of Burgundy.

The house of Burgundy produced a succession of dukes who continued a tradition of book commissioning and book purchases, so that Philip the Bold's grandson Philip the Good, the ruler of nearly all of the principalities of the Low Countries, had probably the most extensive library of any ruler in the middle of the fifteenth century. Philip the Good had a committee of connoisseurs of fine books, great noblemen, who were themselves building up their own smaller libraries, to advise him on purchases for the ducal library. That in Brussels came to be more than Philip's personal library, for courtiers and privileged persons could borrow from it. Much of this library survives today as the inmost core of the national library of Belgium (Bibliothèque Albert I). The place where many of the volumes were illuminated and sold was Bruges. The Bruges book trade supplied workers not only to the Burgundian rulers and the nobility of the Netherlands, but also to those of England and France. By this time the production of books in Paris had collapsed, like that of tapestries, with the disappearance of the home market provided by the court.[67]

In southern Europe, the book trade was equally focused on the same commercial centres in which other works of art were produced, particularly Florence and Venice. When Humphrey of Gloucester, Regent of England for his young nephew, Henry VI, wished to build up his library, and particularly wanted humanist texts, he had them sent from Florentine booksellers and copyists. Florentine booksellers were thus supplying not only the Medici library in Florence itself, but also what became the Bodleian Library in Oxford, as well as the curial library of the Popes, which ended up in the Vatican. Only slightly less lavish copies were being created in large numbers for members of the courtly aristocracies, and cheaper copies still were being written on paper rather than parchment. In retirement, after selling his business in 1480, the best known of the Florentine booksellers, Vespasiano da Bisticci, who is reputed to have employed fifty copyists at a time, wrote brief lives of his most distinguished customers. Although his customers were mostly Italian, they included men from as far away as Portugal, England and Hungary, which gives some indication of the European extent of his market.[68]

Mainz, where printing from moveable type began, lay part way along the newly reviving land route from the Low Countries through southern Germany to northern Italy. It is therefore not surprising that in a very few years printing spread not only to the capital cities of Europe, Rome, Paris and London, but also to the great distribution centres of late fifteenth-century Europe, Nuremberg, Venice, Florence, Lyons and Bruges, in other words, to exactly those places in which the production of manuscripts had previously been concentrated. On a smaller scale, from Strasbourg Johann Mentelin was selling printed romances and epics by the 1470s to some of the same customers who had previously bought manuscript versions of similar light reading copied at the 'book factory' of Diebold Lauber at nearby Hagenau.[69]

In Nuremberg Konrad Zeninger of Mainz already had a press in the 1460s, but the most famous Nuremberg printer was Anton Koberger, who set up shop as printer, publisher and bookseller in 1470. He published more than 200 titles between 1473 and 1513. He was the first printer to operate on a really large scale, and clearly aimed at a Europe-wide market. At the peak of his production he was operating 24 presses, and employing a staff of over 100 – compositors, proof-readers, press operators, illuminators and binders. He even owned his own paperworks. He produced large folios of popular or widely used works, handsomely printed and often beautifully illustrated. The most famous example of this is Hartmann Schedel's great illustrated *Liber chronicarum* (Book of Chronicles), of which he printed both Latin and German editions in 1493. The 1,800 woodcuts include fifty illustrations of fifteenth-century towns. Koberger's Bible of 1483, although not the earliest bible in German (that appeared from Mentelins's press in Strasbourg in 1460–66), was the finest of the early Bibles to be printed in a vernacular. To reach his Europe-wide market, Koberger maintained a full-time agent in Paris, and entered into partnership with other printer-publishers in Basel, Strasbourg and Lyons, who printed for him, as well as selling books he had had printed in Nuremberg. Elsewhere he sold through general commercial channels, in cities such as Antwerp. In 1509, he had unsold stock of Schedel's *Liber chronicarum* not only in Nuremberg itself, and Paris, Strasbourg and Lyons, but also in Milan, Como, Florence, Venice, Leipzig, Prague, Graz and Budapest.[70] Basel, which already had a flourishing paper industry ready to supply its presses, became the centre of scholarly publishing in Europe. Printing was established here in 1467 by a pupil of Gutenberg. Ten years later the scholar-printer Johann Amerbach came from the Sorbonne to set up a press to publish editions of the classics and the Fathers of the Church, edited with scrupulous care and accuracy, as well as fastidious taste. As junior partner he had another scholar-entrepreneur Johannes Froben, who carried on the firm after him. Over sixty years they produced a prodigious number of volumes which 'in their judicious selection, careful editing, and fine workmanship, satisfied the needs and desires of scholars all over Europe'.[71] Their chief literary advisors were in turn Johann Heynlin and Erasmus of Rotterdam. For the latter, they printed not only his influential Greek New Testament, but a host of critical editions of classics and the Fathers, as well as his best-selling *Adagia*, which was revised and republished frequently throughout his life. As well as Nuremberg, Strasbourg and Basel, other 'south German' and Rhineland commercial and industrial cities were also prominent in the early history of printing, particularly Augsburg and Cologne.

Northern Italy was the other principal area for the production of printed books in the fifteenth century, particularly in Milan, Florence and pre-eminently Venice. In Venice printing began in 1469, and thirty years later the

Such was the success of Hartmann Schedel's Liber Chronicarum *that it was reprinted in Augsburg in 1496, but in a smaller format, which meant that the new woodcuts were rather cramped. Fire falling from heaven in 1490, destroying 800 houses, provided the subject for the last of three different woodcuts of Constantinople.*

book trade was being fed by no fewer than 150 active presses there. Most of these produced either short runs of high quality books, or slightly longer runs of rather shoddy books. The firm of Aldus Manutius, set up in 1490, rapidly came to dominate the market. It combined high quality with long runs. By the end of the century, it was producing standard printed texts of the classics in editions of 1,000 copies, instead of the runs of 100, 250 or even 275 copies printed for earlier printer-publishers .

Its fairs made Lyon an obvious early centre for book distribution and therefore for printing, as Koberger recognized. Books had been printed there from 1473 onwards, and in Bruges from the following year. Bruges-printed books entered into north-west European trade, just as Bruges manuscript books were already doing. When Bruges declined, its place as the city for printing for the international market was taken, as in so many other things, by Antwerp, where the Plantin firm was to be particularly notable from the mid-sixteenth century. In its turn, Antwerp was to be replaced as the key city for printing by Amsterdam.

Although printing, like manuscript-production, was soon widely dispersed, the very fact that printed books could be manufactured so much more cheaply and in such large numbers, meant that there could be much more international trade in them than there had been in manuscripts. When Aldus Manutius printed Cicero by the thousand he was aiming not only at the higher nobility, but also at the lower nobility or gentry of the whole of Europe, anticipating that they would pay a ducat a time for his clear, well produced, authoritative texts, rather than pay a larger sum for a locally-printed Cicero, available, if at all, in a short poorly produced run, and lacking in authority. Manuscript production had been more aimed at local markets, either in a capital city, or in a regional centre, like Salisbury, for long the distribution point to the nobility of southern England in the fourteenth and fifteenth centuries. Printing, at least as practised by the leading printers, was no longer a regional affair.

From the beginning publisher-printers used devices to label books as being theirs. The most famous early publishing house, that of Aldus Manutius in Venice, displayed several variants of the dolphin and anchor prominently on the first and last pages of its books for a hundred years. In this version an abbreviated form of his name appears as well: ALDUS MA[nutius] RO[manus].

Imitation

One of the features that has come up again and again in this description of manufacture has been the way in which merchants who have been importing a commodity have then proceeded, once the scale of imports had reached a sufficiently important level, to foster the creation of a similar commodity at home, first to supply the domestic market, then for export onwards to other markets, and sometimes even for export back to the region from which it had once been imported.

We have seen this pattern of imitation repeated over again with the Florentine imitation of the finest woollens of Flanders and Brabant, the Lombard imitation of the cottons of Syria, the Venetian imitation of the glass of Syria, the Brabançon imitation of the carpets of Persia and the Levant, the Lucchese imitation of the silks of Byzantine and the Levant which were themselves derived from Chinese originals, the Fabriano imitation of paper, the Faenza imitations of majolica, and the Venetian imitation of Castilian white soap.

Imitation once achieved was often repeated in other areas, by other merchant entrepreneurs. The Lombard cottons and fustians found south German imitators, Lucca silk found imitations in many parts of Italy, whilst Fabriano paper and Faenza majolica found imitations in south Germany and Antwerp as well as in many parts of Italy. These imitations were often marked by the movement of skilled craftsmen, lured by merchant entrepreneurs and even by city authorities and princes. In this way woollen-weavers from Flanders moved to Brabant and England, as woollen-weavers from Brabant moved to Florence and Silesia. Lucchese silk-workers moved to many parts of Italy, most successfully to Bologna, Florence, Venice and Genoa, while Venetian glass-workers, Faenza potters and Fabriano paper-makers did the same. The same path was followed in the north, where Dinant brass-workers scattered to Mechelen, Aachen, Brussels, Namur and Antwerp. Furthermore, many of the mints of Europe were not only run by north Italian mint masters, but staffed in part by moneyers and mint-workers who had come from north Italian cities, and many of the mines of Europe were worked by miners of 'Saxon' origin.

Many of these imitations depended on the import not only of craftsmen with their essential skills, but also on that of key commodities, often from very far away. The superior Florentine woollens, like their Flemish and Brabançon precursors, depended on the import of high quality wool from England, close to Flanders and Brabant, but distant from Tuscany; the fustians of Lombardy and South Germany had to depend on cotton from distant Syria, the silks of Lucca on silk from Anatolia, and the glass and soap of Venice on alkaline ash, also from Syria. Even when merchants attracted industry to themselves, a former trade in manufactured goods was replaced by one in raw materials. In the next chapter I will look at this trade in the raw materials of industry. I will start with the bulkiest trades of all, those in basic foodstuffs.

In manuscripts, capital letters at the beginnings of sections of a book had frequently been an opportunity for expression of the illuminator's skill and imagination. Early printers carried on this tradition. These large initial capital letters accompany the third fount of type designed by Francesco Griffo for Aldus Manutius and first used by him to print Francesco Colonna's, Hypnerotomachia Poliphili *in Venice in 1499.*

6

Trade in foodstuffs, raw materials and slaves

ONE OF THE MYTHS OF MEDIEVAL HISTORIOGRAPHY is the false contrast between a Baltic trade allegedly concerned only with bulk commodities and a Mediterranean trade allegedly concerned only with luxury goods. In reality Mediterranean trade was even more concerned with bulk commodities than the Baltic, as the south European populations that needed to be fed and fuelled from a distance were so much greater than the north European. Great cities like Venice and even Milan could only be fed for a few weeks each year out of the produce of their immediate hinterlands. Genoa was impossible to feed this way at all. There were not adequate local foodstuffs for these cities. Even second-rank cities in northern Italy, such as Siena, Bologna or Verona, were of the same order of magnitude as capital cities elsewhere, Naples and Palermo, Rome, and later, Avignon. Despite the efforts to cultivate the Lombard plain intensively, or to push cultivation in Tuscany up into the Appenines, it was just not possible to feed these enormous numbers of people and so there was a continuous long-distance trade in huge quantities of heavy foodstuffs. It is little wonder that north Italian maritime traders, the Genoese in particular, developed ships, first the clumsy *bucius*, or *buss*, and then the much more effective *carrack*, that were much larger than any Baltic *cog*, for carrying foodstuffs in bulk to north Italy.

Grain

As the population of Europe grew in the thirteenth century, the standard of living of the bulk of its people declined. They became increasingly dependent for their nourishment on bread, porridge, gruel and other grain-based foods. The import of adequate quantities of grain mattered most in the first half of the fourteenth century. The people of the great cities were the most vulnerable to dearth, and city governments took special care to ensure that adequate quantities of grain were available.

The commune of Florence had a regular office of the Biadaiolo to oversee the grain market and ensure a continuous supply of food. In years of dearth, a special commission, the Abbondanza, was called into being to take emergency measures. In normal years the grain grown in the upper Sieve valley, the Mugello, or around Figline in the upper val d'Arno, played an appreciable part in the feeding of the city. However, when a city had reached the size of Florence it could no longer live on the produce of its own *contado*. In the 1340s, Domenico Lenzi, one of the officials of the Abbondanza, reckoned that the *contado* could only produce enough in a good year to feed the city for five months. The city therefore had always to import grain from outside. Even in normal years a great deal of grain came up the Arno to the highest

A maniere
de labourer
les champs
gaingnables

rement nous dirons del aere
et des garniers qui sont ap
partenans a chascune seme
ce selon sa nature.

t dicte en denoulles m

De laer.

Mediterranean Europe suffered from famine in 1328–30. In Florence, unable to feed itself even in good years, it was particularly bad. In 1329 Domenico Lenzi interrupted his lists of prices in the Specchio Umana, to write a long descriptive passage, with two mournful sonnets and painted scenes of devastation. First he painted the calamitous harvest and then, on the next folio, the effect on the grain market (opposite). Just one small barrel of grain is shown for sale. All the big barrels are empty, and armed men stand behind to prevent famished citizens looting the market. The archangel Michael is leaving his garden, with his trumpets broken, and the devil has taken his place. Lenzi must have realised that worse was to come. In 1330, despite the best efforts of the government, thousands died of famine-related diseases.

The extensive cultivation of grain along the rivers running into the Baltic and the Black Sea increased or diminished in proportion to the demand for bread from the distant inhabitants of cities in the southern Netherlands and northern Italy. The grain trade was organized by merchants at ports at the mouths of these rivers, Hanseatics in the Baltic and Genoese in the Black Sea (see pp. 291–2).

point of navigation, Signa, and from the warehouses there it was carted the last fifteen kilometres into the city. In bad years there was not enough even to feed the inhabitants of the *contado*, and the city was totally dependent on imported grain. The Abbondanza commissioned purchases of grain not only in Sicily, which was normal, but also in North Africa, Greece, and from the Genoese, who acquired it on the shores of the Black Sea.[1] Besides Florence, the other fourteenth-century cities of Tuscany had a similar, although not so acute, problem of provisioning. Prato or Pistoia could not be fed from their tiny *contadi*, nor could Lucca or even Siena from much larger territories – so that the supply of distant grain through Pisa was vital to all of them. Professor Herlihy has suggested that, around 1300, Pisa, despite its possession of the grain lands of the Maremma, itself needed some fifteen large *bucius*-loads of grain from a distance to keep its own citizens fed in normal years.[2]

Europe divided itself in two as far as the grain trade was concerned. There was a semi-integrated northern European grain market, focused on feeding Paris, London and the cities of the Low Countries, that stretched from the grain lands north of the Loire in western France to those of the Baltic river systems. There was another semi-integrated southern European grain market focused on feeding the cities of north Italy, that stretched from the grain lands of Andalusia to those around the Black Sea. The two regions normally remained quite separate. However, in exceptional circumstances grain was carried from one to the other. When torrential summer rains destroyed the harvests right across northern Europe from Ireland to Poland in two successive years, this resulted in the great north European famine. The lack of even the most basic foods was at its worst in the spring and early summer of 1317. Bruges, as a seaport, was marginally better off than Ypres or

Tournai, where a tenth of the population died, since grain imported into Flanders came first to Bruges, but, even there, 5% of its people probably died of starvation and famine-related diseases.[3] The price of grain rose to such a prodigious height in the north that it became, most unusually, worthwhile to bring grain in from the Mediterranean. Giovanni Villani, the prominent Florentine businessman-chronicler, commented that 'the cost of all foods became so high that everyone would have died of starvation, had not merchants, to their great profit, arranged for food to be transported by sea from Sicily and Apulia'.[4] Grain became so expensive that a Genoese galley, not a bulk carrier but a carrier of luxury goods, was chartered in March 1317 in Seville to row across to North Africa and collect wheat to take to England.

It was the turn of Mediterranean Europe to suffer in 1328–30 and twice more in the 1340s. The Abbondanza of Florence organized special shipments of grain for its own citizens at vast public expense, only to see the starving people of Pisa loot it on the way. To prevent this happening in future years they built a prodigious store over the grain market at Or San Michele which could carry enough grain to tide the city through such a crisis if it should recur. However, the crisis of the 1340s did not recur in so acute a form for two and a half centuries, for in 1348 the first of the late medieval waves of bubonic plague reached northern Italy. When population stabilized after the 1438–39 wave of plague Florence and Genoa had only half the number of inhabitants that they had had a century earlier. Moreover the bulk of these inhabitants had a much improved standard of living and were not so dependent on grain for keeping alive.

From the thirteenth to the fifteenth century there was a regular supply of grain for the cities of northern Italy from Sicily and the lands bordering on the Black Sea, and to a lesser extent from southern Italy, Greece, Asia Minor and North Africa. Much Mediterranean trade was thus concerned simply with the movement of grain to northern Italy, and some of the greatest trading companies, like the Peruzzi of Florence, were heavily involved in it.[5]

Sicily, which in classical antiquity had been the 'granary of Rome', became a major supplier of grain to northern Italy once again in the later Middle Ages, and remained so well into the early modern period. Immense quantities of grain came from the Black Sea region, which was one of the prairie frontiers of Europe opened up in the thirteenth century. After having been shipped down the great rivers which flowed into the Black Sea, the grain was bought by Venetians and, even more, by Genoese. After the crushing defeat of Pisa in 1284, the Genoese had taken over shipping goods in and out of Tuscany, so that the grain brought to Florence and Siena, Prato and Pistoia, Lucca and even Pisa itself was carried in Genoese ships. On the Black Sea the Genoese maintained permanent trading posts at or near the mouth of the great rivers, at Kilia on one of the mouths of the Danube and Pruth, at Moncastro (Akerman, the precursor of modern Odessa) at the mouth of the Dnestr and at Ilice near the mouths of the Dnepr and Bug.

The other such prairie frontier was made up of the lands along the south shore of the Baltic in Mecklenburg and Pomerania, which were colonized by

Not all wine was traded over long distances. By the fifteenth century the local trebbiano and sangiovese grapes already provided the white and red wines most drunk in central Italy, as they still do. In the 1390s Franco Sacchetti used witty ripostes in taverns, over a jar of trebbiano, as the punchline to some of his humorous stories. Can we hear a witty riposte in the wall painting (opposite) by the Salimbeni in the fifteenth-century Oratory of St John at Urbino?

A scene from the life of St Nicholas by Fra Angelico. The miracle illustrated above came about when his 'province was beset by a famine. The man of God learned that several ships laden with grain were in the harbour. He begged the ships' people to come to the aid of those who were starving. But they replied "Father, we dare not, because our cargo was measured at Alexandria and we must deliver it whole and entire to the emperor's granaries". The saint answered "Do as I tell you and I promise you in God's power that the imperial customs men will not find your cargo short". The men did so, and when they arrived at their destination they handed over to the imperial granaries the same quantity of grain that had been measured out at Alexandria.'

Germanic farmers, who subdued the indigenous Wends, with great violence, in the early thirteenth century. The grain lands along the Vistula were developed by Polish farmers at the same time. Hanseatic merchants purchased their grain at Torun and Gdansk near the mouth of the Vistula, just as the Genoese did at their Black Sea ports (see map p. 288).

Many of these new lands along the Baltic were temporarily abandoned in the late fourteenth century and the early fifteenth when the demand for grain from the shrunken populations of Western Europe dropped away. However, as the population and the need for bread grew again in the West, at the end of the fifteenth century, these lands were re-cultivated, and the pattern of West European dependence on the Black Sea and Baltic grain trade that was established at the end of the Middle Ages remained until the opening up of the American prairie frontier in the second half of the nineteenth century. (One of my own great-grandfathers was a north Italian importer of Black Sea and Baltic grain to Bristol in the second half of the nineteenth century, who wrote a handbook on the subject!)

As well as the softer European wheat used for bread, hard wheat, *triticum durum*, was also traded in and, by the later Middle Ages, extensively grown in southern Europe. This is the sort of wheat used for cous-cous in North Africa, and for pasta and pizzas in Italy. The earliest surviving references to pasta in Italy come only from the thirteenth century, but by the fourteenth many different kinds were being made. Marchionne di Coppo Stefani, in his *Cronaca Fiorentina*, which covers the years 1362 to 1385, uses a vivid simile when he reports that the burial of the dead in a mass grave during a visitation of plague, first a layer of earth, then a layer of bodies, then another layer of earth, then another was 'just like lasagne'. Whether the Italians or the Arabs invented pasta is not clear, but the hard wheat from which it was made certainly reached Christian Europe from the Islamic Mediterranean.

Rice-growing had already spread from China as far west as the valleys of the Tigris and Euphrates in pre-Islamic times, and its cultivation was gradually extended by the Muslim conquerors to places like the Nile valley and Valencia where there were adequate quantities of water for its cultivation. Rice, purchased by Italians from Muslim sources, or from Christian southern Spain after its reconquest, was distributed through the late medieval trade network, in small quantities, to all parts of Europe. By the fourteenth century it had become possible to buy rice in Scandinavia. It remained, however, a relatively exotic food until, in the fifteenth century, rice-growing began in Italy itself, in the Po valley.

Wine and beer

Amongst 'foodstuffs' wine and beer were second only in bulk to grain and salt. In the thirteenth century almost all the principal centres of population still lay in the wine zone of Europe, but in the course of the fourteenth and fifteenth centuries, partially because of climatic change, the beer/wine line moved southwards, so that the inhabitants of the densely populated southern Netherlands increasingly became beer rather than wine drinkers.

The four principal wine-exporting ports of Europe were Bordeaux in

Gascony, Seville in Andalusia, Naples, and Candia in Crete, and, as with the grain trade, the bulk trade in wine in the Mediterranean was far more important than that elsewhere. Because of its bulk, and frequently its low value, wine, like grain, was generally only worth carrying, except for very short distances, by water, either by sea or by river. It was carried down the Guadalquivir, the Garonne and the Dordogne in river barges, before being shipped out to Seville, Bordeaux and Libourne in sea-going ships.

Although wine was grown extensively there, the countrysides of northern Italy do not seem in general to have been able to supply its great cities with adequate supplies of wine, any more than they could with grain. Liguria seems to have been the sole exception, for its steep hillsides, although totally unsuitable for grain, produced more than enough wine for Genoese consumption. The Genoese, besides exporting their own wine from Liguria, also, after the elimination of Pisa, supplied wine in bulk from overseas for the cities of Tuscany, whilst the Venetians brought in wine in bulk for the cities of Lombardy. The principal source of the wine that the Genoese sold was southern Italy, and it was largely shipped out of Naples. The principal sources of the wine that the Venetians sold were their 'colonial' vineyards in Crete, shipped out of Candia. The Genoese also sold wine that they had shipped out of Corsica, which they had begun to colonize at the end of the twelfth century.

Both Genoese and Venetians maintained trading posts on the shores of Greece and on the Greek islands from which they imported both common table-wines and also some highly prized sweeter luxury wines like the malmsey shipped through Monemvasia, from which it derived its name. When the Genoese assisted the Castilians and Portuguese in developing their Atlantic islands in the fifteenth century, the two principal crops that they thought worth planting for profit were vines and sugar. The 'Monemvasia' vines, transplanted, thus came to produce the malmsey of Madeira, already thought of in the 1460s as 'the best wine in the world'.

Brewing the new style of hopped beer, which would keep and could travel and hence could be traded, extended in the fourteenth and fifteenth centuries from the Bremen–Hamburg area, not only to Holland, and then Brabant, but also to southern England, Poland and southern Germany. The brewery illustrated by Jost Amman in Frankfurt in 1586 (above) was little different from its predecessors except in scale.

In periods of peace the wine trade from Bordeaux to England somewhat recovered, but never again reached the scale of the early fourteenth century. This woodcut of 1580 shows wine ships bound for Hull, Newcastle, London and Bristol. It emphasises how precarious a trade it had become, without credit.
The French vendor states that Bordeaux wine may only be had for ready money. The English purchaser responds 'I bring goulde from England for voynes'. Two men with heavy money bags back up his claim, whilst barrels are being rolled to the gangplank.

After the Castilian reconquest in the thirteenth century, the wine of Andalusia, exported through Seville, went both into the larger Mediterranean wine trade, and into the smaller Atlantic trade. Andalusian wine was carried in many cases by the Genoese, who exploited Andalusian products so considerably, to England, northern France and the Low Countries, as well as to Italy. By the end of the Middle Ages, the English were already beginning to acquire their taste for the sack of Jerez. The English, besides buying Castilian wine from the thirteenth century onwards, also bought Portuguese wines. However, until the dislocations of the trade in the mid-fourteenth century, they relied most heavily on Gascon wines. When the first phase of the Hundred Years' War devastated Gascony in the middle years of the fourteenth century, and destroyed many of its vineyards, England came to rely much more on Iberian wines, but the era of cheap wine in England was over.

Until the mid-fourteenth century Gascony exported wine in great quantities by sea not only to England, but also to Flanders. Gascon merchants chose whether to carry their wines to London or Bruges depending on the level of taxes imposed and the extent of privileges granted by the kings and the counts respectively. Between 1305 and 1336 an average of 83,000 tuns (standard barrels) or approximately 18,000,000 gallons, over 80,000,000 litres, were shipped out of Bordeaux on the Garonne every year. In the best year over 100,000 barrels were shipped out, and in the worst little more than 50,000 tuns. After 1336 the quantities exported were very much smaller. Some were also shipped from Libourne on the Dordogne.[6] To produce so much wine, the small areas of land in Gascony formerly used for growing grain had been turned over to vines. Grain had consequently to be imported to feed its wine-growing inhabitants. Much of the wine grown was cheap, but some notable luxury wines, like that of St Emilion, were already recognized. A whole Biscay shipping industry developed along the coast from Bilbao to Bayonne, largely but not exclusively devoted to the export of Gascon wine. These 'Gascon' shippers also carried woad grown round Toulouse, Iberian produce, especially iron from northern Spain, and Mediterranean goods sent overland by merchants of Montpellier. They brought in not only grain for themselves, and cloth from the Low Countries, but also wool to send back to Montpellier for the Italian textile industries. After 1336, with the outbreak of war, all these trades were much diminished.

Gascon wines, although not the only wines in western France, were the most important. Wines grown in Poitou and along the Loire were also traded. From La Rochelle and Nantes they were despatched to Flanders particularly after the collapse of the Bordeaux wine trade.[7]

France was able to supply its own needs for wine, even that of Paris, by a very considerable internal trade in wine along its rivers. The provisioning of Paris with wine was heavily dependent on barge transport on the Seine. Loire wines were often sent downstream, shipped round the coast and then brought up the Seine by barge, although they could also be taken upstream to Orléans and then taken to Paris by road. Most of the Burgundy drunk in Paris came from the Basse Bourgogne, around Auxerre. Salimbene of Parma reported after staying in the Franciscan friary in Auxerre in 1247: 'The men of this land do not sow or reap, nor do they store anything in barns, but send wine to Paris, because they have a river right at hand that goes to Paris, and they sell it for a good price, from which they get all their food and all of the clothes that they wear'.[8] Some wine from Burgundy was carried downstream past Paris, illegally trans-shipped from river boats to sea-going vessels at the mouth of the Seine, to be taken to Bruges for sale, for consumption in Flanders and elsewhere in the Low Countries. Under Philip IV the Parlement of Paris ordered the *bailli* of Rouen to prevent the transport of Burgundian wine to Flanders by this route and compel it to be taken through Bapaume where it would have had to pay duty to the king.[9]

In the fourteenth century the Burgundy of Haute Bourgogne around Beaune was mostly sent down the Saône/Rhône by barge to the papal capital at Avignon, but some had also been sent to Paris from the thirteenth century onwards. Only the finest wines were worth the additional cost and trouble of transporting by road to the head of navigation on the Seine, for shipping downstream. In the fifteenth century, with the shift of the French court to the Loire valley, the wines of the Loire and Poitou were drunk there, and only negligible amounts shipped any longer to shrunken Paris. In 1458–59, 85% of the wine of known origin brought into Paris came from 'Burgundy', almost entirely from the Auxerrois.[10] Large parts of Germany were also self-sufficient in wine. Rhenish wines were, in addition, shipped down the Rhine to the populous cities of the Low Countries, and thence across the North Sea to London, and around the coast into the Baltic for drinking in Scandinavia and in those parts of northern Germany which were unsuitable for growing grapes.

Inspectors registering wine brought into Paris c. 1500. Registers show that, in the second half of the fifteenth century, wine reaching the city on the Seine overwhelmingly came down the Yonne from the Auxerrois. Chablis today has the only famous vineyards in what was once an enormously important wine growing region.

The long-distance trade in beer was much less developed than that in wine in the Middle Ages. Until the innovation of adding hops, beers had a very short life and had to be drunk where brewed. In so far as beer-drinking stimulated long-distance trade, it merely added to the demand for barley and increased the scale of the grain trade. Adding hops vastly improved the taste. In Holland beer had previously been flavoured with myrtle seeds (*gruit*), which gave it a very sour taste. Hops also gave beer a much longer life, so that a trade in beer itself could begin. The new hopped beers were heavy, strong and as expensive as good wine.

The hopping of beer began in northern Germany. By the early fourteenth century, Bremen, and shortly afterwards Hamburg, were beginning to export beer to the Netherlands. In the 1360s, Hamburg was sending 3,000,000 litres of beer a year to Amsterdam. It was distributed from there by internal waterways throughout the Netherlands, including the cities of Brabant and Flanders. Import substitution had already begun by then and hopped beer was being brewed in Holland itself from the mid-1320s. Soon beer brewed in Holland, particularly in Delft, Haarlem and Gouda, was being exported to Brabant and Flanders. Brabant, and particularly Flanders, proved a growing market for beer, because the climatic changes of the four-teenth and fifteenth centuries meant that, as in England, it ceased to be easy to grow large quantities of grapes there to make cheap wine for local con-sumption. At the end of the fourteenth century, another round of import substitution began in Brabant, at Leuven, although not in Flanders, which went on importing beer from Holland in growing quantities. Professor Aerts has estimated that at Lier in Brabant three-quarters of the beer drunk in 1408–9 had been imported from Holland, whilst in 1473–75 three-quarters of the beer drunk had been brewed in Brabant itself.[11] Nevertheless in the 1480s Gouda still had 350 breweries, and at the end of the fifteenth century beer was second only to textiles among Holland's exports.

The same pattern can be seen in England as in Brabant. At the begin-ning of the fifteenth century England had been importing considerable quantities of beer from Holland. However, by the 1430s brewers from Holland had settled in England. They were not only established in London, and large provincial towns like Boston, but even in tiny towns along the east coast like Scarborough in Yorkshire and Walberswick in Suffolk. Conse-quently, by the 1440s hops, by the hod, were being imported instead of hopped beer, at all the English ports from Southampton round to Hull.[12]

Salt   Salt was, and is, a necessity for everyone. We use it both to flavour our cooking and as a condiment. Bread without salt tastes revolting. It is equally vital for livestock, for whom we continue to provide salt licks. However, until very recently, it was used much more extensively: it was the prime means of preserving meat, fish and vegetables. Until refrigeration, no long-distance transport of fish or meat could be managed without it. Fish was normally carried salted or smoked. Until the first refrigerated ship carried frozen meat to England from New Zealand in 1882, it was normal to butcher animals in the place where they were to be eaten, and then to salt any meat that was not to be consumed immediately. Unlike the market for grain, that for salt was universal. There was no way that men in the country could supply themselves with salt, as they could with food. Salt was amongst the goods that they had to buy from outside their own environ-ment. It was a considerable bulk trade, but not one of the very largest, for although so universally used, salt was not consumed in the great quantities. It made a very considerable third to bread and wine.[13] Many of the coast-lands of Europe, from Norfolk to Cyprus, had salt marshes, which, when properly managed, could be turned into salt pans, from which salt could be obtained by evaporation. In the north, the very slow natural evaporation was accelerated by the use of artificial heat, for example on the island of Walcheren where peat was used as fuel. In the south the sun was enough by itself. Sea water was let into the salt pans at intervals, allowed to evaporate and the salty residue raked into heaps to dry out completely. The same process is still carried out today, as may be seen in the salt flats between the medieval port of Aigues Mortes and the present coast of the Mediterranean.

Although such salt pans were to be found in many places, only a few were so productive that they could supply more than an immediate local market. The most important of these were those controlled by Venice in the Adriatic, particularly those at Chioggia at the southern entrance to its own lagoon; those along the Languedoc and Provence coast; those controlled by Catalans on the island of Ibiza in the Balearics and in Sardinia; and those around the Bay of Bourgneuf just south of the Loire.

In the tenth century the early prosperity of the Venetians lay in large part in the exploitation of the salt of their own lagoon. Their successors, despite the wide extent and the extreme complexity of their commerce in later centuries, never relaxed their hold on the salt trade. In the fourteenth and fifteenth centuries salt still represented 30% to 50% of the volume of goods carried by Venetians by sea. Like grain, it was, of course, carried in 'round' ships, not in galleys. The Venetians gradually extended their control of salt in two directions, production and sale. They tried to acquire as many as possible of the other major salt pans of the Adriatic, and when they could not buy them up, they tried at least to become sole, or at least privileged, purchasers. When they could do neither, they cynically decided to destroy them, as they did those of the Archbishop of Ravenna at Cervia in 1336.

One of the two largest inland sources of salt in late medieval Europe was Hallein, now in Austria. Its civic seal proclaims its Latin name as 'Salina' and shows a man carrying salt in the distinctive conical barrels in which it was shipped down the Salzach.

As well as a monopoly of salt production from the Adriatic coasts, the Venetians strove to exercise a monopoly of sale throughout heavily populated Lombardy. Venetian barges carried the salt up the Po and all its tributaries, even following the Ticino up to Lake Maggiore. The Venetians tried to see that the citizens of Milan, of Verona, of Bologna and indeed of all the cities between the Appenines and the Alps bought Venetian salt or none at all.

In this they were partially frustrated by the Genoese. The Genoese had no salt pans of their own along the Ligurian coast, just as they had no grain. They consequently bought in large quantities of salt from outside, as they did grain. They bought salt from the coastal salt pans of Provence, Languedoc, Spain and Sardinia and above all from Ibiza, the island of salt. Of the 8,000 tons of salt in the warehouses of San Giorgio in Genoa in 1458, three-quarters had come from Ibiza. This more than fulfilled the needs of Genoa and Liguria, so that the Genoese were then able to act as suppliers of salt to others, just as they did with grain. The Papal States, and the Kingdom of Naples bought salt from the Genoese. The Genoese built up the same sort of monopoly on the Tyrrhenian side of Italy that the Venetians had on the Adriatic side. Furthermore, they challenged the Venetian monopoly in Lombardy itself. Genoa regularly sent salt across the mountains to Turin, but this was not all. In 1448 Francesco Sforza contracted to buy 22,000 *mine* (5,100 tonnes) of salt from Genoa for Milan and in 1450 32,000 *mine* (7,400 tonnes). Occasionally Genoese salt was even sent as far as Mantua and Ferrara, even closer to Venice. Salt was the product most often to be found in the passes behind Genoa and Sarzana. Many thousands of mule loads were carried over the mountains to Piedmont and upper Lombardy.

The 'Bay Salt' of Bourgneuf was distributed over an extremely wide area. Much of western and northern France was supplied from this source. It was carried up the Loire, it was taken by sea to Rouen and then by barge up the Seine; it was taken by sea to England and the Low Countries and even as far as Scandinavia. 'Bay Salt' was carried not only by Breton ships, but attracted shippers from as far away as the Hanse.

Salt counted as a 'bulk' commodity, with a relatively low intrinsic value, although its price was often pushed up for fiscal purposes, or by monopolists like the Venetians. As a bulk commodity it was sensible to transport it by sea or river as far as possible. The distribution of 'Venetian', 'Genoese', and 'Bay' salt has already illustrated this preference. That controlled by the Catalans from Ibiza and Sardinia was largely shipped by them to Genoa. Indeed it contributed considerably to the imbalance of trade between Barcelona and Genoa in the fourteenth and fifteenth centuries. The Genoese more than made up for its cost from what they sold onwards. Most of the salt from the salt pans of the Languedoc and Provençal coast that was not bought by the Genoese was taken by extremely slow barges hauled up the Rhône and its tributaries and distributed throughout the Rhône basin. How slow this river transport was when hauled upstream can be illustrated by the estimate that it took six to eight weeks to drag salt up the Rhône from Peccais to Geneva. As with other river systems, once a head of navigation was reached on the Rhône or its tributaries goods had to be unloaded and taken by road to their ultimate destinations. Some of the roads leading up into Dauphiné and Savoy came to be known as *Via Salaria*, salt roads.

This map shows only the most important sources of salt in late medieval Europe. As well as the major groups of salt pans (speckled areas) constructed along the coasts , others were laid out along low lying-coasts, wherever there was adequate sunshine to evaporate salt from sea water. The arrows give an indication of the areas supplied from each of the marked sources, generally over relatively short distances. Dotted lines have been added to indicate the longer distance distribution of salt from the Adriatic (by Venetians), Ibiza (by Genoese), Bourgneuf and Lüneburg.

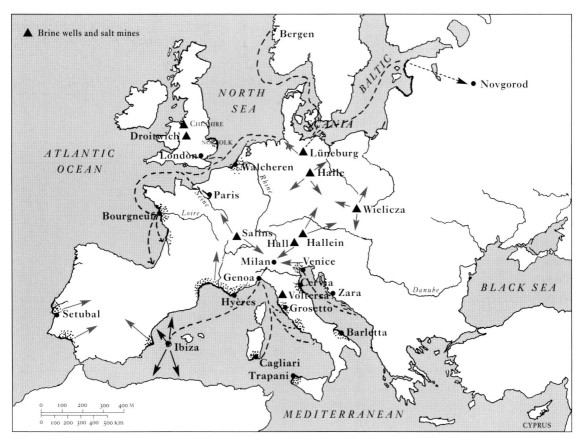

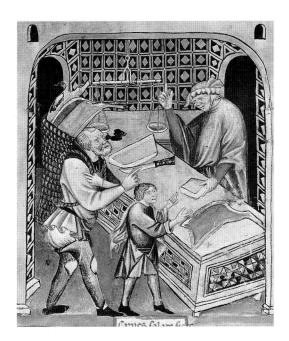

Sea salt was not the only salt of medieval Europe; brine-wells and salt-mines existed in many places. Salt from coastal salt pans often began its journey by water and ended it by road; that from brine-wells and salt-mines generally began its journey by road and sometimes ended it by water. Salt thus provides an excellent example of the interdependence of road and water transport. Water transport, when available, was generally preferred, since salt was a commodity for which speed was not essential, yet it was so much a necessity that the generally higher costs of road transport could normally be absorbed by the eventual purchasers, along with considerable taxation and the profits of middlemen. Because salt was so much needed in West Africa, it was even worth carrying it across the Sahara. It was then paid for in gold.

Many of the brine-wells and salt-mines, like so many of the coastal salt pans, had only a local or regional importance. The salt from the brine-wells of Cheshire, for example, essentially supplied the needs of midland and northern England and did not enter into long-distance commerce, and in the same way the brine-wells of Volterra supplied most of the local needs of Tuscany. Some mineral salt, however, supplied a wider market. Lüneburg in north Germany and Hallein, which produced the *Salz* of *Salz*burg, probably possessed the two largest inland sources of salt in thirteenth-, fourteenth- and fifteenth-century Europe. They were followed in scale by brine-wells and salt-mines at Salins in Franche Comté and Halle on the Saale in eastern Germany. In the second half of the fifteenth century the salt of Hall in the Tyrol and of Wielicza in southern Poland were becoming of increasing importance. By the early sixteenth century, Wielicza rivalled Halle and surpassed Salins, which had begun to be worked out in the fifteenth century (see map). At Wielicza, much of the early modern wooden machinery of salt extraction still survives *in situ* and it is possible to see it and to walk through the galleries from which salt has been taken.

Salt was the key to the availability of meat or fish. Since cattle were driven seasonally into north Italian cities in great droves, often from distant places like Apulia or Hungary, and butchered on arrival, meat could only occasionally be eaten fresh. Cured ham or pastrami was therefore more commonly eaten than fresh pork or beef. In the butcher's shop (above left), a basket of salted and dried meat is being brought in, ready to lay out for customers. At the fishmonger (above right) the fish has been taken from barrels, in which it had been brought, ready salted, from where it was landed: tuna on Mediterranean coasts and cod, stockfish and herring at northern fishing ports. These illustrations are taken from a Milanese Tacuinum Sanitatis, *table of health, of the 1390s.*

Some of these inland sources of salt had been exploited in classical antiquity and may never have been totally abandoned. Others were discovered in the Middle Ages themselves. Salt had been extracted in the Salzburg area since prehistoric times and the town was so called by the end of the eighth century AD. The emblem of its founding archbishop and patron saint, St Rupert, was a barrel of salt. Its salt came from the Dumberg, the salt mountain at Hallein, which continued to belong to its archbishops.

As elsewhere, the work of extraction of the brine and its boiling down into salt was divided up into many small enterprises, the owners of which often formed associations. At Hallein the tenants of the brine-wells of the archbishop of Salzburg formed one of these associations. Production at Hallein was greatly enlarged at the end of the twelfth century and the beginning of the thirteenth. Its salt was taken down the Salzach and Inn to Passau on the Danube and distributed throughout upper Austria and Bohemia. In 1498 nearly 26,000 tons of salt were distributed from Salzburg.

Although production at Lüneburg may not have been quite so large as at Salzburg, its effects were more dramatic. Lüneburg is first heard of as a source of salt in the tenth century. Like the Salzburg mines at Hallein, those at Lüneburg greatly enlarged their production at the end of the twelfth century. It has been estimated that by 1205 over 5,000 tons were being extracted in a year. Considerable thirteenth-century evidence shows production rising to over 15,000 tons annually before the end of the century. The evidence for the fourteenth and fifteenth centuries is much scantier. In 1338, production was a little below 15,000 tons. In 1497 it was over 17,000 tons. At Lüneburg the tenants who operated the salt boiling pans there, the *Sulfmeister*, also formed an association. In a later print of Lüne cburg a thick cluster of chimney stacks marks out the area of the town given over to salt boiling. Once the brine had been evaporated in Lüneburg, the salt was loaded on to barges on the small river Irmenau which runs through the town. The medieval crane for loading the salt barges is one of the few medieval cranes to survive. The barges carried the salt down the Irmenau into the Elbe and the merchants of Hamburg and Lübeck then competed for the profits of distributing it. Hamburg had the initial advantage of being directly accessible by water, but the merchants of Lübeck countered this with an extraordinarily imaginative idea. They proposed in 1336 that a canal should be dug from the Elbe to the Trave which flows past Lübeck.

Such a canal was a truly remarkable concept for it had to be over 50 km (30 miles) long and needed locks both up and down to cope with the rising ground between the two rivers. The canal was actually dug and was a remarkable monument to medieval technology. It took a long time to complete. It was not until 1398 that the first water-borne load of salt arrived in Lübeck. Thirty barges of salt reached the port of Lübeck on 22 July that year and were received with great festivities. From Lübeck the salt of Lüneburg was distributed throughout the Baltic and indeed along Hanseatic routes as far as Novgorod and, very importantly, Bergen, where it was used for salting cod.

The salt crane at Lüneburg is the sole survivor of the great cranes for loading and unloading ships that dominated fifteenth- and sixteenth-century waterfronts. Pictures of those from London, and Antwerp appear on pages 135, and 381-3.

Where water power was not available, horsepower was used to operate complex machinery. A chain of buckets full of brine (opposite) is being drawn up in the Grande Saunerie at Salins under the admiring gaze of a large party of ecclesiastics and well dressed noblemen and women. Such a gigantic industrial enterprise was not only famous enough to attract grand visitors on guided tours, but also to be commemorated in this tapestry woven in Bruges for the ruler of the Netherlands.

Comment la fontaine du puis a nueue fut ydue et cuueut per
huterrellicij de faint anathoille duquel le chief fut deuateut poste
audit puis fut beroubee et fortit icelle fontaine plus bas que y aua

Salted cod and stockfish constituted 90% of Bergen's exports, and were mainly bought by the Lübeck merchants who brought in the salt. The principal purchasers of Lüneburg salt, however, were the herring fisheries of Scania, which took their herring from the Sound between Sweden and Denmark, to produce the huge quantities of salted herring which Hanseatic traders carried in all directions. In 1494 around 60,000 barrels were produced, some 7,600 tonnes of herring.[14] A barrel of salt was needed for every four barrels of herring. The herring, which were caught from August to October, arrived, salted, in the Hanseatic warehouses of Boston and Lynn in November and December. It was when the herring fisheries demanded even more salt than Lüneburg could provide, that Hanseatic merchants went to supplement their Lüneburg salt with that from far-off Bourgneuf.

Production at Salins was still considerable and, at its apogee in the fourteenth century, was well over half that at Lüneburg. There were three separate concerns producing salt at Salins, of which the best records are for the largest, the 'Grande Saunerie'. In 1325, it produced 67,000 *charges*, (mule-loads of around 99 kg) and in 1329 it produced 72,000 *charges*. Between 1458 and 1467 its production had dropped from the 7,000 tonnes of the 1320s to an annual average of 4,500 tonnes. In these years the other two 'sauneries' produced an average of 2,900 tonnes between them. All this had to be carried away by road, either by cart down into the Burgundian plain, or by mule over the Jura. The Salins evidence makes it apparent how enormous a quantity of wood was needed to run a salt-works. In 1459 every 'boiling' of brine at the Grande Saunerie, which produced around 320 kg of salt, needed 11 *stircs* of wood (between 15 and 16 tonnes). The organization of the Grande Saunerie was one of the largest single enterprises in western Europe, only certainly surpassed in scale by the Venetian Arsenal. There were possibly as many as 600 workers, many of them women, under a single management. It was described as the eighth wonder of the world '*Ob salses latices inter miracula mundi ponitur octavum*', and drew sightseers.[15] One such sightseer is represented on an early sixteenth-century tapestry being given a guided tour, just as the most enterprising factories of the industrial revolution, like Wedgwoods, were later to offer guided tours in the eighteenth century. This particular sightseer is improbably identified as Saint Anatolia, a Scottish hermit (ill. p. 301). These large enterprises at Salins were also remarkably profitable undertakings. In 1459, the three *sauneries* made a profit, after paying the enormous bills for wood and wages, of around 58,000 *livres tournois*, a sum comparable to the combined revenues of the county and the duchy of Burgundy together for their duke, Philip the Good.

Olive oil

Although the amount of olive oil carried about Europe and the Mediterranean was less bulky than that of grain, wine, beer, or even salt, the quantities involved were still considerable. Olive oil was a commodity with a multitude of uses – for cooking and as a preservative. Even today, it is surprising how many tinned or bottled products are packed either in brine or in oil.

The Tacuinum Sanitatis *shows some olive oil reaching its eventual customers. In the 1390s a peripatetic oil seller is pouring from his barrel into jugs at a kitchen door in Lombardy. This copy of the* Tacuinum *was made for Verde Visconti, the widowed duchess of Austria.*

It was also one of the key ingredients in making hard white soap (see p. 273), for oiling wool for the manufacture of cloth, and for tawing leather. The greatest production of oil was in southern Italy and southern Spain. In Lombardy and the hinterland of Venice, where so much was used, none was produced; in Tuscany some was produced, but not enough. The plentiful oil of southern Italy, the Regno, was therefore largely exported to northern Italy. From the ports of Apulia it was sent up the Adriatic coast to Ancona, and to Venice, partially for soap-making there. Alternatively it was shipped out of Naples, up the west coast to Pisa, Porto Venere, Genoa and Savona. Some was, of course, used in southern Italy itself in the extensive soap-making at Gaeta. In 1279, a Pisan merchant recorded in his *Memoria* the transport of olive oil from Apulia to Tunis in North Africa where it was used, amongst other things, for preserving fish. The barrels of tuna in oil exported from Tunis, and also Seville, were the southern European equivalent of the barrels of salted Scania herring in northern Europe. The *Memoria* also records the export of Apulian oil to the Levant, to Alexandria and to Acre, the remnant of the Crusader Kingdom of Jerusalem.[16]

An eastern market for European olive oil still survived in the mid-fifteenth century, when Spanish oil, mostly from Andalusia, was being shipped by Genoese and Catalan merchants, to Syria, to the Ottoman Turks

Tacuinum Sanitatis *included a wide variety of commodities. Here a chandler's shop, no doubt drawn from one in Milan in the 1390s, offers a range of candles of different sizes. The beeswax might have been local, but might equally have come from North Africa or Russia.*

in Asia Minor, and to Chios and Phocaea off the west coast of Asia Minor. Evidence from the 1440s suggests the exchange of Spanish oil, for use in making soap in Phocaea, which was mostly distributed in the Middle East, against return cargoes of alum for the large manufacture of cheap cloth in Catalonia. The quantity of oil that might be carried in a carrack was quite considerable. There were 533 huge pottery *jarres* and 42 wooden *fûts* in one ship from Majorca to Phocaea, and 825 *jarres* in another ship from Seville to Chios. Spanish oil, of course, went on being heavily used at home for the production of the prestigious white Castilian soap, but it was also carried to England and Flanders. The Genoese began this trade by picking up Andalusian oil on their way north, but by the 1320s Spaniards were also sailing north with their own oil. By the 1360s Englishmen, particularly Bristol merchants were already coming south to look for olive oil as well as Iberian wines. We have, once again, some notions of the quantities and values from the fifteenth century. The 'Mary Redclyffe' returned from Seville to Bristol in 1473 with 134 tons of oil on board, bought for the equivalent of £536 sterling. The rest of the cargo, 146 barrels of wine, some soap and some sugar, cost only £36–10s. sterling. Olive oil bought for £4 sterling a ton in Seville, could be sold for around £8 a ton in Bristol. Since the costs of carriage, handling and customs duties only came to around £1 a ton, there was a handsome return on the money laid out. Altogether, oil ranked only second to iron in volume among the commodities carried to Bristol from Spain. In England the best oil was used for cooking. Only old oil was used for leather tawing, or preparing washed wool for carding and combing. It was much preferred for this to the local alternatives, rancid butter or pig fat.

Honey and wax

Far less important than these in terms of long-distance trade were honey and wax. There seems to have been relatively little long-distance trade in honey. It was available everywhere and was relatively cheap. However, what was worth carrying long distances was beeswax. Wax candles, as we have seen, provided a superior form of lighting to tallow ones and were much more expensive. They were in demand by the wealthy and by the greater churches. Although beeswax was available everywhere, there was not enough locally available to satisfy the demand of the rich in the great cities. The regions of Europe with a surplus of beeswax over their local needs were the sparsely inhabited forest lands of the east, particularly Russia. Presumably they also had a surplus of honey, but it was just not worth the costs of transport.

Hanseatic merchants bought beeswax from Russians at Novgorod, and from the subjects of the Teutonic Order at Königsburg in Prussia (now Kaliningrad). They carried this around Easter each year, to Bruges, which became the staple for its distribution. The anonymous early fourteenth-century description of the trade of Bruges includes wax among the products coming to Bruges from the kingdoms of Hungary and Bohemia as well as Russia. From Bruges, wax was sent onwards, to Paris for example, and also to London, although not to the latter in very great quantities. A hundred tons or so of beeswax was being imported into London annually at the end of the

fifteenth century, whilst a little more reached Lynn and Boston direct from Lübeck.

The Genoese also bought Russian beeswax at Black Sea ports and carried it back to Italy. More came from Spain. It was carried by the Catalans to Genoa, or bought by the Genoese in Andalusia, or shipped by Castilians in modest quantities, even with a little honey, out of their Basque ports. Yet more came from North Africa, particularly from Bougie, which has given the French their name for candles.

As beeswax was to tallow for lighting, so was sugar to honey for sweetening. But sugar, unlike honey, was not available everywhere. It was a much more expensive commodity than honey. The English customs collectors in the fifteenth century valued imported honey at £2–10s. sterling the ton (i.e. nearly four pounds weight for a penny sterling), but they valued imported sugar at £40 the ton (4 pence sterling for a pound weight). By the time it reached the customer a single pound (0.5 kilo) of sugar would cost a skilled man's wages for a day. It became worth sending long distances, and even arranging the

Two regularly repeated scenes from keeping bees appear on this eleventh-century south Italian Exultet *roll: on the left, extracting honey from a hive; and on the right, coping with a swarm.*

Sugar

Zucharum

From the thirteenth century onwards, European merchants at the ports of the Levant and the Black Sea became increasingly aware of the camel caravans which brought culinary, medical, aromatic and other spices to them across the arid deserts that divided them from fertile Mesopotamia (see pp. 309–16 and 344–6). The camel caravan about to set out (opposite) from the far side of the desert comes from a Baghdad manuscript of the 1230s.

In large cities like Milan the equivalent of sweet shops already existed by the 1390s (above), where expensive Candi *(from the arabic* Kand*) could be bought by weight in small quantities, made of imported cane sugar, melted and crystallized. The* Tacuinum *tells us that the best is translucent, but warns that it is not good for choleric stomachs, unless eaten with gently acidic fruit.*

cultivation of sugar cane specially for export. In the later Middle Ages, it was cultivated in the islands of the Mediterranean and carried by Venetians and Genoese not only to northern Italy but to northern Europe as well.

The Venetians had long been interested in sugar as a part of their oriental spice trade, although by the later Middle Ages sugar was properly more a 'levantine' than an 'oriental' spice. It had been introduced from India into the Levant in the eighth and ninth centuries.[11] By the tenth century, Egypt had become a major producer of sugar, and Egyptian sugar was then exported to all parts of the Mediterranean. By the twelfth century, sugar cane was being grown, wherever practicable, in all the Muslim-controlled lands bordering on the Mediterranean, and even as far away as Morocco and Andalusia. There was a considerable European market for this sugar. It was already used on a large scale in France in the reign of Philip IV, who forbad export in time of famine. The Venetians were the first Christian Europeans to produce sugar. Their first exercise in growing sugar cane was in the Kingdom of Jerusalem in the twelfth century, but it was in the island of Cyprus that they managed to grow it in a large way. It also seems that it was in Cyprus in the mid-thirteenth century that water-power was first applied to the crushing of sugar.[17] The invention of the sugar-mill instantly made the production of sugar much cheaper. The Corner (or Cornaro) family drew a considerable portion of their great wealth from owning particularly extensive sugar plantations in the south of the island around Espiscopi, where their sugar-refinery has recently been excavated.[18] By the fourteenth century,

وَسَكَنِي وَمَسْكَنِي وَحَوْلِي وَحَالِي وَمَآبِي وَمَالِي وَلَا تُلْقِنِي نَغَيْسَ ٣٤ وَلَا

سَلَّطْ عَلَيَّ مُغِيرًا وَاجْعَلْ لِي مِنْ لَدُنْكَ سُلْطَانًا نَصِيرًا اللَّهُمَّ احْرُسْنِي بِعَيْنِكَ وَعِزِّكَ

وَاخْصُصْنِي بِأَمْنِكَ وَمِنَّكَ وَتَوَلَّنِي بِالْأَخْبَارِكَ وَخَيْرِكَ وَلَا تَكِلْنِي إِلَى كِلَاءَةِ غَيْرِكَ

وَهَبْ لِي عَافِيَةً غَيْرَ عَافِيَةٍ وَارْزُقْنِي رَفَاهِيَةً غَيْرَ وَاهِيَةٍ وَاكْفِنِي مُخَازِيَ الْأَوَاخِرِ

Sol in Capricorno

Venice had become the key city for the refining and distribution of sugar in Europe. It was sold throughout Europe in conical 'loaves'. The Genoese encouraged, and participated in, the growth of sugar cane nearer home, providing both expertise and finance for a capital-intensive enterprise. They did so in the fourteenth century in Sicily, in the early fifteenth century in the Algarve south of Lisbon, and in the middle years of the century in Madeira. Don Henrique of Portugal, better known to the English under the strange soubriquet Henry the Navigator, was a partner in the first sugar-mill in the islands in 1452, and two years later the Venetian traveller Alvise da Mosto described Madeira as already a 'land of many canes'. On 26 May 1471 Luca Landucci, a Florentine apothecary, noted excitedly in his diary 'I bought some of the first sugar that ever came here from Madeira; which island was subdued a few years ago by the King of Portugal, and sugar has begun to be grown there; and I had some of the first that came here'.[19] Cultivation increased rapidly. In the Portuguese Cortes of 1481–82, a deputy was able to say that in the previous year 'twenty forecastle ships and forty or fifty others loaded cargoes [in Madeira], chiefly of sugar'.

The Genoese, and others, as well as carrying Madeira sugar to Lisbon and into the Mediterranean, soon took it northwards directly to the Low Countries, first to Bruges and then to Antwerp. Wouter Despars spent seven years in Portugal in the 1480s buying sugar in Lisbon to send to his brother and partner Jacob in Bruges, and selling Flemish tapestries, woollens and fustians.[20] By the end of the century, a third of the Madeira sugar was sent to Antwerp. The quantity of new sugar available was so great that the price on the Bruges and Antwerp markets collapsed. Sugar ceased to be a 'spice' only for the very rich and replaced honey further down the economic scale. Antwerp was rapidly coming to rival Venice as the sugar-refining centre of a Europe that was consuming increasing quantities of sugar. In the 1480s the Genoese of Seville unsuccessfully tried to rival their compatriots in Lisbon by organizing sugar plantations in the Canaries, but their turn came at the beginning of the next century with the sugar plantations of the West Indies. A little of both the Madeira and the Canary sugar was taken to Bristol from the 1470s onwards, a foretaste perhaps of the great imports of sugar to Bristol from the West Indies in the eighteenth century.

Sugar was one of the few 'spices' of which west Europeans even partially controlled the production. However, not all the sugar consumed in western Europe was grown by west Europeans. Even at the end of the Middle Ages some still came from the Muslim lands of the Levant, and from Granada, that survivor of Muslim Spain. The Genoese of Malaga kept agents in Almeria, the sugar port of Granada, to buy it from the Muslim Grenadines.

At the end of the fifteenth century the Bishop of Trent had frescos of the work of each month painted in his castle, the Castello del Buonconsiglio (opposite). That for December shows the felling of timber in his Alpine principality and its transport on huge specially constructed ox-wagons into the city. What was not used for fuel or building in Trent was then sent down the Adige to Verona and beyond, for use in the cities of the Lombard plain and Venice, whose glass industry used a prodigious amount of wood.

At the end of his notebook, Pegolotti jotted down a list of nearly 300 products, representing around 200 sorts of goods that counted as 'spices'. These included many of the foodstuffs and raw materials that are the substance of this chapter. Culinary spices feature in his list, like three sorts of cumin and five sorts of ginger, but other, bulkier, foodstuffs can be found there too. Not

Spices

only fourteen sorts of sugar, but also two sorts of rice, dates, raisins and two other sorts of dried grape. Medical spices are listed too, like borax, aloes and rhubarb from China. Aromatic substances, like camphor and musk, used in perfumes, and frankincense for burning in church, also counted as spices, as did alum and dyestuffs, like five sorts of madder and four sorts of indigo. In the list there is also a range of products totally unexpected by modern readers, whose notions of spice are reduced only to culinary spices, like eleven types of wax, elephant tusks, eight sorts of cotton, copper and tin besides pearls and gems like turquoises. Even a few manufactured articles feature in the list, like four sorts of paper, four sorts of glue and soap.[21]

Alum and sugar were the only 'spices' that were traded in any considerable quantities. Most of the commodities which we still consider as 'spices' were dealt in only in very small amounts. One, rather conservative, estimate of the total quantity of spices brought into Venice around 1400 suggests that it amounted to as little as 500 tons each year, though other estimates suggest twice as much. This is no more than the amount of grain or salt that could be carried in a single large carrack. However, because of the value of many spices, they were worth the high cost of carrying in armed galleys rather than in ordinary 'round' ships. Nevertheless the popular picture of medieval European commerce as predominantly consisting of trade in spices must be corrected. By the beginning of the fifteenth century the Venetian share of the spices brought into Europe probably amounted to three-quarters of the whole. The remainder was divided among Genoese, Catalans, and merchants from Marseilles and Ragusa. Nearly two-thirds of the culinary spices brought into Venice was ordinary pepper, used in small quantities in many noble households throughout Europe, particularly with salted meat. Like ginger, also widely used in Europe, in even smaller quantities, pepper was grown along the western coasts of south India and Sri Lanka. The Franciscan missionary Odoric of Pordenone and the Venetian adventurer Marco Polo were among the few west Europeans who left surviving reports of their visits to south India or Sri Lanka in the Middle Ages. European merchants generally stopped short at the ports of the Mediterranean. When it was possible for them to penetrate Asia, from the mid-thirteenth century to the mid-fourteenth and again, for a short while, around 1400, they mostly only went as far as Persia. If they did travel further, they were more interested in the long steppe journey to China for silk, than in going to India. Those few western merchants that we know about who did go to India did so for precious stones rather than spices. Culinary spices may have been valuable enough to warrant travel by galley, but unlike silk or precious stones they were still not costly enough to warrant the expense of carriage overland.

The spice trade was in effect an Indian Ocean trade run by non-Europeans, and Europeans only joined in to the margins of what was essentially an Asian trade. In the western Indian ocean it was in the hands of Arab and Indian shippers, particularly the Gujarati merchants, many of whom were based at Cambay on the west coast 400 kilometres (250 miles) north of Bombay. From the ports on the Malabar coast, like Calicut, Cochin and

Quilon, they exported the spices grown in south India to the Middle East. In addition Gujarati merchants could buy in Calicut spices grown much further east, like the camphor of Sumatra or cloves from the Moluccas (ill. p. 313). These were largely carried to Calicut, through the straits of Malacca, by Chinese merchants, who in return carried south Indian spices back to China, along with those they bought in the islands that are now Indonesia. Control of the straits of Malacca was so vital to this trade that when, early in the sixteenth century, Tomé Pires, the Portuguese, wrote up his travels in the area in his *Suma Oriental* he concluded 'If Cambay were cut off from trading with Malacca, it could not live'. He went on to underline its long-distance importance even in Europe by adding 'Whoever is lord of Malacca has his hands on the throat of Venice'.[22]

It is hard for Euro-centric readers to see the medieval spice trade as an Asian trade which was primarily in the hands of Asian merchants, with marginal European participation. Our attitudes too easily reflect the intervening centuries in which European interlopers, first the Portuguese, then the Dutch, and finally in India, the British, managed in turn to wrest much of the trade out of the hands of Indian and Chinese merchants.

At the end of the Middle Ages, Gujarati merchants were carrying the spices, whether Indian or Indonesian, by sea either to the Red Sea for the Arabian, Egyptian and Syrian markets, or to the Gulf, for the Persian market and that in the caliphate around Baghdad. In view of the extraordinary difference in costs of carriage by sea and by land, it is surprising that Europeans should have bought any spices other than those shipped to Suez at the north end of the Red Sea for the Egyptian market. Europeans bought their share of these at Alexandria or Damietta at the mouths of the Nile after a short land and river journey from Suez. However, the free action of the market was distorted by the weight of taxes levied in Egypt by the Mamelukes and also by the partially-observed papal interdiction on trade with Egypt after the fall of Acre in 1291, which lasted until the 1340s. As a consequence Europeans also

Cinnamon from Ceylon and pepper from the west coast of India had been available in Europe since classical times, and found their place in Dioscorides' Herbal in the first century, Greek manuscripts of which were available in most of the great libraries of fifteenth-century Italy. During the century it was translated into Latin and Italian. The spice-seller (left), almost overwhelmed by his cinnamon-sticks, comes from one such translation. Marco Polo was only the best known of the medieval Europeans who visited the places where these spices grew. On his protracted return journey from China in 1292–5, he travelled up the west coast of India. When Rustichello wrote up Polo's travels in the Livre des Merveilles *he described the pepper plantations in the kingdoms of Quilon, Ely, Malabar and Gujarat. According to Polo the pepper was mainly sent to south China, although some came west via Aden, and part of this was sold on to Europeans at Alexandria. The fourteenth-century French illuminator has imagined Polo examining the newly harvested pepper (above right).*

bought some of the spices which had been unloaded for Arabia and Syria further south on the Red Sea coast, even at Aden, and reached Palestine and Syria in the caravans from Mecca, along with the frankincense and myrrh of the Arabian peninsula itself. Part of them reached the Mediterranean at Acre, when that was in Christian hands, and later at Beirut. Some of the spices brought into the Persian Gulf and carried up the great rivers to Baghdad were then taken upstream to the head of navigation on the Euphrates and then the relatively short distance overland to the Armenian coast of the Mediterranean, where west Europeans bought them in the second half of the thirteenth century and the first half of the fourteenth.

What is much more surprising is that Europeans also bought anything as bulky as spices at Sultaniyeh and Tabriz in north-western Persia. The purchase of silk, precious stones or pearls there is not surprising, but the Florentine Pegolotti recorded in his notebook that south Indian ginger was also available. In the late thirteenth and early fourteenth centuries there were enough Venetian and Genoese merchants doing business in Tabriz for both nations to have protected *funduks* of their own, with communities regulated by consuls.

The European end of the spice trade, although relatively small in global terms, was nevertheless of great importance to those Europeans who participated in it. The fifteenth century Venetians, who controlled so much of the last, short, leg of the spice trade, from Beirut or Alexandria, could commonly reckon on a profit of 40% merely on bringing spices half the length of the Mediterranean. Earlier the trade had been much more widely shared with merchants from different western cities buying at different Levantine ports. In the earliest surviving merchant notebook, that fair-copied by a merchant from Pisa in January 1279, details were noted of the purchase of spices not only in Alexandria, but also in Acre, and at 'Laiasso in Hermenia' [Lajazzo].

There was no way that Europeans could replace Indian and Indonesian spices, if they wanted them. They did want them. The Pisan merchant noted down a score of spices to be obtained in Lesser Armenia, a client kingdom of the Mongols in the north-east corner of the Mediterranean. A few years later the source of spices in Bruges were still noted down as the Kingdom of Armenia (Lajazzo), the Kingdom of Jerusalem (Acre) and Egypt (Alexandria). There was no notion in Bruges that when the spices had reached the Mediterranean they had already accomplished most of their journey to the west. From Bruges they could be taken further still by Hanseatic merchants, and hence to members of the Swedish nobility, for example. The galleys of Flanders, as well as taking spices to Bruges, also stopped in England on the way. Professor Dyer has shown how common it was in great English households to buy Asian spices, but in very limited quantities.[23] In 1444–45 John Hopton, a Suffolk gentleman, sent his steward to Norwich to buy a range of commodities. It included a small amount of Indian pepper which had thus been sent out from London to an English provincial town for final resale to its eventual customer, a very long way from the Malabar coast.[24] As well as being distributed around Europe by sea by Italians, spices were bought in Venice by

south German merchants, like Hilpolt Kress of Nuremberg, who in 1392 carried Indian pepper and ginger, cinnamon and nutmeg back across the Alps along with textiles and pearls for distribution into Germany and Central Europe (see p. 354). Spices, too, were amongst the goods bought regularly between 1408 and 1412 for the royal household of Navarre, then newly established in Navarre itself, at Olite, rather than in Paris (see p. 137). We have the prices paid, and from them can get some idea of the relative values of different spices. In terms of the day's wages of a journeyman carpenter, unchanged at 8 *sueldos carlines* of Navarre, a Navarrese pound of pepper rose in price during the four years covered by the accounts from around one day's wages to two. A pound of cinnamon or of ginger, however, remained constant at around 3.5 days' wages, and a pound of cardamom at 4.5 days' wages, whilst the price of a pound of cloves, the most distant spice of all, rose from 5 to 6 days' wages for a journeyman carpenter. Expensive, yes, but not astonishingly so considering the distance the cloves had come and the number of hands through which they had passed on their way from the Moluccas to Olite. What is apparent is the remarkable instability of the prices for spices, with the price of pepper doubling between 1408 and 1412. Whereas ginger and cinnamon had much the same price in these Navarrese accounts, two decades earlier, in 1392, the Kress firm had paid twice as much in Venice for its ginger as for its cinnamon. For the ginger it had paid 34 ducats per *centinaio*, or hundredweight, and for the cinnamon only 17 ducats.[25] It is not clear how much these large changes in price were a consequence of the differences in the quantities of each spice harvested from year to year; changes in the

After Marco Polo's lifetime, few Europeans reached the pepper-growing west coast of India between the fourteenth-century collapse of the Mongol empire and Vasco da Gama's landing at Calicut, on the coast of Malabar, on 20 May 1498. Within thirty years so many Europeans, adventurers, merchants and missionaries had been there, that it was possible to produce a realistic woodcut of Calicut in Strasbourg in 1527 and find a market for it.

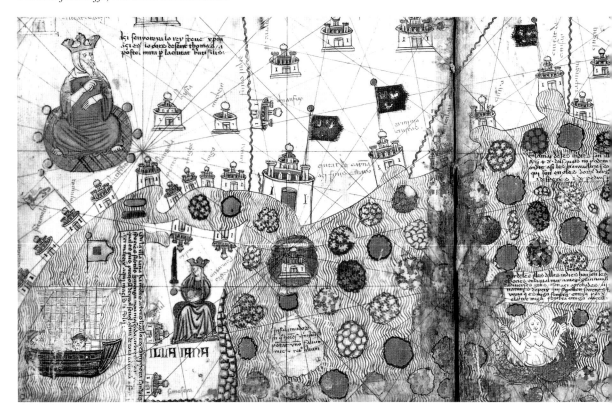

Whereas the Mediterranean sections of the Majorcan Catalan Atlas of 1375 are drawn with great exactitude (see pp. 36 and 55), the Asiatic parts are much more schematic. For example, the Moluccas and other 'spice islands', the source of cloves, mace and nutmeg, appear (above) scattered at random between the Isle of Jana, with its Amazon Queen, the Isle of Trapobana (Sumatra), the source of camphor, and the coast of south China, the source of ginger. Swimming amongst them are not only fish, but also a two-tailed mermaid, and, surprisingly realistically for such a mythicized environment, a Chinese-looking boat, like those that were actually carrying East Indian spices to China or India at this time. On the right the fourteenth-century French illuminator of Polo's travels has imagined Venetians and oriental potentates bartering cloth for spices.

level of customs dues, often very high, to which they were subjected en route; or of political change and instability outside Europe. The end of the fourteenth century and the beginning of the fifteenth witnessed very considerable disturbances in central and western Asia, as Timur built up his precarious Samarkand-based empire, which stretched from Anatolia to the borders of China. Timur's rise both disrupted trade and created opportunities for adventurous west European merchants to go into central Asia for the first time for two generations. However, the equally rapid collapse of his empire abruptly cut those opportunities short. Furthermore, in India itself, the overlordship of the Tuqhluqid sultans of Delhi was greatly disturbed by the incursions of Timur's lieutenants, and was eventually brought to a close shortly after Timur's death.

In Europe, ginger was used for spicing wine, as well as flavouring meat and fish. It could arrive dried, but it was also sent preserved in sugar. Cloves too were used for spicing wine and flavouring food, but they were also used by apothecaries. Indeed oil of cloves is still used today by dentists. Not only cloves but other imported spices, like the herbs grown at home, often had as much a medicinal as a culinary value, like the dried rhubarb and the galingale brought from eastern China, and the aloes brought from Socotra at the entrance to the Red Sea.

Although most 'spices' were of Asiatic origin, some of a very distant provenance, a few others, as well as sugar, were produced by Europeans, like cheap cummin seed and expensive saffron. Cummin was grown in the central

Mediterranean, for example in the islands of the Maltese archipelago, and in the Navarrese accounts was priced at less than a third of pepper.

Saffron, the brilliant orange-coloured stigmas of autumn crocus, was also a plant of Asian origin, much grown in the tenth and eleventh centuries in the mountains of Cilicia in southern Asia Minor. From there it was taken westwards to Byzantium, and southwards through Alexandria to the Indian Ocean. In the thirteenth century, it began to be grown in Europe as well, in Catalonia and on both sides of the Appenines, in eastern Tuscany and above all in the western parts of the Abruzzi around Aquila. It was dried and used not only for colouring and flavouring food, but also medicinally and as a dyestuff for fabrics. It was remarkably expensive. The early fifteenth-century royal household of Navarre paid eight times as much for saffron as for pepper. In 1400 saffron was by far the most expensive commodity imported into Prussia by the Teutonic Order. They were selling it for eleven times the price of pepper. Saffron was sufficiently expensive for it to be worthwhile for Buonocorso Pitti to carry it overland from Venice to Hungary at the end of the fourteenth century. At the same time in eastern Europe saffron was being carried overland from the Black Sea through Lvov to Cracow to supply the Polish market. Catalan saffron, as well as being exported by sea from Barcelona to Flanders, was also carried overland from Saragossa through southern France to the fairs of Geneva and Lyons, and thence onwards to Basel, Constance, Ravensburg and Nuremberg.[26]

Silk

Just as west Europeans took up the cultivation of sugar to supplement and replace sugar grown in the Levant, they also took up the cultivation of the mulberry for the sake of silk. Like sugar, silk had been introduced into the Mediterranean from further east, by its Arab conquerors. The Arabs encountered silk in central Asia and north Persia. Christian Europeans therefore inherited the cultivation of mulberries and silk worms in both Sicily and Andalusia when they reconquered them. Mulberry trees can be much more widely grown than sugar cane, but west Europeans only realized this very gradually, and their introduction further and further north into Europe was correspondingly slow. By the end of the Middle Ages they were still cultivated no further north than Tuscany (see p. 251).

Despite the slowly growing cultivation of mulberry trees and silk worms in Spain and Italy the demand for silk by the manufacturers of damasks and brocades and velvets in late medieval Italy was such that raw silk as well as silk fabrics continued to be imported from and through the Levant. After the defeat of Pisa in 1284 the Genoese took over the import of raw silk to Lucca through Porto Pisano as part of their dominance over the shipping of goods into and out of Tuscany. Much of this originated in Asia Minor and was bought by the Genoese at Pera, the Genoese colony next to Constantinople, and at Phocaea on the west coast of Asia Minor itself.

In the fifteenth century, when the manufacture of silk fabrics spread to other north Italian cities, including Florence and Genoa itself, the Genoese continued to play a very considerable role in the import of silk for this growing industry. By now much of the silk was purchased in Chios and Rhodes. Although Genoa specialized more in bulk carriage by the fifteenth century, it thus still retained some share in the rich trades.

Silk was, of course, one of the most expensive commodities that was traded in. In 1458 a large carrack of 950 tonnes returned to Genoa from a Levantine voyage to Beirut and Rhodes and Chios. There were 6,000 Genoese pounds of silk on board (around 2 tonnes). By weight it only formed a tiny part of the cargo, but by value it was significant. It cost various prices between 6 *li.* and 7 *li. genovese* per pound. Even the pepper on board, a relatively valuable commodity in itself, seemed cheap by comparison. It had cost 67 *li.* 10 *s. genovese* per *centinaio* (100 pounds). In other words, on this occasion silk was priced around ten times as highly as pepper. Other evidence suggests that it was valued at twelve times as much. This made it worthwhile to cross Asia by land to bring the finest quality from China, whilst spices could be carried similarly immense distances only if they were carried most of the way by water. Silk was so highly regarded that it was exceeded in value for its weight only by pearls and precious stones.

Pearls and precious stones

More expensive than any of the eastern 'spices' imported from outside Europe, or even than the silk fabrics and raw silk imported from the East, were the pearls and precious stones which followed some of the same routes, although their high value made them even more appropriate than silk for carriage over long distances by road.

The Pisan merchant's notebook of 1279 noted pearls at Lajazzo in three sizes. Small pearls under 12 carats were sold by the ounce, those between 12 carats and 24 carats were sold in strings of 36, and large pearls over 24 carats were also bought in strings of 36. The small pearls ended up sewn not only on to secular garments (see p. 121-3), but also on to episcopal mitres. The large pearls were used in jewelry, from royal crowns downwards. They were to be found en route not only in the hands of merchants of Pisa returning home from Armenia, but in the hands of merchants from Nuremberg, returning home from Venice. They originally came from pearl fisheries in the Persian Gulf and off the coasts of Ceylon and the nearest point of south India. European and Muslim travellers like Marco Polo, Odoric of Pordenone and Ibn Battutah were sufficiently impressed to describe the fisheries. Western Europeans were therefore not ignorant of the origin of their pearls. From the fisheries off the island of Kich and elsewhere, Gulf pearls were brought to Ormuz, the greatest distribution centre. From Ormuz they were sent to Sultanieh and Tabriz in north-west Persia, where Clavijo saw them being set in jewelry, and to Samarkand in central Asia, but above all to Baghdad. It was in these places that Europeans bought pearls, when they could get to them – but by the fifteenth century the trade in precious stones, like that in 'spices' was virtually reduced to a single Alexandria–Venice axis.

Like the pearl-fisheries, the source of diamonds in south India was also known to west Europeans in the Middle Ages. Niccolo di Conti, who was one of the European travellers who entered Asia during Timur's rule, visited the south Indian Empire of Vijayanagar around 1420 and included it in the account he wrote on his eventual return to Venice. The rulers of Vijayanagar then controlled Golconda, now in Hyderabad, which is still an active source of diamonds. The two most important mines in the area were at Raolconda and Kulur. The mines at Kulur on the middle course of the Kistna were described by Conti as fifteen days' journey north of Vijayanagar itself. They were leased out for limited periods by the ruler to entrepreneurs who operated the mines with an immense number of ill-paid miners. Visitors' narratives suggest there were not less than 30,000. If true, this dwarfs any enterprise in late medieval Europe, and, even if a gross exaggeration, it probably still humbles the largest operations that Europeans could then mount. India and Ceylon also produced the world's emeralds, sapphires and rubies,

Since travellers' reports of the previous century had given vivid accounts of pearl fishing in the straits of Ormuz, at the entry to the Persian Gulf, it was possible in 1375 for the Majorcan creator of the Catalan Atlas *to insert a lively vignette not far from the right place. Are those sharks threatening the divers?*

as they still do. It is no wonder that Italian merchants were prepared to accept the risks and expense of travelling overland to Delhi in the early fourteenth century to buy precious stones. We know about one Genoese partnership engaged in purchasing diamonds and other stones from the litigation that broke out amongst the partners on their return home. Most precious stones came from India itself, but even semi-precious stones came from outside Europe. The less valuable *Balas* rubies, as well as lapis lazuli, came from the area of the upper Oxus in central Asia, whilst turquoise came from Persia. Only for limited periods could Italians get anywhere near their actual sources. Normally they had to purchase them, along with pearls, at places like Alexandria and Constantinople, after they had passed through the hands of many Asian middlemen. As with the spice trade, Italians normally controlled only the last, western, part of the trade. The goldsmiths of Paris, London and the other European capitals who produced all too evanescent masterpieces for rulers and great noblemen were essentially being supplied with Asian commodities conveyed by Asian merchants and carriers. The unit cost of diamonds, emeralds, sapphires and rubies may have been vast, and the eventual products spectacular, but the overall effect on the economy of Europe was far less than the bulk trades in grain, salt, wine, iron and timber or that in textiles.

Venetian, Genoese and other Italian merchants, missionaries and adventurers visited and lived in Persia, India and China in the thirteenth and early fourteenth centuries and again a century later. Their letters home and the accounts of their journeys written after their return to Europe meant that Asia should not have been totally mysterious to Europeans. Unfortunately the fake narrative of de Mandeville, full of strange wonders, was much more widely read than the genuine narratives of Rubruck or Odoric or Conti. Despite the knowledge which was actually available, the sources of spices, dyestuffs, pearls and precious stones still seemed as strange and wonderful as it had done in the late twelfth century when Chrétien could describe the robe given by King Arthur to Erec for his coronation as King of Brittany as lined with fur which 'belonged to some strange beasts…these beasts live in India and eat nothing but spices, cinnamon and fresh cloves'. Surely the height of mysterious luxury!

Raw materials at Bruges

The trade in spices, silks and jewels from the east has taken us far from bulky and less precious foodstuffs and raw materials. It is time to return to the West and to the basics of living. Bruges has appeared already as the key point for the export of manufactured goods from the industrial heartland of medieval Europe (see p. 232). It has also appeared as the key point for the import and distribution of consumer goods for the Low Countries and much of northern and north-western Europe (see p. 113). As the Castilian nobleman, Pero Tafur, who visited Bruges in 1438, commented, 'the products of the whole world are brought here.' He himself only paid attention to the consumer goods, but other descriptions of Bruges make it clear that it was also the key point of entry for many of the raw materials needed by the industries in its hinterland. A hundred years earlier than Pero Tafur an anonymous writer had already spelled out much more fully what 'the products of the whole world' then meant to him. His list contains a very interesting mixture of consumer goods and industrial raw materials:

> From the kingdom of England cometh wool, leather, lead, tin, mineral coal and cheese. From the kingdom of Norway cometh gerfalcons, wood for building, boiled leather, butter, tallow, grease and pitch and goatskins for the making of cordovan leather. From the kingdom of Denmark cometh palfreys, leather, grease, tallow, potash, herring and bacon. From the kingdom of Russia cometh wax, vairs, and greys [both sorts of squirrel]. From the kingdom of Hungary cometh wax, bar gold and silver. From the kingdom of Bohemia cometh wax, silver and pewter. From the kingdom of Germany cometh Rhennish wine, pitch, potash, timber for building, Prussian blue, iron and steel. From the see of Liège and the region adjacent thereto cometh all manner of wares of beaten and wrought copper as also great wooden beams.[27]

I have already quoted his sections about wax from Russia, Hungary and Bohemia, and about spices from the kingdoms of Armenia, Jerusalem and Egypt and the land of Soudan (above pp. 304 and 312), but did not add that he also knew of Armenia as a source of cotton. He continues with the 'kingdom of Scotland', 'the kingdom of Ireland', 'the kingdom of Sweden', 'the kingdom of Poland', 'the kingdom of Bulgaria', 'the kingdom of Navarre', 'the kingdom of France', 'Poitou', 'Gascony' and 'divers other lands also'. And 'from all these kingdoms and all these lands herein before written come merchants and goods to the land of Flanders, wherefore there is no land able to bear comparison with Flanders for the infinite variety of goods to be found there'.

If we go back yet one century earlier, to the early thirteenth century, we have a description of an attack on Damme, which was them already the port of Bruges. In 1213 a French fleet, under Savary de Mauléon, tried, on the orders of Philip II, to capture the outport. Savary reported to his master:

> Urged on by a favourable breeze, the fleet arrived joyfully in that port. The harbour was so wide and so calm that all our ships were able to ride at anchor in it. Here lies the fairly large town called Damme, a pleasant place with its gently flowing river and fertile countryside, happy in its proximity to the sea. Proud of its seaport and the site whereon it is built. And there Savary found wealth beyond all his hopes, brought in by ship from all parts of the world, masses of unwrought silver, and red copper, fine cloth, goods from Cathay and the innumerable hides and fells dispatched hither from Hungary, together with the iron, metals, cloth and other merchandise amassed in this place.[28]

Amongst the consumer goods, a considerable number of raw materials for industry stand out from these descriptions: wool from England; cotton from Armenia; potash from Denmark and Germany; leather, hides and goatskins from England, Denmark, Hungary and Norway; iron and copper from Germany; tin from England; timber from Norway, Germany and the Meuse valley, and mineral coal from England.

Building materials and fuel

The heaviest of all commodities to be carried were building materials. Stone and bricks were worth carrying, even by water, for only limited distances, except for the most luxurious, like marble from the Carrara quarries.[29]

The brick-kilns that served Florence were situated in the valley of the Greve some ten kilometres south of the city, and those that served Bruges were similarly close.[30] Timber, however, was carried a very long way by sea and river. Our list of commodities coming to Bruges therefore included not only great wooden beams from Liège, floated down the Meuse, and wood for building from Germany, floated down the Rhine, but also wood for building brought by sea from Norway.[31] Timber was needed for building ships as well as houses. The reliance of Dutch and English shipbuilders in the seventeenth and eighteenth centuries on timber from the Baltic lands, particularly for masts and spars, can be traced back to the later Middle Ages. Wood was also needed for the innumerable barrels used for transporting grain and salt, furs and fish, besides wine and beer. However, its principal use was as fuel: for domestic heating and cooking and in communal bakeries, and as industrial fuel for industries such as making bricks and tiles, smelting minerals, firing pottery, brewing ale, and evaporating brine.

The demand for timber for some industries was prodigious: the armourers of Milan and Brescia, for example, had an insatiable appetite for charcoal. But the amount of fuel that they consumed paled into insignificance beside the glass-makers of Murano. The consequent deforestation caused alarm in Venice because the supply of suitable timber for ship-building at the Arsenal was affected. In the second quarter of the fifteenth century barge-building had to move inland because of the lack of timber. Furthermore, during the 1450s the Venetians became aware that their lagoon was being endangered by the increasing amount of silt brought down by rivers, when the timber on the land through which they ran had been felled and it was left exposed to erosion. The Venetian Council of Ten ordered a replanting programme and from 1470 vainly attempted to conserve woodlands to increase the supply of oak available for naval purposes. The glass industry was responsible not only for the deforestation in the hinterland of the city, which worried Venetians, but also for rapid and destructive deforestation in Dalmatia, which did not. Glass-making always used prodigious quantities of wood. In sixteenth-century England glass-makers from Lorraine came across to the Weald in 1568, then moved on to Hampshire, and next to Staffordshire, leaving a trail of desolation behind them. Complaints were also made in England against this too exhaustive destruction of woods and forests for fuel. Eventually legislation was passed prohibiting the use of charcoal for the manufacture of glass. In 1615 the woodland furnaces closed for ever, and the glass-makers migrated to Newcastle-on-Tyne and Stourbridge where they could use locally mined coal.[32] This was not an option open to the medieval glass-

When John, Duke of Bedford, wanted a new Book of Hours *of his own in 1423, naturally he commissioned it from one of the best workshops in Paris, where the book trade had not yet totally collapsed. In his* Hours, *the ark that the carpenters are building, under Noah's direction, appears not as a boat, but as a timber-framed house being made ready to float away, which reveals how much large timber was needed for a single substantial house. The illuminator saw the construction of timber houses regularly, since Paris was itself in an area of timber-framed buildings, where only the grandest princely* hôtels *were entirely built of stone.*

makers of Murano, so they continued to draw charcoal from greater and greater distances, eventually even from Crete. Even if pit-coal was not available in Murano, it was available in north-western Europe. Most of the English coalfields were being worked in a small way from the thirteenth century onwards. However, because of the costs of transport, pit-coal was only worth using in the immediate vicinity, except for the coal from the Northumberland coalfield, which was sufficiently near the sea to be shipped around the English coast as far as London and Southampton, or across the North Sea to Flanders and Holland, and even into the Baltic. It has been estimated that in the last quarter of the fourteenth century the coalfield produced around 50,000 tons of coal, of which 20,000 tons were sent around the coast from Newcastle and another 7,000 overseas, for such varied uses as drying madder, smoking fish, burning lime and working iron.[33] It is not clear whether or not production here surpassed that in the Liège and Charleroi coalfields along the Meuse in the later Middle Ages. It certainly did so by the end of the sixteenth century. In the fourteenth century there was already competition for markets in Flanders and Holland between Northumberland and Meuse coal, although the Bruges list of commodities only mentioned that coming by sea from England. In the fourteenth century coal was being carried down the Meuse past Dordrecht and down the Ijssel past Kampen. The earliest surviving reference to coal-mining around Liège dates from

1195, but only relatively small quantities seem to have been mined until the 1270s, when production expanded enormously. In the early fourteenth century a guild of Liège mine-operators, *a métier des houillères* was formed, which even in the slightly contracted circumstances of the early fifteenth century had nearly 2,000 members. The coalfield was thus dotted with a huge number of tiny mines, some owned by partnerships or small companies. In 1356 such a company, with its capital divided into eight shares took on the lease of a mine at Mollins, north east of Liège.[34] Outside north-western Europe even well-travelled people were so unaware of the existence of pit-coal, that when Marco Polo encountered it in Asia, he was recorded by Rustichello of Pisa as describing it as a novelty unknown in Europe!

In addition to timber, charcoal and, in a limited number of places, pit-coal, later medieval Europe also used peat as a source of heat, both for domestic and industrial purposes. For the heat it gave, it was even more expensive to transport than coal and was only used in large quantities very close to the places where it was dug out. When Pero Tafur crossed Brabant in 1438, he observed that, between 'sHertogenbosch and Mechelen, 'instead of wood they burn sods of earth like bricks. They cut them in the summer, each one from his land, and dry them in the sun, and keep them until winter. These sods make a pleasant fire and are said to be very healthy.'[35] Another place that used peat was Bruges itself, where it was the domestic fuel of the poor. In 1449 the magistrates of Bruges ordered peat-tokens to be distributed to 4,000 households, out of around 7,000 in the city. These peat-tokens entitled them to free peat through the winter.

The most widespread industrial use of fuel was for the smelting of metal from its ore, but this did not create much in the way of long-distance trade since only the presence of abundant local timber made it economic to mine copper and iron.

Metals The only unworked metals picked out in the early fourteenth-century Bruges list were iron and copper from Germany and tin from England. However, German iron and copper formed only a very small proportion of the metals mined in late medieval Europe. Because of their weight in relation to their value, metals were rarely carried long distances. There were, however, some exceptions, and metal from mines close to the sea and to navigable rivers naturally had an advantage in this respect, since it was cheaper to carry iron or copper by water.

Copper and iron were not of course carried away from mining areas as ore, but in the form of ingots of metal. To produce these, water-powered stamp mills and blast furnaces with water-powered bellows were to be found in the vicinity of copper and iron mines, which needed plentiful running water and timber as fuel. Like sugar-refiners and cloth-fullers, the metal trades applied water power at an early date. We know of water-powered bellows in the thirteenth century and water-powered stamp mills from the early fourteenth. The earliest known blast furnace was at Liège in 1384.

As with the ores of precious metals, there was a continuous process of discovery, exploitation, and exhaustion of the deposits of iron ore. These deposits were, of course, much more numerous than the deposits of silver or gold. The most productive by the fifteenth century, when we begin to have some statistics, seem to have been those in the Alps and in the Upper Palatinate, east of Nuremberg.[36] Numerous different deposits of iron ore were exploited in the Alps, from Savoy in the west right around to Styria in the east. Some of this iron was brought relatively short distances to Milan and Brescia where it fed the production of arms and armour for an international market (see pp. 259–60). Water transport was used where possible. Iron from the Val Telline, for example, was carried by boat the length of Lake Como.

Georg Bauer, the town physician of Freiberg, where the old silver mines had been revived, wrote extensively on mining under the Latinised form of his name, Georgius Agricola. In his De re Metallica of 1561, the illustrations of mining, and the accompanying text, provide us with some of the earliest exact descriptions of the advances in technology over the previous hundred years. On the right a cut-out view of underground workings reveals a horse drawing a box of ore on wheels (known as a Hund or dog) along a set of rails, which is perhaps the earliest picture of any sort of railway. Other miners are bringing out ore in wheelbarrows, which is then being transferred to a four-wheeled horse-drawn cart. The ore, still uncrushed, is being taken to a water-driven battery mill, to prepare it for smelting (see p. 364).

The mining, smelting and trade in iron from the areas around Amberg and Sulzbach in the Upper Palatinate had been controlled by Nuremberg capital since at least the early fourteenth century. In the fifteenth century there were reputedly 200 water-powered iron hammers at work. This iron principally fed the metal industries of Nuremberg itself, not far distant, which had developed a number of specialist trades. In 1400 there were 141 separate crafts in the city, many of whose members were working in iron, such as locksmiths, tool-makers, wiresmiths, cutlers, bladesmiths, thimble-makers, needle-makers, nail-makers, scale-makers and makers of large clocks. Such iron wares themselves became objects of long-distance trade, carried by road to the Main, and then shipped down to the Frankfurt fairs and so into the Rhineland, the Low Countries and beyond.[37] Nuremberg naturally also used Upper Palatinate iron to become the centre for the south German manufacture of armour in the fifteenth century (see pp. 260–5).

However the unworked iron that was most heavily traded over long distances in northern and western Europe was that from northern Spain: it which was exported in large quantities from the ports of northern Spain to Gascony, Brittany, northern France, the Low Countries and England. The iron-mines in the mountains of north-western Spain lay close to the sea. Those in the hinterland of Bilbao had already been worked in classical antiquity, but there seems to have been no continuity with the medieval exploitation of the ore. Once they were re-opened they soon provided for more than local needs and three centuries of exports followed. By the mid-thirteenth century a considerable iron trade had already grown up between north-west Spain and both the Netherlands and England. The fourteenth century saw a considerable further increase in iron exports to both England and France, allegedly stimulated by the war in France, and the fifteenth century saw fresh mines opened up in the Basque provinces to replace those that had been worked out.[38] Bilbao, already the most important of these iron-exporting ports, obtained the exclusive right to authorize the export of this Cantabrian iron in 1494, at the same time that Burgos obtained control of the inland trade in it.[39]

Even in northern England, where a certain amount of local iron was mined and worked in nearby Weardale, the Durham Cathedral community and its extensive estates were still heavily reliant in the late fifteenth century on imported Spanish iron bought at Newcastle. England's iron imports were indeed overwhelmingly of Spanish iron. However in the fifteenth century high-quality *osmund*, a Swedish form of malleable iron, began to be of importance.[40] Central Sweden was the only significant area for the production of iron on the western and northern periphery of Europe in the later Middle Ages, and even here iron-mining developed rather more slowly and later than in Spain, Italy, or Germany. The first evidence of the export of Swedish iron comes from the earliest surviving Lübeck toll register, of 1368, which records the payment of toll on 19,000 *zentner* of unworked smith's iron from Sweden. Such a quantity suggests that an export trade to Lübeck had already been growing for some time by 1368. However, it was not until the second half of the fifteenth century that a really considerable exploitation of Sweden's iron ores took place. Numerous forges and iron works were then set up along the water routes, particularly on the Mälarsee, which led from the mines to Stockholm, from which Swedish iron was principally exported. Exports of Swedish iron then grew very fast, much of it carried by Hanse merchants and taken by way of Lübeck.[41] Half of all the iron landed at Hull in the fifteenth century was *osmund*. In the early modern period Sweden was to become the most important source of iron in Europe.

Other mining areas also sent iron to northern England. Rather surprisingly, four tons of 'Liège' iron was landed at Newcastle in 1494–45. Although the exploitation of iron in Namur and Liège had begun in the fourteenth century, it was, like most other European iron deposits, almost entirely used locally. Indeed the Low Countries did not have enough iron for their own use and imported considerable quantities of iron from northern Spain.

Since copper was frequently found in combination with silver, most of the discussion of copper-mining, and of the trade in copper, will be found with the discussion of the mining of precious metals in the chapter on the imbalances of trade (see pp. 363-71). Some of the most plentiful supplies of copper came from mining areas better known for their silver: from, for example, around Goslar in the Harz, Kutna Hora in Bohemia and Schwaz in the Tyrol. Sometimes the production of copper continued long after the silver had been exhausted. We have already seen the transport of copper from the Harz to the brass-making areas of the middle Rhine and the middle Meuse, and for sale at Bruges. We have also seen the transport of copper from Slovakia for brass making in south Germany (see pp. 267-70).

At the end of the Middle Ages Venice was the key emporium for the copper trade. At the end of the fourteenth century Venice was still receiving some Harz copper by sea from Bruges, but by far the most important sources were already the copper mines of Slovakia, particularly in and around Banská Bystrica (Neusohl, Fuxine nove). Although there was some direct purchase in Slovakia by Venetians, and some by Viennese merchants, most of the trade between Slovakia and Venice was in the hands of the south German entrepreneurs who had a key role in the operation of the mines themselves. The copper itself could easily be carried down the Hron valley and then shipped up the Danube to Vienna or southern Germany, but then it was heavy and difficult to carry across the Alps to Venice. An alternative to the difficulties of transporting copper across the Alps was to carry it, like the gold of Kremnica, across Hungary and Croatia to the Adriatic at Senj, and then to bring it into Venice by sea. Early in the fifteenth century Slovak copper was temporarily supplemented from the silver mines of Bosnia and Croatia, which also yielded copper for the Venetian market. Only at the very end of the century was Slovak copper eclipsed by new sources in the Tirol and at Mansfeld in Thuringia. In Venice copper was sold by auction at the Fondaco dei Tedeschi. Like silver ingots, copper ingots (*rame di bolla*) had to be stamped with a mark as a guarantee of its fineness before being sold. If necessary, copper had to be re-refined before being sold onwards. From Venice much of

Although by the fifteenth century there were many sheep in England pastured on former arable land, this shepherd is still following an older tradition by driving his flocks up on to the hills to graze. The wool from sheep that had run on English hills was considered the best in Europe. This is from an English fifteenth-century Book of Hours.

the copper was sold to the Levant. The single most important customer for Venetian copper was the government of Mamluk Egypt, which over a long period bought considerable amounts of copper for its mints, in which large quantities of copper *fulūs* were being minted from the thirteenth century onwards, in the place of silver coinage. The vizir of sultan Barḳūḳ (1382–98) even sent agents to Europe to ensure the supply of copper for minting. Further copper was used in Egypt not only for traditional domestic vessels, but also for industrial vessels, such as vats for sugar-boiling. From the mid-fourteenth century onwards the copper trade was both encouraged and regulated by the Venetian Senate. In 1355, for example, it decreed that every galley going to Cyprus (and Beirut) should carry 80 *miglaia* (some 37 tonnes) of copper or tin.[42]

Until the fourteenth century Cornwall had a near monopoly in the large-scale production of tin in Europe. Cornish tin was sent as far afield as Italy, Provence and southern France, as well as to Bruges and Cologne, and through Cologne to the Frankfurt fairs.[43] However, in the course of the fourteenth and fifteenth centuries tin deposits were exploited in Bohemia, Saxony, Silesia and Moravia. This central European tin gradually replaced Cornish tin at the Frankfurt fairs, despite the costs of transport by road.[44]

Wool Apart from building materials, fuel and metals, the most significant raw materials to be carried about Europe were those destined to feed the textile industries, particularly the woollen cloth industry. The cheap cloth produced everywhere in Europe generally relied on local wool, but the huge manufacture of cheap cloth in fourteenth- and fifteenth-century Lombardy, like that of Tuscany, needed more than local Alpine and Appenine sheep could produce (for cloth industries see pp. 232–48 and map on p. 231). Even taking into account wool from the flocks driven north from Apulia, which grew increasingly in the late fourteenth and early fifteenth centuries, it needed to import large quantities of wool from overseas. The north Italian manufacture of cheap cloth came to depend heavily, but not exclusively, on cheap wool shipped in large quantities to Genoa, Venice and Porto Pisano from Iberian east-coast ports like Tortosa and Peniscola. Around 1400 Peniscola was, temporarily, the most important wool port of the Mediterranean. The extent of this dependence became apparent during the 'Catalan Revolution' of 1460–71, a disastrous civil war in Aragon and Catalonia, accompanied by rural revolt, which not only destroyed the Barcelona cloth industry, but, by cutting off vital supplies of wool, brought about a sudden shrinkage in that of Lombardy as well. Aragonese and Catalan wool also supplied the native cloth industry of Barcelona, and was supplemented there, and in northern Italian industry, by wool from Valencia and Murcia further south, from the Balearics, Sardinia and Sicily, and from the wool of the transhumant sheep of North Africa, shipped out of every port from Rabat to Algiers. Lombardy was further supplied through Genoa with wool from the Rhône valley and Provence, also used for the local Provençal manufacture of cheap cloth, and through Venice with wool from 'Romania', what remained of the Byzantine Empire. For the production of the finest woollen cloth in the Low Countries or Florence, however, only English wool was good enough, until Castilian wool improved enough to rival and even supplant it (see map p. 329).

The earliest unequivocal reference to the import of English wool into Flanders only dates from 1113, yet it is a reference that implies that it was an import that was already commonplace.[45] Although it is impossible to know when this import began, some historians believe that it was already established by the late tenth century and began to grow considerably from that period onwards. The early thirteenth-century statutes of the Flemish Hansa in London give a vivid impression of merchants not only from Bruges, but also from Ypres, Dixmude, Aardenburg, Lille, Oostburg, Damme, Furnes, Tournai and a number of other places in Flanders, actively trading in London. In the twelfth and the first half of the thirteenth century, such Flemish merchants were coming to England as great purchasers of English wool. However, in the course of the thirteenth century Italian merchants, with the ability to borrow money at much lower rates of interest than the Flemish, were able to offer English wool-producers better terms, like payment in advance. In this way the Flemings were largely eased out of England as exporters, and their place taken by Italians.[46] At the beginning of the fourteenth century Italian merchants largely sent English wool to the southern Netherlands, particularly to Bruges, but early in the century they began to send large quantities of English wool direct to Italy as well. Thus, in the first half of the century, at its highest point, the export of English wool, whether to Bruges or Italy, was very largely in the hands of great Italian business houses such as the Bardi and the Peruzzi. The quantity of English wool exports reached over 45,000 sacks in the single year 1305. A sack of wool was enormous. It took a whole wagon to hold a single one, although wool was frequently carried as two 'sarplers', half-sacks, each a suitable load for a pack animal. Each sack contained the wool of between 180 and 250 sheep, since fleeces varied greatly in weight. So over 45,000 sacks was the wool from

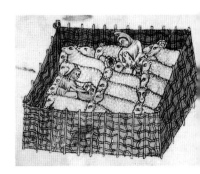

Unlike the circular sheep-fold for grazing (overleaf), this tight, square fold from the Luttrell Psalter was for shearing, marking, sale or slaughter. Sheep shearing in England and Northern Europe took place in June, sale and slaughter around Easter and in the autumn.

Wool from England

327

By the sixteenth century Castile had overtaken England as the principal provider of wool for the industries of the Low Countries. Many Castilian sheep were transhumant for hundreds of miles across the central plateau. Others moved shorter distances, like this flock folded for grazing on arable land outside Ecija in Andalusia from Braun and Hogenberg. Their folds were moved gradually around the fields through the winter, so that their dung would enrich the soil equally.

The map shows the areas which produced the best wool, and the ports through which it was exported from England. From Southampton wool was largely carried to Italy, and from the other ports to the Low Countries. Pickering and Pontefract are marked as the gathering places for wool from the earl of Lancaster's huge Yorkshire sheep ranches, and Clun for the earl of Hereford's. Meaux, another great Cistercian house, like Tintern and Abbey Dore, similarly ran sheep in great numbers (on the Yorkshire Wolds).

between 8,000,000 and 11,000,000 sheep. This was an exceptional year, but 30,000 sacks and more were frequently exported from England until the 1360s.

In the 1340s a wave of bankruptcies hit some of the major Florentine wool-exporters. Native English merchants then took over the export of English wool to the Low Countries. However, at the same time, the English crown began to tax the export of English wool particularly heavily for war purposes. The taxation on English wool, was not an ad valorem tax, but at a fixed rate per sack, so that the consequent price increase afflicted the users of poorer wools much more than those who used the dearest wool from the Welsh Marches or from the Cotswolds. The luxury woollen industry of the Low Countries' cities, the 'Old Drapery' therefore concentrated, as it shrank, more and more on the most luxurious cloths made from the finest wool. It is not surprising that the overall quantity of English wool exported went into decline in the second half of the fourteenth century, or that English cloth exports made a comeback, since the high level of taxation on wool unintentionally acted as a protection to English cloth-making.[47]

Two regions were especially important for high-quality wool, the Welsh Marches which produced the very best wool in western Europe, and secondarily the long ridge which runs from the Cotswolds north-eastwards across Northamptonshire, Leicestershire, into Lincolnshire and then on beyond the Humber into the Yorkshire Wolds and the Yorkshire Moors. In the Welsh Marches and on the Yorkshire Moors, there were great sheep ranches, while in the Cotswolds and Northamptonshire and Leicestershire there were many smaller flocks. Their sheep provided profits for the monastic owners of many large ranches which enabled them to build their splendid conventual buildings, the ruins of which are still impressive today. Pegolotti, who worked for the Bardi, pinpointed what in his opinion were the most important wool-producers of Europe, in the second decade of the fourteenth century. For him the finest wools were those of the Welsh Marches, particularly those on the sheep ranches of the Cistercian abbeys of Tintern and Abbey Dore, which ran their flocks of sheep in the Black Mountains. Pegolotti's opinions on quality can largely be confirmed and even amplified from other records.[48] However, he was not so interested in quantity, and very considerable quan-

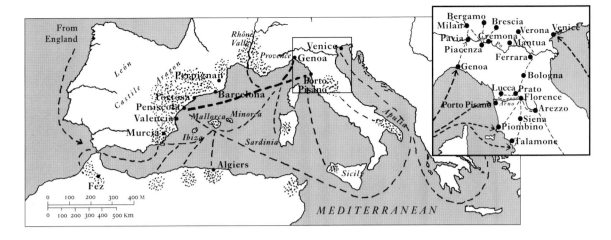

From
England

Rhône
Valley

Provence

Venice

Genoa

Porto
Pisano

Apulia

Perpignan

Barcelona

Tortosa
Peniscola
Valencia

Mallorca   Minorca

Murcia

Ibiza

Sardinia

Algiers

Sicily

Fez

León

Aragon

Castile

MEDITERRANEAN

0   100   200   300   400 M

0   100 200 300 400 500 Km

Bergamo
Milan   Brescia
Verona   Venice
Pavia   Cremona
Piacenza   Po   Mantua
Ferrara
Genoa
Bologna
Lucca Prato
Porto Pisano   Florence
Arno   Arezzo
Siena
Piombino
Talamone

tities of less prestigious wools from other parts of the country were being produced as well, and some exported in his time.

Apart from London, the largest exports of wool from England went out through Hull, Boston and Southampton. In the fifteenth century London more and more monopolized the small remaining wool exports. By this time to there were strict government controls on the wool trade. After the capture of Calais by Edward III, in 1346, in the opening stage of the Hundred Years' War, all wool destined for the Low Countries was compelled to pass through the town, which thus became the principal outport of Bruges for wool, although other commodities continued to come up the canal through Sluys and Damme. Very little of Calais in its great days survives, because of the destruction of wars. All that can now be seen is the thirteenth-century lighthouse built before the English took over the town, but maintained by them, because it was so vital for coming in to Calais Roads. For a time it rivalled Peniscola as one of the great wool ports of Europe. The trade to Calais eventually came into the hands of a closed group of English merchants, mostly London Grocers, and only Italians sending wool direct to Italy, and Hanseatics sending it direct to the Baltic, were permitted to avoid Calais.

In the inset are the principal towns in which the north Italian woollen cloth industry was concentrated around 1400, together with the ports through which wool was imported from overseas. In the main map the areas are speckled which were the principal sources of that wool, with the ports through which it was exported to Italy. The dependence of both Tuscan and Lombard clothiers on wool imported from all parts of the western Mediterranean is very evident. The sea routes from Peniscola have been emphasized to indicate the particular importance of Catalan and Aragonese wool.

Wool from Spain

The only regions of Europe to rival the wool-producing areas of England for the quality of their wool were the hills and plateaux of Castile and León. Many of the sheep here were transhumant, and the basic outlines of Castilian transhumance were drawn during the century and a half after the Christian reconquest of Toledo in 1085. Transhumance was regulated in great detail. Each autumn flocks were gathered together in the mountains and driven down to the plains over immense distances, sometimes over 500 miles (800 kilometres), along a complex network of cañadas, broad, strictly regulated tracks. They then fanned out to graze on arable land after harvest, which they enriched with their dung over the winter. Before the sowing of arable crops in the spring, they were driven back to the mountains, which they normally reached in late May. The sheep were sheared at some point on the journey north. The owners of the transhumant sheep formed a nation-wide corporation, which was given royal protection by Alfonso X in 1273 and subsequently known as La Mesta Real (the royal guild).[49] A similar organization, the Casa de Ganaderos existed in Aragon, where transhumance was also practised, as it was in Catalonia and Valencia. In 1477 nearly 3,000,000 sheep owned by members of the Mesta, were moving across Castile twice a year. In addition there was a large but uncertain number of non-Mesta owned sheep. Some authors believe that they already very greatly outnumbered Mesta sheep as they did in later centuries.

Until the fourteenth century the wool produced in Spain in such large quantities was thought unsuitable for producing fine cloth, but was used extensively both in Spain itself, in Castile and Catalonia, and in Italy for producing cheaper cloth. However, Pedro IV (1336–87) imported sheep from North Africa, called Merino from the Merinid or Marīnīd dynasty which then ruled Morocco and the Atlas. Tens of thousands of flock-owners helped cross-breed them with the native Spanish sheep[50] Over the next century the quality of the finest wool produced in Spain increased enormously to the point where it could compete effectively with English wool in the Low Countries. Spanish merino wools, short-stapled and curly fibred, like the better English wools, and suitable for extensive fulling and felting, were used only in the production of true, heavy-weight woollens.

The merchants of Burgos gradually came to dominate the internal wool trade of Castile. They bought and sold wool throughout Castile, even as far south as Cordoba. When foreign trade in the finer wool of the fifteenth century developed they were well placed to dominate that too, for Burgos lay close to the passes that led through the Cantabrian Mountains to the ports on the Bay of Biscay, Bilbao, Laredo and Santander. The merchants of Burgos had already joined together as a religious confraternity in the thirteenth century, but did not become a chartered corporation until 1494 (the Consulado of Burgos). The charter of 1494 gave the Consulado the exclusive right to authorise wool shipments to Flanders, England, Brittany and the mouth of the Loire.[51]

Northern Spanish merchants were well known in the Low Countries as shippers of their own iron and of Gascon wines long before they became predominant as importers of fine wool. By 1280 Spanish merchants had already been given privileges in Bruges, and by 1348 their privileges were identical to those of Hanseatic merchants. In 1350 forty large Spanish ships were returning from Flanders when they were attacked by an English fleet. Nevertheless in the *Livre des Mestiers*, of about 1369, there was not yet any mention of wool from Castile amongst the types of wool available in Bruges. It was only in the first years of the fifteenth century that the cloth industries of Flanders and Brabant began to use Castilian wool. The earliest reference to the use of Castilian wool in the Low Countries comes from Brabant in 1407. Once it had begun the use of Spanish wool grew very fast. In the second quarter of the fifteenth century the growing 'New Draperies' of the Lys (Leie) valley were already mostly using Spanish wool, although the traditional urban 'Old Draperies' continued to use English wool for much longer. By the late 1430s the *Libelle of Englyshe Polyce* was able to emphasise how closely 'Flanders' and 'Spain' were bound together by the predominant use of Castilian wool in the woollen-manufacture of the southern Netherlands. It is no wonder that Spaniards became the largest foreign community in Bruges. Traditionally the shippers of wine and iron from northern Spanish ports like Bilbao, Laredo and Santander, many of whom were Basques, had lodged in inns for the months that they spent in the city, but by the 1440s the newer group of wool merchants, largely from Burgos, had acquired at least six large houses for permanent residence. The interests of the two groups were rather different, and in 1455 they separated and had separate consulates. After 1494 the wool-merchants' *consulado* was subordinated to the *consulado* of Burgos.[52]

Once Castilian wool had become competitive in quality it supplanted English wool in the Low Countries so rapidly because of fiscal policies in the two countries. Whereas successive English governments responded to the costs of war by imposing heavy taxation on the export of wool, so making English wool dearer, successive Castilian governments responded to the same costs by repeated debasement of the coinage, particularly from 1429 to the 1470s, which each time made exports from Castile cheaper, and consequently gave a continuous series of price advantages to Castilian wool over English. By the early sixteenth century, the quantity of Castilian wool imported into the Netherlands was as large as that of English wool in the early fourteenth century.

Castilian wool was also exported to Italy through Cordoba. At the end of the fifteenth century Burgos merchants had a considerable presence in Cordoba. The names of thirty of them are known, and they jointly built a wool warehouse on the banks of the Guadalquivir. From there the wool was sent downstream to Seville and trans-shipped to sea-going vessels. The commerce in wool was by far the largest of the trades in fibres used in the manufacture of textiles, but there was also a large trade in cotton as well as that in silk.

Cotton was another Indian plant brought to the lands bordering on the Mediterranean by Arab conquerors. Only a little of the cotton brought to Bruges from the 'Kingdom of Armenia' at the beginning of the fourteenth century was actually grown in Armenia. Most came from elsewhere in the Muslim Middle East, but was exported, because of the political circumstances of the time, through Christian Armenia. The most important cotton-growing area seems already to have been 'Syria', but the cotton from Iraq was also accessible in Armenia. Cotton had been grown in Egypt for several centuries, but it only seems to have become a very large-scale producer in the fifteenth century. When, in January 1279, a Pisan merchant made a fair copy of his miscellaneous jottings on Mediterranean trade, he noted cotton from 'Laiasso in Hermenia' [Lajazzo]; and cotton of '*oltramare*', i.e. Syrian–Palestinian cotton. It could then also be transported from Acre as well as Armenia, since Acre was still in the Christian, Crusader, hands, and was carried not only to Pisa itself, but by Pisans to Bougie in the Maghreb (now Algeria). He also noted, nearer home, cotton from Sicily.

The cultivation of cotton had spread to Sicily during the period of Arab occupation, along with that of many other crops from the east that depended

Cotton, flax and hemp

on the special techniques of irrigation that the Arab conquerors had themselves borrowed from the Punjab. In Sicily it was planted as a summer crop to be rotated with winter wheat or barley. Cotton could be transported from its place of origin already spun into yarn. Early in 1272 a Corsican pirate from Bonifacio seized a Sicilian ship, from Syracuse on its way to Genoa loaded with 30 *ruotoli di bombice filate* (30 *rotoli* of ready-spun cotton), together with a mixed cargo of sugar, cheese and wax.

Just as with sugar and silk, west Europeans increasingly grew cotton themselves in areas under their control. In this way Venetians began to grow cotton in Cyprus and Crete to supplement and partially replace their purchases of cotton from Egypt, Syria and Asia Minor. Similarly the cultivation of cotton spread from Sicily to Calabria, Apulia and Malta. The demand by Lombard and Catalan manufacturers of cotton textiles and of fustians, and then by south German and Swiss makers of fustians, for ever-increasing quantities of raw cotton could thus more readily be met from these sources, even when, in the fifteenth century, supplies from lands under Turkish control diminished.

Not all cotton was of the same quality. When, in 1412, Sigismund of Luxemburg, King of Hungary, and newly elected King of the Romans, from whom the Venetians had recently recaptured Friuli and parts of Dalmatia, attempted an economic blockade of Venice, he relied on the ability of the south Germans to obtain everything that they needed from alternative sources. Unfortunately for him, the Genoese suppliers could not replace completely Venetians. They were unable to get cotton to Ulm or Zurich in either adequate quantities or qualities for the fustian-makers in south Germany or Switzerland. The Turkish cotton that the Genoese brought from Chios and could supply was not as good as the cotton that the Venetians had been bringing from their plantations in Cyprus or Crete, let alone the Syrian and Egyptian cotton to which the Venetians had access at Beirut and Alexandria and the Genoese did not.

At the opposite extreme from silk and even cotton, which were worth carrying enormous distances, it was hardly worth carrying flax and hemp any distance at all. The manufacture of linens and fustians, of canvas and of rope, therefore became localized in the particular areas of Europe where flax and hemp could easily be grown. The trade was in the manufactured products, not in the raw materials.

Dyestuffs and alum

The textile industries generated a large trade in other commodities beside the fibres themselves. For luxury fabrics the most expensive part of the manufacturing process was dyeing. It was the consistency and appropriateness of colour that added most to the acceptability and value of the finished product. The popularity of particular colours amongst the eventual royal and noble customers was a combination of tradition and fashion. Some of these colours demanded the use of dyestuffs that had come as far as culinary and medicinal spices. Other colours could be achieved from dyestuffs readily available within western Europe itself.

The most commonly used dyestuff of all was woad. It was used not only for directly producing a vivid blue, but also as a preliminary dye before using other dyes. The textile industries of Italy used the woad of Lombardy, and those of the Low Countries the woad grown in Flanders and Brabant themselves around Lille and St Trond, supplemented by that grown in Picardy. However, the dyers of the Netherlands gradually ceased to use local woad and imported increasing quantities of it, mostly from around Toulouse. Cultivation in Flanders and Brabant consequently diminished. Toulouse woad was carried for Spanish merchants from Burgos and Avila to Bruges, along with iron and wool. When the English cloth industry expanded, woad was shipped out of Bordeaux and the Basque ports by northern Spanish shippers to London and Bristol, as well as to Bruges. Bristol merchants also went to collect woad from this area. Altogether the woad imported into Bristol from Spain exceeded both iron and olive oil in value, although it was not as bulky as either. In addition, Genoese carracks brought Lombard woad to Southampton for English dyers. Lombard woad was also shipped out through Venice, occasionally in galleys. In February 1459, a purchaser in Venice contracted to buy 300 *some*, or pack animal-loads, of woad from Bastida dei Dossi twelve kilometres from Pavia. However, it was not carried on 300 pack animals, but by barge, for Bastida dei Dossi stands on the south bank of the Po. The contract stipulated that the owner would directly defray the Milanese export duties and the costs of loading, and the shipper would pay all the tolls en route out of the freight charges, and would deliver to the owner in Venice, who would then discharge Venetian import dues. The carrier gave the owner 50 gold ducats as bond for performance, to be returned, with the payment for the freight charges, within one month of delivery. Saffron, derived from the crocus, and madder-root, the sources of the common yellow and red dyes, were equally grown in Europe. Madder, although a plant of Persian origin, was extensively grown in France and the Low Countries in the later Middle Ages.

The most expensive of all dyestuffs used was the 'grain' or 'kermes' used for scarlets. In mid-fifteenth-century Flanders, it cost up to twenty-nine times as much as madder, the most commonly used red dyestuff. It came from two species of shield-lice, parasitic on evergreen oak trees, which were found in various parts of the Mediterranean from Portugal and Morocco to Armenia and Crete. The females were collected in May and June before their eggs were laid, killed and dried in the sun. When dried they resembled small seeds or worms, hence the names grain and kermes or *vermiculus* (the Arabic and Latin for small worm).

Not only grain, but all dyestuffs, even woad, were expensive commodities, and used in relatively small quantities. It is little wonder that, like the materials used by apothecaries, they were categorised as spices in medieval merchants' notebooks. The spices imported from Asia therefore included the brazilwood of Java and Ceylon, widely used to give a rich reddish-brown colour. That of Ceylon was reputed to be the best. This was brought to Europe in surprisingly large quantities, for 80% of the examples of red fabrics surviving from the period from around 1100 to around 1450 that have been analysed, prove to have been dyed with at least some brazilwood. Around the middle of the fifteenth century it ceased to be used, presumably because Turkish disruption of trade meant that it was no longer available. Hence the delight of the Portuguese half a century later on discovering a related wood in the country that they consequently called Brazil. This complex use of dyestuffs was one of the approaches to practical chemistry in the Middle Ages, along with the use of 'spices' by apothecaries and of 'ashes'. In the modern world too, dyestuffs, pharmaceuticals and alkalis have been important in the development of chemical industries.

Nearly all colours needed alum as a fixative. Since alum was also used to remove grease and oil from newly made woollens, there was a huge market for it in all the textile-producing areas. The import of alum from Asia Minor was enormously important to the Genoese. Their *mahona* of Chios, a vast trading cooperative, had a near monopoly by the beginning of the fifteenth century. A hundred years earlier, when the *mahona* had not yet acquired such a tight grip, Pegolotti, during his period as branch manager in Cyprus of the Bardi business, had noted down the various places in Asia Minor in which alum was mined, adding the different qualities of the alum from each mine. He presumably had it shipped to Famagusta from the coast of Asia Minor for trans-shipment to Florence. Although much of the alum was already being carried in Genoese bottoms, at least a part of the trade remained in Tuscan hands. The near monopoly of the *mahona*, which shipped alum directly from Chios to Bruges as well as to Tuscany and Lombardy, was abruptly broken by the discovery in 1462 of alum in Italy itself, in the Monti della Tolfa around Tolfa in the papal states, north of Rome. Successive popes, from Pius II onwards, leased out the exploitation of the mines. For a number of years a company in the Medici group held the contract. Under their management the Tolfa alum-mines became an enterprise to rival the Grande Saunerie at Salins in scale. They exported the alum from Civita Vecchia. Various Genoese companies later managed to win the contract, but for the time being the Genoese alum monopoly was broken.

Furs Clothes for the rich involved not only textiles, but furs. They came from the north, not from the fabulous east. The furs used so extensively in western Europe for trimming garments and, more luxuriously, for lining them came largely from the forests of northern and eastern Russia. Many of the cheaper furs, particularly squirrel, came out through Novgorod and the Baltic, whilst the dearer furs, like ermine and sable, came out through Tana and the Black Sea. The late medieval European fur trade, whether of bulk furs, carried by Hanseatics, or of both bulk and luxury furs, carried by Italians, converged on Bruges and, in the fifteenth century, on the fairs of Antwerp and Bergen-op-Zoom.

The actual trappers who hunted down the beasts in the wild largely passed their skins on to their lords, as dues in kind or tribute. These *boyars* in turn sold them to local merchants who carried them to Novgorod, or to a lesser extent, Pskov in northern Russia; or in southern Russia to Tana on the sea of Azov; or to a lesser extent, Kaffa and Soldaia in the Crimea. In the north they were bought by German merchants, particularly men of Lübeck, and in the south by Venetians and Genoese. Amongst the huge variety of merchandise at Kaffa in 1438 Pero Tafur noted: 'above all, from the countries round, come the furs of the whole world and at the cheapest rates'.[53]

In the north, furs were carried the whole length of the Hanseatic network. At Novogorod furs were the principal product bought by Hanseatic merchants, whilst the principal sales were of cloth from the Low Countries. At Bruges they sold the furs and bought the cloth.

We have scattered statistics for the scale of this northern trade. In 1311 the town of Pskov, not only a fur-trading town in its own right, but also on one of the routes from Novgorod to the Baltic, seized nearly 50,000 furs belonging to German merchants. In the winter of 1336–37 there were 160 fur-buying merchants at the Peterhof, the Hanseatic 'factory' or '*kontor*' in Novogorod. The account books survive for 1338–59 for the Wittenborg firm of Lübeck. It was founded by Hermann Wittenborg, a member of a landed patrician family of the city, and carried on by his son Johann, who became *burgomaster* of Lübeck in 1360. Despite his civic eminence, he was summarily executed in the market place there in 1363 because the fleet that he commanded had been defeated by Waldemar IV of Denmark. The Wittenborg purchases of fur in Livonia and Novgorod varied from year to year, but averaged some 20,000 skins annually. For the Wittenborgs, furs were only part of a large-scale business that traded from England and Flanders in the west to Scania in the north, and to Prussia, Livonia and Novgorod in the east, besides investment in real estate and fixed-interest securities. Their purchases of furs in 1358 reached a value of 1,300 Lübeck marks. This can be put in proportion when we see that their purchases of cloth in the west were roughly double the cost of the furs, and of wax in the east roughly half.[54]

The unprepared skins were packed in barrels for the journey. Sometimes these consignments were very large. One ship sailing from Reval to Lübeck in 1368 carried seventeen such barrels, containing between 75,000 and 100,000 furs in all. In 1403 English pirates captured 142,268 furs from Novgorod and Pskov, in two ships, sailing from Riga to Flanders, and in 1441 the city of Novgorod was able to confiscate between 200,000 and 280,000 skins held at one moment by the Hanseatic merchants there. These and other scattered figures suggest that in the fourteenth and early fifteenth centuries this bulk trade in fur probably reached a scale of as many as 500,000 skins a year, mainly of squirrel. The northern fur trade seems to have shrunk in the fifteenth century, possibly because the squirrel population had been reduced by over-hunting.[55]

The forests of northern Russia stretched westwards into Scandinavia and down through the Baltic states to the Prussian lands of the Teutonic knights. Hanseatic merchants could therefore also acquire furs in Sweden or at Königsberg in Prussia, from wild animals hunted down in the wastes of the Prussian hinterland. As well as Hanseatic merchants, the Teutonic Order was

In the second half of the fourteenth century, to celebrate the source of their prosperity, a group of Hanseatic merchants trading with Novgorod commissioned, for their stalls in the Nikolai church in Stralsund, an extraordinarily lively carving of suitably exotic Russians (whether trappers, boyars or merchants is not clear) coming to offer to sell them furs in Novgorod.

itself involved in trading in furs. Between 1390 and 1405 the *Grossschäfferei* of the order at Königsberg sent furs to Flanders, with an average value of 538 Flemish pounds groot [*li. gr. fl.*]. However furs were not the most important export at Königsberg. In the same years the Order also sent out an average of 675 *li.gr.fl.* of amber and 910 *li.gr.fl.* of wax to Flanders, and imported 1,842 *li.gr.fl.* of cloth annually from Flanders.

In southern Russia, the Venetians first appear as purchasers of furs at Soldaia in the Crimea in 1204, soon after the Fourth Crusade and the western capture of Byzantium. After the Palaeologid restoration in 1261 the Genoese joined the Venetians in buying furs at a wide range of Black Sea ports and carrying them back to northern Italy.

Italian purchasers of furs, like their Hanseatic counterparts in the north, preferred to buy skins unprepared so that a greater value could be added to the purchase price of the raw material by their own furriers. In Venice the furriers-of-new-skins consequently became a prosperous guild. At the annual ceremonial greeting of the doge by the guilds, the master furriers-of-new-skins were described, when they called on Lorenzo Tiepolo (doge 1268–75) in the ducal palace, as appropriately 'decked with sumptuous robes of ermine and squirrel and other rich furs of wild animals'. The Ottoman advance in the late fourteenth century put pressure on all western Black Sea trading. However, Timur, although he sacked Tana, the principal fur-exporting port, in 1395, gave the Venetians and Genoese another half-century of trade in the Black Sea by his crushing defeat of the Ottomans at Ankara in 1402. Andrea Barbarigo was still able to buy furs at Tana, for shipping back to Venice, up to his death in 1449.

Although the forests of northern and eastern Europe were the prime sources of furs in late medieval Europe, they were not the only ones. Marten skins from Ireland, for example, were imported into west European commerce through Liverpool, whilst cheap rabbit fur was available from the warrens within western Europe itself.

The two principal regions of fur trading joined together in Bruges. Later, in 1438, Pero Tafur commented that the furs of the Black Sea region, which he had already encountered at Kaffa, were available in Bruges.[56] Yet, at the same time, some of the Russian ermine, fox and squirrel fur that Andrea Barbarigo was importing to Venice came by way of Bruges instead of Tana. As well as Venetians seeking Hanseatic squirrel skins in Bruges, at least one Hanse firm tried to break into the Venetian market itself. At the end of the fourteenth century, the brothers Hildebrand and Sievert Veckinchusen founded a firm at Reval in Livonia, the principal business of which was the export of furs. As the business grew it also diversified, exporting Russian wax as well as Russian furs from Reval, and in return importing cloth, salt and spices. Soon Hildebrand was established at Bruges, whilst the more cautious Sievert was in overall charge of operations at Lübeck from 1400 to 1408, with a new partner at Reval itself. Beside their core business in furs, they sold cloth in Danzig; spices in Novgorod; and Russian wax and Norwegian fish at the Frankfurt fairs. In 1407 they built on success by setting up a fresh company, in partnership with Peter Karbow in Venice. From Bruges, Hildebrand sent on furs, including ermine that he had received from Reval, to Peter Karbow in Venice, who, in return, sent back ginger, nutmeg, mace and cloves, cotton and silk to Hildebrand. The Veckinchusen's Venetian company ran into trouble, however, largely because Karbow bought poor-quality spices and too many of them. In 1411 he sent 70,000 ducats worth of goods to Bruges, over six times the capital of the company. He financed his excessive purchases by drawing more bills of exchange on Hildebrand than the latter could meet. Not all the problems began at the Venetian end however. There were even problems in the fur business itself. On 19 January 1411 Peter Karbow wrote that he had opened some barrels of fur sent to Venice from Bruges. They contained 2,000 skins that were supposed to be lynx, but turned out to be something very inferior. Although the Venetian side of the enterprise collapsed, the main Veckinchusen fur business continued, despite Hildebrand's unwise participation in a large loan to the Emperor Sigismund, who, as well as failing to repay, forbad trade with Venice. In October 1418, Sievert, who was by then in Cologne, wrote to Hildebrand acknowledging the receipt of another small barrel of furs, but pointing out that he did not need to increase his stock any further, because the dearth of silver in Cologne made it totally impossible to sell any goods then for ready money. However he was managing to sell some furs at 87 *gulden* the thousand, to be paid for at the next Lent Fair at Frankfurt, although he would have preferred to sell at 80 *gulden* for ready money. Whilst Sievert was reluctantly selling fur on credit, Hildebrand was foolhardily stocking up with more furs, despite the difficulties in selling them. In that same month, October 1418, he bought 11,000 furs in Lübeck in ten days, all to be paid for later. The firm broke up and the two brothers went their separate ways. They each met an appropriate fate. The rash Hildebrand ended up spending three years in prison in Bruges for debts, whilst the cautious Sievert ended up with enough property in and around Lübeck to be admitted to the patriciate there, a very proper reward for a lifetime of cautious trading in fur.

Although Hanseatic merchants traded directly with England, the supply of furs to England did not depend on direct contact. During the Anglo–Hanseatic hostilities in the 1470s, fur was shipped to England from Bruges and its dependent fairs at Antwerp and Bergen-op-Zoom by merchants from Cologne and the Low Countries as well as Englishmen. Not only fur-traders carried furs to England. Members of the Cely company of wool-staplers were frequently commissioned to buy fur for their English friends and acquaintances whenever they crossed the Channel to sell their wool. Between 1475 and 1486, they were asked to buy at Bruges, calaber (squirrel), fox, twenty mink skins (at 3s. each, or a week's wage for a skilled building craftsman), a mantle of fine black shanks, and a fur of budge 'one of the finest you can find'. The skin of new-born black lambs was also treated as fur, and known to English buyers as 'bugee', 'bogy' or 'budge'. It reputedly owed its name to Bougie in North Africa, one of the places from which it was exported to Italy. The best was that acquired in the Black Sea, later known as

Astrakhan, but, in the far west, Ireland could also supply English buyers with 'black lamb fellow to bogey'. In addition, the Celys bought at the fairs in Antwerp and Bergen-op-Zoom black cat fur for trimming a blue riding gown, a fur of fitchews (polecat), sable, ermine (the winter coat of stoats), lettys (snow weasel), beaver, foins (stone marten), marten, otter, curled budge, marten tails for a long gown, and for one customer as many as sixty budge skins. In Calais they accepted the goods of another stapler as security for a loan, which included his wife's gown of murry (claret-coloured cloth) furred with miniver (another sort of squirrel). If this is what was brought in incidentally, it is not surprising that the gentry of late medieval England were able to have their clothes trimmed with various sorts of Russian squirrel fur, calaber, miniver, grey, or, most expensive of all, vair, with its grey back and white belly. The aristocracy went up-market for marten, sable and Astrakhan budge.

Slaves Apart from precious stones, pearls and the finest silks, the most expensive of all non-manufactured goods dealt in by medieval merchants were human beings themselves. It is impossible for the modern historian to categorize them.

Slavery, which had been ubiquitous in western Europe in classical antiquity, continued to be widespread during the earlier Middle Ages, receiving repeated boosts from the slaving activities of many of the barbarian peoples, particularly the Franks in the expansive phase of the Carolingian period. The Vikings' slaving activities tended to be at the expense of west Europeans. However, in much of western Europe slavery on any considerable scale died out in the eleventh century,[57] perhaps because of the formulation of the doctrine that Christians should not be the slaves of other Christians. For two centuries western European Christians were strangely different from the human norm, by not keeping slaves. Slavery continued unabated in the neighbouring regions of the world, even Christian Byzantium and the Balkans, and as western merchants increasingly dealt with their neighbours in the 'long thirteenth century' they found themselves participating in the slave trade. Early in the century the Genoese, for example, included slaves amongst the goods which they carried between the Maghreb and the Levant, and by the end of the century their colony at Kaffa in the Crimea had become the key entrepot for Asiatic slaves. Slave-owning gradually crept back into southern Christian Europe, particularly in those areas like southern Spain and Sicily that had been in Muslim hands. However, slavery never returned to non-Mediterranean Europe. Slaves are not heard of in late medieval Europe north of Languedoc and Provence.[58]

Since Christians should not be the slaves of other Christians, such slaves had properly to come from outside Christian Europe. The existing slave-traders of Asia and Africa found that they now had a European market as well. West European merchants, particularly the Genoese, had no compunction in importing slaves, generally girls, for the domestic market. The rule about not keeping other Christians as slaves was actually enforced from time to time. Some girls from Bosnia and Albania who had been enslaved by fraud, despite being baptized Christians, and sold to Florentine households managed to claim their liberty in Florentine courts in 1399. Their vendor was sentenced to death. The ownership of slaves, explicitly only of non-Christian origin, had not been legalized in Florence until 1364.[59] Many of these domestic slave-girls inevitably provided more personal services for their owners. The prosperous early fifteenth-century Florentines, Gregorio Dati and Paolo Niccolini, respectively a silk merchant and a successful woollen cloth manufacturer, noted with pride the births of their children by their slave girls in their *ricordanze*. They were baptized and brought up as free Florentines, along with their numerous children by their successive wives.[60] They were not alone. Francesco Datini also had a child by a slave-girl, so did Cosimo dei Medici himself (he had four slave-girls in his household in 1457), and so did Giovanni Benci, the general manager of the Medici group of companies. Since the children of these slave-girls were baptized and free, there was no continuous supply of slaves within European society, unlike the breeding of slaves in plantation America. There was therefore a need to import further domestic slaves in each generation, and this continued until the Turkish closure of the Black Sea cut off the source of supply in the last quarter of the fifteenth century.

A few male slaves were used by Europeans. In fifteenth-century Genoa only one in seven of the slaves sold was male. They were used for non-domestic purposes, for example, in salt extraction on Ibiza and in Andalusia, and in the mills on the sugar plantations of Crete and Cyprus. The Genoese used them in the alum mines of Phocaea, and also supplemented the convicts that they used to row their war galleys with slaves. The Venetians, on the other hand, kept to free, paid, oarsmen for their galleys, although they seriously considered the use of slaves for maintaining the banks of the lagoon and its waterways, but decided against doing so. A very few were also used for agriculture in Cyprus, Andalusia, Valencia, Sicily and the Balearics, particularly to assist in the cultivation of sugar cane and silkworms, as they had been during the Muslim period. Additional workers had to be bought in from time to time. In 1438 the Venetian merchant Giacomo Badoer purchased 346 slaves in Constantinople for delivery to Palma. The model of a sugar plantation entirely reliant on slaves was developed by a Genoese, Antonio da Noli, in the Cape Verde Islands in the 1460s, after he had failed to persuade European settlers to come out freely to work on the normal sharecropping system. The unfortunate success of his experiment provided an unhappy precedent for much plantation slavery in the New World.[61]

The most important source of slaves has always been the capture of children in war, although some entered slavery through sale by hard-pressed parents, or even as adults for debt. Mongol conquests in the thirteenth century and the internecine wars between the peoples of the steppes after the break up of the Mongol hegemony produced abundant supplies of slaves. The most important markets were Tana on the Sea of Azov and Kaffa in the Crimea, where many of them were purchased by the Venetians and Genoese

In 1521 Dürer chose to draw Katherina, the 20-year-old black servant of a Portuguese merchant in Antwerp, because she was an unfamiliar and exotic sight. There were no slaves in northern Europe in the later Middle Ages, let alone black ones. This diversion of the west African slave trade from the Sahara to the Atlantic was a new phenomenon at the end of the fifteenth century.

respectively. After visiting Kaffa in 1437 Pero Tafur expressed the belief that 'In this city they sell more slaves, both male and female, than anywhere else in the world'. He observed, with some repugnance, the sale of children by their parents, but put down the justification: '…They say, further, that the selling of children is no sin, for they are the fruit given by God for them to use for profit.'[62]

His repugnance did not prevent him coming home with useful souvenirs, which obviously gave him pleasure: 'I bought there two female slaves, whom I still have in Cordova, with their children'. The fate of Tafur's girls fitted into a larger pattern, for the slave-girls were mostly shipped to western Europe, although some were made to walk there overland.[63] Many ended up in Genoa or Venice themselves, but most were sold onwards there. The Florentine Cino Rinuccini noted in his *ricordanze* that it was in Venice that he bought his 'Russian' slave girl in 1466. He paid the Medici firm a bargain price of 74½ florins for her, for slave-girls could easily cost over 80 florins, as much as the sort of modest house a weaver might live in, or twice as much as the complex two-man loom which gave him his livelihood. At prices like these, slave-girls were exotic and prestigious objects of luxury consumption.

The Venetians and Genoese mostly carried the boys to Mamluk Egypt, but some to the Ottomans for their army. So great was the slave trade to Egypt that Ashtor, in reckoning up the balances of payments for the Levant, considered that the continual purchase of slave-boys for the Mamluk army was a major factor in passing on the precious metals received from Europe to other regions.[64] West Europeans themselves enslaved the inhabitants of some of their conquests, such as the Moorish inhabitants of Majorca in the thirteenth century, and took others in acts of piracy.

By the late Middle Ages, the internecine wars between the peoples of West Africa had been producing supplies of slaves for many centuries. Many of these were marketed at Timbuktu, and their North African purchasers then walked them across the Sahara. In his travel narrative, completed in 1354, the widely travelled Moroccan, Ibn Battutah, described how he had met strings of young slave-women being driven northwards. The death toll on this long march appears to have been even greater than on the later transatlantic slave ships. The west African slave trade was not an early modern European invention, as is sometimes supposed. West Europeans merely took over, adapted and profited from an already existing trade nurtured by Africans themselves until, for a second time, Christian European scruples turned, once again, against it. Since the nineteenth century Europeans have more or less successfully imposed this view on the rest of the world.

Most of the west African slaves that survived the harsh medieval journey across the Sahara remained in the Maghreb, but others were sold on to the Levant. A modern reader may all too easily unconsciously assume that slaves were necessarily black. In reality in the later Middle Ages only a very few who were brought to Christian Europe were black. Almost all of these came to Spain. As well as Spanish wool and hides, raw silk, Morrocan lace and

When Mantegna painted the Gonzaga family in the Camera degli Sposi in Mantua he enjoyed himself painting a trompe l'oeil *balcony on the ceiling with family servants looking down. Like Dürer, Mantegna was attracted by a black face because it was so exotic. Most slave girls in Italy were Asiatic. Only when the generation of Asiatic slave girls bought at Kaffa before its fall in 1474 had died, was it possible to equate blackness and slavery in Europe.*

cochineal, twelve slaves were picked up in Spanish ports by Florentine galleys on their way home from Flanders and England in the spring of 1467.[65] They were presumably African. An African slave-girl can be seen among the other women servants looking down on the Gonzaga family out of Mantegna's ceiling in the Camera degli Sposi in Mantua (1465–74). However, in general, Asian slave girls were much preferred in European households to African ones. Mongol girls were particularly appreciated for their loyalty and hard work, and Circassians for their beauty. The expansion of the Ottomans, in the fourteenth and fifteenth centuries, provided new sources of slaves from their conquests. The Genoese and the Venetians, already experienced in slave-trading, were quick to take advantage of this opportunity, and Genoese Chios, and Candia in Venetian Crete, became key markets. Since many of them were Balkan Christians, there could be no legal markets for them in Europe, so they were mostly carried to Syria or Egypt, but some ended up in western Europe despite all prohibitions.

The anonymous early fourteenth-century writer describing imports to Bruges was not exaggerating their variety. The medley to be found in this chapter illustrates to the full the enormous variety of foodstuffs and raw materials sucked into a greedy medieval Europe, where trade was far livelier than many people have supposed. The anonymous writer, not surprisingly in view of the place and period in which he was writing, omitted only the human 'raw materials', the slaves. As well as the 'rich' trades in spices, silks and precious stones, of which people do tend to be aware, there were much more vast, less glamorous 'bulk' trades in the necessities of everyday life, grain and timber, salt and iron, wool, wine and beer. Specialization was already old in early modern Europe.

7

Imbalances in trade

Very appropriately, the fifteenth-century artist tried to portray a mint for the frontispiece to a fine copy of Nicolas Oresme's De Moneta *(opposite). Unfortunately he did not have a very clear idea of how a mint worked, and coin could never have been produced in the way he has shown. Oresme's book, in its genesis a radical tract for the times, written first in French in 1355 and enlarged three years later in Latin, argued that control of coinage belonged to the estates not the king, since the actual currency in circulation belonged to the people who used it for trade, amongst other purposes.*

I HOPE I HAVE MANAGED to bring out the importance of the bulk trades in grain and salt and wine throughout much of Europe, particularly Mediterranean Europe, and the importance in scale of trade in such raw materials as wood and wool, iron and alum. I hope I have also emphasized adequately the high values attached to the much smaller-scale trades in the finest woollen fabrics, in silks, in furs, in spices in the broadest sense, in dyestuffs, in slaves and in pearls and precious stones, which meant that the trades in these commodities were disproportionately important in the balances of commercial payments. The prices of these commodities defrayed the high costs of carrying them for long distances by road or of transporting them in heavily manned armed galleys.

Any attempt to understand long-standing imbalances in trade must be based on the values of goods, rather than the weight that was carried. It must also take into account the value added by manufacture, particularly in the southern Netherlands and northern Italy, Tuscany and Lombardy, and, in the fifteenth century, in southern Germany, and finally such invisibles as profits remitted from subsidiaries scattered through Europe to the holding companies in Tuscany, the profits of banking and insurance, and those remitted to distant shareholders from some mining enterprises.

Some imbalances persisted over extremely long periods of time and there were therefore continuous movements of precious metals, of marks of silver in the form of silver ingots, of ounces of gold dust in leather bags, of barrels of silver coins, and of gold coins, sometimes also in sealed leather bags.[1] The difference between the regions west of a line from Antwerp to Nuremberg to Venice and those east of it, was that to the west such movements of bullion represented the balance of very many different transactions in each direction, whilst to the east each movement of bullion was the response to a separate transaction. This was because in the late Middle Ages, virtually all payments east of the line from Antwerp to Venice were made in coin or bullion, and west of that line most separate international commercial payments, and some others as well, were made by bills of exchange provided by north Italian bankers and merchants, and in the fifteenth century by south German ones too. Nevertheless even if individual transactions could be settled in paper, overall imbalances had to be settled in silver or gold.

Even for a single country, as neatly circumscribed, and as well documented as the kingdom of England, it is very difficult to be certain of the balances of trade. Anything that I am now attempting to write about the balances within the whole of western Europe, and between western Europe and the rest of the world, must therefore be treated with the utmost caution.

Nevertheless some impressions do persist. One of these is the large and continuous imbalances between the ports of northern Italy and those of the eastern Mediterranean and the Black Sea. A single example will illustrate this.

The Black Sea and the Levant

In 1360–61 Antonio di Ponzo, a notary at the Genoese colony at Kilia, at the mouth of the Danube, entered in his register contracts for the import of wine and salt, for the export of wheat and of Bulgarian honey and wax, and for the re-export of slaves, who were mostly Mongol girls of twelve or thirteen. Payment for all these was predominantly made in '*virge sommorum argenti*' [silver bars, each weighing a *somme*, around 200 grams].[2]

From the western and northern shores of the Black Sea Italian merchants carried away grain in large quantities, wax in much smaller quantities, a little honey, expensive furs, and, from the mid-fourteenth century, even more expensive slave girls. They brought with them salt and wine, linens and light woollens, but predominantly had to pay for their goods with precious metals, predominantly silver, in the form of *sommi*. These bars were very nearly pure silver, 11 oz 17 dwt. fine, or 0.98 fine by modern reckoning. This was the acceptable standard for trade around the Black Sea, and indeed across the steppes far into Asia. *Sommi* for the Black Sea trade were cast at the mints of Venice and Genoa. Those who carried their silver as far as Constantinople in mark bars of western finenesses, such as the Mediterranean sterling standard, could have it melted down and re-cast at Pera and Galata, the Italian merchant suburbs of Constantinople, into fresh bars of the higher, Asiatic fineness, before entering the Black Sea.[3]

From the mid-thirteenth to the mid-fourteenth century the Crimea and the Sea of Azov formed one of the gateways by which European merchants, almost entirely Italians, could enter directly into Asia. During that period it was possible to travel from Kaffa and Tana onwards into Asia, to Persia, to Transoxiana and even to China to bring back the highest priced oriental goods to justify the long, expensive overland journeys. The round trip to China could take three years. They returned with jewels and pearls, and, above all, the finest silks. All that was carried outwards was superior European linens. These did not balance against the very expensive imports into Europe. The difference was carried in silver *sommi*. Those who did carry western linens were advised to sell them at Urgenj, in central Asia, to the south of the Aral Sea, for *sommi* which they then carried to China, at the frontiers of which silver *sommi* were exchanged for paper money, which was eventually used to purchase silk.[4]

Whether it was at the mouth of the Danube, in the Crimea, on the Sea of Azov, or even further into Asia, this trade was patently imbalanced against western Europe, and absorbed European silver in large quantities.

Even when it was no longer possible for west Europeans to go beyond Kaffa and Tana, they remained termini to a trans-Asiatic trade route in non-European hands. The single commodity that came to dominate the trade here in the fifteenth century was slaves. Girl slaves were in demand for south

a questa carauana es partida del imperi
de sarra p anar ,1alcaca1o :

European households and boy slaves for the Mamluk armies (see p. 338–41). Neither Italians nor Egyptians had much to offer in return except precious metals and linens. After failing to travel beyond Kaffa in 1438 Pero Tafur described it in familiar terms for Castilians: 'The city is very large, as large as Seville, or larger, with twice as many inhabitants, Christians and Catholics as well as Greeks.' After describing the slave trade with fascinated horror, he went on 'They bring there much merchandise, spices, gold, pearls, and precious stones, and above all...furs'.[5] All this added to the imbalance.

When the trade in oriental luxuries through the Crimea and on the Sea of Azov became so attenuated with the disorders in the steppes in the fourteenth century, Trebizond remained a gateway into the East. In the fifteenth century Europeans could still obtain silks and spices here, although a certain amount of trade had been diverted across Asia Minor, newly conquered by the Ottomans, to Bursa. Once again it was an unbalanced trade.

Along the coast of the eastern Mediterranean west Europeans used different ports from time to time. In the thirteenth century, Acre in the crusader states was the key port. Even before Acre fell to the Muslims in 1291, its place was taken by Ayas, or Lajazzo on the gulf of Alexandretta, in the kingdom of Armenia. This benefited from the fact that the Christian king of Armenia was a client of the Mongol khans. In the first half of the fourteenth century Lajazzo was the Mongol window on the Mediterranean. When it too fell to the Mamluks in 1347, its place was taken by Beirut, and to a lesser extent Tripoli. In the fifteenth century Europeans could no longer travel into Asia, but they could still buy Syrian goods from Damascus and Aleppo in Beirut or Tripoli, and some goods from a greater distance, that had come from or through Baghadad, and then via a relatively short overland journey from the upper Euphrates to Aleppo. However, by this time, the Mamluk rulers of Egypt and Syria tried increasingly to concentrate west European trade in Alexandria. Merchants stayed in enclosed communities in these ports, but pilgrims were allowed inland to the holy sites in and around Jerusalem. When

Before the breakdown of Mongol rule in the 1330s and 1340s Pegolotti described the overland journey from Tana to China as safe for European merchants both by day and by night, and gave details of which parts of the journey were by camel wagons, which with pack asses, and which with horses. When Abraham Cresques prepared the Catalan Atlas *in 1375, the overland route was no longer open to Europeans. He compressed all these different sorts of transport into a single vignette of Chinese merchants, with pack camels, returning along the 'Silk Road'.*

the much-travelled Castilian nobleman, Pero Tafur, extended his journey-ings in 1437 to that goal of the most intrepid pilgrims, the monastery of St Catherine at the foot of Mount Sinai, he was fortunate to arrive at the right moment to be able to observe that:

> …the caravan [from 'Greater India'] duly arrived, bringing so many camels with it that I cannot give an account of them, as I do not wish to appear to speak extravagantly. This caravan carries all the spices, pearls, precious stones and gold, perfumes, and linen, and parrots, and cats from India, with many other things, which they distribute throughout the world. One half goes to Babylonia [i.e. Cairo], and from thence to Alexan-dria, and the rest to Damascus, and thence to the port of Beyrout.[6]

In the thirteenth century this trade was shared between the merchants of Pisa, Genoa and Venice, but at the end of the thirteenth century the Genoese destroyed Pisan competition. In the fourteenth they also attempted to destroy Venetian competition and were very nearly successful. However, in the end it was the Venetians who ousted the Genoese from the Levant trade. The whole west-European trade with the Levant was therefore in the fif-teenth century increasingly funnelled into a Venice–Alexandria axis. In one of his earlier books, thirty years ago, Professor Eliyahu Ashtor proposed the following balance for the fifteenth century, which has not since been appre-ciably modified by himself or other scholars.

The Venetians brought back	The Venetians sent out
400,000 ducats of spices from further east	300,000 ducats in coin
80,000 ducats of goods from the Near East	200,000 ducats in goods
20,000 ducats in coin	
Other Europeans brought back	**Other Europeans sent out**
130,000 ducats of spices	100,000 ducats in coin
20,000 ducats of goods from the Near East	60,000 ducats in goods
10,000 ducats in coin	

This gives a net imbalance of 370,000 ducats in coin on a total trade worth 660,000 ducats a year.[7]

By this time the quantity of goods imported from and through the Levant had been much reduced from its highest level at the beginning of the four-teenth century. Not only had the purchasing power of the dominant groups in western European societies diminished, but many of their needs were being satisfied from sources within Europe itself. A vast amount of import substitution had taken place inside western Europe, particularly in Italy. Italian silks, for example, were increasingly substituted for Levantine and ori-ental silks; and Lombard and south German cottons and fustians for Levantine cottons. Although this meant that raw cotton was imported from Syria in increasing quantities, it was of less value than manufactured cotton fabrics. Similarly Italian paper replaced Egyptian paper; and sugar from

Egypt	Venice	Logical action to be taken
1278 (1:9.2)	1285 (1:10.9)	send silver
	1295 (1:11.8)	
	⎡1305–30 (1:14:2)	send silver
1324–36 (1:10.3)	1331–2 (1:13.7)	send silver
	⎣1333 (1:11.5)	send silver
	⎡1346 (1:10.5)	send silver
	1349 (1:10.5)	send silver
1338–59 (1:9.4)	1350 (1:9.4)	send metal available, i.e. gold
	1353 (1:10.5 *market*)	send silver, but none available
	1354–69 (1:9.6 *official*)	send metal available, i.e. gold
	⎣1358 (1:10.5 *market*)	send silver, but none available
1375 (1:11.3)	1374 (1:9.9)	send gold
	1379 (1:10.2)	send gold
	1380 (1:11.4)	
1384 (1:14.7)	1382 (1:10.7)	send gold
	1398 (1:11)	send gold
1399 (1:12.7)	1399 (1:11.3)	send gold
1400–9 (1:14)	1408 (1:11.2)	send gold
1410 (1:11)		send either silver or gold
1415 (1:8.1)		send silver
1416–21 (1:10.7)	1417 (1:12.5)	send silver
1422–4 (1:7)		send silver
1425–38 (1:11)	1429 (1:10.6)	send metal available, increasingly gold
1440s (1:10.1)	1440s (1:10.6)	send silver, if available
1450s (1:10.1)	1450s (1:10.6)	send silver, less and less available
1460s (1:10.2)	1460s (1:10.6)	send silver, none available in mid-1460s
1470s (1:10.3)	1472 (1.:10.7)	send silver

This table (left) gives the different gold–silver ratios in Egypt and Venice from the 1270s to the 1470s. The ratio 1:10.9 means that one mark weight of gold was worth the same as 10.9 marks weight of silver.[8]

The Faenza plate (above) commemorates the aid sent by Venice to Naples in 1495 against French invaders. Doge Barbarigo superintends the loading of a galley with labelled sacks of coin. Coin sent in galleys to the Levant by merchants was packed in similar sacks or groppi.

Italian plantations in Crete and Cyprus, and later in the Madeiras, replaced Egyptian sugar. Venetian glass had also replaced Syrian glass, although the 'soda ash' used in its manufacture was imported instead. Like raw cotton imported instead of manufactured cottons, it cost much less (see p. 254). In addition, some trades, like that in ivory, had unaccountably ceased altogether by the fifteenth century. Ashtor's estimates emphasize how much the trade had shrunk to one in spices, for which there could be no western European substitutes. If Ashtor's estimates are anywhere near correct, by the fifteenth century spices represented 80% of the imports into Europe. What is equally clear is that, even in the reduced trade of the fifteenth century, the drain of precious metal out of Europe in this direction was still enormous, but it was less to Europe's disadvantage, because of the reduction of imports to Europe, and the increase in exports from Europe, for example of cheap Lombard woollens. In the fourteenth century the imbalance had been that much greater. Even Ashtor's 370,000 fifteenth-century gold ducats weighed well over a ton of gold (1,317 kilos).

Although the gold sent in any one year was not so considerable as the amounts of gold involved in some political-cum-military payments, it must be remembered that the gold sent out of Europe to the Levant went out year after year, never to return. Therefore, over time, this drain to the east had a much greater cumulative effect on the monetary circulation of Europe than any political–military payments, however large. It must also be remembered that many political payments returned to the same parts of Europe from which they originated.

Whether gold or silver was sent out of Europe to the Levant depended on the availability of the two precious metals and the consequent ratio in values between them both in Europe and the Levant (see table, previous page). At the lowest silver-gold ratio, the equivalent of 1,300 kilos of gold ducats would have been over twelve tons of silver.

As well as the silver and gold that went out of Europe to the ports of the Black Sea and those between Lajazzo and Alexandria, yet more went out to Asia Minor, Greece and the islands of the eastern Mediterranean. The largest expenditure here was on the alum of western Asia Minor and from the offshore island of Phocaea, but Asia Minor also produced raw silk, as well as manufactured silks and kermes for the dyeing of scarlet, whilst Crete and Cyprus produced sugar and wine, and Greece itself produced more wine and dried fruits. The whole area produced yet more grain for consumption in northern Italy.

Before I come to the problem of where these precious metals came from, to be sent to the Black Sea and the Levant from Venice, Genoa and earlier, Pisa, and, to a much smaller extent, other west European ports like Barcelona, I would like to look at some other imbalances in trade.

The Baltic

The eastern Mediterranean and the Black Sea were not the only directions towards which precious metals flowed out of Europe. They were also carried out through the Baltic. The trade of the Hanse from western Europe to the north and east was also unbalanced. West Europeans bought large quantities of Baltic grain and timber, and slightly smaller quantities of beer, fish, salt, wax and furs, and tiny quantities of expensive amber and falcons. In return they sent textiles and metal wares from the southern Netherlands, Rhenish wine, and, in the fifteenth century, English woollen textiles too, besides a whole range of re-exports that had been brought into Bruges from or through southern Europe – most expensively, spices and silks, but also rice, sugar and soap.

In the later Middle Ages, as in the early modern period, precious metals continually leaked out of western Europe through the Baltic. The mark bars of silver from the west often ended up recast in Novgorod into *grivnas* or *roubles*, bars of approximately the same weight as the *sommi* of the steppes.[9]

North Africa

The only direction from which precious metal came into Europe was from North Africa. The trades across the Sahara were imbalanced in favour of the north, so that west African gold dust, called by Europeans the gold of *paiola*,

The Catalan Atlas *shows how conscious Europeans were of the west African origin of the gold they received from the Maghreb. South of the detailed Mediterranean coastline, Abraham Cresques shows first the mountain barrier of the Atlas, and then our eyes are inevitably drawn down past the named oases, to the trans-Saharan camel-riding trader with his mouth covered against the desert sand, and to the spectacular Musa, the Mansa, or ruler, of Mali at Timbuktu, holding his huge orb of gold. The text behind him translates as 'This negro lord is called Musa Mali, lord of the negroes of Guinea. So abundant is the gold which is found in his country that he is the richest and most noble king in all the land.' In 1375 Mali still dominated west Africa, although Musa had died in 1337.*

was readily available in the Maghreb, the North African coastlands between the Sahara and the sea, from modern Morocco to modern Tunisia. The relative importance of the trans-Sahara routes to Sidjlamassa in the Atlas and to Tunis varied in the late Middle Ages. Once it reached North Africa much of the gold was coined into dinars and double dinars.

The trade between North Africa and western Europe was also imbalanced in favour of the latter. The Maghreb primarily sent raw materials to western Europe, beeswax for candles, unwrought iron, coarse wool for cheap cloth, furs, particularly budge, hides for European leather-working, and the occasional west African slave. In return North Africa imported a much greater value of European goods and services, mainly manufactures, particularly textiles, but also metal wares like copper vessels. It sometimes also imported foodstuffs. In addition west Europeans, particularly Genoese, provided carrying services for North Africans, not only between the Maghreb and the Levant, but also along their own coasts. As a consequence of the difference in value, west African gold dust in sealed leather bags, and North African dinars and double dinars were paid across the Mediterranean from Tunis to Sicily, from Tunis via the Balearics to Catalonia, and from Tangier and Ceuta to Andalusia and Valencia. The augustales of thirteenth-century Sicily and the doblas of late medieval Castile were effectively North African double dinars. At some periods, notably the thirteenth century, the flow of gold into western Europe was further stimulated by a contra-flow of European silver into the Maghreb.[10]

England and Castile

Inside Europe there were also a number of long-standing imbalances. England appears to have had a continuously favourable trade balance from the late twelfth century onwards, primarily based on its position as the producer of the finest wool in Europe, supported by its dominant position in the production of tin until the fourteenth century. England was self-sufficient in foodstuffs. The overall value of the goods, mainly luxuries imported from the Low Countries, Gascony and the Iberian peninsula and by Italians, and Hanseatics from a wide variety of places, was exceeded by the value of the wool and tin.[11]

From the end of the twelfth century there was a considerable stock of silver, and, from the mid-fourteenth century, of gold in England, which was continually replenished, and often increased by a positive balance of trade, however much its successive Kings Richard, John, Edward I, Edward III, Henry V and Henry VI emptied it of treasure for political ends.[12]

From the mid-fourteenth century, the heavy export dues on wool levied to pay for the French wars by the kings of England made English wool uncompetitively expensive in Flanders and Tuscany. The export of English wool consequently fell by three-quarters during the second half of the fourteenth century, between 1361–62 and 1402–3.[13] At the same time the kings of Castile were also in need of money for war purposes. However, they did not solve this by raising customs dues, but by debasing the coinage.

The first wave of debasements began around 1354 to pay the royal troops of Pedro the Cruel in his attempts to suppress the revolts amongst his nobility. Debasement was continued by both sides when these revolts evolved into a fully fledged civil war between Pedro, supported by English troops under the Black Prince and Henry of Lancaster, and his half-brother Henry, Count of Trastamara, supported by French troops under Du Guesclin.[14] Among the effects of these debasements, which went on until 1371, was the reduction in price of Castilian exports on international markets. As the export of English wool fell, so the export of Castilian wool rose. Further waves of debasement, from 1386 to 1391, from 1429 to 1441 and from 1463 to 1471 maintained the price advantage of Castilian wool over English. Castilian wool exports therefore became very considerable in the fifteenth century, particularly for the textile industries of the Netherlands. Northern Castile also exported to northern Europe considerable quantities of iron and wine and smaller quantities of soap, so that Castile too, like England, and basically for the same reason, as a supplier of fine wool, had a positive balance of payments. It too attracted silver, and the availability of adequate quantities of precious metals was particularly noticeable during the bullion famines of the late Middle Ages.

The Southern Netherlands and Northern Italy

Until the fifteenth-century transformation of the economy of south Germany created a third, there were two regions of Europe through which large amounts of precious metals passed. These were the southern Netherlands and northern Italy. The southern Netherlands sent precious metals to the Baltic for a wide range of primary commodities, to England and Castile for wool, to northern France for foodstuffs and to northern Italy as the overall balance in a very complex set of trading relationships. Strictly speaking, only a region in which precious metals were mined could send out bullion over a long period of time without exhausting its stock. Flanders and Brabant, however, maintained such considerable stocks of both precious metals through trade that, except during the harshest phases of the late medieval silver famines, they seemed veritable promised lands to less prosperous areas. They received them in even greater quantities, from Frankfurt through Cologne. In the heavily urbanized belt from Calais to Cologne, as one of only two major industrial areas of Europe until the fifteenth century, the value added by manufacture to raw materials, whether English and Castilian wool, transformed into the whole price range of woollen cloths, or German copper transformed into brass wares, ensured that a comfortable proportion of the precious metals passing through the area remained there.

In Tuscany and Lombardy as well, the value added by manufacture to raw materials, whether English and Castilian wool transformed into woollen cloths, Syrian cotton transformed into cottons and fustians, or silk from Spain, Sicily and Asia Minor transformed into velvets and brocades, ensured that, here too, a comfortable proportion of the precious metals passing through the area remained in it. The profits of commerce, banking and shipping further increased the amount of money circulating in Tuscany and Lombardy.

The southern Netherlands saw precious metals coming in from a single direction, from the Empire, and passing out in many directions. By contrast, northern Italy saw precious metals flowing out in a single direction, to the east, but coming in from many directions: from Spain, from France, from north-western Europe and, above all, across the Alps.

Before turning to the ultimate source of precious metals, the mines of silver and gold in central Europe, I would like to emphasize the long-standing imbalance in trade between north-western Europe and northern Italy. The value of the luxury goods sent to north-western Europe from Italy seems always to have exceeded those taken southwards, even in the heyday of the 'Flemish' manufacture of rich, heavy woollen fabrics. Symptomatic of this imbalance, even at an early date, was what happened to the monetary system and the weight system of the Champagne fairs, at which the merchants of north-western Europe encountered those from northern Italy in the twelfth century and for much of the thirteenth. The money of Champagne, the *deniers provinois*, was carried southwards in large quantities and circulated freely in north and central Italy (see p. 146), to such an extent that when *denari* first came to be minted in Rome they were *denari provisini* made in imitation of those of Champagne. The weight system of Champagne, based on the mark of Troyes, travelled northwards with the goods purchased there, and Troy weight was commonly adopted in north-western Europe.

When in the fourteenth century the Italians began to produce their own 'Flemish' woollens instead of importing them, the imbalance between north and south became even greater. During the silver famines, around 1400 and again around 1450, this drain of specie was particularly noticeable, but it was only the continuation into a more difficult period of an unbalanced pattern of trade that had been established in easier times.

Southern Germany

The clue to what I have to say next lies in my emphasis on the supply of precious metals to the southern Netherlands from Frankfurt through Cologne, and to northern Italy from across the Alps.

A visible reminder of the importance for nothern Italy of traders from across the Alps may be seen in the Fondaco dei Tedeschi in Venice. The first Fondaco had been built by the Venetian state in 1220s in the commercial heart of the city, next to the Rialto bridge, to provide 'German' merchants visiting Venice with lodgings and warehouse facilities. It was a means both of encouraging a trading group that had already become important to the city, and of regulating its activities. From its discovery on a large scale at the end of the twelfth century, silver from the eastern Alps seems to have been the prime commodity brought to Venice by Germans, like the immensely rich Bernardus Teutonicus, who had profited greatly from bringing the silver and copper of Friesach and St Veit in large quantities across the Tarvis Pass and sending Italian and Levantine goods northwards.[15] By the time that the first Fondaco was built, silver was also being brought from the mines at Freiberg in Meissen. For century after century merchants called 'German' in the widest sense, from what are now south Germany, Austria, Czechoslovakia and Hungary, came to Venice with a limited range of commodities and large quantities of silver and, later, of gold from the mines of central Europe.[16]

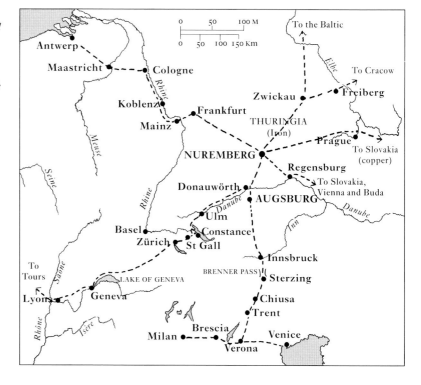

After a century of growth, the increasing industrial and financial importance of Nuremberg and Augsburg made southern Germany the centre for European land trade before 1500. A network of radiating routes (see pp. 391–3) closely connected Nuremberg and Augsburg to the French court on the Loire, the older commercial and industrial centres of northern Italy and the Low Countries, besides the mines which they controlled: iron in Thuringia; copper in Slovakia; silver and gold in Slovakia, Bohemia and Saxony (see p. 373).

This first Fondaco was destroyed by fire and was twice rebuilt; the present building (much restored) dates from the early sixteenth century.

A vivid impression of the range of goods passing over the Alps between Venice and Nuremberg in 1392 is given by the accounts of Hilpolt Kress, who was responsible for the business in Venice of one of the most important firms of fourteenth- and fifteenth-century Nuremberg. Rolls of cloth formed the most important group of goods sent from Venice. In one year 101 rolls of cloth, mainly silk, appeared in his accounts, ranging in value from the rolls of cheap 'Pasthart' which were worth only 3½ florins the roll, up to a single roll of rich blue velvet valued at no less than 40 florins – nearly two years' wages

The 'Rialto' was the financial quarter of Venice. The Loggia dei Mercanti can be seen on the left. At the right-hand end was the 'Fondaco dei Tedeschi' through which precious metal mined in central and eastern Europe arrived in Venice. When Vittore Carpaccio painted the bridge in 1494 in his Miracle of the Holy Cross, *it was wooden with shops on it, and a centre section that opened.*

353

for an ordinary Florentine labourer at this date. Most of the cloth fell into a middle range like brocades at 10 or 14 florins the roll, or taffetas at 7½ florins each. These were still luxury cloths, but not so luxurious as the velvet. By this date most were already woven in northern Italy, but others still came from much farther afield, from Damascus or Baghdad whilst the taffetas even came from Samarkand. Altogether these 101 rolls of cloth were valued at 1,075 florins. Next in value came nearly 880 ducats worth of spices, nearly half of which (by value) was Indian pepper. As well as cloth and spices the third important commodity imported by Kress from Venice was pearls. There were no less than 257¼ ounces of these at seven different prices from 5s 6d to 17s the ounce. No total value for these appears in the accounts, but it cannot have been much less than the total value of spices, and may even have quite considerably exceeded the total value of cloth, depending on how many ounces of each quality were in the total. Far behind silk, spices and pearls in value were a number of other commodities: loaves of sugar for example, from plantations in Sicily or Crete and elsewhere in the eastern Mediterranean, which had been refined in Venice, and bales of raw Syrian cotton, and barrels of soap. Soap must have been near the bottom limit of value of commodities which it was worth transporting the difficult 650 kilometres (400 miles) through the Brenner to Nuremberg. It was only put down in the accounts at 2 ducats per 100 pounds, and the whole half-ton that Kress imported was worth far less than the single roll of blue velvet.

In the opposite direction Kress sent over 3,600 florins worth of silver, about two-thirds in ingot form and one third worked up by Nuremberg silversmiths. The value put on skilled craftsmanship seems surprisingly small to modern eyes, for the silver plate was only valued at a rate some 8% higher than bar silver. By contrast with silver, the value of gold sent to Venice by this route seems small. There was only just over 500 florins worth, and since nearly 140 florins worth of gold was sent in the opposite direction, the net value of gold was not very great.

Of the four other commodities that Kress sent to Venice, only Baltic amber is possibly worth mentioning. However, even this was barely worth more than the sugar sent in the opposite direction. In essence then, Kress' trade with Venice consisted largely of silks, spices and pearls in one direction, but almost exclusively of silver in the reverse direction.[17] On the route from central Europe to the Low Countries the outward trade was as preponderantly one in precious metals as it was from central Europe to northern Italy. This can be illustrated by the way that although the fair at Frankfurt was known to people from central Europe as a *tuchmesse*, a cloth fair, in the Low Countries it was known as a *geldmesse*, a bullion fair.

Silver and gold mines   The land trade routes naturally eventually reached from the southern Low Countries and northern Italy back to the places where the precious metals were actually mined in the later Middle Ages (see map p. 373).

Silver, and later gold, was mined in a large number of places in central Europe, the importance of each of which changed quite rapidly over time.[18]

It must be borne in mind that all mines had a limited lifespan, between the discovery of ore in workable quantities, and the point at which the easily accessible ore had been worked out to the limits of the technology of the period. After that point, any ore left in the ground cost more to get out than it was worth, and mining dropped off abruptly or ceased altogether. It only started again, if at all, when improved technology or falling costs changed the situation. As well as the numerous minor sources of precious metals, there were a handful of places in which mining took place on a large scale in the later Middle Ages. The earliest of the sequence of major sources of silver were the mines in Meissen at what come to be known as Freiberg, where silver was apparently accidentally discovered in 1168. As the German humanist, Georgius Agricola, re-told the story in the sixteenth century:

> It came about by chance and accident that the silver mines were discovered at Freiberg in Meissen. By the river Saale…is Halle…famous and renowned for its salt springs… When some people were carrying salt from there in wagons…they saw lead ore (*galena*) in the wheel tracks,

In his altarpiece for Annaberg in Saxony of 1521 Hans Hesse caught the extreme individualism evident in the mining of a newly discovered source of ore. The hillside is covered with myriad tiny silver mines each owned and operated by a handful of free miners, who have staked out their separate claims. Without the water- or horse-powered apparatus of large-scale mining, they can be seen winding up their own ore, and breaking it down by hand into small enough pieces to take away in wheelbarrows, wearing leather aprons behind them, almost like a uniform.

355

which had been uncovered by the torrents. This lead ore, since it was similar to that of Goslar, they put into their carts and carried to Goslar, for the same carriers were accustomed to carry lead from that city. And since much more silver was smelted from this ore than from that of Goslar, certain miners went at once to that part of Meissen in which is now situated Freiberg, a great and wealthy town; and we are told by consistent stories and general report that they grew rich out of the mines.[19]

The crude woodcut from the title page of Rülein von Calw's Bergbüchlein, *printed in Freiberg around 1500, reinforces the image of the individualistic free miners of the Annaberg altarpiece.*

There had been no major discovery of silver in Europe since that near Goslar in the Harz in the 960s. The mines at Goslar had been producing less and less silver since the 1040s. As a consequence of the lack of fresh supplies of newly mined silver in Europe over the previous century, the continuous export of silver from Europe, particularly pronounced since the first Crusade, had reduced the stock of silver in Europe to a very low ebb by 1168.

The exploitation of the discovery of silver at Freiberg was the first of a sequence of successful mining ventures that multiplied the stock of silver in Europe many times over by the early fourteenth century. For a generation the mines at Freiberg were the major suppliers of silver to Europe. In the 1170s and 1180s more, and probably a great deal more, than four tons of silver were mined there annually. The minting of silver money consequently increased enormously in the Rhineland, in Flanders and Artois, and in England, as well as in central Europe itself and in northern Italy. At the end of the century, the mines at Freiberg were joined as major producers of silver by those at Friesach in the lands of the archbishops of Salzburg in the Eastern Alps, and by those at Montieri in central Italy on the confines of the Sienese and Volterran states. The mines at Friesach lasted for the shortest time. They showed signs of being exhausted around 1230. Those at Montieri were running out

When silver-mining recommenced at Kutná Hora in the late fifteenth century, it was organized by mining companies on a much larger scale. The illuminator of the Kutná Hora Gradual has imagined an underground vision of miners working in the multiple galleries of a large mine.

At the end of the fifteenth century silver-mining, smelting and minting interlocked at Kutná Hora in a complex way (see pp. 365–7). On the right, a sample of unsmelted argentiferous ore is spread out on a large polygonal table. Above: the seal of the moneyers of the Kutná Hora mint, the central mint of Bohemia, who formed a closed corporation.

in the 1250s, and those at Freiberg soon after, well before the close of the thirteenth century.

In the second half of the thirteenth century the most important silver-mines were those at Jihlava on the borders of Bohemia and Moravia, and those at Iglesias in south-west Sardinia. These had been exploited in a large way since the 1220s and 1250s respectively. The mines at Jihlava were possibly producing some four tons of silver annually in the third quarter of the thirteenth century. The discovery of silver at Jihlava attracted miners from Freiberg, in the same way that the Freiberg and Alpine discoveries had attracted 'Saxon' miners from Goslar half a century earlier. These German-speaking miners called the place Iglau. It is therefore hardly surprising that the mining laws of Jihlava, or Iglau, were based on those of Freiberg, which in their turn had been based on those used in Goslar since the tenth century. Nor it is surprising that the king of Bohemia opened a mint at Jihlava, which rapidly became the busiest in his kingdom. At about the same time that the mines at Jihlava were replacing those of Freiberg and Friesach as the principal silver-mines of central Europe, those of Iglesias in Sardinia were replacing those of Montieri as the principal silver-mines of southern Europe.

The discovery of prolific silver at Kutná Hora gave Wenceslas II of Bohemia the opportunity of totally reorganizing his coinage. In 1300 he moved his existing mints to a single large mint complex near the mines. The new mint struck a totally new denomination, the Prague groschen (above). When first issued it was by far the largest denomination in central or eastern Europe and rapidly gained a wide circulation there. Huge numbers were transported to Italy and on to the Levant to pay for Asiatic products.

As well as the new, leading mines at Jihlava and Iglesias, a large number of less successful silver-mines were opened in many parts of Europe in the latter half of the thirteenth century. In all of these 'German' miners were involved, as they were in Sardinia and Bohemia. Men from Jihlava, itself a German enclave in a Slav land, participated in the generally fairly successful mining ventures to its south and east. Sometimes this was at the specific invitation of rulers like Bela IV, King of Hungary from 1235 to 1270, who invited miners from Jihlava to open up silver-mines for him at Banskáštiavnica, in Slovakia, then part of the kingdom of Hungary. The miners called the place Schemnitz and Bela IV granted them a mining code based on that of Jihlava. Schemnitz became the mother town of all the 'Hungarian' mining towns.

At the very end of the thirteenth century, when production at Jihlava was already in decline, the most prolific silver-mines of the whole Middle Ages were opened up at Kutná Hora in Bohemia. Silver was discovered there in 1298 and for at least the next forty years some twenty to twenty-five tons of silver were mined annually at Kutná Hora, known of course to the German-speaking miners by a German name, Küttenberg. Kutná Hora replaced Jihlava as the principal mint for the kingdom of Bohemia. The Prague groschen or *grossus Pragensis*, the first and most prolific of the silver groschen to be struck north of the Alps, began to be minted there in 1300.

The last great sources of precious metal to be exploited on a large scale in the expansive 'long thirteenth century' were the deposits of gold, rather than silver, around Kremnica in Slovakia, which were opened up about 1320, and were only thirty kilometres from the moderately successful silver-mines at Banskáštiavnica. The mining of gold in the kingdom of Hungary was not new in 1320, but the scale of operations changed radically at that point. The first reference to the transit of gold up the Danube through Vienna is as early as 1196 and occasional references all through the thirteenth century indicate that small deposits of gold had been found in several places in 'Hungary', particularly in Transylvania, by those prospecting for silver. Like the silver it passed by way of trade to Bruges and Venice. However, the quantities of Hungarian gold available before 1320 were still insignificant in comparison with west-African gold.

The discovery of gold on a large scale at Kremnitz, as the German-speaking miners called it, was followed by a commercial and monetary treaty between Charles Robert of Hungary and John the Blind of Bohemia. In 1327 both kings agreed upon an identical florin-groschen system of coinage for both countries, drawing on Bohemian silver and Hungarian gold. As a consequence Charles Robert recruited moneyers in 1328 from Kutná Hora, the seat of the Bohemian mints and still the most important mining town of Bohemia, to go to Kremnica, which the recently discovered gold had already made the most important mining town in the Kingdom of Hungary, to work on the new mint there. The first successful minting of gold coins beyond the Alps began there in 1328. They were pieces of virtually the same weight and fineness as the Florentine florins and the Venetian ducat, and the first issues even imitated the Florentine florin in type as well.

The initial transforming surge of gold-mining in 'Hungary' took place in the 1320s and 1330s, but the production of gold continued throughout the next century-and-a-half. Initially much of the gold was sent to Venice unminted.[20] However, under Louis the Great (1342–82), locally mined gold was supposed to be bought up by the '*comes camerarum*' on behalf of the king and sent to the mint. In the second half of the fourteenth century some 400,000 to 500,000 gold florins (or ducats as they came to be called by the end of the century) were struck annually at the Kremnica mint. In 1402 around 400,000 gold ducats were still being struck.[21] This is just under a tonne-and-a-half of gold; then equivalent in value to around 16 tonnes of silver. Minting, of course, only gives a minimum figure for the production of gold, but with gold mined and minted in such quantities, it is no wonder that the Hungarian ducat became, and remained, the favourite means of payment in much of central Europe, and that in the last century-and-a-half of the Middle Ages most countries of western Europe usually had an adequate stock of gold for currency.

The same cannot be said of silver currency, for the stocks of silver in western Europe began to decrease quite markedly from the second half of the fourteenth century. The trouble was that the commercial imbalances between Europe and Asia continued, whilst fresh mining of silver diminished. When the mines at Iglesias in Sardinia went into a rapid decline in the 1340s, no major new source of silver was discovered in southern Europe to replace them. They were finally exhausted around 1365. When the mines at Kutná Hora also declined the problem was compounded, for no major new source of silver was discovered in central Europe either until the 1460s. Whereas the Sardinian mines seem to have been worked out relatively suddenly, the decline at Kutná Hora seems to have been very slow indeed. Silver, which had been produced at the rate of over twenty tons a year in the first half

The gold from Slovak mines, principally those at Kremnica, was largely minted into ducats (above left), bearing as their distinctive type St Ladislas, the patron saint of Hungary. Like Prague groschen before them, they circulated widely in Germany and eastern Europe. Many of those taken to Italy were restruck as Venetian ducats and conveyed onwards to the Levant, to cope with the European imbalance of trade. The late fifteenth-century moneyer (above right) from the Moneyers' Chapel in the church of St Barbara at Kutná Hora is striking Prague Groschen. He placed a blank disc of silver, accurately prepared by other mint workers, on the lower die which was fixed into his work bench, and then holding the upper die exactly on top of the blank, struck it smartly with his hammer.

of the fourteenth century, was probably still being produced at the rate of around ten tons a year throughout the second half of the century. The mines did not close down until the sack of Kutná Hora by Sigismund's troops in 1422 during the Hussite wars. Even then some mines were reopened quite quickly. In many respects the new supplies of gold coming from Hungary did a great deal to make up for the diminution in supplies of silver. For large-scale transactions, and for settling the eventual imbalances from trading with bills of exchange, gold coins were much more convenient than silver ingots. Gold coins were, however, quite unsuitable to cope with the everyday needs of the bulk of the population. The imbalances of payments and the working-out of the mines were in themselves enough to create a critical lack of silver in Europe, and this was exacerbated by two other factors of very different kinds, deliberate hoarding and loss by wear, reminting and accident. The shortage of silver began to be felt in the 1370s, and in some parts of Europe reached famine proportions in the 1390s. Only the Venetians partially escaped the effects of this silver famine, for they had access to the new silver- and gold-mines of Serbia and Bosnia. However, none of the Serbian or Bosnian mines was of the scale of the great discoveries of precious metals of the previous two centuries. The evidence is very ambiguous, but the most important of these mines, at Novo Brdo, may, in the early 1430s, have been producing under 2.5 tonnes of silver, together with half a tonne of gold, annually. Some of these mines had been making a contribution to the Venetian supply of silver from the 1370s. Not all of it went to Venice. Dalmatian silver was included in the Ragusa-Ancona commercial treaty of 1372. The Florentine mint made an arrangement to acquire silver from Ragusa, which was sent through Ancona, and the city of Florence claimed that Ragusan silver had made up most of the 200,000 florins worth used to purchase the city and *contado* of Pisa from Marshal Boucicaut in 1405.[22] Further mines were opened up at the beginning of the fifteenth century. Their production reached its highest point in the 1420s. However, three-quarters of the silver that reached Venice was re-exported at once from Venice to Egypt and Syria and only a little of it entered into circulation in Europe, in England and northern Italy. The Venetian export of Serbian and Bosnian silver to the Levant did, however, mean that the general lack of gold, that had been felt in many parts of Europe from the 1390s as a by-product of the silver famine, was somewhat alleviated, since, until the Serbian and Bosnian production of silver began to decline from around 1430, gold no longer needed to be sent out in such large quantities. As far as Venice and western Europe were concerned supplies of silver and gold from these mines came to an abrupt halt when the Turks overran Serbia, and then Bosnia, in the 1450s and 1460s.

Meanwhile, the production of gold from Kremnica had also diminished. The largest number of Hungarian gold florins to survive are those minted under Louis and his son-in-law Sigismund (1387–1437). However, minting, and probably also mining, was shrinking at the end of Sigismund's reign, from the 1420s onwards. In 1442, only around 24,000 ducats were being struck there, under a sixteenth of the amount forty years before, and minting ceased within the next two years. As a consequence the middle years of the fifteenth century saw a bullion famine even more severe than the silver famine at the beginning of the century. The most extreme difficulties from the dearth of coin, and the accompanying lack of credit, were felt early in the 1460s, but they disappeared very suddenly with the opening up of large new sources of silver. A whole series of new discoveries of silver ore was made in the Alps and in the Erzgebirge, particularly at Schwaz in the Tirol, and at Schneeberg in Saxony. At the same time a series of technical innovations, for example in the development of pumps for draining the mines and in the refining of silver, made it profitable to reopen old mines. These revived mines included those at Kremnica in Slovakia, at Kutná Hora in Bohemia, at Freiberg in Saxony and at Goslar in the Harz, each of which had already possessed the richest mines in Europe in turn. The second period of exploitation of these revived mines produced relatively small amounts, however, compared with their first period of exploitation, or compared with the most important of the new mines being opened up in the second half of the fifteenth century. For example, the production of gold at Kremnica never reached its fourteenth-century levels again. The most numerous surviving Hungarian ducats of the later fifteenth century are those of Matthias Corvinus, yet we know that in the last four years of his reign, i.e. 1487–90, an average of only 72,000 ducats a year was minted at Kremnica. Although this was under a fifth of the fourteenth-century level of striking, it was still the equivalent in value of three tonnes of silver. Kremnica was again making a noticeable contribution to Europe's money supply.

The ore at Schwaz and at Schneeberg had been discovered before 1460, but it was not until well after 1460 that the mines at either place really began to produce silver in important quantities. By the 1480s enough ore was being dug out of the mines at each place to produce between 10 and 11 tonnes of pure silver annually. These were only the two richest of the many groups of mines being opened up in Europe. Such quantities sound enormous to us. In the fifteenth century they gave the same impression, especially when placed against the background of a general dearth of silver throughout Europe. It is always impressive to dine off a table of solid silver, as the Elector of Saxony did in one of his mines, but it is the more impressive when others are altogether lacking any silver at all.

The first generation of the sixteenth century saw an acceleration of the same processes that had marked the end of the fifteenth. The mines of Annaberg in Saxony and those of Jachymov (Joachimsthal) in Bohemia, on the northern and southern slopes of the Erzgebirge respectively, were the most important for this new generation. The latter were as rich as the mines at Kutná Hora had been in their fourteenth-century heyday. At the same time the most important mines of the previous generation, at Schneeberg and at Schwaz, still remained at a high level of production for several decades. The total production of silver in Europe went on growing until it reached a peak around the 1530s and then began to diminish. Whether or not the peak production of the 1530s equalled that two hundred years before is not clear.

For all these places I have written of mines in the plural, for in each place there were numerous small mines scattered about a hillside or along a valley starting where seams of ore came to the surface. The impression given by visiting the remains of the silver-mines at S. Giorgio near Monteponi outside Iglesias in Sardinia is of a landscape that has been intensely bombarded by artillery. Over a thousand separate pits can be made out.[23]

Miners, mine-owners, smelters and mints

In most places the miners themselves owned the mines. Free miners, often from an already existing mining area, rushed to stake out claims when new ore was discovered. Medieval miners, therefore, were generally self-employed men working in small groups for their own benefit. Each partnership owned and operated its own small pit or gallery. Any silver, or at Kremnica any gold, that they took from it was largely their own, although they usually had to pay a royalty to the local prince, a small rent to the surface landlord, and tithes to the church. This tradition of the 'free' miner was an extremely strong one and very widespread. In some places it lasted into modern times, and the earliest gold-miners to arrive in California, Australia, New Zealand or Alaska were still staking out claims to mine on their own account, in this tradition. If the analogy of sixteenth-century Potosi or nineteenth-century California is anything to go by, the majority of miners were hopeful and poor, and a minority were suddenly transformed from paupers to rich men. In California the era of 'free' miners was followed by that of mining companies, and in some places a similar process occurred in the Middle Ages.

In Italy, investment by non-miners in mining had already appeared at a very early date. At the beginning of the thirteenth century a complex, capitalist, form of organization was developing in Tuscany, perhaps not unrelated to the evolution of trading companies there at the same period, and, improbably, comparable to the appearance of dam- and mill-owning companies in the Toulouse area.[24] In the Tuscan silver-mines there were shareholders, *partiarii*, who formed *Le compagnie di fatto d'argentiera* at Montieri, or the *communitates fovee* at Massa. They employed mine-managers, *magistri,* who took on the actual miners, the *laboratores*, as hired men, who worked for wages, not for themselves. There even seems to have been some division of labour amongst the workmen.[25] When the Pisans opened up the mines at Iglesias later in the century, they created a similar organization. As well as numerous small mines owned by the miners themselves, there were in the first half of the fourteenth century a handful of mining companies with *partionarii*.[26] Investment in mining could be treated in just the same way as investment in any other profit-making activity. For example, the notarized inventory of the property of a rich Pisan orphan, drawn up by his guardian in 1318, showed that, amongst other investments, he held shares in no less than six different mines in the vicinity of Iglesias. Not until the fifteenth century did this sort of capitalist investment in mining take place north of the Alps. Edward I of England's attempt to exploit the tiny Beer Alston silver-mines in Devon directly, appears to have been an unique experiment. This was pro-

This late fifteenth-century German drawing by the Master of the Housebook shows a strongly enclosed furnace for smelting, with twin bellows for maintaining the heat. A gutter leans against a wall ready for use in drawing off the molten metal. Similar furnaces were used for both precious and base metals.

voked by the need to spend more money than 'free miners' could provide on digging drainage adits. When direct royal working failed, Edward I persuaded an Italian company to run the enterprise on Italian capitalist lines, but it made a loss and was abandoned. Until the fifteenth century most of Europe's miners were still their own masters, fiercely maintaining the extensive 'liberties' enshrined in their mining codes and with a real chance of becoming, at least temporarily, wealthy men, if they discovered a rich vein of ore. In the fifteenth century, however, capitalist mining companies also appeared north of the Alps, frequently run by south Germans who were fellow citizens of those who were adopting Italian merchant capitalist commercial techniques, or were involving themselves in import substitutes for Italian manufactures. Many of the new mines of the 1460s and the reopened mines of the same period were funded by absentee shareholders who provided the necessary injection of capital, much of it from southern Germany, that enabled expensive new mining equipment to be developed.

As at Beer Alston, it was the costs of drainage that brought the period of 'free' mining to an end at Kremnica. Only mining companies with outside capital could pay the cost of drainage and revive the mines once the ore accessible to 'free' miners had been exhausted. As the historian of Kremnica, Dr Stefan Kazimir, has expressed it, the Klondike gave way to South Africa.[27]

The mining machinery on show at the mining museum at Kutná Hora is from this period, not from the earlier 'free' mining period. Shares in mines, as in other enterprises, could be bought and sold. Occasionally, revealing hints suggest how lively the market in mining shares may have been. In 1477 a confidence trickster persuaded a citizen of Cologne to purchase a shareholding in a non-existent mine. The success of such a confidence trick implies that a market for real mining shares existed at the time in Frankfurt as well as for the silver itself.[28]

Among the key firms in the early development of capitalist silver-mining in central Europe were that of the Stromers of Nuremberg and that of the

Thurzos. The Thurzos originated in Slovakia itself, and not only arranged for much of the south German capital involved in the revival of silver-mining, but were also deeply involved in copper-mining and in trade in silver and copper. The Fuggers of Augsburg at the very end of the fifteenth century were merely following, even more successfully, in an established tradition. When, in the 1520s, a princely and noble attack was made on large companies in Germany, mining companies were excepted from their censure. In 1525 Frederick, the Count Palatine, instructed his proctor to the imperial Diet at Augsburg, 'the best thing would be to abolish and dissolve all firms, large and small, in the Empire, outside the mining districts, where many mining firms are needed.' However, in mining, the big merchants were described as the princes' 'bedfellows'. Frederick's own tin deposits east of Nuremberg were exploited by a stock company, as George, Duke of Saxony's, in the Erzgebirge had been since the 1490s. Tyrolean copper as well as silver, like Slovak copper and Erzgebirge silver, were then being exploited by the capital and organizing ability of urban, mostly south German, investors organized in mining companies. The princes could not deny that mining and selling metals required a concentration of capital.[29]

Even though the mining itself was in many places carried out for so long by 'free' miners, the smelting of the ore demanded the use of capital from the very beginning. The crushing of the ore in preparation for smelting was done in battery works or mills, by sets of hammers driven by water-power. This was yet another application of the same mechanical principle that had first been used in fulling-mills and later in paper-mills (see pp. 244 and 257). The smelting itself demanded the organization of plentiful supplies of fuel and was carried out in foundries, where the bellows might also be water-powered. In Iglesias the entrepreneurs who owned and ran these smelting works were known as *guelchi*. They purchased ore from small individual miners and mining companies alike, and sold lead in large quantities for export from Cagliari, and sold silver to the mint. Their proprietors were amongst the most important men in Iglesias. The most successful of these were the Agliata, Pisan *contadini* by origin, whose rise to wealth, power and status came in large part from owning one of these smelting works and possessing shares in several mines. They were also involved in the Cagliari grain trade, purchased property in both Sardinia and Pisa, and invested in Pisan trading-houses. A few years after the Aragonese conquest of Sardinia, they returned to Pisa, where they were prominent in politics and able to marry into the landed nobility.[30] In 1442 at Kremnica, eight hundred miners were matched by four hundred smelters. At the core of the patriciate that dominated the town were the families of the masters who employed these smelters.

The ores involved were generally complex. The gold-bearing lodes at Kremnica also produced some silver, just as the silver-bearing lodes at Novo Brdo also produced some gold. Silver-bearing ores generally also produced either copper or lead, sometimes in much greater quantities than the silver. The Goslar mines remained one of the key sources of copper in Europe long after the silver there had been effectively exhausted. Slovakia too was

renowned for its copper, as well as for its precious metals, whilst Iglesias produced lead. What was done with the silver or gold that was produced varied from place to place and from time to time.

In the twelfth and thirteenth centuries there seems to have been no compulsion to pass the silver through a local mint. The attempt to do so at Kutná Hora in 1300 was an innovation and a not very successful one at that. The notion of compelling miners and smelters to have their silver minted immediately was obviously under discussion at this time in other places besides Bohemia, for in the first years of the fourteenth century, the miners of the *contado* of Siena took the trouble to obtain confirmation from the city of their traditional liberty to carry their unminted silver wherever they liked. It was not until later in the fourteenth century that further attempts were made to make immediate minting compulsory. At Freiberg, the first attempt to compel the smelters to have their silver minted took place in 1339. It was also in the 1330s that compulsory minting was introduced at Iglesias. Pegolotti recorded, as if it was something distinctive, that Sardinian silver was not available in plates, since it all had to be minted into *grossi affonsini*, or '*anfrusini*', as he called them. These were first minted in 1326–27, but were struck in considerable quantities only in the late 1330s, which suggests that the new regulation was actually enforced. In the Black Forest area the smelters remained free to dispose of their metal. In 1369 silver-smelters could still sell their silver in bar form at Freiburg-im-Breisgau. In the toll-roll of that year the town took a toll of 4d. per mark on unminted silver. At Kremnica the provincial treasury of the King of Hungary tried to exercise a

At the beginning of the sixteenth century the Antwerp master, Herri met de Bles, presents part of the process of turning newly mined ore into usable metal. On the right an overshot waterwheel outside a foundry building is operating bellows to keep the fire at full heat. The newly smelted metal can be seen running out at the extreme right. On the left a variety of activities are set in and around a forge, including the hammering out of some of the freshly smelted metal on a primitive anvil in front. It is all taking place deep in the mountains, next to the mines themselves, and to the battery works where the ore is broken down before being smelted (ill. p. 323). Although concerned with copper, not silver, the processes were much the same. Herri, from near Dinant, was brought up in the Meuse valley where the metal industries still drew a little copper from local mines, although most of their copper came from the Harz Mountains.

Two scenes from the windows of the minster at Freiburg, on the edge of the southern Black Forest, where there were numerous small silver-mines. None were individually very important, but together they formed a major source of silver in the first half of the fourteenth century. The miners are wearing similar white garments to those in use at Kutná Hora, and using similar baskets for sending ore up the shafts.

monopoly of the purchase of gold from 1328, and, even though the fixed price offered was an artificially low one, a large proportion of the gold does seem to have been sold to the treasury, or 'Kammer', which oversaw the running of the mint.

The large mints at the most successful mining towns were themselves considerable industrial enterprises. The state provided the extensive buildings required, as well as the fixed capital. The wealthy entrepreneurs, many of them Italian specialists, who competed to lease the mints for terms of years, provided the working capital, whilst privileged and hereditary corporations of mint-workers and moneyers provided the labour force (ills pp. 357 and 359). In these late medieval factory mints, there was very considerable division of labour amongst a labour force that could be numbered in hundreds.[31] Alongside the large numbers of miners and smelters, there could therefore also be large numbers of mint-workers and moneyers in the rapidly growing towns that grew up around the discoveries of silver- or gold-bearing ores.

Mining towns

What is clear is how rapidly these towns did grow. The growth of Freiberg provides the earliest example. The influx of miners, particularly from Saxony, was such that the village of Christiansdorf, where the initial discovery of ore was made, growing haphazardly like the mining camps of the Californian gold rush, soon became known as Sachstadt, 'the town of the Saxons'. In 1185, Otto, the Margrave of Meissen, deliberately turned this mining-camp into a chartered town, to which he gave the name of Freiberg ('free mountain') presumably in allusion to the freedoms enjoyed by the miners (Bergmänner). Rapid growth continued. By 1218, fifty years after the initial discovery of silver, Freiberg was a substantial walled town, and two very considerable extensions had already been made which more than tripled the area of Otto's Freiberg, by then known as the Altstadt. Other mining towns grew in the same way. Iglesias, Jihlava, Kutná Hora and Kremnica in their turn grew to substantial walled towns.

At Jihlava nothing remains of the late medieval town, except its layout around a vast market square, because of an early sixteenth-century fire, but at Kutná Hora a great deal remains. However, most of this is from the second period of prosperity in the late fifteenth and early sixteenth centuries, and relatively little of the early 'Klondike' period, when, with a few exceptions, the buildings were all of wood. When Kutná Hora was destroyed in the sack of 1422 its first period of prosperity had fizzled out, and it was already a crumbling ghost town.

Even the vast mint complex of 1300, which very early became known as the 'Italian Court', since it was initially run by Italians, was probably largely of wood. The great mint courtyard was rebuilt in stone in the fifteenth century and became the ground floor of one of Wladislaw IV's royal palaces. His private chapel was built above the mint's strong room. Today the mint houses an impressive minting museum. More of it survives than of any other medieval mint in Europe, but how far it reflects and incorporates the first mint of 1300 is not clear.

The core of the 'little fortress' at Kutná Hora does survive from the early fourteenth century, but as seen today it is effectively the elegant later Gothic and early Renaissance house of a capitalist mine-owner. From the same period as the rebuilding of the 'little fortress' is the substantial 'Stone House' of a successful nouveau riche whose fortune stemmed in part from transporting silver for the kings from Kutná Hora to Budapest.

The magnificent Gothic rotunda of the town's late medieval water supply also derives from the second period of prosperity. Even the mine discovered when the city's modern water supply was extended after the Second World War is from the second, capitalist, period. This single mine has thirteen galleries. Visitors are taken into one of its levels dressed in modern versions of medieval miners' outfits, which were white to make them more visible when working underground in the near dark. Our presupposition of blackened miners derives from our thinking primarily of coal miners. The surviving wooden winding gear, in the Kutná Hora mining museum, operated by six pairs of horses, is of the early sixteenth century, and clearly represents the expensive new machinery of the fifteenth century that only capitalist forms of mining enterprise could fund. The Kutná Hora Gradual (ills pp. 356–7) gives a vivid schematic representation of such mines, the miners working within them, and the equipment they used. The Kutná Hora mining museum has gathered together examples of much of this equipment. The mines at Kutná Hora lay in the 'valley of donkeys' on the west side of the town and the richest of them extended under the town itself, which overlooked the valley in a great horseshoe from the 'Italian Court', past the 'Little Fortress' to the church of St Barbara. St Barbara, although begun in the first period of prosperity, is today largely a flying buttressed creation of the second. Its rebuilding was abruptly cut short in the mid-sixteenth century, when the mines were flooded disastrously. It incorporates a miners' chapel, with appropriate wall paintings of mining and of a bullion dealer; a moneyers' chapel, also with appropriate wall paintings of a moneyer striking coins; and a mint-worker preparing the blanks for striking. Even the town's surviving walls are from the second period of prosperity. Since this also came to a sudden and disastrous end, the town has been preserved by poverty, apart from the quarter flattened to make way for the seventeenth-century Jesuit college.

At Kremnica there are also few remains of the first 'gold rush' stage of growth when virtually all the buildings were of wood, except the parish church and the stone-built fortress where the provincial treasurer, the *comes camerarum* lived. Even these incorporated Romanesque stonework from the small town that existed before the discovery of gold. The first provincial treasurer was appointed in 1328 to represent Hungarian royal interests in the area, at the same time that the miners received their privileges and the mint was opened. Below the royal fortress a huge market square was laid out even more immense than at Jihlava. Here the urban patricate slowly began to build themselves stone houses away from the industrial centre by the bridge. By 1379 there were 31 such patrician houses.

The city was dominated by the provincial treasurer in the castle and by a limited number of patrician families, for although the mining itself might be 'free', the processing of the ore in *Bergmühlen*, stamp mills, and foundries was in the hands of those who could lay out the necessary capital. A patrician entrepreneur might need to lay out three to four times as much on one of his *Bergmühle* as on his grand stone house. The same few families also maintained a monopoly on the sale of wine, and the Kremnica miners and smelters are known to have frequently drunk to excess. Yet it is the late Gothic stone houses of the patricians, with their ample wine cellars that have survived, not their industrial buildings. The town was eventually granted the right to govern itself in 1405, around the time that its prosperity was beginning to ebb. It was, of course, self-government by this small oligarchy of entrepreneurs. The patricians nevertheless at once established a town hall and emphasized their autonomy by building a town wall as soon as possible. It joined on to the royal fortress, but only enclosed the great square in which the oligarchs themselves lived, and the huddled wooden houses immediately around them. Most of the town remained outside the walls. Yet the walls survive, with their three towers and their gates. One of the latter was symbolically provided in the sixteenth century with statues of a miner and a smelter. The town had a hospital and a school before the end of the fourteenth century. In the fifteenth century the mint was rebuilt inside the new walls. Stone built fragments of the old fourteenth-century mint in the heart of the town strangely do survive, as well as parts of the new mint of the fifteenth century. The latter have been incorporated into the state mint of modern Slovakia, which still functions on the same site. In 1442–43, when the mines were about to expire for the first time, there were still some 3,000 people crammed into the tiny area within the walls, mostly in fragile wooden houses, besides a larger number outside. However, half the inhabitants within the walls were described as 'poor', presumably since the livelihood of their breadwinners as miners or smelters had vanished away. When the mines declined and the miners left for new mining areas, the formerly prosperous mining towns became ghost towns. Wooden buildings mouldered away, as in the Klondike, but stone buildings, often put up near the end of the period of prosperity, have remained as monuments to it, preserved from subsequent renewal and change by the period of poverty that followed.[32]

Precisely how large the towns had been in their heyday is never clear. Igle-sias before the first wave of plague may have had between 6,000 and 7,000 people.[33] Only in the sixteenth century can we begin to put some figures to this town growth. Jachymov (Joachimsthal) in Bohemia, grew in population from 1,050 to 14,072 in the ten years after the discovery of silver there in 1516. Comparison with the more densely settled parts of western Europe would suggest that it had risen from the size of a market town to that of a major provincial city. None of the major provincial cities of England (York, Norwich and Bristol) had a population quite as large as this in the 1520s, although they were not much smaller. However, in the sparser populations of central Europe, settlements of this size were among the largest east of the Rhine. By comparison the population of Potosi in Peru is reputed to have grown from nothing when the silver was discovered in 1545 to 120,000 when the Spanish governor took a 'census' in 1572. It was by far the largest city in the Americas and ranked in size with the largest capital cities in Europe.

We can also believe, by analogy, that there was an extraordinarily free-spending atmosphere in these mining towns. How the silver was taken out of the hands of the miners and smelters themselves may be judged by the esti-mates that about 1600 there were not only 14 dance-halls and a theatre in Potosi, but also 36 gambling-houses, where the miners might be fleeced by between 700 and 800 professional gamblers, besides the 120 licensed, and the innumerable unlicensed prostitutes. Gold-rush San Francisco was much the same, and it is not hard to believe that Freiberg and Montieri, Friesach and Jihlava, Iglesias and Kutná Hora, Kremnica and Joachimsthal had, in their time, the same free-spending carnival atmosphere. Was it as true there, as in nineteenth-century California, that 'the great profits went to the merchant, the hotel keeper, the transportation company and the gambling house propri-etor' or at least to their medieval equivalents?

In 1493 the woodcut in Schedel's Liber Chronicarum *caught Buda at the height of its development, 30 years before it was burnt by the Turks. The prosperity of the city and of the kings of Hungary both rested on the Kremnica gold mines. A century earlier Sigismund had used some of his mining royalties to build a vast Gothic palace, on the left, on the site of the thirteenth-century castle. With the revival of the mines, Matthias (1458–90) had been able to modernise the palace, and add his famous Renaissance library.*

The miners themselves, together with gamblers, prostitutes and the myriad other hangers-on of a successful mining community, spent lavishly on goods as well as pleasures. Suppliers met this demand with extraordinary speed. Within two years of the discovery of silver, Potosí was the most considerable market for luxuries in the Americas, and continued to be so despite the attempts of the Governor of Peru to restrain what he considered as waste. Silver not only changed hands very fast within Potosí, but soon left it to pay for an extraordinary range of commodities. Fortunes were made dealing in:

> …silks of all sorts, and knitted goods from Granada; stockings and swords from Toledo; clothes from other parts of Spain; iron from Viscaya; rich linen and knitted goods from Portugal; textiles, embroideries of silk, gold, and silver, and felt hats from France; tapestries, mirrors, elaborate desks, embroideries, and laces from Flanders; cloth from Holland; swords and steel implements from Germany; paper from Genoa; silks from Calabria; stockings and textiles from Naples; satins from Florence; cloths, fine embroideries, and textiles of excellent quality from Tuscany; gold and silver braid and rich cloth from Milan; sacred paintings from Rome; hats and woollen textiles from England; crystal glass from Venice; white wax from Cyprus, Crete and the African coast of the Mediterranean; ivory and precious stones from India; diamonds from Ceylon; perfume from Arabia; rugs from Persia, Cairo and Turkey; all kinds of spices from the Malay Peninsula and Goa; white porcelain and silk cloths from China; Negro slaves from the Cape Verde Islands and Angola.[34]

Fortunes were to be made in the supply of basic necessities as well as of luxuries, for in sixteenth-century Potosí, as in nineteenth-century California, the prices of ordinary foodstuffs reached incredible heights.

It would be splendid for medieval historians if a thirteenth- or fourteenth-century chronicler had made a similar list of the goods that flowed to Freiberg, Jihlava, Kutná Hora or Kremnica. We can do little more than assume that these places, each in its own heyday, had the same magnetic attraction for the luxuries of Europe, as well as for very considerable quantities of food. Only for Iglesias do we have a small glimpse of the luxuries flowing to a medieval mining town, silks and linens as well as woollen cloth, olive oil and Greek wine. The swollen population required necessities as well as luxuries. The mining boom provoked a considerable expansion of agriculture in the hinterland, but even this proved inadequate to feed the multitudes drawn by the mines. In the twelfth century, Sardinia had been an exporter of grain, but in 1295 the commune of Iglesias had to make a large bulk purchase of Sicilian grain to keep the people alive. When in 1318 the city of Pisa ordered Sardinian grain to be shipped to the Italian mainland to feed the mother city, the community of Iglesias protested vigorously that they were importers of foodstuffs, not exporters: 'the men devoted their time more to working in silver than in wheat or barley, so that, from experience, they cannot live for a fortnight unless grain is brought to them from outside'.[35]

In their vast study of sixteenth-century Seville, the Chaunus have been able to examine in detail its exports and imports, and to provide precise quantities for a large part of the range of goods passing through the city. They have thus been able to explore and explain the changes in the quantity and nature of goods going to the New World. Domenico Sella has neatly summarized the impact on European industries of this demand and the flow of income involved in it.[36] There are, unfortunately, no statistics for the goods bought at the Champagne Fairs, passed eastwards through Cologne and Frankfurt to Meissen and Bohemia in the thirteenth century, nor is there any means of demonstrating that the thirteenth-century expansion of European industries, for example the textile industry in Flanders, can be closely related to demands generated in Meissen or Bohemia, although it seems highly probable.

Although much of the provisioning of the mining areas of central Europe with both necessities and luxuries was in the hands of 'German', particularly south German, intermediaries, some Italians did take a direct hand in this trade, both at Kutná Hora and at Kremnica. At Kremnica, it was initially Florentines who appeared, but later it was Venetians. In 1331 'Magister' Hippolyt, who was provincial treasurer there, and the dominant figure in the town, was a member of the Bardi family which was then running the largest commercial enterprise in Europe from Florence. A later member of the family, Nofri dei Bardi, was given Hungarian nobility. Some of the early masters of the Kremnica mint, who accounted to the provincial treasurer, were also Florentines, and the Portinari, another Florentine family with commercial interests spread through Europe, was involved at Kremnica as well. In the next century, in additional to individual Venetian merchants, the Venetian Republic was itself involved in the direct purchase of precious metals and of copper from Slovakia.

The mining towns thus provided in turn an extraordinary boost to trade in all sorts of commodities, not only of basic foods, and of large quantities of wine, on which miners, smelters and mint-workers could get drunk, but of rich fabrics and of spices which had come from long distances. Kremnica was known as a market for textiles as well as for cattle. As well as the market provided by the miners and smelters and by the prostitutes and professional gamblers, there was a further market provided by the prince and his court, by landlords and churchmen, which also depended on the productivity of the mines. This secondary market was not to be found necessarily in the mining towns themselves, but in the capital cities of the prince. The spectacular growth of Prague in the fourteenth century, and of Buda only a little later, depended in large part on the mines of Jihlava and Kutná Hora, and of Kremnica.

The share of the proceeds of mining that accrued to the prince varied enormously from place to place, according to local custom, which was not in itself unchangeable. Looked at retrospectively, from the dubious perspective of Agricola's time, the princely share of the mines in German principalities seems generally to have been a tenth – the *Bergzehnten*. In Bohemia the kings received an eighth of the silver, and the kings of Hungary not surprisingly

By the end of the fifteenth century Slovakia had became the most important source of copper in Europe, as well as being known for its gold- and silver-mines. It is entirely appropriate that a church in Spiš in eastern Slovakia, should have had its font made of bronze.

followed this example. In Italy the practice was very varied. At Montieri in the twelfth century, the bishops of Volterra took a quarter of the ore, although this was reduced to an eighth in the thirteenth century when the mines were becoming exhausted. In the thirteenth century, the counts of Savoy took a tenth, an eleventh and a fortieth from mines in different places, whilst the patriarchs of Aquileia took an eighth. When the mines at Iglesias were opened up, the city of Pisa claimed a royalty of a twelfth on all silver mined. It did not waste effort trying to gather it in from the multitude of miners, but simply collected it from the small number of *guelchi*, the proprietors of the smelting works, who were much easier to regulate.[37] It is not clear whether mining royalties were normally collected from smelters elsewhere. The system of royalties continued into early modern times. The kings of Spain took an imperial fifth of the silver from the mines of Potosi in the sixteenth and seventeenth centuries.

This was not, however, all that the miners had to pay out. They also had to make payments to the actual surface-owners. In the Black Forest area, for example, as well as the standard *Bergzehnten* to the bishop of Basel, the abbey of St Trudpert or the count of Freiburg, as prince and thus owner of the *Bergregal* or mining-royalties, the miners also made payments that varied according to individual agreements between mine-owners and landowners. Generally the thirtieth or thirty-first pfennig was paid here, although from a good mine the twentieth pfennig might be paid, or from a poor one the fortieth pfennig, or from a very unproductive mine only the hundredth pfennig. At Friesach, at the end of the twelfth century, the miners paid a ninth to the monastery of Admont, which seems rather a high proportion for a landowner. In some cases the prince and the surface-owner were one and the same. The margraves of Meissen at Freiberg, the bishops of Volterra at Montieri, and the kings of Bohemia at Kutná Hora made sure that they were.

Precious metals and European trade

The sequence of discoveries of precious metals from that at Freiberg to that at Joachimsthal, as well as producing a sequence of temporarily inflated mining towns, each in turn amongst the largest towns of central Europe, and as well as enriching selected rulers and their courts and making them greater poles of attraction for luxuries, also had a generally stimulating effect on the whole economy of central Europe. There was an enlarged demand not only for agricultural products, grain and meat and wine, but also for salt and clothing. As well as the Germanic miners, other Germanic settlers helped open up the country of Spiš (or Zips), in eastern Slovakia for agricultural production, and the area also became an area for fustian weaving, using locally grown flax and cotton imported from Syria through Venice.

Central Europe therefore shared with western Europe in the planting of new towns. In the lands dominated by the kings of Hungary new towns appeared not only in the mining areas of Slovakia and in the county of Spiš. Bela IV, the promoter of silver-mining at Schemnitz, moved his capital from Szekesfehervar to Buda, which naturally grew very rapidly. He planted a new town at Pest across the Danube from it, and another at Visegrad upstream,

The principal mines of silver
and gold, tenth to fifteenth centuries.

SILVER

Goslar: *Tenth to twelfth and fifteenth centuries*

Montieri, Friesach, Freiberg: *twelfth to thirteenth centuries*

Iglesias: *thirteenth to fourteenth centuries*

Jihlava (Iglau): *thirteenth century*

Kutná Hora (Kuttenberg): *fourteenth to fifteenth centuries*

Banska Stiavnica: *fourteenth to fifteenth centuries*

Srebrenica, Novo Brdo: *early fifteenth century*

Schwaz, Schneeberg: *fifteenth to sixteenth centuries*

GOLD

Kremnica: *fourteenth to fifteenth centuries*

Other towns mentioned in the text are in smaller type

half way to Esztergom, the St-Denis of Hungary. In the other direction he opened up a new route to Italy, using the Adriatic coastline of the Kingdom of Hungary, with a new port at Senj (in some ways the precursor of Rijeka) and a major new town at Zagreb in Croatia on the route from Senj to Buda. This supplemented the existing main route to Italy the 'right road', *rechtstrasse*, through Ptuj (Pettau) on the Drava and then around the eastern end of the Alps. Hungarian cattle continued to be driven in increasing numbers to Italy in the later fourteenth and the fifteenth centuries by this route. Around 1478 the traffic had reached around 9,000 to 10,000 head of cattle a year.[38] Hides were also sent this way, but commodities that were not self-propelled were generally taken along the shorter new route to the coast and thence by sea to Italy, principally to Venice.

From Buda, other routes ran overland south-eastwards to Byzantium, north-eastwards to Zips and then through the Carpathians to Cracow and the roads north of the mountains to Lvov (Leopolis) and Kiev. The Danube was of course a major artery in both directions, down to the Black Sea and up through Vienna to southern Germany. Much traffic was carried on the river itself, but in addition Hungarian cattle were driven to southern Germany on a major drove road along its south bank. On this route from Hungary to southern Germany, Vienna also became prosperous. It lay at the river crossing where the main route from Bohemia to Italy crossed this river route. The Viennese took advantage of their situation, by declaring their city a 'staple' city, which meant that all foreign merchants, whether south Germans or Italians, Bohemians or Hungarians had to offer any goods that they brought to Vienna for sale. Only goods which were not sold could be carried onwards. In other words, native merchants had to be given the chance of acting as middlemen for all trade in any direction. The Viennese naturally grew wealthy on this, as did their rulers, the dukes of Austria. They also came to be hated by Italians, Bohemians, south Germans and Hungarians as a consequence. Vienna, as well as acting as a middle point in long-distance transit trades, also dealt in some of the products of Austria itself, and was the key distribution point for foreign wares in the country. The key export from Austria itself was salt, but wine, skins, honey, wax and iron were also produced and exported. The principal imports to Austria were textiles.

From Vienna southwards the main road to Venice ran through the Tarvis pass, and it was along this road that Bohemian silver was carried southwards in the thirteenth century and the early fourteenth, and Italian textiles and levantine and oriental wares were carried northwards. After the opening up of the gold-mines at Kremnica, the Kings of Bohemia and Hungary attempted to do without the Viennese.

The Hungarian–Bohemian monetary alliance of 1327 (above p. 358) was renewed and extended to a general commercial treaty in 1335, in which the King of Poland joined. Both agreements were aggressively directed against Habsburg Vienna, which had in the thirteenth century become such a prosperous intermediary in both Hungarian–German and Bohemian–Italian trade, particularly the precious-metal trade, and had come to be so resented by both Czechs and Magyars. As a result of this commercial treaty, trade through Vienna was for some time boycotted by both countries. For a time Hungary virtually ceased to trade with Germany through Vienna and directed its trade and its gold towards Italy, opening up the routes to the Adriatic coast through Croatia, then, like Slovakia, under Hungarian rule. Hungary's surviving trade to the west was in future to be through Bohemia or Poland. Bohemia similarly virtually ceased to trade with Italy through Vienna and directed its trade, and its silver, through southern Germany to the Low Countries, or else to Italy by way of southern Germany. It was essentially Kutná Hora silver that the Kress company of Nuremberg were sending to Venice in the 1390s (see p. 354). The discoveries of gold at Kremnica generated an enormously increased purchasing-power in Hungary and a greatly increased flow of commodities to the country, focused on the fairs of Buda. Most of these commodities came from Italy around the eastern end of the Alps, or across Croatia. There was consequently a reciprocal flow of gold to Venice, Hungarians being amongst the 'German' merchants whose enhanced prosperity enabled the Fondaco dei Tedeschi to be rebuilt on a much grander scale after the disastrous fire. In return, some of the major business houses of Florence opened branches in Buda for the sale of their goods. Buonaccorso Pitti, a noble Florentine cloth magnate, has left in his *ricordanze* an account of how, as a young man, he had set out in the 1380s for Cracow with a large consignment of saffron, how he had travelled across Croatia on the road from

Senj through Zagreb to Buda, only to fall ill there and be succoured by the Florentine community at Buda, and how he had returned from Buda by the same route with a consignment of Hungarian horses, despite the risks of taking the latter by sea from Senj to Venice.

Much of the gold of Kremnica after being sent down the Hron valley to the Danube, to Esztergom and Buda, was then sent onwards to Venice by this route through Zagreb and Senj. Spices, and above all textiles, were imported in exchange. However, despite all the attempts to bypass it, Vienna remained of great importance as an intermediary.

Other boycotts also had effects on the routes of trade. In 1412 Sigismund of Luxemburg, King of Hungary, attempted an economic blockade of Venice. As ruler of Slovakia, he tried to stop the gold of Kremnica reaching Venice. It still did so, but in a roundabout way, through Milan and even Florence. In 1423 Doge Mocenigo estimated that the possessions of the Duke of Milan sent 1,600,000 gold ducats a year to Venice, over and above 1,200,000 ducats worth of cloth and provisions. At the same time nearly 400,000 ducats of gold a year came from Florence, over and above the value of Florentine textiles. Much of the gold that came to Venice from Milan and Florence had reached Milan from the cities of south Germany, which had received it in their turn from Hungary, by way of Bohemia or Austria. In return, spices and other oriental and Levantine products travelled to Hungary by this roundabout route rather than directly from Venice to the 'Hungarian' coast at Senj. As with the boycott of 1335, south Germans were once again among the beneficiaries. The routes from the mining areas of central Europe to Frankfurt and the Low Countries in any case passed from Prague through south Germany and enriched the burghers of Regensburg and Nuremberg, even when those to northern Italy were not also diverted through south Germany.

From the mines and mints of central Europe, the newly mined silver and gold, whether minted into Meissen pfennigs, Prague groats, Hungarian ducats, or merely sent in the form of ingots, followed the varying routes of trade, across Germany to Flanders and on to England and Castile, over or around the Alps to northern Italy, and on by sea to Kaffa, Trebizond and Brusa, to Acre, Lajazzo, Beirut and Alexandria, and further still to Damascus, Tabriz, Samarkand and Basra to end up in China or India. They ultimately paid for everything.

8 Conclusion: the pattern of trade

Once the canal from the Elbe to Lübeck was completed in 1398, barge-fulls of Lüneburg salt were brought in large quantities to salt warehouses in Lübeck (opposite) before being shipped out to Scania and Bergen.

The scale of commercial activity

IN THIS CONCLUDING CHAPTER I cover three themes: firstly the scale of commercial activity in various parts of Europe, particularly the Baltic, the Mediterranean and the Low Countries; secondly some of the changes in the geographical patterns of trade between the thirteenth century and the fifteenth; and, finally, some of the main themes that have emerged several times in this book.

When I set out to compile this chapter I knew that there were totals for the value of goods going in and out of the harbours of Lübeck and of Genoa to compare, and believed that I would find other figures for comparison. This turned out to be optimistic. Let me therefore begin with the figures that we have for Lübeck, by general agreement the most important Hanseatic trading city.[1] Dr Rolf Hammel-Kiesow has provided the basis from which any comparisons between north and south must start. They are for the minimum value of goods going in and out of the harbour.[2] He gives his figures in Lübeck marks, as in the sources themselves, and then converts them into marks weight of fine silver and of fine gold in order to index them and make comparisons over time. For comparisons between places I shall convert them into Italian florins and ducats.

When I looked at the figures closely I was startled to find that the information available for Lübeck is so extremely limited. It does not start until 1368. There are then only three further figures available for the fourteenth century, from the period 1379 to 1384. After a gap of over a century, figures for Lübeck's seaborne trade also survive from four years in the 1490s. That is all that is known for certain before the 1680s. With such limited evidence it is necessary to look at each figure very carefully to determine whether it may have been typical or atypical.

Dr Hammel-Kiesow's calculations show the remarkable consistency of the volume of trade for the years 1379 to 1384, when the volume of trade was worth between 62,000 and 66,000 marks weight of fine silver.[3] However in 1368 the value of trade had been much greater. It had been worth over 150,000 marks weight of fine silver, nearly two-and-a-half times as much as a decade later. Was 1368 a freak year? or had something changed in between? Dr Hammel-Kiesow believes that 1368 was not an exceptional year. He has disproved the proposed explanation that the larger figures only reflect the reopening of the Sound after a period of closure. There is no other known cause why Lübeck's sea-borne trade should have been specially inflated in that year. It is interesting to note that the normal output of silver *witten* from

Like many other ports, the city of Stralsund put a ship on its seal. Its new seal of 1329 shows the most up-to-date Baltic cog used on long-distance trading voyages between Novgorod and Lisbon. The largest could carry around 250 tons of rye or other grains, herring, salt, wax, timber, cloth and furs. They were very manoeuvrable, with square sails and stern rudders, operated by a helmsman, visible here by the aftercastle.

the Lübeck mint shrank dramatically in these very years. It was well over twice as great in the late 1360s as in the mid-1370s.[4] Except in times of recoinage, mints that were not situated in mining areas normally had to rely on new silver or gold brought in from outside by merchants. Normal mint output can thus be used as a crude barometer for some element, or elements, in trade. This would confirm Dr Hammel-Kiesow's conclusion that 1368 was not a freak year, and that trade had declined very substantially between the late 1360s and the mid-1370s. These years do span the third visitation of bubonic plague, and also the aftermath of it, in which the cumulative depopulating effects of three waves of plague began to bite. This affected the levels of rents and prices in many parts of northern Europe, and also the demand for certain commodities. It would therefore be reasonable to anticipate a very considerable real shrinkage in Lübeck's seaborne trade between 1368 and 1379. It is unfortunately impossible to say whether or not that trade had been even larger before 1368.

The Genoese evidence is much fuller. Figures survive which even suggest total seaborne trade for three years in the expansive thirteenth century itself, for 1214, 1274 and 1293.[5] One of the two late thirteenth-century figures comes from before, and the other from after, the decisive sea-battle of La Meloria at which Genoa utterly defeated Pisa, its arch-rival in the western Mediterranean. Its total victory over Pisa was symbolized by the removal to Genoa of the chains that closed the harbour at Pisa. In practical terms, this victory enabled Genoa to take over Pisa's role as the principal shipper for the rapidly growing economies of Tuscany. As a result the trade of Genoa greatly increased between 1274 and 1293. The figures that we have are of the amount of revenue derived from the *dazio*, the most significant of the *ad valorem* customs dues. The values of the trade corresponding to these sums were 936,000 Genoese lire in 1274 and 3,822,000 lire in 1293. Translating these figures in money of account into gold florins, suggests that, over the years between the two dates, the seaborne trade of Genoa rose in value from well over a million florins to over five million florins.[6] Since these years are isolated ones, we cannot know how typical they were, nor consequently whether or not quadrupling is the real measure of the increase in the volume of trade over the intervening years, that had come about because of the combination of natural growth and the taking over of previously Pisan trade. The 1293 figure may be atypically, and suspiciously, large, for it is much greater than any other thirteenth- or fourteenth-century figures for Genoese trade.[7] For our present purposes, we must ignore all these early figures, since it is unfortunately impossible to compare them with any comparable Lübeck figures, since nothing survives. The 1293 figure must not be compared, as Professor Lopez did,[8] with the figures from Lübeck seventy years later!

From the fourteenth century there are records of the sums for which the customs were farmed: for 1334, and then for 46 years between 1341 and 1406.[9] With this long run of Genoese customs figures in the middle and late fourteenth century we are at last on firm ground and have material for a fair north–south comparison. In 1334 the value of goods shipped has been reck-

Lübeck, the largest city north of Cologne, was the leading member of the Hanseatic League. Considerable ships could come up the deep mouth of the Trave into its harbour. Altdorfer's artistic licence, exaggerated by the printmaker in 1560, has made the Trave look like the distant Baltic, with far too much shipping waiting in it. The city was built on a hill almost entirely surrounded by rivers. There were only two ways into the town by land: a single bridge across the Trave to Holstein, and this road, defended by a double gate, at the castle end of the town, leading to Wismar.

oned as 1,800,000 Genoese lire (1,440,000 *genovini* or florins). In the 1340s their value has been calculated as around 1,700,000 lire (1,360,000 *genovini*), except for much lower values in the crisis year of 1345–46.[10] In the 1350s and 1360s, the value of trade going in and out of the harbour of Genoa generally continued to oscillate about 1,400,000 florins. At the end of the 1360s it rose quite sharply, and in 1371 it exceeded two million gold florins. In 1376–77 the value of Genoese seaborne trade was still at this level, including 370,000 ducats worth of goods imported from the Levant.[11] However in the early 1380s it was below 1,700,000 gold florins and had soon resumed the level of the 1350s and 1360s.

To make valid comparisons with these Genoese figures I have converted the Lübeck figures into Italian terms. In 1368 the gold *gulden* being minted at Lübeck were still as fine and as heavy as the florins, ducats and *genovini* being struck in Italy, principally, but not exclusively, in Florence, Venice and Genoa.[12] The value of the goods being shipped in and out of Lübeck in that year was equivalent to 875,000 Lübeck *gulden* or Genoese florins, *genovini*. The next year, trade through the harbour of Genoa was worth over 1,800,000 *genovini*, just over double the Lübeck figure. However, the figures for 1379 to 1384 show that the Lübeck trade had shrunk to 350,000 gold florins, at a time that Genoese trade was dropping from two million florins to 1,700,000 florins. In other words, the trade through the harbour at Genoa was, at this point in time, shrinking from six times as much as at Lübeck to five times as much. But for the short period for which it is fair to make comparisons, between 1379 and 1384, there is no doubt that trade at Genoa was many times greater than that at Lübeck.

At this time the general, non-statistical, impression is that trade at Venice was of the same order of magnitude as that at Genoa, although possibly slightly smaller. If so, its trade too might have been around five times as great as Lübeck's. For the Mediterranean, there were no other ports as important as Genoa and Venice, not even Barcelona or Porto Pisano, which, although without considerable shipping of its own, was the key port of entry for Tuscany, so that a great deal of seaborne trade consequently passed through it. Moreover Marseilles, Ragusa and even Ancona and Aigues Mortes were not without importance. For the Baltic, there was no other port to rival Lübeck, although places like Gdansk, Rostock, and Torun cannot be ignored. It would probably be an exaggeration, but not a very great one, to double the evidence for Genoa to take account of Venice, and then suppose that other ports in each region ranked in proportion, and therefore to suggest that by the early 1380s, Mediterranean trade was ten times greater than that in the Baltic. However, the very sparse evidence from the late 1360s might be used to suggest that, since Lübeck trade had then been so much larger, Mediterranean trade had then only been five times greater than that in the Baltic. These are very wild and risky extrapolations, but, I believe, of the right order of magnitude.

In the War of Chioggia (1378–81) the Venetians eventually destroyed the naval power of Genoa, although not as completely as the Genoese had destroyed that of Pisa a hundred years earlier. Afterwards Genoese trade went into a marked decline. In 1400 Piero Benintendi gave up the farm of the Genoese customs, on the grounds that the volume of trade had not reached the anticipated level in any of the seven preceding years. He said that he had consequently made a loss on farming the customs. In the next year, 1401, the sum assumed trade had shrunk yet further. In this, the lowest year in the surviving statistics, seaborne trade at Genoa was down below 900,000 florins worth.[13] Even this was still more than two-and-a-half times that at Lübeck between 1379 and 1384. The general indications are that Venetian trade correspondingly gained.

The great boom in Venetian trade with the Muslim Near East began in the late 1380s.[14] I hoped that this increase could be measured more precisely than by the sums paid in Venice at the annual auctions of the galleys bound for Alexandria and Beirut, since I knew that there were wide varieties of dues paid on imports and exports to and from Venice. Unfortunately the whole range of trading statistics that I hoped for could not be derived from the complex range of dues imposed by the Venetians. We therefore have no global figures for Venetian trade. We can work out figures for particular commodities at particular dates. The pepper imported into Venice from Alexandria and Beirut in 1395 was worth 342,562 ducats. We can even rank participation in particular trades. In the last years of the fourteenth century whilst the Venetians were bringing home over 500 tons of pepper each year from Beirut and Alexandria, the Genoese and Catalans came far behind, but on a level with each other. They were each bringing home around 200 tons of pepper.[15] The difficulty of working with only partial figures is exemplified by the

In 1551 Jan Provoost used the waterfront at Antwerp, looking upstream (opposite), as the background for a portrait. The large Antwerp crane, on the left, very clearly derived from that at Bruges. Here men can clearly be seen walking the treadmill that operated the crane. A generation earlier, an anonymous artist caught the busyness of the harbour front of Antwerp (overleaf), including the same crane, on the largest of the wharves between the Scheldt and the town walls, each with its own gate. Amongst the many ships, he captured the last galleys to come from Venice in 1520, and the tall new sailing ship which took pilgrims from the Low Countries direct from Antwerp to the Holy Land.

primo February 1516. Als ich
zw̄ her Jacob fugger kam: doch erst
e. zener 1517. verschriben worden

Rom
Venedig
Offen
Craca

Mayland
Inspruck
Nürmberg
Antorff
Lisbona

HER · IACOB · FVGGER

19. iar 6 mo: 8 tag

rather different pattern obtained by counting ships. In the years 1399–1408, 278 Venetian boats entered the harbour of Beirut, against 264 Genoese boats and 224 Catalan ones.[16] By this time the late fourteenth-century shrinkage in Genoese trade, and the increase in Venetian trade, meant that Venetian trade was larger than Genoese. But was it slightly larger, as the shipping figures suggest? Or a great deal larger, as the pepper figures suggest? Both figures imply that Barcelona, along with its associated ports, was then still in the same league as Genoa and Venice. Professor Melis, in his study of shipping around 1400, found that the combined merchant fleets that he could discover for Barcelona, Valencia, and Majorca were only slightly exceeded in numbers by the combined merchant fleets of Genoa, Savona and other Ligurian ports. He was able to discover records of 921 Ligurian boats and 875 Catalan boats in the period 1383–1411, mainly in the period 1391–1405. However, the Catalan boats were markedly smaller, mostly less than half the size of their Genoese counterparts. The most common size of Catalan boat that Professor Melis found was one with a tonnage of only 300 *botti* (around 200 tonnes), whilst the most common size of Genoese boat that he found had a tonnage of 800 *botti*.[17]

In place of global figures for Venetian trade we have to interpret the partisan information in the famous 'deathbed oration' of 1423 in which the dying Doge, Tommaso Mocenigo, reputedly pleaded, unsuccessfully, for the election of a 'dove' rather than a 'hawk' as his successor. Francesco Foscari, who was elected, was not finally forced out until 1457, but a faction opposed to his pro-Florentine policies compelled him to offer his abdication as Doge of Venice in 1433–34. It was probably as part of this campaign against Foscari that the remarkable 'deathbed oration' of his predecessor Tomaso Mocenigo was invented. In 1929 Professor Luzzatto looked at some of the figures attributed to Mocenigo and on that basis concluded that they were all tolerably accurate.[18] However, more recent scholarship has suggested that many other facts and figures used in the supposed speech, as far as they can be checked, were grossly exaggerated, and some clearly anachronistic.[19] Mocenigo was made to praise himself for the commercial prosperity of the Venetian republic in 1423. The size of the galley fleet, and the huge quantities of gold and silver being brought into Venice to pass through the mint, were used to exemplify the desirable condition of the republic at the time, as well as the scale of silk manufacture and the regularity of payment of interest on the *monte*. In other words Venice was presented, in the 'good old days' before Foscari became doge, as a state run by entrepreneurs for entrepreneurs. The level of trade in various commodities was inflated, particularly that with the Milanese state, described as the 'garden of Venice'. He allegedly listed how many woollens and fustians Venice received from Milan and how much raw material was sent to Milan, wool, cotton, cotton thread, spices, sugar and slaves. He is supposed to have added the admonition, 'If you were to lay waste your garden it would be said that you had become mad.'[20] He was therefore made to say that he wanted another doge who would not get embroiled in war with Milan, as Foscari has since done, and ruin what Foscari's enemies

In his Trachtenbuch *(book of achievements) young Matthäus Schwarz wrote with pride that he came to Jacob Fugger in 1516 at the age of 19. After a year training in each of the Fugger offices in Milan, Genoa, and Venice, he came back to Augsburg, as bookkeeper, in 1520. He put into his memoirs a sketch of Jakob Fugger telling him what to enter in the books (opposite). When Jakob died in 1525, he was head of the first business to grow larger than the Bardi of early fourteenth-century Florence. Schwarz has drawn files, behind his own head, for each of the subsidiary companies in the group: in the left hand column – Rome, Venice, Buda (Ofen), and Cracow; and in the right hand column – Milan, Innsbruck, Nuremberg, Antwerp and Lisbon.*

Although commercially overshadowed by Venice, Genoa was still important at the end of the fifteenth century, and the principal port for the prospering Milanese state, of which it was part from 1464, except for the turbulent period from 1478 to 1487. In these few years, this proud representation of Genoa's independence and naval might was painted. A score of light war galleys in formation occupies the foreground. Genoa no longer had any commercial great galleys, but half a dozen huge bulk-carrying carracks are leaving the safety of the harbour, and, within the mole, numerous lesser boats are drawn up in formation. The city is much less clearly depicted than the parade of shipping.

considered Venice's most important trade, that with Milan. The pre-war figures that they attributed to Mocenigo, for this trade alone, totalled four million ducats. No total was attributed to him for trade with Florence, but he was made to say that the imbalance in favour of Venice was a remarkably precise 392,000 ducats. These are, of course, land trades, like that, unmeasured, with 'Germany'. His figures for seaborne trade begin with trade with the Venetian colonies in the eastern Mediterranean, for which he was made to quote an adverse balance of 100,000 ducats, and then a smaller imbalance still for trade with England. He was not made to suggest a total for the trade with Alexandria and Beirut, but once again the size of the adverse balance was attributed to him, which was of 500,000 ducats. Gino Luzzatto pointed out that the adverse balance on trade with Alexandria and Beirut was actually 460,000 ducats in 1433, at just about the time that the 'deathbed oration' was probably concocted. This makes one wonder if, putting aside the polemically exaggerated figures for trade with Milan, other figures for balances, particularly the precise figure for trade with Florence, also reflected some reality of the 1430s. These hints provide us with no global figures. Although they suggest a trade very much larger than that of Genoa at any previous time, they are probably no more to be trusted than Jacopo Doria's figure for Genoese trade in 1293.

When we again have figures for Lübeck in the 1490s we no longer have any global figures for Genoa or for Venice, so we cannot resume the comparison of the 1380s. We do, however, have figures for one sector of Venetian trade, that with the Levant. The 'Mocenigo' statistics, however, suggest that the trade with Alexandria and Beirut was probably only a very minor part of the total trade of Venice in the first half of the fifteenth century, but that need not have been the case three generations later. Certainly the Venetians had come to dominate the Levant trade from the fourth decade of the fifteenth century onwards at the expense of their Genoese and Catalan rivals.[21]

In 1492 the trade through the harbour at Lübeck was valued at the equivalent of 330,000 Venetian ducats, but in the three subsequent years at only about 240,000 Venetian ducats. The figures for Venetian trade with Alexandria and Beirut for 1497 show that this trade alone was worth around 590,000 ducats. About 475,000 ducats worth of goods, predominantly spices, was imported and 115,000 ducats worth of goods, largely textiles, was exported. The balance was made up by mammoth shipments of bullion. The figures for trade with Alexandria alone in the following year, 1498, suggest that 1497 had not been an abnormal year.[22] Furthermore we know the size of shipments of bullion to Alexandria and Beirut in 1496, and they totalled only very slightly less than in 1497, 340,000 ducats against 360,000 ducats. This adds to our confidence in the 1497 figures. This one segment of Venetian trade was therefore well over double the value of all that passed through the harbour of Lübeck in the three preceding years. The problem is, of course, to know how important the Egyptian and Syrian trade had then become in the whole overseas trade of Venice. Had it grown or shrunk in relative importance in the previous seventy years? It was slightly lower in monetary value than it had been earlier, but the general impression remains that if the Egyptian and Syrian trades alone were well over double the total trade at Lübeck, then Venetian trade overall was by then very many times greater than that at Lübeck.

My attempts to estimate the scale of trade at Bruges proved even more fruitless than for Venice. I knew that tolls were taken at Sluys on goods going in and out of Bruges, and I hoped that these would give me values for imports and exports for Bruges. I deliberately did not look for the numbers of ships passing in and out of Sluys because of the differences in size of vessel over time and place. There was a huge range of sizes of ships entering the port, and even at the top end of the scale, they differed vastly in size. The largest Genoese carracks in 1400 were three times as large as the largest Hanseatic cogs. We have the sums for which the tolls at Sluys were farmed from 1384 to 1540, and can therefore establish approximate trends in the seaborne trade of Bruges. The revenue from the toll was at its highest in the 1430s, when it was farmed for 8,400 *livres parisis* (approximately equivalent to 3,360 Venetian ducats). It shrank slowly to the 1480s, and then dropped suddenly during the civil wars, to 2,800 livres by 1493 (approximately equivalent to 700 Venetian ducats).[23] However, we cannot do the same for these figures as has been done in Genoa, since we lack the multiplier to turn them into even a minimum value of trade, not counting the expenses of collection, the profit of the farmer, and the large number of exemptions from the toll. We cannnot therefore estimate either its value or volume, to compare it with the scale of trade either in the Baltic or the Mediterranean.

Nobody, to my knowledge, has tried to estimate the overall size of trade at either Bruges or Antwerp before 1560. Around 1520 the trade of Antwerp was probably still of much the same sort, and on much the same scale, as that of its predecessor, Bruges, before the civil wars of the 1480s. However, by 1560 the trade of Antwerp had experienced a generation of prodigious growth to a achieve a level quite unknown anywhere in medieval Europe. Professor Brulez estimated the overall trade of Antwerp in 1560 at around 36 million *carolus gulden*, equivalent to some 28 million Venetian ducats.[24] This is a very much greater value of trade than we believe ever passed through Bruges. Even Venice in its fifteenth-century heyday never approached such a scale. For comparison with either the Venetian import of spices, or Lübeck's trade in grain, it is interesting to note that the import of spices stood no higher than seventh in value of the different trades of Antwerp (two million *carolus gulden*, or just over 1½ million Venetian ducats). The import of grain from the Baltic, so important to traders within the Baltic itself, came no higher than fifth in value and made up no more than a twelfth part of the overall trade at Antwerp (three million *carolus gulden*, or 2⅓ million Venetian ducats).[25] The import of spices into Antwerp had declined since the 1540s. By 1560 it ranked no higher than seventh in value. It was still worth two million *carolus gulden* or just over 1.5 million Venetian ducats, in itself a much larger annual value than that of the spices imported into Venice in the previous century.

I also knew that gate taxes were taken on goods going in and out of Florence and I hoped that these would give me some figures for a great inland city. I imagined that I would find something similar elsewhere, perhaps for Milan, or perhaps for one of the major south German commercial centres like Nuremberg or Augsburg. I have almost totally failed. Estimates for inland cities like Florence, Nuremberg or Augsburg turned out to be even less forthcoming than for Bruges.

In the end the only safe comparison that I could make was that between Lübeck and Genoa in the years between 1379 and 1384, when the seaborne trade at Genoa was five or six times greater than that at Lübeck. Since Lübeck is generally conceded to have been dominant on the Baltic and to have had a very large share of Hanseatic trade, whilst Genoa was rivalled, although not yet over-shadowed by Venice, it is clear that Mediterranean trade was many times greater in scale than that on the Baltic.

Nearly twenty years ago, in an essay for John Day's collection of studies, and as I repeated at the beginning of this book, I pointed out, for the Mediterranean, that as the amount of business focused on a limited number of particular places, or rather along a limited number of routes between these places, passed a critical mass, qualitative changes in the nature of commerce began to take place as well as merely qualitative ones. Until the critical scale of operations was reached, on any particular route, all that occurred was an increase in the volume of trade within the traditional framework. However, once the critical volume was reached, the scale of enterprises which became possible allowed for a division of labour. When that point was reached, businesses became large enough and continuous enough to maintain three separate parties, sedentary merchants at home, specialist carriers, and full-time agents.[26] Only now can I see that the difference in scale between Baltic trade, even that of Lübeck, and Mediterranean trade, explains why the division of labour so noticeable in the south hardly occurred in the north. With this sort of difference in the scale of trade it is not surprising that the number of inhabitants who could be supported by it was so different. Historical demographers have estimated that in Lübeck in the late fourteenth century the population was barely more than 25,000, which in itself made it much the largest city on the Baltic, whilst the population of Genoa is supposed to have been four times as great. A century later the population of Lübeck apparently had not changed, whilst that of Venice was well over four times as great.[27]

In the last generation historical demographers have been providing more and more sophisticated estimates of population. I hope that, in the next generation, economic historians will be able to produce some clearer estimates of the scale of trade. We already have a great many pieces of this jigsaw puzzle, although many have been irrecoverably lost. Yet it still remains to try to make an overall picture from them.

Changes in land routes

As well as the general long-term swings in overall European economic activity – expansion to the first half of the fourteenth century, contraction to the mid-fifteenth century, and then again expansion – there were also enormous local variations and shifts, besides much shorter-term transformations. Sudden, short-term changes from expansion to contraction, and back again, are ones with which we were all too familiar in the later twentieth century. Late medieval Europeans also knew these phenomena. The calamities of the 1340s, which in retrospect look like the death knell of the long-thirteenth-century expansion, were followed by a brief recovery. Even in the middle of the century-long contraction which followed, there was a short-lived boom. Indeed, the first twenty years of the the fifteenth century were regarded in Florence as a period of unprecedented prosperity, because by then no-one could remember how rich the city had been a hundred years earlier. This brings up a problem of the definition of wealth. The accumulating capital assets of this society may have continued to grow at the same time as other indicators, industry, trade, and population, were shrinking, just as they did in the Netherlands in the eighteenth century. In this sense Florence may really have been wealthier than a hundred years earlier. Is it more than coincidental that it was in these two optimistic decades at the beginning of the fifteenth century that patronage was available that helped the stylistic transition from late Gothic to early Renaissance to begin?

When, in the second half of the fifteenth century, the European economy eventually recovered from the long period of overall contraction, the 'great depression' of the later Middle Ages, it was no longer the same as it had been.

From the thirteenth century Europe has contained an urban belt stretching from England to Italy. It still persists today, and since the 1990s some urban geographers have given the nickname of the 'blue banana' to the curved backbone of key cities that now runs from Manchester to Milan through modern Belgium and the Netherlands, western Germany, Switzerland and the Rhône valley.[28] At the end of the Middle Ages it included all three principal industrial regions of Europe (see pp. 228–31).

This 'blue banana' itself has varied surprisingly little over the last seven centuries. By 1300 the urban backbone already curved through Europe from London to Siena and Perugia. What has not remained the same is the area of greatest density of the urban fabric within the 'banana'. That has changed frequently, and is still changing in the twenty-first century. In the 1980s the most densely woven part of this urban fabric lay in the Brussels, Cologne, Amsterdam area focused on the Rhine mouth Europoort. However, the most striking region for growth lay farther south in the Frankfurt, Basel, Zurich, Munich area.

Up to the mid-fourteenth century the greatest economic weight lay in the two most southerly segments of the urban belt, the Arno basin and the Po basin, divided by the Appenines. By the end of the fifteenth century the economic focus of Europe had begun its centuries-long journey northwards. In the late fifteenth century the Po basin still retained its economic weight, but the cities south of the Appenines, from Genoa to Perugia, had lost importance. Some, like Siena, once so significant in international trade, had virtually vanished from long-distance commerce, whilst others, like Lucca, still clung to a considerable share in it. On the other hand, cities immediately to the north of the Alps had correspondingly gained in weight. In the fifteenth century, it was the region of new growth, particularly the Augsburg–Nuremberg area, that caught contemporary attention. In 1471, the mathematician Johannes Müller settled there because:

> it is there easiest for me to keep in touch with all the learned of all countries, for Nuremberg, thanks to the perpetual journeyings of her merchants, may be counted the centre of Europe.[29]

The region had been growing in importance since the late fourteenth century, and its accumulated wealth was already such by the middle of the fifteenth century that the Sienese humanist Aeneas Sylvius Piccolomini, later Pope Pius II, had been able to point out that:

> the burghers' dwellings seem to have been built for princes. In truth, the kings of Scotland [which he had visited in 1435] would gladly be housed so luxuriously as the ordinary citizen of Nuremberg.[30]

In the thirteenth century the key trade routes of Europe may be represented as a triangle. On the west lay the route running from Flanders to Tuscany, passing through Champagne, where it connected with Paris, which was then the greatest single consumption centre in Europe, and across the Great Saint Bernard pass, to become the via Francigena in Italy (see Chapter 3). On the east lay the route from Tuscany to the mining areas of Europe, which left Italy by the Tarvis pass and went on through Vienna. The mining areas of Europe were, in turn, linked to Flanders by the road running from Freiberg to Bruges. This northern side of the triangle had already been observed at the very end of the twelfth century by Hendrik van Veldeke, one of the earliest writers of love songs in the German vernacular. Praising his native town of Maastricht, he pointed out that the road, which gave the town

its name, *Trajectum, Tricht*, 'the crossing' (of the Meuse), was that 'from England to Hungary, from the sea coast across the plains of Flanders, and then from Tongres through Tricht into Cologne'.

This triangle of key land routes between Flanders, Tuscany and Hungary, had been replaced by the end of the fifteenth century by a series of key roads radiating outwards from the newly commercially important south German centres. This change in the relative importance of roads vindicated Johannes Müller's comment on Nuremberg, on which it was claimed that twelve major trade routes converged.[31] The geographical centre of this rising region was the bridge at Donauwörth, where the road linking the two principal economic focii, Augsburg and Nuremberg, crossed the Danube.

The most important of these radiating roads was naturally that linking the new centres of south Germany across the Brenner pass with those old centres of northern Italy which remained commercially important. Both Milan and Venice, the two most significant cities, politically as well as economically, could be reached easily from Verona, where the road from the Brenner (or Verona) pass descended to the Lombard plain. Trade along this route had grown to such an extent by 1480 that it had become worthwhile to go to the huge expense of turning the packhorse road across this Alpine pass into one fit for wagons. This naturally made it cheaper to carry goods across the Brenner, and consequently increased the desirability of using it. In turn this made the pass much busier.[32] In the autumn of 1494 the young Albrecht Dürer travelled to Venice by this route, returning to Nuremberg in the

From 1383 Poland and Lithuania were united under one ruler, with twin capitals in Cracow and Vilnyus. The principal road between them crossed the river Nieman at Grodno in the Lithuanian wilderness, and a medium-sized town grew up there, which became a collecting point for furs. In an engraving printed in Nuremberg in 1568, an extraordinary collection of carriages passes along the road in the foreground, whilst men are washing furs in the Nieman.

following spring. He painted a number of watercolours on the way. The painting he made of Innsbruck on his way south has been described by the British art historian Kenneth Clark as 'the first portrait of a town'. On his way back Dürer also painted Arco and Trent (ill. p. 188) besides the new wagon road itself as it climbed to the pass.[33]

The second most important radiating road was that from south Germany to Antwerp, which had come to replace Bruges, during the civil wars of the 1480s, as the economic focal point of the whole Netherlands. This route ran northwards through Frankfurt, notable for its fairs, where central European precious metals and Low Countries' cloth had already for long found a ready market. One spin-off from the fairs was that carrying long-distance freight became a speciality of the men of the Frammersbach district of Hesse, just south of Frankfurt, who used massive four-wheeled wagons on the improved roads, with teams of six to eight horses, to carry goods between southern Germany and Antwerp.[34] This route to Antwerp reached the Rhine at Mainz, where goods were either transferred to the Rhine itself, or crossed the river to the west bank on the lowest Rhine bridge of the Middle Ages. Situated at a key place on this route, Mainz proved a good central point for the invention and dissemination of print in the fifteenth century, as Gutenberg, or rather his grasping backers, well knew.

The four great Rhineland electors, and as many lesser rulers as they could persuade to join them in a series of leagues, contrived to keep traffic flowing safely and profitably from Mainz to Cologne, either on the Rhine or along the main road on its west bank. Naturally, they took numerous tolls to pay for the upkeep of the route, and the protection of those who used it. In the sixteenth century this road from southern Germany to Antwerp was to replace the road from southern Germany to Venice in importance. Even in the wartime conditions of 1585–86, the della Faille firm managed to find carriers in Antwerp, which had itself recently been sacked by the Spanish, who could still reach Cologne by roundabout routes with their freight-wagons in 10 to 21 days, and Augsburg in 60 to 75 days. Even in its decline in 1610, 2,000 long-distance freight wagons were still reputedly reaching Antwerp each week, besides the 1,000 local wagons bringing in provisions.[35]

As well as the two principal radiating routes, to Venice over the Brenner, and down the Rhine valley to Antwerp, other important routes radiated outwards from southern Germany in the fifteenth century (map p. 352).

The main route westwards went by way of the fairs at Geneva or Lyon to the French court, which was by now on the Loire rather than on the Seine. The route to the French court was another of those late medieval routes that mixed road and river transport. Goods from Nuremberg were sent in distinctive large south German four-wheeled wooden carts, with boat-shaped bodies, with canvas roofs stretched over hoops, and with huge rear wheels.[36] They travelled in these along the great south German and Swiss road which led through Ulm and Constance to Zurich and on through the central valley of Switzerland to Geneva and Lyon. From Lyon, the wagoners of Roanne took goods onwards across the watershed to Roanne, where, unless they were taken on by road to Bourges, they were embarked on the upper waters of the Loire, to be carried downstream to the stretch of river between Gien and Chinon, where successive rulers, from Charles VII onwards, chose to continue to live.[37]

In so far as there was a single dominant city in the region, it was Tours. Jacques Coeur of Bourges, *argentier* of Charles VII from 1438 to 1451, who handled most of the funding for driving the English out of France, and provided a considerable amount of it himself, moved his base of operations from Bourges to Tours where he 'ran a sort of bazaar' to supply the king and the court with silks and spices, tapestries, jewels and plate, as well as arms, armour and personal loans. By the time of his disgrace, he was running a multi-branched, multi-function company based in Tours, like a major north Italian or south German business. At the beginning of Charles VII's reign in the 1420s the purchasing power of the French crown and court were insignificant. The greatest princes of France were no longer to be found with their king. Instead they were scattered about France, or even outside France in Navarre, Provence or Brabant. However, by the end of Louis XI's reign, in the 1480s, the French court was again the greatest consumption centre of Europe, and the routes to Tours from south Germany and north Italy, and from the fairs at Lyon, where these routes joined, had grown correspondingly in importance.

Another set of routes ran eastwards from southern Germany. One route led north of the Erzgebirge and the Tatra to southern Poland and beyond, another led into central Bohemia, and a third led south of Bohemia to the Danube at Regensburg and on downriver to Austria, Slovakia, Hungary and beyond. South German merchants trading along these routes could not only reach the consumption centres of Cracow, Prague, Vienna and Buda, but also the rejuvenated mining areas of Europe, from Thuringia to Slovakia, where mining companies, depending on south German capital, had currently replaced the free miners of the past, and controlled large parts of the European production of iron, copper, silver and tin (see pp. 361 and 364).

The new role of south German merchants at the end of the fifteenth century is illustrated by a quick reference book made for use in the Fondaco dei Tedeschi in Venice, which was designed to show at a glance what taxes were to be paid on each commodity, and how much would be charged for carriage and brokerage; what payments had to be made to porters, packers, weighers and spice-garblers (i.e. those who sifted out dirt and foreign bodies or extraneous objects), and what fees were to be paid to the writers of the very numerous official documents required by the Venetian authorities.[38] Around 1500, south German merchants were expected to bring with them a much wider range of goods than the silver and amber of a hundred years before (see pp. 353–4). In the intervening century very considerable changes had also taken place in the geographical area from which this extended range of goods had come. In the course of the fifteenth century the south German manufacture of linen had taken off. At the end of the century, rolls of linen, of various lengths from 50 to 138 yards, were being brought from Constance and

For the pretentious Gothic mansion the French entrepreneur Jacques Coeur built himself in Bourges in 1443 (ill. p. 138), he ordered stained glass paintings, including this delicate cog, the sort of boat that, although initially developed in the Baltic, had become the basic trading vessel along all the coasts of western Europe by the time Coeur was running ships from the mouth of the Rhône.

On his pilgrimage to Jerusalem
and Sinai in 1483, Bernhard von
Breydenbach, the noble
chamberlain of Mainz, took with
him an artist: 'the learned and
ingenious Erhard Rewich, so that
he should cunningly draw and
reproduce upon paper things fair
and lovely to the eye'. On his
return he had his narrative
printed in Mainz, with woodcuts
made by Rewich from his sketches.
When Rewich drew his panorama
of Venice, from the great
Benedictine monastery of San
Giorgio, it reached from the salt
warehouses and customs house on
the left, to the entrance to the
Arsenal on the right. In the centre
is the Doge's Palace, with the
domes of St Mark's visible above
its roof. In the foreground lies the
pilgrim galley they were about to
board for Jaffa.

St Gall and elsewhere in southern Germany. Furthermore, south German capital had gone into iron works in Thuringia and copper mines in Slovakia, so that south German merchants, besides bringing in iron, were making Venice, for the time being, the principal copper market of Europe. Some south German businessmen had extended their operations even further eastwards than Slovakia, and were therefore able to bring Bulgarian and other skins and furs to Venice. These pelts of martens, ermines and even of white wolves, had, before the fifteenth-century Turkish advances, been shipped to Italy from Black Sea ports. As well as those south Germans who had extended their field of activities eastwards, there were those who had extended it northwards to the Low Countries and beyond. From the Low Countries they were sending overland to Venice expensive tapestries and a wide range of qualities of woollen cloth, from those priced at over twenty ducats the piece, down to those valued at under five ducats the roll, and also the new, cheap, light serges. It is not clear if the goods made of latten, the copper-zinc mixture so suitable for tableware, that were brought to Venice were still from the Low Countries, or from the newer latten industry in Nuremberg. As well as bringing goods overland from the Low Countries, south German merchants were also consigning fine white woollen cloth and English wool and tin for delivery to Venice by the long westward sea route, to the galleys of Flanders, so long as they continued to run.

South Germans had also extended their field of activity southwards from Venice itself. As well as buying goods in Venice, they were now themselves engaging in a transit trade through the city. They were carrying home through Venice, saffron and sugar bought further south, and were buying silk directly in Calabria and Messina. From Venetian suppliers they were still

buying silks, pepper and other 'spices', pearls, sugar, cotton and soap, as Kress had done in the 1390s, but in addition they were now paying export dues on oil, and on Greek malmsey and other wines by the amphora that they had bought in Venice, on boxes of salted cod and other fish, and on all manner of other 'mercery', including ivory, mercury and copper wire. The 'spices' which were garbled in Venice, at the cost of the German exporter, before being carried across the Alps included not only oriental 'spices' like ginger, cloves and cinnamon, but also Mediterranean 'spices' like rice and cummin. All this was partially for home consumption in south Germany, but mainly for onward transmission along the routes to the north, west, and east.

The replacement of the triangle of key thirteenth-century land routes by a web of fifteenth-century routes radiating outwards from south Germany was not a direct succession. Although so many goods were carried overland in both the mid-thirteenth century and the late fifteenth century, in the two intervening centuries much trade had been carried by sea.

From the corners of the thirteenth-century triangle of great land routes, further routes extended outwards. Many of them were sea routes. Trade by road and river routes and trade by sea routes were in most cases complementary. The sea routes of the Mediterranean, the North Sea and the Baltic joined the overland routes across Europe. From Bruges, there were not only the short Channel crossings to England, but also the Hanseatic routes through the North Sea and the Baltic. From Genoa, Pisa and Venice, there were sea routes to the Maghreb and the Levant. From the mines of Meissen a route led eastwards, north of the chain of mountains, to Cracow, Kiev and beyond.

Sea routes

The improvements in navigation and the corresponding extension of maritime activity, particularly by Italians, meant that the triangular land routes were partially circumvented by much longer, but still cheaper, sea routes. It became easier to reach Cracow from Italy by travelling to the Black Sea in a Genoese carrack and thence up the Dniester through Lwow, rather than going the whole distance overland. It became easier to reach Cracow from Flanders by travelling to Gdansk or Torun in a Hanseatic cog and thence up the Vistula, rather than going along the 'road from England to Hungary'. Above all, it became easier to go directly by carrack or galley from Genoa or Venice to Bruges itself, rather than travelling overland across the Alps and the Jura, Burgundy and Champagne.

The Atlantic route between north-west Europe and Italy could thus be regarded as an alternative, and a rival, to the land and river routes across Europe. Travel by sea from the north to the Mediterranean had had an intermittent history since Viking times. Some of the English crusaders on the Second Crusade went by sea (and helped in the 'reconquest' of Lisbon in 1147 on the way), as did the ships of Richard I of England for the Third Crusade. He himself went overland to Marseilles and embarked there. However it was only in the course of the thirteenth century that the sea route came to be used frequently for commercial purposes. The successes of the Christian reconquest of the Iberian peninsula provided suitable stopping places to make the journey commercially viable. The capture of Seville in 1248 was the greatest triumph of the mid-thirteenth century *reconquista* of Andalusia by (St) Ferdinand, the king of Castile and León. A Genoese community was known in Seville from the year of its 'reconquest'. Seville became not only a gateway for Italian, particularly Genoese, exploitation of the commercial opportunities provided by Andalusia itself, but also an excellent staging point for journeying onwards into the Atlantic. It was, of course, not the only such staging point. In the fourteenth century the Genoese community in Seville was rivalled in size by that in Cadiz, which had itself been reconquered in 1265. Cadiz possessed a better harbour, but not such a rich hinterland. The Genoese community in Seville was possibly also rivalled by that at Málaga, which had an even better harbour, but lay in the un-reconquered kingdom of Granada and therefore suffered from the insecurity of Muslim–Christian relations. There was yet another, smaller, Geneose community in Lisbon. Genoese ships were soon to be found rounding Spain and trading as far as La Rochelle. The earliest Genoese galleys known to have gone all the way to Flanders did so in 1277, and may have been preceded by Catalan ships. Such trading voyages were initially sporadic, but became more and more common as time went on.

When Philip IV's ill-judged attempt to occupy Gascony led to a fully fledged war against England and her coalition of allies, of which Flanders was the most important, it brought about a severe disruption of the land route across Champagne to Flanders. The falling returns from the tolls at the passes in the Jura and the western Alps indicate how much trade moved away from the traditional route across eastern France. As well as a shift by overland carriers to a Rhineland route, itself partially disrupted after 1313 by civil war in the Empire, a certain number of merchants took advantage of the opportunity of sending goods by the new sea route.[39] As long as this was only a galley route, it was an expensive alternative to carriage by road and river, for galleys with their huge complement of men were very costly to operate. The earliest Venetian 'great galleys', an enlarged mercantile version of the traditional Mediterranean many-oared man-of-war, which was introduced in the 1290s, required nearly 200 crew, predominantly rowers, for only fifty tons of cargo. Galleys normally sailed when out at sea, but the oarsmen gave them greater manoeuverability when winds were contrary, when passing through narrow straits and when entering or leaving harbour. In the course of the next hundred years the Venetians built their 'great galleys' larger and larger until they were threefold their original size. By 1400 they had a second principal mast, and a third, smaller mast at the stern. They nevertheless still carried a large complement of rowers. The regulations of 1412 stipulated that there should be 170 oarsmen, all free, properly paid, Venetians, not convicts or slaves, among a total crew of at least 210.[40] Such manning levels meant that, although they were appreciably less costly to operate than in the 1290s, they were still prodigiously dear to run.[41] Because operating galleys was so expensive, the Genoese soon abandoned their commercial use, but the Venetians kept them on and indeed developed, in the course of the fourteenth century, a pattern of regulated convoys of state-owned galleys (see p. 401).

However, even in Venice, 'great galleys' were only a minor, if the most prestigious, part of the merchant fleet. The larger part of its merchant fleet, and almost the whole of those of Genoa and Barcelona, was made up of sailing ships which grew larger, more efficient and cheaper to run as time went by. In the Mediterranean they carried not only grain, but also wine, oil and salt, timber, cotton and alum.[42]

The galleys from Venice to Flanders and England may have taken spices and other very highly priced commodities off the trans-European trade routes, but the real competition for much land trade was provided by the development of bulk carriers that could take other merchandise between north and south more cheaply. The development of bulk carriers in both the Baltic and the Mediterranean was, of course, related to the grain trade. Carriage of grain by road for any distance added prohibitively to its price, and yet the cities of the southern Netherlands and northern Italy had to be fed with grain grown at a great distance.

In the thirteenth century the Italians used a rather ungainly sailing ship, the *navis* or *bucius*, sometimes called a *buss* in the Mediterranean, and the Hanseatics a much smaller, but rather more efficient cog in the Baltic (ill. p. 378). Both had a greater capacity than even the largest of the great galleys, with crews tiny by comparison. The largest Hanseatic cogs could carry around 250 tons, the largest *bucius* around 800 tons. The *bucius* was useful for carrying people as well as bulky commodities. In the course of the century, in an attempt to improve its sailing abilities, a second and then a third mast were added to the *bucius*, although it still carried triangular, lateen, sails. At the

Before the middle of the fifteenth century Venice was running seven galley routes. Six were known by the principal place for which they were bound (see p. 401). Between them they covered every port of commercial importance between Trebizond and Bruges. At Corfu their routes divided. Those going east called next at Venetian colonies in Greece. The galleys of **Romania** *went to Constantinople, which was virtually all the Roman empire that survived, and often went on into the Black Sea. After Crete, the galleys of* **Alexandria** *split from those of* **Beirut**, *which put in at Rhodes and Cyprus. Those going west from Corfu next stopped in Sicily. The galleys of* **Aigues Mortes** *then called all round the north coast of the western Mediterranean, going past Aigues Mortes as far as Valencia; those going to Flanders also called in Majorca, Andalusia, Portugal and England on the way; the* **Barbary** *galleys continued on from the north African, Barbary, coast to still-Muslim Granada; and the galleys* **al trafego** *pursued a triangular route, first to Tunis, then going eastwards, carrying north African goods to Alexandria, and finally returned to Venice by way of Greece. On all routes frequent stops had to be made to take in water and food for the large crews.*

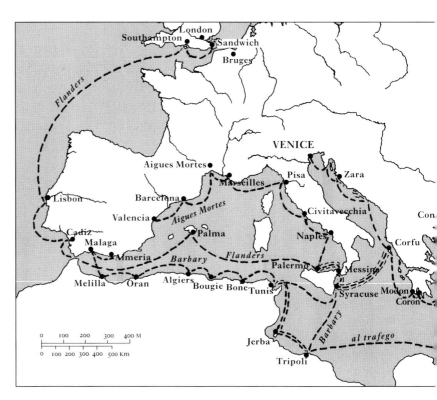

same time it was also built broader, and higher, frequently with three decks. The largest *bucius* could reputedly carry 1,000 pilgrims or 100 crusaders and their attendants, with their horses on the bottom deck.[43]

Around 1300, Hanseatic cogs began to be imitated in the Mediterranean, where they were known as *cocche*. Writing a generation later, Giovanni Villani produced an entertaining account of the change, under the year 1304: 'Certain people from Bayonne in Gascony with their ships which are called *cocche*, passed through the straits of Seville (Gibraltar), and came into our sea as pirates and did a great deal of damage. Immediately afterwards the Genoese, the Venetians and the Catalans began to sail with *cocche* and left off sailing with great *navi* to be able to sail more safely, and less expensively, and this was a great change in our shipping'.[44] Over the next century the carrack was developed in the Mediterranean. It combined the scale of the *buss* with many of the advantages of the cog. The square sails of the cogs were taken over, and stern rudders instead of huge, clumsy oars. Further new features were introduced in the fifteenth century, like the division of the sail area on each mast into two and later three smaller square sails. Not only did subdivision of the sail area give greater flexibility and control, but the smaller sails needed fewer seamen to handle them. Compared with the old *bucius*, a carrack of the same size needed half the number of crew, and the carrack could be built bigger still. The number and size of such ships developed particularly fast in the last years of the fourteenth century and the early years of the fifteenth, particularly, but not exclusively, in Genoa (ill. p. 386). Genoese carracks of 1,000 tons existed by the end of the fourteenth century, and of 2,000 tons in the fifteenth, a size not to be surpassed until the eighteenth century. It is little wonder that Venetian freight rates for bulk cargoes

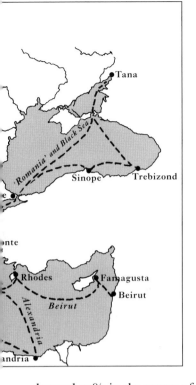

dropped 25% in the course of the fourteenth century, despite the rise in wages, and further still in the fifteenth. As well as carrying the grain of the Black Sea or North Africa back to Italy, the Venetians used their carracks for the carriage of Syrian cotton and Cretan wine, and the Genoese used theirs for alum from Asia Minor and woad from Lombardy or Toulouse, which they took to Southampton or Bruges. A very few carracks were needed to ship the 3,000 ton consignments of alum sent from Phocaea to Southampton in the fifteenth century. In the first half of the fourteenth century Pegolotti recorded that carriage to the north added some 24% to the purchase cost of alum, and 30% to the cost of woad. Less than a hundred years later, Datini only paid 8% of the cost of either for carriage.[45] Unlike galleys, which needed to put in at very frequent intervals for food and, above all, water for their enormous crews, carracks could sail for huge distances without coming into port. Even on such a long journey as that from Phocaea to Southampton they often stopped only once. From Asia Minor they sailed the length of the Mediterranean, until they put in at Málaga or Seville for fresh supplies, before setting sail for England. Although the Genoese no longer carried large numbers of pilgrims to or from the Holy Land, their carracks were still useful for carrying slaves in even larger numbers from Caffa, or Chios, or the ports of North Africa.

The author of the polemic poem *The Libelle of Englyshe Polycye*, composed in the 1430s, had good things to say of the 'Januays and her grette karrekkys' when they arrived in England, although he was very suspicious of the 'Venicyans and Florentynes with there galees'. His approval of the Genoese made him list the necessities for English manufacture that they carried:

Even after both the great galleys used for Venetian trade and the light galleys used for war had abruptly gone out of use around 1500, the shape of a galley survived into the sixteenth century for light craft, such as that depicted on the tomb of Alessandro Contarini in 1535.

...of woad grete plente,
Woll-oyle, wood-aschen by vessell in the see,
Coton, roche-alum and gode golde of Jene.

His disapproval of the Venetians and Florentines made him list the unnecessary luxuries that they brought:

Apes and japes and marmusettes taylede,
Nifles, trifles, that litell have availed,
And thynges wyth whiche they fetely blere oure eye,
Wyth thynges not endurynge that we bye.

He even proceeded to argue against the apothecaries' 'spices' that they brought, on the grounds that English herbs were just as curative:

But that a man may voyde infirmytee,
Wythoute drugges fet fro beyonde the see....
That wee shulde have no nede to skamonye,
Turbit, euforbe, correcte, diagredie,
Rubarbe, sene...

He would only concede that sugar was irreplaceable of all the things they imported. The root of his distrust of the Venetians and Florentines lay in their north-western operations being based on Bruges, since the whole poem is a one-sided attack on Flanders and all those associated with it. He therefore went on to condemn the Florentines and Venetians not only for their slow-ness in paying for the wool they bought in Calais, but also for making what he felt to be excessive profits on bills of exchange. He concluded by condemning them for taking gold out of the country. The Genoese he had already praised for bringing it in:

Than these seyde Venecians have in wone
And Florentynnes to bere here golde sone
Overe the see into Flaundes ageyne;
And thus they lyve in Flaundes, sothe to sayne.

But to what degree was there a switch from land to sea trade? The less bulky commodities like spices, whether culinary spices or apothecaries' spices, had certainly travelled overland at an earlier date, and the return cargoes of the carracks, and indeed of the galleys, often consisted of northern textiles that had also gone previously by land. As the author of the *Libelle* said of the Genoese carracks:

And they be charged wyth woll ageyne, I wene, and wollene clothe of owres of colours all [and of the Venetian and Florentine galleys]...bere hense our beste chaffare, Clothe, wolle and tynne....[46]

The first half of the fifteenth century saw the heyday of sea-borne trade, particularly in the hands of the Venetians, who had gradually extended their shipping, so that by the mid-century there was an annually repeated pattern of regular official sailings from the city, as quoted by Gino Giommini in the 1440s:

Feb. 10–15	Unarmed sailing ships to Syria
Mar. 1–15	Galleys *al trafego* to Tunis and Tripoli
Mar. 15–June 25	Galleys to Flanders
Apr. 22–May 8	Galleys to Barbary and to Aigues Mortes
July 25	Galleys to 'Romania'
July & early Aug.	Unarmed sailing ships to Syria
Aug. 24	Galleys to Beirut
Aug. 30	Galleys to Alexandria[47]

Of the seven routes travelled regularly at fixed times each year by galleys, only that to Flanders and England lay outside the Mediterranean (map p. 398). All the known galley voyages from Venice for every year from 1332 to 1534 have been separately mapped.[48] Two galley routes, to Cyprus and Armenia, and to 'Romania' and La Tana, were already being regulated in 1308, when for the first time galleys were compelled to travel in convoy.[49] Other routes were added in the course of the fourteenth century, but some of the regular Venetian galley services were new in the fifteenth century itself. Venetian galleys first came to Aigues Mortes in 1401, and only regularly did so from 1412. The Aigues Mortes galleys also called at Valencia from 1436, as the Venetians thrust themselves more and more into the traditionally Genoese–Catalan western Mediterranean. It is at first sight a little surprising that not only did carracks continue to sail to Marseilles, but that this new galley route to Aigues Mortes should be opened up after the papacy had removed from Avignon. However there was still the Angevin court at Taras-con on the Rhône itself, and pepper, ginger, sugar, and other spices supplied to the mouth of the Rhône were increasingly carried onwards to the fairs at Geneva, and later Lyon, and thence to the French court, which was to be found on the Loire after the 1420s. As well as considerable quantities of grain and salt from the salt marshes along the coast, Marseilles and the ports of southern France exported honey, wool, the cheap woollen cloths and linens and the rough hempen canvas made in the middle Rhône valley, in Bresse and up the Saône valley as far as Macon and the Charollais.[50] This canvas was also sold at the Lyon fairs.

The Venetian state tried to insist that certain of the most valuable commodities, such as spices, be only carried in its armed 'great galleys', a necessary provision to keep the service running. The galleys themselves belonged to the state, but were run by small shipping companies which leased them from the state.[51] Venice was in a strong position to make such a requirement in the fifteenth century, for in the course of the century the import of spices into Europe was increasingly restricted to Venetian purchasers in Alexandria and Beirut. It was a trade from which the Genoese and Catalans were gradually being excluded, and into which the Florentines and the French failed to make considerable inroads.[54] The carriage of Jerusalem-bound pilgrims to Jaffa also became a Venetian monopoly, and two, or occasionally three, specially appointed pilgrim galleys set out each year from Venice from the late fourteenth century to the early sixteenth.

In the middle of the fourteenth century the Venetians had extended their regulation of galleys to round ships as well, which they also organized into *mude*, regulated convoys, with fixed dates for loading and departure. Unlike the galleys, however, the control of *cocche* did not progress from official regulation to state-ownership. The regulated convoys of *cocche* that they sent annually to Crete and twice yearly to Syria were known from the principal commodities that they brought back, wine and cotton, as the *muda vendemian* and the *muda gotonorum*. The 'Syrian' ships could also, of course, pick up other goods, like sugar in Cyprus, on the way back.[52]

As well as the Venetian galleys and carracks, and the Genoese carracks, sea trade was opening up in other hands. When Florence acquired the city and territory of Pisa in 1405, Porto Pisano remained in Genoese hands for a further twenty years. It was only in 1421 that Florence eventually came to possess its own port. Once it had done so, the Florentine state built a fresh Arsenal on the Arno downstream from Pisa and began to run its own galley fleets from Porto Pisano in the 1430s, not only to Alexandria, but also to England and Flanders. It was a self-conscious revival of the Pisan fleets of two centuries before, carried out in emulation of the Venetian fleets. The Florentine galleys too only carried the highest priced luxuries.[53] In the 1430s the anonymous author of *The Libelle of Englyshe Polycye* commented on those coming to England:

> The grete galees of Venees and Florence
> Be wel ladene with thynges of complacence,
> All spicerye and other grocers ware,
> Wyth swete wynes, all manere of chaffare....

As well as the new Florentine galleys, there were also, occasionally, galleys based in southern France. In the 1420s there was a single 'galley of Narbonne' which traded to Beirut and Alexandria until it was shipwrecked off Corsica in 1432. Between 1444 and his fall in 1451, Jacques Coeur, the French entrepreneur par excellence, ran up to four 'galleys of France' to Alexandria, variously based in Montpellier, Marseilles and Aigues Mortes. Not surprisingly, they aroused violent antipathy in Genoa, whose merchants felt threatened by such enterprise. On one occasion the Genoese seized the galleys in the port of Aigues Mortes itself.[54] After the fall of Jacques Coeur, his galleys were sold in 1454 to a merchant of Montpellier, and the tradition of small numbers of ships going from southern France to the Levant continued with the building of new galleys in 1464.[55] They enjoyed royal protection. Louis XI attempted to give a spice monopoly to the shippers of his own ports, and prohibit foreigners from bringing spices into his kingdom, but the Venetians, Genoese and Florentines continued to bring in pepper, ginger and sugar. They did so by using Marseilles, which was then not yet in France. Besides Jacques Coeur's galleys, there were other local ships based at Aigues Mortes, Montpellier and Marseilles, although they were far from as numerous or as large as those based in Genoa.

Catalan shipping was enormously important not only in the western Mediterranean, but also outside it. As we have seen, Professor Mellis found that the combined fleets of Barcelona, Valencia and Majorca in the period around 1400 numbered something like 875 vessels, though they were smaller than those used by the Italian ports. He found none of the new large 1,000 ton carracks in Catalan service. Catalan shipping was certainly not confined to the Mediterranean, for he found nearly 50 Catalan boats that had sailed to the North Sea in this period.[56]

Northern Spain also had its own shipping. These were the boats of the Biscay coast that were the principal carriers of Castilian wool, local iron, and Gascon wine to the Low Countries and to England (see pp. 294, 324 and 330). These northern Spanish boats were built on the same sort of scale as those from Catalonia and did nothing to rival the larger Genoese bulk carriers. They were one of the most significant segments of the growing amount of shipping at the end of the Middle Ages from Atlantic ports. Other growing Atlantic shipping ports could be found from Portugal northwards to the mouth of the Loire, Brittany, England and Scotland. These Atlantic based boats did not yet enter the Mediterranean, which was still dominated by north Italians and Catalans, or the Baltic, still dominated by the Hanse, but they did compete with Italian, Catalan and Hanseatic shipping on equal terms from the Straits of Gibraltar to the Danish Sound (Øresund). Much of their trade was focussed on Bruges, where, like the various Italian nations, the Catalans and the Hanseatics, they maintained consulates.

The picture normally painted of Bruges is of a passive port, lacking its own shipping. This was a view to which the Castilian nobleman Pero Tafur subscribed after he had visited Bruges in 1438. He wrote:

> It is said that two cities compete with each other for commercial supremacy, Bruges in Flanders in the West and Venice in the East. It

Two Spanish ships. In order to unload a ship not at a proper harbour, it was necessary for it to stand out to sea, and for the cargo to be brought in little by little in a rowing boat, as in the manuscript illustration on the left prepared for Alfonso X 'the Wise', King of Castile 1252–84. The boat is a cog, as used on the Biscay coast. Some dramatic, but now forgotten, story lies behind the model of a Mediterranean carrack on the right. It was left as a votive offering in a Catalan monastery around 1450 in gratitude for rescue from shipwreck.

seems to me, however, and many agree with my opinion, that there is much more commercial activity in Bruges than in Venice. The reason is as follows…thither repair all the nations of the world and they say that at times the number of ships sailing from the harbour at Bruges exceeds seven hundred a day. In Venice, on the contrary, be it never so rich, the only persons engaged in the trade are the inhabitants.[57]

Writing at almost the same time the author of the *Libelle* wrote of the Brabant fairs at Antwerp and Bergen op Zoom:

To whyche martis, that Englissh men call feyres,
Iche nacion ofte maketh here repayeres
Englysshe and Frensh, Lumbardes, Januayes,
Cathálones, theder they take here wayes;
Scottes, Spaynardes, Iresshmen there abydes,
Which grete plente bringen of salte hydes.[58]

The passive nature of the permanent market at Bruges and the dependent fairs in Brabant can be exaggerated. Although Flemish participation in the cross-Channel trade with England diminished when northern Italians arrived in the thirteenth century, it did not vanish. In the second half of the fourteenth century Flemish ships were still carrying English wool out of London, besides the new and growing trade in coal from Newcastle. There was an expansion of shipping from Flanders, Zeland and Brabant to France, Castile and Portugal in the fourteenth century, and even more in the fifteenth. Flemish shippers, as well as Bretons and Biscay shippers, brought back grain from Normandy, wine from the La Rochelle and Bordeaux, salt from Bourgneuf and a wide variety of goods from Bayonne, Biarritz and other Castilian ports. By the second half of the fifteenth century Flemish merchants were to be found in most major towns of the Iberian peninsula.[59] Furthermore, by the 1430s Netherlands shippers from the outports of Bruges and Antwerp, particularly from Walcheren in Zeeland, and from Holland, were again beginning to take an increasing share in north-western Europe's sea-borne trade.[60] The two 'galleys of Burgundy', run for the Burgundian state by the Medici company of Bruges, were far from the only merchantmen based in the Netherlands.

At the same time that Atlantic shipping was growing, Mediterranean-based sea-borne trade was shrinking, and by the end of the fifteenth century was in full retreat. The second half of the fifteenth century, and the first years of the sixteenth, saw the decline in shipbuilding in Venice and the unravelling of the web of Venetian galley routes. The last galleys to the Black Sea rowed out in 1452, the last to Aigues Mortes in 1508, and in 1533 the last galleys set out both to the Barbary coast and Lisbon and to Flanders and England.[61] Thereafter any remaining import of wool from England was left to overland wagoners and carracks. Within Europe itself overland trade had come into its own again, combined with oceanic trade beyond the confines of Europe.

Once sea routes had become practical, the difference in cost was, by itself, enough to account for the transfer of much trade from overland routes to sea routes. The transport of bulky goods became economically possible, but even on higher priced goods there could be some cost advantage. The figures noted down by Francesco Pegolotti around 1336 for the costs of bringing English wool to Italy, by way of Libourne on the Dordogne and Aigues Mortes, indicate the extraordinary difference in cost between land and sea journeys. The costs of carriage of a sack of wool from London to Libourne, in a returning wine boat, came to about one Florentine gold florin, including customs on the Gironde. The costs per sack of transport overland, from unloading the ship at Libourne to loading the galley at Aigues Mortes came to about eight gold florins. The distances involved make the point even more clearly. Libourne is some 500 miles (800 km) due south of London, but the sea journey, around Kent and Brittany, was probably nearly double that. The overland journey from Libourne to Aigues Mortes is some 300 miles (480 km) as the crow flies, but probably nearer 400 miles as the mule trod. The cost was therefore around eight times as much for under half the distance.[62]

A hundred years later the cost of carrying a *cantar* of Lombard woad from Voghera, on the Po opposite Pavia, to Genoa, by mule over the Bocchetta pass, a distance of just over 100 km (around 65 miles) cost ten Genoese *soldi*. Carrying the same woad onwards in a carrack from Genoa to Southampton or Sandwich cost exactly the same, although it was a distance of 4,000 km (2,500 miles). Carriage across the Alps from Asti to Geneva cost 45 Genoese *soldi* per *cantar*, which, bizarrely, meant that it was more than twice as expensive to transport woad from Lombardy to a fair at Geneva as to an English port.[63]

However, even 'cheap' sea transport was 'expensive' for some commodities. At the end of the thirteenth century, shipping from Palermo to Pisa, a distance of about 400 miles (650 kilometres) only added 7% to the cost of cotton or rugs. However it added 39% to the cost of grain. This sort of trans-

Naval warfare developed rapidly around 1500, and a broadside from the new sixteenth-century English man-of-war, with cannon near the water-line, was very destructive. England's growing commercial and naval power went hand in hand. Merchant and royal ships were sometimes interchangeable. Which role were these three vessels performing in Dover harbour late in the reign of Henry VIII (died 1547)?

port cost made trade in grain worthwhile only when there was a huge differential in grain prices between the areas of production and the cities of consumption. It is little wonder that, except in years of exceptional dearth, Europe remained divided into two separate zones as far as the grain trade was concerned, and remained so until the effects of cheapening transport costs in the seventeenth century were felt.[64]

Another, and perhaps more surprising, advantage of some sorts of sea transport was speed, for sea transport need not be slower than land transport. Indeed it was frequently quicker. Galleys in particular were fast. In the 1270s Pisan galleys were reputed to be capable of 100 miles (160 km) a day. Just over a century later, the Datini correspondents enable us to be a great deal more precise. Letters entrusted to ship captains in Alexandria, Beirut or Constantinople were normally delivered to the Datini firm's Pisa office some 1,600 miles (2,500 km) away in 32 to 51 days. Letters from Bruges, only half the distance away, sent overland by the regular commercial courier system, the *scarsalla fiorentina* (the Florence bag) or the *scarsella lucchese* (the Lucca bag), normally took 26 to 30 days to reach Pisa. Sometimes letters from the eastern Mediterranean reached the Datini firm in Pisa quicker than those from Flanders. If even professional couriers who rode regularly between Tuscany and Flanders were slower than ships, carriers of goods were yet slower still, with their combinations of pack animals, wagons and river or lake boats.[65]

There is therefore no problem in understanding why shipping by sea, where appropriate, so largely replaced carriage by land by the mid-fourteenth century. Land transport for higher priced goods did not cease, and even at the end of the century, careful consideration had to be given to the choice between land and sea. In 1397–98, an Italian merchant at Bruges reported that the charges for sending a high quality woollen broadcloth from Wervik, worth 23 francs, to Barcelona were 5 francs by land and 3½ francs by sea. However, this difference in carriage charges was not the sole determinant of the choice of whether to use land or sea transport. Toll charges on roads and customs dues in ports had to be added into the equation, and rapidly varying conditions of security, caused by brigandage by land and piracy by sea had also to be taken into consideration.[66]

There is, however, some difficulty in understanding why carriage by land should have recovered so noticeably in the second half of the fifteenth century. The reduction in the costs of carriage by land, for example by using wagons rather than pack animals on the Brenner pass, although noticeable, cannot in itself provide an adequate solution, for the costs of shipping were also dropping at the same time. The costs of bringing cotton from Syria to Venice, for example, dropped by 50% in the course of the fifteenth century. Cost and speed were in favour of the sea. Safety, however, was a very changeable factor.

Sea voyages were always more at risk of the weather than land voyages, but it was human rather than natural interference that was crucial. Shipwreck and piracy could both be insured against, but the activities of known pirates on a route also had a secondary deterrent effect in increased premiums.

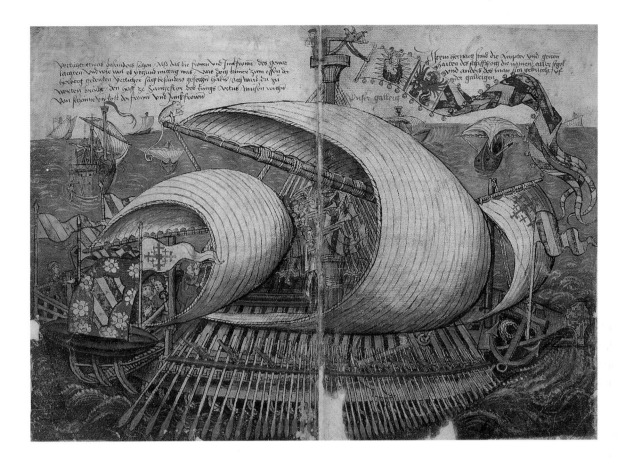

In the second half of the fifteenth century land travel became much safer. The long wars in France ended in 1453 and the new royal standing army meant that this peace did not bring about the wave of disorder from 'free' companies of unemployed soldiers that had come about after the earlier treaties and truces in the 1360s, 1380s and 1430s. The wars in Italy equally ended in 1454, and there too the existence of standing armies meant that *condottiere* were not able to devastate the countryside and impede trade as they had done in earlier periods of truce and demobilization from the 1320s onwards. Even southern and western Germany were increasingly pacified.

On the other hand, travel by sea, particularly in the Mediterranean, became increasingly unsafe. Galleys, although being used less and less for trade, continued to be used for military purposes in the increasingly bitter wars between Muslim and Christian. The Genoese, having largely been ousted from Syrian and Egyptian trades by their Venetian competitors, had no compunction about attacking Muslims in the eastern Mediterranean, whilst on the other hand the Ottoman advance was also accompanied by anti-Christian piracy. In the western Mediterranean the corsairs from the Barbary coast, already based on Algiers, repeatedly attacked Christian shipping, whilst Spanish, and later French, corsairs retaliated. The eastern and western ends of the Mediterranean were, of course, not unconnected. When a Genoese pirate enslaved some Muslims in Syria, the Genoese community in Málaga was victimized by way of reprisal in 1452.

From 1479 to 1494 Agostino Contarini, a notorious patrician profiteer, overcharged pilgrims to Jerusalem on one of the two regular galleys from Venice to Jaffa, 'La Contarina', vividly sketched here by a pilgrim in 1486. Much to the discomfort of his passengers, he then loaded all sorts of goods on the return journey: Syrian cotton at Jaffa; salt and carob beans in Cyprus and malmsey in Crete.

Initially both the large Genoese and Venetian carracks, and the Venetian merchant galleys, all of which carried considerable complements of cross-bowmen, were more or less immune to piratical attacks. Gradually, however, Genoese and eventually even Venetian trade was crippled by piracy.[67] It was of little avail that sea routes were noticeably cheaper and quicker, if the cargo was not likely to arrive.

As well as the negative push of piracy which crippled sea trade, there was also the positive pull of south German merchant capitalism which revived land trade. The rising economic weight of Swabia and Franconia with their new industries, linens, fustians, arms, armour, brass wares, glass, pottery and paper, their control of iron, copper, tin and precious metal mining and processing, their traditional links to Venice and Milan, their newer links to Brabant and Flanders, and to the French court, all combined to revive land trade in south German hands. They adopted and improved on the business techniques of the Italians, for example the combination of capital in companies with multiple shareholders for mining as well as for trade, they enjoyed the availability of capital at lower rates of interest than anywhere else. As Mediterranean trade became increasingly difficult, the south Germans shifted the principal focus of their operations from the road to Venice, to the road to Antwerp. As a consequence, early in the sixteenth century Antwerp came to replace Venice, not only in the distribution of spices and the refining of sugar, but also in the marketing of copper, and in printing for a Europe-wide market. Individual Genoese gained greatly from the new trades with Africa, and at the end of the century with Asia, but it was above all Antwerp and the south German cities that benefited most.

Main themes   Some of the main themes that have come out in writing this book have already been noted more than once.

The so-called 'commercial revolution' of the thirteenth century, described in Chapter 1, with the advances in commercial techniques and organization, has largely been taken for granted in the rest of the book. None of these advances were lost in the long 'depression' of the late fourteenth and early fifteenth centuries. Indeed some additional innovations were introduced, like marine insurance and the holding company. Furthermore these forms of commercial organization were included in the north Italian inheritance of the south German commercial and industrial firms of the fifteenth century. From then on they were no longer a peculiarly north Italian preserve, but becoming part of the common European way of doing things. At Burgos in northern Castile, business houses adopted north Italian models of company structure in the fifteenth century, although it is not clear whether they were copied direct from Italy or by way of Bruges, along with the use of bills of exchange by the 1420s, local banking and double-entry bookkeeping by the 1460s, and marine insurance by the 1480s.[68] A theme emphasized in the second chapter, on courts and capitals, was the importance of the consumer. The emphasis of economic historians and economists looking at the past century or more has been on production, distribution and supply. However it

At the end of most commerce was small-scale retail trade. Four petty chapmen have been sketched into a design for an armorial window at Berne. The figure on the right is staggering under a load of linen, the man on the left is selling cooked food from a brazier, and the man in the centre has a tray of knick-knacks to offer.

is much more evident in the pre-industrial world that the consumer was king, that it was demand that mattered rather than supply. The whims of fashion were created in and by those in court circles, not by skilful advertising. The merchant had to meet the wishes of the customer, the wholesaler those of the retailer, the importer those of the distributor, the manufacturer those of the exporter. Another stage in this theme recurred in the chapter on trade in manufactured goods, in which it became apparent how much manufacture was dependent on trade, and how much those trading in distantly-made goods sought to have imitations made under their own hands, whether they were Florentines having Flemish-style woollen cloths made in Florence for Mediterranean markets; Lucchese having Damascus-style silk cloth made in Lucca; Venetians having Syrian-style glass made in Venice for the whole western European market; or Nuremberg merchants having Milan-style armour made in Nuremberg for north European markets. Import substitution, both for home markets and for re-export, was a corollary of developed trade.

The chapters on the roads to Tuscany (Chapter 3) and on helps and hindrances to trade (Chapter 4) emphasized the way that late medieval commerce was assisted by developments in infrastructure. The most visible of these were the deliberate bridge- and road-building programmes, which, with the opening of passes and improvements in river navigation, made the movement of men and goods increasingly easy and rapid, and considerably cheaper, if not yet cheap. Rulers and others in positions of authority, whether nobles or towns, were also seeing, generally self-interestedly, that wharves and warehouses, trade halls, exchange-places and fairs were available. Of course, they all had to be paid for by their users. Other helpful developments in infrastructure, like the growth in literacy and numeracy, have scarcely been touched on, although the widespread ability to read and to reckon was a necessary pre-requisite for the successful implantation of large-scale trade and industry, whether in fourteenth-century Tuscany and Lombardy, fifteenth-century Swabia and Franconia, sixteenth-century Brabant and Flanders, seventeenth-century Holland and Zeeland, or eighteenth-century England and lowland Scotland. In each period the cities that did most to promote education, like fourteenth-century Lucca, gained correspondingly commercially.

The chapter on foodstuffs and raw materials (Chapter 6) emphasized the importance of the bulk trades as well as the rich trades for north Italian merchants in the later Middle Ages, just as it was to be for Dutch merchants in the early modern period. Indeed many of the themes touched on in this volume as characteristic of later medieval Europe turn out to be characteristic of early modern Europe as well. The actors may have changed, but the text of the play they were performing, although translated, was hardly rewritten from the 'commercial revolution' of the long thirteenth century to the 'industrial revolution' of the eighteenth and nineteenth centuries.

Although in the Middle Ages direct commercial relations with the non-European world were limited in scope and time to the period of the 'Mongol peace', it is clear that the trade of Europe, even the most local, was part of a much wider pattern of trade, as it continued to be in the early modern period, when much stronger direct links were forged, incorporating western and central Europe with the other great centres of human population and activity, focused on northern India and northern China. Until industrialization, Europeans bought much more from other parts of the world than they sold to them, and the secular imbalance of trade meant that the supply of precious metals, acceptable for payment of such adverse balances, was a crucial part of the economy. The continual output of successive mines of silver and gold, either within Europe, or under European control elsewhere, was an essential element in world trade both in the later Middle Ages and the early modern period.

What has not been touched on fully is the way in which ideas as well as goods travelled along the routes of trade. The transmission of the cultivation of sugar from India and of mulberries and silkworms from China has been touched on, but not the basic technology of gunpowder and printing, which came to Europe along trade routes from Asia as much as tapestry-and carpet-weaving. Admittedly when gunpowder and printing arrived in Europe they were both transformed. Black powder was used for gunnery rather than entertainment, and printing was developed from the page-sized blocks suitable for a culture with ideograms which used 2,000 basic characters and many thousands more less basic ones, to moveable type appropriate to a culture with phonetic writing, which used a mere 26 characters repeated in endless combinations. The technology of the western style of printing was itself disseminated within Europe along the routes of trade, just as the printed books themselves became items of continent-wide commerce. More ideas than technological ones could travel along the routes of trade. The dissemination of some sorts of religious belief appears to have done so. The Bogomil dualism of the Balkans, with roots in the Byzantine Empire and perhaps farther east still, was transmitted to the Patarini of northern Italy, particularly around Milan, and then across the Alpine passes to the Cathars of the Rhineland and Champagne and to the Albigenses of Languedoc. The Waldensianism of the Rhône valley crossed the Alpine passes from west to east, and was also carried north-eastward along the great Swiss valley between the Alps and the Jura, to southern Germany and even Bohemia. Later, in the sixteenth century, the 'new heresies' similarly ran along trade routes, both old and new. English sailors out of Hull, carrying home a cargo of grain across the North Sea, picked up Lutheran ideas as well in Bremen. The 'Christian Bretheren' imported forbidden Lutheran texts concealed in rolls of cloth. Later, Hendrick Niklaas' works for the Family of Love similarly travelled outwards from Antwerp hidden in rolls of fustian and say.

Within Europe too, 'plague', like 'technology' and 'heresy' was carried along the routes of trade. Elizabeth Carpentier's dated mapping of the first wave of bubonic plague, at the end of the 1340s, revealed not only the accuracy of Matteo Villani's description of the way that it reached Italy from the steppe route across Asia, but has also shown how its movement around Europe followed the routes of trade within the continent, ending up with the Hanseatic routes into northern Russia. Mapping later waves of plague has shown how successive epidemics continued to be disseminated about late fourteenth- and early fifteenth-century Europe along the routes of trade.

As well as 'technology', 'heresy' and 'plague', 'art' also travelled. Works of art were carried, like books, as items of commerce. In addition, innovations in style, as well as in technique, stimulated further innovation in other places. Artists themselves were called upon to travel long distances from time to time. Italians abroad, not only merchants like Tommaso Portinari in Bruges, but noblemen as well, like Francesco d'Este at the Burgundian court, employed native artists and sent their works home. It was little wonder that Bartolomeo Fazio, secretary to Alfonso V, writing on painters in Naples in 1456, should number Jan van Eyck and Rogier van der Weyden amongst the painters with most influence on the Italian art of his own, early Renaissance, day. Fazio reports the meeting of Rogier van der Weyden with Gentile da Fabriano when Rogier came to Rome in the Holy Year of 1450.[69]

Late medieval, and in continuity with it, Early Modern European trade, thus involved not only the supply of everyday necessities, grain, wine, salt, timber, and that of luxuries, furs, saffron, pearls, silks, but also the dissemination of crops, technology, ideas, heresy, style and even less desirable commodities, like the plague bacillus.

After Constantinople fell in 1453 regular sailings of Venetian galleys to Tana and Trebizond ceased. Genoese continued trading in the Black Sea longer, until they lost Kaffa, their last colony, in 1475. When west European merchants could no longer trade directly in the Black Sea, the Ottoman Sultan encouraged his subjects to take their place. Not only Turks, but also Armenians, Jews and, above all, Greeks, did so, many based in Istanbul. This silver repoussé icon cover shows some Greek successors to the Italians and one of their ships.

Notes to the text · Bibliography
Sources of illustrations
Index

Notes to the text

Chapter 1: The transformation of trade, pp. 12–59

1. Allen, 'The Volume', Mayhew, 'Population'.
2. Ashtor, *Levant Trade*, pp. 551–5.
3. Fernandez-Armesto, *Before Columbus*, pp. 134–48.
4. And also the merchants of Lucca, Milan, Catalonia, Portugal, Castile, Biscay, La Rochelle, Brittany, and Scotland besides the Hanse. de Roover, *Money*, pp. 9–28; van Houtte, *Bruges*, pp. 54–67.
5. van Houtte, *Bruges*, pp. 63–4; de Roover, *The Rise*, p. 300.
6. Abulafia, *A Mediterranean Emporium*, pp. 78–91.
7. Pullan, *Rich*, pp. 476–509.
8. de Roover, 'The Commercial Revolution'. He expressed this insight more fully in his chapter on 'The Organisation of Trade'. It has since become part of the stock-in-trade of medieval economic historians, although the specific role of the money supply in the transformation has not been explored until now.
9. Some of the matter in this section also appears in my 'Access to Credit', which deals with the whole period from the late twelfth century to the early eighteenth.
10. Sapori, *La crisi*, pp. 227–51.
11. de Roover, *The Rise*, pp. 194–224.
12. Lutz, *Die rechtliche Struktur*, pp. 210–11.
13. Braudel, *Civilization*, ii, pp. 436–7.
14. For multi-branched companies in Pistoia, see Herlihy, *Medieval…Pistoia*, pp. 165–6.
15. A former student of mine, Dr Clare Howard, is at present engaged in a study of the early Cerchi and hopes to be able to publish an article on them, and for the Velluti see Davidsohn, *Storia di Firenze*, vi, p.379.
16. Sapori (ed.), *I libri degli Alberti*; Melis, 'Le società'.
17. Berlow, 'Development', p. 21.
18. Melis, 'Intensità'.
19. Hyde, 'Some Uses', pp. 118–9.
20. Hyde, 'The Role', pp. 238–9.
21. Uzzano, 'La pratica' Chapter 10, more easily accessible in Spufford, *Handbook*, pp. 320–1.
22. Brucker (ed.), *Two Memoirs*, p. 49.
23. Melis, 'Intensità'.
24. Hitzer, *Der Straße*, pp. 169–76.
25. *Dispatches*, ed. Kendall and Ilardi. In 1497 the Milanese ambassador to Henry VII wrote to his Duke recommending how he communicate with London: '…the Genoa letter-bag will be of good use, but get more such Florentine merchants as are in your confidence, as their correspondence passes through France without impediment and is but little searched'. Quoted by Beale, *A History*, p. 160.
26. Wiesflecker, *Kaiser Maximilian I*, v, pp. 293–4.
27. McCusker and Gravesteijn, *The Beginnings*.
28. Pacioli, *Summa*. Section 'De Scripturis'; de Roover, 'The development'; Yamey (ed.), *Double Entry Bookkeeping*.
29. Van Egmond, *Practical Mathematics*.
30. Margaret Spufford, 'Literacy'.
31. Grendler, *Schooling*, pp. 74–8.

32. Spufford, 'Spätmittelalterliche Kaufmannsnotizbücher'.
33. Edler de Roover, 'Early Examples'
34. Zeno (ed.), *Documenti*.
35. Stefani (ed.), *Insurance*.
36. de Roover, *The Rise*.
37. del Treppo, *Els Mercaders Catalans*, pp. 339–428.
38. de Roover, *L'Evolution*, and numerous other writings, the most important collected in *Business*. Most, but far from all, the exchange rates collected in Spufford, *Handbook*, fall within the geographical area outlined above. As late as 1491 exchanges from Genoa were still confined within this area, except for exchanges with the Genoese colony on Chios. Giandomenico Dormio in Airaldi and Marcenaro (eds), *Credito*, p. 118.
39. Renouard, *Les Relations*.
40. According to the Florentine Giovanni Villani, *Nuova Cronica*, bk. xi, cap. xcii, presumably relying on news in business letters sent to Florence. Porta edition, ii, pp. 635–6.
41. Sapori, 'Gli Italiani in Polonia fino a tutto il quattrocento', *Studi*, iii, pp. 149–76.
42. Ashtor, 'Banking Instruments', pp. 572–3.
43. de Roover, 'New Interpretations'; Spufford, *Money*, pp. 254–9.
44. Ashtor, 'Banking Instruments', pp. 554–5.
45. Spallanzani, 'A Note'.
46. de Roover, *Money*, pp. 171–344. For some examples of banking at Bruges, see p. 206.
47. Lane, 'Venetian Bankers 1496–1533' (1937) collected in *Venice and History*, pp. 69–86.
48. Usher, *The Early History*, i, pp. 239–42.
49. '*ne puisse tenir table ne banc pour recevoir l'argent des marchans et faire leurs paiemens*'. Mint Ordinance 12 October 1433, article 11.
50. Van der Wee (ed.), *La banque.*
51. Spufford, 'Access to Credit', pp. 320–2.
52. Gilchrist, *The Church*. I have largely followed Gilchrist, but ???
53. Spufford, 'Access to Credit', pp. 317–9
54. Gilchrist, *The Church*.
55. Luzzatto, 'Tasso d'interesse'.
56. Brucker (ed.), *Two Memoirs*, p. 25.
57. Lopez and Raymond, *Medieval Trade*, pp. 355–8, 281–9.
58. Nightingale, *A Medieval Mercantile Community*, passim.
59. In 1299 Jan I made Dordrecht the compulsory '*marct van allen coepwaerlichen ghoede dat de Marwe of de Lecke nedercomt*'. In 1338 Willem IV added a '*Maasrecht*' by which all ships coming into the Meuse from the sea had to offer their goods at Dordrecht. When Willem V renewed the privilege in 1355 he made it quite explicit that it covered all goods going upstream as well as downstream on the '*Rijn, de Marwe, de Waal, die Ysel, die Lecke ende die Merwede*'. Klein, *De Trippen*, p. 46.
60. Verlinden, 'Markets', pp. 126–53.
61. Epstein, 'Regional Fairs'. He has recently expanded this argument in Epstein, *Freedom*.
62. Dubois, *Les Foires de Chalon*. The change from Geneva to Lyon was by no means straightforward. It depended on the attitudes of successive kings of France. In 1462 Louis XI favoured Lyon and forbad Frenchmen to go to Geneva. In 1466 he allied with Savoy and

permitted them to go to Geneva. In 1467 he sold the monopoly back to Lyon. In 1471 he favoured watermen and forbad the import of spices overland through Savoy to Lyon. In 1476 he permitted overland trade. In 1484 Charles VIII closed the Lyon fairs. In 1487 he re-opened two of them. In this case commerce was altogether vulnerable to the priorities of international relations. Blockmans, 'Voracious States', p. 236.
63. The towns of origin of those recorded as renting stalls at the Lendit fair in the late fourteenth century are mapped and discussed in relation to the *Dit du Lendit* in Favier, 'Une ville', pp. 1260–2.
64. Schneidmüller, 'Die Frankfurter Messen'.
65. Blockmans, 'Das westeuropäische Messenetz'; Blockmans, 'Aux origines des foires d'Anvers'.
66. Tafur, *Travels*, pp. 203–4.
67. Most, but not all, of the nations at Bruges transferred to Antwerp in 1488–9, returned to Bruges in the 1490s, and finally moved to Antwerp, to remain there, in the years around 1510. Goris, *Etude*, pp. 25–80. Voet, *Antwerp*, pp. 249–72.
68. Denuce, 'De Beurs van Antwerpen'; Materné, 'Schoon'.
69. Riu, 'Banking', pp. 136, 148–9; Mueller, *The Venetian Money Market*, pp. 37–40.
70. Braudel, *Civilization*, ii, pp. 97–100; Nicholas, *Metamorphosis* discusses the brokers of Ghent at some length, but does not indicate that they had any single regular meeting place.
71. '*hoe dat de plaetze van den borsen, in de Wolstrate gestaen (midts der menichvuldigheyt der coopluyden der voors. stadt ende borse hanterernde meer dan in vorleden tyden) te cleyn was*'.
72. '*dat de selve borsse is ende leeght inde bequemste plaetse daerse ter commoditeyt van de coopman soude moegen liggen te weten in de binnenstadt ende opt hoochste van Antwerpen bijder kercken, by der merckt, by den stadhuys, by de wage, by de panden…ende niet verre vand water*'.
73. '*want die coopman liever hadde datse naerder den water lage gelyck die borsse in andere groote coopsteden liggen, als tot Venegien, te Jennes, Naples, Palerme, Lyons ende principalick te Brugghe*'. All three quotations are from documents printed by Denuce in 'De Beurs van Antwerpen'.
74. Saunders (ed.), *The Royal Exchange*; Spufford, 'Access to Credit', pp. 303–37.
75. Ricci, *Il Manuale di Mercatura*.
76. Canal, *Zibaldone*.
77. [Bona], *La 'Pratica di Mercatura'*.
78 Spufford, 'Spätmittelalterliche Kaufmannsnotizbücher'; Denzel, 'Kaufmannshandbücher'.
79. *El Libro di Mercantie*, ed. Borlandi.
80. Pegolotti, *La pratica della mercatura*.
81. Lane, *Venice: A Maritime Republic*, pp. 119–21.
82. Fernandez-Armesto, *Before Columbus*, pp. 246 and 159.
83. Abulafia, *A Mediterranean Emporium*, pp. 204–5; Campbell, 'Portolan Charts'.
84. Melis, *I trasporti*.
85. Frearson, *The English Corantos*, pp. 30–40.

86. Krüger, *Das Älteste Deutsche Routenhandbuch*.
87. Ghent Univ MS 13, described by Derolez, *The Library*, printed as 'Itinéraire de Bruges'. Sections of this road book have been used repeatedly, e.g. Chapter 3, pp. 140–1, 149, 156, 159, 163, 165, 171 and Chapter 4, pp. 200–1, 207, 210, 216.
88. Harvey, *Medieval Maps*.
89. The information on Benci and Sassetti has been derived from de Roover, *The Rise*.
90. Spufford, 'The Role of Entrepreneurs'.
91. Davidsohn, *Storia di Firenze*, vi, 628–9 (1896–1927), Italian trans. 1956–68, vi, 628–9.

Chapter 2: Courts and consumers, pp. 60–139

1. Botero, *A Treatise*.
2. The main theme of this chapter is a greatly extended version of the argument I first put forward in Spufford, 'La rôle', pp. 355, 362–73, and repeated in Spufford, *Money*, pp. 240–51.
3. Lyon, *From Fief*.
4. Duby, *Le Dimanche*, p. 39.
5. Strayer, *On the Medieval Origins*.
6. Spufford, 'The Role'.
7. Fossier, *La Terre*.
8. Britnell, in his *Commercialisation*, pp. 79–151, spells out the complexity of the transition in one country.
9. Partially brought together by Renouard, *Les relations*, pp. 36–7.
10. Henneman, *Royal Taxation*, pp. 347–53.
11. Abulafia, *Western Mediterranean Kingdoms* quotes Pryor, 'Foreign Policy', as having estimated the income of Robert's grandfather Charles I, at 1,100,000 florins before the kingdom was split. In Robert's time the island of Sicily was a separate kingdom ruled by Frederick II of Aragon (1296–1337). I have no figures for his income, but two generations later his granddaughter Maria, and her husband Martin, had an income from the island in 1400 of only 90,000 florins. The crown had in the meanwhile become increasingly impoverished.
12. Villani, Giovanni, *Nuova Cronica*, bk. xii, cap. xcii.
13. In 1312 the *cortes* estimated that the young Alfonso XI needed a regular income of around 480,000 Florentine florins. The earliest Castilian royal income of which I am aware is that inherited by the young Juan II in 1406. It was by then around 990,000 florins, despite the lavish gifts made by his grandfather, Henry of Trastamara, to his allies in the civil war.
14. Favier, *Philippe*, pp. 60–64.
15. Favier, *Un conseiller*.
16. Favier, *Paris*, pp. 104–5.
17. Dunbabin, *Charles I*, pp. 70–76, 188–9, 210–11 and Runciman, *Sicilian Vespers*, pp. 126–8, 181–2.
18. Colvin (ed.), *History*, i, pp. 491–52 and Plan III.
19. In the first wave of plague in 1348, 93 people died out of the 654 in the papal palace of Clement VI. The 654 were made up of 55 in the personal entourage of the pope, a guard of honour of 207, 311 administrators in various departments, and 81 servants to look after all the rest. Guillemain, *La Cour pontificale*.
20. Deviosse, *Jean*, pp. 175–7.
21. Martindale, in 'Venetian Sala', compares

the Venetian frescoes with contemporary frescoes at Avignon, Paris, Westminster and Karlstejn.
22. Favier, *Paris*.
23. Honeybourne, *Sketch Map*; Barron, 'Later Middle Ages', pp. 49–51; Schofield, *Medieval London Houses*, pp. 3 and 6; Carlin, 'Reconstruction'.
24. Barron, 'Centres', pp. 1–16; Schofield, *Medieval London Houses*
25. Léonard, *Les Angevins*.
26. There was an identical myth in Lucca. Bologna's claim to 180 towers is more believable. Clarke, *Medieval City State*, pp. 60–1. Despite the mammoth rebuilding of Florence, in the nineteenth century, particularly of the area around the market, where many powerful tower families had clustered, the remains of 55 towers still survived and had been identified thirty years ago. Bargellini and Guarnieri, *Firenze*.
27. Brucker (ed.), *Two Memoirs*, pp. 38–43.
28. *providere et procurare decorem et honorem civitatis* was the phrase used when compulsorily purchasing houses for destruction to enlarge the square around the baptistery and the cathedral in 1296, Pampaloni (ed.), *Firenze*, pp. 56–8.
29. Goldthwaite, *Building*.
30. Lane, *Venice: A Maritime Republic*, pp. 151–2, 252–3.
31. Heers, *Gênes*, part 3.
32. Brentano, *Rome*, pp. 13–15, 173–209.
33. Guillemain *La Cour pontificale*.
34. G. Mollat, *Papes*, pp. 307–8.
35. Partner, *Lands*, pp. 396–419.
36. Vaughan, *Philip*, pp. 157–163. A description of the Burgundian court in 1465 is included in Rozmital, *Travels*, pp. 26–42.
37. Guillemain, *La Cour pontificale*.
38. Thrupp, *Merchant Class*, pp. 41–8.
39. Leguay, *La Rue*, pp. 130–3.
40. Abulafia, *Frederick II*, pp. 162–3, 210, 263–4.
41. Villon, *Ballade de bonne doctrine*.
42. Brucker (ed.), *Society*, document 88.
43. For example 40% became destitute in Dixmunde when the linen industry collapsed. Blockmans and Prevenier, 'Poverty'.
44. Henderson, *Piety*.
45. After the introduction of an efficient general tax, the *taille*, Philip VI's grandson, Charles V, had an income of the order of 2,500,000 Florentine florins, much more in keeping with the wealth of the country he ruled. By then Richard II of England had an income of some 800,000 florins a year.
46. Spufford, *Money*, pp. 382–5.
47. Pegolotti, *Pratica* gives details of the south Italian fairs specialising in pecorino, sheep's cheese.
48. Much of the material in the next section is derived from Cazelles, *Paris*, 383 ff.
49. From the sparse evidence on wheat yields summarised by Georges Duby in 1962. In Provence, the Toulousain, Normandy and southern England he found wheat yields were normally 4 to 1 or below, *Rural Economy*, pp. 99–101. Fourquin, *Les Campagnes*, p. 79, confirmed Duby's eightfold yield for the Ile de France, but Bois, *Crisis*, pp. 204–7, suggested yields in Normandy might reach 5 to 1 on better land, but under 4 to 1 on poorer land.
50. Ordonnance of February 1416 n. s. *Ordonnances*, x, p. 269.
51. Laurence, *Practice*, p. 7.
52. *Journal*
53. Chorley, 'Cloth Exports'.

54. A huge quantity of information has recently become available from the project 'Feeding the City: London's Impact on the Agrarian Economy of Southern England, *c.* 1250–1400' directed by Derek Keene and Bruce Campbell. A first summary of findings is to be found in Keene, 'Medieval London', and the grain supply is explored in Campbell et al., *A Medieval Capital*.
55. James, *Studies*.
56. Thoen, *Landbouwekonomie*.
57. Nicholas, *Medieval Flanders*, p. 362; Unger, 'Feeding Low Countries Towns'.
58. Van der Wee, *The Growth*, i, pp. 277–86.
59. Fiumi, 'Economia'.
60. Herlihy and Klapisch-Zuber, *Tuscans*, pp. 67–74; Goldthwaite, *The Building*, p. 33.
61. The complexity of tax incentives in the Florentine *contado* is explored in Cohn, *Creating the Florentine State*.
62. Goldthwaite, *Wealth*, pp. 224–32.
63. Muel, *Tapestry*.
64. Vaughan, *Charles*, pp. 50–1, 146–8, and 377.
65. Heyd, *Histoire*, p. 706.
66. Goldthwaite, *Wealth*, pp. 224–32.
67. Dyer, *Standards*.
68. La Marche, *Mémoires*.
69. *Two Fifteenth-Century Cookery Books*.
70. Tafur, *Travels*, p. 135.
71. Mundy and Riesenberg, *Medieval Town*, pp. 33–4, cite an account book in which one Swedish noble family purchased in 1328 '1 ½ lbs. of saffron, derived from Spain or Italy, 12 lbs. of kummel and 90 lbs. of almonds from the Mediterranean, 4 ¾ lbs. of Indian ginger, a half pound of grains of paradise from west Africa, 1 lb. of Ceylon cinnamon, 6lbs. of pepper from the Malabar coast, 3 lbs. of anis from southern Germany, and 3 lbs of galangal from south Asia, 105 lbs of rice and 4 lbs of sugar from Spain, and 3 barrels of wine, one Rhine and two French'.
72. Tafur, *Travels*, p. 200.
73. Autrand, *Charles VI*, pp. 594–5.
74. Changes of fashion in the Burgundian Netherlands can be seen in Scott, *Late Gothic Europe*, and in Italy in Herald, *Renaissance Dress*.
75. Mazzaoui, *Italian Cotton Industry*, pp. 97–8 has suggested that until the early fourteenth century rich and poor were only distinguished by the quality of the fabrics from which garments were made, and that only in the fourteenth and fifteenth centuries could rich and poor be distinguished by the style of their clothing as well.
76. Brentano, *Rome*, p. 53.
77. van Uytven, 'Cloth', pp. 152.
78. *Idem*, pp. 135, 139, 86.
79. G. Mollat, *Papes*, p. 311.
80. Vaughan, *Charles*, pp. 141–4.
81. Origo, *Merchant*, p. 40.
82. Tafur, *Travels*, p. 200.
83. van Uytven, 'Cloth', p. 152
84. 'The Journey of William of Rubruck' in Dawson (ed.), *Mongol Mission*, p. 157.
85. Alexander and Binski, *Age*, pp. 202–3.
86. Examples of Sienese goldsmiths' work in Cherry, *Goldsmiths*, pls. 69,71,72; Origo, *Merchant*, pp. 38–9.
87. Vaughan, *Philip*, pp. 69–70.
88. Vaughan, *Charles*, p. 36.
89. E.g. in inventory of dowry of Nannina dei Medici in 1466, Rucellai, 'Zibaldone', pp. 32–4.
90. van Uytven, 'Cloth', pp. 151–2.
91. Arano (ed.), *Medieval Health Handbook*; Opsomer (ed.), *L'Art*.

92. Mackenney, *Tradesmen*, pp. 90–3.
93. Origo, *Merchant*, pp. 35–7.
94. Davis, *Medieval Warhorse*, p. 63–4.
95. Brucker (ed.), *Two Memoirs*, p. 27.
96. *Le Registre*, ed. Favier.
97. Melis, *Aspetti*; Origo, *Merchant*.
98. Mancini, *Usurpation*, p. 102.
99. Richmond, *John Hopton*, p. 63.
100. It was an eclectic French and Spanish creation, a moorish-gothic mix, partially modelled on the Castilian Alcázar at Segovia and partially on the royal palaces in Paris. Tapestry workers were brought from Arras, but other walls were painted by Mudejars in gold and vivid colours. The orange parterre was cultivated by Valencian gardeners, but some of the musicians for the chapel came from Flanders. Hillgarth, *Spanish Kingdoms*, ii, pp. 50–1; Javier Fortun (ed.), *Sedes Reales*, pp. 202–25.
101. Favier, *Paris*, p. 103.

Chapter 3: From court to counting house, pp. 140–173

1. This route from Paris to Troyes appears in two sections of the 'Itinéraire de Bruges' in the Ghent University MS 13 on fo. 56 recto, and from Troyes to Dijon in sections on fo. 55 verso, printed in Hamy (ed.), Appendix 4, pp. 180 and 174–5. These sections of the text are used as illustrations on pp. 55, 126 and 147.
2. Vaughan, *Matthew Paris*, pp. 242–50; and Parks, *English Traveller*, i, p. 184.
3. Tyler, *Alpine passes*; and Renouard, 'Routes'.
4. Fawtier, *Capetian Kings*, p. 186.
5. In the summers of 1421 and 1423 and the winters of 1438–9 and 1439–40. *Journal*.
6. Leguay, *La Rue*, pp. 144–5.
7. Spufford, *Money*, p. 141.
8. These fairs all seem to have come into existence at more or less the same time in the middle years of the twelfth century. The earliest surviving reference to the Provins fair of St Ayoul is from 1138, and to the Troyes fair of St Remi from 1147, whilst a papal document of 1153 refers to both Troyes fairs for the first time. Bur, *Formation*, p. 303.
9. Bautier, 'Les foires'; Chapin, *Les Villes*.
10. Giraldus, *Autobiography*, pp. 307–8, 311–2, 318.
11. Fortún, *Sedes Reales*, pp. 151–9.
12. The heyday of the fairs was relatively short lived. Only a century separated their foundation in the mid-twelfth century (note 8), and the first resident representatives of Italian firms in Bruges, Paris and London.
13. Bur, *Formation*, p. 303.
14. Even of the count of Champagne's abbey, only a seventeenth-century building survives. It was in favour of his abbey that the count founded the fair.
15. Extracts from both the *Codex Cumanicus* and the Pegolotti notebook are translated in Lopez and Raymond (eds), *Medieval Trade*, pp. 347–8 and 358.
16. Giraldus, *Autobiography*, pp. 312–8.
17. The author, in 1978, was prevented from crossing the Great Saint Bernard on 1 June, by no less than 3 metres of snow.
18. Part of toll return for July 1341 printed in Lopez and Raymond (eds), *Medieval Trade*, pp. 135–7.
19. Hocquet, *Le Sel et le pouvoir*.
20. Chomel and Ebersholt, *Cinq siècles*.

21. Bergier, 'Péages'.
22. Tyler, *Alpine Passes*, pp. 4 and 9.
23. Beresford, *New Towns*; Phillips and Phillips, *Spain's Golden Fleece*, p. 218.
24. Some of the receipts for tolls on fustians, mercery and spices collected from Milanese merchants on their way to the Geneva fairs in 1423–4 are printed in Lopez and Raymond (eds), *Medieval Trade*, pp. 137–42.
25. Listed in the Appendix to Quaglia, *La Maison*, p. 505.
26. Tyler, *Alpine Passes*, p. 27.
27. Tyler, *Alpine Passes*, pp. 28–9 and Parks, *English Traveller*, i, pp. 196–7.
28. Tyler, *Alpine Passes*, p. 29 and Parks, *English Traveller*, i, pp. 194–5.
29. Brucker, *Two Memoirs*, pp. 49–50.
30. Dubois, *Les Foires*.
31. Grandchamp and others, *La Ville*.
32. Tyler, *Alpine Passes*, p. 30 and Parks, *English Traveller*, i, p. 195.
33. Daviso di Charvensod, *I Pedaggi*.
34. Doehaerd, *Relations commerciales*, i.
35. Tyler, *Alpine Passes*, p. 173.
36. Stopani, *Via Francigena*.
37. Renouard, *Avignon Papacy*.
38. Letter to Francesco Nelli, cited in Wilkins, *Life*, p. 158.
39. Mallett, *Florentine Galleys*.

Chapter 4: Helps and hindrances to trade, pp. 174–227

1. Attwater, *Penguin Dictionary*, pp. 174–5.
2. Boyer, *Medieval French Bridges*.
3. Hitze, *Der Straße*, p. 150.
4. Of these the bridge and chapel at St Ives survive. Other bridges with chapels survive in England at Wakefield over the Calder, at Rotherham over the Don, and at Bradford-on-Avon.
5. In England it was common for towns at key river bridges to administer lands and tenements to support their bridges, as in Cambridge and York.
6. Epstein, *Wills*, pp. 186–7, 195.
7. In 1253 St Louis' emissary to the Great Khan, the franciscan William of Rubruck, met a Parisian goldsmith, William Buchier, at Caracorum who 'thinks he still has a brother on the Grand Pont called Roger Buchier'. Dawson, *Mongol Mission*, p. 157.
8. Kosi, *Potujoči*, p. 302.
9. Wiesflecker, *Kaiser Maximilian I*, v, 601; Hitzer, *Der Straße*, pp. 145–6.
10. Plesner, *Una rivoluzione stradale*.
11. La Roncière, *Florence*, iii, 835–70. This replacement of stone by wooden bridges was a common pattern of improvement throughout Europe. In Bristol the stone bridge, with the chapel on it, replaced an earlier wooden bridge in 1247. Lilley, *Modernising*, pp. 12–14.
12. '*Maxima gentium multitudo consueta erat de partibus Romandiole venive ad civitatem florentie per dictam partem cum frumento et blade et aliis necessariis*.'
13. Szabò, 'La rete stradale'; Waley, *Siena*, 3–5; Bowsky, *Medieval Italian Commune*, pp. 198–202. The Sienese later added a tenth road.
14. De Rosa, 'Land'; Runciman, *Sicilian Vespers*, p. 128.
15. Dickstein-Bernard, *La Gestion Financière*, pp. 97–109 'La Caisse de "la Chaussée"'.
16. Glauser, 'Der Gotthardstransit'.
17. Hitzer, *Der Straße*, 135 ff.
18. Phillips and Phillips, *Spain's Golden Fleece*, pp. 210–6.
19. Lugon, 'Le trafic commercial'; Kosi, *Potujoči*, pp. 300–6.
20. Lilley, *Modernising*, pp. 11–12.
21. Tolls were taken at the bridge at Warneton on both the road and the river. Duvosquel, 'Les Routes'.
22. Numerous other examples are given in Sosson, 'Travaux publics et politiques économiques'.
23. Wiesflecker, *Kaiser Maximilian I*, v, 601.
24. Doria and Piergiovanni, *Il sistema portuale*, pp. 55–107.
25. Carter, 'Settlement'.
26. Glauser, 'Der Gotthardstransit', pp. 21–7.
27. Tafur, *Travels*, p. 193.
28. Sapori, *Una compagnia*.
29. Dubois, *Les Foires*, pp. 451–461.
30. Maschaelle, 'Transport Costs'; Campbell et al., *A Medieval Capital*, pp. 60–3, 193–8.
31. Nicholas, *Medieval Flanders*, pp. 118, 129, and 390; Sosson, 'Travaux publics'.
32. Braunstein, 'Relations d'affaires', pp. 240–1. For comparison with the speeds and costs of carriage by sea, see the Conclusion.
33. Pegolotti, *La pratica*, pp. 257–8; Eng. trans. in Lopez and Raymond (eds), *Medieval Trade*, p. 252–4.
34. Leguay, *La Rue*, p. 156.
35. Hunt and Murray, *A History*, pp. 161–3.
36. Wolff, 'Les Hôtelleries toulousaines'; Leguay, *La Rue*, p. 133.
37. Carlin, *Medieval Southwark*, pp. 191–223; Kelly, 'Bishop'.
38. Hitzer, *Der Straße*, pp. 207–8.
39. Quaglia, *La Maison*, p. 45.
40. Some accounts of expensive pilgrimages are to be found in Labarge, *Medieval Travellers*, pp. 68–95, and Prescott, *Jerusalem Journey* and *Once to Sinai*.
41. Van Heerwaarden, *Opgelegde Bedevaarten*.
42. Künig, *Die walfart*.
43. Cohen, *Gift*, p. 13.
44. Text of register in Archivio di Stato Siena, *Ospedale* 4776 currently being edited by Dr Gabriella Piccinni, with comment on the sums of money involved by Prof. Lucia Travaini.
45. There were 33 dependent hospices in all, but no more than 29 at any one time. Some are mentioned in Chapter 3 above. They are all listed among two hundred properties, churches, fairs, lordships, lands, and priories in the appendix to Quaglia, *La Maison*.
46. Quaglia, *La Maison*.
47. Tyler, *Alpine Passes*.
48. Stopani, *La Via Francigena*, pp. 73–7.
49. McArdle, *Altopascio*.
50. Quaglia, *La Maison*, pp. 143–6.
51. Ricordanze of Buonnaccorso Pitti in Brucker (ed.), *Two Memoirs*, pp. 85–6.
52. La Roncière, *Florence*, iii, pp. 921–36.
53. Epstein, *Wills*, pp. 186–7, 195.
54. De Rosa, 'Land', pp. 342–3.
55. Parks, *English Traveller*, i, p. 545.
56. La Roncière, *Florence*, iii, 938. The end result of this improvement in the safety of the trans-appenine road from Florence to Bologna was not only felt in terms of easing commercial contacts between the Arno and Po valleys, but also in making the journey to Rome so much easier. The road via Bologna and Florence to Rome became known as the 'strada regia Romana' in the fourteenth century, and replaced the old via Francigena as the principal pilgrim route to Rome. Stopani, *Via Francigena*, pp. 100–1.
57. Tyler, *Alpine Passes*, pp. 45–6.

58. De Rosa, 'Land', pp. 342–3 and 349–50.
59. Strauss, *Nuremberg*, pp. 131–2.
60. Brady, *Turning Swiss*, pp. 132–3, 242–5.
61. Jenks, 'Die *Carta Mercatoria*'. Although continuing into the fourteenth century, the practice of reprisal started to erode in Italy at the very end of the thirteenth century. Bowsky, *A Medieval Italian Commune*, pp. 232–46
62. Los Angeles, Huntingdon Library, MS HM 341.
63. The rates of export duties on wool and cloth can be found in Carus-Wilson and Coleman, *England's Export Trade*, Appendix III, pp. 195–7.
64. '*reparacio camini…per quem ducuntur balle lane et alie mercandie de quibus levatur pedagium apud Villam novam*'.
65. Lopez and Raymond (eds), *Medieval Trade*, pp. 137–42.
66. Epstein, *Freedom*, pp. 124–7.
67. Strauss, *Nuremberg*, pp. 128, 133.

Chapter 5: Trade in manufactured goods, pp. 228–285

1. Chorley, 'Cloth Exports'; Munro, 'The Industrial Crisis'.
2. Tafur, *Travels*, p. 199.
3. van Uytven, 'La Draperie brabançonne'.
4. Nicholas, *Metamorphosis*, pp. 135–77.
5. Munro, 'New Institutional Economics', reckons that in the 1350s and 1360s, when the price of a traditional broadcloth of Ghent, Ypres, Bruges, Mechelen, Brussels, or Leuven represented over 170 days' wages for a master mason, the price of one from Wervik represented only 85 days' wages.
6. Melis, 'Mercanti-imprenditori italiani' and 'La diffusione'.
7. Van der Wee, 'Structural Changes'.
8. Munro, 'Symbiosis'.
9. Much of what follows is derived from Hoshino, *L'arte della lana*; and Hoshino, 'Rise'.
10. Melis, 'La lana della Spagna'.
11. Battistini, *La Confrèrie*.
12. *Lettere Volgari*, pp. 13–59. Siena never became a first rank producer of woollen cloth. In the 1340s it never produced more than 10,000 rolls of cloth in any year. Bowsky, *Medieval Italian Commune*, pp. 219–20.
13. Melis, *Aspetti*; Origo, *Merchant*.
14. Chorley 'Cloth Exports'.
15. Munro, 'Industrial Transformations'.
16. Epstein, *Freedom*, pp. 115–27; Mazzaoui, *Italian Cotton Industry*, pp. 62–72.
17. For cloth exports from Barcelona to Italy, del Treppo, *Els Mercaders Catalans*, p. 226–40.
18. The various processes have been most recently discussed in Cardon, *La Draperie*, and are summarised by John Munro in his entry on 'Textile Technology' in Strayer (ed.), *Dictionary*, xi, 1988, pp. 693–711. The various processes, as carried out in the Datini cloth businesses, are discussed in Melis, *Aspetti*. The time taken by the various processes is discussed in Endrei, 'Manufacturing'.
19. Melis, *Aspetti*, 514 ff.
20. One of the earliest written references to the new style of standard *panni* produced by these looms comes in the poem on the *Conflictus ovis et lini* of *c.* 1068–70. Verlinden, 'Marchands'. Archaeological evidence has recently confirmed dating at least as early as the tenth century.
21. Herlihy, *Opera Muliebria*, pp. 189–90. In Florence the proportion of women weavers to men shrank rapidly in the early fourteenth century.
22. For the application of water power Bradford B. Blaine in Strayer (ed.), *Dictionary*, viii, pp. 389–95, Walter Endrei reckoned that for his notional standard cloth (see note 18) the fulling mill used 50 man hours against 1,000 man hours by foot-fulling. Endrei may have exaggerated the saving. John Munro now reckons that foot-fulling a cloth only took a master fuller and two journeymen three to five days. He acknowledged that the charge for this still represented 20% of production costs, whilst he reckons that mechanical fulling cut this to 5% of production costs. 'Industrial Crisis', p. 125, (note 88).
23. Munro, 'Medieval Scarlet'.
24. Dini, 'L'industria serica'.
25. King, 'Types of Silk Cloth', pp. 457–64.
26. Munro, 'Medieval Scarlet', pp. 67–9.
27. Molà, *La comunità*; and, for the events of 1314 in Lucca and their effects on the silk industry, Green, *Castruccio Castracani*, pp. 55–58.
28. Edler de Roover, 'Andrea Banchi'. She includes a useful description of the processes involved in this article.
29. Relevant section, with the Latin translated into English appears in Lopez and Raymond (eds), *Medieval Trade*, as document 174, pp. 346–8.
30. Heyd, *Histoire du commerce*, p. 707.
31. Frescobaldi's narrative is included in *Visit to the Holy Places*.
32. Munro, 'Industrial Transformations', pp. 145–6; Munro, 'Linen', in Strayer (ed.), *Dictionary*, vii, 586 ff.
33. Mazzaoui, *Italian Cotton Industry*, pp. 137–42.
34. Halaga, 'A Mercantilist Initiative'.
35. Waley, *Siena*, pp. 155–6.
36. Basanoff, *Itinerario*, pp. 13–27.
37. Heers, *Gênes*, pp. 177–8; Ashtor, *Levant Trade*, p. 210.
38. Basanoff, *Itinerario*, pp. 27–53 and map facing p. 84.
39. Stromer, 'Ulman Stromer'; von Stromer, 'Die erste Papiermühle'.
40. For example to Bristol in the fifteenth century. Carus-Wilson, *Medieval Merchant Venturers*, p. 51.
41. High quality cutlery was also made elsewhere. In the fifteenth century, knives, razors and shears were exported from Brabant to England. Diest had a particular reputation for its wool-shears. Thielemans, *Bourgogne*, p. 243.
42. Cameron, *A List*.
43. Badham, 'Monumental Brasses'.
44. Marian Campbell, 'Metalwork', p. 163, quoting Uhler, *English Customs Ports*. On 13 October 1465 two ships bound for London from Antwerp were intercepted by French pirates and taken to Honfleur. They contained 13,303 quarters and 16 lbs. (Dinant weight) of brass shovels, basins and cauldrons. Thielemans, *Bourgogne*, p. 244.
45. Gachard (ed.), *Collection de documents*, ii, document lxxxvii, pp. 379–92.
46. Strauss, *Nuremberg*, pp. 135–41.
47. Carlin, *Medieval Southwark*, p. 152.
48. *Czechoslovakian Glass*.
49. Abulafia, *A Mediterranean Emporium*, p. 203.
50. Childs, *Anglo-Castilian Trade*, pp. 110–1.
51. Eliyahu Ashtor has suggested that the decline of Near Eastern soap production was a consequence of increased labour costs and a decrease in olive cultivation because of Mamluk taxation, *Levant Trade*, pp. 208–10.
52. Larner, *Culture*, pp. 312–5.
53. Essays by Nano Chatzidakis and Maria Constantoudaki-Kitromilides in *From Byzantium*, pp. 48–52.
54. Bartolomeo Fazio, *De viris illustribus*, 1456. Section *De pictoribus*, reprinted in Baxandall, *Giotto*, pp. 167, with English translation p. 108; Campbell, *Van der Weyden*, pp. 92–3.
55. Vale, 'England', pp. 209–10.
56. Muel, *Tapestry*, pp. 16–17.
57. Darwin, *Louis d'Orléans*, pp. 98–100.
58. Nicholas, *Medieval Flanders*, p. 381.
59. Tafur, *Travels*, pp. 201–2.
60. Tafur, *Travels*, p. 199.
61. Walter B. Denny, 'Rugs and Carpets' in Strayer (ed.), *Dictionary*, x, pp. 546–52.
62. Peeters, 'De-Industrialization', pp. 171 & 178–9,
63. Staniland, *Embroiderers*, pp. 5–6, 10, 55.
64. South of Cheapside between Cordwainer Street and Bread Street. Fitch, 'London Makers', pp. 288–96.
65. Rubin and Wright, *Renaissance Florence*, pp. 238–43.
66. Rouse and Rouse, *Manuscripts*.
67. Book production in the fifteenth century has most recently been summarised by Vale, 'Manuscripts', pp. 278–86.
68. Vespasiano da Bisticci, *The Vespasiano Memoirs*.
69. Steinberg, *Five Hundred Years*. Printing in the fifteenth century has most recently been summarised by McKitterick, 'The beginning'.
70. Strauss, *Nuremberg*, pp. 251–261. The German version of Schedel's, *Liber Chronicarum*, was reprinted in 2001 as *Chronicle of the World*, with a long and useful critical introduction in English by Stephan Füssel.
71. Steinberg, *Five Hundred Years*, pp. 48–9.

Chapter 6: Trade in foodstuffs, raw materials and slaves, pp. 286–341

1. Lenzi, *Il Libro del Biadaiolo*; and Pinto, 'Firenze e la carestia.'
2. Bowsky, *Medieval Italian Commune*, pp. 202–5; Herlihy, *Pisa*.
3. Jordan, *The Great Famine*, pp. 145–8.
4. Villani, Giovanni, *Nuova Cronica*, bk X, Chapter 80. However, Jordan, *idem*, pp. 159–62 and 173–4 is sceptical about whether the grain brought by Italian merchants to north-western Europe actually originated in the Mediterranean.
5. Hunt, *The medieval super-companies*.
6. James, 'Fluctuations'.
7. Craeybeckx, *Un grand commerce*.
8. Quoted by Little, *Religious Poverty*, p. 11.
9. Craeybeckx, *Un grand commerce*.
10. These figures have to be tentative, since the origins of around a third of the wine brought in was not given precisely. *Le Registre*, ed. Favier, i, esp. table on p. 104.
11. Aerts and Unger, 'Brewing'; Unger, 'Beer imports'.
12. Thielemans, *Bourgogne et Angleterre*, pp. 241–2,295 and 542–3.
13. Much of the following paragraphs is derived from Bergier, *Une histoire du sel*, Fribourg, 1982; and Hocquet, *Le Sel et la fortune* and *Le Sel et le pouvoir*.

14. Bill et al., *Fra stammebåd*, p. 135.
15. Quoted by Jean-Marie Augustin in Cabourdin (ed.), *Le Sel*.
16. Memoria.
17. Bradfield B. Blaine, 'Mills', in Strayer (ed.), *Dictionary*, viii, pp. 389–95.
18. Wartburg, 'Archaeology'.
19. Landucci, *Diario Fiorentino*, p. 10.
20. Nicholas, *Medieval Flanders*, pp. 389–90.
21. Pegolotti's list is translated in Lopez and Raymond (eds), *Medieval Trade*, pp. 108–114, and commented on in Balard, 'L'Impact'.
22. Quoted by Abu-Lughod, *Before European Hegemony*, p. 291.
23. Dyer, *Standards of Living*, pp. 62–7.
24. Richmond, John Hopton, pp. 51 and 145.
25. Braunstein, 'Relations d'affaires'.
26. Hillgarth, *The Spanish Kingdoms*, ii, pp. 8, 21–3.
27. *Cartulaire de l'étape de Bruges*, p. 19.
28. le Breton, 'Phillipidos', pp. 321–2.
29. Klapisch-Zuber, *Les Maîtres de marbre*.
30. Goldthwaite, *Building*, pp. 181–2; Sosson, *Les Travaux publics*.
31. Details of the importance of each sort are given by Sosson, *Les Travaux publics*.
32. Spufford, *Eccleshall*, pp. 27–9.
33. Hatcher, *History*, i.
34. van Houtte, *An Economic History*, pp. 38, 88–9, 93–4,167–70. Kranz, 'Klerus und Kohle'.
35. Tafur, *Travels*, p. 193.
36. Such limited statistics as we do have are tabulated in Sprandel, *Das Eisengewerbe*, pp. 274–7. He discusses Alpine iron pp. 109–18 and141–158, and Upper Palatinate iron pp. 158–77.
37. Strauss, *Nuremeberg*, pp. 135–41.
38. Sprandel, *Das Eisengewerbe*, pp. 93–101.
39. Phillips and Phillips, *Spain's Golden Fleece*, p. 169.
40. Threlfall-Holmes, 'Late Medieval Iron Production'.
41. Sprandel, *Das Eisengewerbe*, pp. 206–11.
42. Ashtor, *Levant Trade*, pp. 156–9; Ashtor, *Les métaux précieux*, pp. 55–64.
43. Hatcher, *English Tin Production*.
44. Stahl, 'Der Zinnhandel'.
45. For English wool see Power, *Wool Trade*; Lloyd, *English Wool Trade*; and Munro, *Textiles*.
46. In1273 licences were given to 681 merchants to export 32,734 sacks of wool from England. Of this, 24% was already being carried by Italians, and33% by men from Flanders and Brabant. Native Englishmen were carrying 35% and Hanseatic merchants 4% of the total. Dollinger, *La Hanse*, p. 78.
47. Carus-Wilson and Coleman, *England's Export Trade*.
48. Munro, 'Wool Price Schedules'.
49. Phillips and Phillips, *Spain's Golden Fleece*, pp. 26–39, and 97–115. They have considerably revised the older standard work in English, Klein, *The Mesta*.
50. Phillips, *Spain's Golden Fleece*, pp. 40–6.
51. Phillips, *Spain's Golden Fleece*, pp. 167–78.
52. Phillips, *Spain's Golden Fleece*, p. 237, also Hillgarth, *Spanish Kingdoms*, ii, pp. 36–7.
53. Tafur, *Travels*, p. 134.
54. Dollinger, *German Hansa*, pp. 169–71.
55. Małowist, 'Trade', pp. 594–6.
56. Tafur, *Travels*, p. 200.
57. Stuard, 'Ancillary Evidence'.
58. Origo, 'Domestic Enemy'; Verlinden, *L'Esclavage*.
59. Texts of lawsuit and decree printed in Brucker (ed.), *Society*, pp. 222–4.
60. *Two Memoirs*, ed. Brucker; Niccolini da Camugliano, *Chronicles*.
61. Balard, 'L'impact', pp. 49–50; Fernandez-Armesto, *Before Columbus*, pp. 200–2.
62 Tafur, *Travels*, pp. 132–3.
63. Małowist, 'The Trade', pp. 587–90.
64. Ashtor, *Les Métaux précieux*, pp. 88–94.
65. Mallett, 'Anglo-Florentine Commercial Relations', p. 264. Michael Mallett comments that many of the Florentine galleys returning from Spain brought some slaves.

Chapter 7: Imbalances in trade, pp. 342–375

1. Some of the material in this chapter has already appeared in Spufford, 'Financial Markets'.
2. Iliescu, 'Nouvelles éditions'.
3. Spufford, *Money*, p. 219.
4. Pegolotti, *La pratica*, pp. 21–5, and Larner, *Marco Polo*, pp. 69–74, 116–9, 187–90.
5. Tafur, *Travels*, p. 132.
6. Tafur, *Travels*, pp. 83–4.
7. Ashtor, *Les Métaux précieux*, p. 96.
8. Table based on Watson, 'Back to Gold'; Spufford, *Money*, pp. 271–2, 353–6 and 370; Lane and Mueller, *Money and Banking*, i, p. 366. When silver became more common, as in the 1280s and 1290s, the value of gold went up in value in terms of silver. When gold became more common, or silver scarcer, as from the 1330s, its value went down. The right-hand column indicates how imbalances in the value of goods between Venice and Egypt should have been paid for. When gold was more highly valued in Venice than Egypt, as in the 1320s, it was sensible to send silver to Egypt, and for the smaller return payments to come back to Venice in gold. When gold was more highly valued in Egypt than Venice, as in 1400–9, it was logical to send gold to Egypt.
9. Spufford, *Money*, pp. 220–1.
10. Spufford, *Money*, pp. 163–86.
11. Bolton, *Medieval English Economy*, pp. 305–14. Dr Bolton is currently (2002) writing on the English balance of trade in the later Middle Ages.
12. Allen, 'The Volume and Composition' and 'The Volume'.
13. Carus-Wilson and Coleman, *England's Export Trade*.
14. Mackay, *Money*.
15. Much information derives from Bernard's disputed will of 1213. He left legacies in Aquileia where he had property, and in Munich, as well as in Venice, which had become the centre of his business operations. Although his investments were primarily in transalpine trade, he also had interests in the Levant trade of Venice. Stromer, 'Bernardus Teutonicus'.
16. Lane and Mueller, *Money and Banking*, i, pp. 136–42.
17. Braunstein, 'Relations d'affaires', pp. 240–1.
18. Much of the material in the remainder of this chapter will be found in an extended form in Spufford, *Money*, where due acknowledgment is made to the underlying sources.
19. Agricola, *De veteribus et novis metallis*, p. 397.
20.Toth, 'The Role'.
21.Kazimír, *Kremnická mincovňa*.
22. 'essi anno ripieno tutto il nostro comune d'ariento, che quasi in gran parte abbiamo fatto l'acquisto della città di Pisa col detto ariento': instructions to Florentine ambassadors seeking release of silver from Ragusa seized en route in 1406. *Monumenta Historica Slavorum Meridionalium*, pp. 118–9, 419–21.
23. Tangheroni, *Città dell'argento*, p. 96.
24. Gimpel, *Medieval Machine*, pp. 17–23. Jean Gimpel, relying on Sicard, *Aux origines*, believed them to be the oldest limited companies in the world, and to date from the twelfth century.
25. Volpe, 'Montieri', p. 370.
26. Tangheroni, *Città dell'argento*, pp. 206–8.
27. Kazimír *et al*, *Kremnická mincovňa*.
28. *Quellen*, ed. Kuske, ii, pp. 653, 659–60, 668.
29. Brady, *Turning Swiss*, pp. 123–30.
30. Tangheroni, *Città dell'argento*, pp. 180–2.
31. Spufford, 'Mint Organisation' and Spufford, 'Conclusioni'.
32. Kazimír, *Kremnická mincovňa*.
33. Tangheroni, *Città dell'argento*, pp. 156–9.
34. The chronicle of Orsúa y Vela, quoted by Hanke, *Imperial City*, p. 28.
35. homines…intendunt magis in laborerio argenterie quam grani et ordei, ita quod de sua recollecta non possent vivere xv diebus nisi aliunde portaretur eis blada.
36. Chaunu, *Séville*; Sella, 'European Industries'.
37. Tangheroni, *Città dell'argento*, pp. 103–7, 194–8.
38. Kosi, *Potujoči*, p. 292

Chapter 8: Conclusion: the pattern of trade, pp. 376–413

1. Dollinger, *German Hansa*.
2. Hammel-Kiesow, 'Hansischer Seehandel'.
3. Hammel-Kiesow, 'Hansischer Seehandel', p. 85.
4. North, *Geldumlauf*, p. 11; Jesse, *Wendische Münzverein*; and Sprandel, *Mittelalterliche Zahlungssystem*.
5. Felloni, 'Struttura'. Some of these figures were also graphed in Robert Sabatino Lopez, 'Market Expansion'.
6. Felloni 'Struttura', p. 175.These are based on the sums for which the Genoese state farmed out the right to collect customs dues, multiplied up to correspond to the number of denari in the lira at which the custom was levied. For the years that he considered, up to 1350, Felloni increased the sums by 30% for the expenses and profits of the customs' farmer.
7. Frederic C. Lane, in his discussion of Lopez, 'Market Expansion', p. 469, pointed out the unsubstantial nature of the figure for 1293, which had been derived by H. Sieveking from the chronicle of Jacopo Doria, who used it to bolster his boasting of the prosperity of the city in the 1290s.
8. Lopez, 'The Trade', 1st edn, p. 315, unchanged in 2nd edn, p. 355.
9. Day, *Les douanes*, i, pp. xvi–xviii, xxvi. Kedar, *Merchants*, p. 19 and Appendix 3, pp. 139–41, has used Day's figures to calculate the minimum values of goods on which the farmer would break even.
10. Felloni, 'Struttura', p. 175.
11. Ashtor, 'Il volume', gives abundant details of the cargoes of individual ships.
12. In the second half of the fourteenth century the Florentine florin, *fiorino d'oro*, was, for a time, very slightly reduced in weight, from 3.52 grams of gold to 3.34 grams, and so was the Lübeck gulden. The

Genoese *genovino d'oro* perhaps remained marginally heavier, as the Venetian *ducato d'oro* did.

13. Day, *Les Douanes*, p. xxvii. In 1393 the *dazio*, then at 4d in the lira, had been farmed for 25,515 lire. In 1400, seven years later, the *dazio*, at the same rate, had been farmed for 15,200 lire. This was the tax on 1,225,000 florins worth of goods, reducing to 730,000 florins worth, without making any allowances for the expense of collection and the ostensibly non-existant profit. Simply to pay his farm in 1401, Benintendi's successor needed to collect the *dazio* on 691,000 florins worth of goods. He needed to collect the tax on further goods to cover his expenses and to make a reasonable profit. Giuseppe Felloni's formula, of 30% for expenses and profit, implies that total trade was expected to reach a little under 900,000 florins worth.

14. Ashtor, 'Observations'.

15. Ashtor, 'The Volume' modifies the statistics for the period around 1400 produced the previous year by Wake, 'The Changing Pattern', pp. 361–71 and 396–9. For his Catalan figures, Wake relied on Carrère, *Barcelone*, pp. 644–5.

16. Melis, 'Note', pp. 371–3, as quoted by Ashtor, 'L'Apogée', p. 308.

17. Melis, 'Werner Sombart'.

18. Luzzatto, 'Sull'attendabilità'. Lane, *Venetian Shipbuilders*, pp. 253–261, built on Luzzatto's acceptance of the Mocenigo oration, albeit with some reservations.

19. Stahl, 'Deathbed Oration'.

20. Version incorporated in Sanuto, *Vitae*, col. 953.

21. Ashtor, 'L'Apogée', pp. 324–6.

22. Ashtor, *Les Métaux précieux*, pp. 79 and 86.

23. Prevenier and Blockmans, *Burgundian Netherlands*, p. 109; Nicholas, *Medieval Flanders*, p. 391.

24. Voet, *Antwerp*, pp. 311–12; Brulez, 'The Balance'.

25. Van der Wee, *Growth*, ii, pp. 153–7.

26. Spufford, 'La Rôle' later elaborated in Spufford, *Money*, pp. 250–3.

27. According to the sources consulted by Bairoch *et al.*, *The Population*.

28. Coined after the publication of Brunet (ed.), *European Cities* with the banana-shaped urban belt printed in blue on the cover.

29. Quoted by Benjamin A. Rifkin in his introduction to Amman and Sachs, *The Book of Trades*.

30. Also quoted by Rifkin, *loc. cit.*

31. Strauss, *Nuremberg*, pp. 127–9.

32. Barbieri, 'L'arteria atesina'.

33. All reproduced in Winkler, *Dürers Zeichnungen* and discussed in Grote, «*Hier bin ich ein Heer*» and Clark, *Landscape*.

34. Voet, *Antwerp*, pp. 315–6.

35. Voet, *loc. cit.*

36. Strauss, *Nuremberg*, p. 128

37. Gascon, *Grand Commerce*.

38. Amsterdam, Netherlands Economic History Archive, MS 349.

39. Van der Wee and Peeters, 'Un modèle dynamique'; Munro, 'Industrial Transformations', pp. 127–8.

40. Doumerc, 'Le galere', pp. 377–8; Lane, *Venetian Ships*.

41. This was not a straightforward change; costs of using galleys rose further in the first half of the fourteenth century, before dropping in the second half of the century. Munro, 'Industrial Transformations', p. 126.

42. Lane, 'Venetian Shipping', Lane, *Venetian Ships*, p. 103, suggested that in the 1420s the tonnage of round ships operated by the Venetians was virtually ten times that of their galleys.

43. Unger, *The Ship*, pp. 123–6; Scammell, *The World Encompassed*, pp. 193–5; Gardiner and Unger (eds), *Cogs*.

44. Giovanni Villani, *Nuova Cronica*, book ix, cap. 77. Although he claims to have begun writing in 1300, this part of his chronicle seems to have been compiled by Villani from other writings, now lost, long after the event. The Genoese were already building *cocche* at least two years before the events he purports to describe.

45. Melis, 'Werner Sombart'.

46. *The Libelle*.

47. Lane, 'Rhythm', p. 110.

48. Tenenti et Vivanti, 'Le Film'.

49. Doumerc, 'Le galere', p. 358.

50. Heers, *L'Occident*, p. 175.

51. These companies generally had 24 shares or *carats*, although individual shareholders, *caratarii*, might hold several shares, or only a fraction of a share. Doumerc and Stöckly, 'L'Evolution'; Stöckly, *Le Système*.

52. Doumerc, 'Le galere', and Lane, 'Fleets'.

53. Mallett, *Florentine Galleys*.

54. Heers, *L'Occident*, p. 175.

55. Ashtor, *Levant Trade*, pp. 344–9.

56. Melis, 'Werner Sombart'. Lane, *Venetian Ships*, p. 102–5 suggested that the Venetians were slower to build larger ships, and that they were never as large of the largest Genoese boats. In the middle decades of the fifteenth century the Venetians still only had half a dozen ships of over 600 tons.

57. Tafur, *Travels*, p. 198.

58. *Libelle*, lines 524–9.

59. Van Werveke, 'Der Flandrische Eigenhandel'; Nicholas, *Medieval Flanders*, pp. 286–9, 383–90.

60. Thielemans, *Bourgogne*, pp. 312–19.

61. Lane, *Venice: A Maritime Republic*, pp. 348–52.

62. Pegolotti, *La pratica*, pp. 257–8 translated in Lopez and Raymond, *Medieval Trade*, pp. 252–4.

63. Heers, *Gênes*, p. 309

64. Braudel and Spooner, 'Prices'.

65. Melis, 'Intensità'.

66. Melis, 'La diffusione'; Munro, 'Industrial Transformations', p. 129.

67. Tenenti, *Piracy*.

68. Phillips and Phillips, *Spain's Golden Fleece*, pp. 168–70, quoting from Casado Alonso, 'El comercio internacional burgalés'.

69. Fazio, *De viris illustribus*, Section *De pictoribus*, reprinted in Baxandall, *Giotto*, pp. 163–8, with English translation and commentary pp. 97–111. Most of the works that he cites in Italian collections of his own day have since been lost.

Bibliography

Primary Sources

Agricola, Georgius, *De veteribus et novis metallis*, Basle, 1546.

Agricola, Georgius, *de Re Metallica*, 1561, trans. and ed. H. C. and L .H. Hoover, London, 1912.

[Bona, Nicolo di], *La 'Pratica di Mercatura' Datiniana*, ed. Cesare Ciano, Biblioteca della Rivista *Economia e storia*, ix, Milan, 1964.

Amman, Jost and Hans Sachs, *The Book of Trades*, Frankfurt, 1568, facsimile edition, ed. Benjamin A. Rifkin, New York, 1973.

Botero, Giovanni, *A Treatise Concerning the Causes of the Magnificence and Greatnes of Cities* [*Delle cause della grandezza delle citta*] (1588), done into English by Robert Peterson], London, T. P[urfoot]. for R.Ockould and H.Tomes, 1606.

Brucker, Gene (ed.), *Two Memoirs of Renaissance Florence. The Diaries of Buonaccorso Pitti and Gregorio Dati*, New York, 1967.

Brucker, Gene (ed.), *The Society of Renaissance Florence: A Documentary Study*, New York, 1971, reprinted Renaissance Society of America, Reprint Texts 8, Toronto, 1998 .

Canal. *Zibaldone da Canal. Manoscritto mercantile del sec.XIV*, ed. Alfredo Stussi, Venice, 1967; *Merchant Culture in Fourteenth-Century Venice: the Zibaldone da Canal*, Eng. trans. with intro. J. E. Dotson, Binghamton, 1994.

Cartulaire de l'étape de Bruges, ed. L. Gilliodts van Severen, Bruges, 1904.

Catalan Atlas. *Mappamundi, the Catalan Atlas of the Year 1375*, ed. G. Grosjean, Zurich, 1978.

Cent Nouvelles Nouvelles, Les, ed. Franklin P. Sweetser, Geneva, 1966.

Dawson, Christopher (ed.), *The Mongol Mission*, London, 1955, reprinted as *Mission to Asia*, Medieval Academy of America Reprints for Teaching, viii, Toronto, 1980.

Dispatches with Related Documents of Milanese Ambassadors in France and Burgundy, 1453–1483, ed. P. M. Kendall and V. Ilardi. 3 vols, Ohio, 1970–81.

Etzlaub, Erhard, *Romweg Karte*, Nuremberg, 1500.

Fazio, Bartolomeo, *De viris illustribus*, 1456.

Gachard, L. P. (ed.), *Collection de documents inédits concernant l'histoire de la Belgique*, ii, Brussels, 1834.

Gail. *Das Älteste Deutsche Routenhandbuch. Jörg Gails "Raißbüchlin"*, ed. Herbert Krüger, Graz, 1974.

Giraldus. *The Autobiography of Giraldus Cambrensis*, ed. H. E. Butler, London, 1937.

'Itinéraire de Bruges', ed. E.-T. Hamy, as Appendix 4 to Gilles le Bouvier, *Le Livre de la description des pays*, Paris, 1908, pp. 157–216.

Journal d'un bourgeois de Paris, trans. and ed. Janet Shirley as *A Parisian Journal 1405–1449*, Oxford, 1968.

Künig, Hermann, *Die walfart und Straß zu sant Jacob*, Strasbourg, 1495, trans. and ed. John Durant, London, 1993.

La Marche, Olivier de, *Mémoires*, ed. H. Beaune and J. d'Arbaument, Société de l'Histoire de France, Paris, 1883–8.

Landucci, Luca, *Diario Fiorentino*, ed. I. del Badia, Eng. trans. *A Florentine Diary from 1450 to 1516*, London, 1927.

Laurence. Brother Laurence, *Practice of the Presence of God*, between 1666 and 1691, Eng. trans., London, 1824, reprinted Oxford, 1980.

le Breton, Guillaume, 'Phillipidos', in *Monumenta Germaniae Historica, Scriptores*, xxvi, Hannover, 1878.

Lenzi, Domenico, *Specchio Umano* published as *Il libro del biadaiolo. Carestia e annona a Firenze dalla metà del 200 al 1348*, Pinto, Giuliano (ed.), Florence, 1978.

Lettere Volgari del Secolo XIII scritte da Senesi, ed. C. Paoli and E. Piccolomini, Siena, 1871.

Libelle of Englyshe Polycye, ed. George Warner, Oxford, 1926.

Libro di mercatantie et usanze de' Paesi, ed. Franco Borlandi, Documenti e Studi per la Storia del Commercio e del Diritto Commerciale Italiano, vii, Turin, 1936.

Lopez, Robert S. and Irving W. Raymond (eds), *Medieval Trade in the Mediterranean World. Illustrative Documents Translated with Introductions and Notes*, New York, 1955.

Mancini, Dominic, *The Usurpation of Richard III*, trans. and ed. C. A .J. Armstrong, 2nd edn, Oxford, 1969, p. 102.

Melis, Federigo (ed.), *Documenti per la storia economica dei secoli XIII–XVI*, Istituto Internazionale di Storia Economica 'F. Datini' Prato, Serie Documenti, I, Florence, 1972.

Memoria. Lopez, R. S. and G. Airaldi (eds), 'Il più antico manuale italiano di pratica della mercatura [Memoria de tucte le mercantie]', *Miscellane di studi storici*, ii, Genoa, 1983, pp. 99–133.

Monumenta historica slavorum meridionalium vicinorumque populorum e tabulariis et bibliothecis italicis deprompta, ed. Vincentio Makuscev, Warsaw, 1874.

Ordonnances des Rois de France de la Troisième Race, 24 vols, Paris, 1723–1849.

Pacioli, Luca, *Summa de arithmetica*, Venice, 1494. Section 'De Scripturis', translated into English by Antonia van Gebsattel, with introduction by Basil Yamey, as *Exposition of Double Entry Bookkeeping*, Venice, 1994.

Pampaloni, Guido (ed.), *Firenze al tempo di Dante. Documenti sull'urbanistica fiorentina*, Rome, 1975.

Pegolotti, Francesco di Balducci, *La pratica della mercatura*, ed. Allan Evans, Medieval Academy of America, Cambridge, Mass., 1936.

Quellen zur Geschichte der Kölner Handels und Verkehrs im Mittelalters, ed. B.Kuske, ii, Bonn, 1917.

Le Registre des compagnies Françaises (1449–1467), ed. Jean Favier, Le Commerce Fluvial dans la Région Parisienne au XVe siècle, i, Paris, 1975.

Rucellai, Giovanni, *Il zibaldone quaresimale*, ed. A. Perosa, Studies of the Warburg Institute, 24, Part 1, 1960.

Ricci. *Il manuale di mercatura di Saminiato de' Ricci*, ed. Antonia Borlandi, Genoa, 1963.

Rozmital. *The Travels of Leo of Rozmital*, ed. Malcolm Letts, Hakluyt Society, 2nd ser., cviii, 1957.

Sanuto, Marin, *Vitae ducum Venetorum*, ed. L. A. Muratori, Rerum Italicarum Scriptores, xxii, 1733.

Schedel, Hartmann, *Liber chronicarum*, Latin and German editions, Nuremberg, 1493.

Stefani, Marchionne di Coppo, *Cronaca fiorentina*, ed. N. Rodolico, *Rerum Italicorum Scriptores*, new series, xxx, part 1, 1927.

Tacuinum. Arano, Luisa Cogliati (ed.), *The Medieval Health Handbook 'Tacuinum Sanitatis'*, London, 1976.

Tacuinum. Opsomer, Carmélia (ed.), *L'Art de vivre en santé*, Liège, 1991.

Tafur, Pero, *Travels and Adventures 1435–1439*, trans. and ed. Malcolm Letts, London, 1926.

Two Fifteenth-Century Cookery Books, ed. Thomas Austin, Early English Text Society, cxi, 1888.

Uzzanno. 'La pratica della mercatura scritta de Giovanni di Antonio da Uzzanno' in G. F. Pagnini della Ventura, *Della decima e delle altre gravezze*, iv, Lisbon/Lucca, 1766.

Vespasiano da Bisticci, *The Vespasiano Memoirs: Lives of Illustrious Men of the XVth century*, Eng. trans. London, 1926, reprinted Renaissance Society of America, Reprint Texts 7, Toronto 1997.

Visit to the Holy Places, trans. and ed. T. Bellorini and E. Hoade, Studium Biblicum Franciscanum, Publications, vi, Jerusalem, 1948.

Villani, Giovanni, *Nuova Cronica*, ed. Giuseppe Porta, 3 vols, Parma, 1990–1.

Villani, Matteo, *Cronica*, ed. Giuseppe Porta, 2 vols, Parma, 1995.

Villon, François, *Ballade de bonne doctrine* in *Oxford Book of French Verse*, ed. St John Lucas, Oxford, 1907, p. 38.

Voragine, Jacobus, *Legenda aurea* (*c.* 1260), Eng. trans. William Granger Ryan, Princeton, 1993.

Zeno, R. (ed.), *Documenti per la storia del diritto marittimo nei secoli XIII e XIV*, Turin, 1936.

Secondary Books and Articles

Abulafia, David, 'Asia, Africa and the Trade of Medieval Europe', in M. M. Postan and E. E. Rich (eds), *The Cambridge Economic History of Europe*, ii, 2nd edn, Cambridge, 1987, pp. 402–73.

Abulafia, David, *Frederick II. A Medieval Emperor*, London, 1988.

Abulafia, David, *Commerce and Conquest in the Mediterranean 1100–1500*, Aldershot, 1993.

Abulafia, David, *A Mediterranean Emporium. The Catalan Kingdom of Majorca*, Cambridge, 1994.

Abulafia, David, *The Western Mediterranean Kingdoms 1200–1500*, London, 1997.

Abu-Lughod, Janet L., *Before European Hegemony, The World System AD 1250–1350*, Oxford, 1989.

Adelson, Candace, 'Documents for the Foundation of Tapestry Weaving Under Cosimo I de' Medici', Andrew Morrogh et al. (eds), *Renaissance Studies in Honor of Craig Hugh Smyth*, Villa I Tatti, vii, Florence, 1985, ii, pp. 3–21.

Aerts, Erik and Richard Unger, 'Brewing in the Low Countries', in Erik Aerts et al. (eds), *Production, Marketing and Consumption of Alcoholic Beverages since the Late Middle Ages*, Leuven, 1990, pp. 92–101.

Aerts, Erik et al. (eds), *Studia Historica Œconomica. Liber amicorum Herman Van der Wee*, Leuven, 1993.

Airaldi, Gabriella and Giuseppe Marcenaro (eds), *Credito e banca dall'Italia all'Europa secoli XII–XVIII*, exhibition catalogue, Genoa, 1992.

Alexander, Jonathan and Paul Binski (eds), *Age of Chivalry. Art in Plantagenet England 1200–1400*, Royal Academy of Arts, London, 1987.

Allen, M. R., 'The Volume and Composition of the English Silver Currency 1279–1351', *British Numismatic Journal*, lxx, 2000, pp. 38–44.

Allen, Martin, 'The Volume of English Currency, 1158–1470', *Economic History Review*, liv, 2001, pp. 595–611.

Ashtor, Eliyahu, *Les Métaux précieux et la balance des payements du proche-orient à la basse époque*, Paris, 1971.

Ashtor, Eliyahu, 'Banking Instruments between Muslim East and Christian West', *Journal of European Economic History*, i, 1972, collected in his *East–West Trade*.

Ashtor, Eliyahu, 'Observations on Venetian Trade in the Levant in the XIVth Century', *Journal of European Economic history*, v, 1976, pp. 533–586.

Ashtor, Eliyahu, 'L'Apogée du commerce vénitien au levant: un nouvel essai d'explication', 1977, reprinted in his *Technology*.

Ashtor, Eliyahu, *Studies on the Levantine Trade in the Middle Ages*, Aldershot, 1978.

Ashtor, Eliyahu, 'Il volume del commercio levantino di Genova nel secondo Trecento', 1978, collected in his *East–West Trade*.

Ashtor, Eliyahu, 'The Volume of Mediaeval Spice Trade', *Journal of European Economic History*, ix, 1980, 753–63.

Ashtor, Eliyahu, *Levant Trade in the Later Middle Ages*, Princeton, N. J., 1983.

Ashtor, Eliyahu and Guidobaldo Cevidalli, 'Levantine Alkali Ashes and European Industries', *Journal of European Economic History*, xii, 1983, pp. 475–522.

Ashtor, Eliyahu, *East–West Trade in the Medieval Mediterranean*, Aldershot, 1986.

Ashtor, Eliyahu, *Technology, Industry and Trade. The Levant versus Europe, 1250–1500*, Aldershot, 1992.

Attwater, Donald, *Penguin Dictionary of Saints*, 1965.

Autrand, Françoise, *Charles VI*, Paris, 1986.

Badham, Sally, 'Monumental Brasses and the Black Death – A Reappraisal', *Antiquaries Journal*, lxxx, 2000, pp. 207–47.

Bairoch, Paul, Jean Batou and Pierre Chèvre, *The Population of European Cities from 800 to 1850*, Geneva, 1988.

Balard, Michel, *La Romanie génoise (XIIe–XVe siècle)*, 2 vols, Rome, 1978.

Balard, Michel, *La Mer Noire et la romanie génoise, XIIIe–XVe siècles*, Aldershot, 1989.

Balard, Michel, 'I pisani in Oriente dalla guerra di Acri (1258) al 1406', *Bolletino Storico Pisano*, lx, 1991, pp. 1–16.

Balard, Michel, 'L'Impact des produits du Levant sur les économies Européennes (XIIe–XVe siècles), in S. Cavaciocchi (ed.), *Prodotti e tecniche d'Oltramare nelle economie Europee secc. XIII–XVIII*, Atti del 'Settimana di Studi', xxix, Istituto Internazionale di Storia Economica 'F. Datini', Prato, 1998, pp. 31–57.

Barbieri, Gino, 'L'arteria atesina nelle sue millenarie premesse storico-mercantile', *Economia e Storia*, xx, 1973, pp. 7–21.

Bargellini, Piero and Ennio Guarnieri, *Firenze delle torri*, Florence, 1973.

Barron, Caroline, 'The Later Middle Ages: 1270–1520' in Mary D. Lobel (ed.), *The City of London From Prehistoric Times to c. 1520*, The British Atlas of Historic Towns, iii, Oxford, 1989.

Barron, Caroline M., 'Centres of Conspicuous Consumption: The Aristocratic Town House in London 1200–1550', *The London Journal*, xx, 1995, pp. 1–16.

Bartlett, Robert, *The Making of Europe: Conquest, Civilization and Cultural Change 9560–1350*, Harmondsworth, 1993.

Basanoff, Anne, *Itinerario della Carta dall'Oriente all'Occidente*, Milan, 1965.

Battistini, Mario, *La Confrérie de Sainte Barbe des Flamands à Florence*, Académie Royale de Belgique, Commission Royale d'Histoire, ser. in 8⁰, xli, Brussels, 1930.

Bautier, R.-H., 'Les Foires de Champagne', *Recueils de la Société Jean Bodin*, v, La Foire, Brussels, 1953, pp. 97–147.

Bautier, R.-H., *The Economic Development of Medieval Europe*, 1966, Eng. trans., London, 1971.

Bautier, R.-H., 'La Circulation fluviale dans la France médiévale', *Recherches sur l'économie de la France médiévale. Les Voies fluviales – la draperie*, Paris, 1989.

Bautier, R.-H., *Sur l'histoire économique de la France médiévale*, Aldershot, 1991.

Bautier, R.-H., *Commerce méditerranéen et banquiers italiens au Moyen Age*, Aldershot, 1992.

Baxandall, Michael, *Giotto and the Orators*, Oxford, 1971.

Beale, Philip, *A History of the Post in England*, Aldershot, 1999.

Beardwood, Alice, *Alien Merchants in England 1350–77. Their Legal and Economic Position*, Cambridge, Mass., 1931.

Beresford, Maurice, *New Towns of the Middle Ages: Town Plantation in England, Wales and Gascony*, London, 1967, reprinted Gloucester, 1988.

Bergier, J-F., 'Péages du XVe siècle au pays de Vaud', in H. Aubin et al. (eds), *Beiträge zur Wirtschafts- und Stadtgeschichte, Festschrift für Hektor Ammann*, Wiesbaden, 1965, pp. 286–95.

Bergier, Jean-François, 'Histoire des Alpes. Perspectives nouvelles', special number of *Revue Suisse d'Histoire*, xxix, 1979.

Bergier, Jean-François, *Une histoire du sel*, Fribourg, 1982.

Berlow, Rosalind Kent, 'Development of Business Techniques at the Fairs of Champagne (End 12th century–13th century)', *Studies in Medieval and Renaissance History*, viii, 1971, pp. 3–23.

Bill, Jan et al., *Fra stammebåd til skib. Dansk Søfarts Historie*, i, indtil 1588, Copenhagen, 1997.

Blockmans W. P. and W. Prevenier, 'Poverty in Flanders and Brabant from the Fourteenth to the Mid-Sixteenth Century: Sources and Problems', *Acta Historiae Neerlandicae*, x, 1978, pp. 20–57.

Blockmans, W. P., 'The Social and Economic Effects of Plague in the Low Countries 1349–1500', *Revue Belge de Philologie et d'Histoire*, lx, 1982, pp. 833–63.

Blockmans, W. P., 'Das westeuropäische Messenetz im 14 und 15 Jahrhundert' in Koch (ed.), *Brücke zwischen den Völkern. Zur Geschichte der Frankfurter Messe*, i, pp. 37–50.

Blockmans, W. P., 'Aux origines des foires d'Anvers, in P. Contamine et al. (eds), *Commerce, finances et société. Recueil de travaux d'histoire médiévale offert a m. le Prof. Henri Dubois*, Paris, 1993, pp. 21–26.

Blockmans, W. P., 'Voracious States and Obstructing Cities: An Aspect of State Formation in pre-Industrial Europe' in Charles Tilly and Wim P. Blockmans (eds), *Cities and the Rise of States in Europe AD 1000 to 1800*, Oxford, 1994.

Bois, Guy, *The Crisis of Feudalism. Economy and Society in Eastern Normandy c.1300–1550*, 1976, Eng. trans. 1984.

Bolton, J. L., *The Medieval English Economy 1150–1500*, London, 1980.

Boutruche, Robert, *La Crise d'une société. Seigneurs et paysans du Bordelais pendant la Guerre de Cent Ans*, Paris, 1947.

Bovill, E. W., *The Golden Trade of the Moors*, 2nd edn, Oxford, 1968.

Bowsky, William M., *A Medieval Italian Commune. Siena under the Nine, 1287–1355*, Berkeley, 1981.

Boyer, Marjorie N., *Medieval French Bridges*, Cambridge, Mass, 1975.

Brady, Thomas A., *Turning Swiss. Cities and Empire, 1450–1550*, Cambridge, 1985.

Braudel, Fernand and F. Spooner, 'Prices in Europe from 1450 to 1750', in E. E. Rich and C. H. Wilson (eds), *Cambridge Economic History of Europe*, iv, Cambridge, 1967, pp. 378–486.

Braudel, Fernand, *Civilization and Capitalism 15th–18th Century*, 3 vols, 1979, Eng. trans., London, 1984.

Braudel, Fernand, *Mélanges en l'honneur de Fernand Braudel*, ii, 'Méthodologie de l'histoire et des sciences humaines', Paris, 1973.

Braunstein, Philippe, 'Relations d'affaires entre Nuremborgeois et Vénitiens á la fin du XIVe siècle' *Mélanges d'archéologie et d'histoire de L'Ecole Française de Rome*, lxxvi, 1964, pp. 227–68.

Brentano, Robert, *Rome Before Avignon*, Berkeley, 1990.

Bresc, Henri, *Un monde méditerranéen. Economie et société en Sicile, 1300–1450*, 2 vols, Rome, 1986.

Bridbury, A. R. *Medieval English Clothmaking*, London, 1982.

Britnell, R. H., *The Commercialisation of English Society 1000–1500*, Cambridge, 1993.

Britnell, R.H., 'England and Northern Italy in the Early Fourteenth Century: the Economic Contrasts', *Transactions of the Royal Historical Society*, 5th ser., xxxix, 1989, 167–83.

Brulez, W., 'The Balance of Trade in the Netherlands', *Acta Historiae Neerlandica*, iv, 1970.

Brunet, Roger, (ed.), *European Cities*, Barcelona, 1989.

Brunschvig, R., *La Berbérie orientale sous les Hafsides, des origines á la fin du XVe siècle*, 2 vols, Paris, 1940.

Bur, Michel, *La Formation du comté de Champagne*, Nancy, 1977.

Cabourdin, Guy (ed.), *Le Sel et son histoire*, Nancy, 1981.

Cameron, H. K., *A List of Monumental Brasses on the Continent of Europe*, London, 1970.

Campbell, Bruce M. S. (ed.), *Before the Black Death. Studies in the 'Crisis' of the Early Fourteenth Century*, Manchester, 1991.

Campbell, Bruce M. S., James A. Galloway, Derek Keene and Margaret Murphy, *A Medieval Capital and its Grain Supply: Agrarian Production and Distribution in the London Region c. 1300*, Institute of British Geographers, Historical Geography Research Series, xxx, 1993.

Campbell, Lorne, *Van der Weyden*, London, 1979.

Campbell, Marian, 'Metalwork in England, *c.* 1200–1400', in Jonathan Alexander and Paul Binski (eds), *Age of Chivalry. Art in Plantagenet England 1200–1400*, Royal Academy of Arts, London, 1987.

Campbell, T. 'Portolan Charts from the Late Thirteenth Century to 1500' in J. B. Harley and David Woodward (eds), *The History of Cartography*, i, Chicago, 1987, pp. 371–463.

Cardon, Dominique, *La Draperie au Moyen Age: essor d'une grande industrie européenne*, Paris, 1999.

Carlin, Martha, 'The Reconstruction of Winchester House, Southwark', *London Topographical Record*, xxv, 1985, 33–57.

Carlin, Martha, *Medieval Southwark*, London, 1996.

Carrère, C., *Barcelone centre économique à l'époque des difficultés, 1380–1462*, Paris, 1967.

Carter, F. W., 'Settlement and Population during Venetian Rule (1420–1797): Hvar Island, Croatia', *Journal of European Economic History*, xxiii, 1994, pp. 7–48.

Carus-Wilson, E. M. 'The Woollen Industry', in M. M. Postan and E. E. Rich (eds), *The Cambridge Economic History of Europe*, ii, 1st edn, Cambridge, 1952, pp. 355–428, reprinted with revised bibliography in 2nd edn, Cambridge, 1987, pp. 614–690.

Carus-Wilson, E. M., 'La Guède française en Angleterre: un grand commerce du Moyen Age', *Revue du Nord*, xxxv, 1953, pp. 89–106.

Carus-Wilson, E. M., *Medieval Merchant Venturers*, London, 1954.

Carus-Wilson, E. M. and Olive Coleman, *England's Export Trade 1275–1547*, Oxford, 1963.

Casado Alonso, Hilario, 'El comercio internacional burgalés en los ss. XV & XVI', in Floriano Ballesteros Caballero (ed.), *Actas del V Centenario del Consulado de Burgos*, Burgos, i, 1994, pp. 175–274.

Cavaciocchi, Simonetta (ed.), *L'Impresa Industria Commercio secc. XIII–XVIII*, Atti del 'Settimana di Studi', xxii, Istituto Internazionale di Storia Economica 'F. Datini', Prato, 1991.

Cavaciocchi, Simonetta (ed.), *Produzione e commercio della cartae del libro secc. XIII–XVIII*, Atti del 'Settimana di Studi', xxiii, Istituto Internazionale di Storia Economica 'F. Datini', Prato, 1992.

Cavaciocchi, Simonetta (ed.), *La Seta in Europa Sec. XIII–XX*, Atti del 'Settimana di Studi', xxiv, Istituto Internazionale di

Storia Economica 'F. Datini', Prato, 1993.

Cazelles, Raymond, *Paris de la fin du règne de Philippe Auguste à la mort de Charles V 1223–1380*, Nouvelle Histoire de Paris, Paris, 1972.

Chapin, Elizabeth, *Les Villes de foire de Champagne*, Paris, 1937.

Chaunu, H. and P., *Séville et L'Atlantique*, 12 vols, Paris, 1955–60.

Cherry, John, *Goldsmiths*, British Museum Medieval Craftsmen Series, London, 1992.

Chiapelli, Fredi (ed.), *The Dawn of Modern Banking*, New Haven, Conn., 1979.

Childs, Wendy R., *Anglo-Castilian Trade in the Later Middle Ages*, Manchester, 1978.

Childs, Wendy R., 'Anglo-Portuguese Trade in the Fifteenth Century', *Transactions of the Royal Historical Society*, 6th series, ii, 1992, pp. 195–219.

Childs, Wendy R., 'Commerce and Trade', in Christopher Allmand (ed.), *New Cambridge Medieval History*, vii, *c.* 1415–*c.* 1500, pp. 145–60.

Chomel, V. and J. Ebersholt, *Cinq siècles de circulation internationale vue de Jougne*, Paris, 1951.

Chorley, Patrick, 'The Cloth Exports of Flanders and Northern France during the Thirteenth Century: a Luxury Trade?', *Economic History Review*, xl, 1987, pp. 349–79.

Clark, Kenneth, *Landscape into Art*, London, 1949.

Clarke, M. V., *The Medieval City State*, London, 1926.

Cohen, Esther, *Gift, Payment and the Sacred in Medieval Popular Religiosity*, Uhlenbeck – Lecture IX, Netherlands Institute for Advanced Study, Wassenaar, 1991.

Cohn, Samuel Kline, *Creating the Florentine State: Peasants and Rebellion, 1348–1434*, Cambridge, 1999.

Colvin, H. M. (ed.), *The History of the King's Works*, i, 1963.

Craeybeckx, J. *Un grand commerce d'importations: les vins de France aux anciens Pays-Bas (xiiie–xvie siècle)*, Paris, 1958.

Czechoslovakian Glass 1350–1980, exhibition catalogue, Corning Museum of Glass, New York, 1981.

Darwin, F. D. S., *Louis d'Orléans (1372–1407)*, London, 1936.

Davids, Karel and Jan Lucassen (eds), *A Miracle Mirrored; The Dutch Republic in its European Context*, Cambridge, 1995.

Davidsohn, Robert, *Geschichte von Florenz*, 4 vols, Berlin, 1896–1927, Italian trans. *Storia di Firenze*, 8 vols, 1956–68.

Davis, R. H. C., *The Medieval Warhorse*, London, 1989.

Daviso di Charvensod, M. C., *I Pedaggi delle Alpi Occidentali nel Medio Evo*, Deputazione Subalpina di Storia Patria, Turin, 1961.

Day, John, *Les Douanes de Gênes 1376–7*, 2 vols, Paris 1963.

Day, John, (ed.), *Études d'histoire monétaire, XIIe–XIXe siècles*, Lille, 1984.

Day, John, *The Medieval Market Economy*, Oxford, 1987.

Day, John, *Monnaies et Marchés au Moyen Age*, Comité pour l'histoire économique et financière de la France, Paris, 1996.

Day, John, *Money and Finance in the Age of Merchant Capitalism*, Oxford, 1999.

De Clercq, Geert (ed.), *Ter Beurze/A la Bourse*, Bruges/Antwerp, 1992.

del Treppo, Mario, *Els Mercaders Catalans i*

l'expansió de la Corona Catalano-Aragonesa al segle XV, Barcelona, 1976.

Denuce, J., 'De Beurs van Antwerpen. Oorsprong en eerste Ontwikkeling 15e en 16e eeuwen', *Antwerpsch Archievenblad* 2nd ser., vi, 1931, pp. 81–141.

Denzel, Markus A., 'Kaufmannshandbücher als Quellengattung zur vergleichenden europäischen Überseegeschichte', in Thomas Beck et al. (eds), *Überseegeschichte*, Beiträge zur Kolonial- und Überseegeschichte, lxxv, 1999, pp. 120–34.

Derolez, R., *The Library of Raphael de Mercatelis*, Ghent, 1979.

de Roover, Raymond, 'The Commercial Revolution of the Thirteenth Century', *Bulletin of the Business Historical Society*, xvi, 1942, pp. 34–9, republished in Frederic C. Lane and Jelle C. Riemersma, *Enterprise and Secular Change*, Homewood, Illinois, 1953, pp. 80–85.

de Roover, Raymond, *Money, Banking and Credit in Medieval Bruges: Italian Merchant Bankers, Lombards and Money-Changers*, Medieval Academy of America, Cambridge, Mass., 1948.

de Roover, Raymond, *L'Evolution de la lettre de change (XIVe–XVIIIe siècles)*, Paris, 1953.

de Roover, Raymond, 'New Interpretations of the History of Banking', *Journal of World History*, ii, 1954, pp. 38–76, reprinted in his *Business*, pp. 200–38.

de Roover, Raymond, 'The Development of Accounting Prior to Luca Pacioli According to the Account Books of Medieval Merchants', in A. C. Littleton and B. S. Yamey (eds), *Studies in the History of Accounting*, London, 1956, pp. 114–74, reprinted in his *Business*, pp. 119–180.

de Roover, Raymond, 'The Organisation of Trade', *Cambridge Economic History of Europe*, iii, Cambridge, 1963, 42–118.

de Roover, Raymond, *The Rise and Decline of the Medici Bank, 1397–1494*, Harvard University Press, Cambridge, Mass., 1963.

de Roover, Raymond, 'Le Marché monétaire à Paris du règne de Philippe le Bel au début du XVe siècle', *Académie des Inscriptions et Belles-Lettres, comptes rendus*, 1968.

de Roover, Raymond, *The Bruges Money Market Around 1400*, Brussels, 1968.

de Roover, Raymond, *Business, Banking, and Economic Thought in Late Medieval and Early Modern Europe, Selected Studies of R. de Roover*, ed. Julius Kirshner, Chicago, 1974.

De Rosa, Luigi, 'Land and Sea Transport and Economic Depression in the Kingdom of Naples from the XIVth to the XVIIIth Century', *Journal of European Economic History*, xxv, 1996, pp. 339–68.

Deviosse, Jean, *Jean le Bon*, Paris, 1985.

Dickstein-Bernard, Claire, *La Gestion financière d'une capitale à ses débuts: Bruxelles, 1334–1467*, Brussels, 1977.

Dini, Bruno (ed.), *Una Pratica di Mercatura in Formazione 1394–5*, Florence, 1980.

Dini, Bruno, 'L'industria serica in Italia Secc. XIII–XV', in Simonetta Cavaciocchi (ed.), *La Seta in Europa Sec. XIII–XX*, Atti del 'Settimana di Studi', xxiv, Istituto Internazionale di Storia Economica 'F. Datini', Prato, 1993, pp. 91–123.

Doehaerd, Renée, 'Les Galères génoises dans la Manche et le Mer du Nord à la fin du XIIIe et au début du XIVe s.', *Bulletin de* l'*Institut Historique Belge de Rome*, xix, 1938, pp. 5–76.

Doehaerd, Renée, *Les Relations commerciales entre Gênes, la Belgique, et l'Outremont au XIIIe et XIVe siècles*, Brussels–Rome, 1941.

Dollinger, Philippe, *La Hanse (XIIe–XVIIe siècles)*, Paris, 1964; Eng. trans., *The German Hansa*, 1970.

Doria, Giorgio and Paola Massa Piergiovanni, *Il sistema portuale della repubblica di Genova*, Genoa, 1988.

Doumerc, Bernard, 'Le galere da mercato', in Alberto Tenenti and Ugo Tucci (eds), *Storia di Venezia*, xii, Il Mare, Rome, 1991, 357–95.

Doumerc, Bernard and Stöckly, Doris, 'L'Evolution du capitalisme marchand à Venise: les financements des *galere da mercato* à la fin du Xve siècle', *Annales H. S. S.*, l, 1995, 133–57.

Dubois, Henri, *Les Foires de Chalon et le commerce dans la vallée de la Saône à la fin du Moyen Age (vers 1280–vers 1430)*, Paris, 1976.

Dubuis, Pierre (ed.), *Ceux qui passent et ceux qui restent, Etudes sur les trafics transalpins et leur impact local*, Grand Saint-Bernard, 1989.

Duby, Georges, *Rural Economy and Country Life in the Medieval West*, 1962, Eng. trans., London, 1968.

Duby, Georges, *Le Dimanche de Bouvines*, Paris, 1973, Eng. trans., *The Legend of Bouvines*, London, 1990.

Dunbabin, Jean, *Charles I of Anjou*, London 1998.

Duvosquel, Jean-Marie, 'Les Routes d'Ypres à Lille et le passage de la Lys au Moyen Age ou de l'économie domaniale aux foires de Flandre', in Erik Aerts et al. (eds), *Studia Historia Œconomica. Liber amicorum Herman Van der Wee*, Leuven, 1993, pp. 93–110.

Dyer, Christopher, *Standards of living in the Later Middle Ages. Social Change in England c. 1200–1520*, Cambridge, 1989.

Edler, Florence, *Glossary of Medieval Terms of Business. Italian Series 1200–1600*, Medieval Academy of America, Cambridge, Mass., 1934.

Edler de Roover, Florence, 'Early Examples of Marine Insurance', *The Journal of Economic History*, v, 1945.

Edler de Roover, Florence, 'Andrea Banchi setaiolo fiorentino del Quattrocento', *Archivio Storico Italiano*, cl, 1992, 877–963.

Endrei, Walter, 'Manufacturing a Piece of Woollen Cloth in Medieval Flanders: How Many Work Hours?' in Erik Aerts and John Munro (eds), *Textiles of the Low Countries in European Economic History*, Leuven, 1990, pp. 14–23.

Epstein, Steven A., *Wills and Wealth in Medieval Genoa, 1150–1250*, Harvard Historical Studies, 103, Cambridge, Mass., 1984.

Epstein, Steven A., *Genoa and the Genoese, 958–1528*, Chapel Hill, 1996.

Epstein, S. R. 'Cities, Regions and the Late Medieval Crisis. Sicily and Tuscany compared', *Past and Present*, cxxx, 1991, pp. 3–50.

Epstein, S. R., *An Island for Itself. Economic Development and Social Change in Late Medieval Sicily*, Cambridge, 1992.

Epstein, S. R., 'Regional Fairs, Institutional Innovation, and Economic Growth in Late

Medieval Europe, *Economic History Review*, 2nd ser., xlvii, 1994, 459–82.

Epstein, S. R., *Freedom and Growth. The Rise of States and Markets in Europe, 1300–1750*, London, 2000.

Favier, Jean, *Un conseiller de Philippe le Bel: Enguerran de Marigny*, Paris, 1963.

Favier, Jean, *Les Finances pontificales à l'èpoque du grand schisme d'Occident 1378–1419*, Bibliothèque des Ecoles Françaises d'Athènes et de Rome, ccxi, 1966.

Favier, Jean, 'Une ville entre deux vocations: la place d'affaires de Paris au XVe siècle', *Annales E. S. C.*, xxviii, 1973, pp. 1245–79

Favier, Jean, *Paris au XVe siècle, 1380–1500*, Nouvelle Histoire de Paris, Paris, 1974.

Favier, Jean, *Philippe le Bel*, Paris, 1978.

Favier, Jean, *Gold and Spices, The Rise of Commerce in the Middle Ages*, 1987, Eng. trans., New York, 1998.

Fawtier, Robert, *The Capetian Kings of France*, 1941, Eng. trans., London, 1960.

Felloni, Giuseppe, 'Struttura e movimenti dell'economia genovese tra due e trecento: bilanci e prospettive di recerca', *Genova, Pisa e il Mediterraneo tra due e trecento*, Società ligure di storia Patria, Genoa, 1984, pp. 153–77.

Fernandez-Armesto, Felipe, *Before Columbus. Exploration and Colonisation from the Mediterranean to the Atlantic, 129–1492*, London, 1987.

Fitch, Marc, 'The London Makers of *Opus Anglicanum*', *Transactions of the London and Middlesex Archaeological Society*, xxvii, 1976, 288–96.

Fiumi, Enrico, 'Economia e vita privata dei fiorentini nelle rilevazione statistiche di Giovanni Villani. Indagine sulle condizioni alimentari', *Archivio Storico Italiano*, cxi, 1953, pp. 207–41.

La Foire, Recueils de la Société Jean Bodin, v, Brussels, 1953, reprinted Paris, 1983.

Fortún, L. J., *Sedes Reales de Navarra*, Pamplona, 1991.

Fossier, Robert, *La Terre et les hommes en Picardie jusqu'à la fin du XIIIe siècle*, Paris – Louvain, 1968.

Fourquin, Guy, *Les Campagnes de la région parisienne à la fin du Moyen Age*, Paris, 1964.

From Byzantium to El Greco Greek Frescoes and Icons, exhibition catalogue, ed. Myrtali Acheimastou-Potamianou, Royal Academy of Arts, London, 1987.

Fryde, Edmund B., *Studies in Medieval Trade and Finance*, London ,1983.

Fryde, Edmund B., *William de la Pole. Merchant and King's Banker (†1366)*, London and Ronceverte, 1988.

Gardiner, Robert and Richard W. Unger (eds), *Cogs, Caravels and Galleons. The Sailing Ship 1000–1650*, London, 1994.

Gardiner, Robert (ed.), *The Age of the Galley*, London, 1995.

Gascon, R., *Grand commerce et vie urbaine au XVIe siècle. Lyons et ses marchands*, Paris, 1971.

Gilchrist, John, *The Church and Economic Activity in the Middle Ages*, London and New York, 1969.

Gimpel, Jean, *The Medieval Machine*, 2nd edn, Eng. trans., Aldershot, 1988.

Glauser, Fritz, 'Der Gotthardstransit von 1500 bis 1660', in Jean-François Bergier (ed.), *Histoire des Alpes. Perspectives Nouvelles*, special number of *Revue Suisse*

d'*Histoire*, xxix, 1979, pp. 16–52.

Goldthwaite, Richard A., *The Building of Renaissance Florence*, Baltimore, 1980.

Goldthwaite, Richard A., *Wealth and the Demand for Art in Italy 1300–1600*, Baltimore, 1993.

Goris, J.A., *Etude sur les colonies marchandes méridionales (portugais, espagnols, italiens) à Anvers de 1488 á 1567*, Louvain, 1925.

Grandchamp, P. G. et al., *La Ville de Cluny et ses Maisons: XIe–XVe siècles*, Paris, 1997.

Graus, František, 'Die Handelsbeziehungen Böhmens zu Deutschland und Österreich im 14. und zu Beginn des 15. jahrhunderts', *Historica*, ii, Prague, 1960, pp. 77–110.

Green, Louis, *Castruccio Castracani*, Oxford, 1986.

Grendler, Paul F., *Schooling in Renaissance Italy 1300–1600*, Baltimore, 1989.

Grote, Ludwig, «Hier bin ich ein Heer» Dürer in Venedig, Munich, 1956.

Guillemain, Bernard, *La Cour pontificale d'Avignon, 1309–76*, Paris, 1962.

Haedeke, Hans Ulrich, *Metalwork*, Eng. trans., 1970.

Halaga, Ondrej R., 'A Mercantilist Initiative to Compete with Venice: Kaschau's Fustian Monoploy (1411)', *Journal of European Economic History*, xii, 1983, pp. 407–35.

Hammel-Kiesow, Rolf, 'Hansischer Seehandel und wirtschaftliche Wechsellagen. Der Umsatz im Lübecker Hafen in der zweiten Hälfte des 14. Jahrhundert, 1492–6 und 1680–2', in Stuart Jenks and Michael North (eds), *Der hansische Sonderweg? Beiträge zur Sozial- unt Wirtschaftsgeschichte der Hanse*, Quellen und Darstellungen zur hansische Geschichte, n. s., xxxxix, Cologne/Vienna, 1993, pp. 77–94.

Hanke, L., *The Imperial City of Potosi*, The Hague, 1956.

Harrison, D. F., 'Bridges and Economic Development, 1300–1800', *Economic History Review*, 2nd ser., xlv, 1992, pp. 240–61.

Harte, N. B. and Ponting, K. G. (eds), *Cloth and Clothing in Medieval Europe*, London, 1983.

Hartt, Frederick, *History of Italian Renaissance Art: Painting, Sculpture, Architecture*, 4th edn, revised David G. Wilkins, London, 1994.

Harvey, Paul, *Medieval Maps*, British Library, London, 1991.

Hatcher, John, *English Tin Production and Trade Before 1550*, Oxford, 1973.

Hatcher, John, *The History of the British Coal Industry. Vol. 1: Before 1700: Towards the Age of Coal*, Oxford, 1993.

Haverkamp, Alfred, *Herrschaftsformen der frühstaufer in Reichsitalien*, Trier, 1971.

Heers, Jacques, *Gênes au XVe siècle. Activite économique et problèmes sociaux*, Paris, 1961 (shortened version *Gênes au XVe siècle*, Paris, 1971).

Heers, Jacques, *L'Occident aux XIVe et XVe siècles. Aspects économiques et sociaux*, Paris, 2nd edn, 1966.

Heers, Jacques, *Esclaves et domestiques au Moyen Age dans le monde méditerranéen*, Paris, 1981.

Henderson, John, *Piety and Charity in Late Medieval Florence*, Oxford, 1994.

Henneman, John Bell, *Royal Taxation in Fourteenth-Century France. The Development of War Financing 1322–1356*,

Princeton, 1971.

Herald, Jacqueline, *Renaissance Dress in Italy 1400–1500*, History of Dress Series, London and New Jersey, 1981.

Herlihy, David J., *Pisa in the Early Renaissance; a Study of Urban Growth*, New Haven, Conn., 1958.

Herlihy, David J., *Medieval and Renaissance Pistoia: the Social History of an Italian Town, 1200–1450*, New Haven, Conn., 1967.

Herlihy, David and Klapisch-Zuber, Christiane, *Tuscans and their Families*, 1978, abbreviated Eng. trans., New Haven and London, 1985.

Herlihy, David, *Opera Muliebria. Women and Work in Medieval Europe*, New York, 1990.

Heyd, W., *Histoire du commerce du Levant au Moyen Age*, French edn, 2 vols, Leipzig, 1885–6.

Hilario Casado Alonso, 'El comercio internacional burgalés en los ss. XV & XVI', in Floriano Ballesteros Caballero (ed.), *Actas del V Centenaio del Consulado de Burgos*, Burgos, i, 1994, pp .175–274.

Hillgarth, J. N., *The Spanish Kingdoms 1250–1516*, 2 vols, Oxford, 1978.

Hitzer, Hans, *Der Straße*, Munich, 1971.

Hocquet, Jean-Claude, *Le Sel et la fortune de Venise*, 2 vols, Lille, 1978–9.

Hocquet, Jean-Claude, *Le Sel et le pouvoir*, Lille, 1985

Hocquet, Jean-Claude (ed.), *Le Roi, le marchand et le sel*, Lille, 1987.

Holmes, G., 'Florentine Merchants in England 1346–1436', *Economic History Review*, 2nd ser., xiii, 1960, pp. 193–208.

Honeybourne, M. B., *Sketch Map of London Under Richard II*, London Topographical Society, xciii, 1960.

Hoshino, Hidetoshi, *L'arte della lana in Firenze nel basso medioevo. Il commercio della lana e il mercato dei panni fiorentini nei secoli XIII–XV*, Biblioteca Storica Toscana, xxi, 1980.

Hoshino, Hidetoshi, 'The Rise of the Florentine Woollen Industry in the Fourteenth Century', in N. B. Harte and K. G. Ponting (eds), *Cloth and Clothing in Medieval Europe*, London, 1983, pp. 184–204.

Hunt, Edwin S., *The Medieval Super-Companies. A Study of the Peruzzi Company of Florence*, Cambridge, 1994.

Hunt, Edwin S. and James M. Murray, *A History of Business in Medieval Europe 1200–1500*, Cambridge, 1999.

Hyde, J. K., 'Some Uses of Literacy in Venice and Florence in the Thirteenth and Fourteenth Centuries' in his *Literacy*, pp. 112–135.

Hyde, J. K., 'The Role of Diplomatic Correspondence and Reporting: News and Chronicles', in his *Literacy*, pp. 217–59.

Hyde, J. K. (ed. Daniel Waley), *Literacy and its Uses. Studies on Late Medieval Italy*, Manchester, 1993.

Iliescu, Octavien, 'Nouvelles éditions d'actes notariés instrumentés au XIVe siècle dans les colonies génoises des bouches du Danube', *Revue des Études Sud-Est Européennes*, xv, 1977, 113–29.

Irsigler, F., *Die Wirtschaftliche Stellung der Stadt Köln im 14. und 15. Jahrhundert*, Vierteljahrschrift fur Sozial- und Wirtschaftsgeschiche, Supplement 65, 1979.

James, Margery K., 'The Fluctuations of the Anglo-Gascon Wine Trade During the Fourteenth Century', *Economic History Review*, 2nd ser., iv, 1951–2, pp. 170–196.

James, Margery K., *Studies in the Medieval Wine Trade*, Oxford, 1971.

Javier Fortun, Luis (ed.), *Sedes Reales de Navarra*, Pamplona, 1991.

Jenks, Stuart, 'Die *Carta Mercatoria*: ein "Hansisches" Privileg', *Hansische Geschichtsblätter*, cviii, 1990, pp. 45–86.

Jenks, Stuart, *England, die Hanse und Preußen: Handel und Diplomatie; 1377–1474*, 3 vols, Quellen und Darstellungen zur hansische Geschichte, n. s., xxxxviii, Cologne/Vienna, 1992.

Jesse, Wilhelm, *Der Wendische Münzverein*, Lübeck, 1928.

Jordan, William Chester, *The Great Famine. Northern Europe in the Early Fourteenth Century*, Princeton, New Jersey, 1996.

Kazimir, Stefan et al., *Kremnická mincovňa 1328–1978*, Kremnica 1978.

Kaye, Joel, *Economy and Nature in the Fourteenth Century. Money, Market Exchange and the Emergence of Scientific Thought*, Cambridge, 1998.

Kedar, Benjamin Z., *Merchants in Crisis: Genoese and Venetian Men of Affairs and the Fourteenth-Century Depression*, New Haven, Conn., 1976

Keene, Derek, 'Medieval London and its Region', *The London Journal*, xiv, 1989, pp. 99–111.

Kelly, H. A., 'Bishop, Prioress and Bawd in the Stews of Southwark', *Speculum*, lxxv, 2000, pp. 342–88.

King, Donald, 'Types of Silk Cloth Used in England 1200–1500' in Simonetta Cavaciocchi (ed.), *La Seta in Europa Sec. XIII–XX*, Atti del 'Settimana di Studi', xxiv, Istituto Internazionale di Storia Economica 'F. Datini', Prato, 1993, pp. 457–64.

Klapisch-Zuber, Christiane, *Les Maîtres de marbre: Carrare 1300–1600* , Paris, 1969.

Klein, Julius, *The Mesta: A Study in Spanish Economic History*, Cambridge, Mass., 1920.

Klein, p. W., *De Trippen in de 17e eeuw*, Assen, 1965.

Koch, Rainer (ed.), *Brücke zwischen den Völkern. Zur Geschichte der Frankfurter Messe*, 3 vols, Frankfurt, 1991.

Kosi, Miha, *Potujoči srednji vek [Roads, Travellers and Traffic in Slovenian Territory]*, Ljubljana, 1998, with English summary.

Kranz, Horst, 'Klerus und Kohle, ein Lütticher Fördervertrag von 1356', *Vierteljahrsschrift fur Sozial und Wirtschaftgeschchte*, lxxxv, 1998, pp. 461–76.

Krüger, Herbert, *Das Alteste Deutsche Routenhandbuch. Jörg Gails "Raißbüchlin"*, Graz, 1974

Labarge, Margaret Wade, *Medieval Travellers. The Rich and the Restless*, London, 1982.

Lane, Frederic C., 'Venetian Shipping during the Commercial Revolution', *American Historical Review*, xxxviii, 1933, reprinted in his *Venice and History*, pp. 3–24.

Lane, Frederic C., *Venetian Ships and Shipbuilders of the Renaissance*, Baltimore, 1934.

Lane, Frederic C., 'Rhythm and Rapidity of Turnover in Venetian Trade of the Fifteenth Century', *Studi in onore di Gino Luzzatto*, i, Milan, 1949, translated and collected in Lane, *Venice and History*, pp. 109–27.

Lane, Frederic C., 'Fleets and Fairs', *Studi in oonore di Armando Sapori*, i, Milan, 1957,651–63, reprinted in his *Venice and History*, pp. 128–41.

Lane, Frederic C, 'The Economic Meaning of the Invention of the Compass', *American Historical Review*, 1963, pp. 605–17.

Lane, Frederic C., *Venice and History*, Johns Hopkins Press, Baltimore, 1966.

Lane, Frederic C., *Venice. A Maritime Republic*, Johns Hopkins Press, Baltimore, 1973.

Lane, Frederic C., *Studies in Venetian Social and Economic History*, Aldershot, 1987.

Lane, Frederic C. and Reinhold C. Mueller, *Money and Banking in Medieval and Renaissance Venice*, i, Johns Hopkins Press, Baltimore, 1985.

Larner, John, *Culture and Society in Italy 1290–1420*, London, 1971.

Larner, John, *Marco Polo and the Discovery of the World*, New Haven, Conn., 1999.

La Roncière, Charles de, *Un changeur Florentin du Trecento: Lippo di Fede del Sega (1285 env.–1363 env.)*, Paris, 1973.

La Roncière, Charles de, *Florence, centre économique régional au XIVe siècle*, 5 vols, Aix-en-Provence, 1976. A compressed and slightly revised version, published as *Prix et salaires à Florence au XIVe Siècle (1280–1380)*, Collection de l'École Française de Rome, lix, Rome, 1982.

Laurent, Henri ,*Un grand commerce d'exportation au Moyen Age. La Draperie des Pays-Bas en France et dans les pays méditerranéens (XIIe–XVe siécle)*. Paris, 1935.

Le Goff, Jaques, *Marchands et banquiers du Moyen Age*, 7th edn, Paris, 1986.

Leguay, Jean-Pierre *La Rue au Moyen Age*, Rennes, 1984.

Leguay, Jean-Pierre, 'Urban Life' in Michael Jones (ed.), *New Cambridge Medieval History*, vi, Cambridge, 2000, pp. 102–23.

Léonard, E., *Les Angevins de Naples*, Paris, 1954.

Liagre-de Sturler, Léone, *Les Relations commerciales entre Gênes, la Belgique, et l'Outremonet d'après les archives notariales génoises (1320–1400)*, 2 vols, Brussels and Rome, 1969.

Lightbown, R. W., *Secular Goldsmiths' Work in Medieval France: A History*, Reports of the Research Committee of the Society of Antiquaries of London, xxxvi, 1978.

Lilley, Keith, *Modernising the Medieval City: Urban Design and Civic Improvement in the Middle Ages*, Royal Holloway, University of London, Department of Geography, Research Papers, 1999.

Little, Lester K. *Religious Poverty and the Profit Economy in Medieval Europe*, Ithaca, N. Y., 1978.

Lloyd, T. H., *The English Wool Trade in the Middle Ages*, Cambridge, 1977.

Lloyd, T. H., *Alien Merchants in England in the High Middle Ages*, Brighton, 1982, pp. 83–93.

Lloyd, T.H., *England and the German Hanse 1157–1611*, Cambridge, 1991.

Lopez, Roberto, *Genova marinaria nel Duecento: Benedetto Zaccaria*, Messina, 1933.

Lopez, Robert Sabatino, 'Market Expansion: The Case of Genoa', *Journal of Economic History*, xxiv, 1964, pp. 445–464, with critical comment by Frederic C. Lane, pp. 465–9.

Lopez, Robert S., 'The Trade of Medieval Europe: The South', in M. M. Postan and E. E. Rich (eds), *The Cambridge Economic History of Europe*, i, Cambridge, 1952, pp. 257–354, reprinted ii, 2nd edn, Cambridge, 1987, pp. 306–401.

Lopez, Robert S., *The Commercial Revolution of the Middle Ages, 950–1350*, Englewood Cliffs, 1971.

Lucas, Henry S., 'The Great European Famine of 1315, 1316 and 1317', *Speculum*, v, 1930, pp. 343–77, reprinted in E. M. Carus-Wilson, *Essays in Economic History*, ii, London, 1962, pp. 49–72.

Lugon, Antoine, 'Le Trafic commercial par le Simplon et le désenclavement du Valai oriental (fin du XIIe – milieu du XIVe siècle), in Dubuis, Pierre (ed.), *Ceux qui passent et ceux qui restent, Etudes sur les trafics transalpins et leur impact local*, Grand Saint-Bernard, 1989, pp. 87–99.

Lutz, Elmar, *Die rechtliche Struktur süddeutscher Handelsgesellschaften in der Zeit der Fugger*, Tübingen, 1976.

Gino Luzzatto, 'Sull'attendabilità di alcune statistiche economiche medievali', *Giornale degli Economisti*, 1929, reprinted in his *Studi di Storia Economica Veneziana*, Padua, 1954, pp. 271–84.

Luzzatto, Gino, 'Tasso d'interesse e usura a Venezia nei secc. XIII–XV', *Miscellanea in onore di Roberto Cessi*, Rome, 1958.

Luzzatto, Gino, *An Economic History of Italy*, 1958, Eng. trans. 1961 (*Breve storia economica d'Italia*, 2nd edn, 1965, not translated).

Lyon, Bryce D., *From Fief to Indenture*, Cambridge, Mass., 1957.

Mackay, Angus, *Money, Prices and Politics in Fifteenth-Century Castile*, Studies in History, xxviii, Royal Historical Society, 1981.

Mackenney, Richard, *Tradesmen and Traders. The World of the Guilds in Venice and Europe, c. 1250–c. 1650* (Totowa, New Jersey, 1987)

McArdle, Frank, *Altopascio: A Study in Tuscan Rural Society, 1587–1784*, Cambridge, 1978.

McCusker, John J. and Cora Gravesteijn, *The Beginnings of Commercial and Financial Journalism*, Amsterdam, 1991.

McKitterick, David, 'The Beginning of Printing', in Christopher Allmand (ed.), *The New Cambridge Medieval History*, vii (*c. 1415–c. 1500*), Cambridge, 1998, pp. 287–98.

Mallett, M. E., 'Anglo–Florentine Commercial Relations, 1465–91', *Economic History Review*, 2nd ser., xv, 1962–3.

Mallett, Michael, *Florentine Galleys in the Fifteenth Century*, Oxford, 1967.

Małowist, Marian, 'The Trade of Eastern Europe in the Later Middle Ages', in M. M. Postan and Edward Miller (eds), *The Cambridge Economic History of Europe*, ii, 2nd edn, Cambridge, 1987, pp. 525–612.

Maréchal, Joseph , 'La Colonie espagnole de Bruges du XIVe au XVIe siècle', *Revue du Nord*, 35, 1953, pp. 5–40.

Martindale, Andrew, 'The Venetian Sala del Gran Consiglio and its Fourteenth-Century Decoration', *Antiquaries Journal*, lxxiii, 1993, pp. 76–124.

Marx, Anna Vannini (ed.), *Trasporti e sviluppo economico secoli XIII–XVIII*, Atti del 'Settimana di Studi', v, Istituto

Internazionale di Storia Economica 'F. Datini', Prato, 1986.

Masschaele, James, 'Transport Costs in Medieval England', *Economic History Review*, 2nd ser., xlvi, 1992, pp. 266–79.

Masschaele, James, *Peasants, Merchants and Markets: Inland Trade in Medieval England, 1150–1350*, Basingstoke, 1997.

Materné, Jan, 'Schoon ende Bequaem tot versamelinghe der cooplieden' in De Clercq (ed.), *Ter Beurze*, pp. 51–85.

Mayhew, N. J., 'Population, Money Supply, and the Velocity of Circulation in England, 1300–1700', *Economic History Review*, xlviii, 1995, 238–57.

Mazzaoui, Maureen Fennell, *The Italian Cotton Industry in the Later Middle Ages 1100–1600*, Cambridge, 1981.

Melis, Federigo, 'Mercanti-imprenditori italiani in Fiandra alla fine del '300', 1958, collected in his *I mercanti Italiani*, pp. 297–316.

Melis, Federigo, 'La diffusione nel Mediterraneo occidentale dei panni di Wervicq e delle altre città della Lys attorno al 1400' (1962), collected in his *I mercanti Italiani*, pp. 317–344.

Melis, Federigo, *Aspetti della vita economica medievale – studi nell'Archivio Datini di Prato*, Monte dei Paschi di Siena, 1962.

Melis, Federigo, 'Werner Sombart e I Problemi della Navigazione nel Medioevo' in *L'opera di Werner Sombart nel centenario della nascita*, supplement to *Economia e Storia*, viii, 1964, reprinted in his *I trasporti*.

Melis, Federigo, 'Le società commerciali a Firenze dalla secondo metà del XIV al XVI secolo', 1965, reprinted in his *L'Azienda*, pp. 161–78.

Melis, Federigo, 'Note sur le mouvement du port de Beyrouth d'après la documentation florentine aux environs de 1400', in *Sociétés et compagnies de commerce en Orient et dans l'Océan Indien. Actes du huitième colloque international d'histoire maritime*, Paris, 1970.

Melis, Federigo, 'Intensità e regolarità nella diffusione dell'informazione economica generale nel Mediterraneo e in Occidente alla fine del Medioevo', in *Mélanges en l'honneur de Fernand Braudel. Histoire économique du monde méditerranéen 1450–1650*, Toulouse, 1973, i, pp. 389–424.

Melis, Federigo, 'La lana della Spagna Mediterranea e della barberia occidentale nei srecoli XIV–XV', in Marco Spallanzani (ed.), *La lana come materia prima. I fenomeni della sua produzione e circolazione nei secoli XIII–XVII*, Istituto Internazionale di Storia Economica 'F. Datini', Prato, Atti delle 'Settimane di Studio', i, Florence, 1974, 241–51, reprinted in his *I mercanti italiani* pp. 233–49.

Melis, Federigo, *I trasporti e le communicazioni nel medioevo*, Florence, 1984.

Melis, Federigo, *I vini Italiani nel medioevo*, Florence, 1984.

Melis, Federigo, *La banca pisana e le origini della banca moderna*, Florence, 1987.

Melis, Federigo, *Industrie e commercie nella Toscana medievale*, Florence 1989.

Melis, Federigo, *I mercanti Italiani nell'Europa medievale e rinascimentale*, Florence, 1990.

Melis, Federigo, *L'Azienda nel Medioevo*, Florence, 1991.

Miskimin, H., *The Economy of Early Renaissance Europe 1300–1460*, Cambridge, 1975.

Miskimin, H., *Cash, Credit and Crisis in Europe, 1300–1600*, Aldershot, 1989.

Molà, Luca, *La comunità dei lucchesi a Venezia. Immigrazione e industria della seta nel tardo Medioevo*, Venice, 1994.

Mollat, G., *Les Papes d'Avignon (1305–1378)*, Paris, 1920, Eng. trans. *The Popes at Avignon, 1305–78*, 1963.

Mollat, Michel, *Le Commerce maritime normand à la fin du Moyen Age*, Paris, 1952.

Mollat, Michel, *Le Rôle du sel dans l'histoire*, Paris, 1968.

Muel, Francis, *The Tapestry of the Apocalypse at Angers, Front and Back*, abbreviated English translation of *La Tenture de l'apocalypse d'Angers*, Nantes, 1996.

Mueller, Reinhold C., 'The Spufford Thesis on Foreign Exchange: the Evidence of Exchange Rates', *Journal of European Economic History*, xxiv, 1995, pp. 121–9.

Mueller, Reinhold C., *The Venetian Money Market. Banks, Panics, and the Public Debt 1200–1500*, Baltimore, 1997.

Mundy, John H., and Peter Riesenberg, *The Medieval Town*, Princeton, 1958.

Murray, Alexander, *Reason and Society in the Middle Ages*, Oxford, 1978.

Munro, John H., *Wool, Cloth and Gold. The Struggle for Bullion in Anglo–Burgundian Trade 1340–1478*, Brussels and Toronto, 1973.

Munro, John H., 'Wool Price Schedules and the Qualities of English Wools in the Later Middle Ages', *Textile History*, ix, 1978, pp. 118–69.

Munro, John H., 'The Medieval Scarlet and the Economics of Sartorial Splendour' in N. B. Harte and K. G. Ponting (eds), *Cloth and Clothing in Medieval Europe*, 1983, pp. 13–70.

Munro, John H. 'Industrial Transformations in the North-west European Textile Trades c. 1290–1340: Economic Progress or Economic Crisis?, in Bruce M. S. Campbell (ed.), *Before the Black Death. Studies in the 'Crisis' of the Early Fourteenth Century*, Manchester, 1991. pp. 110–48. All three reprinted in his *Textiles*.

Munro, John H., *Bullion Flows and Monetary Policies in England and the Low Countries, 1350–1500*, Aldershot, 1992.

Munro, John H., *Textiles, Towns and Trade: Essays in the Economic History of Late Medieval England and the Low Countries*, Aldershot, 1994.

Munro, John H., 'The Industrial Crisis of the English Textile Towns, c. 1290–c. 1330', in Michael Prestwich, Richard Britnell and Robin Frame (eds), *Thirteenth-Century England*, vii, Woodbridge, 1999, pp. 103–42.

Munro, John H., 'The Symbiosis of Towns and Textiles: Urban Institutions and the Changing Fortunes of Cloth Manufacturing in the Low Countries and England, 1270–1570', *The Journal of Early Modern History: Contacts, Comparisons, Contrasts*, iii, 1999, pp. 1–74.

Munro, John H., 'The "New Institutional Economics" and the Changing Fortunes of Fairs in Medieval and Early Modern Europe: The Textile Trades, Warfare and Transaction Costs', *Vierteljahrschrift für Sozial- und Wirtschaftgeschichte*, lxxxviii, 2001, pp. 1–47.

Nef, John U., 'Mining and Metallurgy in Medieval Civilisation', in M. M. Postan and E. E. Rich (eds), *The Cambridge Economic History of Europe*, ii, 2nd edn, Cambridge,

1987, pp. 693–761.

Niccolini da Camugliano, Ginevra, *The Chronicles of a Florentine Family, 1200–1400*, London, 1933.

Nicholas, David, 'Economic Reorientation and Social Change in Fourteenth-Century Flanders', *Past and Present*, lxx, 1976, pp. 3–29, collected in *Trade, Urbanisation and the Family. Studies in the History of Medieval Flanders*, Aldershot, 1996.

Nicholas, David, *The Metamorphosis of a Medieval City – Ghent in the Age of the Arteveldes 1302–1390*, University of Nebraska Press, Lincoln, Nebraska, 1987.

Nicholas, David, *Medieval Flanders*, London and New York, 1992.

Nightingale, Pamela, *A Medieval Mercantile Community. The Grocers' Company and the Politics and Trade of London, 1000–1485*, New Haven and London, 1995.

North, Michael, *Geldumlauf und Wirtschaftskonjunktur im sudlichen Ostseeraum an der Wende zur Neuzeit (1440–1570)*, Kieler historische Studien, 35, Sigmaringen, 1990.

Ohler, Norbert, *The Medieval Traveller*, 1986, Eng. trans. Woodbridge, 1989.

Origo, Iris, 'The Domestic Enemy: the Eastern Slaves in Tuscany in the Fourteenth and Fifteenth Centuries', *Speculum*, xxx, 1955, 321–66.

Origo, Iris, *The Merchant of Prato. Francesco di Marco Datini*, London, 1957.

Parks, G. B., *The English Traveller to Italy*, i, The Middle Ages to 1525, Rome, 1954.

Parsons, E. J. S., *The Map of Great Britain circa AD 1360, known as the Gough Map*, Oxford, 1958.

Partner, Peter, *The Lands of St Peter*, London, 1972.

Patrone, Anna Maria, *Le Casane astigiane in Savoia*, Deputazione Subalpina di Storia Patria, Turin, 1959.

Peeters, J. P. , 'De-industrialization in the Small and Medium-sized Towns in Brabant at the End of the Middle Ages', in Herman van der Wee (ed.), *The Rise and Decline of Urban Industries in Italy and in the Low Countries*, Leuven, 1988, pp. 165–86.

Phillips, Carla Rahn and William D. Phillips Jr., *Spain's Golden Fleece: Wool Production and the Wool Trade from the Middle Ages to the Nineteenth Century*, Johns Hopkins, Baltimore, 1997.

Pinto, Giuliano, 'Firenze e la carestia del 1346–7', *Archivio Storico Italiano*, cxxx, 1972, pp. 3–84, reprinted in: Pinto, Giuliano, *La Toscana nel tardo medioevo*, Florence, 1982.

Plesner, Johan, *Una rivoluzione stradale del Dugento*, Acta Jutlandica, Copenhagen, 1938.

Postan, M. M., 'The Trade of Europe: The North', in M. M. Postan and E. E. Rich (eds), *The Cambridge Economic History of Europe*, ii, 2nd edn, Cambridge, 1987, pp. 168–305.

Pounds, N. J. G., 'Europe in the Early Fourteenth Century' in *An Historical Geography of Europe 450 BC to AD 1330*, Cambridge, 1973.

Power, Eileen, *The Wool Trade in English Medieval History*, Oxford, 1941

Prescott, H. F. M., *Jerusalem Journey. Pilgrimage to the Holy Land in the Fifteenth Century*, London, 1954.

Prescott, H. F .M., *Once To Sinai: The Further Pilgrimage of Father Felix Fabri*, London, 1957.

Prevenier, Walter and Blockmans, Wim P., *The Burgundian Netherlands*, Antwerp, 1983, Eng. trans., Cambridge, 1986.

Pryor, John H., 'Foreign Policy and Economic Policy of the Angevins of Sicily and the Economic Decline of Southern Italy', in L. O. Frappell (ed.), *Principalities, Powers and Estates. Studies in Medieval and Early Modern Government and Society*, Adelaide, 1980, pp. 43–55.

Pryor, John H., *Geography, Technology and War. Studies in the Maritime History of the Mediterranean, 649–1571*, Cambridge, 1988.

Pryor, John H., *Commerce, Shipping and Naval Warfare in the Medieval Mediterranean*, London, 1987.

Pullan, Brian, *Rich and Poor in Renaissance Venice*, Oxford, 1971.

Quaglia, Lucien, *La Maison du Grand-Saint-Bernard*, Martigny, 1972.

Renouard, Yves, *Les Relations des papes d'Avignon et des compagnies commerciales et bancaires de 1316 à 1378*, Bibliothèque des Ecoles Françaises d'Athènes et de Rome, cli, Paris, 1941.

Renouard, Yves, *The Avignon Papacy 1305–1403*, 2nd edn, 1962, Eng. trans., 1970.

Renouard, Yves, 'Routes, étapes et vitesse de marche de France à Rome au XIIIeme et au XIVeme siècle d'aprés les itinéraires d'Eude Rigaud (1254) et de Barthélemy Bonis (1350), in *Studi in onore di Amintore Fanfani*, iii, Milan, 1962.

Renouard, Yves, *Les Hommes d'affaires italiens du Moyen Age*, Paris, 1968.

Renouard, Yves, *Les Villes d'Italie de la fin du Xe siècle au debut du XIVe siècle*, ii, 2nd edn, 1969.

Reyerson, Kathryn L., 'Medieval Silks in Montpellier: The Silk Market *ca.* 1250–*ca.* 1350', *Journal of European Economic History*, xi, 1982, pp. 117–40, collected in *Society, Law and Trade in Medieval Montpellier*, Aldershot, 1995.

Reyerson, Kathryn L., *Business, Banking and Finance in Medieval Montpellier*, Toronto, 1985.

Reyerson, Kathryn L., 'Commerce and Communications', *New Cambridge Medieval History*, v, Cambridge, 1999, 50–70.

Richmond, Colin, *John Hopton. A Fifteenth-Century Suffolk Gentleman*, Cambridge, 1981.

Riu, Manuel, 'Banking and Society in Late Medieval and Early Modern Aragon', in Chiapelli (ed.), *The Dawn of Modern Banking*.

Robinson, Jancis (ed.), *The Oxford Companion to Wine*, Oxford, 1994.

Rörig, Fritz, *The Medieval Town*, 4th edn, 1964, Eng. trans., London, 1967.

Rouse, Richard H. and Mary A., *Manuscripts and their Makers, Commercial Book Producers in Medieval Paris 1200–1500*, London, 2000.

Rubin, Patricia Lee and Alison Wright, *Renaissance Florence. The Art of the 1470s*, National Gallery, London, 1999.

Ruddock, A. A., *Italian Merchants and Shipping in Southampton, 1270–1600*, Southampton, 1961.

Runciman, Steven, *History of the Crusades*, 3 vols, Cambridge, 1951–4

Runciman, Steven, *The Sicilian Vespers*, Cambridge, 1958.

Sapori, Armando, *La crisi delle compagnie mercantili dei Bardi e dei Peruzzi*, Florence, 1926.

Sapori, Armando, *Una compagnia di Calimala ai primi del Trecento*, Biblioteca Storica Toscana, vii, Florence, 1932.

Sapori, Armando, (ed.), *I libri di commercio dei Peruzzi*, Milan, 1934.

Sapori, Armando, (ed.), *I libri degli Alberti del Giudice*, Milan, 1943.

Sapori, Armando, *Le Marchand Italien au Moyen Age*, Paris, 1952; abbreviated Eng. trans.: *The Italian Merchant in the Middle Ages*, New York, 1970.

Sapori, Armando, *Studi di storia economica medievale…secoli XIII–XIV–XV*, 3rd edn, 3 vols, Florence, 1955–67.

Saunders, Ann (ed.), *The Royal Exchange*, London Topographical Society, 152, 1997.

Scammell, G. V., *The World Encompassed. The First European Maritime Empires c. 800–1650*, London and New York, 1981.

Schneidmüller, Bernd, 'Die Frankfurter Messen des Mittelalters – Wirtschaftliche Entwicklung, herrschaftliche Privilegierung, regionale Konkurrenz' in Koch (ed.), *Brücke zwischen den Völkern der Frankfurter Messe*, i, pp. 67–84.

Schofield, John, *Medieval London Houses*, New Haven and London, 1994.

Scott, Margaret, *Late Gothic Europe, 1400–1500*, History of Dress Series, London and New Jersey, 1980.

Sella, Domenico, 'European Industries 1500–1750', in Carlo M. Cipolla (ed.) *Fontana Economic History of Europe*, ii, 1974, pp. 354–426.

Sicard, G., *Aux origines des sociétés anonymes. Les Moulins de Toulouse au Moyen Age*, Paris, 1953.

Sosson, Jean-Pierre, *Les Travaux publics de la ville de Bruges, XIVe–XVe siècles. Les Matériaux. Les Hommes*, Brussels, 1977.

Sosson, Jean-Pierre, 'Travaux publics et politiques économiques. L'Example de quelques villes des anciens Pays-Bas (XIVe–XVe siècle)', in Eric Aerts et al. (eds), *Studia Historia Œconomica. Liber amicorum Herman Van der Wee*, Leuven, 1993, pp. 239–58.

Spallanzani, Marco (ed.), *La lana come materia prima. I fenomeni della sua produzione e circolazione nei secoli XIII–XVII*, Atti delle 'Settimane di Studio', i, Istituto Internazionale di Storia Economica 'F. Datini', Prato, Florence, 1974.

Spallanzani, Marco (ed.), *Produzione commercio e consumo dei panna di lana (nei secoli XII–XVIII)*, Atti delle 'Settimane di Studio', ii, Istituto Internazionale di Storia Economica 'F. Datini', Prato, Florence, 1976.

Spallanzani, Marco, 'A Note on Florentine Banking in the Renaissance: Orders of Payment and Cheques', *Journal of European Economic History*, vii (1978), 145–65.

Spallanzani, Marco, 'Il piatto islamico Venier-Molin del Bargello', Andrew Morrogh et al. (eds), *Renaissance Studies in Honor of Craig Hugh Smyth*, Villa I Tatti, vii, Florence, 1985, ii, pp. 465–76.

Sprandel, Rolf, *Das Eisengewerbe im Mittelalter*, Stuttgart, 1968.

Sprandel, Rolf, *Das Mittelalterliche Zahlungsystem nach hansisch-nordischen Quellen des 13.–15. Jahrhunderts*, Stuttgart, 1975.

Spufford, Margaret, 'Literacy, Trade and Religion in the Commercial Centres of Europe', in Karel Davids and Jan Lucassen (eds), *A Miracle Mirrored; The Dutch Republic in its European Context*, Cambridge University Press, 1995, pp. 229–83.

Spufford, Peter and Margaret, *Eccleshall*, Keele, 1964.

Spufford, Peter, 'La Rôle de la monnaie dans la révolution commerciale du XIIIe siècle' in John Day (ed.), *Etudes d'histoire monétaire, XIIe–XIXe siècles*, Lille, 1984, pp. 355–95.

Spufford, Peter, *Handbook of Medieval Exchange*, Royal Historical Society, Guides and Handbooks 13, London, 1986.

Spufford, Peter, 'Coinage and Currency' in M. M. Postan and E. E. Rich (eds), *The Cambridge Economic History of Europe*, ii, 2nd edn, Cambridge, 1987, pp. 788–873.

Spufford, Peter, 'Mint Organisation in Late Medieval Europe' in Peter Spufford and N. J. Mayhew (eds), *Later Medieval Mints: Organisation, Administration and Techniques*, British Archaeological Reports, International Series, Oxford, 1987, pp. 5–27.

Spufford, Peter, *Money and its Use in Medieval Europe*, Cambridge University Press, Cambridge, 1988.

Spufford, Peter, 'Spätmittelalterliche Kaufmannsnotizbücher als Quelle zur Bankengeschichte. Ein Projektbericht', in Michael North (ed.), *Kredit im spätmittelalterlichen und frühneuzeitlichen Europa*, Quellen und Darstellungen zur Hansischen Geschichte, n. s. xxxvii, Hansischen Geschichtsverein, 1991, pp. 103–20.

Spufford, Peter, 'Financial Markets and Money Movements in the Medieval Occident', in *Viajeros, peregrinos, mercaderes en el Occidente Medieval*, Actas de la XVIII Semana de Estudios Medievales de Estella, Pamplona, 1992, pp. 201–16.

Spufford, Peter, 'Access to Credit and Capital in the Commercial Centres of Europe', in Karel Davids and Jan Lucassen (eds), *A Miracle Mirrored; The Dutch Republic in European Perspective*, Cambridge University Press, Cambridge, 1995, pp. 303–37.

Spufford, Peter, 'The Role of Entrepreneurs in State Formation in Late Medieval Europe', in Simonetta Cavaciocchi (ed.), *Poteri Economici e Poteri Politici secc. XIII–XVIII*, Atti del 'Settimana di Studi', xxx, Istituto Internazionale di Storia Economica 'F. Datini', Prato, 1999, pp. 483–500.

Spufford, Peter, 'Trade in Fourteenth-Century Europe', *New Cambridge Medieval History*, vi, Cambridge, 2000, 155–208.

Spufford, Peter, 'Conclusioni', in Rina La Guardia (ed.), *I Luoghi della Moneta*, Milan, 2001, pp. 157–72.

Stahl, Alan, 'The Deathbed Oration of Doge Mocenigo and the Mint of Venice', *Mediterranean Historical Review*, x, 1995, pp. 284–301.

Stahl, Patricia, 'Der Zinnhandel auf der Frankfurter Messe', in Rainer Koch (ed.), *Brücke zwischen den Völkern. Zur Geschichte der Frankfurter Messe*, ii, Frankfurt, 1991, pp. 147–58.

Staniland, Kay, *Embroiderers*, British Museum Medieval Craftsmen Series, London, 1991.

Stefani, Giuseppi (ed.), *Insurance in Venice from the Origin to the end of the Serenissima*, Trieste, 1956, Eng. trans. 1958.

Steinberg, S. H., *Five Hundred Years of Printing*, 2nd edn, Harmondsworth, 1961.

Stöckly, Doris, *Le Système de l'Incanto des galères du marché à Venise (fin du XIIIe – milieu du XVe siècle*, Leiden, 1994.

Stopani, Renato, *La Via Francigena. Una Strada europea nell'Italia del Medioevo*, 2nd edn, Florence, 1992.

Strauss, Gerald, *Nuremberg in the Sixteenth Century*, New York, 1966.

Strayer, Joseph R., *On the Medieval Origins of the Modern State*, Princeton, 1970.

Strayer, Joseph R. (ed.), *Dictionary of the Middle Ages*, New York, 12 vols, 1982–9.

Stromer, Wolfgang von, *Oberdeutsche Hochfinanz 1380–1450*, 3 vols, Wiesbaden, 1970.

Stromer, Wolfgang von, *Die Gründung der Baumwollindustrie in Mitteleuropa: Wirtschafts-politik im Spätmittelalter*, Stuttgart, 1978.

Stromer, Wolfgang von, 'Bernardus Teutonicus und die Geschäftbeziehungen zwischen den Deutschen Ostalpen und Venedig vor ausbruch des Fondaco dei Tedeschi', in P. W. Roth (ed.), *Beiträge zur Handels- und Verkehrgeschichte*, Grazer Forschungen zur Wirtschfts und Sozialgeschichte, iii, 1978, pp. 1–15.

Stromer, Wolfgang von, 'Ulman Stromer (1329–1407), das Handelshaus Stromer und die Papiermühle', in Wolfgang von Stromer and Jürgen Franzke (eds), *Zauberstoff Papier. Sechs Jahrhunderte Papier in Deutschland*, Munich, 1990.

Stromer, Wolfgang von, 'Die erste Papiermühle in Mitteleuropa: Ulman Stromeirs 'Hadermühle' Nürnberg 1390–1453, an der Wiege der Massenmedien', in Simonetta Cavaciocchi (ed.), *Produzione e commercio della cartae del libro secc. XIII–XVIII*, Atti del 'Settimana di Studi', xxiii, Istituto Internazionale di Storia Economica 'F. Datini', Prato, 1992, pp. 297–311.

Stuard, Susan Mosher, 'Ancillary Evidence for the Decline of Medieval Slavery', *Past and Present*, 149, 1995, 3–28.

Szabò, T., 'La rete stradale del contado di Siena', *Mélanges de l'Ecole Française de Rome*, lxxxvii, 1975, pp. 141–86.

Tangheroni, Marco, *La città dell'argento. Iglesias dalle origini alla fine del Medioevo*, Naples, 1985.

Tenenti, Alberto and Vivanti, Corrado, 'Le Film d'un grand système de navigation: les galères marchandes vénitiennes xive–xvie siècles', *Annales E. S. C.*, xvi, 1961, pp. 83–86 and map.

Tenenti, Alberto, *Piracy and the Decline of Venice*, London, 1967.

Thielemans, Marie-Rose, *Bourgogne et Angleterre. Relations politiques et economiques entre les Pays-Bas bourguignons et l'Angleterre 1435–67*, Brussels, 1966.

Thoen, Erik, *Landbouwekonomie en bevolking in Vlaanderen gedurende de late Middeleuwen en het begin van de Moderne Tijden*, Ghent, 1988.

Threlfall-Holmes, Miranda, 'Late Medieval Iron Production and Trade in the North-East', *Archaeologia Aeliana*, 5th ser., xxvii, 1999, pp. 111–22.

Thrupp, Sylvia L., *The Merchant Class of Medieval London (1300–1500)*, Ann Arbor, 1948.

Toth, Csaba, 'The Role of the Hungarian

Gold Coinage in Europe', in *XII Internationaler Numismatischer Kongress Berlin 1997, Akten*, ed. Bernd Kluge and Bernhard Weisser, ii, Berlin, 2000, pp. 1095–7.

Touchard, Henri, *Le Commerce maritime breton à la fin du Moyen Age*, Paris, 1967.

Tyler, J. E., *The Alpine Passes 962–1250*, Oxford, 1930.

Unger, Richard W., *The Ship in the Medieval Economy 600–1600*, Montreal, 1980.

Unger, Richard W., 'Feeding Low Countries Towns: the Grain Trade in the Fifteenth Century', *Revue Belge de Philologie et d'Histoire*, lxxvii, 1999, pp. 329–358.

Unger, Richard W., 'Beer Imports into the Low Countries', in Nils Jörn, Werner Paravicini and Horst Wernicke (eds), *Hansekaufleute in Brügge*, iv, Berne, 2000, pp. 205–14.

Usher, A. P., *The Early History of Deposit Banking in Mediterranean Europe*, Cambridge, Mass., 1943.

Vale, Malcolm, 'England, France and the Origins of the Hundred Years' War' in Michael Jones and Malcolm Vale (eds), *England and her Neighbours, 1066–1453*, London, 1989.

Vale, Malcolm, 'Manuscripts and Books', in Christopher Allmand (ed.), *The New Cambridge Medieval History*, vii (c. 1415–c. 1500), Cambridge, 1998, pp. 278–86.

Van der Wee, Herman, *The Growth of the Antwerp Market and the European Economy (Fourteenth – Sixteenth Centuries)*, 3 vols, The Hague, 1963.

Van der Wee, Herman, 'Structural Changes and Specialisation in the Industry of the Southern Netherlands, 1100–1660', *Economic History Review*, 2nd ser., xxviii, 1975, pp. 203–21, reprinted in his *Low Countries*, pp. 201–22.

Van der Wee, Herman (ed.), *The Rise and Decline of Urban Industries in Italy and in the Low Countries*, Leuven, 1988.

Van der Wee, Herman (ed.), *La Banque en Occident*, Antwerp, 1991.

Van der Wee, Herman and T. Peeters, 'Un modèle dynamique de croissance interseculaire du commerce mondiale, XIIe– XVIIIe siècles' *Annales, E. S. C.*, xv, 1970, pp. 100–28.

Van Egmond, Warren, *Practical Mathematics in the Italian Renaissance*, Annali dell'Istituto e Museo di Storia Scienza, Supplement 4, Florence, 1980.

Van Heerwaarden, Jan, *Opgelegde Bedevaarten*, Assen/Amsterdam, 1978.

van Houtte, J. A., 'The Rise and Decline of the Market of Bruges', *Economic History Review*, 2nd ser., xix, 1966, pp. 29–47.

van Houtte, J. A., *Bruges*, Brussels, 1967.

van Houtte, J. A., *An Economic History of the Low Countries 800–1800*, London, 1977.

van Uytven, Raymond, 'La Draperie brabançonne et malinoise du XIIe au XVIIe siècle: grandeur éphémère et décadence', in Spallanzani, Marco (ed.), *Produzione commercio e consumo dei panna di lana (nei secoli XII–XVIII)*, Atti delle 'Settimane di Studio', ii, Istituto Internazionale di Storia Economica 'F. Datini', Prato, Florence, 1976, pp. 85–97.

van Uytven, Raymond, 'Cloth in Medieval Literature of Western Europe' in N. B. Harte and K. G. Ponting (eds), *Cloth and Clothing in Medieval Europe*, London, 1983, pp. 151–83.

van Uytven, Raymond, *Liber Amicorum*, *"Proeve 't al, 't is prysselyck"*. Consumption in European Towns (13th–18th Century). *Bijdragen tot de Geschiedenis*, lxxxi, 1998.

van Werveke, Hans, 'Der Flandrische Eigenhandel im Mittelalter', *Hansische Geschichtsblätter*, lxi, 1936, pp. 7–24, reprinted in his *Miscellanea*, pp. 45–59.

van Werveke, Hans, 'De omvang van de Ieperse lakenproductie in de veertiende eeuw', *Mededelingen van de Koninklijkse Vlaamse Academie, Klasse der Letteren*, ix, 2, 1947.

van Werveke, Hans, 'La Famine de l'an 1316 en Flandre et dans les régions voisines', *Revue du Nord*, xli, 1959, pp. 5–14, reprinted in his *Miscellanea*, pp. 326–38.

van Werveke, Hans, *Miscellanea Mediaevalia*, Ghent, 1968.

Vaughan, Richard, *Matthew Paris*, Cambridge, 1958.

Vaughan, Richard, *Philip the Good*, London, 1970.

Vaughan, Richard, *Charles the Bold*, London, 1973.

Veale, Elspeth M., *The English Fur Trade in the Later Middle Ages*, Oxford, 1966.

Verlinden, Charles, *L'Esclavage dans l'Europe médievale*, i, Bruges 1955, ii, Ghent, 1977.

Verlinden, Charles, 'Markets and Fairs', *Cambridge Economic History of Europe*, iii, Cambridge, 1963, 126–53.

Verlinden, Charles, 'Marchands ou tisserands? A propos des origines urbaines', *Annales, E. S. C.*, xxvii, 1972, pp. 396–406.

Voet, Leon, *Antwerp. The Golden Age*, Eng. trans. Antwerp, 1973.

Volpe, G., 'Montieri: costituzione politica, struttura soziale e attivita economica d'una terra mineraria toscana nel XIII secolo', *Vierteljahrschrift für Sozial- und Wirtschaftsgeschichte*, vi, 1908.

von Wartburg, Marie-Louise, 'The Archaeology of Cane Sugar Production: A Survey of Twenty Years of Research in Cyprus', *Antiquaries Journal*, lxxxi, 2001, pp. 305–35.

Wake, C. H. H., 'The Changing Pattern of Europe's Pepper and Spice Imports. ca. 1400–1700', *Journal of European Economic History*, viii, 1979, pp. 361–403.

Waley, Daniel, *Siena and the Sienese in the Thirteenth Century*, Cambridge, 1991.

Watson, Andrew, 'Back to Gold – and Silver',

Economic History Review, 2nd series, xx, 1967, pp. 1–34.

Wiesflecker, Hermann, *Kaiser Maximilian I*, 5 vols, Vienna, 1971–86.

Wilkins, E. H., *Life of Petrarch*, Chicago, 1961.

Winkler, Friedrich, *Dürers Zeichnungen*, i, 1484–1502, Berlin, 1936.

Wolff, Philippe, *Commerces et marchands de Toulouse (vers 1350–vers 1450)*, Paris, 1954.

Wolff, Philippe, 'Les Hôtelleries toulousaines au Moyen Age', *Bulletin Philologique et Historique*, 1960, pp. 189–205.

Yamey, Basil S. (ed.), *Double Entry Bookkeeping in Western Europe, 1300 to 1800*, Routledge, London, 2000.

Unpublished Ph. D. theses

Frearson, Michael C., *The English Corantos of the 1620s*, University of Cambridge, 1993.

Uhler S., *English Customs Ports 1275–1323*, St Andrews, 1975.

Sources of illustrations

Angers, Royal Museum of Fine Art 382–3
Antwerp, Musée des Tapisseries 110, 264
Athens, Byzantine Museum 413
Avignon, Musée de Villeneuve-Avignon 85
Berlin, Kupferstichkabinett 27, 98; Nationalgalerie 18, 236
Braunschweig, Herzog Anton Ulrich Museum 384
Bruges, Groeningemuseum 89, 270, 381; University Library 35, 55, 286
Cambridge, Fitzwilliam Museum, 347
Dijon, Archives Départementales 153; Musée des Beaux Arts 190, 205
Dresden, Sächisches Hauptarchiv 357 left
Dublin, National Gallery of Ireland 268
Florence, Biblioteca Laurenziana 80, 248, 289; Biblioteca Riccardiana 86–87, 240; Bargello 258; Uffizi 277, 339
Genoa, Museo Navale 386
Glasgow, University Library 203
Hallein, Keltenmuseum 297
Hamburg, Museum für Kunst und Gewerbe 269
Heidelberg, University Library 17
Issogno, Val d'Aosta, Castello 130
Karlsruhe, Badische Landesbibliothek 407
Koblenz, Landeshauptarchiv 167
Leeuwarden, Fries Museum 59
Liège, University Library 117; Cathedral Treasury 128
London, British Library 15, 140, 224, 225, 243, 247, 321, 326, 327, 404; British Museum 14, 145, 358, 361; National

Gallery 131 top, 270, 267; Victoria and Albert Museum 124, 262–3
Los Angeles, Paul Getty Museum, 272, 271
Lübeck, Stadtarchiv 378
Lyon, Musée Historiques des Tissus 127
Modena, Biblioteca Estense 311
Montefiore dell'Aso, Santa Luccia 125
Munich, Bayerische Staatsbibliothek 2, 7
Naples, Capodimonte Museum 21, 36
New York, Metropolitan Museum of Arts 275, 258
Nuremberg, Germanisches Nationalmuseum 54, 218
Oxford, Ashmolean Museum 135
Paris, Bibliothèque Nationale 36, 49, 61, 79, 92, 100–1, 124, 126, 164, 193, 223, 299, 303, 306, 307, 311, 314–5, 317, 343, 345, 349; Bibliothèque de l'Arsenal 112, 102, 113; Musée Cluny 35, 301; Musée du Louvre 13, 67, 131 left, 142; Archives Nationales 1
Perugia, Collegio della Mercanzia 235
Prato, Dantini Archives 29, 34; Palazzo Comunale 233
Rome, Biblioteca Apostolica Vaticana 305; Pinacoteca Vaticana 292
Rotterdam, Boyman van Beuningen Museum 229, 403
Siena, State Archives 62
St Gallen, Historisches Museum 252
Turin, Museo Civico 111
Urbino, Palazzo Ducale 123, 74
Venice, Biblioteca Marciana 394–5; Galleria

dell'Accadémia 353
Verona, Museo di Castelvecchio 142
Vienna, Österreichische Nationalbibliothek 28, 204, 304, 356, 357
Waldsee, Kunstsammlung Waldburg-Wolfegg 362
Warsaw, National Museum 391
Zürich, Centralbibliothek 217

With special thanks to Madame M. T. Hirschkoff in Paris

Photographic credits

ACL, Brussels 234, 267; AKG, London 300, 353, 379; Alinari 39, 365, 399; Alleman, A. 44; Archives Photographiques, Paris 279, 393; Austin, James 73; Bridgeman Art Library 190; Bruckner, Georgina 21, 77; Delvert, Ray 172; Department of Environment 69; Edimund 208; Florence Soprintendenza delle Gallerie 108, 109; Francassetti, Martha 179 top; French Government Tourist Office 145, 157 both, 178; Giraudon 122, 138, 161; Giusti 178; Hirmer Verlag 126; Italian Government Tourist Office 82, 208, 245; Lane, Emily 173; Querezi, Cremona 83; RMN, Paris 201, 301; Roger-Viollet, Paris 71, 76, 151, 154, 170; Scala 90–91, 125, 174, 231, 233, 235, 243, 261, 290, 308; Schelling, Lubeck 377; Spufford, Peter 176, 179, 234, 245, 359; Webb, John for Thames and Hudson 14, 74, 262–63, Van der Veer, J. 59; Zodiaque 169 both.

Index